THAYER'S
LIFE OF BEETHOVEN
VOLUME II

THAYER'S
LIFE OF
BEETHOVEN

REVISED AND EDITED BY
ELLIOT FORBES

II

PRINCETON, NEW JERSEY
PRINCETON UNIVERSITY PRESS
1967

First Princeton Paperback Printing, 1970
Third Printing, 1973
Ninth Printing, 1989
Tenth paperback printing, for the first
time in two volumes, 1991

19   18   17   16   15   14   13   12   11

Princeton University Press books are printed on acid-free
paper, and meet the guidelines for permanence and durability
of the Committee on Production Guidelines for Book
Longevity of the Council on Library Resources.

Printed in the United States of America

LIST OF ABBREVIATIONS

A Emily Anderson, *Letters of Beethoven*. Three volumes. London, 1961.

AMZ *Allgemeine Musikalische Zeitung*. Leipzig. Also referred to as *Allg. Mus. Zeit.*

Beeth. Gustav Nottebohm, *Beethoveniana*. Leipzig, 1872.

II Beeth. Gustav Nottebohm, *Zweite Beethoveniana*. Leipzig, 1887.

BJ *Beethovenjahrbuch*, Theodor von Frimmel, editor. Two volumes. Leipzig, 1908-1909.
Beethoven-Jahrbuch, Paul Mies and Joseph Schmidt-Görg, editors. Volumes 1953/54, 1955/56, 1957/58, 1959/60.

Biographie Anton Schindler, *Biographie von Ludwig van Beethoven*. Third edition, two volumes in one. Münster, 1860. Anton Schindler, *Biographie von Ludwig van Beethoven*, first edition, Münster, 1840, is occasionally cited and is indicated by *Biographie*, 1840 or first edition.

DM *Die Musik*. Berlin and Leipzig.

FRBH Theodor von Frimmel, *Beethoven-Handbuch*. Two volumes. Leipzig, 1926.

GA *Beethovens Werke. Kritische Gesamtausgabe*. Twenty-five volumes. Breitkopf and Härtel, Leipzig, 1866-1868, 1888. Also referred to as Collected Works Edition.

Kerst Friedrich Kerst, editor, *Die Erinnerungen an Beethoven*. Two volumes. Stuttgart, 1913.

KHV Georg Kinsky, *Das Werk Beethovens. Thematisch-bibliographisches Verzeichnis seiner sämtlichen vollendeten Kompositionen*. Completed and edited by Hans Halm, Munich, 1955.

KK Kastner-Kapp, *Ludwig van Beethovens sämtliche Briefe*, Emerich Kastner, editor. Revised and enlarged by Julius Kapp. Leipzig, 1923.

MQ *The Musical Quarterly*. New York.

NBJ *Neues Beethoven-Jahrbuch*, Adolph Sandberger, editor. Augsburg and Braunschweig.

Notizen Franz Wegeler and Ferdinand Ries, *Biographische Notizen über*
(*Not.*) *Ludwig van Beethoven*. Coblenz, 1838. With a supplement (Nachtrag) by F. Wegeler. Coblenz, 1845.

Schünemann Georg Schünemann, editor, *Ludwig van Beethovens Konversationshefte*. Three volumes. Berlin, 1941-1943.

TDR   Alexander Wheelock Thayer, *Ludwig van Beethovens Leben*, Hermann Deiters, editor. Revised and completed by Hugo Riemann. Five volumes. Leipzig, 1907-1917.

TK   Alexander Wheelock Thayer, *The Life of Ludwig van Beethoven*, Henry Edward Krehbiel, editor. Three volumes. New York, 1921.

Other abbreviations

CM   Convention Money or Coin (Konventions-münze).

VS   Vienna Standard (Wiener Währung).

WoO   Werke ohne Opuszahl (Works without opus number). Cf. KHV.

CONTENTS

VOLUME II

THAYER'S

LIFE OF BEETHOVEN

VOLUME II

From the oil portrait by W. J. Mähler (1804)
Courtesy of the New York Public Library

After the bust by Franz Klein (1812)

Used with permission of the Beethoven-Haus, Bonn

CHAPTER XXVIII

THE YEAR 1815

RESOLUTION OF ANNUITY PAYMENTS— DEATH OF CARL VAN BEETHOVEN— GUARDIANSHIP OF THE NEPHEW

BEETHOVEN might well have adopted Kotzebue's title: "The Most Remarkable Year of my Life" and written his own history for 1814, in glowing and triumphant language; but now the theme modulates into a soberer key.

In a letter of early December to the Archduke, who was then in Prague attempting to hasten a settlement of the Kinsky payments, Beethoven writes; "—then there is the *matter of a new opera*—the *subject* of which I must decide in the next few days—" The *Sammler* of December 13th explains the allusion to an opera: "It is with great pleasure that we inform the music-loving public that Herr van Beethoven has contracted to compose an opera. The poem is by Herr Treitschke and bears the title: *Romulus und Remus*." The notice was based upon this note to Treitschke: "I will compose Romulus and shall begin in a few days, I will come to you in person! first *once*—then *several times* so that we may discuss the whole matter with each other."

Now here was a promising operatic project; but before six weeks had passed came the *Allg. Mus. Zeitung* bringing Johann Fuss's musical "Review of the month of December," wherein among the items of Vienna news was a notice that "Hr. Fuss had composed an opera in three acts entitled *Romulus und Remus* for the Theater-an-der-Wien"! And this was so; portions of it were afterwards sung by a musical society of which Dr. L. Sonnleithner was a member, and in Pressburg it was put upon the stage in 1818;—but it never came to performance in the theatres of Vienna, perhaps in consequence of measures adopted after the following letter to Treitschke:

I thought I could expedite the matter by sending Herr. v. Schreyvogel a copy of this letter—but no.

You see this Fuss can attack me in all the newspapers, unless I can produce some written evidence *against him*, or [unless] you—or the director of the theatre undertake to make a settlement with him. On the other hand the business of my contract for the opera is not concluded.

I beg of you to write me an answer especially as regards Fuss's letter; the matter would be easily decided in a court of *art*, but much as we should like it to be, this is not the case . . .

The matter was so arranged with Fuss as to leave the text in Beethoven's hands; but how, and on what terms, is not known.

Of the many poets whose names became associated with Beethoven, here might be mentioned the Prussian Imperial Government Councillor Sack from Liegnitz who sent, along with a long letter, the text to his oratorio *Das Weltgericht.*[1] Beethoven does not appear to have even considered the subject.

It was about this time (precisely when the painter could not remember when speaking of it in 1860), that Beethoven sat again for his friend Mähler, who wished to add his portrait to his gallery of musicians. In his *Beethoven Handbuch*, Frimmel writes:[2] "It is a half-length portrait in three, or perhaps four copies, of which one is in Freiburg while others have been preserved by the Karajan family and in the Gesellschaft der Musikfreunde Collection."

On the 25th of January, a grand festival took place in the Burg on the occasion of the Russian Empress's birthday, which in part consisted of a concert in the Rittersaal. The last piece on the program was the canon in *Fidelio*: "Mir ist so wunderbar," and by a whimsical stroke of fortune Beethoven himself appeared, and, to the audience of emperors and empresses, kings and queens, with their ministers and retinues, played once again in public! Wild, who dates the concert a month too soon, gives an account of it in which, after telling of his own success with "Adelaide," he says: "It would be as untruthful as absurd were I to deny that my vanity was flattered by the distinction which the gathered celebrities bestowed upon me; but this performance of 'Adelaide' had one result which was infinitely more gratifying to my artistic nature; it was the cause of my coming into closer contact with the greatest musical genius of all time, Beethoven. The master, rejoiced at my choice of his song, hunted me up and offered to accompany me. Satisfied with my singing he told me that he would orchestrate the song. He did not do this, but wrote for me the cantata 'An die Hoffnung' (words by Tiedge) with pianoforte accompaniment, which, he playing for me, I sang at a matinée before a select audience."[3]

---

[1] For Sack's letter and libretto see W. Virneisel, *op.cit.*, pp. 368-75.

[2] I, p. 44; see also *Beethoven Studien*, I, pp. 59ff.

[3] Although the song was already composed in 1813, Thayer believes that he revised it for

By far the most important event in Beethoven's history during these months, was the final settlement, by compromise, of the annuity affair with the Kinsky heirs, on the 18th of January. So soon as the legal formalities could be ended and communicated to Beethoven, he issued in autograph a power of attorney to Baron Josef von Pasqualati in Prague to collect the money due, and act for him in all things necessary. On March 26th, Pasqualati acknowledged the receipt of 2479 florins V.S. (Vienna Standard) as payment on the annuity in full up to the end of March, 1815. In this instance "W.W." (*Wiener Währung*) meant notes of redemption, since the bank-notes had been retired from circulation in 1812. The compromise decree arrived at through the ministration of Dr. Kanka fixed the original annuity of 1800 florins at 1200 florins, beginning on November 3d, 1812. There was therefore due to Beethoven, for the period from November 3d to the end of March, 1815, 2890 florins, from which was deducted 411 florins, as the equivalent of the 60 ducats paid to Beethoven by Prince Kinsky in October, 1812, leaving 2479 florins as aforesaid. The decision in the case with Lobkowitz also soon followed. According to the judgment of the Court, entered on April 19, 1815, the future annual payments were fixed at 700 florins (the equivalent of 280 fl. conventional coin, silver), and the 2508 fl. arrears were ordered paid in notes of redemption within two months. Payments were made accordingly and (as Dr. v. Köchel reported in a private note to the author), from 1811 up to his death, Beethoven received on the annuity contract the following sums every year:

From Archduke Rudolph .... 1500 fl.
From Prince Kinsky 1200
From Prince Lobkowitz 700

Total .... 3400 fl.

This sum, 3400 florins in notes of redemption, was the equivalent of 1360 florins *Conventions Münze*, silver, or 952 Prussian thalers.

Notwithstanding that Prince Lobkowitz's financial affairs had been satisfactorily ordered, his return to Vienna was delayed until the spring of 1815, one reason being that (as he states in a letter to Archduke Rudolph, dated Prague, December 29, 1814) an opinion prevailed in the Austrian capital that his presence would be "unseemly." In this letter he gives expression to his feelings toward Beethoven as follows: "Although I have reason to be anything but satisfied with the behavior of Beethoven toward me, I am nevertheless rejoiced, as a passionate lover of music, that his assuredly great works are beginning to be appreciated. I heard 'Fidelio' here[4] and barring the book, I was extraordinarily pleased with the music, except the two

Wild in 1815 before its publication in April, 1816. Wild performed it a month later. (Cf. TDR, III, 550, n. 2.)
[4] *Fidelio* had its first performance in

Prague on November 21, 1814. Liebich was the director of the theatre and C. M. von Weber, Kapellmeister. (TDR, III, 492, n. 1.)

finales, which I do not like very much. I think the music extremely effective and worthy of the man who composed it."

Is this not nobly said?

Consider these facts: Lobkowitz was now deprived of the control of his revenues; those revenues, in so far as they were based upon contracts, were subject to the *Finanz-Patent* of 1811; the curators of his estates were also bound by it; and the General Court (*Landrecht*) had no power arbitrarily to set it aside. What that tribunal could and did do was, by its assent and decree, to give binding force to such agreement between the parties in principal, as had obtained the sanction of the curators, with, probably, the consent of the principal creditors of the Prince. It follows then that the concession of Beethoven's full demand of 700 fl. in notes of redemption *could* have been obtained only through the good will and active intervention of Lobkowitz himself, using his personal influence with the other parties concerned. Schindler incidentally confirms this.

Will the reader here pause a moment and think what impression the aspersions on Lobkowitz's character in Beethoven's letters have left upon his mind? Have they not begotten a prejudice so strengthened by "damnable iteration" that it is now hardly possible to overcome it, and believe it unfounded? Lobkowitz, young, generous to prodigality, rendered careless by the very magnitude of his possessions, had, in the lapse of some twenty years, so squandered his enormous resources, as to fall into temporary embarrassments, which threw the responsibility of meeting his pecuniary engagements upon others, who were bound by the nature of their office to pay none but strictly legal claims. Thus Beethoven became a loser in part of what was originally no debt, but a gift—or rather would have been so, but for the interference of Lobkowitz.

We have here another warning of the great caution to be exercised when using private correspondence for purposes of biography. In writing of Beethoven this is especially necessary, because so large a proportion of it consists of confidential notes and communications containing the ebullitions of splenetic moments, and not seldom hasty charges and mistaken accusations, such as he gladly withdrew on learning the truth. To accept all this without question is preposterous; to use it as authentic historic matter without scrupulous examination, is to do great injustice to the dead.

The proof is ample, that Beethoven was already fully convinced of the entire innocence of both Prince Kinsky and Prince Lobkowitz of all desire to escape any really just demands upon them: yet the memory of those noble and generous personages has been made to suffer on the authority of Beethoven's hasty expressions.

A letter written in English, probably by his friend Häring, who had been much in England, and signed by Beethoven, marks the progress of his business with Thomson:

Address.

> Mr. George Thomson, merchant in the musical line.
> Edingbourgh, Scotland.

Sir,

Many concerns have prevented my answers to your favors, to which I reply only in part. All your songs with the exception of a few are ready to be forwarded. I mean those to which I was to write the accompagnements, for with respect to the 6 Canzonettes, which I am to compose I own that the honorary you offered is totally inadequate. Circumstances are here much altered and taxes have been so much raised after the English fashion that my share for 1814 was near 60 £. Besides an original good air,—and what you also wish—an Overture, are perhaps the most difficult undertakings in musical compositions. I therefore beg to state that my honorary for 6 songs or airs must be 35 £ or seventy Impl. Ducats—and for an Overture 20 £ or 50 Impl. Ducats. You will please to assign the payment here as usual, and you may depend that I shall do you justice. No artiste of talent and merit will find my pretentions extravagant.

Concerning the overture you will please to indicate in your reply whether you wish to have it composed for an easy or more difficult execution. I expect your immediate answer having several orders to attend, and I shall in a little time write more copiously in reply to your favors already received. I beg you to thank the author for the very ingenious and flattering verses, which I obtained by your means. Allow me to subscribe myself

> Sir,
> your very obedt. & humble servt.
> Ludwig van Beethoven.

Vienna, Feb. 7, 1815.

——There is a sketchbook in the Berlin Library, described by Nottebohm, which shows in part what compositions employed Beethoven's thoughts about this time.[5] It contains sketches for marches; an unfinished piano concerto in D;[6] the canon, "Kurz ist der Schmerz"; the last movement of the Violoncello Sonata, Op. 102 No. 1; the last part of the Overture in C, Op. 115 (evidently at the time of preparing the score); a second version of "Merkenstein"; the canon, "Lerne schweigen"; a "Symphony in B minor"; a "Sonata pastorale" for pianoforte and violoncello; a "Sonata in C minor"; the second part of "Meeresstille und glückliche Fahrt"; the last movement of the Violoncello Sonata, Op. 102 No. 2; and various projected fugal movements.—— The date of these sketches is fixed by a memorandum of Beethoven on the seventh leaf, referring to Smart's production in London of "Wellington's Victory":[7] "In Drurylane Theatre on February 10th, and repeated by general request on the 13th, *Wiener Zeitung* of March 2nd." This led to inquiry, and Sir George Smart's name, as leader of the Lenten concerts in London, became known to Beethoven, who engaged his friend

---

[5] See *II Beeth.*, pp. 314-20.

[6] For an extended sketch for this work, see *ibid.*, pp. 321-22.

[7] Sir George Smart also introduced to England Beethoven's oratorio (in English and entitled *The Mount of Olives*) and the Mass in C. The oratorio was first performed on February 25, 1814, the mass in its entirety not until somewhat later. (TK, II, 310, see also n. 1.)

Häring, who knew Smart intimately, to write the following English letter in his behalf:

To Sir George Smart,
    Great Portland St., London.

My Dear Sir George:

I see by the papers that you have brought forth in the theatre Beethoven's battle and that it was received with considerable applause. I was very happy to find that your partiality to Mr. B.'s compositions is not diminished and therefore I take the liberty in his name to thank you for the assistance you afforded in the performance of that uncommon piece of music. He has arranged it for the pianoforte, but having offered the original to his R. H. the Prince Regent, he durst not sell that arrangement to any Editor, until he knew the Prince's pleasure, not only with respect to the dedication, but in general. Having waited so many months without receiving the least acknowledgment, he begged me to apply to you for advice. His idea is to dispose of this arrangement and of several other original compositions to an Editor in London—or perhaps to several united— if they would make a handsome offer— They would besides engage to let him know *the day of the appearance for sale* of the respective pieces, in order that the Editor *here*, may not publish one copy before the day to be mentioned. At the end of this letter follows the list of such compositions, with the price, which the Author expects. I am persuaded, Sir George, you will exert yourself to benefit this great genius. He talks continually of going to England, but I am afraid that his deafness, seemingly increasing, does not allow him the execution of this favorite idea. You are informed without doubt that his opera: Fidelio, has had the most brilliant success here, but the execution is so difficult, that it would not suit any of the English houses.

I submit here his list with the prices. None of the following pieces has been published, but No. 2, 4 and 9—have been performed with the greatest applause—

1. Serious Quartetto for 2 violins, tenor and bass.................................40 guineas.
2. Battle of Vittoria—Score...70 guineas.
3. Battle of Vittoria arranged for the pianoforte................................30 guineas.
4. A Grand Symphony—Score...70 guineas.
5. A Grand Symphony arranged for the pianoforte..............................30 guineas.
6. A Symphony—Key F—Score...40 guineas.
7. A Symphony, arranged for the pianoforte...................................... 20 guineas.
8. Grand Trio for the pianoforte, violin and violoncello.....................40 guineas.
9. Three Overtures for a full Orchestra......................................each 30 guineas.
10. The Three Arrangements for Pianoforte..................................each 15 guineas.
11. A Grand Sonata for the pianoforte and violin..............................25 guineas.

The above is the produce of four years labour.

Our friend Neate has not yet made his appearance here—nor is it at all known where he is roving about. We—I mean mostly amateurs—are now rehearsing Handel's Messiah—I am to be leader of the 2d violins; there will be this time 144 violins—first and second altogether, and the singers and remainder in proportion. I have been so unfortunate, as not to receive a single line or answer from England since my stay in Vienna, which is near three months; this discourages me very much from writing, for I have dispatched immediately after my arrival several letters and have been continuing to send letters, but all in vain. Amongst those to whom I wrote about two months ago, is our friend Disi—pray if you meet him give him and his very respectable family my best regards. I have passed so many happy hours in his house, it would be highly ungrateful for me to forget such an amiable family.

Beethoven happening to call on me just now, he wishes to address a few lines to you which you will find at the bottom of this. My direction is Monsieur Jean de Häring, No. 298 Kohlmarkt, Vienne.

Poor B. is very anxious to hear something of the English editors, as he hardly can keep those of this city from him, who tease him for his works.

Häring now writes the following for Beethoven to sign:

Give me leave to thank you for the trouble you have taken several times, as I understand, in taking my works under your protection, by which I don't doubt all justice has been done. I hope you will not find it indiscreet if I solicit you to answer Mr. Häring's letter as soon as possible. I should feel myself highly flattered if you would express your wishes, that I may meet them, in which you will always find me ready, as an acknowledgment for the favors you have heaped upon my children.

Yours gratefully,

Vienna 16. March, 1815.   Ludwig van Beethoven.

And now I shall beg, my dear Sir George, not to take this long letter amiss, and to believe that I am always with the greatest regard,

Your most humble and obedient servant,

Vienna 19. March, 1815.   John Häring.

The works enumerated in this letter, taking them in the same order, are Op. 95, 91, 92, 93, 97, 113, 115, 117 and 96. Häring was evidently ignorant that all of Beethoven's new works were even then sold, except for England. Steiner had purchased them, which introduces the consideration of Beethoven's most recent important publisher.

The "K. K. Priv. Chemische Druckerey," the property of Rochus Krasinzky and Sigmund Anton Steiner, passed about 1810 into the hands of Steiner alone. In that year Tobias Haslinger (of Zell in Upper Austria), who had been one of Kapellmeister Glöggl's singing-boys at Linz and assistant in his music-shop, came to Vienna with the design of establishing himself in business, and there soon became acquainted with Steiner. He detailed to Steiner his purposes and plans and induced him to withdraw his prints and other wares from Grund's bookstore in the Singerstrasse, to open a shop of his own in the narrow passage then existing at the northeast corner of the Graben, known as the Paternoster-Gassel, and to employ him (Haslinger) as bookkeeper and manager.[8] From this position he soon rose to be partner

---

[8] Unger dates Haslinger's association with the firm, and thus with Beethoven, as probably in early 1814. See *Ludwig van Beethoven* *und seine Verleger* (Berlin and Vienna, 1921), pp. 5-6.

in the firm, S. A. Steiner and Co. Beethoven conceived an odd and whimsical liking for the young man, and for a few years his relations to the firm became very much the same as those which formerly existed between him and the Kunst- und Industrie-Comptoir. Haslinger had learned divers instruments in Linz, had begun the study of composition there and continued it in Vienna. His Opus 10, "Ideal einer Schlacht," for the pianoforte, had just been published—the subject of Homeric laughter to Jupiter-Beethoven and the other gods. He made his place of business attractive and it became a favorite resort of composers, musicians, singers, writers for the theatre, the public press and the like. In Beethoven's correspondence with the firm the composer was "Generalissimus," Steiner "Lieutenant-General," Haslinger "Adjutant," or rather the diminutive of Adjutant, "Adjutanterl." Their assistants were "Subalterns" and the shop, "Office of the Lieutenant-General."

It will be remembered that in the fall of 1813 Beethoven had arranged for a loan for his brother Carl through Steiner, and that part of the agreement stated that if the repayment of the loan [1814] reverted to Beethoven, he could have an extension in return for granting Steiner certain privileges with a new unpublished sonata. Thus it would seem that this formed the beginning of their relationship in a business way, since beginning with Op. 90, Steiner published a substantial number of Beethoven's works, as is seen in the list below. The actual terms of contract for these works have not been discovered, but the fact that there was a contract, and that Beethoven for some time remained in debt to the publisher, is evident from the correspondence of the next few years.

Our first letter to Steiner is dated February 1, 1815, and shows that Carl van Beethoven was somehow involved.

Most Wellborn Lieutenant General!

I have received today your letter to my brother and am satisfied with it, but must beg of you to pay *the costs of the pianoforte arrangement in addition*. As I am obliged to pay for *everything* in the world and *more dearly than others*, this would be a hardship for me. Besides I don't believe you can complain about the honorarium of 250 ducats— But neither do I want to complain; therefore arrange for the transcriptions yourself. But all must be looked over by me and if necessary improved. I hope that you are satisfied with this.— In addition to this you might *give my brother the collected pianoforte works of Clementi, Mozart and Haydn*. He needs them for *his little son*. Do this, my dearest Steiner, and be not stone,[9] as stony as your name is—Farewell excellent Lieutenant-General, I am always,

Yours truly, General-in-Chief,

Ludwig van Beethoven

The works purchased by Steiner are named in a list, bearing the date of April 29, 1815, which is a copy of an unsigned memorandum,[10] evidently proceeding from Beethoven, which runs thus:

[9] German: *Stein* =English: stone. (TK, II, 313, n. 1.)

[10] Sent by Nottebohm to Thayer along with the letter just cited. (TDR, III, 499.)

NOTE

Concerning the following original musical compositions, composed by the under-signed, and surrendered as property to the licensed art dealer H. S. A. Steiner.

1st. Score of the opera Fidelio.

2d. Score of the cantata Der glorreiche Augenblick.

3d. Score of a quartet for 2 violins, viola and basso.

4th. Score of a grand Trio to be sung with pianoforte arrangement.

5th. Score of the Battle of Vittoria with pianoforte arrangement.

6th. Pianoforte arrangement and score of a Symphony in F.

7th. Pianoforte arrangement and score of a Symphony in A major.

8th. Grand Trio for pianoforte, violin and basso in score.

9th. Grand Sonata for pianoforte and violin in score.

10th. Score of a Grand Overture in E-flat major.

11th. Score of a Grand Overture in C major.

12th. Score of a Grand Overture in G major.

13th. 12 English songs with pianoforte accompaniment and German text.

For all of these works[11] which H. Steiner may use as his property in all places except England, I have been wholly recompensed.

Vienna, April 29, 1815.

The correspondence with Steiner and Co. indicates that the task of arrang-ing the orchestral works for the pianoforte was performed by Haslinger and Anton Diabelli, with occasional assistance from Carl Czerny, under Beet-hoven's superintendence.

Diabelli, born near Salzburg in 1781, had now been for some years one of the more prolific composers of light and pleasing music, and one of the best and most popular teachers in Vienna. He was much employed by Steiner and Co., as copyist and corrector, and in this capacity enjoyed much of Beethoven's confidence, who also heartily liked him as a man. In the composer's comical military staff, he was the "General Profoss," and in the correspondence his name becomes "Diabolus"—for Beethoven could never resist the temptation to a play upon words.

About the first of April Beethoven received a package which proved to be an opera text by Rudolph von Berge, sent to him with a letter by his old friend Amenda from Courland.[12] While this letter was under way Beethoven received a visit from a friend of Amenda's who, on his departure from Vienna, carried with him a letter for Amenda from Beethoven:

Vienna, April 12, 1815.

My dear, good Amenda!

The bearer of this, your friend Count Keyserling, visited me and awoke in me memories of you. You live *happily*, you have *children*, neither of which is true

---

[11] No. 3, Op. 95; No. 4, "Tremate, empi, tremate," Op. 116; No. 8, Op. 97; No. 9, Op. 96; No. 10, *König Stephan*, Op. 117; No. 11, "Namensfeier," Op. 115; No. 12, *Ruinen von Athen*, Op. 113. (TDR, III, 499, nn. 1-7.)

[12] This letter is given in TDR, III, pp. 501-503.

of me. To discuss this would make it too long-winded. More about this another
time when you write to me again.— You are one thousand times in my mind
with your patriarchal simplicity, and how often I have wanted to have people
like you around me.— Unfortunately for my good or that of others, fate denies
my wishes in this respect. I can say that I live almost *completely alone* in this
greatest city of Germany, since I must live almost in estrangement from all persons whom I love or could love— On what kind of footing is music with you?
Have you ever heard any of my great works there? *Great* say I—but compared
with the works of the Highest, everything is small— Goodbye, my dear good A,
think sometimes of your friend

Ludwig van Beethoven

When you write to me, the only address you need is *my name*.

The opera book sent by Amenda was entitled *Bacchus*, a "Grand Lyric
Opera in Three Acts." The libretto was preserved among Schindler's papers
in the Berlin Library. It seems likely that Beethoven gave some thought to
the opera and experimented with some themes. There are interesting notes
on a work with a classical subject, the words apparently the beginning of an
invocation to Pan, in a sketchbook of 1815, which Nottebohm[13] describes
without deciding whether they belong to Treitschke's *Romulus und Remus*
or von Berge's *Bacchus*:

not quite so characteristic, it must be evolved out of the B.M.[14] where the
dance only intermittently—

Throughout the opera probably dissonances, unresolved or very differently,
as our refined music cannot be thought of in connection with those barbarous
times.—Throughout the subject must be treated in a pastoral vein

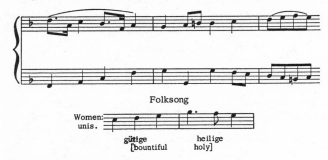

---

[13] *II Beeth.*, pp. 329-30. (TDR, III, 503.)
[14] Dr. Riemann suggests that "B.M." stands for "Bachus Motive." (TK, II, 315, n. 1.)

gütiger   schützender   segnender   Pan
[bountiful   protecting   blessed   Pan]

                                                        ...."

Of some minor compositions belonging to this spring, this is the story:
The Prussian King's Secretary, Friedrich Duncker, brought to Vienna, in
the hope of producing it there, a tragedy, *Leonore Prohaska*, "which tells
the story of a maiden who, disguised as a soldier, fought through the war of
liberation." For this Beethoven composed a Soldiers' Chorus for men's voices
unaccompanied: "Wir bauen und sterben"; a Romance with harp, 6/8 time,
"Es blüht ein Blume"; and a Melodrama with harmonica. Also he orchestrated the March in the Sonata, Op. 26,[15] Duncker preferring this to a new
marcia funebre.

On the approach of warm weather the Erdödys removed for the summer
to Jederslee, never to return to the Schottenbastei; and as Lichnowsky was
dead, Beethoven had no inducement to remain in that vicinity and therefore
departed from the Mölkerbastei—also never to return. The new lodging was
in the third story of a house then belonging to Count Lamberti, in the
Sailerstätte, with a double number 1055, 1056, near which he had lived a
dozen years before, having the same sunny aspect and the glorious view
across the Glacis from the Karlkirche and the Belvidere Gardens, away
across the Danube to the blue Carpathian mountains in the distance.

In this house, about the first of June, Häring introduced to Beethoven the
very fine English pianist and enthusiastic musician Charles Neate, who
after five months' study with Winter in Munich had come to Vienna in the
hope of obtaining instruction from the great symphonist. To his application, Beethoven replied in substance: "I cannot teach, but I will give you
an introduction to my master, Förster" (which he did by letter), "and you
may bring your compositions to me for inspection, and I will examine and
remark upon them." In consequence of this permission Neate saw him
almost daily. Beethoven spent a part of this summer in Baden, and Neate
took a room very near him. There the composer was in the habit of working
all the forenoon, dining early at twelve or one o'clock, and, towards evening,
walking with Neate—sometimes up the Helenen-Thal, oftener through the

[15] The autograph of this version is in the
Library of the Paris Conservatory of Music.
It is published in the Complete Works Edi-
tion, Ser. 25, No. 272. (TDR, III, 482.)

Kinsky-Halm (p. 553) dates the music to
Leonore Prohaska, fall, 1815—an advance
over Thayer's date of spring, 1814.

fields. Neate, in the course of his long life—he was nearly eighty in 1861 when he related these things to the author—had never met a man who so enjoyed nature; he took intense delight in flowers, in the clouds, in every-thing—"Nature was like food to him, he seemed really to live in it." Walking in the fields, he would sit down on any green bank that offered a good seat, and give his thoughts free course. He was then full of the idea of going to England, but the death of his brother and the adoption of his nephew put an end to the project. Neate remembered the boy as a very beautiful, intelli-gent lad. Beethoven, at that time, and as Neate knew him, was charmingly good-tempered to those whom he liked—but his dislikes were so strong, that to avoid speaking to persons to whom he was not well affected, he would actually increase his pace in the street to a run. At this time, his dark com-plexion was very ruddy and extremely animated. His abundant hair was in an admirable disorder. He was always laughing, when in good humor, which he for the most part was, as Neate saw him. In their conversations Neate spoke clearly and found no difficulty in making himself understood if he spoke into his left ear.

One day Neate spoke to him about the popularity of his Sonatas, Trios, etc., in England, and added that his Septet was very much admired:— "That's damned stuff" (or "a damned thing"), said Beethoven, "I wish it were burned!" or words to this effect, to Neate's great discomfiture. Another time, walking in the fields near Baden, Neate spoke of the "Pastoral" Symphony and of Beethoven's power of painting pictures in music. Beethoven said: "I have always a picture in my mind, when I am composing, and work up to it."

Neate brought to Beethoven an order from the Philharmonic Society of London—obtained by the exertions of Ries—for three concert overtures, of which we shall hear more hereafter. It is sufficient to say here, that instead of composing new ones as expected, he gave Neate the overtures to *König Stephan*, the *Ruinen von Athen* and the so-called "Namensfeier," and received for them 75 guineas.

The destruction of Razumovsky's palace suspended the quartets, and Linke, the violoncellist, passed the summer with the Erdödys at Jedlersee. This gave the impulse to Beethoven to write the principal works of this year: the two Sonatas for Pianoforte and Violoncello, Op. 102. The first bears his date: "Towards the end of July"; the second: "Beginning of August." While he was employed upon them, Treitschke called upon him for a closing chorus, "Es ist vollbracht," to a little dramatic piece similar to the *Gute Nachricht* entitled *Die Ehrenpforten*, and prepared to celebrate the second capitulation of Paris. It was performed July 15, 16 and 23; and, on the occasion of the Emperor's name-day, was revived "with appropriate changes" October 3rd and 4th; but (according to the theatre bills) with the chorus "Germania" substituted for "Es ist vollbracht."

This was the last year of Beethoven's personal intercourse with the Erdödys, a very interesting memorial of which, namely, a series of notes and letters, has been preserved and made public by the coolness and decision of Otto Jahn. Being in Munich in 1852, or about that time, he learned that this correspondence was in the hands—if our memory serve—of the widow of Brauchle,[16] and obtained permission to read it in the presence of the possessor. Suddenly starting up, he exclaimed (in effect): "I will copy this at the hotel," and before the lady, in her amazement and perplexity, could refuse or prevent, he was away, and made the only copies then known to be in existence.[17] Several of these papers are only Beethoven's apologies for not coming to Jederslee "today" or "tomorrow"—but all are interesting in the glimpse which they give of the affectionate intimacy which they show as existing between Beethoven and the family. The following undated letter to Countess Erdödy is a sample:

My dear and honored Countess!

You have already given me repeated gifts and that is not right. You deprive me thereby of the credit of having been able to do the least thing for you— It is uncertain whether I can come to see you tomorrow, however much I may want to; but certainly it will be in a few days, but only in the afternoon. My affairs have become very complicated at present; more of this when I see you— Give my regards to your children, who are dear to me and press them all to your heart—for the Magister a slight box on the ears, for the chief bailiff a ceremonious bow. Let the violoncello apply himself; starting on the left bank of the Danube he is to play until everyone has crossed from the right bank of the Danube. In this way the population will soon be increased. What's more I am confident of the route over the Danube that I have already set; with *courage* one may gain any objective if *righteous*. I kiss your hands many times over. Remember with favor your friend

Beethoven

Do not send a carriage, then; I'd rather *risk* it than a *carriage! The music that I promised is coming from the city.*

—The Magister was the tutor, Brauchle, and the chief bailiff, or steward, a man named Sperl.[18] The violoncellist was, of course, Linke, whose name probably inspired the drollery about the left (*linke*) bank of the Danube. The postscript has another play on words: *Wagen* (carriage) as a verb means "to risk."

A letter to Brauchle is important from a biographical point of view. It reads:

I had scarcely returned home before I found my brother making lamentable inquiries about the horses— Please do me the favor to go to Lang-Enzersdorf

---

[16] Brauchle was the tutor of the Erdödy children.

[17] Jahn related this incident to the writer [Thayer] with much humor, in the autumn of 1860. (TDR, III, 508, n. 1.)

[18] TDR, III, p. 509, cites some verses written by Sperl on July 20, 1815, a poetical invitation to Beethoven, as probably relating to this letter.

about the horses; take horses *at my expense* in Jederslee, I'll gladly reimburse
you— His sickness (my brother's) is accompanied by a sort of unrest— Let us
be of help where we can, I am *obliged to act thus and not otherwise!*— I await
a speedy fulfillment of my wishes and a friendly answer on the subject from
you— Do not spare expenses; I'll willingly bear them. It is not worth while to
let anyone suffer for the sake of a few dirty florins.

Hastily your friend Beethoven

Best wishes to the dear Countess.

Some time around October 15, Beethoven had returned to Vienna from
Mödling where he had been intermittently during the later summer. And
now another bitter parting: the Erdödys, accompanied by Brauchle, Sperl
and Linke, departed to Croatia.

Turning back to Beethoven's interest in an English market for his compositions, we begin with a letter to an old Bonn acquaintance, Johann Peter
Salomon, who since 1781 had been active in London as composer, conductor
and violinist:

Vienna, June 1, 1815.

My respected countryman!

I have long hoped for the fulfillment of a wish to see *you* in person in London,
and to hear you; but the wish has always been frustrated by manifold hindrances—
And for this reason, since it is not to be the case, I hope you will not deny my
request, which is that you speak with some publisher there, and offer him the
following works for me: a Grand Trio for pianoforte, violin and violoncello (80
ducats); Sonata for pianoforte and violin (60 ducats); Grand Symphony in A
(one of my most excellent); smaller Symphony in F—a Quartet for 2 violins,
viola and violoncello in F minor—a Grand Opera in score, 30 ducats—a Cantata
with choruses and solo voices 30 ducats.—the score of the Battle of Vittoria on
Wellington's victory, 80 ducats and also the pianoforte arrangement (if it has
not, as I am assured, already been published)— I have set down the honorarium
of a few works which I think fair for England, but leave it to you in the case
of these as well as the others, to do what you think best as to my fee.

I hear, indeed, that *Cramer* is also a publisher[19] but my pupil Ries wrote me
recently that he *had publicly expressed himself against my compositions*, I hope
for no other reason than *the good of art*, wherefore I have no objection to offer.
However if Cramer wants any of these injurious works of art, he is just as agreeable to me as any other publisher.— I only reserve to myself the privilege of also
giving the same works to my local publisher so that the works will appear in
London and *Vienna* only and simultaneously.—

Perhaps you may be able to point out to me in what manner I may get from
the Prince Regent at least the copyist's charges for the *Battle Symphony* on
Wellington's Victory at the Battle of Vittoria, which I gave him, for I have long

[19] Johann Baptist Cramer (1771-1858), the
well-known pianist, had long dabbled in
publishing ventures: in 1805 as Cramer and
Keys, in 1812 with Samuel Chappell, and in
1824 as Cramer, Addison and Beale.

ago abandoned all hope of ever getting anything more, I was not even vouchsafed an answer as to whether I might dedicate the work to the Prince Regent when I publish it. I hear even that the work has already been published in London in pianoforte arrangement,[20] what a fate for a composer!!! While the English and German newspapers are full of reports concerning the success of this work as performed at the Drury Lane Theatre, and the theatre itself has had some takings from it, the composer does not even have a friendly line to show touching it, not even the expense of copying. Besides all this, he has been denied all profit; for if it is true that the pianoforte arrangement is already published, no German publisher will take it. It is probable that the pianoforte arrangement will soon appear in a reprint by a German publisher and I will lose honor and honorarium.— Your well-known noble character bids me hope that you will take an interest in the matter and show yourself active in my service. The wretched paper money of our country has already been reduced to one-fifth of its value, so I was treated according to the scale. But after much urging I received the full standard though with a considerable loss. But now we have again reached a point where the currency is worth much less than one-fifth of its value, and I am confronted for the second time with the prospect that my salary will be reduced to *nothing* without recourse of any kind.— My only earnings now come from my compositions. If I could count on their sale in England it would be very advantageous to me.— Count on my boundless gratitude. I hope for a speedy, a very speedy answer from you.

Your admirer and friend Ludwig van Beethoven.

The letters to Smart, Salomon and Ries were not in vain; through their efforts, especially Salomon's, Mr. Robert Birchall, Music Publisher of No. 133 New Bond St., was induced to purchase four of the works enumerated by Häring, viz., the pianoforte arrangements of the "Wellington's Victory," Op. 91, and Symphony in A, Op. 92; the Trio in B-flat, Op. 97, and the Sonata for Pianoforte and Violin, Op. 96, for "the sum of one hundred and thirty gold Dutch ducats—value in English currency, sixty-five pounds." The correspondence between the composer and publisher begins with a letter from Beethoven, dated October 28th, in which he informed Birchall that the Battle Symphony in pianoforte arrangement had been sent ahead of the other three works. He urged him to print it speedily for reasons which "Hr. Salomon will have the goodness to explain."

We now reach one of the most important and at the same time most melancholy events in Beethoven's life—an event which exerted the profoundest influence on the rest of his life—the death of his brother Carl Caspar. We introduce it with that brother's last will and testament:

Certain that all men must die and feeling that I am near this goal, but in the full possession of my understanding, I have freely and voluntarily deemed it good to make these, my last dispositions.

[20] According to Kinsky-Halm (KHV, p. 255), the first publication of Op. 91 was not until January, 1816, by Birchall in London, in pianoforte transcription.

1. I commend my soul to the mercy of God, but my body to the earth from which it came and desire that it be buried in the simplest manner in accordance with the rites of Christian Catholicism.

2. Immediately after my death, four holy masses are to be said, to which end I set apart 4 florins.

3. My heirs general are commanded to pay the pious legacies according to law.

4. As my wife at our marriage brought me and paid over 2000 fl. in B. bonds, for which I gave no receipt, I acknowledge receipt of these 2000 fl. in B. bonds and desire that these 2000 fl. in B. bonds as also the deposit be rectified in accordance with the existing marriage contract.

5. I appoint my brother Ludwig van Beethoven guardian. Inasmuch as this, my deeply beloved brother has often aided me with true brotherly love in the most magnanimous and noblest manner, I ask, in full confidence and trust in his noble heart, that he shall bestow the love and friendship which he often showed me, upon my son Karl, and do all that is possible to promote the intellectual training and further welfare of my son. I know that he will not deny me this, my request.

6. Convinced of the uprightness of Hrn. Dr. Schönauer, Appellate and Court Advocate, I appoint him Curator for probate, as also for my son Karl with the understanding that he be consulted in all matters concerning the property of my son.

7. The appointment of heirs being the essential matter in a testament, I appoint my beloved wife Johanna, born Reiss, and my son Karl, heirs general to all my property in equal portions after the deduction of my existing debts and the above bequests.

8. The wagon, horse, goat, peacocks and the plants growing in vessels in the garden are the property of my wife, since these objects were all purchased with money from the legacy received from her grandfather.

In witness whereof, I have not only signed this, my last will with my own hand, but to aid in its execution have also called in three witnesses.

Thus done, Vienna, November 14, 1815.

Carl van Beethoven,
m. p.

Carl Gaber, m. p.
House owner, Breitenfeld No. 9.
Benedikt Gaber, m. p.
House owner, Breitenfeld No. 25.
Johann Naumann, m. p.
House No. 5, Breitenfeld.
("This testament was delivered under seal to the R. I. L. Austrian General Court, by the Karl Scheffer Solicitor Dr. Schönauer, on November 17, 1815, etc.")

The autograph preserved in the City Archives in Vienna shows that the first sentence in Section 5 read originally: "Along with my wife I appoint my brother Ludwig van Beethoven co-guardian." The phrase "Along with my wife" and the "co-" were crossed out. The following fragment in Beethoven's writing, preserved at the Beethoven-Haus in Bonn explains the reason for the change: "I knew nothing about the fact that a testament had been made; however, I came upon it by chance. If what I had seen was really to be the *original text*, then passages had to be stricken out. This I had my brother bring about since I did not wish to be bound up in this with such a bad woman in a matter of such importance as the education of the child."[21]—

CODICIL TO MY WILL

Having learned that my brother, Hr. Ludwig van Beethoven, desires after my death to take wholly to himself my son Karl, and wholly to withdraw him from the supervision and training of his mother, and inasmuch as the best of harmony does not exist between my brother and my wife, I have found it necessary to add to my will that I by no means desire that my son be taken away from his mother, but that he shall always and so long as his future career permits remain with his mother, to which end the guardianship of him is to be exercised by her as well as my brother. Only by unity can the object which I had in view in appointing my brother guardian of my son, be attained, wherefore, for the welfare of my child, I recommend *compliance* to my wife and more *moderation* to my brother.

God permit them to be harmonious for the sake of my child's welfare. This is the last wish of the dying husband and brother.

Vienna, November 14, 1815.

Carl van Beethoven

m. p.

We, the undersigned, certify in consonance with truth that Carl van Beethoven declared in our presence that he had read the statement on the opposite page and that the same is in accordance with his will, finally we certify that he signed it with his own hand in our presence and requested us to witness the act.

Thus done on November 14, 1815.

Carl Gaber, m. p.

Benedikt Gaber, m. p.

Johann Neumann, m. p.

("This codicil was delivered under seal to the R. I. L. Austrian General Court by the Karl Scheffer Solicitor Dr. Schönauer, on Nov. 17, 1815, etc.")

On November 20, 1815, the *Wiener Zeitung* printed the announcement that Hr. Carl van Beethoven, Cashier in the R. I. Bank and Chief Treasury, aged 38 years,[22] died of consumption on November 16. And so in his own house died the brother Carl whose last moments came with a suddenness which aroused his brother's suspicions that the end had been hastened by poison! Nor would he be satisfied upon the matter until his friend Bertolini had made a post mortem examination "whereby the lack of foundation for the suspicion was proved."

A few weeks before his death, Carl had applied for leave of absence from

[21] See Dr. Dagmar Weise, "Beethoven, Entwurf einer Denkschrift," in *Veröffentlichungen des Beethoven-Hauses in Bonn*, III, No. 1 (1953), p. 13.

[22] Actually he was 41½ years old since he was baptized on April 8, 1774. (TDR, III, 519, n. 1.)

his office on the score of his feeble condition; but his petition was refused in a document on which Beethoven afterwards wrote: "This miserable financial product caused the death of my brother, since he was really so sick that he could not carry out his occupation without hastening his death;—a beautiful testimony to this rough high official. L. van Beeth."[23] In fact, however, it made probably little difference; his was evidently one of those common cases of phthisis, where the patient, except to the experienced eye, shows no signs of immediate danger; who at the last moments finds himself free from pain and blessed with a buoyancy of spirit that gives him vain hopes of a prolonged life. It is the last flickering of the flame, as the skillful physician well knows.

As above noted, Carl van Beethoven's will was deposited with the proper authorities on the 17th, and "the R. I. L. Austrian Landrecht [General Court] on November 22, 1815, appointed the widow of the deceased, Johanna van Beethoven, guardian, the brother of the deceased, Ludwig van Beethoven, associate guardian of the minor son Karl." And so, for the present, we will leave the matter.

There is a striking incongruity between Beethoven's pleas of poverty in his letters to correspondents in England at this period and the facts drawn from official and other authentic sources. Let us tarry a moment on this point.

He was now, at the end of 1815, in the regular receipt of his annuity, 3400 florins in notes of redemption; in March and April the arrears, 4987 florins in such notes, had been paid him; the profits of his concerts since January 1, 1814, with presents from crowned heads and others were, if we may trust Schindler, who appears to speak from accurate knowledge, sufficient in amount to purchase somewhat later the seven bank-shares, which at his death, "according to the price current on the day of his death," had a value in convention-coin of 7441 florins; Neate had paid him 75 guineas; for the works sold to Steiner and Co. he had "been wholly compensated"; in March (1816) he received from Mr. Birchall 65 pounds sterling; and there were payments to him from Thomson and others, the aggregate of which cannot be determined.

This incongruity is not essentially diminished either by his taxes—sixty pounds for 1814, he tells Thomson—nor by the 10,000 florins V.S. expended for the benefit of his brother, whether the "Vienna Standard" in the letter to Ries given below be understood as the old five for one, or the new in notes of redemption; for this fraternal charity extended back over a series of years. In this letter to Ries, the reader will observe also a remarkable instance of its writer's occasional great carelessness of statement, where he speaks of

[23] Beethoven's note, given in full (Thayer had quoted only the first phrase) and the answer of October 23rd by Carl's employers to his petition have been published by Schiedermair, "Neue Schriftstücke zu Beet- hovens Vormundschaft über seinen Neffen," NBJ, VIII (1938), pp. 59-60. While the request for leave was refused, his employers considered favorably the idea of lightening his duties.

his "entire loss of salary" for several years; for the Archduke's share had throughout been punctually paid; not to mention again the receipt of what had for a time been withheld of the Kinsky and Lobkowitz subscriptions. The omission of these facts in this and other letters, imparted to Ries an utterly false impression; and on their publication in 1838, to the public also. Hence the general belief that Beethoven was now in very straitened circumstances, and that Carl's widow and child had been left in abject poverty. The truth as to them was this: that the property left them produced an annual income, which with the widow's pension amounted at this time to above 1500 florins. From the day that Beethoven assumed the office of guardian and took possession of the child, he had a valid claim upon the mother for a part of the costs of maintaining him—a claim soon made good by legal process. If he afterward elected to suffer in his own finances rather than press his sister-in-law, this is no justification of the heedless statements in some of his letters now—a truth to be held in mind. And now the letter to Ferdinand Ries:

Wednesday, November 22, Vienna, 1815.

Dear R!

I hasten to write you that today I sent the pianoforte arrangement of the Symphony in A by post to the house of Thomas Coutts and Co. As the Court is not here, couriers go not at all or seldom, and this besides is the safest way.— The Symphony should appear around March; I will fix the day. It has occupied too much time for me to make the term shorter. More time may be taken with the Trio and the Sonata for violin, and both will be in London in a few weeks— I urgently beg of you, dear Ries, to make this matter your concern and to see that I get the money. It will cost a great deal before everything gets there and I need it— I had to lose 600 fl. annually of my salary— At the time of the banknotes it was nothing,—then came the notes of redemption and because of them I lost the 600 fl. with several years of vexation and entire loss of salary— Now we have reached a point where the notes of redemption are worse than the bank-notes were before. I pay 1000 fl. for house-rent; imagine for yourself the misery caused by paper money— My poor unfortunate brother has just died. He had a bad wife. I may say he had consumption for several years, and to make life easier for him I gave what I may estimate at 10,000 fl. V. S. True that is nothing for an Englishman, but very much for a poor German, or rather Austrian. The poor man had changed greatly in the last few years and I can say that I sincerely lament him, and I am now glad that I can say to myself that I neglected nothing in respect of care for him— Tell H. B[irchall] to repay H. Salomon and you the cost of postage for your letters to me and mine to you. He may deduct it from the sum which he is to pay me. I want those who labor for me to suffer as little as possible—
Wellington's Victory at the Battle of Victoria (this is also the title on the pianoforte arrangement) must have reached Th. Coutts and Co. long ago. Herr Birchall need not pay the honorarium until he has received all the works— Make haste so that I may know the *day* when H. B. will publish the pianoforte arrangement— For today, no more except the warmest commendation of my affairs to

you; I am always at your service in all respects.— Affectionately Farewell, dear R!
Your friend Beethoven

On the same day he wrote to Birchall concerning the shipments—promising "the Trio and the Sonata in a fortnight" and asked that the sum of 130 gold ducats be paid to Thomas Coutts and Co. The Trio and the Sonata, however, were not forwarded until the 3rd of February—a decidedly long "fortnight."

In those days £65 was no small sum for the mere right of republication in England of these pianoforte works and arrangements, and Ries richly merited these words of his old master:[24] "And now my heartiest thanks, dear Ries, for all the kindness you have shown to me, and particularly for the corrections. Heaven bless you and make your progress even greater, in which I take the most heart-felt interest." Ries, writing on September 29th for Salomon, who had broken his right shoulder in a fall from his horse, informed Beethoven that at that date the three overtures purchased by Neate for the Philharmonic Society had not reached London. Beethoven, in December, repeated this to Neate, who was still in Vienna, adding, in substance, his readiness to make any desired written agreement about these things in England. Salomon's misfortune occurred in August; he lingered only until the 28th of November. No higher proof of his reputation in England can be given than the fact that the remains of this Bonn violinist rest near those of Handel in Westminster Abbey.

About the first of December, "a magisterial deputation solemnly delivered" into the hands of Beethoven a certificate conferring upon him the citizenship of Vienna in acknowledgement of his benevolent services on behalf of St. Mark's Hospital.

Schindler somewhere censures the Gesellschaft der Musikfreunde for its long delay in making Beethoven an honorary member. It did what was better. Hardly was it organized, when its directors turned their attention to him; and, in the second year of its legal existence, proposed to him through Zmeskall to compose an oratorio for its use. On the 22d of December, Count Appony reported: "that Hr. L. v. Beethoven, through Hr. v. Zmeskall, had declared his readiness to deliver a large work to the society and that the Board of Management were awaiting his conditions." It was but the course of common propriety—of ordinary delicacy—to leave him free of all obligation to the society until this matter of business should be settled; indeed, that Streicher was one of the principal founders and most influential members of the society is a sufficient pledge, that no disrespect for, nor indifference to, his great merits, had aught to do with the delay, which Schindler blames. We shall find that, so soon as it was certain that Beethoven could not live to fulfill his engagement, the society sent him its honorary diploma. Could it well do this before?

[24] In a letter dated January 20, 1816.

Of noteworthy new friends and acquaintances may be mentioned here Peters, tutor of the young Princes Lobkowitz, and Joseph Karl Bernard, a young literateur and poet—the reviser of Weissenbach's poem—a great admirer of Beethoven's music, soon to be appointed Editor of the official *Wiener Zeitung*. He is the "Bernardus non Sanctus" of the Conversation Books; and the two are the friends whom Beethoven set to music in the text:

Sanct Petrus was ein Fels !	Saint Peter was a rock!
Bernardus war ein Sanct??	Bernardus was a saint??

Another was Anton Halm, "in whose fresh military nature Master Ludwig took delight," says Schindler. He was a native of Styria, and now but twenty-six years of age. After some years' service against Napoleon, he had resigned (1812) his lieutenancy in the 44th Regiment. He was a pianoforte player of very respectable rank, and even before entering the army had appeared in public in Beethoven's C minor Trio, Op. 1, and the C major Pianoforte Concerto, Op. 15. He had now been three years in Hungary, living during the third with his friend, Brunsvik, who gave him a letter to Beethoven upon his departure for Vienna, whither he had come to be tutor in a Greek family named Gyike. "Halm once brought a sonata of his own composition to him," says Czerny, "and when Beethoven pointed out a few errors, Halm retorted that he (B.) had also permitted himself many violations of the rules, Beethoven answered: 'I may do it, but not you.'"

Young Schindler's acquaintance with Beethoven had now advanced a step: He writes:[25]

"Toward the end of February, 1815, I accepted an invitation to become tutor at Brünn. Scarcely arrived there, I was summoned before the police officials. I was questioned as to my relations with some of the tumultuaries of the Vienna University as also certain Italians in whose company I had often been seen in Vienna. As my identification papers, especially the statement concerning the different lectures which I had attended, were not in good order, the latter really faulty—through no fault of mine—I was detained, notwithstanding that a government officer of high standing offered to become my bondsman. After several weeks of correspondence back and forth it was learned that I was not a propagandist and was to be set at liberty. But a whole year of my academic career was lost.

"Again returned to Vienna, I was invited by one of Beethoven's intimate acquaintances to come to an appointed place, as the master wanted to hear the story of the Brünn happening from my own lips. During the relation, Beethoven manifested such sympathetic interest in my disagreeable experiences that I could not refrain from tears. He invited me to come often to the same place and at the same hour, 4 o'clock in the afternoon, where he was to be found nearly every day—reading the newspapers. A handgrasp said still more. The place was a somewhat remote room in the beer-house

[25] I, pp. 230-31.

'Zum Rosenstock' in the Ballgässchen. I was there right often and came to know the place as a quasi-crypt of a number of Josephites of the first water, to whom our master presented no discordant note, for his republican creed had already received a considerable blow through a more intimate acquaintance with the English Constitution. A captain of the Emperor's bodyguard and Herr Pinterics, widely known in musical Vienna, who played an important role in the life of Franz Schubert, were the closest companions of the master and, in the exchange of political views, his seconds actively and passively. From this place I soon began to accompany him on his walks."

But Schindler's intimacy with Beethoven was not yet such as to save him from errors when writing of this time. Thus he gravely assures us that a concert which took place on the 25th of December "provided the impulse which led the Magistracy of Vienna to elect our master to honorary citizenship." And yet the "solemn delivery" of the diploma is already an item of news in the Vienna newspapers of December 15. This concert, in the large Redoutensaal, conducted by Beethoven was for the benefit of the *Bürgerspitalfond* (Citizens' Hospital Fund) and the works performed were "an entirely new overture" (that in C, known as the "Namensfeier"); "a new chorus on Goethe's poem 'Die Meeresstille'"; *Christus am Ölberg.* Between the cantata and the oratorio, Franz Stauffer, "the twelve-year-old son of a citizen of Vienna," played a "Rondo brillant" by Hummel.

The compositions which are known or, on good grounds, are supposed to belong to the year 1815 are:

Canon. "Brauchle, Linke," WoO 167.[26]
Canon. "Glück zum neuen Jahr," for Baron Pasqualati, WoO 165.
Canon. "Kurz ist der Schmerz" (Schiller's *Jungfrau von Orleans*), WoO 166, 2nd version, for Ludwig Spohr's album. At the end is written "Vienna, March 3rd, 1815." The dedication reads: "May you always remember me with affection, dear Spohr, wherever you find true art and true artists, from your Ludwig van Beethoven."[27]
"Das Geheimnis" (Wessenberg), WoO 145.
"Es ist vollbracht" for Bass, Chorus and Orchestra, closing song for Treitschke's *Die Ehrenpforten*, WoO 97.
"Meeresstille und Glückliche Fahrt" for Chorus and Orchestra (Goethe), Op. 112.
"Merkenstein" for Two Voices and Pianoforte (Rupprecht), Op. 100.
Music for Friedrich Duncker's tragedy *Leonore Prohaska*, WoO 96: (1) Krieger-Chor (2) Romanze (3) Melodram (4) Trauermarsch (orchestration in B minor of March from Op. 26).

[26] This canon, written on the names of two of the Erdödy circle, the tutor Brauchle and the cellist Linke, was probably written this summer when Beethoven was seeing a good deal of the Countess and her family at their home in Jederslee. See G. Haupt, "Grafin Erdödy und J. X. Brauchle" in *Der Bär* (Leipzig, 1927), p. 81.

[27] See Spohr's *Selbstbiographie* (Cassel, 1860), I, pp. 213 and 216 opp.

Overture "zur Namensfeier," Op. 115.

Twelve Folk Songs, WoO 157: 2 English, 5 Irish, 1 Jacobean, 2 Scottish, 1 Sicilian, 1 Venetian. Kinsky-Halm believes that some of these songs were written in 1814 or earlier.[28]

Two Sonatas for Pianoforte and Violoncello, Op. 102.

The ascertained publications of the year are:

By Mechetti:

"Des Kriegers Abschied" (Reissig), WoO 143.

Polonaise for Pianoforte, Op. 89, dedicated to Empress Elisabeth Alexiewna of Russia.

By *Selam*, almanac edited by I. F. Castelli:

"Merkenstein" (Rupprecht), WoO 144.

By Steiner:

"Es ist vollbracht" for Bass, Chorus and Orchestra, closing song for Treitschke's *Die Ehrenpforten*, WoO 97.

Sonata for Pianoforte, Op. 90, dedicated to Count Moritz Lichnowsky.

[28] KHV, p. 657.

CHAPTER XXIX

THE YEAR 1816

THE NEPHEW IN GIANNATASIO
DEL RIO'S SCHOOL—NEGOTIATIONS WITH RIES,
BIRCHALL AND NEATE

COMPARED with the years immediately preceding, the year 1816 is comparatively barren of large incidents in the life of Beethoven; its recorded history, therefore, is to be found to a still larger extent than before in the composer's extended correspondence together with explanatory annotations. Some of the letters, especially those written to his English friends, are likely to make a somewhat melancholy, and to that extent erroneous, impression. The real record of the writer finds expression in the letters which he wrote to Steiner and Co. and Zmeskall. These are bubbling over with playfulness and jocularity, proving that the writer was generally in a cheerful humor and in this year was anything but the melancholy Beethoven of the romance writers. He seems to have endured the rapid and disquieting increase in his malady, an inevitable consequence of the exertions and excitement attending the rehearsing and conducting of so many large concerts, with surprising patience and resignation. And why not? His pecuniary affairs were in good condition, notwithstanding his lamentations to Ries and others; he had won his lawsuit with his brother's widow, and his artistic ambition must have found complete satisfaction in the great fame which he had won. A letter concerning a new operatic project first invites attention. The eight roles which Madame Milder had played in the past summer in Berlin, had given such keen delight that she had been reengaged for a second and much longer series. Domestic troubles and sorrows, in which her husband, the jeweler Hauptmann, appears to have been entirely the guilty party and which embittered all her future life, rendered her utterly unable for the present to appear upon the stage; and "because of illness and weakness" it was not until several weeks after her return from the baths at Pyrmont that she could begin the new engagement on October 3rd. Meantime, in Berlin *Fidelio* had been put upon the boards and "given for the first time on October 11th with great success." "This opera," said the Berlin *Dramaturgisches Wochenblatt* in its notice of the event, "bears within itself the seeds of a dramatico-musical reformation and will hasten the end of the bastard music." And yet on this evening, the Leonore was Mme. Schultze—Schuppanzigh's sister-in-law. When, three days after, Mme. Milder took the part, its greatness was for the first time fully appreciated; and of the twenty-four evenings to which her engagement extended, this greatest representative then living of Gluck's grandest inspirations devoted eleven to *Fidelio*. This triumph of his opera in Berlin drew from the composer a letter (dated January 6, 1816) full of expressions of gratitude and enthusiastic appreciation of the singer's talents, and giving voice, too, to a rekindled dramatic ambition. He says:

... If you were to beg Baron de la Motte Fouqué[1]—in my name—to invent a grand opera subject which would at the same time be adapted to *you*, it would do a great service to me and the German stage.— I should like, moreover, to compose it exclusively for the *Berlin stage* as I shall never bring about another opera for the parsimonious management here. . . .

The letter ends with a musical joke on the name "Hauptmann."[2]

ich küs - se sie   drück - te sie an   mein Herz
[I   kiss ___ you   press ___ you to   my   heart.]

Ich   der   Haupt - man der   Hauptman
[I'm   the   head - man the   headman

(Fort mit allen übrigen falschen Hauptmännern)
[Away with all other false headmen]

The next letter relates to the oratorio for the Gesellschaft der Musikfreunde:

Friday, February 9th, 1816.

My dear Zmeskall!

With dismay I observe for the first time today that I have not yet answered the application of the Gesellschaft der Musikfreunde of the Austrian capital for an oratorio. The death of my brother two months ago, the guardianship of my nephew which thereby devolved upon me, together with many other unpleasant circumstances and occurrences are the cause of my tardy reply.— Meanwhile the poem by Herr von Seyfried is already begun and I shall also soon set the same to music. That the commission is highly honorable, I scarcely need tell you; that is self-evident, and I shall try to execute it as worthily as my small

---

[1] Friedrich de la Motte-Fouqué (1777-1843), author of "Undine."

[2] The musical reference in the first measure

to the *Fidelio Overture* in E is undoubtedly intentional.

powers will allow— As regards the *artistic means* to be employed in the performance I shall be considerate, but wish to be allowed to depart *from those already
introduced*. I hope that I have made myself understood in this matter. As they
insist upon knowing what honorarium I ask, I inquire in turn whether the
Society thinks 400 ducats in gold agreeable for such a work. I again beg pardon
of the Society for the tardiness of my answer; meanwhile, you, my dear friend
have at least reported by word of mouth my readiness to compose the work,
before now, which sets my mind measurably at ease— My dear Z. I am with
great esteem your friend

Ludwig van Beethoven

The next selections require the preliminary statement of certain facts.
Beethoven's dissatisfaction at the appointment (on November 22, 1815) of
his sister-in-law as the guardian of her son—now nine years old—was expressed in an appeal to the Upper Austrian *Landrecht* on the 28th,[3] to transfer
the guardianship to himself. Next day, the 29th, that tribunal ordered the
petitioner and Dr. Schönauer to appear before it in this matter on December
2nd at 10 o'clock a.m. At that time the subject was deferred to the same
hour on the 13th. Beethoven then appeared and declared that he could
produce "weighty reasons why the widow should be entirely excluded from
the guardianship." Whereupon, on the 15th, it was ordered that he produce
those grounds within three days, "failing which, the preparation of the
guardianship decree to the widow would be proceeded without further
delay." The same day Beethoven signed a petition to the City Magistrates
for an official certificate concerning the "condemnation of his [Karl's]
mother, Johanna van Beethoven, on an investigation for infidelity." The
magistrate answered him on the same day through their secretary that they
could not legally grant him a copy of the judgment against her, but would
communicate the "necessary disclosures" to the tribunal. This was done on
the 21st. —⊷{The day before, December 20th, Beethoven wrote a long document to the *Landrecht* presenting his case.[4] In it he emphasized that the
codicil of his brother's will, which divided the guardianship between Johanna
and himself, had been forced behind his back upon the dying man for
signature by his wife.}⊷— Then came the Christmas holidays, and no further
action was taken until the 9th of January, when a decision was rendered
in Beethoven's favor, and he was ordered to appear on the 19th to take the
"vows for the performance of his duties." He complied, and on the outside of
this order is written: "Today appeared Ludwig van Beethoven as the legally
appointed guardian of his nephew Karl and vowed with solemn handgrasp
before the assembled council to perform his duties."

This document also empowered the new guardian to take possession of

[3] First published by O. E. Deutsch, "Drei
neue Beethoven-Briefe" in *Österreiche Musikzeitschrift*, VIII (1953), pp. 79ff. In *The
Letters of Beethoven* Miss Anderson gives all
the documents relating to Beethoven's litigation over the guardianship of his nephew from
1815 to 1820, in Vol. III, Appendix C.

[4] First published by Schiedermair, *NBJ*, VIII
(1938), pp. 62ff.

the boy, who of course was still with his mother. But what to do with him? Beethoven could not take him into his own lodging; a child of that age needs a woman's care and tenderness.

A certain Cajetan Giannatasio del Rio was at that time proprietor and manager of a private school in the city for boys, which enjoyed a high and deserved reputation. His family consisted of his wife and two highly accomplished daughters, Fanny and Anna (Nanni), young women of fine talents, of much musical taste and culture, and—especially the elder—enthusiasts for Beethoven's music. The composer, accompanied by his friend Karl Bernard and the boy, visited and inspected the school, and was so much pleased with it and the family, that he determined to withdraw his nephew from the public school, and place him there as pupil and boarder. On February 1st, he wrote to Giannatasio:

With sincere pleasure I inform you that at last on tomorrow I shall bring to you the precious pledge that has been entrusted to me.— Moreover I beg of you again under no circumstances to permit the mother to exercise any influence. How or when she may see him, all this I will talk over with you tomorrow— You may impress this also on your servants, for *mine* in another matter was *bribed by her!*— More about this will follow by word of mouth, though silence would be preferable to me— But for the sake of your future citizen of the world, this melancholy communication is necessary. . . .

[In Karl's hand]: I am very glad to come to you, and am your Karl van Beethoven.

The next day, February 2, the boy was taken from his mother. The intolerable annoyance caused by her appearing in person or sending a messenger daily to take him from the school, drew from Giannatasio on the 11th a written application to the guardian for "a formal authority in a few lines for refusing without further ado to permit her to fetch her son." In his reply, Beethoven writes: "as regards the mother I request that on the plea that he is busy you do not admit her to him at all." He then consulted Joseph Edler von Schmerling, a member of the *Landrecht*, upon the measures proper for him to adopt, and communicated that gentleman's advice to Giannatasio by letter. The same day, taking Bernard with him, he went to the school, and there meeting Giannatasio, the three prepared a formal petition to the *Landrecht*, praying that tribunal to grant the guardian plenary authority to exclude the widow and her agents from all or any direct communication with the boy. This was signed by Beethoven and immediately presented. On the 20th, the *Landrecht* granted, essentially, this petition; but its decree contained this proviso: that the mother might still visit her son "in his leisure hours, without disturbing the course of his education or the domestic arrangements, in the company of a person to be appointed by the guardian or the director of the educational institution." Armed with this authority, Giannatasio on March 8th informed in writing "Madame Jeannette de Beethoven, Vorstadt, Alsergasse, No. 121," that she has in future "to apply solely to the uncle as to whether, how and when" she can see her son. And thus this wretched business again for the present rested. In these days belongs a letter by Beethoven to Giannatasio which begins:

The Queen of Night surprised us yesterday and also delivered a veritable anathema against you; she showed her usual impertinence and malice against me and set me back for a moment and I almost believed that what she said was right; but when I reached home later I received the result of the decision of the *Landrechte* which turns out to be just *what was desired*. I communicate the most necessary points although you will probably *receive a copy of it* towards evening. . . .

Neate was now gone to London. On his departure Beethoven wrote in his album two canons entitled "Das Schweigen" (Silence) and "Das Reden" (Speech), adding, with the date, "January 24, 1816," the words: "My dear English compatriot in *silence* and in *speech* remember your sincere friend Ludwig van Beethoven."

The document concerning the sale of the three overtures to the Philharmonic Society, which Beethoven promised to give Neate, ran as follows:

Hr. Neate has received from me in the month of July, 1816 [*sic*] three overtures in the name of the Philharmonic Society in London and has paid me an honorarium of 75 guineas for the same in consideration of which I bind myself to permit them *nowhere else* to be published in parts[x] although I have the right to perform *the same* wherever I please as well as to publish them in pianoforte arrangement, though not before Hr. Neate shall have written me that they have been performed in London:— Moreover, Hr. Neate has assured me that he will kindly take it upon himself that the Philharmonic Society after a period of one or two years will permit me to engrave and publish these three overtures *in score and in parts*, inasmuch as I can do this only with their consent—with which I present my compliments to the P. S.

Vienna, February 5, 1816.   Ludwig van Beethoven[5]

       [x] or in score

The three overtures had already been sold to Steiner, but were not published until many years later.[6] The works entrusted to him, as remembered by Mr. Neate forty-five years afterwards, were: 1) a copy of the Violin Concerto, Op. 61, with a transcription of the solo for Pianoforte on the same pages, which Beethoven said he himself had arranged and was effective; 2) the two Sonatas for Pianoforte and Violoncello, Op. 102, with a dedication to Neate; 3) the Seventh Symphony in score; 4) *Fidelio* in score; and 5) the String Quartet in F minor, Op. 95—all in manuscript.[7] There is some reason to think that besides these works Neate also took a copy of *Der*

---

[5] In the first sentence Beethoven, of course, meant 1815. For a facsimile of the autograph and the history of this letter see Sonneck, *Beethoven Letters in America*, p. 88.

[6] The Overture to the *Ruinen von Athen* in 1823, the "Namensfeier" Overture in 1825, and the Overture to *König Stephan* in 1826. (Cf. TDR, III, 544-45.)

[7] Why the concerto was supposed to be in manuscript is not clear since it was published in both forms in 1808. (TDR, III, 543.)

glorreiche Augenblick. On January 20, Beethoven wrote the following letter to Ries in London:

Vienna, January 20, 1816

My dear Riess I see from your letter of January 18[8] that you have safely received both works[9]— As no couriers are going, the *post* is probably the safest, but it costs a great deal. I will send you the bill for what I have paid here for *copying* and *postage* soon. It is very little for an Englishman but much more for a *poor Austrian musician!* See that Hr. B[irchall] recompenses me for this, since *for England* he has the compositions very cheaply—Neate, who has been about to go every moment, but always remains, will bring the overtures with him. Over and over again I have explained to him the injunctions touching them given by you and our deceased S[alomon]—

The symphony will be dedicated to the *Empress of Russia*— The *pianoforte arrangement of the Symphony in A* must not be published before the *month of June,* however, since the *local publisher* cannot do so before this— Tell this at once to Hr. B., my good R.—

The Sonata with violin, which will go from here by the next post, may also *be published* in London *in the month of May*—but the Trio later. (It will also arrive by the next post), I will fix the date myself later.—

And now my heartiest thanks, dear R, for all the kindness you have shown to me and particularly for the corrections.— Heaven bless you and make your progress ever greater in which I take the heartiest interest— Commend me to *your wife.*

As always, your sincere friend,
Ludwig van Beethoven

It is necessary here to state certain facts, both to explain the failure of Mr. Neate to sell any of these works to the London publishers, and to render some of the letters to come intelligible.

The Philharmonic Society was an association of the first musicians of London and its vicinity, and no city on earth could at that time present such an array of great names. Here are a few of them taken alphabetically from its roll: Attwood, Ayrton, Bridgetower, Clementi, Cramer, Carnaby, Dragonetti, Horsley, Lindley, Mazzinghi, Mori, Naldi, Novello, Ries, Shield, Smart, Spagnoletti, Viotti, Watts, S. Webbe, Yaniewicz. Imagine the disappointment of these men, fresh from the performance of the C minor Symphony, when they played through the overtures to *Die Ruinen von Athen* and *König Stephan,* which, however interesting to a Hungarian audience as introductions to a patriotic prologue and epilogue in the theatre, possess none of those great qualities expected from Beethoven and demanded in a concert overture! Nor was the "Namensfeier" thought worthy of its author. Ries speaks thus of the matter: "After I had with much trouble persuaded the Philharmonic Society to permit me to order three overtures from him, which should remain its property, he sent me three, not one of which, in

---

[8] Miss Anderson notes that Ries's reply was actually on December 18th from his own notation on Beethoven's letter to Birchall on November 22, 1815 (*A,* II, p. 534, n. 2).
[9] Op. 91 and 92.

view of Beethoven's great name and the character of these concerts, could be performed, because expectation was tense and more than the ordinary was asked of Beethoven. A few years later he published all three and the Society did not think it worth while to complain. Amongst them was the overture to *Die Ruinen von Athen*, which I consider unworthy of him." But when it became known that none of the three—Op. 115 possibly excepted—was new, and that not one of them had been composed to meet the Society's order, is it surprising that this act of Beethoven's was deemed unworthy of him, disrespectful, nay, an insult to the Society, and resented accordingly?

Another matter was personal with Mr. Birchall. That publisher, having at last (early in February) received the last of the works published by him,[10] immediately deposited with Coutts and Co. the sum agreed upon, to the composer's credit, and forwarded the following "Declaration" to Vienna for signature, leaving the day of the month blank—as it still remains—to be inserted when signed:

Received . . . . March, 1816, of Mr. Robert Birchall—Music Seller, 133 New Bond Street, London—the sum of One Hundred and thirty Gold Dutch Ducats, value in English Currency Sixty-five Pounds, for all my Copyright and Interest, present and future, vested or contingent, or otherwise within the United Kingdom of Great Britain and Ireland in the four following Compositions or Pieces of Music composed or arranged by me, viz.:

1st. A Grand Battle Sinfonia, descriptive of the Battle and Victory at Vittoria, adapted for the Pianoforte and dedicated to his Royal Highness, the Prince Regent—40 Ducats.

2nd. A Grand Symphony in the Key of A, adapted to the Pianoforte and dedicated to

3rd. A Grand Trio for the Pianoforte, Violin and Violoncello in the Key of B-flat.

4th. A Sonata for the Pianoforte with an Accompaniment for the Violin, dedicated to

And, in consideration of such payment I hereby for myself, my Executors and Administrators promise and engage to execute a proper Assignment thereof to him, his Executors and Administrators or Assignees at his or their Request and Costs, as he or they shall direct. And I likewise promise and engage as above, that none of the above shall be published in any foreign Country, before the time and day fixed and agreed on for such Publication between R. Birchall and myself shall arrive.

Instead of *this* document, so indispensable for his security, the publisher received a new demand from Beethoven!—one for five pounds additional, as per memorandum:

Copying	1.10.0
Postage to Amsterdam	1. 0.0
Trio	2.10.0
	£5.0.0

[10] Through Ries. See *A* 609.

--⚜{This was transmitted through a letter to Ries dated February 10. On February 28 and April 3 he reiterated his demand for the additional ten ducats, equivalent to five pounds.}⚜-- Then he wrote the following letter in May, portions of which were suppressed when printed by Ries:

Vienna, May 8, 1816.

My dear Ries:

My answer to your letter comes somewhat tardily; but I was ill, had much to do and it was impossible for me to answer you sooner.— Now only the most necessary things—not a heller of the 10 ducats in gold has as yet arrived, and I am already beginning to believe, that the Englishmen, too, are only magnanimous in foreign lands; so also with the *Prince Regent* from whom I have not even received the copyists' fees for *my Battle which was sent* to him, nor even written or oral thanks.[11] *Fries deducted 6 fl.* Convention money here from the amount received from Birchall as well as 15 fl. Convention money for postage. Tell B this—and see that you yourself get the draft for the 10 ducats, otherwise it will be like the first time— What you *tell me about Neate's undertaking would be desirable for me.* I need it; my salary amounts to 3400 florins in paper, I pay 1100 house-rent, and my servant and his wife nearly 900 fl., you can figure out what remains. Moreover, I have got to care wholly for my little nephew. Till now he has been in an Institute; this costs me close to 1100 fl. and thus is hard for me, so I must establish myself in decent housekeeping and have him live with me— How much one must earn in order to live here! And yet there is never an end for—for—for—you know it already— As to the dedications, I will wait for another time— A few orders as well as an Akademie would also be welcome from the Philharmonic Society— Besides my dear pupil Ries ought to sit down and dedicate *something good* to me to which the *master would also respond and repay in kind— How shall I send you my portrait?* I hope to have news from *Neate too; urge him on a bit.* Be assured of my sincere interest in your future. *Urge Neate to get to work and to write— My best regards to your wife.* Unfortunately I have none. I found *only one*, whom I shall doubtless *never possess; but I am not a woman-hater* on that account.

Your true friend, Beethoven

The £5 had been deposited with Coutts and Co. on March 15, and the money order was received by Fries and Co. on May 13, as we shall see later, but month after month passed and still the "Declaration" with Beethoven's signature did not arrive. Of the justice, propriety, delicacy of this new demand, nothing need be said; its historical importance is due entirely to the very unfavorable effect which it and the correspondence relating to it produced upon the minds of the London publishers. Mr. Neate was in some degree prepared for the coldness with which those gentlemen received his proposals in Beethoven's behalf, by a letter written to him after the trial of the overtures. One sentence in it he remembered word for

---

[11] The Prince Regent never ordered this work, nor had his permission to present and dedicate it to him been asked before sending it. Beethoven resented the fact that he had not been recompensed until the day of his death. (TK, II, 336, n. 1.)

word: "For God's sake, don't buy anything of Beethoven!" But he was not prepared for the utter refusal in all quarters to listen to him. He besought Mr. Birchall to purchase the overtures. The reply was: "I would not print them, if you would give me them gratis."

As to the score of the Symphony in A (the Seventh), it was folly to expect that the Philharmonic Society would pay a large sum for the manuscript of a work already (March 6) advertised in Vienna for subscription at the price of twenty-five florins.

It is another instance of Beethoven's unlucky tendency to suspect the conduct and motives of others, that seeing in a newspaper a notice of the production of one of his Symphonies by the Philharmonic Society, he at once assumed that it was the Seventh and that Neate had given the use of his manuscript!

Under such circumstances Neate *could* do nothing for Beethoven; nor could he well disclose the true causes of his failure; so the composer characteristically assumed that he *would* do nothing, and, as will be seen, gave vent to his wrath in terms equally bitter and unjust. The letters selected pertaining to these transactions are reserved for their places in chronological order.

Linke's departure with the Erdödys to Croatia was noted in the last chapter; he returned to Vienna in the autumn of 1815 in season to enable Schuppanzigh to begin his winter season of quartets in November. They were given in the hall of the hotel "Zum Römischen Kaiser," and had now ended. So, too, had ended the engagement of Schuppanzigh, Weiss and Linke with Razumovsky. The destruction of his palace, the approach of old age, and failing sight, induced him now to dismiss them with suitable pensions from his service. Schuppanzigh went to Russia; Linke returned to the Erdödys and Weiss remained in Vienna. Before their departure the first two gave each a farewell concert. Schuppanzigh's took place in the palace of Count Deym, the programme being made up entirely of Beethoven's works, viz: Quartet in C major, Op. 59, No. 3; Quintet for Wind-instruments and Pianoforte, Op. 16, Carl Czerny, pianist; and the Septet, Op. 20. Beethoven "entered at the beginning of the quartet" and shared in the deafening applause of the crowded audience.[12]

Concerning this concert Czerny relates the following: "When once, for instance, I played the Quintet with Wind-Instruments with Schuppanzigh, I permitted myself, in a spirit of youthful carelessness, many changes, in the way of adding difficulties to the music, the use of the higher octave, etc.— Beethoven quite rightly took me severely to task in the presence of Schuppanzigh, Linke and the other players. The next day I received the following letter from him, which I copy carefully from the original draft:

[12] See the *Lpz. AMZ*, XVIII (1816), p. 197.

Dear Czerny!

Today I cannot see you, but tomorrow I will call on you myself to have a talk with you.— I burst forth so yesterday that I was sorry after it had happened; but you must pardon that in a composer who would have preferred to hear his work exactly as he wrote it, no matter how beautifully you played in general.— I shall make amends *publicly* at the Violoncello Sonata. Be assured that as an artist I have the greatest wishes for your success and will always try to show myself—

Your true Friend Beethoven

"This letter did more than anything else to cure me of the desire to make changes in the performance of his works, and I wish that it might have the same influence on all pianists."[13]

Linke's concert took place on the 18th of February in the hall of "Zum Römischen Kaiser," the programme, except a Rondoletto for the Violoncello by Romberg, being also entirely Beethoven. Stainer von Felsburg played "a new Pianoforte Sonata,"[14] and Czerny the pianoforte part of the Violoncello Sonata, Op. 69, on which occasion the composer "made amends publicly." And so, except for an occasional visit to Vienna by Linke, two more of our old acquaintances disappear for several years; also Hummel and Wild. Hummel we shall meet again beside Beethoven's deathbed; Wild no more. An album-leaf containing a canon was the farewell to the pianist and composer.

A happy journey, my dear Hummel, think occasionally of your friend, Ludwig van Beethoven, Vienna, April 4, 1816.

On the 20th, Wild gave a little musical festival "in the home of an art-lover," at which he sang the "Adelaide" and "An die Hoffnung," Op. 94. Beethoven was present and played the accompaniments. And this was his farewell to the singer.

On May 15, a letter of condolence to Countess Erdödy was called out by the sudden death of her son in Padua. The lad burst one morning into his

[13] *Allgemeine Wiener Musik-Zeitung*, September 20, 1845. Czerny notes that he was to play the Violoncello Sonata, Op. 69, with Linke the next week.

[14] *Lpz. AMZ, op.cit.*; "A new pianoforte sonata by this master, heard here for the first time, surprised all of his numerous admirers." Which sonata was played is unclear; Schindler (*Biogr.*, I, pp. 240-41) identifies it specifically as Op. 101, but the date on the autograph of this sonata is November, 1816. In his correspondence Beethoven mentioned it for the first time in a letter to Härtel dated July 19, 1816 (*A* 542). Frimmel (*FRBH*, II, pp. 242-43) believes that the sonata played was Op. 90. (Cf. TDR, III, 480 and 586.)

sister's room and, complaining of his head, with a cry of anguish sank dead at her feet. Beethoven labored sadly in his effort to find words of comfort for the stricken mother. On May 13, before he heard the news, he had already written the Countess, so he sent the two letters together. The later letter follows:

Vienna, May 15, 1816.

Dear honored friend!

This letter was already written when today I met Linke and heard of your lamentable fate, the sudden loss of your dear son[15]— How is comfort to be given? Nothing is more painful than the quick unforeseen departure of those who are near us; thus likewise I cannot forget the death of my poor brother. Nothing except—that one can imagine that those who depart quickly suffer less—but I have the deepest sympathy for your irretrievable loss.— Perhaps I have not written you yet that I have not been well for a long time, to this reason for my long silence is to be added the care for my Karl whom I had often contemplated as a companion to your dear son.— I am seized with grief on your account and on my own since I loved your son.— May heaven watch over you, whose state of health may have failed still further, and not increase your suffering which is already so great. Reflect that your son might have been forced to go into battle and might then, like millions of others, have met his death. Besides you are still *mother* to two dear hopeful children.— I hope soon to have word from you. I weep here with you. Do not, however, listen to all the gossip concerning why I have not written you, nor to Linke, who is certainly devoted to you but *very much of a gossip*—and I feel that no go-between is needed between you dear Countess and myself

in haste and respectfully your friend
Beethoven

A few days later the following letter to Neate was written in English, probably by Häring, and only signed by Beethoven:

Vienna, May 18, 1816.

My dear Neate!

By a letter of Mr. Ries, I am acquainted with your happy arrival at London. I am very well pleased with it, and still better I should be pleased if I had learned it by yourself.

Concerning our business, I know well enough that for the performance of the greater works, as: the Symphony, the Cantata, the Chorus, and the Opera, you want the help of the Philharmonic Society, and I hope your endeavour to my advantage will be successful.

[15] There is some confusion about this event. According to Thayer it was Fritzi who died, and in Croatia. However Gunther Haupt in his article "Gräfin Erdödy und J. X. Brauchle" (*Der Bär*, Lpz., 1927, pp. 70ff.) points out (1) that if the death had been in Croatia, it would have had to occur in late 1815 before the trip to Padua, and (2) that of the three children only one was a *son*, August. Marie (Mimi) and Friederike (Fritzi) were the names of the daughters. In another letter to the Countess, Beethoven sends regards to "the daughters" (*A* 722). In a Conversation Book of July-August, 1820, there is the enigmatic entry: "der kleine Gustav in Italien Stad Padua"—["the small Gustav (August) in the Italian city of Padua"]. See Schünemann, II, p. 214.

Mr. Ries gave me notice of your intention to give a concert to my benefit. For this triumph of my art at London I would be indebted to you alone; but an influence still wholesomer on my almost indigent life, would be to have the profit proceeding from this enterprise. You know that in some regard I am now father to the lovely lad you saw with me; hardly I can live alone three months upon my annual salary of 3400 florins in paper, and now the additional burden of maintaining a poor orphan—you conceive how welcome lawful means to improve my circumstances must be to me. As for the Quatuor in F minor, you may sell it without delay to a publisher, and signify me the day of its publication as I should wish it to appear here and abroad on the very day. The same you be pleased to do with the two Sonatas, Op. 102, for pianoforte and violoncello; yet with the latter it needs no haste.

I leave entirely to your judgement to fix terms for both works, to wit, the Quatuor and the Sonatas. The more the better.

Be so kind to write to me immediately for two reasons; 1st, that I may not be obliged to shrink up my shoulders when they ask me if I got letters from you; and 2ndly, that I may know how you do, and if I am in favour with you. Answer me in English if you have to give me happy news (for example, those of giving a concert to my benefit), in French if they are bad ones.

Perhaps you find some lover of music to whom the Trio and the Sonata with the violin, Mr. Ries had sold to Mr. Birchall, or the Symphony arranged for the harpsichord might be dedicated, and from whom there might be expected a present. In expectation of your speedy answer, my dear friend and countryman, I am wholly yours,

Ludwig van Beethoven

We can follow the progress of the business in connection with the compositions to be published in London from the following excerpt from a letter to Ries, which was dated June 11, 1816:

The publisher here has applied to me to have the Trio *published in London on the last day of August,* for which reason I beg of you kindly to speak with Herr B— H. B. can get himself in readiness concerning the pianoforte arrangement of the Symphony in A, since as soon as the publisher here tells me the day I shall immediately let you or B. know—

As I have not heard a syllable from Neate since his arrival in L., I beg you to tell him to give you an answer whether he has sold the Quartet in F minor as I want to publish it here simultaneously, and what I may expect in reference to the Violoncello Sonatas. Of all the other works which I sent by him I am almost ashamed to speak, even to myself for having again been so trustful as to give them to him wholly without conditions trusting that his friendship and care for my interests would find a way— I was given to read a translation of a report in the *Morning Cronigle* about the performance of the Symphony. The same thing will probably happen to this as well as all the other works which I gave to N. as happened to the Battle; I shall probably get nothing for them as I got nothing for that work except to read about the performance in the newspapers. . . .

Here is the place for some excerpts from the diary of Dr. Karl von Bursy, a Courlander, who at this time visited Beethoven with a letter of introduction from his friend Amenda:[16]

"Vienna, June 1.

. . . Beethoven strongly resembled Amenda, especially when he laughed. He enquired most of all about him and expressed feelings of the warmest friendship for him. 'He is a very fine man,' he said. 'I have the misfortune of having all my friends far away from me and I remain alone in hateful Vienna.' He asked me to speak loudly to him because now he was again having particular difficulty in hearing; for that reason he wanted to be in Baden and the country for the summer. He has not been really well for a long time and has composed nothing new. I asked him about Berge's libretto[17] and he said it was very good and with a few changes would probably be suitable for composition. Until now his illness has not permitted this kind of labor and he wishes to write Amenda himself about it. I shouted in his ear that for such work one really has to have leisure and work full time. 'No,' he said, 'Nothing I create is done so continuously without interruption. I always work at several things at a time, first I take up this and then that.' He misunderstood me very often and, when I spoke, had to pay the greatest attention in order to understand me. Naturally this troubled and embarrassed me very much. He also felt the pressure and spoke up himself that much more and indeed very loudly. He told me a great deal about Vienna and his life here. Venom and rancor raged within him. He defies everything and is dissatisfied with everything and blasphemes against Austria and especially against Vienna. He speaks fast and with great animation. Often he beat his fist upon the piano so violently that it made a clear echo in the room. He is not discreet for he quickly confided in me concerning his personal relations and recounted many things about himself and his friends. . . . He had complaints on several counts of the present times. Art no longer stands so high above the ordinary, is no longer so respected and above all is no longer valued in terms of recompense. Beethoven also complained over the bad times in pecuniary matters. . . . 'Why do you remain in Vienna when every foreign ruler would have to make a place for you near his throne?' 'Conditions hold me here,' he said, 'but here things are shabby and niggardly. It could not be worse, from top to bottom everyone is a scoundrel. There is nobody one can trust. What is not down in black and white is not observed by any man, not even by the one with whom you have made an agreement. Moreover one has nothing in Austria, since everything is worthless, that is, paper.' At the time of the Congress Beethoven composed an occasion cantata. The text, he said, was cut and trimmed like a French garden. And yet it never got a definite performance. After many cabals he gave a concert in the Redouten-Saal and received an entrance

---

[16] The diary was first published, with certain passages censored, in the St. Petersburg *Zeitung* in 1854. (TDR, III, 556.)

[17] It will be remembered that in the previous year Amenda sent Beethoven Rudolph von Berge's libretto entitled *Bacchus*.

.ee of 10 ducats from the King of Prussia. Very shabby! Only the Emperor of Russia paid respectably for his ticket with the sum of 200 ducats. The fact that the general manager of the Imperial Theatre, Count Palfi, received a little rebuke for this pleased him very much. He particularly dislikes this man. . . . He is delighted that his Fidelio is given in Berlin so often and with such success. He is saddened by the loss of Milder-Hauptmann. 'Her place is irrecoverable for us,' he said, 'the way she sings cannot be matched by any of the local singers. We could not pay her, therefore she decided to go to Berlin. Music here is very much on the decline. The emperor does nothing for art and the general public puts up with anything. . . .' "

Beethoven had now made up his mind to take his nephew from Giannatasio's care and make a home for him with himself. The removal was to be made at the end of the approaching quarter, and meanwhile Karl was to remain where he was so that he might have proper care during his recovery from the effects of an operation for hernia. Beethoven notified his purpose to Giannatasio on July 28, 1816, and admonished his friend that in the interim the old strictness was to be observed touching the mother's visits. The following passage is from the letter:

As regards the Queen of Night, matters will remain as they have been, and even if the operation should be performed at your place, as he will be ill for a few days and consequently more susceptible and irritable, she is all the less to be admitted to him since all impressions might easily be renewed in K. which we cannot permit. How little we can hope for improvement in her case is shown by the enclosed insipid scrawl which I send you only that you may see how right I am in pursuing the plan against her that was adopted; but this time I did not answer her like a Sarastro but like a sultan.

The surgical operation on the boy was performed by Dr. Smetana; and under the affectionate care which he received at the hands of the Giannatasios he quickly recovered and in September visited his uncle at Baden, going thither with the Giannatasios. Fräulein Fanny tells the story of the visit simply and gracefully:[18]

"While his nephew was still with us, Beethoven once invited us to visit him at Baden where he was spending the summer months, my father and we two daughters with Karl. Although our host had been informed of our coming we soon noticed that no arrangement had been made for our lodging. B. went with us in the evening to a tavern where we were surprised to note that he dickered with the waiter about every roll, but this was because owing to his bad hearing he had frequently been cheated by serving-people. For even then one had to be very close to his ear to make him understand and I recall that I was often greatly embarrassed when I had to pierce through the grayish hairs which concealed his ear. He himself often said:

[18] First published in *Grenzboten* (Leipzig) 1857, Nos. 14 and 15.

'I must have my hair cut!' Looking at him cursorily one thought that his hair was coarse and bristly, but it was very fine and when he put his hand through it, it remained standing in all directions which often looked comical. (Once when he came we noticed a hole in the elbow when he was taking his overcoat off; he must have remembered it for he wanted to put it on again, but said, laughing, taking it completely off: 'You've already seen it!')

"When we came to his lodgings in the afternoon a walk was proposed; but our host would not go along, excusing himself saying he had a great deal to do; but he promised to follow and join us, and did so. But when we came back in the evening there was not a sign of accommodations for our lodging to be seen. B. muttered excuses and accusations against the persons who had been charged with the arrangements and helped us to settle ourselves; O how interesting it was! to move a light sofa with his help. A rather large room in which his pianoforte stood, was cleaned for us girls to use as a bedroom. But sleep remained long absent from us in this musical sanctuary. Yes, and I must confess to my shame that our curiosity and desire to know things led us to examine a large round table which stood in the room. A note-book in particular received our attention. But there was such a confusion of domestic matters, and much of it which to us was illegible that we were amazed; but, behold, one passage I still remember—there it stood: 'My heart runs over at the sight of lovely nature—although she is not here!'—that gave us a great deal to think about. In the morning a very prosaic noise roused us out of our poetical mood! B. also appeared soon with a scratched face, and complained that he had had a quarrel with his servant who was leaving, 'Look,' he said, 'how he has maltreated me!' He complained also that these persons, although they knew that he could not hear, did nothing to make themselves understood. We then took a walk through the beautiful Helenenthal, we girls ahead, then B. and our father. What follows we were able to overhear with strained ears:

"My father thought that B. could rescue himself from his unfortunate domestic conditions only by marriage, did he know anybody, etc. Now our long foreboding was confirmed: he was unhappy in love! Five years ago he had made the acquaintance of a person, a union with whom he would have considered the greatest happiness of his life. It was not to be thought of, almost an impossibility, a chimera—'nevertheless it is now as on the first day.' This harmony, he added, he had not yet discovered! It had never reached a confession, but he could not get it out of his mind! Then there followed a moment which made good for many misunderstandings and grievous conduct on his part; for he acknowledged my father's friendly offer to help him as much as possible in his domestic troubles, and I believe he was convinced of his friendship for him. He spoke again of his unfortunate loss of hearing, of the wretched physical existence which he had endured for a long time. He (B.) was so happy at the noonday meal (in the open air in Helena) that his muse hovered around him! He frequently turned aside and wrote a few measures with the remark: 'My promenade with you cost me some notes but brought in others.' All this happened in September of the year 1816."

That brilliant youth Alois Jeitteles of Brünn, now a student of medicine at Vienna, wrote when hardly twenty-one years of age the beautiful series of songs "An die ferne Geliebte," so exquisitely set to music by Beethoven. Schindler states that the composer thanked the young poet for the happy inspiration; but whether he had found them in a handbook, which is probable, or received them in manuscript, does not appear. But no one can hear them adequately sung without feeling that there is something more in that music than the mere inspiration of the poetry. It was completed not many weeks before the time he wrote in his letter of May 8 to Ries: "I found *only one*, whom I shall doubtless never possess"; and but six months before the above conversation with Giannatasio.

Beethoven's project now was, upon returning to the city, to abandon his tavern life and so arrange his domestic affairs as to have his nephew with him and attend school or study with private tutors—perhaps both. As usual Zmeskall was charged with looking after servants, discovering their qualifications, etc. After Karl should come there would be need of a housekeeper, but meanwhile Beethoven suggested to Zmeskall that he find for him a servant who should be "good, of· decent deportment, well recommended, married and not murderous so that my life may be safe." He returned to Vienna near the end of September.

Peter Joseph Simrock[19] of Bonn, then 24 years of age, was now in Vienna. He was often with Beethoven, in Baden, in his lodging in the Sailerstätte and in the inn "Zur goldenen Birn," where Beethoven often dined after the removal of Giannatasio to that quarter. Mr. Simrock also told the writer that he had no difficulty in making Beethoven understand him if he spoke into his left ear; but anything private or confidential must be communicated in writing. On one occasion the composer handed him paper and pencil, remarking that his servant was an eavesdropper, etc. A few days afterwards when Simrock called again, "Now," said Beethoven, "we can talk, for I have given my servant 5 florins, a kick in the rear and sent him to the devil." Everywhere in public, said Simrock, Beethoven railed at Emperor Franz because of the reduction of the paper money. "Such a rascal ought to be hanged to the first tree," said he. But he was known and the police officials let him do what he pleased. He ate extravagantly at the tavern because he ordered haphazard and sent away what was not to his taste.

Another of Beethoven's visitors just now was Alexander Kyd. This gentleman, since July 25, 1810, a Major-General in the East India Company's Engineer Corps, paid the usual tribute to the climate, and, broken down in health, came to Vienna to put himself under the treatment of Malfatti. He

[19] Simrock (1796-1870) was the son of the Bonn publisher, Nikolaus Simrock, and became his successor in the firm. His Bonn accent undoubtedly facilitated his conversations with Beethoven. (Cf. TDR, III, 566.)

thus made the acquaintance of Dr. Bertolini, who gave to Jahn and the present writer the following details:

Kyd was a great lover of music, and, after his long residence in India, enjoyed to the utmost his present opportunities of hearing it. Bertolini took him to Czerny, who during several visits played to him all the pianoforte works of Beethoven then in print. The General was ravished with these compositions, asked for a complete thematic catalogue of the composer's works, and besought Bertolini to introduce him to their author. This took place on the 28th of September "in the house next to the Colorado Palace," said Bertolini. They found him shaving and looking shockingly, his ruddy face browned by the Baden sun variegated by razor cuts, bits of paper, and soap. As Kyd seated himself crash! went the chair. In the course of the interview, the General, showing the common belief of Beethoven's poverty, proposed to him through the Doctor, to compose a symphony for which he would pay him 200 ducats (£100), and secure its performance by the London Philharmonic Society, not doubting that the profits of the work to the composer would thus amount to £1000. He offered also to take him himself to London. To Beethoven's leaving Vienna just now there really seems to have been no serious impediment, other than his nephew; and the boy was certainly in the best of hands so long as he remained with Giannatasio. However, he did not accept the proposition, nor even the order for the Symphony, because Kyd desired to have it rather like the earlier, than the later ones—that is, somewhat shorter, simpler, and more easy of comprehension than these last. The conclusion of the story as told in the Fischoff manuscript corresponds entirely with the Doctor's relation: "When Bertolini related all this to his friend with sympathetic joy the latter received it in an entirely different spirit. He declared that he would receive dictation from no one; he needed no money, despised it and would not submit himself to the whim of another man for half the world, still less compose anything which was not according to his liking, to his individuality. From that time he was also cool toward Bertolini and remained so."

When he afterwards quarrelled with and insulted Malfatti he broke entirely with Bertolini; but both those gentlemen were too honorable ever to disclose the details of this breach. Simrock writes in an autograph notice for this work: "When I visited Beethoven in Vienna on September 29, 1816, he told me that he had had a visit on the day before from an Englishman who on behalf of the London Philharmonic Society had asked him to compose a symphony for that institution in the style of the first and second symphonies, regardless of cost. . . . As an artist he felt himself deeply offended at such an offer and indignantly refused it and thus closed the interview with the intermediary. In his excitement he expressed himself very angrily and with deep displeasure towards a nation which by such an offer had manifested so low an opinion of an artist and art, which he looked upon as a great insult. When we were passing Haslinger's publishing house in the

Graben in the afternoon he stopped suddenly and pointing to a large, power-fully built man who had just entered, cried out: 'There's the man whom I threw down stairs yesterday!'" "Whom I threw down stairs" was, of course, meant metaphorically. It is pretty evident that Beethoven in some degree misunderstood General Kyd's proposition and that this ebullition of spleen was rather directed against Neate and the Philharmonic Society than the General. It is greatly to be regretted that this artistic pride had so little restraining effect upon his correspondence when pecuniary matters form the topic—which remark brings us again to Mr. Birchall. Beethoven had at last discovered the £5 to his credit in the bank of Fries and Co., and signed a receipt for it on August 3d—too late to prevent the following letter being sent to him:

August 14, 1815.

Sir:

Mr. Birchall received yours of the 22d of last month and was surprised to hear you have not yet received the additional £5.0.0 to defray your expenses of copy-ing, etc. He assures the above sum was paid to Messrs. Coutts and Co., March 15th last, to be transmitted to Messrs. Fries and Co., of Vienna for you, which he supposed you would receive as safe as the previous sum. In consequence of your last letter, inquiry has again been made at Messrs. Coutts and Co., respecting it and they have referred to their books and find that Messrs. Fries and Co., were written to on the 13th of May, and in that letter the following extract respecting you was contained.

London, May 13, 1816.

"To Messrs. Fries and Co.:

"We have received from Mr. Birchall a further sum of five pounds [£5] on your account for the use of Mr. Beethoven. You will therefore please to account to that gentleman for the same and include the amount in your next bill upon us.

"Coutts and Co."

If Mr. Beethoven will call on Messrs. Fries and Co., and get them to refer to that letter, no doubt it will be immediately paid, as there is a balance in their favour at Messrs. Coutts and Co., of £5.0.0, which was not included in their last Bill on London.

Mr. Birchall is sorry you have not received it so soon as you ought, but he hopes you will be convinced the fault does not lay [sic] with him, as the money was paid the day after Mr. Ries spoke about it.

Mr. Birchall wished particularly to have the Declaration returned to him as soon as possible and likewise wishes you to favour him with the Dedications and opus numbers, which are to be put to the Trio, Sonata and the Grand Symphony in A. The publication of the Sonata has been delayed a long time in consequence of that, but he hopes you will not delay forwarding *all on the receipt of this.* When you write again Mr. Birchall will be glad to know your sentiments respecting writing Variations to the most favourite English, Scotch or Irish airs for the Pianoforte with an accompaniment either for the violin or violoncello— as you find best—about the same length as Mozart's airs "La dove prende" and "Colomba o tortorella" and Handel's "See the Conquering Hero Comes"; with your Variations, be so good, when you oblige him with your terms, as to say whether the airs need be sent you; if you have many perhaps mentioning the name will be sufficient. In fixing the price Mr. Birchall wishes you to mention a sum that will include Copying and Postages.

For R. Birchall.
C. Lonsdale.

Beethoven's reply in English bears all the marks of Häring's pen, being only signed by himself:

Vienna, October 1, 1816.

My dear Sir:

I have duly received the £5, and thought previously you would not increase the number of Englishmen neglecting their word and honour as I had the misfortune of meeting with two of this sort. In reply to the other topics of your favour, I have no objection to write Variations according to your plan and I hope you will not find £30 too much, the accompaniment will be a flute or violin or a violoncello; you'll either decide it when you send me the approbation of the price, or you'll leave it to me. I expect to receive the songs or poetry—the sooner the better, and you'll favour me also with the probable number of works of Variations you are inclined to receive of me.

The Sonata in G with the accompaniment of a violin is dedicated to his Imperial Highness, Archduke Rudolph of Austria—it is Op. 96. The Trio in B-[flat] is dedicated to the same and is Op. 97. The Piano arrangement of the Symphony in A is dedicated to the Empress of the Russians—meaning the wife of the Emp. Alexander—Op. 98.

Concerning the expenses of copying and posting, it is not possible to fix them beforehand, they are at any rate not considerable and you'll please to consider that you have to deal with a man of honour, who will not charge one 6d [sixpence] more than he is charged for himself. Messrs. Fries and Co., will account with Messrs. Coutts and Co. The postage may be lessened as I have been told.

I offer you of my works the following new ones. A grand Sonata for the pianoforte alone £40. A Trio for the Piano with accompt. of Violin and Violoncello for £50. It is possible that somebody will offer you other works of mine to purchase: for ex. the Score of the Grand Symphony in A. With regard to the arrangement of this Symphony for the piano, I beg you not to forget that you are not to publish it until I have appointed the day of its publication here in Vienna. This cannot be otherwise without making myself guilty of a dishonourable act—but the Sonata with the violin and the Trio in B-flat may be published without any delay.

With all the new works which you will have of me or which I offer you, it rests with you to name the day of their publication at your own choice. I entreat you to honour me as soon as possible with an answer having many orders for compositions and that you may not be delayed. My address or direction is:

Monsieur Louis van Beethoven,
No. 1055 and 1056 Sailerstätte, 3te Stock,
Vienna.

You may send your letter if you please direct to your,

Most humble servant,
Ludwig van Beethoven.

Beethoven not only complained of Neate to Ries, but now wrote to Smart of him in such bitter terms that that gentleman suppressed the letter entirely except to show it to Neate himself, whose grief and astonishment at the injustice done him are but partly expressed in this next letter:

London, October 29, 1816.

My dear Beethoven:

Nothing has ever given me more pain than your letter to Sir George Smart. I confess that I deserve your censure, that I am greatly in fault; but must say also that I think you have judged too hastily and too harshly of my conduct. The letter I sent you some time since, was written at a moment when I was in *such* a state of mind and spirits that I am sure, had you seen me or known my sufferings, you would have excused every unsatisfactory passage in it. Thank God! it is now all over, and I was just on the point of writing to you, when Sir George called with your letter. I do not know how to begin to answer it; I have never been called upon to justify myself, because it is the first time that I ever stood accused of dishonor; and what makes it the more painful is "that I stand accused by the man who, of all the world, I most admire and esteem, and one also whom I have never ceased to think of, and wish for his welfare, since I made his acquaintance." But as the appearance of my conduct has been so unfavorable in your eyes, I must tell you again of the situation I was in previous to my marriage.

Until the question upon which my whole happiness depended was decided, whether I should be permitted by the family to marry my wife, which I did on October 2nd, I was not able to appear as an artist. Now I remain a musician. Also I did not want someone else to negotiate for you from the fear that it would not happen as it should. I am notified that I have not kept my word with you, which is untrue; but I have neglected everyone, everything including myself.

I remain in my profession, and with no abatement of my love of Beethoven! During this period I could not myself do anything publicly, consequently all your music remained in my drawer unseen and unheard. I, however, did make a very considerable attempt with the Philharmonic to acquire for you what I thought you fully entitled to. I offered all your music to them upon condition that they made you a very handsome present; this they said they could not afford, but proposed to see and hear your music, and then offer a price for it; I objected and replied "that I should be ashamed that your music should be put up by auction and bid for!—that your name and reputation were too dear to me"; and I quitted the meeting with a determination to give a concert and take all the trouble myself, rather than that your feelings should be wounded by the chance of their disapproval of your works. I was the more apprehensive of this, from the unfortunate circumstances of your Overtures not being well received; they said they had no more to hope for, from your other works. I was not a Director last season, but I am for the next, and then I shall have a voice which I shall take care to exert. I have offered your Sonatas to several publishers, but they thought them too difficult, and said they would not be saleable, and consequently made offers such as I could not accept, but when I shall have played them to a few professors, their reputation will naturally be increased by their merits, and I hope to have better offers. The Symphony you read of in the "Morning Chronicle" I believe to be the one in C minor; it certainly was not the one in A, for it has not been played at a concert. I shall insist upon its being played next season, and most probably the first night. I am exceedingly glad that you have chosen Sir George Smart to make your complaints of me to, as he is a man of honor, and very much your friend; had it been anyone else, your complaint might have been listened to, and I injured all the rest of my life. But I trust I am too respectable to be thought unfavorably of by those who know me. I am, however, quite willing to give up every sheet I have of yours, if you again desire it. Sir George will write by the next post, and will confirm this. I am sorry you say that I did not even *acknowledge* my obligation to you, because I talked of nothing else at Vienna, as every one there who knows me can testify. I even offered my purse, which you generously always declined. Pray, my dear Friend, believe me to remain,

Ever yours, most sincerely,

C. Neate.

Zmeskall, whose patience and forbearance were inexhaustible, had again provided his friend with servants—a man and his wife—and something was done towards making the lodging in the Sailerstätte ready to receive the nephew at the end of the quarter. But this was not yet to be. The circumstances explain the following little letter to Zmeskall of date November 3, 1816:

Dear Z. Your non-recommendation of the servants engaged by me I can also not recommend—I beg of you at once to hand over to me through Hr. Schlemmer the papers, testimonials, etc., which you have from them.—I have reason to suspect them of a theft.—I have been continually ill since the 14th of last month and must keep to my bed and room.—All projects concerning my nephew have foundered because of these miserable persons.—

As ever yours,

L. v. Beethoven

Further information is provided by the following letter to Giannatasio:

Valued friend!

My household greatly resembles a shipwreck, or threatens to. In brief I have been swindled in reference to these people by one who affects to be a connoisseur. Moreover, my recovery seems to be in no hurry. Under such circumstances, to engage a tutor whose inner and outer life is unknown to me and to leave the education of my Karl to chance I can never do, great as are the sacrifices which in many respects I shall again be called upon to make. I therefore beg you, respected G, to keep my Karl again for this quarter. I shall accept your suggestion regarding his cultivation of music to this extent, that two or even three times a week Karl shall leave you at six o'clock and stay with me until the next morning when he shall return to you again by about 8 o'clock. Every day would be too taxing for K. and, since it would always have to be at the same hour, too wearisome and restricting for me— We shall discuss more in detail during this quarter what would be most practicable for K. and considerate also of me, for, in view of the fact that unfortunately my circumstances are continually getting worse, I must refer to this. If your residence in the garden had been better adapted to my health, everything could have been arranged easily— As regards my debt to you for the present quarter I must beg you to bring this to me to be discharged, as the bearer of this has been blessed by God with a certain amount of stupidity which one might not begrudge him if others were not affected by it— Regarding the other expenses for Karl during his illness or matters connected with it, I beg of you to have patience for a few days as I have large expenditures just now on all sides—

I should like also to know how matters stand between me and Smetana in view of his successfully accomplished operation. So far as his compensation is concerned if I were rich or not in the condition of all (except the Austrian usurers) whom fate has bound to this country, I would not ask at all. I mean only an approximate estimate— Farewell, I embrace you with all my heart, and will always look upon you as the friend of myself and of my Karl.

Respectfully, Your L. v. Beethoven

In November, Mr. Lonsdale wrote as follows in behalf of Mr. Birchall:

London, November 8, 1816.

Sir:

In answer to yours of the 1st October, I am desired by Mr. Birchall to inform you, he is glad to find you are now satisfied respecting his promise of paying you £5 in addition to what you before received according to agreement; but he did not think you would have delayed sending the receipt signed after the receipt of the 130 ducats merely because you had not received the £5 . . . , which latter sum was not included in the receipt. Till it comes Mr. Birchall cannot, at any rate, enter into any fresh arrangement, as his first care will be to secure those pieces he has already paid you for, and see how they answer his purpose as a Music Seller and without the receipt he cannot prevent any other Music Seller from publishing them. In regard to the airs with variations, the price of £30, which is supposed you mean for each, is considerably more than he could afford to give, ever to have any hopes of seeing them repay him. If that should be your lowest price—Mr. Birchall will give up his idea of them altogether. The Symphony in A will be quite ready for publication in a week; Mr. Ries (who has kindly undertaken the inspection of your works) has it now looking over— but it will not come out *till the day comes* you may appoint.

Mr. Birchall fears the Sonata in G and the Trio in B-flat have been published in Vienna before his[20]— He will be obliged to you to inform him of the day, when you write, that they were published. I am sorry to say, that Mr. Birchall's health has been very bad for two or three years back, which prevents him from attending to business and as there are, I fear, but little hopes of his being much better, he is less anxious respecting making *any* additions to his catalogue than he otherwise would have been; he is much obliged to you for the offer of the Sonata and the Trio, but he begs to decline it for the reasons before mentioned.

Hoping to hear soon respecting the paper sent for your signature,

I am Sir, for Mr. Birchall, etc.

C. Lonsdale.

P.S. The Sonata in G is published and the Trio will be in a few days. Is Mr. Beethoven's opera of Fidelio published? Where and by whom?

[20] According to KHV, pp. 270, 272, both were advertised on July 29th.

To this letter Beethoven sent an answer addressed to Mr. Birchall dated December 14, 1816, as follows:

Vienna, December 14, 1816.—1055 Sailerstätte.

Dear Sir:

I give you my word of honor, that I have signed and delivered the receipt to the house, Fries and Co., some day last August, who, as they say, transmitted it to Messrs. Coutts and Co., where you'll have the goodness to apply. Some error might have taken place that instead of Messrs. C. sending it to you, they have been directed to keep it till fetched. Excuse this irregularity, but it is not my fault, nor had I ever the idea of withholding it from the circumstance of the £5 not being included. Should the receipt not come forth at Messrs. C., I am ready to sign any other and you shall have it directly with return of post—

If you find variations—in my style—too dear at £30, I will abate, for the sake of your friendship, one-third—and you have the offer of such variations as fixed in our former letters for £20 each air—

Please to publish the Symphony in A immediately, as well as the Sonata—and the Trio—they being ready here.

The grand opera Fidelio is my work. The arrangement for the pianoforte has been published here under my care, but the score of the opera itself is not yet published. I have given a copy of the score to Mr. Neate under the seal of friendship and whom I shall direct to treat for my account in case an offer should present—I anxiously hope your health is improving. Give me leave to subscribe myself, Dear Sir,

Your very obedient serv't,

[Postmark, Dec. 31, 1816.]   Ludwig van Beethoven.

This letter closed the correspondence, for upon the death of Mr. Birchall his successor, Mr. Lonsdale, did not deem the connection with the composer to be worth retaining.

In marked contrast to the sombre tone of his letters to England is the playful character of almost all of the numerous notes to Steiner during the year. Here is a sample:[21]

Here is a small piece of field equipment which I am sending over— (as a present)—so that it may march right into your arsenal. As for Herr Diabolus, hold on to him for what abilities he has left; whatever has to be changed can be done as it was in the past with the Symphony in F— Concerning a new sonata for pianoforte, present me with 60 well-armed men and the same could be published at once. I also have some variations in mind which would suit a special holiday, and they also could be made to appear with the help of only 40 well-armed men— Now as regards the state debt of 1300 fl., payment of this cannot yet be considered, moreover the 1300 fl. would look best if they were transformed into the following figure o o o o—

I am astonishingly respectful of the Lt. Gl.

L. v. Beethoven

[21] In Appendix IV of TDR, III are given 34 letters to Steiner and Haslinger of the period 1815-17.

First, it is worth noting the size of Beethoven's debt to Steiner during this period, which was not to be paid off for some years. Second, the humorous reference to a number of "well-armed men" is Beethoven's military paraphrase for the price in ducats.

According to Kinsky-Halm,[22] the "small piece of field equipment" was the song "Der Mann von Wort" on a poem by Kleinschmid. Steiner obliged and the piece did "march into his arsenal" and appeared in print in November. The new sonata was Op. 101, the first of the great set of late pianoforte sonatas for which, as we shall see, Beethoven was to ponder as to the best word for hammer-action when printing the title. Preliminary sketches for the sonata were probably made in the years preceding, but the working out was done in the summer of this year. There are no sketches for the first movement; but sketches for the second appear in a sketchbook formerly belonging to Eugen von Miller of Vienna and now a part of the Koch collection. Before these sketches, come some detailed work on the song-cycle "An die ferne Geliebte," and after, first, work on an incompleted Trio in F minor and then on "Der Mann von Wort."[23] Sketches for the last movement appear in a sketchbook belonging to the Berlin Library. Here also appears, Kinsky-Halm believes, a clue to the variations for "a special holiday" mentioned in the above letter; for after the sonata sketches appears a sketch entitled "Christ ist erstanden Variations" which Beethoven was evidently contemplating as an Easter theme.[24]

The following four letters tell of incidents which make up the history of the latter part of the year 1816. The first is to Zmeskall, dated December 16:

Here dear Z. you will receive my friendly dedication[25] which I hope will be a precious souvenir of our long-continued friendship and be accepted as a proof of my respect and not as the end of a long-spun thread (for you are among my earliest friends in Vienna).

Farewell— Abstain from the decaying fortresses, the attack is more costly than from those well preserved.

As ever, Your friend, Beethoven

N.B. If you have a moment's time please tell me how much a livery will cost now (without cloak) with hat and boot money. The most extraordinary changes have taken place; the man, thank God, has gone to the devil, but on the other hand the wife seems disposed to attach herself here all the more closely.

The next is to Sir George Smart in London, dictated to Häring:

Vienna, December 18, 1816—1055 Sailerstätte, 3rd Floor.
My dear Sir:
You honor me with so many encomiums and compliments that I ought to blush, tho' I confess they are highly flattering to me and I thank you most heartily for the part you take in my affairs. They have rather gone a little back through

22 KHV, p. 277.
23 See II Beeth., pp. 334-46.
24 Ibid., pp. 553-55; KHV, p. 354.

25 To the Quartet in F minor, Op. 95.
(TDR, III, 576, n. 1.)

the strange situation in which our lost—but happily recovered—friend, Mr. Neate, found himself entangled. Your kind letter of 31 Oct. explained a great deal and to some satisfaction and I take the liberty to enclose an answer to Mr. Neate, of whom I also received a letter, with my entreaties to assist him in all his undertakings in my behalf.

You say that the Cantata might serve your purpose for the oratorios and I ask you if you find 50 £ too much to give for it? I have had no benefit for it whatever until now, but I still should not wish to ask of you a price by which you might be a loser. Therefore we shall name 40 £, and if your success should be great, then I hope you will have no objection of adding the 10 £ to make the sum as mentioned. The *Copyright* would be *yours*, and I should only make the condition of my publishing it *here* at a period which *you will be pleased* to appoint and not before.

I have communicated to Mr. Häring your kind intentions and he joins with me in the expression of the highest regard, which he always entertained for you.—

Mr. Neate may keep the different works, except the Cantata if you accept it, and I hope he will have it in his power with your assistance to do something for me, which from my illness and from the state of the Austrian finances would be very welcome.— Give me leave to subscribe myself with the greatest esteem and cordiality—

Ludwig van Beethoven

The following, to Mr. Neate in London, was written in English by Mr. Häring, at Beethoven's dictation:

Vienna, December 18, 1816.

My dear Sir:

Both letters to Mr. Beethoven and to me arrived. I shall first answer his, as he has made out some memorandums, and would have written himself, if he was not prevented by a rheumatic feverish cold. He says: "What can I answer to your warmfelt excuses? Past ills must be forgotten, and I wish you heartily joy that you have safely reached the long wished-for port of love. Not having heard of you, I could not delay any longer the publication of the Symphony in A, which appeared here some few weeks ago.— It certainly may last some weeks longer before a copy of this publication appears in London, but unless it is soon performed at the Phil[harmonic], and something is done for me afterwards by way of benefit, I don't see in what manner I am to reap some good. The loss of your interest last season with the Phil[harmonic], when all my works in your hands were unpublished, has done me great harm—but it could not be helped,—and at this moment I know not what to say. Your intentions are good, and it is to be hoped that my little fame may yet help— With respect to the two Sonatas, Op. 102, for pianoforte and violoncello, I wish to see them sold very soon, as I have several offers for them in Germany, which depend entirely upon me to accept; but I should not wish, by publishing them here, to lose all and every advantage with them in England. I am satisfied with the ten guineas offered for the dedication of the Trio, and I beg you to hand the title immediately to Mr. Birchall, who is anxiously waiting for it; you'll please to use my name with him.— I should be flattered to write some new works for the Philhar[monic]— I mean Symphonies, an Oratorio, or Cantatas, etc. Mr. Birchall wrote as if he wished to purchase my Fidelio. Please to treat with him, unless you have some plan with it for my benefit concert, which in general I leave to you and Sir George Smart, who will have the goodness to deliver this to you. The score of the opera Fidelio is not published in Germany or anywhere else. Try what can be done with Mr. B or as you think best. I was very sorry to hear that the three Overtures were not liked in London. I by no means reckon them amongst my best works, (which, however, I can boldly say of the Symphony in A), but still they were not disliked here and in Pest, where people are not easily satisfied. Was there no fault in the execution? Was there no party spirit?

And now I shall close, with the best wishes for your welfare, and that you enjoy all possible felicity in your new situation of life—

Your true friend,
Louis van Beethoven

On December 28 Beethoven wrote to Dr. Kanka in Prague urging him to accept the appointment, about to be offered by the town of Retz, as curator for a certain Johann Lamatsch in Prague. ⸺{According to Frimmel,[26] Johanna Reiss van Beethoven's grandfather on her mother's side was a Lamatsch. Beethoven's interest in the matter was that Karl as Johanna's son could "receive a small fortune, and the Retz affair might enable me to spend a few hundred florins more on the education of my dear nephew." In the spring Beethoven wrote to Kanka that he had received good news from a Retz official named Bayer; and in his draft of a memorandum to the Vienna Court of Appeal, February 18, 1820, concerning his nephew he wrote "in connection with his property I traveled to Retz etc."}⸺

The second of the three supporters of Beethoven's annuity disappears at this time from our history. Prince Franz Joseph Lobkowitz, who was born on December 7, 1772, died on December 15, 1816. A reference to the fact occurs in the following letter from Beethoven to Dr. Karl Peters, tutor of the Lobkowitz children:

January 8, 1816
[Should be 1817]

Dear Sir:

Only yesterday did I hear from Herr von Bernard, who met me, that you are here. Therefore I send you these two copies, which unfortunately were not finished until just at the time when the death of our dear Prince Lobkowitz was reported. Do me the favor to hand them to his Serene Highness, the firstborn Prince Lobkowitz, together with this writing. Just today I intended to look up the cashier to ask him to undertake their delivery in Bohemia, not having, in truth, believed any of you to be here. If I may speak of myself, I hope soon to be in a state of tolerably good health and wish you the same— I dare not ask you to come to me for I should be obliged to *tell you why*, which I cannot presume to do just now, any more than why you *do not come* or *do not*

---

[26] See *FRBH*, ii, p. 481.

wish to come— I beg of you to write the inscription to the Prince on the letter as I do not know his given name—the third copy please keep for your wife. Farewell.

Your friend and servant
L. v. Beethoven

The music that Beethoven refers to was undoubtedly the song-cycle "An die ferne Geliebte," which was dedicated to Prince Lobkowitz.[27] The letter he mentions is one to the young Prince which, according to Miss Anderson,[28] is misdated in the same way as the one to Peters.

To the few names which this year have appeared in our narrative, there is still to be added one worthy of a paragraph: that of a wealthy young man from Graz, an amateur musician and composer of that class whose idol was Beethoven—Anselm Hüttenbrenner, who came to Vienna in 1815 to study with Salieri, and formed an intimate friendship with Franz Schubert. His enthusiasm for Beethoven was not abated when the present writer, in 1860, had the good fortune to enjoy a period of familiar intercourse with him, to learn his great and noble qualities of mind and heart, and to hear his reminiscences from his own lips. That these, in relation to Beethoven, were numerous, no one will expect; since no young man of twenty-two years, and a stranger, could at the period before us be much with the master except as a pupil—and he took none—or in the position lately occupied by Oliva and soon to be assumed by Schindler: this of course was completely out of the question with Hüttenbrenner. He relates: "I learned to know Beethoven through the kindness of Hr. Dr. Joseph Eppinger, Israelite. The first time Beethoven was not at home; his housekeeper opened to us his living-room and study. There everything lay in confusion—scores, shirts, socks, books. The second time he was at home, locked in with two copyists. At the name 'Eppinger' he opened the door and excused himself, having a great deal to do, and asked us to come at another time. But, seeing in my hand a roll of music—overture to Schiller's 'Robbers' and a vocal quartet with pianoforte accompaniment, text by Schiller—he took it, sat himself down to the pianoforte and turned all the leaves carefully. Thereupon he jumped up, pounded me on the right shoulder with all his might, and spoke to me the following words which humiliated me because I cannot yet explain them: 'I am not worthy that you should visit me!' Was it humility? If so it was divine; if it was irony it was pardonable."

And again: "A few times a week Beethoven came to the publishing house of Steiner and Co. in the forenoon between 11 and 12 o'clock. Nearly every time there was held there a composers' meeting to exchange musical opinions. Schubert frequently took me there. We regaled ourselves with the pithy, often sarcastic remarks of Beethoven particularly when the talk was about Italian music."

[27] See Ludwig Nohl, *Neue Briefe Beethovens* (Stuttgart, 1867), p. 122.

[28] See *A* 734a, notes 1 and 3.

Hüttenbrenner remembered as a common remark in Vienna in those days that what first gave Beethoven his reputation on coming there twenty-four years before, was his superb playing of Bach's *Well-Tempered Clavichord*.

Two or three minor notes will close the story of the year. In the concert for the Theatrical Poor Fund, in the Theater-an-der-Wien, September 8th, one of the finales to Beethoven's *Prometheus* music was revived: "A glorious piece worked out in a masterly manner," says a reporter; and the concert for the Hospital of St. Mark was opened with his "Symphony in A, one difficult of execution, which was performed with the greatest precision under the direction of this brilliant composer."[29] More important was a proposition made early in the year by his old friend Hoffmeister in Leipzig for a complete edition of his pianoforte works, which came to nothing and concerning which more in another connection. In July he received another series of songs from Thomson which, according to a letter in French to Thomson, dated January 18, 1817, he had already finished by the end of September.

The works composed in 1816 were:

1815-16. "Sehnsucht" (Reissig), WoO 146.[30]
Sonata for Pianoforte, Op. 101.
Twenty-five Scottish Songs with accompaniment for piano, violin and violoncello, Op. 108.
Two Canons. "Das Schweigen" and "Das Reden," WoO 168, for Charles Neate on January 24.

1816. Canons.
"Ars longa vita brevis," WoO 170, for Johann Nepomuk Hummel in the beginning of April.
"Ich küsse Sie," WoO 169, for Anna Milder-Hauptmann on January 6.
"Der Mann von Wort" (F. A. Kleinschmid), Op. 99.
March in D for Military Band, WoO 24. The autograph is dated June 3, 1816. In Schindler's papers was found a note from Lieutenant Commander Franz Xaver Embel of the Civil Artillery Corps to Beethoven asking for a "March for Turkish Music"; to which, according to Schindler's notation Beethoven responded with the March in D.[31]
"Ruf vom Berge" (Treitschke), WoO 147.
Song cycle: "An die ferne Geliebte" (Jeitteles), Op. 98. On the autograph: "1816 in the month of April."
Variations for Piano, Violin and Violoncello on the song "Ich bin der Schneider Kakadu" from Wenzel Müller's *Die Schwestern von Prag,* Op. 121a. In a letter to Gottfried Härtel of July 19, 1816, one of the works offered by Beethoven was the "Variations . . . on a Müller theme, composed earlier, but nevertheless not to be rejected."[32]

[29] On December 26, according to Orel, *Ein Wiener Beethoven Buch*, 1921, p. 103.
[30] For sketches see *II Beeth.,* pp. 332-33.
[31] See TDR, IV, p. 476, n. 1.
[32] See *A* 642.

The publications for the year were:

By Artaria:
"Sehnsucht" (Reissig), WoO 146, in a set of three songs from "Blümchen der Einsamkeit" by Beethoven, Gyrowetz and Seyfried.

By Birchall in London:
"Beethoven's Grand Battle Sinfonia. . . . Descriptive of the Battle and Victory at Vittoria," Op. 91, dedicated to Prince Regent George of England, in transcription for pianoforte, in January. See Steiner, below.

By J. Riedl:
Canon. "Glück zum neuen Jahr," WoO 165 as a supplement to "Songs by Goethe and Matthisson Set to Music by L. van Beethoven."

By Steiner:
"An die Hoffnung" (Tiedge), Op. 94.
"Der Man von Wort" (Kleinschmid), Op. 99.
"Merkenstein" (Rupprecht), Op. 100 (2nd version for two voices), dedicated to Count Joseph Karl von Dietrichstein.
Sonata for Pianoforte and Violin, Op. 96, dedicated to Archduke Rudolph.
Song-cycle. "An die ferne Geliebte" (Jeitteles), Op. 98, dedicated to Prince Franz Joseph von Lobkowitz.
String Quartet, Op. 95, dedicated to Nikolaus Zmeskall von Donamovecz.
Symphony No. 7 in A major, Op. 92, dedicated to Count Moritz von Fries.
Trio for Pianoforte, Violin, and Violoncello, Op. 97, dedicated to Archduke Rudolph.
"Wellingtons Sieg oder die Schlacht bey Vittoria in Musik gesetz von Ludwig van Beethoven 91tes Werk," dedicated to Prince Regent George of England, in score and in parts,[33] in February.

By Thomson in Edinburgh and Preston in London:
"A Select Collection of Original Irish Airs," Vol. II, WoO 153, Nos. 5-20; WoO 154, Nos. 1, 3-6, 8-12; WoO 157, Nos. 2, 6, 8, 11.

By the *Wiener Modenzeitung* (February 29) as a supplement:
"Das Geheimnis" (Wessenberg), WoO 145.

[33] According to Kinsky-Halm (KHV, p. 253), this was the first of Beethoven's publica-tions to appear simultaneously in score and in parts.

CHAPTER XXX

THE YEAR 1817

BEETHOVEN AND THE PUBLIC JOURNALS OF VIENNA—AN OFFER FROM THE PHILHARMONIC SOCIETY OF LONDON— BEETHOVEN AND THE METRONOME

BEETHOVEN'S splenetic remarks to strangers in his last years upon the music, musicians and public of Vienna have given rise to widely diffused but utterly false conceptions as to the facts. Thus William Henry Fry, a leading American writer on music in the middle of the nineteenth century,[1] did but express a common opinion in the following: "That composer [Beethoven] worked hard for thirty years. At his death, after the cup of glory had overflowed, his name resounding through Christendom, he left in all a beggarly sum of two or three thousand dollars, having lived as any one acquainted with his career knows, a penurious life, fitted to his poverty and servile position in Vienna."

The popular want of appreciation of his merits "doomed Beethoven to a garret which no Irish emigrant would live in." It is altogether unnecessary to argue against such statements, as the whole tenor of this biography refutes them; but the public press of Vienna deserves a vindication, and the appearance of a new *Allgemeine Musik-Zeitung* on January 2, 1817, affords a suitable opportunity for the little that need be said on the subject. This journal, conducted "with particular reference to the Austrian Empire," and published by Steiner and Co., was, during the first two years, without the name of any responsible editor; the volumes for 1819 and 1820 announce Ignaz von Seyfried as holding that position; the others, up to 1824, bear the name of Friedrich August Kanne. A leading writer in the earlier volumes

---

[1] Mr. Fry was for many years editorial writer and music critic of the *New York* *Tribune*, with which Mr. Thayer was also associated for a time. (TK, II, 358, n. 1.)

was Hofrath Ignaz von Mosel, who already had some local celebrity for his articles on musical topics in the *Vaterländische Blätter* and other periodicals, and who continued a prolific contributor to musical journals to the end of his life in 1844. Beethoven valued him as a writer; but Mosel had the temerity to undertake, like Mozart, the task of revising and modernizing Handel. Of his eight mutilations of that great man's works, two, *Samson* and *Belshazzar*, were printed and, for some fifty years, adopted for performance throughout Austria and Germany—a remarkable proof of the general ignorance which prevailed concerning the works of the greatest oratorio composer; for two such monuments of arrogant presumption, of incompetency to comprehend his author and of a false and perverted taste, probably do not exist unless, perhaps, among the other six works which were not printed. One of Beethoven's sarcasms, remembered by Carl Czerny, indicates his opinion of Mosel's dilettantism. Reading a newspaper once at Artaria's, he saw that Mosel "had been ennobled, particularly because of his services in behalf of music." "The Mosel is muddy where it flows into the Rhine" (*Der Mosel fliesst trüb in den Rhein!*), said Beethoven, laughingly. Kanne ranked with the best musical journalists of the day; and, to use the words of Hanslick, his labors and influence as a critic were considerable, especially because of his enthusiasm for Beethoven.

Taking 1821-1822 as a medium date, the leading political and literary journals in Vienna in those years were the *Wiener Zeitung*, Joseph Karl Bernard, editor; the *Wanderer*, Ignaz von Seyfried, editor; the *Beobachter,* Joseph Pilat, editor; the *Sammler*, Portenschlag and Ledermeyer, editors; the *Wiener Zeitschrift (Modenzeitung)*, Johann Schickh, editor; and the *Theater-Zeitung,* Adolph Bäuerle, editor. Most of these editors were personal friends of Beethoven; and whoever performs the weary task of looking through their myriads of pages sees that all were his admirers and let no opportunity pass unimproved of adding a leaf to his laurels. Still, disappointment at the comparative paucity of matter relating to him follows such an examination. The cause, however, lay in himself; in the small number of his new compositions of high importance, and in the rarity of his appearance before the public. True, there were newspapers, and in divers languages, that took no note of Beethoven and his works because music and musicians were not within their scope; but not one of them was hostile. In short, whether the periodical press be considered as the exponent or the guide of public opinion, in either case its tone at Vienna during the ten years which remained of Beethoven's life is ample refutation of the so oft asserted disregard for and contemptuous neglect of their great composer on the part of the Viennese.

The correspondence of this and the next two or three years is very voluminous. Schindler says most pertinently of it: "During these years our composer, instead of writing many notes, as had been his wont, wrote many letters, referring in part to his domestic affairs, in part to the litigation and in part to the education of his nephew. These letters are, in general, among the least encouraging and most deplorable testimonials to the excitement which attended his passionate prosecution of these objects. Those of his friends and nearer acquaintances who permitted themselves to be drawn into these three matters were so overwhelmed with documents and communications that they blessed the hour in which the lawsuit was brought to a conclusion."[2]

There are few men of whom a most false and exaggerated picture may not be presented by grouping together their utterances, spoken or written at long intervals and in the most diverse moods and states of mind. Thomas Carlyle says: "Half or more of all the thick-plied perversions which distort the image of Cromwell will disappear if we honestly so much as try to represent them in sequence as they were, not in the lump as thrown down before us." Hence, strict chronological order must not lightly be abandoned—never when distortion of the image is thereby produced. But there are series of letters covering comparatively short periods of time, which may be grouped and placed apart with no ill consequence. Such is the series to Steiner and Co.; and such to the Streichers and Zmeskall, which are too unimportant to place in the text. An abstract or analysis of them would serve but a small purpose; but they should be read despite their triviality, for they show, better than any description would, the helplessness of their writer in all affairs of common life; also, by implication, the wretched prospect of any good result to his undertaking the supervision and education of a boy more than usually endowed with personal attractions and mental capacity, but whose character had already received a false bias from the equally indiscreet alternate indulgence and severity of his invalid and passionate father and of his froward and impure mother. Moreover, this undertaking rendered necessary a sudden and very great change in the domestic habits of a man nearly fifty years of age, who, even twenty years before, had not been able, when residing in the family of his Mæcenas, Lichnowsky, to bear the restraints imposed by common courtesy and propriety. It is obvious that there was but one course to be taken for the boy from which a good result might reasonably have been expected; and this was to send him at once to some institution far enough from Vienna to separate him entirely, vacations excepted, from both mother and uncle; to subject him there to rigid discipline and give him the stimulus of emulation with boys of his own age. When it was too late, as will be seen, this idea was entertained, but not sanctioned by the civil authorities. That such a course with the boy would have resulted well, subsequent events leave no doubt; for we know this: that after his uncle's death, although his bad tendencies of character had been strengthened and intensified by the lack of efficient, consistent, firm and resolute restraint from 1815 to 1827, yet a few years of strict military discipline made of him a good and peaceable citizen, a kind and affectionate husband and father. Had Beethoven's wisdom and prudence equalled his boundless affection

[2] *Biographie*, I, pp. 263-64. (TDR, IV, 6, n. I.)

for his nephew, many painful pages in this work would have no place; many which, if the truth and justice to the dead permitted, one would gladly suppress. But it must not be forgotten that Beethoven, on his death-bed, as Schindler relates, expressed "his honest desire that whatever might some day be said of him, should adhere strictly to the truth in every respect, regardless of whether or not it might give pain to this or the other person or affect his own person."

Let us again take up the thread of our narrative. We are still to imagine Beethoven living in the lofty, narrow house, No. 1055-6 Sailerstätte, entered from the street, but its better rooms on the other side looking over the old city wall and moat and out across the Glacis and little river Wien to the suburb Landstrasse, where, fronting on the Glacis, stood the institute of Giannatasio in which his nephew was a pupil, having been placed there in February, 1816.

From the reminiscences of Carl Friedrich Hirsch, as related to Theodor Frimmel, there is reason to believe that Beethoven spent a good deal of time and maybe lived for awhile as well at the hotel "zum Römischen Kaiser" during the winter of 1816-1817. The following is based on Frimmel's account of this conversation.[3] Hirsch was born in 1801, the youngest son of Anna Albrechtsberger. His grandfather was J. G. Albrechtsberger, Beethoven's old teacher in counterpoint. At this time the Hirsch family lived in the Renngasse close by the hotel "zum Römischen Kaiser" where the young Hirsch became acquainted with Beethoven. Due to the family relation to Beethoven's former teacher, Hirsch's father mustered up the courage to approach Beethoven and arrange that his son take lessons from him two or three times a week in what would now be called harmony. These lessons were given free out of respect for the deceased Albrechtsberger and lasted from November, 1816 to the beginning of May, 1817.[4]

According to Hirsch, Beethoven's deafness had advanced to the point where one had to speak to him very loudly. Beethoven watched his student's hands closely and when a mistake was made he would get very angry, become red in the face, and the vein in his temples and forehead would become swollen; he would also give his pupil a severe pinch through indignation or impatience, and once even bit him in the shoulder. He was very strict during the lesson, and burst forth in anger particularly over "false fifths and octaves," at which he would spurt out in a great rage "Well, what are you doing?" After the lesson he was again very "charmant."

Hirsch also described Beethoven's appearance in detail. Of powerful build, his face was a healthy red, his eyebrows very thick and his brow low. His nose was very big and broad, especially the nostrils which were finely "shaped." His bushy thick hair was already partly gray and stood up from

---

[3] *Beethoven Studien*, II, pp. 55-69.
[4] This date is determined by Hirsch's recollection that the lessons were broken off at the time when one of Beethoven's friends met a sudden death. This must have been Wenzel Krumpholz, whose sudden death on May 2, 1817, is soon to be mentioned.

his face. His hands were "coarse and stout," his fingers short, the veins on the back of his hands thick, and the nails cut short.

Hirsch gave the following account of Beethoven at his lodgings, which he remembered as at the "zum Römischen Kaiser": "At home Beethoven worked in a flowery dressing-gown, outside the house he wore a dark green or brown coat with gray or dark trousers to match." For his head he had a kind of low top-hat or in warmer weather a brown or dull gold straw hat. In his whole dress Beethoven was very slovenly. "In his rooms there was the greatest disorder, notes, sheets, books lying partly on the desk, partly on the floor. Now and then the master used spectacles for reading but he did not wear them continuously." The pianos upon which Hirsch was taught at Beethoven's were "first an old five-octave, two stringed instrument made of cherry wood then a six-octave mahogany one that was completely out of tune."

Whether Beethoven lived or merely gave lessons at the "zum Römischen Kaiser"—a matter that remains in doubt since the only evidence is from the recollections of one man sixty-three years later—Beethoven's permanent quarters were in the Sailerstätte until April 24th, when once again he changed dwellings.

There is no record, nor do the sketchbooks show, that in the first half of this year the composer's mind was occupied with any important composition; on the contrary, his time and thoughts were given to the affairs of his nephew, to his purposed housekeeping and to quarrels with his servants, as the frequent letters to the Streichers and Zmeskall show *ad nauseam*.

A curiously interesting picture of the man and his moods is disclosed by the records of Fanny Giannatasio. Of all the members of this family it was the daughter Fanny who recorded the most tender feelings for Beethoven and the most reverence, judging by numerous entries in her diary, of which the following should be quoted here. On March 1 [1817] she writes:

The fact that Beethoven is angry with us is something which has troubled me a lot ever since, although the way he showed it transformed a sad feeling into one more bitter. It is true that Father has not treated him politely, but to people like us who have shown their respect and love for him every time he should not want to retort with biting sarcasm. He probably wrote that letter[5] in one of his man-hating moods and I excuse it willingly. We have not seen him since that evening when Nanni and I lay sick in bed.

On March 6 she writes further:

. . . Moreover, I feel really hurt on account of Beethoven's behavior towards us, my bitterness towards him has gone completely and I have only the anxious wish that the stupid affair be cleared up, and that even were I not to see him often, yet I would know that he was thinking of us with a friendly loving heart. I don't know that now and it disturbs Nanni and me in our dreams! The wicked man! If he knew how many troubled moments he has already given us and could

---

[5] This letter, which caused such an unhappy reaction, was probably either destroyed, or sent back to the composer, since it does not exist in the letter collections. (TDR, IV, 10.)

understand that in no way have *either of us* deserved this from him and that we have always loved him—he would be compelled in accordance with his affectionate heart—to come here and make everything good between us!

On the 15th of March:

I read over these last lines with an extremely pleasant feeling; for he came—and all is well again. How sorry I am to have to note that Karl is very much to blame for this misunderstanding and sorrier still to see some new signs of his thoughtlessness towards his fine uncle carried out, which were new to him and hurt him all the more.—

When Nanni asked Beethoven if he was still angry, he replied: I think much too little of myself to get angry. Nevertheless he relaxed after an exchange of explanations, whereupon it was found that the cause of this petty coolness was only a misunderstanding. The lack of delicacy in the way Father had fetched Karl, the reminder of the payment which Karl had delivered to him in front of the piano teacher,[6] along with the lie of the latter [Karl] that he had been forbidden to practice the piano; all these things together so affected his already harassed disposition that, forgetting the confidence he had placed in us, he trusted in appearances rather than lovingly turning to his friends. But he came—he even looked embarrassed; he was probably sorry now about his letter and I am living again in the soothing conviction that he cares about us as much as he used to. Altogether my expectations have never been so fully realised as now. If my fulfilled wish—that Beethoven could understand that we cared for him and then love us in return—if this wish could be extended, it would be to live near him and to be able to brighten whenever possible the many gloomy hours of his life.

--⊷{This wish was partially realised on the 24th of the next month when Beethoven moved to the Landstrasser Glacis No. 268, on the second floor, which was not far from either the Streichers or the Giannatasio family. Among Thayer's papers was found the complete transcript of Fanny's diary which he had received from Nanni Giannatasio's daughter, Frau Pessiak. A warm friendship developed between Thayer and Frau Pessiak, and in two letters to him she imparted further information concerning Beethoven and his relationship with her family.}⊷--

While at a picnic party in the environs of Vienna, Beethoven stood beside Frau Pessiak's mother on the most beautiful observation point. Suddenly he took out his notebook, tore out a leaf, drew a staff upon it, jotted down the melody of the song "Wenn ich ein Vögelein wär" (Treitschke's "Ruf vom Berge") and handed it to his companion with the words: "Now, Miss Nanni, you write the bass for it." Frau Pessiak continues: "My mother cherished the leaf as a precious souvenir for a long time, then gave it to me because, as she said, I was the most musical one of the family, and would best appreciate the treasure. I have it preserved under a glass and frame." On another day Beethoven brought with him a number of songs, including the one from *Faust* beginning: "Es war einmal ein König der hatt' einen grossen Floh" ("Once upon a time there was a king who had a large flea"). Laughing,

[6] Carl Czerny.

Beethoven "took his seat at the pianoforte and played them the conclusion in which he pressed down two adjacent keys with his thumb at the same time and said: 'That's the way to kill him!' Mother and Aunt also had to have a try at this thing which had amused him so." On the occasion of Anna Giannatasio's birthday, Beethoven came and offered a musical congratulation. Approaching her he sang with great solemnity the melody of a canon to the words: "Above all may you lack happiness and health too—." Then he stopped and the lady protested that the wish that she might fail in happiness and health was scarcely a kind one; whereupon Beethoven laughed and finished the sentiment with "at no time!" Here is the canon:

Glück fehl Dir vor al lem, Ge - sund - heit auch_ nie - ma - len!

Chiefly from letters written in this year, do we learn a sequence of other happenings. Early in January, as has already been mentioned at the end of the last chapter, Beethoven sent copies of the song-cycle "An die ferne Geliebte," to Court Councillor Peters, tutor in the house of Prince Lobkowitz, for the new prince whose Christian name he did not know.

In December, it will be remembered, he sent Zmeskall the dedication of the String Quartet, Op. 95, for which apparently Zmeskall sent him a gift. On January 30th he wrote the following lines to his friend:

Dear Z;

You want to have me keep company with Schuppanzigh, etc., and thereby you have defaced my pure genuine work. You are not in my debt, but I in yours; and now you have gone and made it still more for me. I cannot write how much this present pains me, and yet I am so honest that I must add that I cannot grant you a friendly glance *in return*. Although you are only a performing musician, you have several times exercised the power of imagination, and it seems to me that it has occasionally put unnecessary whims into your head. At least so it seemed to me from your letter after my dedication. Good as I am and much as I appreciate all the good in you, I am yet angry, angry, angry—

your new debtor
who knows, however, how to avenge himself
Beethoven

But the very next day a note to Zmeskall resumes the habitual vein— jocularity combined with further requests for help in the search for competent servants.

Letters to Steiner at this time refer to the Pianoforte Sonata in A, Op. 101, which was then in the hands of the printers and appeared in February with a dedication to Baroness Ertmann. The suggestion had gone out that German composers substitute German terms in music in place of Italian. With characteristic impetuosity, Beethoven decided to begin the reform at once, although it seems to have involved the reengraving of the title page of the new Sonata. He wrote to Steiner in the military style with which we are already familiar:

To the Wellborn Lieut[enant] Gen[eral] von Steiner for his own hands.

Publicandum

After individual examination and taking the advice of our council we have determined and hereby determine that hereafter on all our works with German titles, in place of pianoforte, *Hammerclavier* be printed; our best Lt. Gen. as well as the Adjutant and all others concerned will govern themselves accordingly at once and put this order into effect.

Instead of Pianoforte, Hammerclavier,—which settles the matter once for all.
Given, etc., etc.   by the
on January 23, 1817.   G[eneralissimu]s

Beethoven was in doubt as to the correctness of "Hammerclavier," thinking that it might better be "Hämmerclavier," and said the matter must be referred to someone versed in languages.[7] In another letter he offered, if necessary, to pay for the engraving of a new title, adding that perhaps the old one might be utilized for another sonata. He based his acceptance of the new word on the belief that the instrument itself was a German invention—a theory long ago disproved as far as the priority of the invention is concerned. He asked that the dedication remain secret as he wanted it to be a surprise.[8]

Baroness Ertmann now lived at St. Pölten, where the command of her husband lay quartered, and thither Beethoven sent a copy of the "Hammer-clavier" sonata accompanied by the following letter:

Vienna, February 23, 1816 [*sic*][9]
My dear, valued Dorothea-Cäcilia!

You must often have misunderstood me while I was obliged to appear displeasing to you. This was caused to a great extent by my circumstances, particularly in the days when my muse was less appreciated than it is now. You know the interpretations of the uncalled for apostles who helped themselves along with quite other means than the holy Gospel; I did not want to be counted among them. Receive now what was often intended for you and what may be to you a proof of my affection for your artistic aspirations as well as your person— That I did not hear you play at Cz[erny]'s recently was due to my ill-health which at last seems to be giving way before my strength— I hope soon to hear from you, how it goes at Pölten with the Muses, and whether you care anything for your

admirer and friend
L. van Beethoven, m.p.

All things lovely to your worthy *husband and consort*.

[7] *A* 746.
[8] *A* 742.
[9] Another obvious blunder of the kind to which Beethoven was prone—it should, of course, be 1817. According to Nottebohm (*II Beeth.*, p. 344) the autograph of the Sonata bears the following inscription: "Neue Sonata für Ham. . . . , 1816, im Monath November." Its forthcoming appearance in print was announced by Steiner in Kanne's *Musik-Zeitung* in January, 1817, and it was published a month later. (Cf. TK, II, n. 1.)

Schindler has written of the role that the Baroness played—now so soon to be ended—in the performance of Beethoven's music:[10] "Through the years—until Colonel von Ertmann became a general in 1818 and was transferred to Mailand—she gathered together around her either at her own place or at other places such as Carl Czerny's a circle of true music-lovers and made the greatest contribution generally among the elite of society to the preservation and cultivation of the purest taste. She was a conservatory all by herself. Without Frau von Ertmann Beethoven's piano music would have disappeared much earlier from the repertory in Vienna; this lady, who was beautiful besides with a tall, fine figure, possessed with the loftiest purpose a feeling for the better things, and resisted the pressure of the new direction in the composition and playing of Hummel and his followers. Thus Beethoven had a double reason to honor her as a priestess of music and call her his 'Dorothea-Cäcilia.' "

Beethoven's correspondence of the winter is full of references to his continued ill-health. In several letters he described the "feverish cold" with which he had been afflicted in October, 1816, the effects of which hung on during the winter and spring, limited his activities in the summer, and made his domestic difficulties seem the more intolerable. The picture of his domestic affairs will gain in vividness by imagining the following extracts from the so-called "Tagebuch" of the Fischoff manuscript to be scattered through these preceding pages. Dates are nowhere given; but memoranda of letters to Brentano in April follow which prove these notes to belong to the previous months:

Never again live alone with a servant; there is always danger, suppose, for instance, the master falls ill and the servant, perhaps, also.

He who wishes to reap tears should sow love.

The Compassionate Brothers [the monks] in Tell, form a semi-circle around the dead man and sing in deep tones:

Rasch tritt der Tod den Menschen an	Quick comes the Death of Man
Es ist ihm keine Frist gegeben	For him is granted no delay
Er stürzt ihn mitten in der Bahn	Down he is thrust amidst his span
Es reisst ihn fort vom vollem Leben	From a full life he is torn away
Bereitet oder nicht zu gehn!	To go, prepared or not!
Er muss vor seinen Richter stehen!	Before his judge he must learn
	his lot![11]

Vidi malum et accepi—(Plinius)

Tametsi quid homini potest dari maius quam gloria et laus et aeternitas.—(Plinius)

What more can be given to man than fame and praise and immortality?

Audi multa loquere pauca.

Something must be done—either a journey and to this end the writing of the necessary works or an opera—if you are again to remain here during the coming

[10] I, p. 242.   [11] End of Act IV.

summer an opera would be preferable in case of circumstances that are only tolerable—if the summer sojourn is to be here, a decision must be made, where, how?

God help me, Thou seest me deserted by all men, for I do not wish to do wrong, hear my supplication, but to be with my Karl in the future, when now no possibility can be found. Oh harsh fate, Oh cruel destiny, no, no, my unhappy condition will never end.

This one thing I feel and clearly comprehend, possessions are not the highest things in life, but guilt is the greatest evil.

There is no salvation for you except to go away, only thus can you swing yourself up to the summits of your art again, while here you are sinking into vulgarity, and a symphony . . . and then away—away—away—meanwhile collect the salary which can be done yet for years.

Work during the summer for the journey, only thus can you carry out the great task for your poor nephew, afterward wander through Italy, Sicily, with a few artists—make plans and be of good cheer for the sake of C.[12]

In my opinion, first the saline baths, like those of Wiesbaden, etc., then the sulphur baths like Aix-la-Chapelle were everlastingly cold. Spend evenings and afternoons in company, it is uplifting and not wearying and live a different life at home.

Sensual enjoyment without a union of souls is bestial and will always remain bestial; after it, one experiences not a trace of noble sentiment but rather regret.

Beethoven's mind was engrossed with the plans of travel indicated in these excerpts throughout the year; he considered a tour of some kind essential to the restoration of his health and the recovery of his creative powers. A remittance from the Kinsky estate falling due in April, he wrote a letter to Kanka asking him to make the collection for him and enclosed a receipt. He complained of still feeling the effects of the inflammatory catarrh with which he had been attacked in the previous October, and ended by asking what would be the consequence if he were to leave the Austrian Empire; would a signature sent from a foreign place be valid?—meaning, probably, would such a signature be looked upon as evidence of a violation of the contract which he was under to his noble patrons not to take up a residence outside the Austrian dominions. His chronic dissatisfaction with the conditions which surrounded him in Vienna, as well as the moody mind in which his illness had left him, also breathes through the following letter (written in German) to Charles Neate in London:

My dear Neate!   Vienna, April 19, 1817.

Since the 15th of October I have had a severe sickness and I am still suffering from the consequences and not quite recovered. You know that I must live from my compositions alone. Since the time of this sickness I have been able to compose but very little, and therefore to earn almost nothing. It would have been all the more welcome had you done something for me—meanwhile I suspect that the result of everything has been—*nothing*.

[12] According to Jahn; others read "L." (TDR, IV, 21, n. 1.)

You have even written *complainingly of me to Häring*, which my straight-forwardness with you does not deserve in the least— Meanwhile I must justify myself in this, namely: the opera Fidelio had been written for several years, but the book and text were very faulty. The book had to be thoroughly remodeled, wherefore several pieces of the music had to be extended, others shortened, others newly composed. Thus, for instance, the overture is entirely new, as well as various other numbers, but it is possible that the opera may be found in London as it was *at first*, in which case it must have been stolen as is scarcely to be avoided at the theatre.— As regards the Symphony in A, as you did not write me a satisfactory reply, I was obliged to publish it. I should as willingly have waited 3 years if you had written me that the Philharmonic Society would accept it—but on all sides nothing—nothing. Now, regarding the *Pianoforte Sonatas* with *Violoncello*, for them I give you *a month's time*; if after that I have no answer from you, I shall publish them in *Germany*, but having heard as little from you about them as about the other works, I have given them to a German publisher who importuned me for them. *But I have bound him in writing (Häring has read the document) not to publish the sonatas until you have sold them in London.* It seems to me that you ought to be able to dispose of these 2 sonatas for 70 or 80 ducats in gold at least. The English publisher may fix the day of *publication* in London and they will appear *on the same day in Germany*. It was in this manner Birchall bought and got the Grand Trio and the Violin Sonata from me. I beg you as a last favor *to give me an answer touching the sonatas as soon as possible*. Frau v. Jenny[13] swears that *you have done everything for me*, I too, that is to say I swear that *you have done nothing* for me, are doing *nothing* and will do *nothing*—summa summarum, *Nothing! Nothing! Nothing!!!*

I assure you of my most perfect respect and hope *as a last favor a speedy reply*.

Your sincere servant and friend
L. v. Beethoven

On May 2nd Beethoven's old friend, the violinist Wenzel Krumpholz died very suddenly of apoplexy while walking on the Glacis. Beethoven commemorated the event by writing his "Gesang der Mönche" (from Schiller's *Tell*) for three male voices with the superscription: "In memory of the sudden and unexpected death of our Krumpholz on May 3rd, 1817." --•☞{The twelve-measure composition with its superscription was written out for the musical scholar, Franz Sales Kandler (1792-1831), who, with a letter of introduction from Beethoven[14] was leaving Vienna for Italy. The autograph was later acquired by Alois Fuchs and is now a part of the Koch Collection.[15]}☜•--

After the composer's removal to the suburb Landstrasse, his mind was

<hr>

[13] According to Kalischer (*Briefe*, III, p. 170) this was the Countess von Genney mentioned in the Conversation Book of 1823, through whose aid Beethoven rented rooms in a villa in Hetzendorf owned by Baron von Pronay. (TDR, IV, 23, n. 2.) O. E. Deutsch believes rather that this was one of the two sisters, Therese and Susanna v. Jenny, who were pianists in Vienna and members of the Gesellschaft der Musikfreunde. See *Schubert, a Documentary Biography*, London, 1946, p. 61.

[14] See *A*, III, p. 1415.

[15] See KHV, pp. 566-67.

much occupied with a new matter between himself and the widow van Beethoven, namely, her bearing a share of the expenses of her son's education. This was concluded by a contract signed by both parties on May 10, 1817, binding her to pay at once into court 2,000 florins for the lad's education and support, and in the future to pay to the same tribunal every quarter at least one-half of the pension which the widow was to receive, as well as other contributions. Reference is made to this agreement in the following entries in the Fischoff "Tagebuch" in January or February of the next year:

Karl's mother asked for the contract, the basis of which was that the house should be sold. From the proceeds of the sale it might be counted upon that all debts could be paid out of the one-half and also the half of the widow's income besides the money for Karl's needs and desires, so that she might live not just decently but very well, but inasmuch as the house is not to be sold! which was the chief consideration for the signing of the contract since it was alleged that execution had already been levied against it, my scruples must now cease, and I can well imagine that the widow has cared pretty well for herself, which I most cordially wish her. My duty, O Lord, I have done.— —

It would have been possible without offending the widow, but that was not so, and Thou, Almighty one, seest into my heart, knowest that I have sacrificed the best of my own for the sake of my precious Karl, bless my work, bless the widow, why cannot I wholly follow my heart's inclinations and hereafter for her the widow—

God, God, my refuge, my rock, my all, Thou seest my inmost heart and knowest how it pains me to be obliged to compel another to suffer by my good labors for my precious Karl!!! O hear me always, Thou Ineffable One, hear me—thy unhappy, most unhappy of all mortals.

This was the barren result of negotiations which had cost Beethoven, as to any important work, the first half of the year.

In May, the composer took rooms in Heiligenstadt[16] to try the baths for his illness, of which he speaks in the following letter to Countess Erdödy:

My dear suffering friend,
My most revered Countess!

Too much of the time I have been upset and overloaded with too many cares. Since the 6th of October, 1816, I have been constantly ill, and since October 15 a severe and feverish catarrh has developed because of which I have had to stay a good deal in bed, and it was several months before I could go out even for a bit. *Up until now* I was *still bothered by the effects.* I changed doctors, since mine, a crafty Italian,[17] had strong designs on me and lacked honesty as well as intelligence; this happened in April, 1817. Then every day from April 15 to

[16] The building in which Beethoven stayed is still standing today, now Pfarrplatz No. 2 in the 19th district. It is a double house with a courtyard in between; his quarters were in the left wing on the first story. A tablet has been placed under one of the windows from which there is a fine view of the Kahlen—and Leopoldsberg to the north.

[17] More likely Dr. Malfatti than Dr. Bertolini. (Cf. TDR, IV, 27, n. 3.)

May 4 I had to take 6 powders, 6 cups of tea; this lasted until May 4. From this time on I had a kind of powder that had also to be taken 6 times a day, and I had to rub myself three times with a volatile salve, thereupon I traveled here where I am taking the baths. Since yesterday I have been taking a new medicine, namely a tincture of which I must take 12 spoonfuls per day— Each day I hope for the end of this troublesome condition. Although it has improved somewhat, still it seems as though it is going to be a long time before I am completely recovered. How much all of this affects my life you can imagine. My hearing has become worse; and where before I was unable to look after myself and my requirements, now it is even more so. And my cares are still greater because of my brother's child— I have not yet found proper lodgings here; since it is difficult for me to take care of myself, I turn first to this person and then to that, and always I am left as before, and the victim of wretched people. A thousand times I have thought of you dear beloved friend as I do now, but my own misery has depressed me. S[18] has delivered Linke's letter to me; he is staying with Schwab. I have written him briefly to find out what would be the probable cost of journeying to you, but I haven't received any answer. Since my nephew has *vacation time from the last of August* until the end *of October,* it would be *after* that that I *could* visit you if it turns out that I am *cured.* We would of course have rooms for study and would have a comfortable existence, and I would be once again after such a long time among old friends who, unaffected by one or another diabolical human trait, have always sustained *me.* Thus perhaps joy and good health would return to me— Linke must write me in what way I can make the trip with the least cost. For unfortunately my expenses are so great and my income small because of my illness, during which time I have been able to compose but little. And the small capital for the possession of which I am indebted to my deceased brother, I must not lay ahold of. Since my salary grows always smaller and is now almost nothing, I must as a result preserve this capital— Since I write to you, dearest Countess, so candidly, for that reason do not misunderstand me. Regardless of this I need nothing and certainly would not accept anything from you. It is merely a question of the best and most economical way of coming to *you.* Everyone without distinction has to think along *these lines,* so my friend is not to be concerned about this— I hope that your health is in a consistently better state than I was made to believe earlier. May heaven preserve this *most excellent mother* for her children, yes, even if—only for them would you deserve the fullest amount of health— Farewell, best and most beloved Countess, let me hear from you soon—

Your true friend
Beethoven

Heiligenstadt June 19, 1817.

Christoph Kuffner, a poet, afterwards Court Secretary, who, according to Czerny (though Nottebohm questioned it) gave poetical form to the text for the Choral Fantasia,[19] also spent some time in the summer of 1817 in Heiligenstadt, and, as he told Music Director Krenn, often went with Beet-

---

[18] Thayer read this letter "C"; according to Miss Anderson (II, p. 684) this is "S," which, of course, would be the Erdödy steward, Sperl.

[19] Kinsky-Halm support Nottebohm's doubt since the text does not appear in Kuffner's complete works. See KHV, p. 212.

hoven of an evening to Nussdorf for a fish supper in the tavern "zur Rose." On one of these occasions, when Beethoven was amiably disposed, Kuffner began:

K.—Tell me frankly, which is your favorite among your symphonies?
B.—[in great good humor] Eh! Eh! The "Eroica."
K.—I should have guessed the C minor.
B.—No; the "Eroica."

Long years afterwards, in 1826, when Kuffner was negotiating with Beethoven for an oratorio text, he recalled the meetings in Nussdorf and wrote in Beethoven's Conversation Book: "Do you remember the fisherman's house in Nussdorf, where we sat till midnight in the light of the full moon on the terrace, before us the rushing brook and the swollen Danube? I was your guest."

Beethoven soon had his fish with less trouble; he moved to Nussdorf, where he remained till the beginning of October. ⸻⟨The move was made probably in late June, for on July 7th Beethoven writes to Nanette Streicher from Nussdorf: ". . . the bad weather kept me from visiting you the day before yesterday when I was in the city; yesterday morning I hurried back here again, but found my servant not at home; he had taken the key to the house along with him. It was very cool, I had nothing to wear from the city but a thin pair of trousers; and so I had to wander about for three hours. This was bad for me and I felt poorly the whole day.— There you see what housekeeping with servants is like! . . ."⟩⸻

Here, too, he received the following highly important letter from Ferdinand Ries, written in London on June 9, 1817:

My dearest Beethoven.

For a very long time I have been forgotten by you, although I can think of no other cause than your too great occupation, and, as I was compelled to hear from others, your serious illness. Truly, dear Beethoven, the gratitude which I owe you and always must owe you—and I believe I may honestly say I have never forgotten it—although enemies have often represented me to you as ungrateful and envious—is unalterable, as I have always ardently desired to prove to you in more than words. This ardent desire has now (I hope) been fulfilled, and I hope to find again in my old teacher, my old and affectionate friend. The Philharmonic Society, of which our friend Neate is now also a director, and at whose concerts your compositions are preferred to all others, wishes to give you an evidence of its great respect for you and its appreciation of the many beautiful moments which your great works have so often provided for us; and I feel it a most flattering compliment to have been empowered with Neate to write to you on the subject. In short, my dear Beethoven, we should like to have you with us in London next winter. Friends will receive you with open arms; and to give you at least one proof of this I have been commissioned on behalf of the Philharmonic Society to offer you 300 guineas on the following conditions:

1st. You are to be here in London next winter.

2nd. You are to write two grand symphonies for the Philharmonic Society, which are to be its property.

3rd. You must bind yourself not to deliver any composition for grand orchestra for any concert in London, nor direct any concert before or during our eight concerts, which begin towards the end of February and end in the first half of the month of June (without the consent of the Philharmonic Society), which certainly will not be difficult.

Do not understand by this that we want to tie your hands; it is only in case an opposition which we have once put down should again arise, since the gentlemen might plan to have you for themselves against instead of for us. At the same time it might call up many enemies against you to decline something when the responsibility would rest entirely with us directors, and we should not be obliged to give heed to the matter. We are all cordially disposed in your favor and I believe that every opportunity to be helpful to you in your plans would sooner give us pleasure than any desire to restrict you in the least.

4th. You are not to appear in the orchestra at any concert until our first two concerts are over, unless you want to give a concert yourself, and you can give as many of your own concerts as you please.

5th. You are to be here before the 8th of January, 1818, free from all obligations to the Society except to give us the preference in the future in case we meet the same conditions offered you by others.

6th. In case you accept the engagement and need money for the journey you may have 100 guineas in advance. This is the offer which I am authorized to make to you by the Society.

All negotiations with publishers are left to you as well as those with Sir G. Smart, who has offered you 100 guineas for an oratorio in one act, and who has specially commissioned me to remind you of an answer, inasmuch as he would like to have the work for next winter. The intendant of the grand opera, G. Ayrton, is a particular friend of ours. He does not want to commit himself, but he promised us to commission an opera from you.

Your own concert, or as many concerts as you choose to give, may bring in a handsome sum to you as well as other engagements in the country. Neate and I rejoice like children at the prospect of seeing you here and I need not say that I will do all in my power to make your sojourn profitable and pleasant. I know England, too, and do not doubt your success for a moment.

Moreover, we need somebody here who will put life into things and keep the gentlemen of the orchestra in order.

Yesterday evening our last concert took place and your beautiful Symphony in A-sharp [B-flat] was given with extraordinary applause. It frightens one to think of symphony writers when one sees and hears such a work. Write me very soon an explicit answer and bid me hope to see you yourself here before long.

I remain always

Your thankful sincere friend

Ferd. Ries

My hearty greetings to Herr v. Zmeskall, Zizius, Krumpholz and other friends.

Beethoven was prompt with his answer, but wishing to send a fair copy to Ries and having his own reasons for not wanting Häring's handwriting to appear in the correspondence he sent his letter to Zmeskall for transcription and posting. The letter, which was promptly forwarded to London, was as follows:

Vienna, July 9, 1817.

Dear Friend!

The propositions made in your letter of the 9th of June are very flattering. You will see by this how much I appreciate them; were it not for my unlucky affliction which entails more attendance and cost than ordinary, particularly while travelling and in a strange land, I would accept the Philharmonic Society's offer *unconditionally*. But put yourself in my place; reflect how many more hindrances I have to contend with than any other artist, and judge then if my demands be unfair. Here they are and I beg of you to communicate them to the directors of the said Society.

1) I shall be in London in the first half of the month of January, 1818, at the latest.

2) The two grand symphonies, newly composed, shall then be ready and become and remain the exclusive property of the Society.

3) For them the Society is to give me 300 guineas and 100 guineas for travelling expenses, which will be much more, since I must necessarily take a companion with me.

4) Inasmuch as I shall go to work on the symphonies at once, the Society is to advance me (on the acceptance of this offer) 150 guineas here so that I may provide myself with a carriage and other necessaries for my journey without delay.

5) The conditions respecting my not appearing with another orchestra in public, my not conducting and my preferring the Society under equal conditions are accepted by me and in view of my sense of honor would have been understood as a matter of course.

6) I shall rely upon the support of the Society in the projection and promotion of one, or, if circumstances justify, more benefit concerts. The particular friendship of some of the directors of your esteemed group as well as the kind interest of all artists in my works are a guarantee for this and will increase my zeal to fulfil all their expectations.

7) In conclusion I ask that the consent or agreement to the above be written out in English and sent to me with the signatures of three directors of the Society.

You can imagine that I heartily rejoice at the prospect of becoming acquainted with the estimable Sir George Smart and of meeting you and Mr. Neate again. Would that I might fly to you instead of this letter!

Your sincere admirer and friend,
L. v. Beethoven

To this Beethoven appended an autograph postscript as follows:

I embrace you with all my heart; I purposely employed the hand of another in the above so that you might the more easily read it to the Society. I am convinced of your kind feelings toward me and hope that the Philharmonic Society will approve of my proposition, and you may rest assured that I shall exert all my powers worthily to fulfil the honorable commission of so select a body of artists.—

How numerous is your orchestra? How many violins, etc., etc., *single or double wind-instruments?* Is the hall large, acoustically good?

Your sincere admirer and friend,
L. v. Beethoven

Efforts of the widow van Beethoven to keep in touch with her son, and questions of discipline in his bringing-up and education, were matters which weighed heavily on Beethoven's mind during the summer of 1817, and occasioned more misunderstandings between Giannatasio and the composer, as also much distress in the minds of the former's daughters, especially the solicitous Fanny, as is evidenced by entries in her diary under dates June 25, July 8 and 21, and August 10.[20] In an undated letter which seems to belong to this period, Beethoven explained to Giannatasio that the mother had expressly asked to see Karl at his, the composer's, house and that certain evidences of indecision on his part which his correspondent had observed (and apparently held up to him) had not been due to any want of confidence, but to his antipathy to "inhuman conduct of any kind," and the circumstance that it had been put out of the power of the woman to do the lad harm in any respect. On the subject of discipline he writes:

As regards Karl, I beg of you to hold him to strict obedience and if he does not obey you (or any of those whom he ought to obey) to *punish* him at once, treat him as you would your own child rather than as a pupil, for as I have already told you, during the lifetime of his father he could only be forced to obey by blows; this was very bad but it was unfortunately so and must not be forgotten.

He requested that the letter be read to his nephew. Beethoven's "antipathy to inhuman conduct of any kind" seems to have led him to make concessions to the widow of which he soon repented. In a letter to Zmeskall dated July 30, he says: "After all, it might pain Karl's mother to be obliged to visit her son at the house of a stranger and, besides, there is more harshness in this affair than I like; therefore I shall permit her to come to me tomorrow"; and he urgently begged his friend to be a witness of the meeting. In a note to Giannatasio he informed him of his intentions to take Karl to see his mother at her home, because she was desirous to put herself in a better light before her neighbors, and this might help. But a fortnight after the letter to Zmeskall he changed his mind, as witness a letter to Giannatasio dated August 14, in which he writes:

I wanted this time to try an experiment to see if she might not be bettered by greater forbearance and gentleness and I informed H. v. S[chmerling] of this idea of mine. But it has foundered, for on *Sunday* I had already determined to *adhere to the old necessary strictness,* because in a moment's time she had communicated some of *her venom* to Karl— In short we must stick to the zodiac and permit her to see Karl only twelve times a year, and then so hedge her about

[20] See TDR, IV, pp. 34-7.

that she cannot secretly slip him even a pin. It is all the same to me whether it be at your house, at mine, or at a third place. For once I had believed that by yielding wholly to her wishes she might be encouraged to better her conduct and appreciate my utter unselfishness.

Notwithstanding the jeremiads in Beethoven's letters this year, and the annoyance caused him by his sister-in-law, there are indications in plenty that he was not on the whole in that state of dejection which one might suppose. One of these indications is a work which amused him during the summer, the story of which the careful Dehn admitted into the *Cäcilia*. A musician, whose name is not mentioned, brought to Beethoven the Pianoforte Trio, Op. 1, No. 3, which he had arranged for string quintet (two violins, two violas and violoncello). Though the composer, no doubt, found much to criticize in the transcription it seems to have interested him sufficiently to lead him to undertake a thorough remodelling of the score, on the cover of which he wrote the whimsical title:

Arrangement of a Terzett as a
3 voiced Quintet
by Mr. Goodwill
and from the appearance of 5 voices
brought to the light of day in 5 real voices
and lifted from the most abject *Miserabilität*
to moderate respectability
by Mr. *Wellwisher*
1817
August 14.

N.B. The original 3 voiced Quintet score has been sacrificed as a burnt offering to the gods of the Underworld.

The score of the arrangement is in the handwriting of a copyist with corrections by Beethoven; the title, however, is his autograph. ──⁂A humorous letter to Steiner undoubtedly refers to this work and the possible identity of Mr. Goodwill:

Here follows the quintet *for the L—t G—l's office*. I shall know presently what conditions to make pertaining to it. Nothing about this is to be imparted to Hr. Kaufmann for the day after tomorrow I shall write him a letter concerning it, wherewith the whole affair will be finished up. For Hr. K. *has given me nothing other than the opportunity to make this complete revision*—Here is my present to the office of the l—t g—l whereby I insist at this time on some shooting and *advance payment*[21] most especially and therewith punctum—

The G[eneralissimu]s
(in thunder and lightning yet somewhat
feebler than usual.)

[On the outside] To the devil's office of the L—t G—l.

[21] Beethoven's pun: *schiessen* (shooting) and *Vorschiessen* (advance payment) is lost in translation.

Steiner, however, did not take the work. ▧•— Instead, it was published by Artaria in February, 1819, as Op. 104. Beethoven evidently attached considerable importance to it. He referred to it in letters to Frau von Streicher, Zmeskall and Ries; and it was performed at a musical entertainment of the Gesellschaft der Musikfreunde in Vienna in December, 1818.

Beethoven having obtained possession of his nephew and placed him in Giannatasio's institute, very naturally took measures that he should have systematic instruction in music; to this end he employed Carl Czerny as teacher, and to him we now turn for information on this point.[22] Czerny writes: "In the year 1815 [1816] at his request I began teaching his nephew Karl, whom he had already adopted, and from that time I saw him almost daily, since for the greater part of the time he brought the little fellow to me. From this period I still have many letters written by him, one of which I reproduce here with absolute fidelity because it is musically noteworthy:

My dear Czerny!

I beg of you to have as much patience as possible with Karl even if matters do not go now as well as you and I might wish; otherwise he will accomplish even less; for (but this he must not know) he is already subjected to too great a strain because of the improper division of his studies. Unhappily this cannot be changed at once. Therefore treat him with as much loving consideration as possible, but with seriousness; *then you will have* better success with Karl in spite of the unfavorable conditions.— In regard to his playing for you, I beg that once he has acquired the correct fingering and can play in time and reads the notes with reasonable correctness, you then direct his attention to the matter of interpretation; and when you have gotten *that far* don't stop him *because of trifling mistakes* but point them out after he has finished the piece. Although I have given but few lessons I have always followed this method, it soon makes *musicians* which, at the last, is one of the first purposes of art, and gives the minimum of weariness to master and pupil.— In certain passages like

I wish that he would use all the fingers occasionally as well as in such as these

so that they may be played in a gliding manner. True, such passages sound "pearly" as the phrase goes (played with few fingers) or "like a pearl," but at times other jewels are desirable.— More at another time.— I hope that you may receive all this in the loving spirit in which it is expressed and intended— At any rate I am and will always remain your debtor— May my sincerity be a pledge for future payment so far as possible.—

Your true friend Beethoven

[22] The principal contributions to Beethoven's biography from Czerny's pen are in Schmidt's *Wiener Allg. Mus. Zeitung*, 1845, No. 113; Cocks's *Musical Miscellany* (London, 1852); and manuscript notes in Jahn's papers. (TDR, IV, 46, n. 2.)

Czerny comments:

"Noteworthy in this interesting letter is the very correct view that one ought not to weary the talent of a pupil by too much petty concern (wherein much depends on the qualities of the pupil, it is true) as well as the singular fingering and its influence on interpretation.

"Much more valuable were Beethoven's oral remarks about all kinds of musical topics, other composers, etc., touching whom he always spoke with the greatest positiveness, with striking, often caustic wit and always from the lofty point of view which his genius opened to him and from which he looked out upon his art. His judgment even concerning classic masters was severe, as a rule, and uttered as if he felt his equality. At one lesson which I gave his nephew he said to me: 'You must not think that you will do me a favor by giving him pieces of mine to play. I am not so childish as to desire that. Give him what you think good for him.'

"I mentioned Clementi. 'Yes, yes,' said he; 'Clementi is very good,' adding, laughingly 'For the present give Karl the regular things so that after a while he may reach the irregular.'

"After such conceits, which he was in the habit of weaving into nearly every speech, he used to burst into a peal of laughter. Since irregularities used to be charged against him by the critics in his earlier days he was wont often to allude to the fact with merry humor. At that time (about 1816) I began to have musical entertainments at my home for my very numerous pupils every Sunday before a very select circle. Beethoven was almost always present, he improvised many times with kindly readiness and with that wealth of ideas which always characterized his impromptu playing as much, or often more, than his written works. As his compositions were chiefly played at these meetings and he indicated the tempo, I believe that in this respect I am intimately acquainted with his wishes regarding his works (even his symphonies, which were frequently played in arrangements for two pianofortes)."

No animadversion upon the venerable Carl Czerny is intended in remarking that both in his memoirs and in the language in which he has sometimes recorded them there is occasionally a very disturbing inexactness. "Beethoven was almost always present" at the Sunday music meetings, which can have been true only of the first months, and the words "he improvised many times," must not be understood too literally. Schindler, in whose hands Jahn placed Czerny's notes and other manuscripts for examination and remark, observes touching this improvising: "Only twice; the first time when Frau von Ertmann played one of his sonatas, the other time when Czerny performed Op. 106, which he had repeatedly gone through with him. In the year 1818, and those that followed, Beethoven never improvised outside of his own dwelling." Schindler was certainly mistaken upon this last point, and, very possibly, upon the other.

In August and September the after-effects of the attack of catarrh and the state of Beethoven's health generally were so distressing and so depressing upon his spirits that he seemed to be on the verge of despair. A letter which Zmeskall noted as received by him on August 21 says:

I am sorry to hear of your illness— As for me, I am in despair so often and would like to end my life, for there is never an end to all these afflictions. God have pity on me, I consider myself as good as lost— I must talk with you also about other things. This servant *steals*, I have no doubt about this. So he must go. Because of my health I must *eat at home* and with greater ease. I would like to know your opinion about this— If my condition does not improve I shall not be in London next year but perhaps in my grave— Thank God, the part is nearly played—

In haste
Your L. van Beethoven

On September 11, Beethoven was able to report to Zmeskall that the reply to his letter had been received from the London Philharmonic Society the day before. There was no tone of elation in his note; it merely mentioned the arrival of the letter and a request for the name of someone who could translate it for him, it being in English. As might have been expected the Philharmonic Society rejected the new terms demanded by him, but, as the Society's records show, repeated the old. These were now at once accepted by Beethoven.

And did he now sit himself down zealously and perseveringly to work on a ninth and tenth symphony? Not at all. His thoughts had become engaged upon a new pianoforte sonata—the great one in B-flat, Op. 106. According to Nottebohm, sketches were made for the first movement and the scherzo of the Ninth Symphony during the composing of the sonata between the fall and spring of 1817-1818;[23] and these will be discussed when the history of the symphony is told.

That "indecision in many things," noted by Breuning a dozen years before, was only aggravated by the lapse of time; and this now was his bane. There was really nothing to prevent his departing at once except that the new symphonies were still to be written. If his nephew must remain in or near Vienna, he could nowhere be so well placed as in the school and family of the excellent Giannatasios, who had all the necessary legal power to save the boy from the bad influence of his mother. The effects of such a journey; of a stay of some months in England; of the intercourse of cultivated people; of the enthusiastic admiration which awaited him there, and of the great pecuniary rewards for his labors which were certain, could only have been propitious in the highest degree to both his physical and mental health. There was, too, just now a new and powerful motive for accepting and fulfilling this engagement.

Though the depreciation of the redemption certificates never quite touched the point feared by him in his letter to Ries in 1815, it did once amount to 4

[23] *II Beeth.*, pp. 159-64, and pp. 121-37.

for 1; and the Government was again forced to repudiate its obligations in part. It founded that National Bank (eight shares in which Beethoven soon afterwards purchased), and made a contract with a new institution by which the bank assumed the obligation of redeeming the redemption certificates at the rate of 2½ for 1. It went into full operation July 15, 1817, and thenceforth Beethoven's annuity remained instead of 3,400 florins in that paper, 1,360 florins in silver. But this fatal indecision! Could he have but resolutely taken up any two of the many new symphonies which he had planned, as the sketchbooks show, and once fairly engaged himself upon them, he could not have rested until they were finished; he could, and doubtless would, then have redeemed his promises; and like Handel, Haydn and many other German musicians of far less note, have secured from an admiring and generous London public an ample sufficiency for the future. The standard of excellence was high and catholic in London and musical taste pure and exalted. True, at the first trial of the C minor Symphony by the Philharmonic Society a part of it only was played, for the leader of the violins—really the conductor, as the orchestras were then constituted—declared it "rubbish." But this leader was a German—our old Bonn acquaintance J. P. Salomon. He, however, repented and made amends. At another trial of it, two or three years afterwards, after the first movement, Salomon laid his violin upon the pianoforte, walked to the front and, turning to the orchestra said (through his nose): "Gentlemen, some years ago I called this symphony rubbish; I wish to retract every word I then said, as I now consider it one of the greatest compositions I ever heard!"

We have had occasion heretofore to refer to several young British Beethoven enthusiasts; another is now added to the list—Cipriani Potter[24]—who came just at this time to Vienna, bringing letters to the composer from Neate, Ries, Rode, Dragonetti and others. He heard so much of Beethoven's rudeness of manners and moroseness of disposition, and so often noticed how people shook their heads when he or his music was mentioned, that he hesitated to visit him. Two weeks had thus passed when one day, at Streicher's, he was asked if he had seen Beethoven and if he had letters to him. He therefore explained why he had not seen him. He was told this was all nonsense; Beethoven would receive him kindly. He exclaimed: "I will go out at once!" which he did. He presented a letter or two, one of the first being that of Dragonetti. Upon opening that Beethoven also opened his heart to his visitor and demanded immediately to see some of his compositions. Potter showed him an overture—probably one that had been commissioned and played by the London Philharmonic Society in 1816. Beethoven looked through it so hurriedly that Potter thought he had only glanced at it out of politeness and was greatly astonished when Beethoven pointed to a deep F-sharp in the bassoon part and said it was not practicable. He made

[24] Potter (1792-1871) was Director of the Royal Music Academy in London, esteemed as conductor, pianist and composer. (TDR, IV, 55, n. 1.)

other observations of a similar nature and advised him to go to a teacher; he himself gave no lessons but would look through all his compositions. In answer to Potter's question as to whom he would recommend, Beethoven replied: "I have lost my Albrechtsberger and have no confidence in anybody else"; nevertheless, on Beethoven's recommendation Potter became a pupil of Aloys Förster, with whom he studied a long time until one day the teacher said to him that he had now studied sufficiently and needed only to practise himself in composition. This brought out the remark from Beethoven that no one ought ever to stop studying; he himself had not studied enough: "Tell Förster that he is an old flatterer!" Potter did so, but Förster only laughed. Beethoven never complimented Potter to his face; he would say: "Very good, very good," but never give unequivocal praise. Once Beethoven advised him never to compose sitting in a room in which there was a pianoforte, in order not to be tempted to consult the instrument; after a work was finished he might try it over on the instrument, because an orchestra was not always to be had.

Beethoven used to walk across the fields to Vienna very often and sometimes Potter took the walk with him. Beethoven would stop, look around and give expression to his love for nature. One day Potter asked: "Who is the greatest living composer, yourself excepted?" Beethoven seemed puzzled for a moment, then exclaimed "Cherubini." Potter went on: "And of dead authors?" Beethoven answered that he had always considered Mozart as such, but since he had been made acquainted with Handel he had put him at the head. The first day that Potter was with Beethoven the latter rushed into politics and called the Austrian government all sorts of names. He was full of going to England and said his desire was to see the House of Commons. "You have heads upon your shoulders in England," he remarked. One day Potter asked him his opinion of one of the principal pianists then in Vienna (Moscheles). "Don't ever talk to me again about mere passage players," came the answer. At another time Beethoven declared that John Cramer had given him more satisfaction than anybody else. According to the same informant, Beethoven spoke Italian fluently but French with less ease. It was in Italian that Potter conversed with him, making himself heard by using his hands as a speaking-trumpet; Beethoven did not always hear everything, but was content when he caught the meaning. Potter considered *Fidelio* the greatest of all operas and once remarked to Beethoven that he had heard it in Vienna, which brought out the remark that he had *not* heard it, as the singers then at the opera-house were not able to sing it. He was asked if he did not intend to write another opera. "Yes," replied Beethoven, "I am now composing *Romulus*;[25] but the poets are all such fools; I will not compose silly rubbish." Potter told him of the deep impression made upon him by the Septet when first he heard it; Beethoven replied in effect that

[25] Treitschke had provided the libretto of *Romulus*; it does not appear that Beethoven ever began its composition. (TDR, IV, 57, n. 2.)

when he wrote the piece he did not know how to compose; he knew now, he thought, and, either then or at another time, he said, "I am writing something better now." Soon after, the Pianoforte Sonata in B-flat (Op. 106) was published.

Another visitor now, and probably occasionally during the winter following, was Heinrich Marschner, who had come from Carlsbad to Vienna on the invitation of Count Amadée. He was 21 years old, ambitious and eager to get Beethoven's judgment on some of his compositions, which he carried to the great master in manuscript. Beethoven received him, glanced through the music hurriedly, handed it back with a muttered "Hm," in a tone more of satisfaction than dispraise, and the words: "I haven't much time—do not come too often—bring me something again." The young man was grievously disappointed; he had expected so much more. He did not understand Beethoven's sententious manner, and not until he told the story of his reception to his patron and Prof. Klein of Pressburg, did he recall that Beethoven had looked kindly upon him when he spoke the words and had given him his hand at parting. He had gone to his lodgings in a passion of despondency, torn up the manuscripts, packed his trunk with the resolve to abandon music and return to Leipzig to continue his studies for the profession for which he had been designed. But now, on the advice of his friends, he took a different view of Beethoven's actions, and continued his intercourse with him. The great man was always gracious, and even occasionally let fall a word of encouragement; but an intimacy never sprang up between them.

Beethoven's intercourse with a third new acquaintance was, doubtless, far more delightful than any other. This was Frau Marie Pachler-Koschak, who visited him in August or September, 1817.[26] Beethoven had already heard from Prof. Schneller, whose pupil she had been, of her extraordinary beauty, talents, intellectual culture and refinement, and of her genius for music. He had unconsciously the year before borne testimony to this last in this wise: Her brother-in-law, Anton Pachler, *Dr. jur.* in Vienna, had at her request shown him for an opinion a fantasia composed by her, but without disclosing the author's identity. Beethoven looked at the piece carefully and said that it was a good deal from one who had not studied composition, and if the composer were present he would point out the faults in it; it would take too much time to do this in writing and the composer would find them out for himself if he studied diligently.

Marie Leopold Koschak was born on October 2, 1794, in Graz, the daughter of a respected lawyer, and she attracted attention early in life by her pianoforte playing and talent for composition. In a concert on December 22, 1811, she played Beethoven's *Choral Fantasy* and for a long time intended to devote herself completely to the art; but she gave this up in the interests of her family. In 1816 she married the lawyer, Dr. Carl Pachler in Graz. Her

[26] See *Beethoven und Marie Pachler-Koschak* (Berlin, 1866), by her son, Dr. Faust Pachler, for a discussion of their relationship. (TDR, IV, 59, n. 1.)

house became the center of a cultivated circle, and she continued to keep up her music as much as her domestic duties would allow. Anslem Hütten-brenner wrote of her: "The daughter of the lawyer Koschak was the most beautiful maiden and later for several years the most beautiful woman in Graz and was called 'heaven's daughter.' She glowed with admiration for Jean Paul, Goethe and Schiller, for Beethoven, Mozart and Schubert."

In 1817 her wish to meet Beethoven personally was fulfilled; her brother-in-law Anton brought her to him in August or September (according to her son). She had never been in Vienna, Beethoven never in Graz, so they, of course, had never met previously. But when they did, it could not be as strangers; for his music had been to her like a new divine revelation, and such noble mental and personal qualities as distinguished her always awakened in him feelings akin to worship. Unfortunately absolutely nothing is known of their personal association except that she wrote ten years later that "they were often in each other's company," and that Beethoven wrote her two notes "in pencil"—one utterly illegible, and the other in terms placing her as a player of his pianoforte music even higher than Frau von Ertmann. He wrote:

I am greatly delighted that you will remain another day; we will make a lot more music, you will play the sonata in F major and C minor for me, will you not? I have never yet found anybody who plays my compositions as well as you do, not even excepting the great pianists, for they either have nothing but technique or are affected. You are the true guardian of my intellectual offspring—

Her son has so fully exploded Schindler's assumption that she was the object of Beethoven's "autumnal love" that no words need be wasted upon it. It was, no doubt, upon seeing in Beethoven's papers the letter "M"[27] in this outburst of feeling:

Love alone—yes, only love can possibly give you a happier life— O God, let me—let me finally find the one—who will strengthen me in virtue—who will *lawfully* be mine.
Baden on July 27
when M drove past and seemed to give a glance at me—

A consideration of the dates given in Dr. Pachler's pamphlet proves conclusively, however, that this "M" cannot refer to Marie Pachler, for its writer could never have seen her "drive past" on any 27th of July!

There are few unmarried men of highly sensitive nature who have not had the bitter experience of a hopeless passion, who have not felt how doubly grateful at such times is intercourse with a glorious creature like Madame Pachler, and how beneficial in preventing the thoughts from continually dwelling on the impossible, and thus aiding reason and conscience to gain the victory over the heart and fancy. Now it happens that one of Beethoven's

---

[27] The letter, which is reproduced in *fac-simile* in Schindler's biography, is a more or less fantastic scrawl or flourish which may be read as an "R" as well as an "M."

transient but intense passions for a married woman, known to have occurred in this period of his life, has its precise date fixed by these passages in the so-called "Tagebuch" from the years 1816 and 1817. "In the case of T. there is nothing to do but to leave it to God, never to go where one might do a wrong through weakness—to Him, to the all-knowing God, be all this committed." And again: "But as kind as possible to T. her attachment deserves never to be forgotten even if the results could never prove advantageous to you." Let the reader recall the passages in his letters showing a strong desire to leave Vienna and read again: "Work during the summer for the journey, only thus can you carry out the great task for your poor nephew, afterwards wander through Italy, Sicily, with a few artists—make plans and be of good cheer for the sake of C. . . ." The last initial is uncertain. Other copies have "L."; what the original was in Beethoven's handwriting is not now to be determined. No instance, however, is known of his writing his nephew's name with a C, and this "C" or "L" was probably T. As the family name of this lady, whose husband was a man of high position and distinction though not noble by birth, is known, it is certain that the T in the above citations is not Therese Malfatti, now Baroness Drosdick; but as her baptismal names have eluded search one can only hint the possibility that the "T" and "M" may indicate the same person, and that this last cry of anguish was written a year or two afterwards when the sight of "M" again, for a moment, tore open a half-healed wound.

In numbers 5 to 8 inclusive of the *Neue Musik-Zeitung* appeared, from the pen of J. S. Kandler, a long article containing historical notices of various attempts to produce a satisfactory instrument for measuring time in music, and closing with an account, taken from the English, of Mälzel's metronome. To No. 25 (June 19) of the same journal, Gottfried Weber contributed a paper "On a chronometric tempo designation which makes Mälzel's metronome, as well as all other chronometric instruments, unnecessary," in which he repeated his idea, already put forth in the Leipzig *Musikzeitung* in 1813, that the simplest and most correct chronometer is a simple pendulum, a bit of thread with a bullet at the end, whose oscillations would mark the duration of measures according to the length of the thread. This article pleased Beethoven, and in one of his variations on the theme of pens he commended it to his "clarissime amice" Zmeskall, as the best invention yet made. Zmeskall took up the subject with interest and in two articles in the same journal called attention to the fact that Neate, in London, had described a time measurer of the same kind which was known in England, but had not remained long in use—"a little ball hanging at the end of a thread and below it a line divided into a scale of inches." Zmeskall approved of Weber's suggestion in principle but improved upon it by proposing that the oscillations of the pendulum indicate the duration of a note instead of a measure, and that the varying lengths of the pendulum be marked by knots in the thread. Beethoven, to whom Zmeskall seems to have sent his contrivance, was interested and lauded its simplicity, playfully wondering whether or not it might be used in measuring from time to eternity.

Music had already come from the press with Mälzel's tempo marks, and Weber, who seems to have had no kindly feeling for him, printed an article, in the number of the journal following Zmeskall's, entitled "Mälzel's Metronome to be had gratis everywhere," and gave a table showing the lengths of a pendulum in Rhenish inches and French centimetres corresponding to all the numbers on the metronome. As the months passed, the metronome had come largely into use in England, France and the United States, but not in Germany and Austria. It was of high importance to the manufacturers of the instruments to obtain the countenance and good will of the composers in those countries also—Salieri, Weigl, Beethoven, etc.— and Mälzel came back to Vienna to try the effect of personal effort, taking the risk of any serious consequences arising from the lawsuit between him and Beethoven. But there were none. The matter was amicably adjusted, each party paying half of the legal expenses which had been incurred. This would be incredible had Beethoven had any substantial grounds for the action; for his sanction of the metronome was of such value that Mälzel would readily have conceded much to obtain it; and the whole tone of the composer's correspondence in this period, so far as relates to his pecuniary affairs, shows how little likely he was to sacrifice any just claim.

Beethoven was at first not well disposed to the instrument, notwithstanding he had joined Salieri and the other composers in strongly recommending the "chronometer" in 1813, which certificate had been used in England *a fortiori* for the new metronome. In a letter[28] Mr. Joseph J. Mickley, of Philadelphia, writes: "Mr. Mälzel, with whom I was well acquainted,[29] told me that he had been particularly anxious Beethoven should mark his music by his metronome, and to get his recommendation; that he (B) refused and became quite indignant, saying: 'It is silly stuff; one must feel the tempos'"; but Beethoven soon yielded to the obvious considerations in favor of the invention. These were presented to the public together with the objections to Weber's and Zmeskall's pendulums, clearly, explicitly and cunningly by Mosel in an article in Steiner's *Musik-Zeitung* on November 27, which put an end to controversy on the topic.

Meanwhile, Beethoven had prepared a table of tempos for his eight symphonies which was printed in the Leipzig *Allgemeine Musik-Zeitung* on December 17 (copied, says Nottebohm, from a little pamphlet published by Steiner and Co. in which also tempos of the Septet were included), and followed this up with a general metronomizing of his works. On the autograph of his song, "Nord oder Süd," he wrote: "100 according to Mälzel; but this must be held applicable to only the first measures, for feeling also

[28] The letter to Thayer is dated May 21, 1873. (TK, II, 385, n. 1; TDR, IV, 65.)
[29] Mälzel lived in Philadelphia for some time before his death at sea on July 21, 1838. (TK, II, 385, n. 1.)

has its tempo and this cannot entirely be expressed in this figure (i.e., 100)."[30]

If the picture of Mälzel drawn by Schindler and his copyists is true, even the most Christian and forgiving spirit could scarcely have demanded more of Beethoven than this public acknowledgement of the value of the metronome by way of heaping coals of fire upon his head; but he did more, by writing to Mosel this very valuable and for us very interesting letter:

I am heartily rejoiced that you agree with me in the opinion touching the time designations which date back to the barbarous period in music. For what, for instance, can be more nonsensical than Allegro, which always means *merry* and how often are we so far from this conception of time that the piece says the very *opposite of the designation*.— As regards these 4 chief movements, which by no means have the correctness or truthfulness of the chief winds, we gladly *put them aside*. It is a different matter with the words used to designate the character of the composition; these we cannot give up, since time is really more the body while *these have reference to the spirit*. So far as I am concerned I have long thought of giving up the nonsensical designations Allegro, Andante, Adagio, Presto; Mälzel's metronome gives us the best opportunity to do this. I give you *my word* that I shall *never use them again* in my new compositions— It is another question whether we shall thereby accomplish the necessary *universal* use of the M[etronome]. I do not think so. But I do not doubt that we shall be decried as *taskmasters*. If the cause might thus be served it would still be better than to be accused of feudalism—I therefore think that it would be best, especially in our countries where music has become a national need and every village schoolmaster ought to use the metronome, that Mälzel try to dispose of a certain number of metronomes by subscription at higher prices, and that as soon as his expenses are thus covered he will be in a position to furnish the needed metronome for the national need so cheaply that the greatest *universality* and *widest distribution* may be expected—It is self-evident that somebody must take the initiative in this matter so that zeal be aroused. As for me you may count on me, and I await with pleasure the post of duty to which you will assign me—

Still more: he joined with Salieri in a public announcement which was printed in the *Wiener Allgemeine Musikalische Zeitung* of February 14, 1818, setting forth that the metronome would attest its utility forever and was indispensable to all students of singing, the pianoforte or other instruments, etc. On one of the last days of December, Beethoven writes to Frau Streicher: "Day before yesterday I was busy with Mälzel, who is in a hurry as he is soon to leave here." What had he so important to do with this "rude fellow, wholly without education or breeding," to cite his own words? Was it in contemplation to make this sudden zeal for the metronome a source of pecuniary profit? No one knows.

On October 2nd, Beethoven wrote a letter to Nanette Streicher from Nussdorf which ends: "Tomorrow I hope to see you for sure, for I am coming in from the country to the Landstrasse just for that reason." One of

---

[30] Thus copied by Fischoff. (TDR, IV, 66, n. 3.)

the matters to be discussed was a move to the Gärtnergasse which Beethoven had mentioned frequently in his letters to Frau Streicher during the summer. He left Nussdorf for good on October 14. At some point after this date he left the dwelling on the Landstrasse (No. 268) for one in the house "zum grünen Baum," first *étage*, 2nd story, No. 26 in the Gärtnergasse, also in the suburb Landstrasse.—— He was again near both his nephew and the Streichers (in the Ungargasse), and, with the aid of Frau Streicher, he at last brought his domestic arrangements into such a condition that he might take his nephew to himself. About this time he wrote his friend:

I am occupied in going over my papers to consider what is necessary for the coming move. That your accounts have not been discharged and that I have not visited you can all be ascribed to this. To bring such things as my papers into order demands *dreadful patience*; but we *must cling to it* once it is present because ordinarily there is none. Associated with this is the question of what we need in the way of utensils— Many thanks for your recommendation of the new h[ousekeeper] and for your continuing willingness to give us help, *without which* I would be completely distrustful of everyone. But with three people everything is more easily figured out. I hope to see you tomorrow or the day after tomorrow. In haste

Your friend Beethoven

On one side of a large sheet of paper (it is now preserved in the Berlin Library) he wrote a list of questions which were painstakingly answered on the opposite page by the friend to whom they were addressed (presumably again Frau Streicher). The questions were as follows:

What ought one to give 2 servants to eat at dinner and supper both as to quantity and quality?
How often ought one to give them roast meat?
Ought they to have it at dinner and supper too?
That which is intended for the servants, do they have it in common with the victuals of the master, or do they prepare their own separately, i.e., do they have different food from the master?
How many pounds of meat are to be reckoned for 3 persons?
What allowance per day do the housekeeper and maid receive?
How about the washing?
Do the housekeeper and maid get more?
How much wine and beer?
Does one give it to them and when?
Breakfast?

Beethoven announced his intention to take his nephew to himself at the end of the current quarter in a letter to Giannatasio dated November 1, 1817. The step involved not only an increase in his expenses, but also an abandonment of his engagement with the London Philharmonic Society and of all the profits which might thence arise. Giannatasio, moved by his complaints of poverty, and probably also by a desire to aid him in the proposed visit to London, kindly offered to keep the boy at a much reduced rate of remuneration for board and instruction. Beethoven's reply shows him to be still undecided as to his movements in the coming spring, and it is possible, could he have made ready the required symphonies, that he might have gone to England; but now the new Sonata had got possession of his imagination, and the symphonies must wait.

Brief mention should be made at this point of Beethoven's increasing deafness. Czerny, who saw Beethoven frequently during these particular years, told Jahn that between 1812 and 1816 it gradually became more and more difficult to make oneself understood without shouting. "But it was not until 1817 that the deafness became so extreme that he could no longer hear music either, and this condition persisted for about 8 or 10 years until his death." And further: "Up to 1816, he was still able (with the aid of machines) to hear himself play, but later even this became more and more difficult, and he had to rely on his inner hearing, his imagination, and experience." This may be compared with Schindler's comments in the *Niederrheinische Musikzeitung* 1854, No. 28, where he enlarges somewhat further on Beethoven's hearing ability as regards music and then goes on to say: "During 1818, Beethoven's hearing became too poor for oral conversation, even with the aid of a speaking trumpet, and he was forced to resort to writing."

There is an interesting passage in a letter dated "Nussdorf, July 7th" from Beethoven to Frau Streicher concerning his hearing at the piano: "Now here is a big request for Streicher. Ask him for my sake to do me the favor of adjusting one of your pianos for my weakened hearing so that it is as loud as possible. I need it. For a long time I have had the intention to buy one for myself, but at the moment it would be very difficult for me. Perhaps somewhat later, though, it will be more easily possible; but until then I want to *have one on loan* from you. I refuse completely to accept it free. I am ready to pay the going price for it within six months in Convention Coin. Perhaps you do not know, that although I have not had one of your pianos all the time, yet I have preferred your make especially ever since 1808— Streicher is the one person who is in the position to send me the kind of piano that I need—"

On November 15, Anton Halm gave a concert for the benefit of the poor in the Kärnthnerthor-Theater at which the Choral Fantasia was performed. The composer and pianist Johann Peter Pixis (1788-1874) was at the performance and recorded in his reminiscences that at the point where the chorus enters, the audience's attention was shattered by horrible inappropriate sounds coming from the piano. The efforts of the conductor to avoid the chaos which followed were to no avail and amid grumbles and hisses from the audience the musicians had to come to a halt before continuing the piece. The next day Pixis was stopping in at Steiner's to buy a copy of the Fantasy. "At that point Beethoven entered the store with his usual dark look. I seized the silver horn which was placed here for him, held it to his ear and asked him: 'Were you at the concert yesterday?' His face became darker than before and in a real rage he said, 'The dirty fellow came to me to learn the tempi; I gave them to him and warned him about the passage just before the chorus comes in; I told him that he should pay attention there, otherwise he would get thrown off, and that's exactly what happened to him!' Then I was called by Steiner into his office and when I came back into the store, Beethoven was gone, but several customers who had come in were standing by the table and observed with animated expressions the words which Beethoven had written with a pencil on the white margin of my copy: 'Nicht jeder Halm gibt Ähren!' " (Not every stalk has ears of corn.) [31]

It is probable that to this time is to be assigned a portrait in oils painted by Christoph Heckel, who was a student at the Royal Imperial Academy in Vienna from 1814 to 1818. Beethoven, it is said, made the acquaintance of the painter in Streicher's pianoforte wareroom.

But one public appearance professionally of Beethoven is recorded this year. At the concert for the Hospital Fund on December 25, the first part was devoted to the Eighth Symphony, which was conducted by the composer. In the second part Seyfried produced C. P. E. Bach's oratorio, *The Israelites in the Wilderness*, which he had revised, adding to the accompaniments, curtailing the airs, prefixing it with the well-known fugue on B-A-C-H (orchestrated by himself), and concluding it with the double chorus "Holy, holy, holy." Nottebohm has shown that the sketches for the overture on the name of the great Leipzig cantor which Beethoven once thought of writing, belong to a later period; but it is yet possible, if not likely, that he conceived the idea at this concert.

There is but little to be added to what has been said about the compositions of this almost sterile year. The transcription of the Pianoforte Trio as a quintet (which was the largest work of the year), and the "Song of the Monks," written on the death of Krumpholz, have been mentioned. Besides these we have a few short songs with pianoforte accompaniment. "Nord oder Süd" (also known as "So oder So"), the poem by Karl Lappe, was known and widely liked in a setting by K. Klage. Beethoven's setting seems to have been less well known. "Resignation" ("Lisch aus mein Licht"), words by Count Paul von Haugwitz, was composed in the second half of the year, and the sketches show that Beethoven contemplated a setting for four voices. The year also saw work done on the Pianoforte Sonata in B-flat, Op. 106, and the beginning of the Symphony in D minor.

Lastly there was the composition of a Fugue in D major for five stringed instruments, which was completed on November 28, 1817. This piece was written especially for a manuscript collection of Beethoven's works projected

---

[31] The pun on the name of the pianist, Halm, is lost in translation. See Willi Reich, "Ein übersehenes Gespräch mit Beethoven," *Schweizerische Musikzeitung*, Vol. 91 (1951), p. 170.

by Haslinger, to be discussed below, and was published by him in the fall of 1827 as Op. 137. Beethoven was particularly interested in fugues at the time. "To *make* a fugue requires no particular skill," he said later to Holz, "in my study days I made dozens of them. But the fancy wishes also to assert its privileges, and today a new and really poetical element must be introduced into the old traditional form." The sketches for the conclusion of the Quintet fugue are mixed with notes from Bach and others showing how zealous were his studies in the form of that time.[32]

In a Conversation Book of January, 1820, one of Beethoven's friends (probably Oliva) writes: "Today I met Haslinger of Steiner's;—he has had your works made into magnificent copies in score."[33] This collection was in the making, according to Unger,[34] from 1817 to 1823 and during this time Haslinger engaged the services of two expert calligraphists, Mathias Schwarz and Friedrich Warsow to make copies of Beethoven's works on beautiful English vellum-paper. The result is a deluxe collection in sixty-two volumes. Originally planned as a preparation for a published edition of the complete works, which was never realised because of difficulty in negotiating with other publishers concerning the rights of particular works, the collection was sold to Archduke Rudolph in 1823 for a sum of 4000 fl. C.M. and after his death was inherited by the Gesellschaft der Musikfreunde, where it may still be seen.[35]

The compositions for the year were:

Canon. "Glück fehl' dir vor allem," WoO 171, for Anna del Rio.
Fugue in D for String Quintet, Op. 137.
"Gesang der Mönche" for Two Tenors and Bass (from Schiller's *Wilhelm Tell*), WoO 104.
"Resignation" (Haugwitz), WoO 149.
"So oder so" (Carl Lappe), WoO 148.
String Quintet, Op. 104, arrangement of the Trio, Op. 1, No. 3.

The publications were:

By Simrock:
"Das Geheimnis" (Wessenberg), WoO 145. Also "An die Geliebte," 2nd version, WoO 140.
Two Sonatas for Pianoforte and Violoncello, Op. 102, without dedication to Countess Marie von Erdödy.
By Steiner:
Sonata for Pianoforte, Op. 101, dedicated to Baroness Dorothea Ertmann.
Symphony No. 8 in F major, Op. 93.
By Thomson in Edinburgh and Preston in London:
"A Select Collection of Original Welsh Airs," Vol. 3, WoO 155 (containing 26 airs by Beethoven and four by Haydn).

[32] See Nottebohm, *II Beeth.*, pp. 349-52. (TDR, IV, 76, n. 4.)
[33] Schünemann, I, p. 200.
[34] *Ludwig van Beethoven und seine Ver-* *leger*, pp. 10-14.
[35] See O. E. Deutsch, "Beethovens gesammelte Werke," in *Zeitschrift für Musikwissenschaft*, XIII (1930), pp. 60-79.

By Wallishauser, as a musical supplement to *Gedichte von Friedrich Treitschke*: "Ruf vom Berge" (Treitschke), WoO 147, for which it was composed on December 13, 1816.

By *Wiener Allegemeine Musikalische Zeitung*, March 6th, as a supplement: Canon. "Das Schweigen," WoO 168. In the issue of June 5th appeared the solution to this riddle canon by Hieronymous Payer, accompanied by a humorous canon of his own on the words "Herr Beethoven's Canon is at the 5th below and at the octave."[36]

By *Wiener Modenzeitung*, February 17, as a musical supplement: "So oder so" (Lappe), WoO 148 (also published singly by Simrock).

[36] See KHV, p. 676, and L. Misch, *Beethoven Studies* (Norman, 1953), pp. 124-26.

CHAPTER XXXI

THE YEAR 1818

A MOTHER'S STRUGGLE FOR HER SON— THE PIANOFORTE SONATA OP. 106

AN ENTRY in an old "Porter's Book" of John Broadwood and Sons, manufacturers of pianofortes in London, offers an agreeable starting-point for the story of Beethoven's life in 1818. In this book the porter of the firm signs his name, Millet, to the record that on December 27, 1817, he took from the warehouse "A 6 octave Grand Pianoforte, No. 7362 tin and deal case, Thomas Broadwood, Esq., marked $\boxed{\text{v. b.}}$ care of F. E. J. Bareaux and Co., Trieste (a present to Mr. van Beethoven, Viene), deliv'd to Mr. Farlowes to be shipped." Some time previously Mr. Thomas Broadwood, the then head of the house, with a Mr. Goding (probably the rich brewer), visited the principal cities of the continent and doubtless became acquainted with Beethoven and offered to present to him one of the firm's pianofortes. On January 3, 1818, Mr. Broadwood seems to have informed Beethoven that the instrument had been shipped, and exactly one month later Beethoven sent the following acknowledgment to the generous donor:

Mon très cher Ami Broadwood!

Jamais je n'eprouvais pas un grand Plaisir de ce que me causa votre Annonce de l'arrivée de cette Piano, avec qui vous m'honorès de m'en faire present, je regarderai comme un Autel, ou je deposerai les plus belles offrandes de mon esprit au divine Apollon. Aussitôt comme je recevrai votre Excellent Instrument, je vous enverrai d'en abord les Fruits de l'inspiration des premiers moments, que j'y passerai, pour vous servir d'un Souvenir de moi à vous mon très cher B., et je ne souhaits ce que, qu'ils soient dignes de votre instrument.

Mon cher Monsieur et ami recevés ma plus grande consideration de votre ami et très humble serviteur

Louis van Beethoven.

Vienne le 3me du mois Fevrier, 1818.

This letter was sent to Broadwood by Joseph Anton Bridi of the firm of Bridi, Parisi and Co., in Vienna, who had evidently been commissioned to look after the delivery of the instrument to Beethoven after its arrival in Trieste. At least Bridi, in transmitting the letter to Broadwood under cover and date February 5, informs the latter that he had taken the proper steps to have the pianoforte sent to Vienna by Bareaux (or Barraux) and Co., and asks for instructions how to carry out what he understands to be the donor's desire that the instrument be delivered to Beethoven without his being put to any expense whatever, not even for the import duty. The latter charge must have been in the mind of Beethoven when he wrote a letter, without date, to Count Lichnowsky enclosing a document bearing on the case expressing the hope that he be permitted to receive the instrument and proposing to apply by word of mouth to Count Stadion, the Austrian Minister of Finance. Frau Streicher was also appealed to in the matter, Beethoven begging her in a letter to ask her "Cousin from Cracow" to get from the chief customs official in Vienna an order for the forwarding of the pianoforte, which could be sent to the custom house in Trieste. But neither Broadwood nor Beethoven was called on to pay the duty, the Austrian Exchequer remitting the charge. After some delay the pianoforte was delivered at Streicher's wareroom and later sent to Beethoven at Mödling. While it was still in his possession, Streicher asked Potter to try it, saying that Moscheles and others could do nothing with it—the tone was beautiful but the action too heavy. Potter, who was familiar with the English instruments, found no difficulty in disclosing its admirable qualities. He told Beethoven, however, that it was out of tune, whereupon the latter replied in effect: "That's what they all say; they would like to tune it and spoil it, but they shall not touch it." Beethoven's delight in the pianoforte must have been great. Bridi reports to Broadwood that the composer already rejoiced in it in anticipation and expressed a desire to dedicate the first piece of music composed after its reception to the donor, "convinced that it would inspire something good." His jealousy of it seems to have been so great that he would not permit anybody to tune it except Stumpff, of London, who came with a letter of introduction from Broadwood.

The case of the instrument, simple, plain but tasteful in design, is of mahogany and the structure generally of a solidity and strength paired with grace which caused no little surprise at the time. The compass is six octaves from C, five leger-lines below the bass staff. Above the keys is the inscription: *Hoc Instrumentum est Thomæ Broadwood (Londini) donum, propter Ingenium illustrissimi Beethoven.* On the board, back of the keys, is the name "Beethoven," inlaid in ebony, and below this the makers' mark: "John Broadwood and Sons, Makers of Instruments to His Majesty and the Princesses. Great Pulteney Street. Golden Square. London." To the right of the keyboard are the autograph names Frid. Kalkbrenner, Ferd. Ries, G. G. Ferrari, J. B. Cramer and C. Knyvett; the names of the virtuosi were no doubt scratched upon the instrument as a compliment to Beethoven and an evidence that they had played upon it. Beethoven kept the instrument as long as he lived. At the sale of his effects it was bought by Spina, the music publisher, for 181 florins; Spina gave it to Liszt, in whose house at Weimar it was up to his death. In 1887, Princess Marie Hohenlohe, daughter of Liszt's friend, the Princess Sayn-Wittgenstein, presented it to the National Museum in Buda-Pesth.

Beethoven's London trip had been abandoned without notice or explanation to the Philharmonic Society, apparently; but Ries must have written to him, renewing the offer previously accepted, for on March 5 Beethoven writes to his old pupil as follows:

In spite of my desire, it was impossible for me to come to London this year; I beg of you to say to the Philharmonic Society that my poor state of health hindered me; but I hope that I may be entirely well this spring and then take advantage of the renewed offers of the Society towards the end of the year and fulfil all its conditions. Please ask Neate in my name not to make use, at least not in public, of the many compositions of mine which he has until my arrival in person; no matter what the conditions of his affairs may be I have cause of complaint against him.

Botter [Cipriani Potter] visited me several times, he seems to be a good man and has talent for composition— I hope and wish that your prosperity may grow daily; unfortunately I cannot say that of myself. My unlucky connection with this Archduke has brought me to the verge of beggary. I cannot endure the sight of want. I must give; you can imagine how my present conditions increase my sufferings. I beg of you to write to me soon. If it is at all possible I shall get away from here sooner in order to escape total ruin and will then arrive in London in the winter at the latest.

I know that you will stand by an unfortunate friend; had it only been in my power, and had I not been fettered, as always here, by circumstances, I would surely have done much more for you—A hearty farewell, give my greetings to Neate, Smart, Cramer—although I hear that he is a counter-subject to you and me, yet I already know something of the art of treating such and we shall produce an agreeable harmony in London after all.

I greet and embrace you from my heart.

Your friend Ludwig van Beethoven

All that is lovely to your dear and (as I hear) beautiful wife.

Ries's reverence for royalty, apparently, led him to omit Beethoven's unkind allusion to his august patron and pupil, Archduke Rudolph; Schindler, writing much later, printed it and admitted, very properly, as we know from other instances of the same kind, that Beethoven sometimes used his friends as whipping-boys, and that his words and deeds were not always consistent with each other.

The time had come for Beethoven to take his nephew from the home and institute of the Giannatasios. On January 6 he wrote to inform the director that Karl would leave his "admirable institute" at the expiration of the month and that Giannatasio might rest assured of his and the lad's life-long gratitude: "I have observed in Karl that he already feels grateful, and this is a proof that though he is frivolous he is not malicious, and least of all is he bad at heart. I have hopes of all manner of good from him, all the more because he had been under your excellent care for nearly two years."

After taking Karl to his own home the composer engaged a tutor to prepare him for matriculation at the gymnasium. This tutor, whose name has not been learned, was a professor at the Vienna University and had evidently agreed not only to look after all of the lad's intellectual needs but also to have an eye on some of the domestic affairs and to that end to become a member of the Beethoven household. On this point, Beethoven enjoined secrecy upon Frau Streicher. How long the service of this "steward," as he playfully called him to Frau Streicher, continued is not known, nor how satisfactory it was. He does not become a subject of Beethoven's correspondence beyond a single reference to the fact that he once stayed out all night.

Ill-advised and full of evil consequences as was Beethoven's step in taking personal charge of his nephew, it was yet creditable to his heart and bears strong witness to his high sense of duty. His purpose was pure and lofty, and his action prompted by both love and an ideal sense of moral obligation. It was a woeful mistake, however; Beethoven sadly misjudged his fitness to fill the delicate and difficult rôle of guardian and parent. In all his life he had never had occasion to give a thought to the duties which such an office involved. In the conduct of his own affairs he had always permitted himself to be swayed by momentary impulses, emotions and sometimes violent passions, and he could not suddenly develop the habits of calm reflection, unimpassioned judgment and consistent behavior essential to the training of a careless and wayward boy. In his treatment of him he flew from one extreme to the other—from almost cruel severity to almost limitless indulgence, and, for this reason, failed to inspire either respect for his authority or deep affection for his person, to develop the lad's self-control or a desire for virtuous living. Very questionable, too, if not utterly unpardonable, were the measures which Beethoven took to separate the boy from his mother in spite of the dying wishes of the father. We have seen his protestations at times of his unwillingness to give her pain. When he was cruel in his own confession it was because he imagined himself constrained to be so by a high obligation of duty. There can be no doubt that the woman whom Beethoven called "The Queen of Night" was wicked and vicious, and that his detestation of her was as well founded as his wish to save his nephew from evil communications and influences.

Thayer's opinion of Beethoven's motives in taking charge of his nephew and of the character of his sister-in-law represents the prevailing view on this subject until recent years. But there has come a reexamination of this phase in Beethoven's life by certain writers from the psychological viewpoint. The most thorough of these studies is a book entitled *Beethoven and his Nephew* by E. and R. Sterba,[1] which attempts to analyse the relationship with the psychoanalytic approach of Freud. Beethoven's love for his nephew was an almost all-consuming emotional preoccupation from the time he became Karl's guardian to his death. From all that we know concerning this relationship, Beethoven's possessive instinct and craving for love from this boy was more decisive in guiding his actions than his objective sense of duty. An antipathy to his sister-in-law that had already existed deepened into a hatred when she became the logical person with whom to divide care for the boy, which represented for Beethoven the complete resolution of his life-long craving to love and cherish another. With the existence of this conflict within him it is problematical to what extent many of his opinions concerning her, be they based on suspicion or gossip, can be accepted. Certainly to name Johanna "wicked and vicious" must be accepted as Beethoven's view but not, as Thayer implies, necessarily the truth.

A memorandum in the *Tagebuch* after February 20th reads: "Karl's mother has not seen him since August 10"—a period of more than six months. How often she was allowed to see him during the following months is not of record; we only know from Beethoven himself, in his letters to Frau Streicher, that the mother's instinct drove her to employ the only means by which she could know the condition of her son during the summer in Mödling—i.e., bribing or feeing the servants. That at least is Beethoven's accusation, and exceedingly wroth he was. We have contented ourselves mostly with mere references to Beethoven's letters to Frau Streicher in this period. They are in the main brief notes monotonously asking help in domestic affairs, and though frequently interesting because of their exhibition of characteristic traits and moods, too insignificant to justify the cumbering of these pages with their literal contents. The following letter, however, deserves to be given in full.

Best Frau Streicher!

It was not possible to reply to your last letter sooner. I would have written to you a few days ago when the servants were sent away, but hesitated in my determination until I learned that it was Frau D. in particular who hindered Karl from making full confession. *"He ought to spare his mother,"* she told him; and Peppi cooperated with her.[2] Naturally they did not want to be discovered; they worked together shamefully and permitted themselves to be used by Frau v. Beethoven; both received coffee and sugar from her, Peppi *money* and the *old one* probably also; for there can be no doubt that she was *herself at the house of Karl's mother*; she said to Karl that *if I drove her away* from my service *she would go straight to his mother*. This happened at a time when I had reproved her for her conduct with which I had frequent occasion to be dissatisfied; Peppi who often played the eavesdropper when I spoke with Karl appears to have tried

---

[1] Pantheon, N.Y., 1954.

[2] Frau D. and Peppi were the new housekeeper and cook, engaged some time early in the year. The former is also called "the old woman" by Beethoven in his letters. Beethoven wrote to Frau Streicher in the early winter and referred to Peppi as "a *good* cook." See *A* 894.

to tell the truth; but the old one *accused her of stupidity and scolded her stoutly*— and so she remained silent and tried to throw me off the trail— The story of this abominable deception may have lasted about six weeks—they would not have got off *so easy* with a less magnanimous man. Peppi borrowed 9 or 10 florins for stuff for shirts and I afterwards made her a present of the money and instead of 60 she got 70 florins; she might have denied herself these wretched bribes. In the case of the old woman, who was always the worse, hate may have played a part as she always thought herself slighted (although she got more than she deserved) for the *scornful smile on her face* one day when Karl embraced me, made me suspect *treachery* and how shameless and deceitful such an old woman could be. Just imagine, 2 days before I came here K. went to his mother one afternoon without my knowledge and both the old woman and P. knew it. But now listen to the triumph of a hoary-headed traitress: on the way hither with K. and her, I spoke with K. about the matter in the carriage, although I did not know all; and when I expressed the fear that we should not be safe in Mödling, she exclaimed "*I should only rely upon her.*" O the infamy of it! This was only the 2nd time in the case of a person of such venerable age that *such a thing* happened to me— A few days before when I sent both away I had told them in writing that under no circumstances were they to accept anything for Karl from his mother. Instead of repenting, Peppi tried secretly to take revenge on K., after he had confessed all. This they knew from the fact that in the note mentioned above, I had written that *all had been discovered*— I expected that they would both beg my pardon after this, instead of which they played me one wicked trick after the other. As no betterment was to be expected in such obstinate sinners and I had every moment to fear another piece of treachery, I decided to sacrifice my body, my comfort in order to better my poor misguided Karl; so out of the house they went as a *warning example* to all those servants who may come after—I might have made their certificates of character a little less favorable; but rather I set down the time of service of each at full six months although it was not true. I never practice *vengeance*; in cases where I act *against* the interest of other people, I never do more *against them* than is necessary to protect myself against them or to prevent them from doing further harm.— On account of Peppi's honesty in general I am sorry to have lost her, for which reason I made her certificate more favorable than that of the old woman; also she appears to have been led astray by the old woman. That P.'s conscience was not at ease, however, she showed by saying to Karl that "*she did not dare go back to her parents,*" and, *in fact, I believe she is still here*— I had suspected treachery for a long time until one evening before my departure I received an anonymous letter the contents of which filled me with dread; but they were only suspicions. Karl, whom I took to task in the evening confessed at once but not everything. As I often treat him harshly though not without cause, he was much too afraid to admit everything completely. In the midst of the struggle we reached here. As I often questioned him, the servants noticed it, and the old woman in particular tried to persuade him *not to admit the truth*. But when I gave Karl my sacred assurance that all would be forgiven if he would but confess the truth, while lying would plunge him into a deeper abyss than that in which he already was, everything came to the light of day— Add to this the other data which I gave you before concerning the servants and you will have the shameful story of the two traitresses clearly before you— K. did wrong, but—mother—mother—even a bad one remains a mother— To this extent he is to be excused, particularly by me who knows his intriguing, passionate mother *much too well*.— The priest here knows already that I know about him, for K. had already told me. It is likely that he was not fully informed and that he will be careful; thus we'll guard against K's being mistreated by him, since he appears to be rather a rough man. Enough of that for now. But as K's virtue was put to the test, for there is no virtue without temptation, I will purposely let the matter go by until it happens again (which I do not expect), in which case I will so bethwhack his reverence with such spiritual cudgels, amulets with my sole guardianship and consequent privileges, that the whole parish will shake— My heart has been terribly shaken up by this affair and I can scarcely recover myself— Now to the housekeeping; it needs your help— How necessary this is to us you already know. Do not be frightened away, such a thing might happen anywhere; but if it has once happened and one is in a position to hold it up to one's new servants, it is not likely that it will occur again— You know what we need, perhaps a French woman, and whatever can be found in the way of a chambermaid; good cooking remains the principal thing—also the matter of economy. For the present we have a person who cooks for us, but badly. I cannot write you more today. You will see that *in this matter* I could not act differently; things had gone too far— I cannot yet invite you to visit me here for everything is still in confusion; *nevertheless it will not be necessary to send me to a lunatic asylum*— I can say that I already suffered fearfully from this thing while I was in Vienna, though I kept silence— Farewell; do not let any of this be known as someone might think prejudicially of K. *Only I* who know all the driving wheels here can testify *for him* that he was terribly misled— I beg of you soon to write us something comforting touching the art of cooking, washing and sewing. I am feeling very ill and in need of a stomach restorative.

In haste, your friend

Mödling, June 18, 1818.   Beethoven

"K. did wrong, but—mother—mother—even a bad one remains a mother." Why did he not follow this thought to its ultimate conclusion? Why did he permit, if indeed, he did not encourage the lad to speak disrespectfully of his mother?

Beethoven removed to Mödling on May 19, taking with him his nephew and the two servants referred to in the letter above. He found lodgings in the so-called Hafner House in the Hauptstrasse, now ornamented by a memorial tablet. --◦❧{It was on the Ungargasse (now Hauptstrasse No. 79). Beethoven had quarters on the first floor, which consisted of a large room with a view on to the court, two small rooms with a view on to both court and garden, and a small dark kitchen where both servants presumably slept.[3]}❧◦-- He began taking the baths two days after his arrival and, the

---

[3] The present editor is grateful to the late Dr. Kurt Smolle for these details. The memorial tablet, which is to the right of the front door, bears the incorrect date of 1820, in which year Beethoven visited Mödling but no longer lived in the Hafner House.

desire and capacity for work soon returning, he took up energetically the Pianoforte Sonata in B-flat. Karl was placed in a class of boys taught by the village priest, named Fröhlich,[4] who dismissed him a month later for reasons which became a matter of judicial record before the end of the year. In a document filed as an appendix to Frau van Beethoven's application for the guardianship, Fröhlich set forth that Beethoven had encouraged his nephew to revile his mother, applauding him when he applied vile epithets to her either in writing or by shrieking them into his ear, "thus violating the fourth divine commandment"; that the boy had confessed to him that while he knew that he was doing wrong he yet defamed his mother to curry favor with his uncle, and dared not tell him the truth because he would only believe lies. "This he once told his mother and would have said more had he not feared being found out and maltreated by his uncle." Once, too, Beethoven came to him (the priest) and in a tone of malicious joy told him that his nephew had that day called his mother a "Ravenmother" (*Rabenmutter*—meaning a wicked and unnatural mother). Since Karl's training was thus contrary to all moral principles, since he had also displayed indifference to religious instruction, been guilty of unruly conduct in church and in the streets, so that many of the inhabitants of the village had come to him with complaints, and since admonitions to the boy and appeals to the uncle had borne no fruit, the priest had been constrained to dismiss him for the sake of his other twelve pupils, who had said "they did not want to study with the unruly Karl van Beethoven." These unfortunate first-fruits of Beethoven's error in undertaking personal and sole care of his nephew will call for more attention before the history of the year 1818 is closed, and may be dismissed for the present for more cheerful topics.

Towards the end of the year 1815 the Gesellschaft der Musikfreunde had instituted inquiries through Zmeskall touching Beethoven's willingness to compose a work of magnitude for the Society. Beethoven signified his assent to the project and in turn asked Zmeskall whether or not the Society would allow him 400 ducats as an honorarium. There the matter seems to have rested until May, 1818, on the 17th of which month Vincent Hauschka, a violoncello player and member of the governing committee of the Society, was authorized by his associates to offer Beethoven from 200 to 300 "pieces of gold" for the music to a "heroic oratorio" to be the exclusive property of the Society for one year after the date of its first performance. Hauschka wrote to Beethoven at Mödling and received a droll letter in reply. It bears no date:

First and best member of the Society of Enemies[5] of Music in the Austrian Empire!

---

[4] It was this priest, evidently, against whom Beethoven threatened to launch the thunderbolts of his wrath, as he told Frau Streicher in the letter above. (TK, II, 396, n. 1.)

[5] The play on the words *Freunde* and *Feinde* is impossible in English. (TK, II, 397.)

Ich bin be - rei - - - - t !
[I am a gree - - - - d !]

Ich bin be - rei - - - - t !
[I am a gree - - - - d !]

I have only a *sacred* subject at hand; but you want a heroic one, which is all right by me. But I think to mix in something sacred besides would be suitable for such a crowd.

A - - - - - men!

Herr v. Bernard would suit me very well, but please pay him as well. I will not speak of myself; since you call yourselves music friends, so it is natural that you will settle this account generously——!!! Now farewell, best fellow, I wish you open bowels and the handsomest of close-stools. As for me, I am wandering about here amongst mountains, hollows and valleys, with a piece of music-paper scribbling down many a thing for the sake of bread and money— For to such a pitch have I been brought in this all-powerful *land of the Phaeacians* that in order to gain a little time for a work of magnitude I must always scribble first a great deal for money so that I may hold out during a large work— For the rest, my health is much better and if haste is necessary I can still serve you well—

Ich bin be rei t ! Ich bin be -
A men !
rei t !

If you need to talk with me, write me, whereupon I will make all the arrangements about it— My compliments to all of the Society of Enemies of Music—

In haste your friend
Beethoven

The tone and contents of this letter show that it was not designed as an official communication to the Society, but merely as a friendly negotiation. Further correspondence on the matter occurs in the next year.

The same summer saw the beginning of the most widely distributed portrait of Beethoven. At the instance of his uncle, Baron von Skrbensky, a young painter named August von Klöber (born at Breslau in 1793), who was continuing his artistic studies in Vienna, undertook to paint a portrait of the composer. His own account of his acquaintance with Beethoven and the incidents connected with the painting of the portrait (or rather with the original sketch) were published in the *Allgemeine Musikalische Zeitung* of 1864 (p. 324). From it we learn that the artist was introduced to Beethoven by a letter written by Dont.[6] He visited Beethoven at Mödling, after receiving permission to make a drawing of him and found him giving a lesson to his nephew on the Broadwood pianoforte. This fact fixes the date of the picture. Though the artist found it impossible to make himself understood unless he wrote his words or spoke them into an ear-trumpet, Beethoven corrected the errors in the lad's playing, compelled him to repeat passages apparently without difficulty. Klöber's account continues:

"After approximately three-quarters of an hour, he grew uneasy; following Dont's advice I knew that it was time to stop and asked him only for permission to come again tomorrow since I lived in Mödling myself. Beethoven was very understanding and said, 'Then we can meet often because I do not like to sit long. You must take a good look at Mödling for it is very beautiful here, and, as an artist you must be a lover of nature.' On my walks in Mödling I met Beethoven repeatedly, and it was most interesting to see how frequently he stopped, with a sheet of music-paper and a pencil-stump in his hands, as if listening, looked up and down and then scribbled notes on the paper. Dont had told me that if I met him thus I should never address him or notice him because he would then become either embarrassed or disagreeable. Once, just when I was sketching a piece of woods, I saw him climb up a hill from the hollow which separated us, with his broad-brimmed felt hat pressed under his arm; when he got there, he threw himself down at full length under a pine-tree and for a long time stared heavenwards.— Every morning he sat for me awhile. When Beethoven saw my picture he remarked that the treatment of the hair pleased him very much, the other painters hitherto had always made him look so *well-groomed*. . . .

"Beethoven's residence in Mödling was extremely simple as, indeed, was his whole nature; his garments consisted of a light-blue frockcoat with yellow buttons, white waistcoat and necktie, as was the fashion at the time, but everything *negligée*. His complexion was healthy and tough, the skin somewhat pock-marked, his hair was of the color of slightly bluish-gray and very animated—when his hair was tossed by the wind there was something Ossianic-demoniac about him. In friendly converse, however, his expression became good-natured and gentle, particularly when the conversation pleased him. Every mood of his soul found powerful expression instantly in his features."

Klöber's original painting has disappeared. It was a full-length portrait with a bit of Mödling landscape as a background. The nephew Karl was included, reposing under a tree. The composer was depicted with note-book and pencil. ––A drawing of the head, presumably as it was in the painting, has survived and is owned by the publishing house of C. F. Peters in Leipzig.––

---

[6] Joseph Valentine Dont, a violoncellist, was a member of Beethoven's circle of friends. (Cf. TK, II, 399; TDR, IV, 104, n. 1.)

We now reach an incident in the story of Beethoven's life concerning which much has been written from the biased and frequently erroneous, because uninformed or ill-informed, point of view adopted by Schindler and which it becomes a duty to rectify not only so that the picture of Beethoven as he was may be kept true, but that the better motives and impulses which prompted the woman whom he so cordially detested be placed in their proper light also. The rights of a woman and the honor which a world has always accorded to the strongest, noblest, divinest instinct of woman—maternal love—were at stake. The mother of Karl, though she had been convicted and punished for adultery at an earlier period, and though she might not have proved a safe mentor for her son, was yet a mother, his mother. That fact Beethoven was willing to recognize as palliating the conduct of the boy, but he could not bring himself to recognize that it might also palliate if it did not justify the steps which his harshness compelled a mother to take to gratify the need implanted by nature. Johanna van Beethoven is at least entitled to the same hearing at the bar of posterity that she received in the tribunals of her day, and it is the duty of Beethoven's biographer to strip the story of the quarrel between her and her brother-in-law of the romantic excrescences which many writers have fastened upon it. In this narrative the truth will be told, perhaps for the first time, as it is disclosed by the documents, the evidence and the judicial decrees in the case. To set forth these documents in full in the body of the text would call for the sacrifice of much space and sadly interrupted the story; what is essential in them will be given literally, or in outline, whenever it becomes necessary.[7]

After his dismissal from the class of the parish priest at Mödling, Karl van Beethoven was placed in the hands of a private tutor to be prepared for admission to one of the public schools of Vienna—no doubt that known as the Academic Gymnasium. To enter this school the boy had to pass an examination, and for this purpose Beethoven brought him to Vienna about the middle of August. Frau van Beethoven was now determined to wrest from her brother-in-law the authority, which was his as sole guardian, to keep the boy in his care and to direct his training. She took to her aid Jacob Hotschevar, a *Hofconcipist* (clerk or scrivener in the government service), and petitioned the *Landrecht* of Lower Austria to take from Beethoven the authority to direct the future training of his ward. The *Landrecht* was a tribunal with jurisdiction in litigations and other matters affecting the nobility. Acting on the assumption that the Dutch "van," like the German "von," was a badge of noble birth, it had listened to Beethoven's plea and appointed him sole guardian of his nephew, removing the widow from the joint guardianship directed in the will of the boy's father on the score of her immorality, as we already know.

[7] Thayer made or procured transcripts of the tribunals in which the struggle for the possession of Karl van Beethoven were made. Readers whose curiosity is not satisfied by these pages are referred to Appendix III of Vol. IV of TDR. (TK, II, 401, n. 1.) See also *A*, III, Appendix C.

The proceedings were begun in September and were dismissed, as the records show, on the 18th of that month. Three days later, that is, on September 21, she applied to the court again, this time for permission to place her son in the Royal Imperial Convict, where he would have board, lodging and instruction. She and Beethoven as "coguardian" were commanded to appear in court on September 23, and the latter was directed to bring the report of the lad's examination with him. There was a postponement of the hearing till September 30, and on October 3d the widow's application was rejected. Thus far victory had gone to Beethoven.

The postponement of the hearing was made in great likelihood to enable Beethoven to change his residence from Mödling to the city (the house on the Gärtnerstrasse). At any rate, Karl was a public school scholar on November 6th, as Fanny Giannatasio records in her diary on that day, together with the fact that her father had met Beethoven, who had shortly before returned from the country. That the boy was in the third grammar class and remained there during the months of November and December, receiving also instruction in pianoforte playing, French and drawing from a private teacher, is known from the court proceedings which were held later. The lad made good progress in his studies, all seemed well and something of the old cordial relations seemed again to be established between Beethoven and the Giannatasios. Fanny writes: "Yesterday Beethoven was with us once again. We have secured a housekeeper for him. He was here three hours and since his hearing was especially bad this day, we wrote everything down. One cannot be in his company without being impressed with his admirable character, his deep sense of what is good and noble. If Karl would but recompense him for the many sacrifices which he makes for his sake! My hopes are intermingled with serious doubts. He will probably make a journey to London this spring. It might be advantageous to him financially in many ways."

Before long Beethoven was at the Giannatasio house again, according to an entry dated November 20. He became interested in the singing of the sisters, singing with them, which produced a comical effect, as he seldom was in tune; but he helped them to give the correct expression to the music. Fanny now deplored that their childish timidity had so long deprived them of such a pleasure, which would now perhaps be of short duration, since he had received a second invitation from England. Within a fortnight the diary chronicles the severest trial that the boy had yet caused his uncle: he ran away from home and sought a haven with his mother. The sympathetic Fanny wrote later:[8] "One day B. came in great excitement and sought counsel and help from my father, saying that Karl had run away! I recall that on this occasion amid our expressions of sympathy he cried out tearfully: 'He is ashamed of me!'" The incident is recorded in her diary under date of December 5; it occurred, apparently two days before. The diarist's

[8] *Grenzboten*, XVI Jhrg. (1857), p. 31. (TDR, IV, 110, n. 3.)

entry is as follows: "Never in my life shall I forget the moment when he came and told us that Karl was gone, had run away to his mother, and showed us his letter as an evidence of his vileness. To see this man suffering so, to see him *weeping*—it was touching! Father took up the matter with great zeal, and with all my sorrow I feel a pleasurable sensation in the consciousness that now we are *much* to Beethoven, yes, at this moment his only refuge. Now he surely perceives his error if he has wronged us in his opinions. Ah! he can never appreciate how highly we esteem him, how much I should be capable of doing for his happiness! How the uniqueness of his character shows itself once again. The naughty child is again with him with the help of the police—the Ravenmother! Oh! how dreadful it is that this man is compelled to suffer so on account of such outcasts. He must go away from here, or she; that will be the outcome. For the present B. will give him into our care; it will be an act of great kindness on my father's part if he receives him, as he will have to look upon him as one under arrest. . . . It did me good when he went away to note that his thoughts were more diverted. He told me that he had been so wrought up by the matter that it took him some time to gather his thoughts. During the night his heart had beat audibly. Alas! and there remains nothing for me to say except that all that we can do is so little! I would give half my life for the man! He always thinks of himself last. He lamented that he did not know what would become of his housekeeping when Karl was gone."

Beethoven went to the mother immediately in the morning to bring back the boy; she promised to release him in the evening; and since Beethoven feared that she would send him away (to Linz or Hungary), he employed the police to get the boy back and turned him over temporarily to Giannatasio again. He was to remain there apparently for the winter.

At the same time the mother was working for her own interests; and on December 7th made a third application to the court:

Johanna van Beethoven (living at Tiefer Graben No. 238 on the second floor) declares to the R. I. Landrecht of Lower A[ustria] that her son Karl van Beethoven *ran away from his uncle and guardian, Hr. Ludwig van Beethoven, without her knowledge and participation, but the same was again returned to him by her through the R. I. chief of police*. At the same time she requested that, since Ludwig van Beethoven according to report intends to send her son to a school and indeed far away from here, perhaps even abroad, he be denied the permission of chief guardianship and that she *once again* will request the sanction to be permitted to send her son to the R.I. University Convict for education and board.

She repeated this request in a petition of December 10th and added the following points. A letter of Giannatasio's dated March 8, 1816, showed that she had to forgo her desire to visit her son or satisfy it once a month and then "like a thief." After Beethoven took the boy, and especially after his removal to Mödling, she was not permitted to see him at all. She had been assured that her son would be admitted to the Convict, but his testimonials had been withheld from her and so she had been unable to file them with her application for a scholarship. His expenses were 750 florins per year for board, lodging, clothes, books, medicines, etc., to pay which 2,000 florins had been deposited in Court and yielded 100 florins interest per annum. She had pledged herself to give one-half of her pension of 333 florins, 20, that is 116 florins, 40 kreutzers towards his education. This amounted to 380 florins V.S., including the interest on the deposit; and she would gladly pay the difference between this sum and 750 florins until she should get the promised scholarship for her son.

Hotschevar supported these petitions in a document like a modern law brief, explaining his interest in the matter on the grounds that his wife was a stepsister of Frau van Beethoven's deceased mother, that the law permitted such an act in all cases where human rights were concerned and that he, having had experience for several years as instructor in the houses of the aristocracy, could not be blamed if he put the knowledge of pedagogics and psychology thus acquired at the service of a lad to whom he bore a family relationship and brought to the attention of the supreme guardian matters which it (the *Landrecht*) could not possibly know concerning its wards unless proceedings were brought before it. He admitted that Frau van Beethoven had years before been guilty of a moral delinquency for which she had been punished, but asserted her right to a standing in court; he then contended: (1) that the mother had illegally been denied all influence over her son partly with, partly without the knowledge of the court, and (2) that her son could not remain under the sole influence of his uncle and guardian without danger of suffering physical and moral ruin. In support of these contentions he recited that the brothers van Beethoven were eccentric men, so often at odds with each other that they might better be called enemies than friends, Carl van Beethoven being pleasantly disposed toward his brother only when he was in need of money from him, and that the suspicion lay near that the boy had been an object of traffic between them, inasmuch as an agreement touching the payment of 1,500 florins had been made only on condition that Ludwig van Beethoven surrender a document which appointed him guardian. Carl van Beethoven, moreover, knowing the animosity which his brother felt towards his wife, had in a codicil to his will expressly said that he did not want Ludwig van Beethoven to be sole guardian of his son but joint guardian with the mother, and had, for the sake of the boy, admonished more compliancy on the part of the mother and more moderation on that of the brother. Although the Court had deprived the mother of the guardianship over her son, it had granted permission to her to visit him; but this privilege had been withheld from her. The statement of the village priest Fröhlich (which has already been given in these pages) was appended to the widow's application as evidence of the physical and moral degeneration of the boy, and for himself Hotschevar says that he had observed after the boy had run away from his uncle that his hands and feet were frostbitten, that he had no seasonable clothing and that his linen and baths had been neglected. The priest's statement was also appealed to to show that the boy had been led into unfilial conduct, indifference toward religion, hypocrisy, untruthfulness and even theft against his guardian—in short, was in danger of becoming a menace to society. He willingly granted Beethoven's readiness and desire to care for his ward, but maintained that his hatred of the mother, his passionate disposition inflamed by the talebearing of others (once naming Giannatasio), made it difficult for him to employ the proper means. Conceding Beethoven's magnanimity, he yet urged that in view of the danger in which the lad was, he ought to forgo the guardianship or associate with himself either the mother or some other capable person, it appearing from the facts in the case that he was "physically and morally unfit" for the post.

Already on December 9th the court had summoned the petitioner and also Beethoven and his nephew to appear in court on the afternoon of December 11th at 4 o'clock. Beethoven brought Karl Bernard with him, no doubt to protect him in his deafness. On the same day the widow appealed to the court that in case the guardian of her son should make application touching the plans for his future training, it be not granted without giving her a hearing. All three were examined. We quote from the minutes of the *Landrecht*:

The ward Carl v. Bethoven appeared, age 12 years, student in the 3rd Latin class, and was questioned:
Had he received good testimonials?
"Eminent" in Latin, "1st class" in other studies.
Why had he left his uncle?
Because his mother had told him she would send him to a public school and he did not think he would make progress under private instruction.
How did his uncle treat him?
Well.
Where had he been of late?
He had been in hiding at his mother's.
Where would he rather live—at his mother's or his uncle's?
He would like to live at his uncle's if he but had a companion, as his uncle was hard of hearing and he could not talk with him.
Had he been prompted by his mother to leave his uncle?
No.
When did he leave him?
Eight days ago.
How could he say that he could not succeed under private instruction when he had made such good progress?
This had been the case since he had studied in public; before that he had received 2nd class in mathematics and had not made it up.
Had his mother commanded him to return to his uncle?

She had wanted to take him back to him herself, but he had resisted because he feared maltreatment.

Had his uncle maltreated him?

He had punished him often, but only when he deserved it; he had been maltreated only once, and that after his return, when his uncle threatened to throttle him.

How long had he been with his mother?

Two days.

Who had given him instruction in religion?

The same teacher who taught him other subjects, formerly the priest at Mödling, who was not kindly disposed towards him because he did not behave himself in the street and babbled in school.

Had he indulged in disrespectful remarks about his mother?

Yes; and in the presence of his uncle, whom he thought he would please in that way and who had agreed with him.

Was he often alone?

When his uncle was not at home he was left wholly alone.

Had his uncle admonished him to pray?

Yes; he prayed with him every morning and evening.

Ludwig v. Bethoven and Joseph Carl Bernhard appeared. Ludwig v. Bethoven was questioned:

How did his nephew Carl leave him?

He did not know exactly; his nephew had made himself culpable; he had charged him with it and the same day in the evening he had received a note of farewell. He could not tell the cause of his departure; his mother may have asked him to come to her the day before, but it might have been fear of punishment.

What had his nephew done?

He had a housekeeper who had been recommended to him by Gianastasio; two of her letters to Frl. Gianastasio and one of the latter's had fallen into his hands; in them it was stated that his nephew had called the servants abusive names, had withheld money and spent it on sweetmeats.

In whose care was his nephew?

He had provided him with a *Correpetitor* for pianoforte playing, French and drawing who came to the house; these studies occupied all the leisure time of his nephew so completely that he needed no care; moreover, he could not trust any of his servants with the oversight of his nephew, as they had been bribed by the boy's mother; he had placed him in the hands of a priest for the development of his musical talent, but the mother had got into an agreement with him also. He would place his ward in the Convict, but the oversight was not strict enough there among so many pupils.

Did he have any testimonials touching his nephew's studies?

He had appended them to his last examination.

Had his nephew not spoken disrespectfully of his mother in his presence?

No; besides, he had admonished him to speak nothing but the truth; he had asked his nephew if he was fond of his mother and he answered in the negative.

How did he get the boy back?

With the help of the police. He had gone to the mother in the forenoon to demand him of her, but she would promise nothing except that she would deliver him back in the evening; he had feared that she intended to take him to Linz, where his brother lived, or to Hungary; for that reason he had gone to the police; as soon as he got him back he placed him in the care of Gianastasio.

What were his objections to having his nephew sent to the Convict?

It was not advisable at present because, as the professor had said, there were too many pupils there and the supervision over a boy like his ward was not adequate.

What means did he purpose to employ in the education of his ward?

His ward's greatest talent was in study and to this he would be held. His means of subsistence were the half of his mother's pension and the interest on 2,000 florins. Heretofore the difference between this sum and the cost had been paid by him and he was willing to assume it in the future if the matter could but once be put in order. As it was not practicable to place his nephew in the Convict now, he knew only of two courses open to him: to keep a steward for him who should always be with him, or to send him for the winter to Gionastasio. After half a year he would send him to the Mölker Convict, which he had heard highly commended, or if he were but of noble birth, give him to the Theresianum.

Were he and his brother of the nobility and did he have documents to prove it?

"Van" was a Dutch predicate which was not exclusively applied to the nobility; he had neither a diploma nor any other proof of his nobility.

Johanna v. Bethoven appeared.

How did her son come to her from the house of his guardian?

He had come to her in the evening for fear of punishment and because he did not like to live with his uncle.

Had she advised him to return to his uncle?

Yes, but her son did not want to do so because he feared maltreatment.

It looked as if she had concealed her son?

She had written to her brother-in-law that she would send her son back to him, but she had not seen him for a long time and was therefore glad to have him with her for awhile, and for this reason she had not sent him back at once.

Had she been forbidden to see her son?

Her wish to do so had been frustrated by telling her of different places where she might see him, but when she went to the places he was not there.

Had her son been taken from her by the police?

She had herself taken him to the police at 4 o'clock.

How did she learn of the plan to send her son out of the country?

Gionastasio had disclosed the project to the police.

Did she consider that her son had been well treated at his uncle's?

She thought it unsuitable for the reasons given in her former application. She wished to say in particular that v. Bethoven had only one servant and that one could not rely on servants; he was deaf and could not converse with his ward; there was nobody to look after the wants of her son satisfactorily; his cleanliness was neglected and supervision of his clothing and washing; persons who had brought him clean linen had been turned back by his guardian.

What prospects had she for caring for her son?

She had previously had the assurance of Count von Dietrichstein that her son would be accepted at the Convict; she had not been to him since because her application [to the Court] had been rejected.

In whose presence had her son spoken disrespectfully of her?

She had not herself heard him do so, nor could she mention the names of persons who had heard him.

From what source would she meet the deficiency in her income which would have to be applied to the support of her son?

She had no fortune herself but the Hofconcipist Hotschevar would defray the expenses.

Was her husband of noble birth?

So the brothers had said; the documentary proof of nobility was said to be in the possession of the oldest brother, the composer. At the legal hearing on the death of her husband, proofs of nobility had been demanded; she herself had no document bearing on the subject.

Hereupon Ludwig v. Bethoven was called up again to produce those letters of the housekeeper and of Frln. Gionastasio of which there was mention in the record, and to deliver all the school reports of his ward.

It remains a mystery, if Johanna spoke the truth in answering the final question, how the case ever got into the *Landrecht* in the first place. As a matter of fact, it deserves to be mentioned that, as later events showed, the lower court espoused the cause of Frau van Beethoven with something like the zeal of an advocate. Beethoven's last statement that "van" was a Dutch predicate not confined to the nobility and that he had no proof of noble birth, is all that the minutes of the court show bearing on this question. His answer, no doubt, raised a doubt in the mind of the court touching its jurisdiction. While both parties were awaiting the results of their efforts, the *Landrecht* made a decision which cut Beethoven to the quick: on December 18th it sent the proceedings to the Vienna Magistracy.

Schindler's comments on the effect of the reference of the case to the Civic Magistrates demand a moment's attention. Schindler says:[9] "The transfer of the case to the Magistracy was felt as an overwhelming blow by Beethoven. It would be difficult to maintain that Beethoven attached importance to appearing in the public eye as of noble birth, his origin as well as family conditions being well known—especially the latter by reason of the humble social position of his brothers. But it is certain that he laid great weight upon having his lawsuit adjudicated by the exceptional upper court, partly because as a matter of fact there was in that tribunal a better appreciation of his importance (as Dame Giannatasio has noted quite correctly), partly because the lower court had an unfavorable reputation which could not inspire in him a hope for the desired outcome. But nevertheless it may be said as sure that neither his genius nor his works of art would have

[9] *Biogr.*, I, pp. 257-58. (TDR, IV, 114.)

given him the privileged position which he occupied in the circles of the nobility had there not been a presumption that he was an equal. This was variously demonstrated as soon as the occurrence in the aristocratic court became known to the public. Not in the middle classes, but in the upper, the little word 'van' had exercised a palpable charm. It is a settled fact that after the incident in the Lower Austrian *Landrecht* the great city of Vienna became too small for our aggrieved master, and had he not been restrained by his sense of duty which was placed upon him by his brother's will, the projected journey to England would have been undertaken and his sojourn there perhaps become permanent."

In one of the Conversation Books used by Beethoven in 1820, there occurs this remark in Beethoven's handwriting: ". . . when it [*sic*][10] learned that my brother was not of the nobility. It is singular, so far as I know, that there is a hiatus here which ought to be filled, for my nature shows that I do not belong among this plebeian m[ass]"; and, in February, 1820, when Peters had observed his dissatisfaction: "The common citizen should be excluded from higher men, and *I* have *gotten amongst* them."[11]

It is also certain that Schindler was not as well informed as he ought to have been in the premises and that his memory often left him in the lurch, as we have frequently seen already and shall see again. Not exact knowledge but an amiable bias in favor of his hero speaks out of his recital. It is scarcely conceivable that Beethoven should have cherished the thought that possibly he was of noble birth or that he seriously encouraged such a belief among his exalted friends.

The nephew's stay at the Giannatasios was not of long duration and the signs of an imminent disruption of a beautiful and profitable friendship soon showed themselves, though for the nonce amiable relations between Beethoven and the Giannatasio family were continued. Yet Fanny saw her lovely illusions melting away. It had been agreed that Karl should not associate with the other pupils at the institute. Willing, perhaps desirous at first, that such an arrangement should be made, it seems that Beethoven felt his *amour propre* hurt by it as soon as the first fit of resentment against the lad gave way before one of his tender moods; now there ensued one of the old fits of moroseness, dissatisfaction and suspicion. He wrote to Gianna-tasio that Karl's room should be better heated—that he had never had frostbitten hands and feet when living with him (Hotschevar's accusation was evidently rankling in his breast); moreover, too much importance was being attached to his act, and the consequences to the delinquent were being carried too far. In her diary under date December 14, Fanny recognizes "that his moodiness and his weakness for the lad have taken possession of him again and induced him to believe the *liar* rather than his tried friends"; she concludes with the lamentation "that it will never be possible

[10] Schünemann believes that Beethoven meant "he" for the second word (*er* rather than *es*). See Schünemann, I, p. 215.
[11] *Ibid.*, p. 247.

to gain Beethoven's entire confidence . . . as to what will happen in the future one can only fear the worst."

Let the rest of the year's history be devoted to Beethoven's creative work. Considering the revival of interest and desire on the part of the composer, the net result, as measured by finished products, was not as large as might have been expected. Two explanations for these circumstances may be offered: the first lies in his domestic miseries and the frame of mind in which they kept him for long stretches at a time—that is obvious; the second may be read in his compositions. He was growing more and more prone to reflection, to moody speculation; his mental processes, if not slower than before, were more protracted, and also more profound, and they were occupied with works of tremendous magnitude. The year produced the Sonata in B-flat, Op. 106 and sketches and partial developments of the Symphony in D minor. The Sonata, so two sketchbooks carefully analysed by Nottebohm[12] show, was begun in 1817, and occupied much of the composer's time during 1818.

In a letter to Archduke Rudolph written in June, 1819, Beethoven shed light on the progress of the sonata the year before: ". . . I enclose two pieces[13] in a fair copy which I wrote already last year [1818] before the name-day of Your Imperial Highness [April 17], but despondency and so many sad circumstances, and my health so bad at the time all made me so *discouraged* that only with the greatest anxiety and embarrassment could I approach Your Imperial Highness. From the time I moved to Mödling until nearly the end of my visit there my health improved, but how many calamities confronted me! Meanwhile many things gathered on my writing desk, from which fact I can assure you that I thought of Your Imperial Highness. . . . To the two pieces which I wrote down in manuscript for the name-day of Y. I. H. two others have been added, the last of which is a large Fugato, so that it constitutes a Grand Sonata which will soon be published and long ago *in my heart* was intended for Y. I. H. . . ."

That work continued on the Sonata during the summer of 1818 at Mödling is also shown by a remark that occurs in the middle of the sketches: "A small house there, so small that one has only a little room— Just a few days in this heavenly Briel— Yearning or longing—fulfillment or deliverance."[14] According to Schindler the work was completed in the autumn of this year. Czerny played it in Beethoven's presence in the spring of 1819, and even earlier in the year a copy had been sent to Ries for sale and publication in England, along with the arrangement for quintet of Op. 1, No. 3. In a letter dated January 30, 1819, he writes Ries:

. . . Do everything *for* me that you can; for I need it. Commissions from the Philharmonic Society would have been very welcome. *The reports which Neate*

[12] *II Beeth.*, pp. 123ff., 352. (TDR, IV, 117, n. 1.)

[13] These were the first two movements.

[14] *II Beeth.*, p. 132. Briel or Brühl is a valley in Mödling. (TDR, IV, 117, n. 3.)

sent me about the near failure of the three overtures were vexing to me; *here each of them not only pleased each in its own way* but those in E-flat and C major made a great impression. The fate of these compositions with the P.S. is incomprehensible to me— You will have by now received the arranged quintet and the sonata. See to it that both works, especially the quintet, are engraved at once. More leisure may be taken with the sonata but I should like to have it published inside of two months, or three at the latest. Your earlier letter referred to I did not receive; wherefore I had no hesitation selling both works here—but that is only for Germany. Moreover it will be three months also before the sonata will appear here; but make haste with the quintet. . . .[15]

The Sonata was sold to Artaria in Vienna for 100 ducats. The publisher sent the proofs to Beethoven on July 24, and announced it in the *Wiener Zeitung* of September 15, 1819 with the following words: "Now we shall put aside all the usual eulogies which would be superfluous anyway for the admirers of Beethoven's high artistic talent, thereby meeting the composer's wishes at the same time; we note only in a few lines that this work, which excels above all other creations of this master not only through its most rich and grand fantasy but also in regard to artistic perfection and sustained style, will mark a new period in Beethoven's pianoforte works." It appeared under both French and German title; the latter follows: "Grosse Sonate für das Hammerklavier Seiner Kais: Königl.: Hoheit und Eminenz, dem Durchlauchtigsten Hochwürdigsten Herrn Herrn Erzherzog Rudolph von Oesterreich Cardinal und Erzbischoff von Olmütz, etc., etc., etc., in tiefster Ehrfurcht gewidmet von Ludwig van Beethoven, Op. 106."

Soon after its publication (on October 1st) Beethoven in a jocose letter asked for six copies of the Sonata and six of the Variations on Scottish songs. Beethoven informed Ries of its publication in a letter dated November 10th and wanted to send him a copy to aid him in correcting the English edition, which was not ready. The Sonata Op. 106 was, therefore, the chief product of the year 1818. Beethoven told Czerny that it was to be his greatest; and so it is, not only in its dimensions but also in its contents. "The Sonata was composed under distressful circumstances," said Beethoven in a letter to Ries (March, 1819), "for it is hard to write almost for the sake of bread alone, and to this pass I have come."

Simultaneously with the Sonata, Beethoven was at work on the Ninth Symphony during a large portion of the year. Not alone the Ninth Symphony, a Tenth also was before his fancy, but with neither of them had Schiller's "Ode to Joy" been brought into association, though the employment of the human voice in one of them was already under consideration. Notes in the *Tagebuch* and sketchbooks which, to judge by their context, were written during the summer sojourn in Mödling show the trend of Beethoven's thoughts on religious subjects which were crystallizing or about to crystallize in the idea of writing a great mass.

[15] The Quintet was published in Vienna by Artaria in February, 1819.

In order to write true church music . . . look through all the monastic church chorals and also the strophes in the most correct translations and perfect prosody in all Christian-Catholic psalms and hymns generally.

Sacrifice again all the pettinesses of social life to your art. O God above all things! For it is an eternal providence which directs omnisciently the good and evil fortunes of human men.

> Short is the life of man, and whoso bears
> A cruel heart, devising cruel things,
> On him men call down evil from the gods
> While living, and pursue him, when he dies,
> With cruel scoffs. But whoso is of generous heart
> And harbors generous aims, his guests proclaim
> His praises far and wide to all mankind,
> And numberless are they who call him good.
>
> —*Homer.*

Tranquilly will I submit myself to all vicissitudes and place my sole confidence in Thy unalterable goodness, O God! My soul shall rejoice in Thy immutable servant. Be my rock, my light, forever my trust!

Among the sketches for the Sonata in B-flat are memoranda of vocal pieces which came into his mind during his wanderings in the environs of Mödling. Goethe's "Haidenröslein," to which his mind several times turned, occupied him again. His spiritual exaltation finds expression in fragments which he notes as "written while walking in the evening between and on the mountains," among them this:

Gott al - lein ist un - ser Herr.   Er al - lein
[God a - lone is God our Lord.   He a - lone]

In his letter to Hauschka Beethoven remarked that he was compelled to do a lot of "scribbling" for the sake of money in order to procure leisure for great works. One such pot-boiler was a pianoforte piece in B-flat which bears the inscription "written upon request on the afternoon of August 14, 1818 by Beethoven." There are sketches for the piece, however, among those for the last movement of the B-flat Sonata.[16] Added to the inscription are the words "written upon the request of a lady unknown to him." According to A. B. Marx,[17] this lady was the Polish pianist, Marie Szymanowska. Published first as a supplement to the Berlin *Allgemeine Musikalische Zeitung* in 1824, it did not receive its strange title of "Dernière pensée musicale" until 1840 when it was published separately by Schlesinger in Berlin.

Further "scribbling" may be explained by the fact that he was still engaged

---

[16] *II Beeth.*, p. 137. (TDR, IV, 131, n. 2.)

[17] *Ludwig van Beethoven, Leben und Schaffen* (Berlin, 1875), I, p. 75.

upon arrangements of folk-songs for Thomson (WoO 156), which were published in Thomson's Vol. vi.[18]

With the folksongs must be associated the Variations for Pianoforte alone, or Pianoforte and Flute (or Violin), which he wrote in this and the preceding year and which were published as Op. 105 and 107. —C. B. Oldman has established the history of these variations[19] which may be summarized here. On January 1, 1816, Thomson asked the composer to send him specimen airs from Germany, Poland, Russia, the Tyrol, Venice and Spain. From his work on British airs for Thomson, Beethoven's interest in folk-songs had been stimulated and previously he had formed the plan to choose his own songs from different countries and arrange them with accompaniment for trio. Thus Beethoven was willing to fall in with this suggestion and sent eighteen such airs on July 8th, followed by one more air shortly afterwards. Thomson failed to find suitable English verses for these melodies, however; and when he made the naive proposal that Beethoven compose for 36 ducats six potpourri overtures for the pianoforte with these melodies as a basis, Beethoven naturally declined the offer. A request from Birchall for variations to favorite English, Scottish and Irish airs also came to naught. Then on June 25, 1817, Thomson offered 72 ducats for variations (not more than 8) on any twelve of the airs "in an agreeable style, and not too difficult." Beethoven did not answer until February 21, 1818, when he made a counter-proposal: "I am willing to write twelve overtures for you for an honorarium of 140 gold ducats, I am willing to write twelve themes with variations for 100 gold ducats, but if you would like me to write twelve overtures and twelve themes with variations *together* or at the same time, I am ready to ask no more for the twelve overtures and the twelve themes varied than 224 ducats." Thomson replied on June 22nd suggesting that Beethoven could choose the majority of the themes from the Scottish airs that he had already harmonized and add a flute part *ad libitum* to the accompaniment. He added: "And it would be quite desirable if you wrote the variations in a style that is *familiar* and *easy* and a bit brilliant, so that the majority of our ladies may play them and relish them." On November 18, Beethoven acknowledged receipt of 140 ducats in gold for the variations upon the twelve themes and arrangement of eight Scottish airs to be sung or played as trios. Thomson received the twelve sets of variations on December 28th, and he published nine of them in 1819,[20] after Beethoven had made certain revisions in response to Thomson's criticisms. — Beethoven composed sixteen Themes and Variations on folk-song material in all; six of them were published by Artaria in Vienna (Op. 105) and the other ten by Simrock in Bonn (Op. 107).

[18] See KHV, p. 655.

[19] "Beethoven's Variations on National Themes: Their Composition and First Publication," *Music Review*, xii (1951), pp. 45-51.

[20] Entitled "Twelve National Airs with Variations," they were published in three volumes of three each (Op. 105, Nos. 1-6 and Op. 107, Nos. 2, 6, 7). See D. W. MacArdle, "A Checklist of Beethoven's Chamber Music," *Music and Letters*, xxvii (1946), p. 53.

--- ⚞Mention has already been made of Beethoven's plan to select songs of different continental countries to supply with his own accompaniment. Besides the eighteen airs sent to Thomson in 1816, Beethoven sent six more within the next two years and granted the publisher the exclusive right to sell them all in his letter of November 18, 1818. However, of these twenty-four airs[21] only three were used for keyboard variations: WoO 158, Nos. 5, 6 and 16 in Op. 107 as Nos. 1, 5 and 7. Only one is represented in the Collected Works Edition (the Venetian song "La gondoletta," WoO 157, No. 12). The other twenty-three (WoO 158) were published in 1941 by Breitkopf and Härtel.[22]

The compositions for the year were:

1816-18. Twenty-three songs of Different Countries, WoO 158; 1 Danish, 2 German, 1 Hungarian, 1 Italian, 2 Polish, 2 Portuguese, 4 Russian, 3 Spanish, 2 Swedish, 5 Tyrolean.

1817-18. Six Varied Themes for Pianoforte, with optional accompaniment of flute or violin, Op. 105.

Sonata for Pianoforte in B-flat major, Op. 106.

Ten Varied Themes for Pianoforte with optional accompaniment of flute or violin, Op. 107.

Twelve Scottish Airs, WoO 156.

About 1818. Canon. "Ich bitt' dich, schreib' mir die Es-Scala auf," WoO 172, for Vincenz Hauschka.

1818. "Ich bin bereit," WoO 201, in a letter to Hauschka.

"O Hoffnung," WoO 200, 4-measure theme for Archduke Rudolph, who wrote variations on this theme, which were published in December, 1819.

Piece for Pianoforte in B-flat major, WoO 60.

The publications for the year were:

By Thomson in Edinburgh and Preston in London:
"A Select Collection of Original Scottish Airs with Introductory and Concluding Symphonies and Accompaniments for the Piano Forte, Violin and Violoncello by Haydn and Beethoven." Of the thirty songs, twenty-five were by Beethoven (Op. 108) and five by Haydn.

By *Wiener Modenzeitung,* March 31, as a musical supplement:
"Resignation" (Count Paul von Haugwitz), WoO 149.⚟

---

[21] In the letter Beethoven writes "twenty-five melodies" (See *A,* III, p. 1424), but Kinsky-Halm (KHV, p. 663) argue that Beethoven should have written "twenty-four," since on June 17, 1823, Thomson turned the publishing rights of *twenty-four* Beethoven airs over to the publishers Paine and Hopkins.

[22] Ed. by G. Schünemann with the title "Neues Volksliederheft." Previously, two songs, "Bolero a solo" and "Schwedisches Wiegenlied," were published singly. See KHV, p. 664.

CHAPTER XXXII

THE YEAR 1819

KARL'S EDUCATION—THE CONVERSATION BOOKS— COMPOSITION OF THE *MISSA SOLEMNIS* BEGUN

T H E key-note for much that must occupy us in a survey of the year 1819 is sounded by two letters to Archduke Rudolph. The first is a New Year's greeting:

Everything that can be gathered up into one wish and be called salutary; wealth, happiness and a blessing, is included in my wish which is offered to Y. I. H. on this day. May a wish for myself also be graciously entertained by Y. I. H.; namely, that I may continue to enjoy the grace of Y. I. H. in the future.— A terrible event took place recently in my family affairs, which for a time robbed me of all my reasoning powers; and to this must be charged the circumstance that I have not called upon Y. I. H. in person nor made mention of the masterly Variations of my highly honored and exalted pupil, the favorite of the Muses. I do not dare to express either by word of mouth or in writing my thanks for the surprise and favor with which I have been honored, inasmuch as I occupy *much too humble* a position, nor dare I, much as I would like and ardently as I long to do so, *repay like with like*. May the heavens hear and fulfil my wishes especially for the health of Y. I. H. In a few days I hope to hear the masterpiece that was sent to me performed by Y. I. H. himself; and nothing can give me greater joy than to have contributed towards Y. I. H.'s speedy assumption of the position already prepared for Your Highness atop Parnassus.

Beethoven, it will be remembered, had composed a four-measure theme "O Hoffnung" in the preceding year for the benefit of his patron's creative efforts. The Archduke responded to this assignment from his teacher by writing forty variations on this theme and dedicating the work to Beethoven. Of the publishers' interest in this exceptional work we shall hear anon.

The events of the final months of 1818 had indeed been devastating ones for Beethoven, and the "terrible" one was of course Karl's running away to his mother in early December, which to the uncle was not the natural result of a boy of twelve having been forcibly separated from his mother, but a terrible misfortune and personal affront. Unfortunately the struggle between the mother and the uncle over the boy must occupy many pages in the account of the years ahead.

The second letter to the Archduke, however, takes us to a topic of the highest creative endeavor. It was written in early June, and we quote the pertinent passages:

Your Imperial Highness!
On the day when Y. I. H. most graciously sent for me, I was not at home, and immediately thereafter I contracted a violent cold, so that I must write to Y. I. H. reclining near my bed— Despite the mass of congratulations which may have been pouring in to you, my most gracious Sir, I know full well that it will not be without *sacrifice to Y.I.H.* that this new honor is bestowed. But I think of what a widening sphere of action will be opened thereby for you and for your great noble-mindedness. So I can only extend my congratulations about this honor to Y. I. H. along with the others. There is almost nothing that is good—without sacrifice, and this appears to apply directly to the nobler, superior man more than others, thereby his virtue becomes tested.

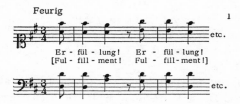

This I might sing out now from the bottom of my heart, were Y. I. H. completely recovered; but the new sphere of action, the transformation, the subsequent travels will certainly bring back soon the priceless health of Your Imperial Highness to a perfect state; and then I shall elaborate on the above theme with a hearty A—men or Allelujah— . . . .

Beethoven returns to this subject later in the letter:

The day when a High Mass of mine shall be performed at the ceremonies for Y. I. H. will be for me the most beautiful day of my life, and God will inspire me so that my weak powers may contribute to the glorification of this solemn day— . . . .

The new honor "bestowed" upon the Archduke was first his elevation to Cardinal and then to Archbishop of Olmütz. He was officially informed of the first on April 24, 1819, and of the second on June 4, 1819, and the date of his installation was set for March 9, 1820. The following testimony of

---

[1] MacArdle discusses the musical transformation of Beethoven's theme for the Archduke "O Hoffnung" (WoO 200) to the expression "Erfüllung" (WoO 205e) quoted here. See MacArdle and Misch, *New Beethoven Letters* (Norman, 1957), p. 248, n. 4.

Schindler is responsible for the confusion in determining just when Beethoven started composing his great work which was to be known as the *Missa Solemnis*. Schindler writes:[2] "Without invitation of any kind Beethoven resolved to compose a mass for the solemnity, thus turning again after the lapse of many years to that branch of his art towards which, after the symphonies— as he himself often said— he felt himself most drawn. . . . I saw the score begun late in the autumn of 1818, after the gigantic Sonata in B-flat major, Op. 106, had just been finished."

However, in the first edition of his biography (p. 113) Schindler writes: "He began to labor on the new work in the winter of 1818-19." A sketchbook in the Wittgenstein Collection in Vienna has helped to show that Schindler's earlier statement was closer to the mark. This is the first known sketchbook to contain work on the Mass. From pages 4 to 15 there are sketches for variations on a waltz by Diabelli, immediately followed by sketches for the *Kyrie* of the Mass. In discussing the sketchbook, Unger writes:[3] "Until now it had been assumed that the beginning of 1820 was the earliest point of time to date the start of work on the variations—but this sketchbook refers it back to the first months of the year 1819; for the choice of Archduke Rudolph as Archbishop of Olmütz took place on June 4, 1819, and the approaching appointment was certainly known some months earlier, that is, probably in the beginning of 1819. Since the installment was to be solemnized in March, 1820, and the master had decided on this work for that purpose, it may be accepted that the preliminary work fell in the first months of the year 1819."

A pocket sketchbook, filled mostly with sketches for the Mass was acquired by the Beethoven-Haus at Bonn in 1899. It has been transcribed and published by Dr. Joseph Schmidt-Görg, who dates it from December, 1819, to about the middle of April, 1820. The 44 page book (there was originally another sheet) contains a few sketches for the second part of the *Gloria* and all parts of the *Credo*. There are a few ideas for the *Sanctus* and one for the *Agnus Dei*. Thus the *Kyrie* and the *Gloria* were the work of the main part of the year, whereas work on the *Credo* did not begin until well into the fall.

Now to return to the first topic, the family struggle. The long court procedures had been wearing, and the final blow had been the transfer of the case to the City Magistracy because Beethoven was not of the nobility. Doubtless he was also filled with fear as to what the decision of the new tribunal would be.

At this point a few official data are wanting, but the suspension of Beethoven from the guardianship of his nephew can only be stated as having been determined by the magistrates immediately after the beginning of the new year. In consequence of this, the boy was for a few weeks with his

[2] *Biogr.*, I, p. 269. (TDR, IV, 326, n. 2.)
[3] "Die Beethoven-Handschriften der Familie W. in Wien" in *NBJ*, VII, pp. 167-68.

mother. On January 10, Fanny Giannatasio writes in her diary: "What Müller tells me about Beethoven pains me deeply. The wicked woman has finally succeeded in triumphing over him. He has been removed from the guardianship,[4] and the wicked son returns to the source of his wickedness. I can imagine Beethoven's grief. It is said that since yesterday he has been entirely alone and eats apart from the others. He ought to know that Karl is glad to be with his mother; it would ease the pain of the separation."

On January 7 the magistrates summoned Beethoven (who still lived in the Gärtnergasse), the boy, the mother, Hotschevar and the curator, Dr. Schönauer, to appear before them on January 11. Of what action was taken that day there is no record, but Hotschevar's attack brought out a vigorous defense in the shape of a letter sent by Beethoven to the Magistracy,[5] in which he maintained the superiority of the educational plan which he was pursuing over that which had been proposed by the mother, proclaimed the magnanimity and virtuousness of all his acts and discharged a broadside of accusation and insinuation against Frau van Beethoven and the priest who had come to her help. We can make room for only a few passages: "His exceptional capacity, and partly also his peculiarities, call for exceptional measures; and I never did a more beneficial or magnanimous act than when I took my nephew to myself and personally assumed charge of his education. Seeing that (according to Plutarch) a Philip did not think it beneath his dignity to direct the education of his son Alexander and give him the great Aristotle for a teacher because he did not consider the ordinary teachers suitable, and a Laudon[6] looked after the education of his son *himself*, why should not such beautiful and sublime example be followed by others? Already during his lifetime his *father* entrusted my nephew to *me* and I confess that I feel myself better fitted than anybody else to *incite my nephew to virtue and industry by my own example*. . . . Had the mother been able to subdue her wicked disposition and permitted my plans to take their quiet development, a very favorable result would have followed; but when a *mother of this sort* seeks to involve her child in the secrets of her own vulgar and evil surroundings, and in his tender years leads him astray to deception (a plague for children!!!), to bribery of my servants, to *untruthfulness*, by *laughing at him* when he tells the truth, yes, even *giving him money* to awaken in him lusts and desires which are harmful, tells *him* that such things are trifles which *by me and others would be accounted* grave faults, the already difficult task becomes more difficult and dangerous. . . . Gifts of fortune may be acquired; *morality* must be *implanted* early (particularly when a child has had the misfortune to suck in *such mother's milk*, was in her care for several years, was put to thoroughly *bad uses, even* had to help

[4] He had not been removed, but only temporarily suspended; he retained the supervision of the boy's education. (TK, III, 2, n. 1.)

[5] The letter was dated erroneously February 1, 1818, instead of 1819. (TK, III, 2, n.2.)

[6] Field Marshal, Baron Gideon Ernst von Laudon (1717-90) according to his biographer Wilhelm von Janko, was educated solely by his father, Gerhard Otto von Laudon.

deceive his father). Furthermore, he will inherit from me; and even now I could leave him enough to *keep him from want* while continuing his studies until he should receive an appointment. We need only *quiet and no more interference from the mother,* and *the beautiful goal which I have set* will be attained. . . . Ought I now to reply to the intrigues of a Hr. Court-scrivener Honschova [Hotschevar] *against me,* or to the *priest of Mödling,* who is despised by his congregation, who is suspected of being guilty of *illicit intercourse,* who lays his pupils military fashion on a form to be thrashed and who could not forgive me because I kept watch on *him* and would not permit my nephew to be caned like a brute— Ought I? No, the association of these men with Frau van Beethoven bears *witness* against *them both,* and *only such* could make common cause *with her against me.* . . ."

From the records of the Magistracy and his own words it follows that Beethoven did not send his nephew to a public school, but engaged a private tutor under whose care he continued his studies in an institute conducted by Johann Kudlich.[7] Beethoven held this man in great esteem judging by his letter to the Magistracy (of February 1, 1819) in which he says "That Herr v. Kudlich teaches and practices himself the basic methods of the university which all connoisseurs consider the best as I do myself." Besides the ordinary subjects, Karl received instruction from Kudlich in French, drawing and music; his religious training was entrusted to a priest. This state of affairs lasted till the end of March, when Beethoven announced a desire to resign the guardianship—persuaded to take this step, it is fair to presume, by the magistrates, who, in the end, would have been obliged to remove him. Karl was living with his mother at the time. According to the court records, Beethoven left the matter of education "entirely to Kudlich," but it was given to him to propose the name of a guardian, either in place of himself or as an associate. He consulted earnestly with his friends as to what was to be done with the boy and who would be his guardian, and they were sorely tried by his constitutional indecision.

The friend who was the most helpful and influential in these affairs was the writer and editor, Joseph Karl Bernard. He was born at Horatitz in Bohemia in 1775 and studied in Prague and Heidelberg. In 1800 he became an officer in the Hofkriegsrat at Vienna, from where he worked slowly into the profession of author. He became an editor of the *Modenzeitung* in 1818, and in the fall of the next year assumed the head-editorship of the *Wiener Zeitung.* His acquaintance with Beethoven started at the time of the Vienna Congress, and by 1819 his name was appearing regularly in the Conversation Books. While other members of the circle, such as Oliva, were given the perfunctory jobs of taking dictation and running errands, Bernard was

[7] Johann Kudlich's institute was on the Erdbergerstrasse No. 91, in the Landstrasse (TDR, IV, 138, n. 1), the same district in which Beethoven lived at the time. According to Frimmel (*FRBH,* I, p. 308), it was not developed enough to become a school until the following year.

entrusted with a real responsibility: the reworking of the contents of Beethoven's documents until they were legally acceptable. His friendship and advice were invaluable at this time.[8]⸎—

In the Conversation Books for March and April, 1819, Bernard writes:[9]

What must be done is to select as guardian a man who has your entire confidence both as respects morality and pedagogical skill, and with whom you may always remain on friendly terms concerning the affair. Since Kudlich has more influence on Karl than . . . Giànatassio [Giannatasio], it is my opinion that you seek no further for someone who would meet every requirement.— It would merely be very troublesome for you.

Beethoven seemed to be in doubt, for he had a preference for his friend the magisterial Councillor Tuscher.[10] In these consultations, the project of sending the boy away from Vienna was discussed, and in that connection the name of Sailer in Landshut[11] was suggested, which appealed to the composer. Bernard says again:

If you want peace of mind I think it wise that you name a guardian as you were willing to do yesterday. But if it is possible to send the boy to Sailer at Landshut, it would, of course, be better still, since then you could feel assured that he was in the best of hands. Even if you have Tuscher as co-guardian, your case will not be bettered, inasmuch as all cares will still rest on you. Perhaps Tuscher and Kudlich might jointly assume the guardianship—this might be very advantageous. All the same, everything will remain as heretofore, even if you send him away he will remain with Kudlich until a change has been made. So long as you are guardian and Karl remains here, you will not only have all the cares as heretofore, but also be compelled to fight the mother and all her intrigues. Have Karl sent for the present again to Kudlich, meanwhile the matter may be straightened out.[12]

Beethoven seems to have expressed a doubt as to Tuscher's willingness to serve as guardian. Bernard continues: "Perhaps he might be more easily persuaded if a co-guardian like Kudlich were appointed.— It is not necessary to settle everything by tomorrow. If we go to Omeyer[13] tomorrow morning, then to Tuscher and Kudlich, we can come to an understanding as to what will be the best thing to do."

Tuscher, if we are correct in recognizing his handwriting, permitted himself to be persuaded, though a bit under protest; he foresaw difficulties. The

[8] See Max Unger, "Beethovens Konversationshefte als biographische Quelle," *DM*, Vol. 34 (1942), p. 382.

[9] See Schünemann, I, pp. 30-32.

[10] It was at the request of Matthias von Tuscher that Beethoven wrote the "Abschiedsgesang" in 1814 for the farewell party of Dr. Leop. Weiss.

[11] Professor Johann Michael Sailer at Landshut University in Bavaria. A famous Catholic orator, Sailer later became a bishop at Regensburg. (Cf. TDR, IV, 140, n. 2.)

[12] At the time of this consultation the boy was with his mother. Later, he was with Kudlich and remained there perhaps until Beethoven went to Mödling. Kudlich was instructed not to permit any communication between him and his mother. (TDR, IV, 139, n. 2.)

[13] Joseph von Ohmayer was of noble birth and a doctor of law. He appears in a Conversation Book of 1820 (Schünemann, II, 30).

Magistracy at the suggestion of Beethoven thereupon appointed the Magisterial Councillor Matthias von Tuscher guardian of the boy on March 26. He was commanded to place his ward, then "living with his mother, Johanna van Beethoven," in another place for bringing up and education under proper care, and submit his opinion touching the proposition of the mother and Hotschevar that he be entered in a public institute of learning before the expiration of the second school semester, that Beethoven contribute to the cost and that the share of the mother's pension and the interest on the money deposited for the boy be applied to this end. Tuscher was decidedly of the opinion that the boy must be sent away for a time and was agreed with the plan of placing him with Prof. Sailer in Landshut after it had been broached to him. For this the consent of the Magistracy and the police authorities and a passport were necessary. In the opinion of one of Beethoven's advisers (Bach) Tuscher was to be informed of the plan only after the passport had been obtained, but before the mother, who had already found "a channel," could take steps to communicate with Tuscher. Beethoven applied to the city authorities for a passport for two years for his ward. On April 23, the authorities asked of the Magistracy if there were any objections to the proposed step. The Magistracy objected to the boy's being sent into a foreign country, but asked Tuscher if he were not willing to withdraw his application and name an institute in Austria. Tuscher declined and set forth the great hopes which he placed in the training to be had of a man like Sailer, who, "because of his reverence for the talents of the composer, Beethoven, was especially bound to him," and hence would bestow upon his charge the strictest oversight and care, which was of great importance in the case of a boy who was "extremely cunning and an adept in every sort of craftiness." In replying to the municipal authorities the Magistracy (on May 7) conceded the necessity of withdrawing the boy from his mother's influence, but thought it unnecessary to send him out of the country on this account, against which the mother had protested and the curator of the ward, Dr. Schönauer, had declared himself. The passport was therefore refused. Beethoven had taken a step which seems to have been made to prevent the widow from securing help for her plans from a source higher than any that had yet been invoked and to enlist that higher power in his own behalf. He appealed to Archduke Rudolph to use his influence with Archduke Ludwig, next younger brother of Emperor Franz I, to aid him in his project of sending his nephew far away from the mother's influence. In the letter written to the Archduke[14] he stated that it had been his intention to petition Archduke Ludwig in the premises, but there had thitherto appeared to be no occasion for so doing for the reason that all the authorities who had jurisdiction in the matter were convinced of the advisability of the step, viz.: the Police, the Supervisory Guardianship Court and the guardian.

[14] It is undated, but to judge from the contents and the sequence of events it was written in May. (TDR, IV, 142.)

He had heard, however, that the mother intended to seek an audience of Archduke Ludwig to prevent the execution of his plan. Convinced that she would stop at nothing in the way of calumniation, he expressed the hope that his reputation for morality would suffice as a refutation of her slanders, and that Archduke Rudolph would bear testimony in his behalf.

The plan to send the nephew out of the country had been frustrated and had to be abandoned; what further could be done? His mind being filled with artistic projects of the greatest magnitude, Beethoven was desirous to pass the summer months again in Mödling, where he moved on May 12th; but after the experiences of the preceding year nothing could be hoped for his nephew in that quarter. Now he came to a realization of the advantages which Giannatasio's institute had offered and in a letter to Giannatasio asked him again to take the lad till other arrangements had been made. The Giannatasio family were fearful lest such a proceeding might work harm to their institution, and on June 17 visited Beethoven at Mödling to tell him that his wishes could not be complied with. "Grievously as it pained us," Fanny writes in her diary, "to refuse Beethoven anything, I am yet so convinced of the necessity of the step and that it could do us no good, but on the contrary harm, that I prefer to have it so."

Thereupon the lad was sent to the institute of Joseph Blöchlinger.[15] Claudius Artaria, who was one of the teachers there (1821-1824), recalled in later years that Karl was one of the older scholars, "naturally talented, but somewhat conceited because he was the nephew of Beethoven." He also saw the mother there a few times, but remembered nothing in particular in connection with her visits. The lad appears to have prospered during the early part of his stay at the school. In December, 1819 Peters (?) writes in a Conversation Book.[16]

A great deal has been gained in that the boy has again become orderly in his public studies— Plöchlinger [*sic*] moreover, though not exactly brilliant, seems to be good.

The public school system acts as a restraint on him. . . .

Your nephew looks well, handsome eyes—charm, a speaking physiognomy, and excellent bearing. I would continue his education for only two years more. . . .

⸙

He is always present, and thus she can do him no harm. However he is agreed that she spoils the boy—

⸙

When you have acquired the sole guardianship, then do you decide and he will obey.

⸙

Your views are admirable but not always reconcilable with this wretched world.

[15] Joseph Blöchlinger (1788-1855) opened his school in 1814 in the Landstrasse suburb on the Kaiserstrasse No. 26 (now Josephstadt-strasse). He had studied with the famed Swiss teacher, Pestalozzi.

[16] Schünemann, I, pp. 128-29.

Tuscher, a member of the Magistracy, was compelled to recognize that his colleagues were wholly under the influence of Frau van Beethoven and Hotschevar, and that he could do no service to his friend or his friend's ward; on July 5, he applied to be relieved of the guardianship which, he said, had become "in every respect burdensome and vexatious," on the ground that "the multiplicity of official duties as well as various other considerations would not permit him longer to administer the office." Beethoven took this action in very bad part, and Tuscher shared the fate of many others of being for a space an object of the composer's critical ill-will. Beethoven now served notice on the Magistracy that he would resume the guardianship under the testamentary appointment and that he had placed his ward in Blöchlinger's institution. On July 15 he wrote to Archduke Rudolph that confusion still reigned in his domestic affairs, no hope or comfort was in sight, all of his structures were blown away, as if by the wind. He adds: "The present proprietor of the institute in which I have placed my nephew, a pupil of Pestalozzi, is of the opinion that it will be difficult for him and my poor nephew to achieve a desirable outcome— But he is also of the opinion that there could be nothing more profitable than removal of my nephew abroad."

Beethoven continued, during the summer and fall, to bombard his friends and those who were helping him with many long letters, containing directives and invectives. Evidently Blöchlinger allowed the boy's mother to visit him at the school, a fact which infuriated Beethoven. Blöchlinger received several violently worded epistles from him on the subject, in which Beethoven refers to himself as "sole guardian" though he had not been legally appointed as such after Tuscher's resignation. Johann apparently entered the controversy in the summer, for in one letter of the summer to Bernard, Beethoven says: "And my worthy brother has become involved (he has just bought an estate worth 20,000 thalers or gulden, and you can be sure that he now helps to corrupt) in that he wants him [Karl] to become an Apothecary, etc." In another letter he says "On no account must my brother be admitted, for he will *only* talk about all that he can have with him. . . ." On Sept. 14 he wrote Blöchlinger: "*Only the following individuals have free access to my nephew, Herr von Bernard, Herr von Oliva, Herr von Piuk, the Referent.*" This last was Franz Xaver Piuk, who was Referent, or Recording Secretary for the court in this affair. Beethoven had written him fully and at the time seemed to have enlisted his support. Further in the letter to Blöchlinger he continues: "*My nephew is not to go out of the house without my written permission*—from which it is plain what course is to be followed towards the mother— I insist that in this respect *strict obedience* be given to what the authorities and I have ordained." Since these letters are highly repetitive in style and content, one should suffice us here, in order to show the composer's distraught state of mind. This is a letter to Bernard in which the recipient, Oliva (who had recently returned to Vienna) and Blöchlinger all come in for chastisement because they took a more moderate view of the boy's mother:

I cannot hide the fact that ever since we have known each other your conduct has often caused me grief. You seem to pay attention to the flattery of poor wretched people and thereupon act the protector; by this means you injure your friends because by this same protection you are hoping to find everything good and for the best. The present affair shows again how false is your stand and how without regard for me you have added new vexations to the old ones— This man is coarse, I might say a very coarse person— You have given your approval to his miserable ideas and betrayed a friend. Only too well did I notice how carelessly everything was arranged with regard to this evil person. Oliva was not smooth enough, and you were not rough enough for this *non-Swiss* lout, for he is, no matter where he may be from, a lout.[17]— *Out of esteem for me he speaks of my unreasonableness*—what logic— On the other hand he solicits *your good will* again— You should not be contagious to this, there *is no honor* from such a creature— But—I must say it occurs to me that you are as much my enemy as a bit my friend— So my nephew should be really hostile to me, and, if so, then he should be allowed to continue so? or attempts could be made to see whether *he loves this raven mother more than me?* You gave your approval to these miserable ideas of this wretched pedagogical creature, without thinking of the complete injustice of it. You yourself a few days ago in the city gave me to understand clearly enough that my nephew hates me—oh, may the whole miserable mob be cursed and damned—

It is not known whether the Magistracy was immediately informed of all of the new steps which Beethoven had taken, though in his draft of the memorandum to the Court of Appeal Beethoven states that he "wrote" to them that he had resumed the guardianship. There is reference in a letter to Bernard dated August 2 that Johanna had forwarded a statement "against me" to the Magistrate.┇━ Be that as it may, as chief guardian the court determined if possible to put an end to the continual friction and undertook an investigation of all the educational experiments which had been made, arriving at the conclusion that the boy had been "subject to the whims of Beethoven and had been tossed back and forth like a ball from one educational institution to another." For this reason it decreed, on September 17, that Tuscher's request for relief be granted, but that the guardianship should not again be entrusted to Beethoven but to the mother, the natural guardian under the law, with a capable and honest man as coguardian. To this office Leopold Nussböck, municipal sequestrator, was appointed.

Beethoven protested against the action in a letter which the Magistracy received on October 31. Having been absent from the city at the time, "on a matter of business," he had made no objection to the appointment of Herr Nussböck as guardian of his nephew, but, returning with the intention of remaining in Vienna, he wished to resume the guardianship, as this was

[17] Blöchlinger was born in Gobelingen, Switzerland (*FRBH*, I, p. 50).

essential to the welfare of the boy, the mother having neither the will nor the strength to look after his training. He was the more insistent on a resumption of this duty since he had learned that owing to lack of money the boy was to be removed from the institution which he had selected for him. He charged that the mother wished to take her son to her home so that she might be able to expend his income, including the half of her pension which she was obliged to devote to his education, upon herself. He asked that the intermediary guardianship be taken from Nussböck and be restored to him without delay.

Acting as a legal advisor to Beethoven at this time was Johann Baptist Bach, who had helped him since 1816 in his dealings with the authorities concerning his nephew. A distinguished Vienna lawyer, Schindler describes him as "a man of many accomplishments including a practising lover of music, who was active on more than a dilettante basis, particularly as violon-cellist in a quartet. The high respect which Dr. Bach enjoyed is demonstrated by the fact that three times he was elected Dean of the Faculty of Law at the University of Vienna."[18] Concerning his petition to the Magistracy, Beethoven wrote to Dr. Bach at great length on October 27:

You will have already received the communication from Frau van Beethoven. That person is too lacking in moral worth for me to refute her attacks against me. His Imperial Highness, Eminence and Cardinal, who treats me as a friend and not as a servant, would unhesitatingly bear witness to my morality, and to all the silly twaddle about Olmütz, not a word of which is true. So far as one knows, His Highness himself will spend at most six weeks of the year there. . . . [Johanna had charged that Beethoven as the Archduke's teacher would now be obliged to spend most of his time at Olmütz.]

The chief points are that I be recognized at once as sole guardian; I will accept no coguardian; that the mother be excluded from intercourse with her son *in the Institute* because in view of her *immorality* there cannot be enough watchmen there and she confuses the master by the false statements and lies which she tells him. Also she has led her son to tell shameful lies and make charges *against me*, and she herself accuses me of having given him too much or too little; I will substantiate all these statements with evidence— But that the claims of humanity may not be overlooked, she may see her son occasionally at my home in the presence of the master and other eminent people. . . . It is my opinion that you should insist stoutly and irrevocably that I be *sole* guardian and that this un-natural mother shall see her son only *at my house*. My well known humanity and culture as well as my accustomed humaneness towards others are a guarantee that my treatment of her will be no less generous than that given her son. Moreover I think that all this should be done quickly and that if possible we ought to get the Appellate Court to assume the superior guardianship. Since I have brought my nephew into a higher category, neither he nor I belong to the M[agistracy] under whose guardianship are only innmakers, shoemakers and tailors—

[18] *Biogr.*, I, p. 257.

As regards his present maintenance, it shall be cared for as long as I live, for the future he has 7,000 florins V.S. of which his mother has the usufruct during life—also 2,000 fl. (or a little more since I have reinvested it for him), the interest on which belongs to *him*, and 4,000 florins in silver *of mine* are lying in the bank; as he is to inherit all my property this belongs to his capital. . . .

The sum of 4,000 florins in silver mentioned in the letter had had an interesting history. The money was presented to Beethoven by the nobility at the Congress of Vienna, but he considered it as savings earmarked for his nephew and therefore untouchable. The money was first deposited with Steiner in July, 1816, at an interest of eight per cent. Three years later Beethoven withdrew it from Steiner and on July 13, 1819, he used it to buy eight shares of bank stock, on the advice of Baron von Eskeles, director of the Viennese bank, Arnstein and Eskeles.[19]

The Magistracy disposed of Beethoven's protest and application on November 4, by curtly referring him to the disposition made of his petition in September, when he was removed from the guardianship. Beethoven asked for a reconsideration, but without avail, and the only recourse remaining to him was the appeal to the higher court which had already been suggested to Dr. Bach. The story of that appeal belongs to the year 1820.

Meanwhile the association of Councillor Peters with him in the guardianship had been broached and was the subject of discussion with his friends. In December the following is written in a Conversation Book:

[Bernard] The Magistracy has till now only made a minute of the proceedings and will now hold a session to arrive at a decision. It is already decided that you shall have the guardianship, but a 2nd is to be associated with you. Since no one still has any objection to Peters, there will be no difficulty in this.
[Peters] The matter will be ordered according to your wishes and my humble self will take care of Herr Plechlinger [*sic*]. The mother will not be admitted to the institute unless you are present, 4 times a year is enough.
[Bernard] Nor the guardian either?— The Magistracy has compromised itself nicely.

Further along in the same Conversation Book, Dr. Bach writes: "If we are willing to let the widow be named coguardian, there will be less difficulties in the affair.—As coguardian she will have no authority, only the honor of being associated in the guardianship. She will be a mere figurehead."[20] Whether the conversations noted at the time referred to the case on appeal or to the application still pending before the Magistracy, or some to the one, some to the other, it is impossible to determine. The record of the refusal of the Magistracy has not been procured, but the decree of the Appellate Court gives December 20 as its date.

[19] See the letter from Steiner to Beethoven dated December 29, 1820. See also Max Reinitz, *Beethoven im Kampf mit dem Schicksal* (Vienna, 1924), p. 110; and Max Unger, "Beethoven als Kapitalist," *Schweizerische Musikzeitung*, Vol. 65 (1925), pp. 57ff.
[20] Schünemann, I, pp. 113, 119.

Frequent citations from the so-called "Conversation Books" made in the course of the narrative touching the later phases of the controversy over the guardianship call for some remarks upon this new source of information opened in these years. In the *Niederrheinische Musikzeitung*, No. 28 of 1854, Schindler wrote: "Beethoven's hearing had already become too weak for oral conversation, even now with the help of an ear-trumpet, in 1818, and recourse had now to be had to writing.[21] Only in the case of intercourse with Archduke Rudolph, and here because of his gentle voice, the smallest of the ear-trumpets remained of service for several years more." That he was, partly by the ear and partly by the eye, to judge of the correctness of the performance of his music, Schindler stated in the same article—a fact also known from many other sources; this was the case even to his last year. When after the death of Beethoven, such of his manuscripts and papers as were thought to be salable were set apart, there remained in the hands of von Breuning a lot of letters, documents and Conversation Books. The estimated value in the inventory of the manuscripts and the price obtained for them at the auction sale, indicate how utterly worthless from a pecuniary point of view that other collection was thought to be; as, however, they might be of use to some future biographer, it was well to have them preserved, and doubtless a small gratification to Schindler for his great sacrifices and very valuable services to Beethoven in these last months, the only one which he as guardian to the absent nephew could make; so Breuning gave them to him. The Conversation Books, counting in as such those which were really nothing but a sheet or two of paper loosely folded, were only about 400 in number, or less than fifty per annum for the last nine years of Beethoven's life—that being the period which they cover. There is no source of information for the biographer of Beethoven which at first sight appears so rich and productive and yet, to the conscientious writer, proves so provokingly defective and requires such extreme caution in its use as these Conversation Books. Schindler, who spoke on this as on so many other topics frankly and without reserve, said that he long preserved the books and papers intact, but not finding any person but himself who placed any value upon them, their weight and bulk had led him in the course of his long unsettled life by degrees to destroy those which he deemed to be of little or no importance.

The earliest surviving Conversation Book, which can be dated late February to early March, 1818, was acquired by the Beethoven Archives at Bonn.[22] Another Conversation Book, written in early September, 1825, a part of the Bodmer Collection, is also at Bonn.[23] The remainder were,

[21] A few conversation sheets may be dated as early as the spring of 1816. See Max Unger, DM, *op.cit.*, p. 377.

[22] *Beethoven-Haus Katalog*, ed. by W. Schmidt-Görg (Bonn, 1935), p. 20. See Ludwig Schiedermair, "Beiträge zum Leben und Schaffen nach Dokumenten des Beethoven-Hauses" in *Veröffentlichungen des Beethoven-Hauses in Bonn*, VI (1930), pp. 12ff.

[23] *Eine Schweizer Beethoven-sammlung, Katalog*, ed. by Max Unger, Zurich, p. 80.

in 1845, transferred to the then Royal Library in Berlin, and, in 1855, when they were examined for this work, numbered one hundred thirty-eight.

Thayer's industry in the gathering and collecting of material for this biography, let it be remarked here in grateful tribute, is illustrated in the fact that he made practically a complete transcript of the Conversation Books, laboriously deciphering the frequently hieroglyphic scrawls, and compiled a mass of supplementary material for the purpose of fixing the chronological order of the conversations. The dates of all concerts and other public events alluded to were established by the examination of all newspapers and other contemporary records and the utility of the biographical material greatly enhanced. ──⟨This tribute to Thayer was reworded by Krehbiel from one first written by Riemann.[24] The present editor can add that with the disappearance of the Thayer papers, referred to in the preface, the nearest to a basic source for the Conversation Books is the incomplete transcription in three volumes by Schünemann which covers the period from 1818 (February, March) to July, 1823. For the benefit of the reader, references to this source have been given.

To return to the one hundred thirty-eight books used by Thayer,⟩── the oldest of these belongs to the period now before us (1819) and was evidently preserved by Schindler on account of the protracted conversations on the topic of the nephew. We have already made several citations from it and shall have frequent occasion to have recourse to it in the progress of this narrative. The period in which it was used is approximately fixed by a reference to a concert given by the violinist Franz Clement, at which he played an introduction and variations on a theme by Beethoven. This concert took place on April 4, 1819. Apparently in reply to a question put by Beethoven, an unidentified hand writes: "Poor stuff—empty—totally ineffective— your theme was in bad hands; with much monotony he made 15 or 20 variations and put a cadenza [*fermate*] in every one, you may imagine what we had to endure—he has fallen off greatly and looks too old to entertain with his acrobatics on the violin."[25] The last conversations in the book took place about the time of Beethoven's removal to Mödling—shortly before and after.

It was but natural that the Conversation Books preserved are such as place Schindler's relation to the master in the strongest light and those deemed by him essential to the full understanding of the more important events of Beethoven's last years. Most of them bear evidence of the deep interest with which Schindler, while they remained in his possession, lived over the past in them. In many cases he appended the names of the principal writers; so that one soon learns to distinguish their hands without difficulty; and occasionally he enriched them with valuable annotations. The larger of them—

See Th. v. Frimmel, "Ein Konversationsheft Beethovens aus dem Jahre 1825," in *BJ* (Munich, 1909), II, pp. 161ff.

[24] TK, III, p. 12, n. 1; TDR, IV, p. 155, n. 1.

[25] Schünemann, I, pp. 35-6.

ordinary blank note-books—are only of a size and thickness fitted to be carried in the coat pocket. It is obvious, therefore, on a moment's reflection, that at a single sitting with a few friends in an inn or coffee-house, the pages must have filled rapidly as the book passed from hand to hand and one or another wrote question or reply, remark or statement, a bit of news or a piece of advice. A few such conversations, one sees, would fill a book, all the sooner as there is no thought of economizing space and each new sentence is usually also a new paragraph. It strikes one, therefore, that the whole 400 could have contained but a small portion of the conversations of the period they covered. This was so. At home a slate or any loose scraps of paper were commonly used, thus saving a heavy item of expense; moreover, many who conversed with Beethoven would only write upon the slate in order to obliterate it immediately, that nothing should remain exposed to the eyes of others. The books, therefore, were for the most part for use when the composer was away from home, although there were occasions when, it being desirable to preserve what was written, they were also used there. Hence, the collection in Berlin can be viewed as little more than scattered specimens of the conversations of the master's friends and companions, most unequally distributed as to time. For months together there is nothing or hardly anything; and then again a few days will fill many scores of leaves. In a few instances Beethoven has himself written—that is, when in some public place he did not trust his voice; and memoranda of divers kinds, even of musical ideas from his pen, are not infrequent. One is surprised to find so few distinguished names in literature, science and art— Grillparzer's forms an exception and he appears only in the later years; as for the rest, they are for the most part of local Vienna celebrities.

This explanatory digression may serve as a modulation to more cheerful themes than that which has occupied us of late.

Though Karl was no longer a member of the Giannatasio household or pupil of the institute, and though there were, in consequence, fewer meetings between Beethoven and his self-sacrificing friends, their relations remained pleasant, and early in 1819 Beethoven found occasion to supplement his verbal protestations of gratitude with a deed. Nanni, the younger daughter of Giannatasio, was married on February 6, 1819, to Leopold Schmerling. When the young couple returned to the house after the ceremony they were greeted by a wedding hymn for tenor solo, men's voices and pianoforte accompaniment. The performers were hidden in a corner of the room. When they had finished they stepped forth from their place of concealment. Beethoven was among them and he handed to the bride the manuscript of the music which he had written to words of Prof. Stein.[26]

26 Professor Anton Joseph Stein (1759-1844) had been Professor of Classical Literature at the University in Vienna since 1806; he was also tutor in the imperial household. Madame Pessiak-Schmerling, a daughter of Nanni, recounted this incident twice in her letters to Thayer. See TDR, IV, pp. 518 and 521.

--❦⟮The version for men's voices in unison and tenor solo is in C major and is probably the second version. The autograph, which was found in the archives of Breitkopf and Härtel and is now in a library at Darmstadt,[27] is inscribed "On January 14th, 1819— For H. v. giannattasio del Rio from l. v. Beethoven." Another version of the song, which is in A major for mixed voices also with piano accompaniment, is owned privately in England. This version has been established as another authentic one by Oldman,[28] who suggests that Beethoven originally intended to include ladies in a harmonized setting for the performance but that this proved impractical. From the description of the event it is clear that the version in C major was the one used.❦⟯--

Beethoven made a single appearance as conductor in this year. It was on January 17 at a concert given for the benefit of the Widows and Orphans of the Juridical Faculty of the University. The orchestra was largely composed of amateurs and the programme began with the overture to *Prometheus* and ended with the Seventh Symphony. Among the listeners was P. D. A. Atterbom, the Swedish poet, who wrote a sympathetic account of it.

In the midst of the worries occasioned by the guardianship, Beethoven was elected Honorary Member of the Philharmonic Society of Laibach, an institution which had been founded in 1702 and revived, after repeated interruptions, in 1816. The project of giving him the distinction had been broached in the councils of the society in 1808, but Anton Schmith, a physician in Vienna, whose opinion had been asked, had advised against it, saying: "Beethoven is as freakish as he is unserviceable." Eleven years later the men of Laibach had more knowledge or better counsel, and they sent him a diploma on March 15 through von Tuscher. Acknowledging the honor on May 4, Beethoven stated that as a mark of appreciation he was sending, also through the magistrate, an "unpublished" composition and would hold himself in readiness to serve the society should it ever need him. There is no direct evidence as to what composition he had in mind; but in the archives of the Laibach society there is a manuscript copy of the Sixth Symphony. It is not an autograph except as to its title, Beethoven having written "Sinfonia pastorale" on the cover in red crayon, and corrections in lead pencil in the music.[29]

The time for Beethoven's annual summer flitting had come. Mödling was chosen again for the country sojourn as we already know and Beethoven arrived there on May 12, taking lodgings as before in the Hafner house on the Hauptstrasse. He had, evidently, brought a housekeeper with him and now engaged a housemaid. On the blank leaves of an Almanac for 1819, such as used to be bound in those useful household publications for the reception of memoranda, Beethoven notes: "Came to Mödling, May 12.!!! *Miser*

[27] See KHV, p. 568.
[28] C. B. Oldman, "A Beethoven Friendship," *Music and Letters*, XVII (1936), pp. 328-36.

[29] See F. Keesbacher, *Die philharmonische Gesellschaft in Laibach* (Laibach, 1862), pp. 49-51. (TDR, IV, 158, n. 1.)

sum pauper. . . ." "On May 14 the housemaid in M. came, to receive 6 florins a month. . . . On 29th May Dr. Hasenöhrl made his 3rd visit to K[arl]. Tuesday on the 22nd of June my nephew entered the institute of Hr. Blöchinger with a monthly payment in advance of 75 florins V.S. Began to take the baths here regularly [?] on 28th Monday, for the first [?] time daily." Schindler adds: "On July 20 gave notice to the housekeeper."

In 1810 Adolf Martin Schlesinger had opened his own book store in Berlin. Starting with a music lending library, he soon developed what was to be Berlin's first music publishing house. A few years later his son, Moritz, followed in his father's footsteps and opened a music publishing house in Paris. Father and son worked closely together and often published simultaneously. The Schlesingers were intelligent enough to cultivate Beethoven's friendship and eventually they were to be rewarded with the publication of, among other things, his last three pianoforte sonatas and the string quartets, Op. 132 and Op. 135.[30] In 1819 the father sent Moritz to Vienna to become acquainted with Beethoven. According to young Schlesinger's reminiscences written forty years later,[31] he was first introduced to the composer by Haslinger in the Steiner shop in Vienna, and Beethoven asked him to visit him in Mödling,[32] which happened a few days later.

"After getting out of the wagon I went to the inn and found Beethoven there, who came out the door in a fury and slammed it hard behind him. After I had dusted off a bit I went to the house which was designated as his dwelling. His housekeeper told me that it would be better not to speak to him as he had returned home in a rage. I gave her my visiting card which she brought to him, and after a few minutes to my great astonishment she came out again and bade me enter. Inside I found the great man at his writing desk. Immediately I *wrote* that I was glad to make his acquaintance. This (the fact that I *wrote*) made a favorable impression. He let himself go immediately and told me that he was the most miserable man in the world; a minute ago he came out of the inn where he had asked for a piece of *veal* which he especially desired; but *there was none there*—all this with a very serious and dark expression. I comforted him; we spoke (I always writing) of other things and so he detained me for two hours; then feeling that I would tire or upset him I wanted often to get up but he always held me back. After leaving him I hurried back to Vienna in my wagon and asked my inn boy if there was any roast veal available. Upon finding there was I left it on the platter, well covered up, and, without writing a word, I gave it to the man waiting with the carriage to take to Baden [Mödling] and present to Beethoven in my name. One morning soon afterwards I was still lying in bed when in came Beethoven, who kissed and embraced me and

---

[30] For a description of the Schlesingers see Max Unger, *Beethoven und seine Verleger* (Berlin and Vienna, 1921), pp. 24ff.

[31] For the second edition of A. B. Marx's

Ludwig van Beethoven Leben und Schaffen, 1863. (Unger, *op.cit.*, pp. 25-6.)

[32] Schlesinger writes "Baden" but this is obviously wrong for the year 1819.

said I was the best fellow he had ever met; never had anything made him so happy as this veal for which at that moment he had had such a longing." ⁊⹋–

Beethoven, as letters to the Archduke dated July 15 and August 31 show, was not in the best of health, but was hard at work on the Mass, with an excursion now and then into the Symphony (Ninth). Schindler presents us with a pathetic, impressive, almost terrifying picture of the state to which his labors lifted him:[33] "Towards the end of August, accompanied by the musician Johann Horzalka still living in Vienna, I arrived at the master's home in Mödling. It was 4 o'clock in the afternoon. As soon as we entered we learned that in the morning both servants had gone away, and that there had been a quarrel after midnight which had disturbed all the neighbors, because as a consequence of a long vigil both had gone to sleep and the food which had been prepared had become unpalatable. In the living-room, behind a locked door, we heard the master singing parts of the fugue in the *Credo*—singing, howling, stamping. After we had been listening a long time to this almost awful scene, and were about to go away, the door opened and Beethoven stood before us with distorted features, calculated to excite fear. He looked as if he had been in mortal combat with the whole host of contrapuntists, his everlasting enemies. His first utterances were confused, as if he had been disagreeably surprised at our having overheard him. Then he reached the day's happenings and with obvious restraint he remarked: 'Pretty doings, these [*Saubere Wirthschaft.*], everybody has run away and I haven't had anything to eat since yesternoon!' I tried to calm him and helped him to make his toilet. My companion hurried on in advance to the restaurant of the bathing establishment to have something made ready for the famished master. Then he complained about the wretched state of his domestic affairs, but here, for reasons already stated, there was nothing to be done. Never, it may be said, did so great an artwork as is the *Missa Solemnis* see its creation under more adverse circumstances!"

The incident doubtless occurred, but Schindler's memory as to his companion was in error. F. Luib brought Horzalka's attention to Schindler's story; the result was recorded by Luib in Thayer's copy of the Schindler biography: "Horzalka knows nothing of this." ⹋⹌ Schindler's account must be questioned further, however. In his introduction to the already mentioned "Missa Solemnis" sketchbook at Bonn, Schmidt-Görg sums up that, with a collation of Conversation Books, letters and the notation "still in 1819," on the first page of this sketchbook, the sketches for the *Credo* may be dated for the most part in November-December, 1819.[34] If Schindler is correct in dating his description of the creative struggle late August, 1819, it is much more likely that Beethoven was working on some section of the *Gloria*. It could well have been the final fugue "In Gloria Dei Patris," for in the Bonn

[33] I, pp. 270-71. (TDR, IV, 161.)
[34] Schmidt-Görg, *Ein Skizzenbuch aus den Jahren 1819/20*, p. 16.

sketchbook there are sketches for passages which precede and the *presto* section which ends the fugue, but not for the main fugue subject.

In a conversation of late March or early April, someone, probably Oliva, writes:

— Is the oratorio finished?
I cannot understand how he is so occupied; his professional work amounts to nothing and other than that he does nothing, and yet he talks all the time about so much work and business.[35]

The author in question was Bernard, who had been designated to write the text for the oratorio which Beethoven had been commissioned to write for the Gesellschaft der Musikfreunde. As we shall see, the writing of the libretto remained an obstacle for this project. Meanwhile, on June 15 Beethoven had received an advance payment for the work, for on this date he wrote the following note to the society:

Dear esteemed Sir!
I am lying in bed and from here cannot immediately elaborate on the subject of the oratorio— Meanwhile I shall write to you about it in a few days or speak to you in person. I confirm for you herewith by virtue of my own signature that I have received 400 fl. V.S.
Respectfully and most sincerely
Beethoven[36]

There was a meeting of the Society on November 22 at which Landgraf von Fürstenberg reported that on the written application of Prince von Odescalchi, representing the President, Beethoven had replied that he had long been desirous to compose a work which would reflect honor on the society and that he would do his best to expedite it.[37] That seems to have been the end of the matter for the time being.

There was also during the Mödling sojourn a continuation of the negotiations with Thomson. A Mr. Smith visited Beethoven bearing a letter from the Scottish publisher which called out a playful rejoinder in which Beethoven sought to turn an easy play upon German words into French. Thomson suggested that the introductions and accompaniments to the Scottish songs be made easier ("lighter," in the German idiom); they would be so, Beethoven replied, if the compensation were made more difficult ("heavier" would have been his word had he been permitted to use the German equivalent). As it is, Beethoven's humor becomes rather ponderous, as see the letter which was written in French by Beethoven apparently without assistance:

[35] Schünemann, I, p. 35.

[36] First published by Sonneck (*op.cit.*, p. 92) from the autograph in the Gardner Museum in Boston. See Miss Anderson's com-

ment on the addressee, *A*, p. 816, n. 1.

[37] Karl Ferdinand Pohl, *Die Gesellschaft der Musikfreunde* (Vienna, 1871), pp. 9-10. (TDR, IV, 161, n. 1.)

Vienne le 25me Maj, 1819.

Mon cher Ami!

Vous ecrivés toujours facile très facile—je m'accomode tout mon possible, mais—mais—mais—l'honorare pourroit pourtant être plus difficile, ou plus-tôt pesante!!!! Votre ami Monsieur Smith m'a fait grand plaisir a cause de sa visite chez moi—en hâte, je vous assure, que je serais toujours avec plaisir de votre service—comme j'ai à present votre Adresse par Mr. Smith, je serai bientôt en Etat de vous écrire plus ample—l'honorare pour un Thême avec variations j'ai fixé, dans ma derniere lettre à vous par Messieurs le Fries, a moien dix Ducats en or c'est, je vous jure malgré cela seulement par complaisance pour vous, puisque je n'ai pas besoin, de me mêler avec de telles petites choses, mais il faut toujours pourtant perdre de temps avec de telles bagatelles, et l'honneur ne permet pas, de dire à quelqu'un, ce qu'on en gagne,—je vous souhaite toujours le bon goût pour la vrai Musique et si vous crie facile—je crierai difficile pour facile!!!!!

Thomson endorsed on this letter: "25 May, 1819. Beethoven. Some pleasantry on my repeated requests to make his Symphs and accompgnts. to our National Airs Easy. sent by Mr. John Smith of Glasg."

There are two entries in a Conversation Book which refer to another British commission that was offered him about a month earlier:

[1]

. . . Another commission was brought by the other Englishman, the friend of Smith.— A Mr. Donaldson in Edinburgh wants to know if you will not write a Trio for 3 pianofortes that is difficult and in the style of your Quintet in E-flat.— He wants to announce it as his property.— The remuneration which you demand is to be paid to you in any way you may select.— All three parts of the Trio must be obligato. If perhaps you don't want now to determine the price, you could simply fix a time when it is ready and write to Donaldson in Edinburgh direct.—

These Englishmen speak of nothing else than your coming to England;—they give assurance that if you were to come for a single winter, from September until sometime in May, to England, Scotland and Ireland, you could earn so much that you could live the rest of your life on the interest.

[2]

Today the gentleman is going to write to Donaldson in Edinburgh—the answer can be here in 4 weeks and the gentleman can also be here that long—

•~•

. . . .

Tell him how much you want;—when it might be finished and how you want the payment made.

He is very desirous to have a composition from you and there is no reason to think that it would be returned—

Moreover it is a big work

If you can get 40 ducats for the Sonata he can doubtless pay 100

•~•

By that time the answer may be here from Edinburgh.[38]

Great Britain's monetary reward, had Beethoven accepted all its invitations, would no doubt have been all that the friend of "Mr. Donaldson of Edinburgh" stated and in proportion would have been the appreciation which Beethoven would have found at the hands of the English professional musicians, amateurs and musical laity.

Pathetic and diverting are the incidents which Karl Friedrich Zelter relates in letters to Goethe of his attempts to form a closer acquaintance with Beethoven. On July 29 he writes the following in his letter to Goethe concerning his journey to Austria: "Beethoven, whom I would like to see once during my lifetime, lives in the country and no one can tell me where." On August 16 he writes: ". . . It is said that he is intolerably *maussade*. Some say he is a lunatic. It is easy to talk. God forgive us all our sins! The poor man is reported as being totally deaf. Now I know what it means to see all this digital manipulation around me while my fingers are becoming useless one after the other. Lately Beethoven went to an eating-house; he sat himself down to a table and lost himself in thought. After an hour he calls the waiter: 'What do I owe?' 'The gentleman has not eaten anything yet, what shall I bring?' 'Bring anything you please, but let me alone!' "

Zelter stayed in Vienna from July to September, but saw nothing of Beethoven. Then on September 14 he writes: "The day before yesterday I wanted to pay a visit to Beethoven in Mödling. He wanted to go to Vienna, so we met en route, climbed out and embraced one another affectionately. The poor fellow is practically stone deaf and I could hardly restrain my tears. Then I went on to Mödling and he to Vienna.— — I must tell you about an episode that amused me considerably.— With me on this trip was Steiner, the music publisher, and since it is rather hard to converse with a deaf man on a country road, we arranged a proper meeting with Beethoven at four o'clock in the afternoon in Steiner's music store. After eating we drove back to Vienna at once. Full as a badger and tired as a dog I lay down and slept away the time, slept so soundly that not a thing entered my mind. Then I went to the theatre and when I saw Beethoven there I felt as if I had been struck by lightning. The same thing happened to him at sight of me, and this was not the place for explanations with a deaf man. Now comes the point: In spite of the things of which Beethoven is accused justly or unjustly, he enjoys a popular respect such as is bestowed only upon the most excellent. Steiner had given it out that Beethoven would appear in his little office, which will hold only six or eight persons, for the first time in person at 4 o'clock, and invited guests so generously that in a room crowded to the street, half a hundred brilliant people waited in vain. I did not get an explanation till next day, when I received a letter from Beethoven in

[38] Schünemann, *op.cit.*, I, pp. 48-9, 60-61. Schünemann believed that the handwriting was Oliva's; Thayer assumed it was Schindler's.

which he begged my pardon, for he, like me, had passed the time set for the meeting in blissful sleep."

Zelter's letter calls for a slight rectification. It was not the next day but four days later that Beethoven wrote him the letter of explanation, and Zelter's statement that Beethoven had overslept himself was pure presumption—unless he learned it from another source. Beethoven wrote:

Highly respected Sir!

It is not my fault that you were lately besmeared[39] by me, as people say here. Unforeseen circumstances robbed me of the pleasure of passing a few lovely and enjoyable hours with you, which would have been profitable to our art. I hear that you are already leaving Vienna day after tomorrow. On account of my weakened health, my life in the country this year has not been as beneficial to me as usual. It may be that I shall come in again the day after tomorrow, and if you have not already left by afternoon I hope to tell you by word of mouth with really true cordiality how much I esteem you and wish to be with you.

In haste your most faithful friend

Vienna, September 18, 1819. Beethoven

The autograph of this letter contains what appears to be either a transcript or a draft of a letter which Zelter either sent or planned to send to Beethoven. In view of the fact that it shows a different feeling towards the great composer than that formerly entertained by the teacher of Mendelssohn, it is given here:

To see once more, face to face, in this life the man who brings joy and edification to so many good people, among whom I of course am glad to count myself— this was the purpose, worthy friend, for which I wished to visit you at Mödling. You came to meet us, and my aim was at least not wholly frustrated, for I saw your face. I know of the infirmity which burdens you and you have my sympathty, for I am similarly afflicted. On the day after to-morrow I go from here to resume my labors, but I shall never cease to hold you in high respect and to love you.

Your Zelter

Friedrich Schneider, of Dessau, visited Vienna in the fall of the year and caused a sensation by his organ-playing. He reported that Beethoven had received him graciously and that he, in turn, had heard the master play the pianoforte, his improvisation being the most marvellous thing he had ever listened to.[40]

In August, Johann van Beethoven bought the Wasserhof estate near Gneixendorf. This would bring the brothers closer together in the period to follow. That Beethoven was also interested in acquiring some property at this time is shown by a letter which he wrote to Steiner:

[39] *Angeschmiert*, that is, "deceived" or "cheated."

[40] Nohl, *Beethovens Leben*, III, p. 856. (TDR, IV, 164, n. 3.)

Mödling, October 10, 1819

Dear Steiner!

The day before yesterday I left you a note asking you to come here before the sale of the house; you would really be doing me a great kindness. The sale is on the 13th, thus next Wednesday. It is not possible for me to undertake anything to do with this without your help. The capital cannot be in any way reduced through this since naturally my nephew, who will devote himself to learning, needs support after my death for the continuation of his studies.— If you have had the record of baptism made through a notary, I will gratefully repay you the expense of it.—

To the WORTHY

LITTLE TOBIAS[41]

I have spoken about the Archduke var., I have proposed *you* for them since I do not believe that you will incur a loss from them and it is always honorable to print something from such a Principe Professore.— As to the corporal I beg you to tell him that he is not to sell anything of which I have notified him until I come to the city; also he must not forget to notify those who are moving and the landlady at the Landstrasse that the bell and window shades are mine.— I hope to see you tomorrow or the day after; mornings are the best since we must talk with H. v. Carbon, at which time we could also get a look at the house; and you could examine everything, if necessary also at the registry, and you could act as a judex since my decision will be based completely upon your judgement.— . . . .

--{Frimmel[42] has shown that the house in question must have been an old ecclesiastical house called "Christhof" which was in secular possession by 1819 and advertised for sale in August. Beethoven was evidently outbid by Johann Speer, who bought the house and rented the apartment on the first floor to Beethoven the following summer. Carbon can have been no other than Captain Franz Ludwig Carbon who was registered as an owner of property in Mödling.}--

The variations composed by the Archduke were, it will be remembered, on a theme composed by Beethoven and given to his imperial pupil as a lesson, and had called forth the obsequious remarks previously quoted in his New Year's letter to the Archduke. His remark to Steiner is explained by the fact that on August 31 he had written to the Archduke as follows:

. . . . As regards the masterly variations of Y. I. H. I think they might be published under the following title, namely:

Theme, or Task
set by L. v. Beeth.
forty times varied
and dedicated to his teacher
by the *Most Serene Author*

---

[41] The letters E[hrenwerthen] T[obiasserl] are large and ornamented. See Max Unger, *Ludwig van Beethoven und seine Verleger*, p. 63.

[42] Theodor von Frimmel, "Beethoven in Mödling," *Beethoven-Forschung*, VIII (1918), pp. 130-39.

There are so many requests for them, and eventually this honorable work will reach the public in garbled copies. Y. I. H. will yourself not be able to avoid presenting copies here and there; therefore, in the name of God, among the many consecrations which Y. I. H. is receiving and of which the world is being informed, let the consecration of Apollo (or in Christian terms Cäcilia) also be made known. True, Y. I. H. may accuse me of *vanity*; but I can assure you that although this dedication is precious to me and I am really proud of it, this is not at all my ultimate aim. Three publishers have appealed for it; Artaria, Steiner and a third whose name does not come to me. Considering but the first two, to which shall the Variations be given? On this point I await the commands of Y. I. H. Both of them have offered to print the variations at *their own cost*. The question now is whether Y. I. H. is *satisfied with the title*? To the question whether or not the variations ought to be published, Y. I. H. ought to close your eyes; if it is done, Y. I. H. *may call it* a misfortune; but *the world will think the contrary* . . . .

Steiner printed the archducal work in the seventh number of his *Musée musical des Clavicinistes* under a slightly changed title, viz.: "Theme [*Aufgabe*] composed by Ludwig van Beethoven, varied forty times and dedicated to the author by his pupil R[udolph], A[rch-] D[uke]." Other evidences of Beethoven's interest in Archduke Rudolph's studies in composition are shown by a letter to his patron dated July 29, 1819. It deserves to be given in full because of passages which, although vaguely worded, give some indication of Beethoven's attitude towards his art.

Your Imperial Highness!
I was indeed sorry to receive the news of a new indisposition of Your Highness; and since I have had no further definite news, I am very much upset— I was in Vienna in order to look in the library of Y. I. H. for some things most useful for me. The central plan is a *quick recognition* of the essential coupled with a *greater artistic unity*[43] in respect of which practical considerations sometimes compel an exception as we may learn in a twofold way from the old composers, where we find stress laid chiefly upon the artistically valuable (among these only the *German Händel* and *Sebastian Bach* had genius). But *freedom, progress*, these are the aims in the world of art as in the whole great universe. Even if we moderns are not so far advanced in *sound technique* [*Festigheit*] as our *forefathers*, yet refinement in manners has opened many new things to us. My exalted pupil in music, already a fellow-contestant for the laurel of fame, must not subject himself to the accusation of one-sidedness—et iterum venturus judicare *vivos*—et *mortuos*.— Here are three poems of which Y. I. H. could perhaps set one to music. The Austrians now know already that the *spirit of Apollo* has newly awakened in the Imperial family. From all quarters I receive requests for something [by you]. The *proprietor of the Modenzeitung* will appeal to Y. I. H. *in writing*, I hope I *shall not be accused of bribery*—at *court and no courtier, what possibilities??*!!! In my search for music in Vienna I found some resistance from *His Excellency the Chief Steward*. It is not worth the trouble to burden Y. I. H. in writing about it; I only must say this much, that because of this, many talented, good and noble

---

[43] (I.e., text and music.) For a short discussion by Deiters of this letter see TDR, iv, p. 169.

men would be frightened away from Y. I. H., who did not have the good fortune to become acquainted with your excellent qualities of spirit and heart— I wish Y. I. H. a speedy, speedy recovery and some news of it for the sake of *my peace of mind.*—

Your Imper. Highness's most obedient and faithful servant

L. V. Beethoven

That his mind was full of his Mass is indicated by the quotation from the text of the *Credo* and that he was consulting authorities on ecclesiastical music for this purpose is suggested by his reference to Bach and Handel.

It is time to consider further biographical events in chronological order. From the Fischoff manuscript we learn that on October 1 Beethoven was made an honorary member of the Mercantile Association (*Kaufmännischer Verein*) in Vienna.

In the fall of this year was painted probably the best known portrait of Beethoven: the oil painting by Ferdinand Schimon (1797-1852). At a later date it came into the possession of Schindler who deposited it in the Berlin Library; ─·❧{now it is the property of the Beethoven-Haus in Bonn where it can be seen on the third floor.}❧·─ Concerning the origin of this picture Schindler has this explanation.[44] Schimon had permission through Schindler to set up his easel in the chamber adjoining Beethoven's workroom, the composer resolutely having refused a sitting because he was busy on the Mass. From this point of vantage he made his studies and had finished all but the eyes—the most striking feature in the portrait. Out of this dilemma Beethoven unconsciously helped him. He had evidently been impressed with the discretion, or independence, of the young artist who came without a "good morning" and went without a "good evening," and invited him to coffee. Thus Schimon had ample opportunity to supply the one deficiency in his sketches. Schindler adds: "From an artistic point of view Schimon's work is not a distinguished work of art, yet full of characteristic truth. In the rendering of that particular look, the majestic forehead, this dwelling-place of mighty, sublime ideas, of hues, in the drawing of the firmly shut mouth and the chin shaped like a shell, it is truer to nature than any other picture."

─·❧{According to Schindler it was at the end of October that Beethoven returned to Vienna from Mödling. His new lodging is described by him in a Conversation Book of March, 1820, as "opposite the Auersperg palace in the same house where the coffeehouse is in the Josephstadt Glacis."[45] Since in front of the palace there was nothing but clear expanse all the way to the wall of the inner city, the dwelling would have been more accurately described as to the side of the palace. This move was made so that he could be near the Blöchlinger institute; and Fanny Giannatasio del Rio writes in

---

[44] *Biogr.*, II, p. 288-89. (TDR, IV, 170, n. 3.)

[45] Schünemann, I, p. 325. The house was owned by a Baron August von Fingerling and had the nickname "Zur goldenen Birne."

Alois Trost has identified the lodging in greater detail. See "Über einige Wohnungen Beethovens" in *Ein Wiener Beethoven-Buch* (Vienna, 1921), pp. 206-208.

her diary on December 1, 1819: "Beethoven, whom we do not hear of now at all lives . . . in the Josefstadt naturally because of the boy." But Beethoven may have had a second lodging at the same time since his home is recorded in two court records dated October 30, 1819, and January 7, 1820, as "im Blumenstöckel" near the newspaper office. This house was on the Ballgasse, No. 986 and was known as "Zum alten Blumenstock."[46] Considering Beethoven's constant association with Jos. Karl Bernard in the guardianship matter, which was again occupying his attention, it is not surprising that he should have had quarters here near the editor's office in the Rauhenstein-gasse. At the same time he was tormented by spells of indisposition; furthermore, financial distress so threatened him that he attempted to negotiate a loan from the banker Henikstein, and he borrowed 750 florins from Steiner.

It is remarkable that Beethoven, under the circumstances which have been set forth in this chapter, could continue his labors on the Mass which were his principal occupation during the year; it was but another proof of the absorbing possession which the composition of a great work took of him when once fairly begun. So diligently did he apply himself that he had hopes not only of finishing it in time for the installation of the Archduke as Archbishop of Olmütz, but he wrote to Ries on November 10 that he had already nearly completed it and would like to know what could be done with it in London. To Schindler, however, in expressing a doubt that he would have it done in time for the ceremonial, he said that every movement had taken on larger dimensions than had originally been contemplated. Schindler says also that when the day came, not one of the movements was finished in the eyes of the composer.

That the *Gloria* was near its final shape is a fair deduction from a Conversation Book of the same period. Bernard (presumably) writes: "It was decided yesterday that you give a concert either on Christmas or some other day. Count Stadion will give the use of the room, and Schick, Czerny and Janitschek will care for the rest. The programme is to include a symphony, the *Gloria* from your mass, the new Sonata played by you and a grand final chorus. All your works. 4,000 florins are guaranteed. Only one movement of the mass is to be performed."[47] The project is mentioned again by another friend,[48] and Beethoven remarks: "It is too late for Christmas, but it might be possible in Lent."

That he worked occasionally on the Ninth Symphony, especially in the early part of the year, has already been said. —Another work which was not to be completed until a later time was probably conceived in this year. In a letter to Simrock dated February 10, 1820, Beethoven offered his wares which included, characteristically, works that were far from completion. On

[46] For this information I am indebted to the late Dr. Kurt Smolle.

[47] Schünemann, I, p. 123. The Conversation Book belongs to early December, 1819.

[48] According to Schünemann, I, p. 126, this was Janitschek.

this list besides the Mass, which he was offering for an honorarium of 125 Louis d'or, Beethoven mentions some "big variations on a well known 'Deutsche,' which, however, I cannot promise you as yet and if you wish them will notify you later of the honorarium." This refers to the variations on a waltz by Diabelli, who conceived the idea of inviting several composers to contribute variations to his theme for a collection to be published as a monument to Austrian talent. Beethoven was not to complete his variations until 1823, but as already mentioned there are sketches for the work alongside those for the *Kyrie* of the Mass, which may be dated 1819.

He also, as Schindler tells us, composed a set of waltzes for a band of seven men who played at an inn in the valley of the Brühl near Mödling, and wrote out the parts for the different instruments. In 1905 Riemann found the parts of these dances in the Archives of the Thomasschule in Leipzig. There are eleven of them in all and they are scored as follows: Nos. 1, 3-8 are for two violins, bass and two clarinets; Nos. 9-11 substitute two flutes for the clarinets; and No. 2 is for flute, clarinet, bassoon and two horns. They were published by Breitkopf and Härtel in 1907.

He wrote a canon for Steiner in the summer, as appears from a conversation recorded in a book of March 20, 1820. An unidentified hand writes:

Last summer you sent a *canon infinitus a due* to Steiner from Mödling

Nobody has solved it, but I have solved it. The second voice enters on the second:

it is infinite.
Go to the devil [Hol Euch der Teufel!]
God protect you [B'hüt Euch Gott!]
was the text.[49]

On September 21 he wrote a canon to the words "Glaube und hoffe" for Moritz Schlesinger, as Beethoven's inscription on the autograph shows.[50] Countess Erdödy was in Vienna at the end of the year, and he sent her a note on December 19, in which he promised to visit her soon, and then scratched down the beginnings of a musical phrase. On December 31 he

[49] According to Schünemann (1, pp. 384-85), this was Czerny. For solutions in four parts to this riddle canon see Ludwig Misch, *Beethoven-Studies* (Norman, 1953), pp. 135-36.

[50] See Misch, *ibid.*, pp. 129-30.

wrote her a New Year canon: "Glück, Glück zum neuen Jahr," which starts approximately with this idea.[51]

--⚜{The completed compositions of the year were few:

Canons: "Glaube und hoffe," WoO 174, for Moritz Schlesinger, on September 21.
    "Glück, Glück, zum neuen Jahr," WoO 176, for Countess Erdödy.
    "Hol' euch der Teufel!" WoO 173, for Steiner.
    "Hochzeitslied" (Stein), WoO 105, for Anna Giannatasio del Rio. Version 1
    for Tenor, Men's Voices and Pianoforte; Version 2 for Mixed Chorus and
    Pianoforte.
Eleven Dances for Seven Instruments, WoO 17.}⚜--

The publications of the year were:

By Artaria:
    Six Themes varied for Pianoforte with optional accompaniment of flute or
    violin, Op. 105.
    Sonata for Pianoforte, Op. 106, dedicated to Archduke Rudolph; in two
    separate editions, one with French and one with German titles.
    String Quintet, Op. 104, arrangement of the Trio, Op. 1, No. 3.
--⚜{By Schlesinger in Berlin:
March No. 1 for Military Band in F, WoO 18.
[By Steiner in *Musée Musical des Clavicinistes* No. 7:
    Forty Variations by Archduke Rudolph on a Theme by Beethoven (WoO 200),
    dedicated to Beethoven.]
By Thomson in Edinburgh and Preston in London:
    "12 National Airs with Variations for the Piano and an Accompaniment for
    the Flute." Of the four projected volumes only three were published with
    three airs apiece. These consisted of Op. 105, Nos. 1-6 and Op. 107,
    Nos. 2, 6, 7.}⚜--

[51] The countess also received the dedication of the Violoncello Sonatas, Op. 102, published by Artaria in January, 1819. They had been previously published by Simrock without dedication. (TDR, IV, 177.)

CHAPTER XXXIII

THE YEAR 1820

END OF THE GUARDIANSHIP LITIGATION—
MISSA SOLEMNIS NOT READY
FOR INSTALLATION CEREMONY—PIANOFORTE
SONATA IN E MAJOR, OP. 109

ALMOST involuntarily, in passing in review the incidents of the year whose story has just been told and projecting a view into the near future, the question arises: Where, in these moments of doubt, ill-health, trial, vexation of spirit and torment of body were the old friends of Beethoven who in the earlier years had stood by him faithfully and lovingly? Where was Stephan von Breuning? Alas! he seems to have been an early sacrifice to Beethoven's obstinate course in respect of his nephew. Schindler says that he had advised against the adoption of the boy and thus wounded Beethoven in his most sensitive part. The temporary estrangement began in 1817. Some others of the old friends may have been rebuffed in like manner; some, like the faithful seneschal, Zmeskall, were ill; some were absent from Vienna—Count Brunsvik, Schuppanzigh; some were dead; in some the flames of friendship may have died down because there was so little in Beethoven's public life to challenge their sympathy and support. Count Lichnowsky has dropped out of the narrative and does not appear for some years. What had happened to the ardent friend of the youthful days, Count Waldstein? An entry from a Conversation Book of December, 1819 awakens curiosity and a hope:

Do not speak so loud. Your situation is too well known;—that is the inconvenience of public places, one is completely limited; everybody listens and hears.

Count Waldstein was also sitting nearby.

Does he live here?[1]

¹ Schünemann, I, p. 138.

Beethoven's answer is unrecorded and thus passes the only opportunity which the known material offers from which it might have been learned what caused the death of that beautiful friendship. ⸺Joseph Heer[2] attributes the rift first to Waldstein's absence from Vienna until 1809, during which time he was in military and then the foreign service; second, to the difference in their political views: Waldstein was a zealous Austrian patriot who continued to agitate against the French "usurper" after the war was ended; and third, to Waldstein's carelessness in business matters, which resulted in his going bankrupt soon after his wife's death in 1816, and in his death as a pauper in 1823.⸻

Beethoven was become a lonely man—an enforced seeker of solitude. No doubt many who would have been glad to give him their friendship were deterred by the widespread reports of his suspicious, unapproachable, almost repellent nature. But a miracle happened. Driven in upon himself by the forces which seem to have been arrayed against him, introspection opened wider and wider to him the doors of that imagination which in its creative function, as Ruskin tells us, is "an eminent beholder of things when and where they are not; a seer, that is, in the prophetic sense, calling the things that are not as though they were; and forever delighting to dwell on that which is not tangibly present." Now he proclaimed a new evangel, illustrated a higher union of beauty and truthfulness of expression, exalted art till it entered the realm of religion.

In a Conversation Book of February, 1820, there stands a bold inscription in Beethoven's hand: "The moral law in us, and the starry sky above us— Kant!!!"[3] This and two other citations, the second of which Beethoven surely culled from some book, also deserve to be set down here as mottoes applicable to the creative work which occupied his mind during the year and thereafter:

⸺

The world is a king and desires flattery in return for favor; but true art is perverse and will not submit to the mould of flattery. Famous artists always labor under an embarrassment;—therefore their first works are the best, although they may have sprung from dark ground.

⸺

'Tis said that art is long and life is fleeting:—
Nay: life is long and brief the span of art!
If e'er her breath vouchsafes with gods a meeting,
A moment's favor 'tis of which we've had a part.[4]

---

[2] See "Der Graf von Waldstein und sein Verhältnis zu Beethoven," *Veröffentlichungen des Beethoven-Hauses,* IX (Bonn, 1933).

[3] "Two things fill the soul with ever new and increasing wonder and reverence the oftener the mind dwells upon them—the starry sky above me and the moral law within me."—Kant's *Criticism of Practical Reason.* (TK, III, 25, n. 1.)

[4] Schünemann, I, p. 322. Since the translations are free, no attempt has been made to reproduce Beethoven's illogical punctuation.

Beethoven began the year 1820, as he had begun its immediate predecessor, by sending a New Year's greeting to the august pupil who was now almost continually in his mind—Archduke Rudolph, soon to be Archbishop and Cardinal. The greeting was in the form of a four-part canon beginning with a short homophonic chorus, the words: "Seiner Kaiserlichen Hoheit! Dem Erzherzog Rudolph! Dem geistlichen Fürsten! Alles Gute, alles Schöne!"

Now to take up the story of the incubus which oppressed the composer's mind, the clog which impeded his creative activities much of the year—the legal proceedings concerning the guardianship of nephew Karl. Fortunately for the tinge of these pages the end is not distant.

Two applications made by Beethoven to the Court of Magistrates had been denied and he now asked for a review of these decisions by the Court of Appeals. The action of the Magistracy had grievously pained him, so he informed the superior tribunal, and not only had his rights been set aside, but no regard had been shown for the welfare of his nephew. Against this he now sought relief, and he set forth his grievances: (1) He was testamentary appointee and the *Landrecht* had confirmed him and excluded the mother; circumstances compelling his absence from Vienna, he had arranged that Herr Nussböck should be appointed guardian *ad interim*; back permanently in the city, his nephew's welfare required that he resume the guardianship; (2) The higher education which his nephew's talents demanded neither the mother nor Nussböck could direct—the former because she was a woman and had conducted herself in a manner which had led the *Landrecht* to exclude her, Nussböck because he was too much occupied with his duties as Municipal Sequestrator and, having been no more than a paper-maker, he did not possess the insight and judgment essential to the scientific education of the ward. (3) Having no child of his own, his hopes were set on the boy, who was unusually talented, yet he had been told that he had been held back a year in his studies and that owing to a lack of funds he was to be taken from the institution in which he had been placed and given in the care of his mother; by her mismanagement the boy would be sacrificed, it being the aim of the mother to expend his share of the pension money on herself. He had declared to the Magistracy his willingness to defray the costs at the institute and also to engage other masters for the boy. Being "somewhat hard of hearing" communication with him was difficult and therefore he had asked that a co-guardian be appointed in the person of Herr Peters, councillor to Prince Lobkowitz, whose knowledge and moral character would assure such a training and education as were justified by the boy's capacity. "I know of no more sacred duty than the care and education of a child," he observes. He would offer no objection to the mother's having a "sort of joint-guardianship," but its duties and privileges should be limited to her visiting him and learning what plans were being made for his education; to permit more would be to compass the ruin of the boy.[5]

[5] For the documents concerning Beethoven's litigation about the guardianship of his nephew

This petition was filed on January 7, 1820; three days later the Appellate Court commanded the Magistracy to file a report of the proceedings held before it, together with all minutes and documents. The Magistracy complied on February 5, citing its decision of September 17, 1819, and defending its action on the grounds that (a) Beethoven, owing to his deafness and his hatred of the mother of the ward, was incapable of acting as guardian; (b) the guardianship belonged to the mother by right of law; (c) the commission of an act of infidelity against her husband in 1811, for which she had suffered punishment, was no longer a bar; (d) none of the alleged "injurious disturbances and interferences" had been definitely set forth or proven:

If under injurious disturbances we are to understand that the mother is desirous to see her child once every 14 days or 4 weeks, or to convince herself about the wear and cleanliness of his clothing, or to learn of his conduct toward his teachers, these can appear injurious only in the eyes of the appellant; the rest of the world, however, would find it amiss in a mother if she made inquiry concerning her child only once a fortnight or month.

Answering the second charge, the magistrates showed that the appellant seemed to demand of the mother and other guardian that they themselves should educate the boy in the sciences while at the same time he found them unsuited for the job. For this not even the appellant was fitted, at least he had not demonstrated such a fitness; he had left the preparation for the higher studies to others and this the mother and guardian could also do, having, indeed, a better plan, which was to send the boy to the R. I. Convict, where he could surely make better progress at smaller expense. *Ad tertium*, the failure of the boy to advance in his classes could not be laid to the mother or guardian, but must be charged against the appellant, who had taken the boy away from his studies for the university for two months, kept him at home three months, and sent him to another institution of learning at the end of June; naturally enough he lost a school year.

In a Conversation Book at the beginning of the year, Bernard writes: "The case will soon reach a firm decision since the Appellate Court has intervened."[6] To strengthen his case for this court, Beethoven spent several weeks on a "memorial" which describes the history of the case from his point of view. In turning to Bernard for help in the editing of this document, Beethoven was also confident of its success in the near future. He writes:

Dear Bernard! As I find myself alone again today in these to me confusing circumstances, a true understanding of my memorial has come to me for the first time. Without wishing to be resplendent in another person's feathers, still I believe I should leave it to your discretion to handle everything according to your superior judgement, since you in a few words can say as much or more

see TDR, IV, App. 3 (from 1817 to 1820), and *A*, III, App. C (from 1815 to 1820).
[6] Schünemann, I, p. 181.

as I can in sheets. The case would become more forceful and intelligible for the judges as a result. But this must be completed soon. Consider that you are laboring for Karl's happiness and for the only possible state of contentment for me and contributing to it for *the last time*—Once again do as you like with my raw material according to your judgement. In any case you write more clearly than I and the copy would soon be ready.

Your friend and admirer Beethoven

There has survived only Beethoven's sketch[7] of this memorial dated February 18, 1820, and there is no evidence as to whether it was ever presented in court. It is the longest piece of writing in Beethoven's hand, and is divided into seven parts. The first part, entitled "Information concerning Frau B." contains exaggerated charges against Johanna the most serious of which was that her illicit relations with another man in 1811 was the direct cause of her husband's sickness resulting in death.[8] In the second part entitled "Information concerning the supreme guardianship of the Vienna Magistracy" there is a detailed review of the "evil consequences" resulting from the transfer of the case from the *Landrecht* to the Magistracy: and in particular the inconsistencies in Beethoven's eyes of one of their number, Herr Piuk, in his handling of the case. The give and take between Beethoven and Johanna of charges of misconduct with the boy continues. For example, to answer an accusation of violence Beethoven confesses that "once in a passion I dragged my nephew from the chair because he had done something very wicked; and since has had to wear a truss ever since his hernia operation of two years before, the swift pulling consequently caused him some pain in the *most tender place* whenever he turned around quickly. I summoned Herr v. Smetana immediately and he declared that it didn't amount to anything and that not the least damage was done." Beethoven in turn accused Johanna of having fed the child strong drinks when he paid her a visit on her name-day, which resulted in an illness causing his confinement in bed for a period of three weeks. The third part, "Information concerning my nephew and his school-certificates," merely describes the benefits to the child's growth from being removed from the influence of his mother to his uncle's care and to Giannatasio's school. The fourth and fifth part give an account respectively of the educational costs and the nephew's estate. In the "conclusion" Beethoven appeals to the Appellate Court to grant his request; "—*the decision will bring* to my nephew *weal* or *woe*, the latter certainly if it is decided *against me*; for *my nephew needs*

---

[7] This document was found among the letters preserved in Bernard's estate by his daughter. It was first published in the Viennese *Zeit.* in December, 1907. It passed through many hands until it was acquired by H. C. Bodmer, who permitted the manuscript to be facsimiled and transcribed in the Beethoven Archives in Bonn. See Dagmar Weise, "Beethoven—Entwurf einer Denkschrift an das Appellationsgericht in Wien von 18 Februar 1820" in *Veröffentlichungen des Beethoven-Hauses in Bonn* (1953), Dritte Reihe, 1.

[8] There is no evidence to support the fact that Carl Caspar's health in this year or the next gave way to sickness.

me, not I him." Then follows a supplement in which Beethoven first brings charges of misconduct against Father Fröhlich as an answer to Fröhlich's earlier testimony concerning Beethoven's method of educating his nephew. Then he re-emphasizes charges already stated in the first section: 1) that Johanna conspired with Karl in the spring of 1819 that he do badly in his studies at Kudlich's institute and receive a second or third class so that he would not be removed from Vienna, which aim was realised in the Easter examinations; and 2) that she persuaded the Magistracy to have Beethoven removed from the guardianship. The memorial ends: "Finally I must say that it appears to me that it still has not been clear whether I am to recognize the Magistracy as a competent authority for the guardianship."

The Court of Appeals demanded a more explicit report. The Magistracy complied on February 28, taking advantage of the opportunity to review the proceedings held before the *Landrecht* from the beginning, and to make severe strictures on the conduct of Beethoven in filing an exhibit (F) with his petition in support of which no evidence was offered, though because of it the *Landrecht* was asked to exclude the mother from the guardianship which belonged to her under the law. Again we quote:

This exclusion can have nothing for its foundation except the misdemeanor of which the mother was guilty in 1811, for all the rest contained in appellant's exhibit F is unproven chatter to which the *Landrecht* could give no consideration, but which gives speaking proof of how passionately and inimically the appellant has always acted, and still acts, towards the mother, how little he recks of tearing open wounds that were healed, since after having endured punishment she stood rehabilitated; and yet he reproaches her with a transgression for which she had atoned years before, which had been pardoned by the injured husband himself who petitioned for leniency in her sentence and who had declared her capable and fit for the guardianship of his son in his last will and testament, directing that the son be not taken away from his mother. Regardless of this the appellant last year, certainly not in the interest of the boy's welfare, inasmuch as we have excellent educational institutions here, but only to pain the mother, to tear the heart out of her bosom, attempted to send him out of the country to Landshut. Fortunately the government authorities, acting on information derived from this court, frustrated the plan by refusing a passport.

Let us try now to take a dispassionate view of the case as thus far presented in the pleadings and documents. Not only the law of nature but the laws of the land justified the mother in asserting her right to look after the physical well-being of her child and seeking to enforce it. Dr. Bach seems to have impressed that fact upon Beethoven, wherefore he declared his willingness in the bill of appeal to associate her with himself in the guardianship to that extent. That the Magistrates displayed unusual, not to say unjudicial, zeal in her behalf while defending their own course is indubitable; but we are in no position to judge of the propriety of their course, which seems to have been in harmony with the judicial procedure of the place and period, least of all to condemn them, so long as it was permitted them so to do, for having made a stout resistance when their acts were impugned in the appeal to the higher court.

The "Exhibit F," filed in the proceedings before the *Landrecht*, has not been found and its contents can only be guessed at from the allusions to it in the documents. Obviously it contained aspersions on the moral character of Frau van Beethoven, and it probably was true that they were unsupported by evidence and therefore undeserving of consideration in a court either of law or equity. In a Conversation Book of this year (1820) Beethoven writes of her that she was "born for intrigue, accomplished in deceit, mistress of all the arts of dissimulation." On the other hand, it is singular that the Magistrates in their final effort to justify their course had nothing to say about the present moral standing of the woman whose legal and natural right they claimed to be upholding. Were they in ignorance of what we now know, that her conduct had not only been reprehensible in 1811 (though condoned by her husband) but continued so after her husband's death? Schindler says that she gave birth to a child while the case was pending, and that is confirmed by a statement of nephew Karl's widow to Thayer that in her old age Frau van Beethoven lived in Baden with this illegitimate daughter, who was also a dissolute woman.

But there are many anomalous things to the studious mind in the proceedings which we are reporting, which differ greatly from anything which could happen in a court of chancery or probate in Great Britain or America today. It is certainly repugnant to our present legal ethics that having filed a petition to reverse the action of one court Beethoven should not only have written private letters to a judge of the court of review, pleading his case on personal grounds, but that his counsel should have advised him to visit members of the higher court to present arguments in his behalf. But, no doubt, this was consistent with the customs of contemporary Austria; and it is what happened.

On March 6 Beethoven writes to Karl Winter, a Councillor of Appeal: "I have the honor of informing you that I have written a memorial consisting of information about Fr. van Beethoven, about the Magistracy, about my nephew, about myself, etc. which I will send you within a few days. I *believed* that I owed this to myself to expose the falsity of the many slanders which have been uttered *against me* and to lay bare the intrigues of Frau van Beethoven *against me* to the injury of her own child, as also to place in its proper light the conduct of the Magistrate's Court." He charged that the Magistrates had summoned the widow and her son to a hearing without his knowledge and, as his nephew had told him, the boy had been urged and led on by his mother to make false accusations against him. He had also forwarded a document which proved the wavering and partisan conduct of the Magistrates. He repeated the charge about his nephew's failure to advance in his studies and added that the boy had had a hemorrhage which, had he not been on hand, might almost have cost him his life. These things were not attributable to Herr Tuscher for the reason that the Magistrates had given him too little support and he could not proceed with sufficient energy—this the writer could do in his capacity of uncle, guardian and defrayer of expenses. He asked that the charges against him be re-examined. He cited his expenditures to keep the boy two years in an educational institution, saying that for a period of fourteen months he had received nothing from the widow and after that only a small yearly contribution. Without the guardianship, he would feel relieved of the duty of taking further interest in the boy, but as guardian he would continue to pay all the cost unselfishly in the future. Moreover, he claimed that he had set apart 4,000 florins which was on deposit in bank and was to go to his nephew on his death. Finally, he expressed his hopes and expectations resulting from his relations with the Archbishop of Olmütz.

The case was prepared shrewdly, carefully and most discreetly by Dr. Bach, who seems to have exerted an admirable influence on Beethoven at this crisis. The nature of his advice may be learned from an entry in the Conversation Book by Bernard, who is evidently giving the result of a consultation with Dr. Bach:[9]

He [Dr. Bach] has already discussed the case with the official, Councillor of Appeal Winter, who was already informed by the *Landrecht* where he had been earlier. Now the Magistracy is being asked for a report of its proceedings, and hereupon the case will be decided by the Court of Appeals. He asked if Hr. Nusbeck [*sic*] has already resigned; if not, it would be good if Doct. Bach were to add a statement of resignation in writing from the same as a supplement to the statement already delivered. Doct. Bach has already said that Nusbeck would willingly resign and so the affair runs into no difficulty from this quarter. At this point there is still to be mentioned whether you have given up the guardianship altogether or only in favor of Tusch[er] in order better to effect the removal of the mother thereby. . . .[10] Furthermore it is necessary to proceed as moderately as possible in all things so that it does not appear as if there were malice; also the mother only in the most extreme cases is to be assailed on a point of honor. The whole [question] shall be connected with the reasoning that she cannot now be given any influence over the education because for a boy of this age a woman is not at all suitable. Furthermore it is necessary for you, if you should be asked, to explain that you will continue to bear the education costs,[11] whereupon if worst came to worst you could follow with the threat to withdraw your support altogether. He believes that reproaches might be made over the amount of time that you have had Karl with you[12] because the priests have become involved and the opposition has seized on this to increase the trouble. . . .

9 Schünemann, I, pp. 184-85.

10 Beethoven adds on the margin: "I appointed Tuscher guardian of the robbed ["des beraubten" is followed by an illegible word]— on the same day that Tuscher resigned I took up the guardianship again." (TDR, IV, 185, n. 2.)

11 Beethoven adds on the margin: "This is self-evident." (TDR, IV, 185, n. 5.)

12 Beethoven's comment on the margin is partly illegible: "would not the mother and in part the investments of the boy himself be indebted. . . ." (TDR, IV, 185, n. 6.)

I believe that in order to avoid all subterfuge at this time you should not take Karl into a tavern for a meal, because immediately it means that you lead him into a public place, because you are noticed by everyone and everything will be misrepresented by gossip and false interpretation.

Bach seems to have advised Beethoven to visit two of the judges, Winter and Schmerling, and himself had an interview with the boy, who told his uncle what the advocate had questioned him about.

For the nonce Karl was on his good behavior. Blöchlinger reported favorably on his studies to Bernard, and in a Conversation Book the boy apologized to his uncle for some statements derogatory to him which he had made to the Magistrates. "She promised me so many things," he said, "that I could not resist her; I am sorry that I was so weak at the time and beg your forgiveness; but I will certainly not again permit myself to be led astray—I did not know what results might follow when I told the Magistrates what I did. But if there is another examination I will retract everything that *I said* at the time which was *untrue!*"[13]

The magisterial commission which followed on March 29, had plainly been held at the instance of the Appellate Court. Beethoven was solemnly admonished, and in answer to questions declared: (1) that he still demanded the guardianship of his nephew under the will and would not relinquish his claim; (2) that he requested the appointment of Councillor Peters as associate guardian; (3) that he demanded that Frau van Beethoven be excluded from the guardianship as she had been by the *Landrecht*, and (4) he reiterated his readiness to provide financially for the care of his ward; he would accept an associate guardian, but not a sole guardian, as he was convinced that no guardian would care for his nephew as well as he.

In insisting on a renewed declaration on these points it is likely that the Court of Appeals had some hope that Beethoven might voluntarily renounce or modify his claims or the Magistrates recede from their attitude. Neither contingency occurred, however, and on April 8 the reviewing court issued its decree in Beethoven's favor, he and Peters being appointed joint guardians (*gemeinschaftliche Vormünde*), the mother and Nussböck being deposed. The widow now played her last card:—she appealed to the Emperor, who upheld the Court of Appeals. There was nothing for the Magistracy to do except to notify the result of the appeals to Beethoven, Frau van Beethoven, Peters and Nussböck. This was done on July 24.

Beethoven had won at last. But at what a cost to himself, his art, the world! What time, what labor, what energy had he not taken away from his artistic creations! What had he not expended in the way of peace of mind, of friendship, of physical comfort, of wear of brain and nerve-force, for the privilege of keeping the boy to himself, of watching unmolested over his physical welfare and directing his intellectual and moral training

[13] Schünemann, I, p. 195.

unhindered! At the present moment, however, his joy was unbounded, and he gave it expression in the following letter to Karl Pinterics:[14]

Dear Herr v. Pinterics!

I am reporting to you that the civil senate was authorized by the high Appellate Court to inform me of their decision which gives me complete satisfaction.— Dr. Bach was my representative in this affair, and this *brook* [in German: Bach] was joined by the sea, with lightning, thunder and storm, and the magisterial brigantine suffered complete shipwreck.

Yours faithfully,
Beethoven

Schindler says that "his happiness over the triumph which he had won over wickedness and trickery, but also because of the supposed salvation from physical danger of his talented nephew, was so great that he worked but little or hardly at all all summer—though this was perhaps more apparent than real, the sketchbooks disclosing from now on only empty pages."[15] A wise qualification, for though the sketchbooks may have been empty, there is evidence enough elsewhere of hard work. Yet the Mass was not finished, and for this unfortunate circumstance the guardianship trial was no doubt to blame. To this subject we shall return presently.

Peters, who was appointed joint guardian with Beethoven of the nephew, was a tutor in the house of Prince Lobkowitz and had been on terms of friendship with Beethoven since 1816. His appointment by the court is a confirmation of Beethoven's tribute to him as a man of intellectual parts and of good moral character. His wife had a good voice and was a great admirer of Beethoven, who had presented her with a copy of the song cycle "An die ferne Geliebte."

Bernard and Peters were the subjects for some humor in the Conversation Books and sketchbooks of this time. In the first *Missa Solemnis* sketchbook, now at Bonn, Beethoven wrote out a three-voiced piece on these words:[16]

Sanctus petrus ist ein Fels	Saint Peter is a rock
Auf diesen kann man bauen.	On this one can build.

The next reference is in a Conversation Book of January, 1820.[17] Bernard writes:

Sankt Petrus ist kein Fels	Saint Peter is no rock
Auf ihn kann man nicht bauen.	On him one cannot build.

---

[14] Pinterics was Count Palffy's private secretary. A friend of Beethoven's during these years, he became a much closer friend of Schubert's. He was widely cultured, and an excellent piano player; and it will be remembered that he sang bass in the "Ta, ta, ta" canon in honor of Mälzel. (Cf. TDR, IV, 188, n. 1.)

[15] *Biogr.*, I, pp. 271-72. (TDR, IV, 188.)

[16] Schmidt-Görg, *op.cit.*, p. 45.

[17] Schünemann, I, p. 183.

Bernardus war ein Sankt	Bernardus was a saint
Der hatte sich gewaschen,[18]	Who washed away the mottles
Er hat der Hölle nicht gewankt,	In front of hell he did not faint
u nicht zehntausend Flaschen	Nor with ten thousand bottles.

Peters answers: "Too bad about your canon which has probably vanished. It would have immortalized me." A month later Peters writes:[19] "The two beautiful canon[s] have certainly been erased" and Bernard answers "Saint Peter is a rock, on this one must . . . [build?]." The first of these canons was probably the one on the name of the poet Wähner, "Wähner es ist kein Wahn,"[20] and an idea of the second is suggested in an undated letter to Peters which follows.

How are you? Are you well or ill? How is your wife?— Permit me to sing something for you:

How are your young princes?

If you are at home this afternoon around 5 o'clock, perhaps I'll visit you together with my *state burden*.

In haste
your Beethoven

Nephew Karl remained at Blöchlinger's institute and continued to cause worry and anxiety to his uncle. Reports to Beethoven concerning his conduct and studies were variable from different persons and at different times. According to Blöchlinger he was unsteady and inclined to be lazy, and it was with great difficulty that he had again been made to work. He writes in March: "Since he has been with us, he had always been treated strictly, otherwise we would not have progressed as far as we now have." In April a cleric declared that he was at heart not a bad child but had been harmed by bad examples. There must have been further bad experiences for again in April someone writes: "Karl has little spirit and NB. despite the knowledge for which he is praised, little intelligence,—that is probably the key to this otherwise unpardonable behavior."[21]

[18] Figuratively: "who was first-rate."
[19] Schünemann, I, p. 240.
[20] See Schmidt-Görg, *op.cit.*, p. 45.
[21] Schünemann, I, p. 380; II, pp. 37, 88. The cleric referred to as "Der Probst von

Michaelern," Schünemann (I, p. 152) identifies as Joh. Michael, curate of the Augustinian order at St. Florian who was also Director of the Linz Gymnasium.

--ॐ{Meanwhile, the conversation was frequently about Johanna's immorality and the necessity of Karl's understanding this. Blöchlinger seems to have come around completely to Beethoven's point of view. In June he writes:

She is simply a canaille, I am amply convinced of it, and unfortunately the boy also appears to be becoming one.

•~•

The boy lies every time he opens his mouth. His laziness, for which naturally he must be punished strictly, leads him astray continually. Will you please speak to him? — —

•~•

Perhaps if he could be taken to Salzburg or to some distant place, he could perhaps improve, removed from the influence of his mother. . . .

•~•

. . . It has seemed to me of late that the Beethoven woman was expecting. I would be very glad to know for sure, one would have new evidence for saying to Karl that his mother was immoral, moreover he will have observed it when he was with her. I would like to know it for certain. Karl must get a clear understanding as regards his mother, as you have said yourself; for if he depends on her, he is lost, and to alienate him from her, he must have proof that she is immoral. The other day I also told him that she had been in a house of correction and let him judge whether what his mother had done till now was good for him.[22]

Blöchlinger reports in the same June Conversation Book: "Today we have had a new incident. Karl had his oral examinations today but ran early in the morning again to his mother because yesterday and today he had not learned his lessons."}ॐ--- Frau Blöchlinger had to take a coach and servant and bring him back to school; and to get him away from Frau van Beethoven, who was disposed to keep him in concealment, had to promise to see to it that he should not be punished. "I went along to the examination in which he did rather well." Blöchlinger continued with sharp words against the mother saying that her presence in his house brought him shame. He asked for a power of attorney to call in the help of the police every time that Karl should go to his mother.[23] Beethoven went for advice to Bach, who told his client that it was impracticable to get a judicial writ against the mother enjoining her from meeting her son, and impossible to prevent secret meetings and secret correspondence. The practical solution of the problem was to have Blöchlinger refuse to admit the woman to his institute and compel her to see Karl at his uncle's home. This would serve the purpose to some extent, as the mother did not like to meet her brother-in-law.[24]

Meanwhile work on the Mass was continuing, as the sketchbooks show. Exactly what condition it was in at that time we have no means of knowing;

[22] *Ibid.*, II, p. 153.   [23] *Ibid.*, pp. 175-77.   [24] *Ibid.*, p. 202.

it was, however, in a sufficient state of forwardness to enable Beethoven to begin negotiations for its publication. —❧In a letter to the firm of Simrock on February 10th Beethoven offered the Mass for 125 Louis d'or. He repeated the offer in a letter of March 9 and suggested on March 14 that perhaps he could ask for a lower figure. What was offered by Simrock as a counter-offer is made clear from Beethoven's answer which follows:❧—

Vienna, March 18, 1820

Dear Herr Simrock!

I don't know whether I discussed everything completely in my last letter— I am writing you briefly therefore that I can extend the date for the edition of the variations,[25] if you find it necessary.— As regards the mass, I have pondered the matter carefully and might give it to you for the honorarium of 100 Louis d'or which you offered me, provided you agree to a few conditions which I shall propose and which, I think, you will *not* find burdensome. We have gone through the plan for publication here and believe that with a *few modifications* it can be put into effect very soon. This is very necessary, wherefore I shall make haste to inform you of the necessary changes soon— Since I know that dealers like to save post money, I enclose 2 Austrian folktunes here as change with which you can do what you like. The accompaniments are mine— I think a folk-song hunt is better than a man hunt of such exalted heroes— My copyist is not here now; I hope you will be able to read it—in fact you could have many things from me, for which you could show me another favor—

In haste   Yours
Beethoven

Enclosed were the songs "Das liebe Käzchen" and "Der Knabe auf dem Berge."

The enthronement of Beethoven's imperial pupil as Archbishop of Olmütz took place on March 20. The Mass which was to have been the composer's tribute was still unfinished. It may have been for the purpose of offering an explanation to the new dignitary of the church, that Beethoven sought an audience as he states in a letter of April 3:

. . . But now I wish that Y. I. H would kindly tell me how long you have decided to stay in O[lmütz]. Here they say that Y. I. H. would return here at the end of May; yet I heard a few days ago that Your Highness will remain in O *for another year and a half*. Perhaps I have taken the wrong measures, certainly *not as regards Y. I. H*., but as regards myself. As soon as I have a report about it I will explain everything further. As for the rest I beg Y. I. H. not to give credence to the many reports about me, I have already learned of many which can be called gossip and with which people believe they can please even Y. I. H. If Y. I. H. calls me one of your most treasured objects, I can honestly say that Y. I. H. is to me one of the most treasured objects in the universe. Although I am no *courtier*, I believe that Y. I. H. has learned to know *me well enough* to know that no cold interest, but a sincere affection, has always attached me to yourself and inspired me; and I might well say that Blondel was found

[25] Op. 107; underneath Beethoven adds: "i.e., longer than 6 months." (TDR, iv, 193, n. 3.)

long ago, and if no Richard is to be found in the world for me, God will be
my Richard— It appears to me that my idea to maintain a quartet will certainly be the best thing to do. Even if there are already productions on a large
scale in O[lmütz], something admirable might arise in Moravia through such a
quartet—Should Y.I.H. come here again in May as reported above, I advise
you to save the children of your muse for me until then, because it is better
if I hear them performed first by you. But if there is really to be a longer stay in
Olmütz, I will receive them with the greatest pleasure and seek to guide Y.I.H.
to the highest peak of Parnassus. . . .

A reference to himself as one who was at court yet not a courtier (*Hofmann*) had been made by Beethoven in an earlier letter. This play on words
seems to have been much in his head about this time and it is small wonder
that when an opportunity offered for the employment of the pun it should
have been embraced. In the Conversation Book used in March, 1820,[26] a
strange hand writes: "In the *Phantasie-Stücke* by Hoffmann, you are often
spoken of. Hoffmann was musical director in Bamberg; he is now Government Councillor.— Operas of his composition are performed in Berlin."
Beethoven remarks, in writing: "Hofmann [*sic*] du bist kein *Hof-mann*."—
This may have been what gave Beethoven the impetus to read the essays on
his works by E. T. A. Hoffmann and to write the following lines to him.
--◦◦{His love of punning has another outlet here in "unser schwach (weak)
starke (strong)."}◦◦-- The letter follows:

Vienna, March 23, 1820

I am seizing the opportunity through Herr Neberich[27] to approach a man so
full of life and wit as you are— Also you have written about my humble self.
Also our *weak Herr Starke* showed me some lines of yours about me in his
album. Thus I am given to believe that you take some interest in me. Allow me
to say that this from a man with such distinguished gifts as yourself pleases
me very much. I wish you everything that is beautiful and good and remain

with high esteem yours faithfully

Beethoven

--◦◦{Further instances of the play on words occurred in the Conversation
Books during March. For instance, Beethoven writes: "nein, nein ich ich
heisse Hofmann u. bin kein Hofma[nn] sondern ein Elen[der] schuft"
["No, I am called Hofmann and am no courtier but a wretched fellow"]
for which he supplies the sketch of a canon.[28]}◦◦-- Beethoven kept the canon
in his mind or had a copy of it, and printed it in 1825, when B. Schott's
Sons in Mainz asked him for a contribution to their newly formed musical
journal *Cäcilia*.

--◦◦{At this time some new portraits were made of the master. Frimmel
has brought to light a half-length drawing in chalk by the artist Hippius

[26] Schünemann, I, p. 314.
[27] Neberich was a wine dealer whom Beethoven had known since at least 1816, when

in a letter to Franz von Brentano he is called
"Europe's first wine artist."
[28] Schünemann, I, p. 334. See also p. 384.

which, according to his family, was based on a sitting with the composer. It is almost life-size and is similar to the Schimon in the interpretation of Beethoven's features.[29]

Another of the portraits of Beethoven which have been made familiar by reproductions was begun in 1819. Joseph Stieler, who enjoyed wide reputation as a portrait painter, had come to Vienna from Munich to paint the portrait of Emperor Franz in the latter year. He remained till some time in 1820 and made the acquaintance of Beethoven through a letter of introduction probably given to him by Brentano. Beethoven took a liking to him and gave him three sittings, but because Beethoven refused to sit longer, Stieler had to exercise his imagination or memory in painting the hands. In fact, the painting never received the finishing touches but remained, as those who have seen it testify, "sketchy." In April, 1820, Stieler asks the question: "In what key is your mass? I want to write on the sheet Mass in—." Beethoven writes the answer "D, Missa solemnis in D," and Stieler: "A quarter hour after it has been exhibited I shall send it to Brentano— I thank you thousands and thousands of times for so much patience." Beethoven's friends refer frequently to the picture in their written conversations with Beethoven. Schindler writes that he prefers the portrait by Schimon: "There is more character in it—all agree on that— You were very well two years ago; now you are always ailing." J. Czerny writes: "We were just talking about your portrait.— Oliva thinks it is a very good resemblance." The artist visited Beethoven again at Mödling in July and writes: "Before the exhibition I shall paint your portrait again, but full life-size. Your head makes an excellent effect full face, and it was so appropriate because Haydn was on one side and Mozart on the other."[30] Stieler dated the canvas "1819," but this can only refer to the time when it was begun. Schindler says it reproduces Beethoven's characteristic expression faithfully and that it met with approval, though fault was found with the pose. Beethoven's contemporaries were not used to seeing him with his head bowed down as Stieler represents him; on the contrary, he carried his head high even when suffering physical pain. A lithographic reproduction of the portrait was made by Fr. Dürck and published by Artaria in 1826.

The portrait remained for awhile in the possession of the family of the painter, then passed through several hands by purchase until it reached those of Countess Sauerma in Berlin, in whose possession it was when Frimmel and Kalischer inspected it for purposes of description. Comparing it to the mask of 1812, Frimmel writes: "The lower third of the face with its broad mouth and irregular cicatrized chin makes a passably good resemblance. But the nose is too broad, the forehead much too high. Only

[29] The drawing of the head is reproduced in Frimmel's *Beethoven im zeitgenössischen Bildnis* (Vienna, 1923), p. 40. According to this source the drawing was last known to be in the possession of the artist's grandson, Ed. Hippius in Moscow.

[30] Schünemann, II, p. 37; I, p. 371; II, pp. 42, 180.

the root of the nose with its small cavities and brows is Beethoven's, but the eyes are placed so high above the cheekbone that their position is uncommon in any face and completely out of the question for Beethoven."[31] Frimmel also criticizes the weakness of the hands but cites the thoughtful expression of the face as perhaps the best thing about the painting. He adds that Stieler, who was an excellent portrait painter, would have undoubtedly corrected many of the errors if he had had the opportunity. According to Frimmel, the portrait is now in the possession of Herr Geheimrat H. Hinrichsen, who acquired it from the music publishing firm of C. F. Peters in Leipzig.

By February Beethoven had returned to live in the house on the Josephstädter Glacis where he stayed until May. ⟩⟨— In this period the Giannatasio family followed up their intention to visit Beethoven. On April 19, 1820, Fanny writes in her journal: "Tonight we visited Beethoven after not seeing him for almost a year. It seemed to me that he was glad to see us again; on the whole things seem to be going well for him now, at least it is a period in which he is free from the vexations of Karl's mother. I lament exceedingly that every connection with this excellent man has been given up; I was stirred more and more by his genuineness in every regard. His hearing has become a little worse. I wrote everything. He gave me a new beautiful song: 'Abendlied unter dem gestirnten Himmel' which gave me very much pleasure." This setting of a text by Goeble was published in the same year and was dedicated to the distinguished doctor, Anton Braunhofer, with whom Beethoven first became associated in this year.

In the summer of 1820[32] Beethoven went to Mödling again, but he did not take lodgings in the Hafner house for the very sufficient reason that the proprietor had served notice on him in 1819, that he could not have it longer on account of the noisy disturbances which had taken place there. He took a house instead in the Babenbergerstrasse and paid twelve florins extra for the use of a balcony which commanded a view which was essential to his happiness.[33] Here again he took the baths. He worked chiefly on the Mass, which was far from finished. His friends thought that he was further along than he was, and he was frequently asked if it was finished and when it would be performed. Some hurried sketches belonging to the *Credo* are found amongst the remarks of his friends, and also sketches for the *Agnus Dei*. Schindler asks him in August: "Is the *Benedictus* written out in score?— Are those sketches for the *Agnus*?"[34]

In the second *Missa Solemnis* sketchbook at Bonn there is a start to a "Sonate in E moll," which is not further developed. At this same time the

[31] *Op.cit.*, p. 45.

[32] The move to Mödling is referred to in a Conversation Book of early May and appears to have taken place at that time.

[33] Babenbergerstrasse No. 116, called

"Christhof," which he had contemplated buying in the fall of 1819. See preceding chapter.

[34] Schünemann, II, p. 201.

last three piano sonatas (Op. 109-111) were projected, to which we can return. Along with sketches to the E major Sonata (Op. 109) there are sketches for the Bagatelles Op. 119, Nos. 7 to 11 inclusive. Their story is known. Friedrich Starke, Kapellmeister of an Austrian regiment of infantry, had undertaken the publication of a pianoforte method which he called the "Wiener Pianoforteschule." Part III of the work, which appeared early in 1821, contained these five Bagatelles under the title "Trifles" (*Kleinigkeiten*).[35] Above them Starke printed: "A contribution from the great composer to the publisher." They must have been asked for in 1820. Somewhere about February of that year an unidentified hand writes in the Conversation Book: "Starke wants a little music-piece by you for the second part of his *Klavierschule*, for which he has contributions from the leading composers besides short notices. . . . We must give him something. Notwithstanding his great deserts in music and literature he is extremely modest, industrious and humble. . . . He understands the art of compiling well. There are now weaklings everywhere even among the strong."[36] To this appeal Beethoven yielded. He wrote the five Bagatelles.

Schindler relates that when Beethoven heard that it was bruited about that he had written himself out, his invention was exhausted, and that he had taken up Scottish melodies like Haydn in his old age, he seemed amused and said: "Wait awhile, you'll soon learn differently." Schindler then adds: "Late in the fall (1820), returned from his summer sojourn in Mödling, where like a bee he had been engaged busily in gathering ideas, he sat himself down to his table and wrote out the three sonatas Op. 109, 110, 111 'in a single breath,' as he expressed it in a letter to Count Brunsvik in order to quiet the apprehension of his friends touching his mental condition." Schindler was dubious about the "single breath" and, indeed, there was considerable lapse of time between the completion of the first of the three sonatas and the last two.[37] But Beethoven's correspondence with the Berlin publisher Adolf M. Schlesinger, shows that from the start he considered writing three in a row. On April 30 he writes: ". . . Also I will be willing to hand over to you new sonatas,—but at no other price than 40 ducats per piece, thus a sort of enterprise of three sonatas for 120 ducats." On May 31 he agreed to write them within three months at a fee of 90 ducats. And on September 20 he writes: "The three sonatas are going faster— the first is about ready for proof, and now I am working on the last two without respite." The Sonata in E belongs unquestionably to the year 1820. The first theme of the first movement is found in the Conversation Book of April;[38] the work was sketched in part before he began the *Benedictus,* in part while he was at work on this section, the *Credo,* the *Agnus Dei* and the

---

[35] See Frimmel, "Ein unbeachtetes Klavierstück von Beethoven," *Der Merker,* VIII (1917), p. 24, for more on Beethoven's contributions to Starke's publications.

[36] Schünemann, I, pp. 241, 297.
[37] *Biogr.,* II, pp. 2-3. No such letter to Franz Brunsvik has survived.
[38] Schünemann, II, p. 44.

Bagatelles for Starke. It was dedicated to Maximiliane Brentano, and published in November, 1821, by Schlesinger in Berlin.

There was at this time considerable talk in the Conversation Book[39] of publishing a complete edition of Beethoven's works. Bernard told him that Steiner was already counting on it, and Schindler, who was enthusiastic over the project, gave it as his opinion that arrangements must be made with a Vienna publisher so as to avoid voluminous correspondence. Bernard remarks: "Eckstein will so arrange it that you will always get all the profits and will also publish your future works as your property. He thinks that every fourth or fifth piece should be a new one." —Since the beginning of the year, there had also been negotiations with Simrock concerning this idea. A letter written to this firm on August 5 from Vienna shows that Beethoven had just made one of his short visits to the city. He writes: ". . . Regarding the edition of my complete works we believe here that it would be good to add a *new work* to each type of composition; e.g., to the variations a new work of this kind, to the sonatas, each etc. etc. . . . ." The plan appealed strongly to Beethoven, but nothing came of it at the time, though we shall hear of it later.

It was the discussion of it by his friends which brought out a letter from Beethoven to Haslinger, "best of Adjutants," asking him to decide a bet. Beethoven had wagered 10 florins that it was not true that the Steiners had been obliged to pay Artaria 2000 florins damages for having published Mozart's works, which were reprinted universally.[40]

Archduke Rudolph, now Archbishop of Olmütz, left his residence for some time, having communicated to his teacher his intention to spend a part of the summer in Mödling. Beethoven wrote to him on August 3 making apologies for apparent neglect in not waiting upon him, which he blamed on the lack of a carriage. He wrote again on Saturday, September 2:

Your Imperial Highness!
Ever since Tuesday evening I have not been well but thought that certainly on Friday I would have the pleasure of coming to Y. I. H. But I was mistaken and now today I can inform Y. I. H. that next Monday or Tuesday I definitely hope to be able to pay a visit again to Y. I. H. which will be early in the morning— My indisposition comes from taking an open post carriage in order not to miss Y. I. H. The day was rainy and almost *cold* here in the evening. Nature almost seems to have taken amiss my openness or boldness and punished me for it— The heavens send down to Y. I. H. all that is good, beautiful, and holy, and for me Your good graces!— *But still sanctioned by justice!*—
Your Imperial Highness's ever most obedient and most faithful servant
L v. Beethoven

—Misfortune in the Erdödy family is referred to by an unidentified writer at the end of a Conversation Book dated July-early August: "For

---

[39] *Ibid.*, pp. 57, 85-6, 96.   [40] See *A* 1025.

some time curious things have been reported. Brauchle was imprisoned by the police, and the *Comtesse* Mimi[41] has gone some days ago to the St. Pölten Cloister, on account of the young count[42] that he mistreated so; and he is charged with beating him to death. Sperl[43] and the servant together with the chambermaid have been very often questioned about the murder; generally Sperl has been present all the time at Brauchle's trial in the Waag Gasse 274 on the ground floor and also in the old Wieden; they are telling the police in person everything possible about their lives."[44]

It will be remembered that the death of the boy August (who died at his sister's feet complaining of a pain in his head) brought forth from Beethoven the moving letter of condolence to the Countess Erdödy on May 15, 1816. The Conversation Book entry quoted above shows that four years later in 1820, Brauchle, tutor in the Erdödy household and friend of Beethoven, was implicated in this death. The evidence concerning this case is incomplete, but Gunther Haupt[45] has investigated the family correspondence and the police records that were available and comes to the following conclusions. In April there were already charges against the Countess and Brauchle for mistreatment of Mimi and a recommendation that Mimi "be freed" from them. Investigation showed that the Countess was unusually strict in the supervision of the children's education and that Brauchle was an excellent manager of domestic affairs for the Countess and a very able tutor for the children, especially in music. Letters written by Mimi and the Countess indicated love for each other and penitence for past frictions,[46] and Mimi's references to Brauchle showed friendship and respect. The records showed further that the interference by the police was at the written request of the widow, Countess Sigismund Erdödy, who was not on good terms with her sister-in-law. The attempt to separate mother and daughter appears to have been in order to secure Mimi for her son and Brauchle for herself. That the threat continues in 1821 is shown by letters written by both the Countess and Mimi; neither objective, however, was attained. Whether in 1820 Countess Marie Erdödy was banished from the country, as Thayer was led to understand, or whether she left of her own accord to still the gossip and calumny concerning her and her family is not clear. At any rate, she moved to Munich in 1824 where she died thirteen years later; already in 1830 Brauchle joined her there where he was survived by his wife. Thus ends the incomplete story of a member of the aristocracy, who was Beethoven's particularly close friend and helper.

Karl came to visit his uncle in Mödling, presumably during his school vacation. When the Giannatasio family made a visit to Mödling on October 5, they saw "our good Beethoven" returning Karl to the city.

[41] Nickname of Countess Erdödy's daughter Marie.

[42] To the right is added the word "Gusti"; nickname for the son, August.

[43] Sperl was the steward.

[44] Schünemann, II, pp. 213-14.

[45] "Gräfin Erdödy und J. X. Brauchle," in *Der Bär* (Lpz., 1927), pp. 70-91.

[46] Mimi had attempted suicide, whereupon she was sent to the St. Pölten Convent.

Towards the end of October, Beethoven returned to Vienna and took lodgings at No. 244 Hauptstrasse in the Landstrasse, "the large house of the Augustinians" beside the church.[47] There he was visited by Dr. W. Chr. Müller of Bremen, a philologist and musical amateur who had long admired Beethoven and, with the help of his "Family Concerts," established in 1732, had created such a cult for Beethoven's music as existed in no city in Germany in the second decade of the nineteenth century—according to Schindler. Müller's daughter Elise played the sonatas exceptionally well and was largely instrumental with her father in creating this cult. On his journey to Italy, Müller came to Vienna where he was in October and early November, 1820. He not only visited Beethoven but also saw and observed him from a distance as is shown by an article which he published entitled "Some Things about Beethoven," from which we quote:[48] "This sense of cosmopolitan independence and consideration for others[49] might have been the reason why over and over again he continued a conversation, already started, in restaurants, where he often had his frugal lunch, and expressed opinions freely and candidly about everything, the government, the police, the manners of the aristocracy in a critical and mocking manner. The police knew it but left him in peace either because he was a fantastic or because he was a brilliant artistic genius. Hence his opinion and assertion that nowhere was speech freer than in Vienna. His ideal of a [political] constitution was the English one."

It was through Dr. Müller that we know somewhat of Beethoven's views on the subject of analytical programmes. Among the zealous promoters of the Beethoven cult in Bremen, was a young poet named Dr. Karl Iken, editor of the *Bremer Zeitung*, who, inspired by the *Familien-Concerte*, conceived the idea of helping the public to an understanding of Beethoven's music by writing programmatic expositions of the symphonies for perusal before the concerts. Some of his lucubrations were sent to Beethoven by Dr. Müller, and aroused the composer's ire. Schindler found four of these "programmes" among Beethoven's papers, and he gave the world a specimen. In the Seventh Symphony, Dr. Iken professed to see a political revolution. "The sign of revolt is given; there is a rushing and running about of the multitude; an innocent man, or party, is surrounded, overpowered after a struggle and haled before a legal tribunal. Innocency weeps; the judge pronounces a harsh sentence; sympathetic voices mingle in laments and denunciations—they are those of widows and orphans; in the second part of the first movement the parties have become equal in numbers and the magistrates are now scarcely able to quiet the wild tumult. The uprising

---

[47] According to Frimmel (*FRBH*, II, p. 458), on the basis of a recollection of Karl van Beethoven's daughter, Frau G. Heimler, Beethoven lived for a short time at Alt-Lerchenfeld No. 8 (now Josefstädter Strasse No. 57) in order to be near the Blöchlinger Institute.

[48] *AMZ* (May 23, 1827), No. 21, p. 350.

(TDR, IV, 206, n. 3.)

[49] Müller had just referred to Beethoven's refusal in the last years to accept help, kindnesses, or even an invitation to a meal from friends of his own class, who knew his circumstances, for fear of limiting his freedom and burdening others with his deafness.

is suppressed, but the people are not quieted; hope smiles cheeringly and suddenly the voice of the people pronounces the decision in harmonious agreement. . . . But now, in the last movement, the classes and the masses mix in a variegated picture of unrestrained revelry. The quality still speak aloofly in the wind-instruments,—strange bacchantic madness in related chords—pauses, now here, now there—now on a sunny hill, anon on flowery meadow where in merry May all the jubilating children of nature vie with each other with joyful voices—float past the fancy."

It is scarcely to be wondered at that such balderdash disgusted and even enraged Beethoven. In the fall of 1819, he dictated a letter to Müller—it has, unfortunately been lost—in which he protested energetically against such interpretations of his music. He pointed out, says Schindler, who wrote the letter for him, the errors to which such writings would inevitably give rise. If expositions were necessary, they should be confined to characterization of the composition in general terms, which could easily and correctly be done by any educated musician.[50]

Beethoven's complaints concerning his financial condition were chronic and did not cease even in periods where extraordinary receipts make them difficult to understand. That the lamentations in his letters during the two years which we have in review were well-founded, however, is no doubt true. With so engrossing a work as the *Missa Solemnis* on hand there could not have been much time for such potboilers as he mentions and the other sources of revenue were not many. From the records which are at hand, we know something about a few of his monetary transactions. On October 26, 1820, he collected 300 florins on account, apparently, from Artaria and Co., through his old friend Oliva.

On December 17th he again applied to Artaria as follows:

While I thank you most sincerely for the 750 fl. C.M. already lent me for which I handed over to you the receipt from H. Imperial Highness the Cardinal, I am requesting anew, since I am in danger of losing one of my 8 bank shares, the loan of a further 150 fl. C.M. which I promise to pay back to you by 3 months from today at the latest. But in order to show you my gratitude, I am promising in writing to send you presently one of my compositions consisting of one, two or several movements as your property without asking for any kind of honorarium.

ever your obliging
Beethoven

It is not known whether Beethoven delivered any work of this kind. These shares, it will be remembered, had been set apart by him as his nephew's legacy, and he clung to them as a sacred pledge.

Meanwhile a letter from Steiner to the composer shows that he had sent Beethoven a dun, or at least a statement of account, and Beethoven had evidently been unreasonable in his reply. The letter follows:

[50] *Biogr.*, I', pp. 208-11. (TDR, IV, 206.)

Vienna, Dec. 29, 1820

Most highly esteemed Sir and friend Beethoven!

Enclosed are the three overtures in score with the request that you go through them at your convenience as you yourself suggested and correct any errors that may have crept in.— As soon as we have received these corrections we will proceed to engrave and print them in order to bring out the first edition as quickly as possible.

I cannot rest content with your remarks concerning the account sent you; for the cash money loaned you I have charged you only 6% interest, while for the money which you deposited with me I paid you 8% promptly in advance and also repaid the capital promptly. What is sauce for the goose is sauce for the gander (*Was also dem Einen recht ist, muss dem Andern billig sein*). I am not in a position to lend money without interest. As a friend I came to your help in need, I trusted your word of honor and believe that I have not been importunate, nor have I plagued you in any way; wherefore I must solemnly protest against your upbraidings. If you recall that my loan to you was made in part 5 years ago, you will yourself confess that I am not an urgent creditor. I would spare you even now and wait patiently if I were not on my honor in need of cash for my business. If I were less convinced that you are really in a position to give me relief and able to keep your *word of honor* I would, difficult as it would be for me, right gladly remain patient a while longer; but when I remember that I myself returned to you 4,000 florins, conventional coin, or 10,000 florins, Vienna Standard, as capital 17 months ago and at your request did not deduct the amount due me, it is doubly painful to me now to be embarrassed because of my good will and my trust in your word of honor. Every man knows best where the shoe pinches and I am in this case; wherefore I conjure you again not to leave me in the lurch and to find means to liquidate my account as soon as possible.

As for the rest I beg you to accept from me the compliments of the season together with the request that you continue to give me your favor and friendship. It will rejoice me if you keep your word and honor me soon with a visit; it rejoices me more that you have happily withstood your illness and are again restored to health. God preserve you long in health, contentment and enjoyment, this is the wish of your wholly devoted

S. A. Steiner.

The letter contains pencil memoranda by Beethoven. He had evidently added together the various sums which he owed Steiner and they amounted to 2420 florins V.S. He remarks: "The 1300 florins V.S. were probably received in 1816 or 1817— 750 fl. V.S. still later, perhaps in 1819—the 300 fl. are debts which I assumed for Frau van Beethoven and can be chargeable for only a few years—the 70 florins may have been for myself in 1819.— Payment may be made of 1200 florins a year in semi-annual payments."[51] A further memorandum on the cover notes Steiner's willingness to accept payments on April 15 and October 15, 1821. -⸰⸰In a letter to Haslinger written on September 5, presumably in 1822, Beethoven writes: "I beg Steiner

---

[51] For a discussion of the financial transactions between Beethoven and the Steiner firm see Max Unger, *Ludwig van Beethoven und seine Verleger*, pp. 15-17.

to go to Dr. Bach tomorrow afternoon where the 600 fl. C.M. may be received, the other 600 will be available also from Dr. Bach as soon as possible." But the conflict between Steiner and Beethoven was again to come to a head in the year 1823. The three overtures mentioned in Steiner's letter were undoubtedly those to the *Ruinen von Athen* and *König Stephan,* and the "Namensfeier" overture. The increasingly strained relations between Steiner and Beethoven are demonstrated by the fact that after the Symphonies No. 7 and No. 8 and the Pianoforte Sonata in A, Op. 101, no big works were given to Steiner and by the fact that as a result these three overtures were not published right away but in 1823, 1826 and 1825 respectively.}

The negotiations for the publication of the Mass had already begun; as we know from the letter of March 18 to Simrock, the Bonn publisher was supposed to receive it for 100 Louis d'or along with certain conditions. —But entries in the Conversation Books show that in Beethoven's circle there was decreasing enthusiasm for the offer, yet increasing need for the money. Already in the latter part of March, soon after the original letter had been mailed, Oliva writes:

> 100 Louis d'or would be 200 ducats, that would be little. 1 Louis is 2 ducats, one Louis is worth 12 g[ulden] or somewhat more in gold;—Prussian Friedrichs d'or are worth less, I am sure of it. How much have you asked from Simrok? At least 150 Louis d'or? 125 is 250 ducats. I told you that before you came out.[52]

In business transactions with Bonn Franz Brentano in Frankfurt was authorized to act as agent. In April Oliva writes again:}— "Have you written to Simrok that he must not publish the mass *at once* as you want first to send it or hand it to the Archduke?" Again: "If you send the Recepisse on the stage-coach he will certainly send you the money *at once.*" And later: "It would be quicker to give the music to the stage-coach and send Brentano the receipt—at the same time informing Simrok that Brentano had been assured of its dispatch; then Brentano can send you the money *at once* without waiting to receive the music." In April again: "But he has not yet replied to your last offer of the mass? I mean Simrock—200 ducats could help you out greatly— Because of your circumstances. You must not delay writing to Simrock or Brentano;— Brentano can send you the money *at once*—or at least very soon.— I am surprised that Simrock has not answered yet."[53]

—On April 23 Beethoven asked again that the 100 Louis d'or be sent to Brentano and stated that Simrock would receive the Mass "by the end of May or beginning of June." The next letter concerning the Mass is dated July 23 and shows that Simrock had written on July 10 questioning the meaning in monetary terms of the Louis d'or. In his reply, Beethoven held to the value of 2 ducats or the various florin equivalents of one Louis d'or

---

[52] Schünemann, I, p. 377.   [53] *Ibid.,* II, pp. 11, 32, 33, 79.

and added "—Herewith if everything is settled, I assure you that you will receive the Mass next month."

The contents of Simrock's next letter, which was written undoubtedly in August are suggested by some more of Oliva's entries in the Conversation Books at the end of August.}— "Leave Simrok's letter with me, I'll answer it and give you the letter this afternoon;—if you are satisfied with it sign it and I will post it tomorrow. There must be no delay." "He says the Mass can be used only by Catholics, which is not true. He is paying too little rather than too much with 200 ducats."[54] —}{In his answer of August 30, Beethoven established the florin exchange at 9 per Louis d'or and asked for 900 florins. Beethoven also corrected Simrock as regards the use of the Mass by pointing out that his first mass was supplied in the Breitkopf and Härtel edition with an additional German text and was performed in Protestant cities, and that he would be willing to supply a German text for his new mass.}—

The difficulty that had developed is explained in a letter from Simrock to Brentano dated November 12, 1820. It was a misunderstanding concerning the price of the "new grand musical mass" which the composer wished to sell for 100 Louis d'or. The publisher had agreed to the price, understanding Louis d'or to mean what the term meant in Bonn, Leipzig and throughout Germany, namely, the equivalent of Friedrichs d'or, pistoles. In order to avoid unpleasantness after the reception of the Mass he had explained this clearly to Beethoven and in a letter, dated September 23, had repeated that by Louis d'or he meant Friedrich d'or; he was not in a position to give more. He would hold the sum in readiness against the receipt of the Mass, which Beethoven had promised to provide with German as well as Latin words. He was also under the impression that he had asked a speedy decision, as he did not want to keep his money tied up in Frankfurt. Hearing nothing for four weeks he had quit counting on the Mass and made other use of his money. Learning, however, from Brentano's letter of November 8th that Beethoven had agreed to let him have the Mass, he now found himself in the embarrassment of not having the gold Louis d'or on hand; but as Brentano had said nothing on the subject he would in the meantime try to secure the coin, unless Brentano were willing to take the equivalent in florins at the rate of 9.36. He asked to be informed of the arrival of the music so that he might instruct Heinrich Verhuven to receive it on paying the sum mentioned.

Simrock had waited four weeks before abandoning hope that Beethoven would send the Mass; it was ten weeks and more before Beethoven answered Simrock's letter. Then he sent his reply enclosed in a letter to Brentano dated November 28. —}{The letter follows:

[54] *Ibid.*, pp. 238, 240.

Vienna, November 28, 1820

My dear Simrock!

I received your last letter in the country. After His Imperial Highness the Cardinal returned to his residence and I had to betake myself to him in the city two or three times weekly during the whole summer, my country life which is dear to me was very much disturbed. Not until October was I able to retrieve some of the country life that I'd missed. Your letter arrived at this time, but going back and forth first here then there I did not read it right away. Since I understand nothing about business affairs, I waited for my friend who, nevertheless, has not been here up until now. In the meantime I could not help learning from others that I would lose at least 100 fl. C.M. Being frank, I must confess to you that earlier I could have had 200 ducats in gold, yet your offer was preferable since 100 l[ouis d'or] according to information was supposed to be worth still more. Now it is too late to change since the firm that was supposed to receive the great Mass has commissioned another big work from me, and I would not like to have appeared to have given out on any kind of a proposal—which you will find natural enough. As soon as the Mass is supplied throughout with a German text, I will send it to Hr. F. Brentano in Frankfurt where you can then transfer 100 pistoles instead of Louis d'or according to your interpretation. The translation is costing me at least 50 fl. V.S., I hope at least that you will provide this amount, and so requiescat in pace— I would rather write 10,000 notes than one letter, especially when it's a question of taking *this* and not *that*. Therefore I hope that much more for your favor in the edition of my complete works, which, as you know, means a great deal to me. Since Bonn is regarded as out of the country, the edition there could extend *my leave of absence* out of the country, which is what I want. All good wishes and regards to Wegeler and his whole family. As soon as I find a beautiful Bohemian goblet, I will send him *one again*.

In haste your Beethoven ——

Thus matters stood with the Mass at the end of 1820, and thus they seem to have remained throughout the next year. Simrock always was to be but never was blest with the score.

Of the performances of Beethoven's music during the year, the following should be mentioned. At the concerts of the Gesellschaft der Musikfreunde the *Eroica* was performed on February 20, the Symphony in C minor and a chorus from *Christus am Ölberg* on April 9, Symphony No. 8 in F major on November 19. On April 17 Fanny Giannatasio records in her diary: "Yesterday I heard once again the harmonies of the two rulers in the realm of tones, a new overture by Beethoven and the overture to *Figaro* by Mozart." The concert was for the benefit of Widows and Orphans; the overture was undoubtedly Op. 115, "Zur Namensfeier."

On October 1, 1819, a new concert series was started, soon to be known as the *Concerts spirituels*. Its founder was Franz Xaver Gebauer (1784-1822), choir director at the Augustinian church. His idea was to enlarge the choir rehearsals into meetings of music-lovers in which was performed not only a choral work in preparation for the next feast day but also a whole symphony. Concerning the founding of these concerts, Mosel writes in the Vienna *Allg. Mus. Zeitung* (April 5, 1820) that "musical jugglery has taken the place of sensitive performance, everywhere the symphonies of Mozart, Haydn, Beethoven have disappeared— Now *Herr Gebauer* makes the proposal to form a special society of a moderate number to bring to performance only symphonies and choruses excluding all virtuoso music (*Concertmusik*) and bravura singing." These concerts were on the one hand more strict in program than those at the Gesellschaft[55] and on the other hand more faulty in performance since the performers were amateurs reading at sight. In the 18 concerts of the first season (1819/20) were performed Beethoven's first four symphonies, the "Pastoral," the Mass in C, and *Meerestille und Glückliche Fahrt*, the last twice. The second season (1820/21) again consisted of ten concerts which included the Symphonies in C minor, A major, and F major (No. 8) and *Christus am Ölberg*.[56]

In Beethoven's circle, Gebauer's choir seems to have been more highly regarded than his new concert series. In a Conversation Book in April Beethoven makes one of his familiar plays on names: Oliva—"Concerning Gebauer"—Beethoven—"Geh! Bauer." [Go! peasant]. Soon Oliva remarks: "Since Gebauer has taken over, the music at the Augustin has improved very much and now the best church music is there." In contrast, Oliva comments on the performance on April 9th: "I forgot to tell you that the dilettantes scraped through your symphony yesterday."[57] And Beethoven wrote the following note in connection with one of these concerts:

To the most famous music store in Europe, Steiner and Company (Pater noster miserere gässel)
I request some tickets (2) from Geh Bauer since some of my friends wish to go to this *musical obscurity* [*Winkelmusik*]—perhaps you have some of these *privy tickets* [*Abtrittskarten*] if so send me one or two—

Your

The score belongs to   Animus
the chorus for which   Beethoven
der *Bauer* has the voice parts.

This year a furore was created in Vienna by an eight-year-old pianist, Leopoldine Blahetka. She was a pupil of Joseph Czerny,[58] who also taught Beethoven's nephew. He helped her rehearse Beethoven's Concerto in B-flat which she played in public on April 3.

[55] The program for the Gesellschaft concert of April 5, for instance, was: Beethoven, Symphony in C minor; Niccolini, Soprano Aria with Chorus from *Il Carlo Magno*; Worzischek, Song for four voices "Gott im Frühling"; Keller, Polonaise for Flute; Beethoven, Chorus from *Christus am Ölberg*.

[56] For further information concerning the Concerts spirituels see Eduard Hanslick, *Geschichte des Concertwesens in Wien* (Vienna, 1869), I, pp. 185-90. (TDR, IV, 218, n. 2.)

[57] Schünemann, II, pp. 40, 41.

[58] Joseph Czerny (1785-1842), not a relative of Carl Czerny, was his successor as teacher of Beethoven's nephew Karl. He was a composer, pianist and pianoforte teacher.

An event at the end of the year which could not fail to affect Beethoven was the departure of his friend Oliva, who had been his faithful helper in all kinds of external matters for a number of years. In December, 1820, he took his passport and moved to St. Petersburg, where he settled as a teacher of languages. From now on, Schindler was to become a closer friend and factotum to Beethoven.

The compositions of the year were:

"Abendlied unterm gestirnten Himmel," WoO 150.
Canons:
"Alles gute, alles schöne" (Goeble), WoO 179, New Year's greeting to Archduke Rudolph.
"Bester Magistrat, Ihr friert," WoO 177 [around 1820]. Eight measures for four bass voices with accompaniment of violoncello or double bass.
"Hoffman, sei ja kein Hofmann," WoO 180, probably inspired by the name E. T. A. Hoffmann.
"Sankt Petrus war ein Fels, Bernardus war ein Sankt," WoO 175, inspired by the names of Karl Peters and Karl Bernard.
"Wähner es ist kein Wahn," for Friedrich Wähner, Hess Verzeichnis No. 301.
Sonata for Pianoforte, Op. 109.
Around 1820: Three Canons: "Gedenket heute an Baden," "Gehabt euch wohl," and "Tugend ist kein leerer Name," WoO 181, amidst sketches for the *Missa Solemnis*.[59]

The publications of the year were:

By Simrock:
Ten Themes, Russian, Scottish and Tyrolean, Varied for Pianoforte with optional accompaniment for flute or violin, Op. 107.
By the *Wiener Modenzeitung* as a supplement, March 28:
"Abendlied unterm gestirnten Himmel," WoO 150, dedicated to Dr. Anton Braunhofer.

[59] See *II Beeth.*, p. 152.

CHAPTER XXXIV

THE YEAR 1821

ATTACKS OF RHEUMATISM AND JAUNDICE—THE
PIANOFORTE SONATAS OP. 110 AND OP. 111

THE information in 1821 concerning Beethoven's life is comparatively meagre. Not only have no Conversation Books of this year survived but also the number of letters existent is very small. Consequently certain portions of the all too rich offerings of the Conversation Books from the past year may be reserved to serve as an introduction to this year. Not all the entries are concerned with the nephew, the price of a commodity, some local news, or a recent musical performance; there are also remarks on topics of general concern—politics, philosophy, literature—which might well be cited as typical for these years. Here are isolated examples drawn from various periods:

[Janitschek][1] If N[apoleon] had come back now, he would have had a better reception in Europe. He understood the spirit of the age and knew how to hold the reins. Our descendants will know better how to estimate him. As a German I was his greatest enemy but as time goes on, I have become reconciled. Dedicated ideals and beliefs are there—his word was worth far more. He had a taste for art and science and hated ignorance. He would have appreciated the Germans more and would have protected their rights. At the end he was surrounded with traitors and the spirit of the generals declined. His best marshals had withdrawn.

The children of the Revolution and the spirit of the age demanded such an iron will. He certainly destroyed the Feudal system everywhere and was the protector of law and justice. His marriage to Princess Louise was the highest culmination point. To give the world peace and good laws was what mattered, and not to want to make more conquests.— Because of pride the greatest fortune became the greatest misfortune. An old torn piece of cloth that can never be

---

[1] Nothing is known of Herr and Frau Janitschek beyond the fact that their names appear frequently along with those of Bernard and Peters during the conversations of 1820. See *FRBH*, I, pp. 238-39.

mended. Instead of being sensible as a result of the experience, they have become still more foolish— That's what happens with privileges. How can one inherit nobleness of the heart? The privileged first of all have established a social contract and then they speak of rights.[2]

[Peters] Kaiser Leopold was a 7 month old child. In order to let him ripen properly he was firmly planted in a freshly slaughtered pig and the meat was subsequently given to the poor which they named Kaiser meat.[3]

[Blöchlinger] Man is living to excess in nature's lap; here he is too much occupied with conceit and with his stomach to realize it. Man should be able to give up everything to preserve himself, otherwise man is lost. There is such a menace, it is a fateful period; we must wait patiently to see what is to be the end of it all and each tend to our own business.

•~•

Meanwhile religion has been pulled into play and the so-called Ligorians[4] have again begun the old Agnosticism and that is respected and called good because there is no alternative. •~•

It seems to me that we Europeans are going backwards, and America is raising itself in culture. The present relationship at least is not favorable; the just claims of Americans to independence, on the contrary, support this.

•~•

The saddest tendency of this new revolutionary spirit is an egotism poorly demonstrated or rather too clearly shown. What purpose is gained by the murder of Kotzebue? Although he was no moral luminary in the world, yet he was opposed to many a priest's tale (*Bonzengeschichte*) and would have been again probably if he were living. •~•

What man is in a position to estimate the results of such an act and consequently consider it as good and necessary.[5]

[Kanne] An excellent work, but only the first part concerning Greek history has been published. By Otfried Müller in Göttingen.[6] Buy it. As soon as possible I will send to you a little work by Schleiermacher in Berlin. Fichte!—Schelling! Would you like to read something intelligible by Schelling? about art and academic study?[7] Winckelmann[8] said: one must sketch with fire and work out with sluggishness. . . . You must read Plato in the German translation by Schleiermacher. You must, I will bring it for you. He and Schelling are the greatest! Veneration to their spirits! The matter not the form. The idea is splendid and very original.[9]

[2] Schünemann, 1, pp. 206-207.

[3] *Ibid.*, p. 243.

[4] Liguorians belonged to the Congregation of the Most Holy Redeemer founded by Alfonso Maria de Liguoris in 1732.

[5] Schünemann, 1, pp. 323-24.

[6] Karl Otfried Müller, *Geschichten hellenicher Stämme und Städte* (Breslau, 1820),

Vol. 1.

[7] Fr. Wilh. Jos. von Schelling, *Vorlesungen über die Methode des akademischen Studiums* (Tübingen, 1803).

[8] Johann Joachim Winckelmann, German archaeologist of the 18th century.

[9] Schünemann, 1, pp. 344-46.

[Bernard on the subject of inflation]

All Europe is in the same condition. In Spain it was the worst. For 2 years the poor received no wages, the officers had to beg and in the navy they have been dying of hunger. They should go to Armenia to fight in order to gain their back wages. It was the same in France before the Revolution. Because of the bad management of finance, the spending of the court and the excessive demands from the poor, the whole of Europe has become like Spain—no states can any longer save themselves from debts.

It is as with families and single men where no more means of help are at hand. Palfy has instituted a lottery, Stadion also.[10] The whole of Europe is going to the dogs. N[apoleon?] should have been let out for 10 years. Germany must be maintaining 38 courts and perhaps a million princes and princesses, the soldiers who work here on the earthworks receive six groschen V.S. daily even though we have received so many millions in contributions from France. As with the gentleman so with the laborers. They have certainly survived. There still is a pride and an ambition to oppose foreign countries. One simply will not yield, the nobility especially—

Also religion is having to become constitutional; the *Concilien,* common gathering of the bishops, must again be inaugurated to regulate the religious needs of each race according to the degree of its culture, instead of through an absolute judgement of the pope or of the Roman See. All in all we have come down in the world.[11]

Before recounting what is known concerning Beethoven in 1821, a final word should be said concerning his old love, Josephine née Brunsvik, since 1810 Baroness von Stackelberg. After the financial misfortunes which followed his marriage, Stackelberg's situation improved at the end of 1815 when he inherited his brother's property in Russia. Josephine refused to leave Vienna, and he departed with their three daughters who were left with their governess with the Dean of Trautenau in Bohemia. Stackelberg returned with the children to Vienna in 1817 and then left Austria for good. Josephine died on March 31, 1821. Her sister Therese wrote in her journal on July 12, 1817: "If Josephine doesn't suffer punishment on account of Luigi's woe—his wife! What wouldn't she have made out of this hero!" During all of these years did the two meet again? There is no known evidence of any communication after Ludwig's poignant close to their correspondence in 1807; it is known only that Josephine's last years were years of suffering from ill health.[12]

The beginning of the year 1821 found Beethoven still at his home in the suburb Landstrasse, and, it would seem, working as hard as his health permitted. In the *Novellistik* section of the *Allgemeine Musikalische Zeitung,* January 10, 1821, appears: "Herr von Beethofen was sick with a

[10] Prince Palffy and Count Stadion.
[11] Schünemann, II, pp. 58-9.
[12] *Beethoven-Dreizehn unbekannte Briefe an* *Josephine Gräfin Deym geb. v. Brunzvik,* ed. Joseph Schmidt-Görg (Beethovenhaus: Bonn, 1957), pp. 34-5.

rheumatic fever. All friends of true music and all admirers of his muse feared for him. But now he is on the road to recovery and is working actively."[13] A letter of March 7 to Adolf M. Schlesinger in Berlin starts:

Noble Sir!

Perhaps you are thinking disparagingly of me, but you may soon change when I tell you that for six weeks I have been laid up with a severe rheumatic attack; but now it is much better. You can imagine how many things have come to a standstill. Soon I shall catch up with everything. . . .

Instructions follow concerning the publication of Op. 108 (referred to here as "107. Werk") and Op. 109. Beethoven adds: "Will you add the year number as I have often wished, but no publisher has been willing to do it? Both of the other sonatas will follow soon. . . ."

On February 18 Beethoven wrote a little Allegretto in B minor for the album of his new friend, Ferdinand Piringer. Piringer (1780-1829) was a music-lover who was associated with Gebauer and acted as assistant conductor for the *Concerts spirituels* at the Landhaussaal. The Conversation Books of the next year show that he became one of Beethoven's closer friends.[14]

In April, 1860, the author had a conversation with Horzalka[15] in which the latter spoke very highly of Schindler and his disinterested fidelity to Beethoven. Horzalka also said that in 1820 or 1821, as near as he could recollect, the wife of a Major Baumgarten took boy boarders in her house. Her sister, Baroness Born, lived with her. Frau Baumgarten had a son who studied at Blöchlinger's Institute, and Beethoven's nephew was amongst her boarders. One evening Horzalka called there and found only the Baroness Born at home. Soon another caller came and stayed to tea. It was Beethoven. Among other topics, Mozart came under discussion, and the Baroness asked Beethoven, in writing of course, which of Mozart's operas he thought the most of. "*Die Zauberflöte*," said Beethoven and, suddenly clasping his hands and throwing up his eyes exclaimed, "Oh, Mozart!" As Horzalka had, as was the custom, always considered *Don Giovanni* the greatest of Mozart's operas, this opinion by Beethoven made a very deep impression upon him. Beethoven invited the Baroness to come to his lodgings and have a look at his Broadwood pianoforte.[16]

For the summer he went first to Unterdöbling. He had suffered from rheumatism during the preceding winter and now became a victim of

[13] See Frimmel, *Beethoven-Forschung*, VIII, p. 117.

[14] See *FRBH*, II, pp. 21-2.

[15] Johann Friedrich Horzalka (1778-1860), composer and pianist, was born in Triesch in 1778, came to Vienna in 1799, and studied harmony and counterpoint with Emmanuel Förster. He died but a few months after his conversation with Thayer.

[16] In the Conversation Books Baroness Born is mentioned already in the early part of 1820, but it is not until late summer that Horzalka is identified by Oliva: "His name is Horschalka, he is a pupil of Moscheles" (Schünemann, II, p. 234). This suggests that the scene in Vienna described above did not take place until the next winter—1820-21.

jaundice. This attack may have been an *avant-courier* of the disease of the liver which brought him to the grave six years later. He wrote the following letter to the Archduke on July 18:

Your Imperial Highness!

I heard yesterday of the arrival here of Your Highness, which would have given me so much pleasure, but now has become a sad event for me since it may be a rather long time before I can be lucky enough to wait upon Y. I. H. After feeling poorly for a very long time, a *full case of jaundice* finally developed, a disease that is extremely loathsome to me. I hope at least that I will be cured enough to see Y. I. H. before your departure— Also last winter I had a very bad rheumatic fever— Much of this is linked up with the sad situation as regards my economic circumstances. Up until now I had hoped by struggling to the utmost to emerge finally victorious over it. God, who knows my heart and knows how sacredly I as a man fulfill all the duties imposed upon me by humanity, God and nature, will some day free me from this affliction— The Mass will be delivered to Y. I. H. while you are here. Please let me spare Y. I. H. the causes of its delay. The details might prove anything but pleasant to Y. I. H— . . . .

The rest of the letter consists of further expressions of concern about his relationship with his patron.

--•❧In order to take a cure prescribed by his physician, Dr. Staudenheim, Beethoven moved to Baden on September 7, where he stayed in the Rathausgasse No. 94.[17]❧•--

In 1820 Professor Höfel, who lived at Salzburg in the last years of his life and who engraved the Latronne portrait of Beethoven for Artaria, was appointed to a professorship of drawing in Wiener Neustadt. A year or two afterward, as he said,[18] he was one evening with Eisner and other colleagues in the garden of the tavern "Zum Schleifen," a little way out of town. The Commissioner of Police was a member of the party. It was autumn and already dark when a constable came and said to the Commissioner: "Mr. Commissioner, we have arrested somebody who will give us no peace. He keeps on yelling that he is Beethoven; but he's a ragamuffin, has no hat, an old coat, etc.—nothing by which he can be identified." The Commissioner ordered that the man be kept under arrest until morning, "then we will examine him and learn who he is." Next day the company was very anxious to know how the affair turned out, and the Commissioner said that about 11 o'clock at night he was awakened by a policeman with the information that the prisoner would give them no peace and had demanded that Herzog, Musical Director in Wiener Neustadt, be called to identify him. So the Commissioner got up, dressed, went out and woke up Herzog, and in the middle of the night went with him to the watchhouse. Herzog, as soon as he cast eyes on the man exclaimed, "That *is* Beethoven!" He took him

---

[17] See Th. Frimmel, "Beethoven im Kurort Baden bei Wien" in *NBJ*, IV (1930), p. 73.
[18] This anecdote is recorded in Thayer's notebook as a memorandum of a conversation he had with Höfel on June 23, 1860. (TK, III, 42, n. 2.)

home with him, gave him his best room, etc. Next day came the burgomaster, making all manner of apologies. As it proved, Beethoven had got up early in the morning, and, slipping on a miserable old coat and, without a hat, had gone out to walk a little. He got upon the towpath of the canal and kept on and on; seemed to have lost his direction, for, with nothing to eat, he had continued on until he ended up at the canal-basin at the Ungerthor. Here, not knowing where he was, he was seen looking in at the windows of the houses, and as he looked so like a beggar the people had called a constable who arrested him. Upon his arrest the composer said, "I am Beethoven." "Of course, why not?" (*Warum nicht gar?*) said the policeman; "You're a tramp: Beethoven doesn't look so." (*Ein Lump sind Sie; so sieht der Beethoven nicht aus.*) Herzog gave him some decent clothes and the burgomaster sent him back to Baden in the magisterial state-coach.

A letter written from Baden on September 10, 1821, to Tobias Haslinger accompanying a canon on the words "O Tobias dominus Haslinger, O, O!" deserves to be given here to show that Beethoven's high spirits could at times dominate him in spite of his general misery.

Very best fellow!

Yesterday, in the carriage on the way to Vienna, I was overcome by sleep, naturally enough, since (because of my early rising here) I had never slept well. While thus slumbering I dreamed that I had made a long journey—to no less distant a country than Syria, then to India, back again, even to Arabia; finally I reached Jerusalem. The Holy City aroused in me thoughts of Holy Writ and small wonder that the man Tobias now occurred to me, and how natural that our little Tobias should enter my mind and the pertobiasser, and now during my dream journey the following canon came to me:

But scarcely awakened, away went the canon and nothing of it would come back to my memory. But when, next day, I was on my way hither in the same conveyance (that of a poor Austrian musician) and continued the dream journey of the day before, now awake, behold, according to the laws of association of ideas, the same canon occurred to me again. Now fully awake I held it fast, as once Menelaus held Proteus, only allowing it to change itself into 3 voices.

Farewell. Presently I shall send you something on Steiner to show you that he has no stony [*Steinernes*] heart. Farewell, very best of fellows, we ever wish that you will always belie your name of publisher [*Verleger*] and never become embarrassed [*verlegen*] but remain a publisher [*Verleger*] never at a loss [*verlegen*] either in receiving or paying—Sing the epistles of St. Paul every day,

Alternative[19] with a 3rd voice

go to pater Werner,[20] who will show you the little book by which you may go to heaven in a jiffy. You see my anxiety for your soul's salvation; and I remain with the greatest pleasure from everlasting to everlasting,

Your most faithful debtor   Beethoven.

The reference to the Mass in the letter of July 18 to the Archduke could suggest that it was almost ready; but unfortunately that was not the case, for he was working on it constantly during this and the following year. The slow progress is explained partly through his illnesses and partly that he had taken up other composition projects simultaneously. Back in Vienna Beethoven wrote the following letter to Franz Brentano which sheds light on these matters:

Vienna, November 12, 1821

Honored friend!

Don't consider me a shabby or thoughtless genius— For the past year up to the present I have been continually ill; likewise during the summer I had an attack of jaundice, which lasted until the end of August. Following Staudenheim's order I had to go to Baden in September. Since it soon became cold there I was overtaken by a case of diarrhoea that was so violent that I could not keep up the course of treatment and had to flee here. Now thank God things are better and it appears that I am to be cheered up by the return of health and may live again for my art, which for the last two years has certainly not been the case

[19] Beethoven writes "offen" which can mean "alternative" or "open," the latter being the opposite of "verschlossen"—"closed" of the first version.

[20] The dramatic poet Zacharias Werner, who had become a convert to Roman Catholicism and, now an ordained priest, was preaching to great crowds of Viennese. The puns on the German words *Verleger* and *verlegen* are untranslatable. (TK, III, 44, n. 1.)

not only from lack of health but also on account of many other human miseries— The mass might have been sent before this, but had to be *carefully looked through,* for the publishers in other countries do not get along well with my manuscript, as I know from experience. A copy for the engraver must be examined note by note. Moreover, I could not do this because of illness, the more since despite everything I have been compelled to make a considerable number of *potboilers* (as unfortunately I must call them)— I think I am justified in making an attempt to get Simrock to reckon the Louis d'or at a higher rate, inasmuch as several applications have been made from other quarters, concerning which I shall write you soon. As for the rest, do not question my honesty; frequently I think of nothing except that your kind advance may soon be repaid—
with sincere gratitude and respect your friend
and servant Beethoven.

It seems a fair inference from his concluding remark, together with the advice of his friend or friends in the Conversation Book of the previous summer concerning a collection through Brentano as soon as the Mass had been handed over to the stage-coach, that Beethoven had got an advance from Brentano on the money which was awaiting the arrival of the work in Frankfurt. The following letter to Brentano strengthens the inference:

Noble man!   Vienna, December 20, 1821.

I am awaiting another letter respecting the mass, which I shall send you to give you an insight into the whole affair. In any event the honorarium will be paid to you whereupon you will please deduct the amount of my indebtedness to you. My gratitude to you will always be unbounded— I was so presumptuous as not to ask before dedicating a composition of mine to your daughter Maxe. Please accept the deed as a mark of my continual devotion to you and your entire family—do not misinterpret the dedication as prompted by my own interest or as a recompense—this would pain me greatly. There are nobler motives to which such things may be ascribed if reasons must be found—

The new year is about to begin; may it fulfil all your wishes and daily increase your happiness as pater familias in your children. I embrace you cordially and beg you to present my compliments to your excellent, one and only glorious Toni—

Your most respectful faithful Beethoven

I have received from here and elsewhere offers of 200 ducats in gold for the mass. I think I can get 100 florins V.S. more. On this point I am waiting for a letter which I will send you at once. The matter might then be presented to Simrock, who certainly will not expect me to lose so much. Till then please be patient and do not think that you have acted towards an unworthy man.

Brentano informed Simrock of the situation; but the subject is now carried over into the next year and must be left for the nonce, while we return to the history of some other compositions.

Beethoven's dedication of his Pianoforte Sonata in E major, Op. 109, to Maximiliane Brentano was accompanied by the following letter to her:

A dedication!!!—well this is not one that is misused as in many cases— It is the spirit which holds together noble and better men on this earth and which can *never* be destroyed by *time*. This is what is now addressed to you and what recalls you to me as you were in your childhood years, so equally your beloved parents, your admirable and gifted mother, your father filled with truly good and noble qualities, and ever mindful of his children. Thus at this very moment I am on the Landstrasse—and see all of you before me. While I am thinking of the excellent qualities of your parents, there are no doubts in my mind that you have been striving to emulate these noble people and are progressing daily— My memories of a noble family can never fade, may your memories of me be frequent and good—
Affectionately farewell, may heaven always bless you in all your ways—
sincerely and always your friend Beethoven
Vienna
December 6, 1821

Meanwhile Beethoven was writing the two other sonatas concerning which he himself left data. On the autograph of that in A-flat major, Op. 110, he wrote the date "December 25, 1821." Sketches for it follow sketches for the *Agnus Dei* of the Mass, which were begun in 1821. It was published by Schlesinger in Berlin and Paris in 1822 without dedication. There is evidence in a memorandum to Schindler found among the latter's papers that Beethoven intended to dedicate both of the last sonatas to Madame Brentano. "Ries-nichts" ("nothing for Ries"), says the memorandum significantly.[21] Ideas utilized in the C minor Sonata, Op. 111, are found among those for Op. 110 and particularly among some for the *Agnus Dei*. It is noteworthy, as shown by Nottebohm, that in the middle of sketches of Op. 110 there appears the first theme of the first movement of Op. 111, which was designated as a "3tes Stück presto" for the "2te Sonate."[22]

The autograph of the last Sonata, Op. 111, bears the inscription "Ludwig Ludwig am 13ten Jenner [January 13] 1822," and it is plain that most of the work was done in 1821. It was published by Schlesinger at the latest in April, 1823, after Beethoven had offered it to Peters of Leipzig. In a letter of May 1, 1822, Beethoven had left the matter of the dedication up to the elder Schlesinger, but on August 31 of the same year he wrote to the son that it was to be dedicated to Archduke Rudolph. In a letter to the Archduke on July 1,[23] 1823, he writes: "Y. I. H. seemed to find pleasure in the Sonata in C minor, and therefore I feel that it would not be presumptuous if I were to surprise you with its dedication." —Corrections for these three sonatas occupied a great deal of Beethoven's time. The difficulties with

[21] See *A* 1118.

[22] *II Beeth.*, pp. 467-68. The theme had figured twenty years before in a sketchbook used when the Sonata in A major, Op. 30, No. 1, was in hand. Its key was F-sharp minor, and it may once have been intended

for this work. See Nottebohm, *Ein Skizzenbuch von Beethoven* (Leipzig, 1865), p. 19. (TK, III, 49, n. 4.)

[23] Beethoven dated the letter June 1st, but since he refers to an "accompanying receipt of June 27th" he must have meant July 1.

Op. 109 are the subject of letters to Schlesinger throughout the year. The history of the printing of Op. 111 will be told in the chapter for the year 1823.

The compositions completed during the year were:

1820-21. Bagatelles for Pianoforte, Op. 119, Nos. 7-11.
1821.   Canon. "O Tobias," WoO 182, in a letter to Tobias Haslinger.
          Piece for Pianoforte in B minor, WoO 61, for Friedrich Piringer.
          Sonata for Pianoforte, Op. 110. According to Kinsky-Halm, the final
          movement was revised early in the next year.[24]

The publications of the year were:

By Schlesinger in Berlin:
   Sonata for Pianoforte in E major, Op. 109, dedicated to Maximiliane Brentano.
By Starke:
   Five Bagatelles for Pianoforte, Op. 119, Nos. 7-11 as Nos. 28-32 in *Wiener Piano-Forte-Schule von Frd. Starke Kapellmeister 3te Abtheilung.*

[24] See KHV, p. 314.

CHAPTER XXXV

THE YEAR 1822

THE *MISSA SOLEMNIS*—BEETHOVEN AND THE PUBLISHERS—THE LAST PIANOFORTE SONATA— MUSIC FOR VARIOUS OCCASIONS

THE events in the year 1822, in which the composition of the great Mass in D comes to an end except for corrections and improvements with which Beethoven never felt that he was done, will be told in a sequence that is as chronological as possible without breaking the individual threads.

At the beginning of 1822, Beethoven still lived at No. 244 Hauptstrasse, Landstrasse, Vienna. The first significant happening to him in the new year was his election as honorary member of the Musik-Verein of Steiermark in Graz, whose diploma, couched in the extravagantly sentimental verbiage of the day and country, bore date January 1.

Beethoven noted the conclusion of the C minor Sonata (Op. 111) on the autograph manuscript on January 13.

Bernard Romberg, Beethoven's old colleague and friend in Bonn, was in Vienna at the beginning of the year, giving concerts with his daughter Bernhardine and his 11-year-old son, Carl, who was also a violoncello virtuoso. Concerning one of the last of these concerts Beethoven wrote to him on February 12:

This last night I have again been *suffering from one of my earaches* which habitually occur in *this season, even your tones* would *today* be merely *painful to me*; this alone is to blame if you do not see me in person— Perhaps I shall be better in a few days in which case I shall still be able to say goodbye to you— Moreover, if you have not received a visit from me, remember the remoteness of my house, my almost ceaseless[1] affairs, all the more since I have been ill for the whole past year, because of which I have been held up on so many works already begun— And, after all, between us there is no need for superficial

---

[1] I am indebted to Miss Anderson for the reading of these two words which were illegible to Thayer. See *A* 1072.

compliment— I wish for a full tribute of applause to you for your high art and also a *metallic recognition* which nowadays is seldom the case— If I can for a little while, I will see you together with your wife and children whom I greet affectionately herewith.

Farewell   great artist
                                       as always your Beethoven

The "metallic recognition" was made, and according to Hanslick, Romberg's earnings during the Vienna season amounted to 10,000 florins.

And now to resume the story of the Mass. At the beginning of 1822 the work was completed in sketch form, by the end of the year the autograph score was made, and on March 19, 1823, a beautiful copy was sent to the Archduke. Meanwhile negotiations for the publication of the Mass continued not only with Simrock but with a number of other firms as well.

On May 13, 1822, Simrock became impatient and wrote the following letter from Bonn:

To Herr Louis van Beethoven!
      in Vienna!

It is now a year since you promised me for sure that I would receive the mass completely finished at the end of April. Since October 25, 1820, I have had 100 Louis d'or on deposit in Frankfurt from which you should have received your payment immediately. On March 19th you wrote me expressly that you had been bedridden for 6 weeks and had not yet fully recovered. I was supposed to be completely assured; you wrote this only so that I should think nothing differently. Next I asked Brentano [about it] at the autumn fair and again at this Easter fair, but nothing has arrived as usual. So I beg you now to write some words about it once and for all: I write about this so that you will not believe that I have died, which nearly happened this past winter!

Every so often I have taken up the idea of publishing your six symphonies in score, which by now should have been done several times—even publicly advertised; but had not been done because there was no profit in it. I know this very well; but I have wanted to make a worthy monument to my worthy old friend and I hope that you will be satisfied with the edition since I have done all I can with it! I have had the first two appear at the same time and will send you a copy along with the first shipment to Vienna!

We thought that we would see you here during the past summer as you had promised in your letter of March 19, but this has not happened either.

We all greet you sincerely.

                                       N. Simrock

What Beethoven said in reply to this letter is not known, his answer not having been given to the world; it can be surmised, however, from the recital given to Brentano in a letter from Beethoven dated May 19. He had been troubled by "gout in the chest" for four months, he said, and able to do but little work; nevertheless the Mass would be in Frankfurt by the end of the next month, that is, by the end of June, 1822. There was another reason for the delay. Cardinal Rudolph, strongly disposed in favor of his music at all times, did not want the Mass published so early and had returned to the composer the score and parts only three days before. Here we have a very significant statement. What may be called the official copy of the Mass in D was formally presented to Archduke Rudolph on March 19, 1823; here, ten months earlier, he speaks of a score and parts which the Archduke had returned to him three days before. The Mass, therefore, must have had what, for the time being (Beethoven never considered it finished so long as it was in his hands), was looked upon as a definitive shape at the time when Beethoven promised to send it to Brentano for Simrock. The Archduke returned it, as Beethoven says, so that the publication might not be hindered. How long it had been in the hands of the Archduke no one can tell. Now, said Beethoven to Brentano, the score will be copied again, carefully examined, which would take some time owing to his ill health, but it would be in Frankfurt at the end of June "at the latest," by which time Simrock must be ready to make payment. He had received better offers from Vienna and elsewhere, but had rejected all of them because he had given his word to Simrock and would abide by the agreement even if he lost money, trusting to make his losses good by other sales to Simrock who, moreover, might be disposed to make a contract for the Complete Edition. Brentano communicated with Simrock at once and received a letter from the publisher on May 29 expressing regret that sickness had been partly responsible for the delay. He had been expecting the Mass every day for more than a year, during which time the money had lain with Heinrich Verhuven because he did not want Beethoven to wait a single day for it.

Thus on May 19, Beethoven told Brentano that he would keep the faith with Simrock even at a sacrifice. On May 1, however, he had written to Schlesinger in Berlin:

. . . In regard to my health, things are better again, thank God; as to the Mass I beg of you to get everything in readiness as other publishers have asked for it and many approaches have been made to me, especially from here; but I resolved long ago that it should not be published *here*, as the matter is a very important one for me— For the present I ask of you only that you signify to me whether you accept my last offer of the Mass together with the two songs. As regards the payment of the honorarium, it may wait for no more than four weeks. I must insist upon an early answer, chiefly because two other publishers who want to have it in their catalogues have been waiting for a definite answer from me for a considerable time— Farewell, and write to me at once, it would grieve me very much if *I could not give you just this particular* work.

Respectfully yours   Beethoven

Schlesinger, as we learn from a letter dated July 2, 1822, had received letters from Beethoven under date of April 9, May 1 and May 29.[2] He answered the three at once, excusing his delay on the ground that he had attended the

[2] The letter of May 29 has not survived. For Schlesinger's letter see Unger, *Ludwig van Beethoven und seine Verleger*, No. 121.

fair in Leipzig, where he fell ill, and had remained under the weather for several weeks after his return to Berlin. Meanwhile business had accumulated. He continues:

. . . Everything is in order about the Mass, and I beg you to send it and the two songs as soon as possible and draw on me at fourteen days' sight for 650 R.T., I will honor the draft at once and pay it, for I have no opportunity to make payment to you there [Vienna]; although several music dealers there are extensively in my debt, I cannot count on prompt payment from any of them. These gentlemen have two very ugly traits: 1) they do not respect property rights and 2), it is with difficulty that they are brought to pay their accounts. The book dealers are much sounder. . . .

Schlesinger's son, who had established himself in business in Paris, wrote to Beethoven on July 3rd and in the course of the letter asked him if a third movement of the Pianoforte Sonata in C minor (Op. 111), which he was publishing, had not been forgotten at the copyists. He, like his father a little later (letter of July 13), evidently suspected that they had not received as much music, measured in detached movements, as they had paid for; they missed a rondo finale! The incident may have amused, or (which is more likely) even angered Beethoven; but there must have been a further incursion of Beethoven's displeasure to account for the fact that Beethoven resolved about this time to have nothing more to do with Schlesinger *père*. On June 26 he wrote to Peters of Leipzig, with whom he had now entered into negotiations and to whom he had just offered the Mass, "In no event will Schlesinger ever get *anything more from me*; he has played me a Jewish trick, but aside from that he is not among those who might have received the Mass." When Beethoven was conducting the negotiations with Schott and Sons in Mainz which resulted in the firm's getting the work, he recurred to the Schlesingers in a letter of January 22, 1825, and said: "Neither is Schlesinger to be trusted, for he takes where he can. Both *père et fils* bombarded me for the mass, but I did not deign to answer either of them, since after thinking them over I had cast them out long before." Beethoven's threats were frequently mere *brutum fulmen*; the Schlesingers, *père et fils*, remained his friends to the end and got two of the last Quartets.

On August 22, 1822, Simrock wrote to Beethoven again. Beethoven's answer followed on September 13 and, as it contains more than a mere implication why he refused to abide by his contract, it is given in full here:

Baden, September 13, 1822

My dear and valued Simrock:

You will receive this letter from Baden, where I am taking the baths, as my illness which has lasted two and a half years has not yet ended. Much as I should like to write you about many things I must yet be brief and only reply to your last of August 22nd. As regards the Mass you know that at an earlier date I wrote you that a larger honorarium had been offered me. I would not be so sordid as to haggle with you for a few florins, but my poor health and many other unpleasant circumstances compel me to insist upon it. The minimum that at least four publishers have offered me for the Mass is 1000 florins C.M. at the rate of twenty, or counting the florin at 3 Austrian C.M. at twenty. Much as I shall regret it if we must part just because of this work, I know that your loyalty [*Biederherzigkeit*] will not allow me to lose money on this work, which is perhaps the greatest that I have composed. You know that I am not boastful and that I do not like to show the letters of others or even quote from them; if it were not so I might submit proofs from far and near. But I very much wish to have the matter about the Mass settled as soon as possible, for I have had to endure plots of all sorts on account of it. It would be agreeable if you would let me know as soon as possible if you will pay me this honorarium. If you will, you need only deposit the difference with Brentano, whereupon I will at once send you a well corrected score of the Mass which will suffice you for the engraving. I hope, my dear Simrock, whom I consider the richest of all these publishers, will not permit his old friend to go elsewhere for the sake of a few hundred florins. Concerning all other matters I shall write you soon; I am staying here till the beginning of October. I shall receive all letters which you may write, safely as I did your last, only I beg of you to write soon. Farewell, greet the family cordially for me; as soon as I can I shall write to them myself.

Cordially your old friend, Beethoven

This was evidently answered by Simrock, who, despairing of ever getting the Mass, may have suggested that he would accept other works in lieu of it, for on March 10, 1823, Beethoven wrote again saying (as he had said to Peters in November, 1822) that he should surely receive *a* mass, for he had written two and was only undecided which one to send. He asked Simrock to be patient until Easter, when he would send one of them to Brentano. He intended also to write a mass for the Emperor. As to other works, he offered "a new overture, which I composed for the opening of the new Josephstadt Theatre,"[3] the music to the *Ruinen von Athen*, to *König Stephan*, some songs and "Kleinigkeiten" for the pianoforte. Only for the new overture did he fix a price (50 ducats), but he adds: "You will surely receive one of these two grand masses which are already composed; only be patient until after Easter, by which time I shall have decided which to send." This is the last letter between Beethoven and Simrock which has been found. It leaves the composer promising *a* mass instead of delivering *the* Mass, and that promise unfulfilled;—of a necessity, for the work, though described as "already composed," was never written.

In 1814 C. F. Peters had purchased the Bureau de Musique founded in 1798 by Hoffmeister and Kühnel, publishers of a number of Beethoven's compositions, including the First Symphony, between 1800 and 1805. On May 18, 1822, Peters addressed a letter to Beethoven in which he said that he had long wished to publish some of his compositions but had refrained from applying to him because he did not wish to offend the Viennese publishers; seeing now, however, that he was going outside with his composi-

---

[3] The *Weihe des Hauses* Overture, Op. 124.

tions and giving them "even to the Jew Schlesinger," he would no longer give heed to such considerations. He had spoken to Steiner on the subject at the last fair, who had offered no objections, had, indeed, said that he would be glad if he (Peters) got the works instead of Schlesinger, and had offered his services as intermediary between him and Beethoven, and asked for a list of compositions which he wanted. Thereupon he had given Steiner such a list: symphonies, pianoforte quartets and trios, pianoforte solos "among which there might be small pieces," songs, etc.—anything, in short, which Beethoven should send him would be welcome, for he wanted honor, not profit, from the association. Beethoven replied on June 5:

Sirs!

You have honored me with a letter, and since I am very busy now and have been ill for 5 months, I will answer you concerning only the most necessary matters— Although I met *Steiner* several days ago and asked him jocularly what he had brought for me from Leipzig, he mentioned not a *syllable* about your *commission* or about *you*, but earnestly pleaded with *me to assure him* that *I would give to him alone both my present and future works* and this *in the form of a contract*; I declined— This trait suffices to show you why I often prefer foreign publishers to local; I love straightforwardness and uprightness and am of the opinion that the artist ought not to be belittled; for alas! glittering as is the external aspect of fame, he is not permitted to be Jupiter's guest on Olympus every day; too often and too repulsively vulgar mankind drags him down from the pure ethereal heights.— The *biggest* work that I have written up until now is a great mass with chorus, 4 solos obbligato and large orchestra. Several people have sought to obtain it; I have been offered 100 Louis d'or in hard cash for it; I want however at least 1000 fl. C.M. at the 20 gulden rate—for which I would prepare the pianoforte arrangement myself— Variations on a waltz for pianoforte alone (there are many) for the price of 30 ducats in gold, that is Viennese ducats. Concerning songs I have worked out some longer ones, thus for example a comic aria with full orchestra on a Goethe text, "Mit Mädeln sich vertragen," etc., again another aria of the same genre[4] for each of which I want 16 ducats (pianoforte arrangement upon request)—

For several extended songs with pianoforte, 12 ducats apiece, among which there is also a small Italian cantata with recit.— Also among my German songs there is a song with recitative— A song with pianoforte 8 ducats. For an elegy for four voices with accompaniment of 2 violins, viola and violoncello the price is 24 ducats. For a chorus of Dervishes with full orchestra 20 ducats.[5] Also the following instrumental music would be available: a grand march for full orchestra with pianoforte arrangement written for the tragedy Tarpeja 12 ducats— A romance for violin (solo with full orchestra) for 15 ducats.[6]

A big trio for 2 oboes and one English horn (could be transcribed also for other instruments) for 30 ducats.[7] Four military marches with Turkish music, upon

---

[4] "Prüfung des Küssens," WoO 89.

[5] Op. 118 and Op. 113, No. 3.

[6] The Romances for Violin, Op. 40 and Op. 50 having been published long before, Beethoven must have had another one in mind. (TK, III, 59, n. 1.)

[7] The Trio for wind instruments, Op. 87, was already in print. Beethoven had composed variations on "La ci darem" from *Don Giovanni*, WoO 28, for the same instruments and

request I will determine the price— Bagatelles or trifles for pianoforte alone, price upon request— All of the works mentioned above are ready. For a solo sonata for pianoforte 40 ducats, which you could have soon.[8]— A quartet for 2 violins, viola and violoncello 50 ducats, which you could have soon.[9] What I wish for more than all these is an *edition of my complete works* which I could superintend myself. Indeed I have received many propositions, but there were conditions which are hardly ones for me to meet and which I could and would not fulfill. I myself would superintend and edit the whole edition in two, even possibly one or one and a half years with the necessary help, and supply for each composition category a new work. For example, for the variations a new set of variations, for sonatas a new example of a sonata and so on; for each type in which I have, I would supply a new work; and for all this together I would ask for ten thousand florins C.M. at the 20 fl. rate.

I am not a businessman and I would prefer it to be otherwise in this matter, however since it cannot be otherwise my conduct is guided by competition.

I beg you to observe complete silence since otherwise I shall be exposed to many harassments as you already can observe from dealings with these men. Once something is published by you, then I would no longer be bothered by them—

I would welcome a relation developing between us, for from hearing many good things I have been assured about you. Then you would also find that I prefer dealing with someone of this kind rather than with those of the ordinary type of which there are so many— I beg a quick answer from you since just now I must decide about the publication of many works. [I am very sorry that Steiner who has estimable qualities has shown himself again to be but a common tradesman.][10] If you care to, please send me a copy of the catalogue which you gave to Herr Steiner— In expectation of a speedy reply

Yours respectfully Beethoven

—·⚜The pianoforte variations referred to were those on a waltz theme by Anton Diabelli. The full story of this work which dates back to 1819 will be told in the account of 1823, the year in which the variations were completed. During 1822, suffice it to say, the main work on what were to become thirty-three highly original variations was taking place.⚜·—

Beethoven was not kept waiting for an answer; Peters' reply is dated June 15. He regretted to hear of Steiner's duplicity and expressed hope that his conduct might have been harmless in intention and caused by his weakness. The works which he wanted and of which he had given a list to Steiner were a quartet for strings, a trio of the same kind, a concert overture for full orchestra, songs, and some small solos for pianoforte "such as

---

the composition was called a Terzetto when performed in 1797. This was probably what he had in mind here and in a similar offer to Peters on November 22. (TK, III, 59, n. 2.)

[8] Since Op. 109-111 were already sold to Schlesinger, Beethoven must have thought himself in readiness to write another if it was desired; there was no lack of material in his sketchbooks. (TK, III, 59, n. 3.)

[9] This suggests that he had already begun work on the Quartet in E-flat, Op. 127. (TDR, IV, 251, n. 6.)

[10] The passage in brackets was in Beethoven's draft of the letter but not in the one that was sent. (TDR, IV, 252, n. 1.)

capriccios, divertissements," etc. Then he took up Beethoven's detailed offer of compositions:

The most admirable among them is your Grand Mass, which you offer me together with the pianoforte arrangement for one thousand florins C.M. which I admit I am ready to accept at this price. . . . Between honest men like us there is no need of a contract, but if you want one send it to me and I will return it *signed*. If not, please state to me in writing that I am to receive the *Mass in question* together with the *pianoforte score* for *1000 florins* at the 20 florin rate and indicate when I am to receive it and that it is to be my *sole* property *for ever*. I want the first so that I may look upon this transaction as *concluded*, and the time I want to know so that I can arrange about the publication. If I were a rich man I would pay you very differently for this Mass, for I suspect that it is something really excellent, especially because it was composed for an occasion; but for me 1000 florins for a Mass is a large expenditure and the entire transaction, *on my word*, is undertaken only in order to show myself to you and to the world as a publisher who does something for art. I must ask another consideration, namely, that *nobody* learn how much I have paid for the Mass— at least not for some time. I am not a man of large means, but must worry and drudge; nevertheless I pay artists as well as I can and in general better than other publishers. . . .

For the present, Peters added, he did not want to publish larger vocal works by Beethoven nor the Mass singly but along with other works, to show the Viennese publishers that there was a contract between him and Beethoven which obliged the latter to send him compositions. To that end he asked for some songs, a few bagatelles for piano solo, the four military marches. He said that he would be glad also to take the new string quartet, but that 50 ducats was beyond his means. Beethoven was at liberty to tell Steiner that he had applied to Beethoven with his knowledge and consent.

Beethoven's answer (incorrectly dated July instead of June 26) may be summarized. He agreed to give him the Mass, which he would receive by the end of July, for the stipulated fee, and enclosed an agreement form which had been prepared by Steiner. Beethoven emphasized that he had never sought commissions from Steiner or any other publisher "because I want to see how extended is the province which my fame has reached." He offered three songs and four marches for 40 ducats and asked for more news on the project of a complete edition of his works.

Peters answered this letter on July 3. He was willing to pay 40 ducats for the songs and marches and to remit part of the honorarium in advance. He was distressed about Beethoven's financial affairs and wanted to help him. "It is wrong that a man like you is obliged to think about money matters. The great ones of the earth should long ago have placed you in a position free from care, so that you would no longer have to live on art but only for art."

Before this letter was received Beethoven had written a second and supplementary reply to the letter of June 15; it is dated July 6. He had reread his letter and discovered that Peters wanted some of the bagatelles and a quartet for strings. For the former he asked 8 ducats each. The quartet was not fully completed, work on it having been interrupted. Here it was difficult to lower the prices, as such works were the most highly paid for—he might almost say, to the shame of the general taste, which in art frequently falls below that of private taste. "I have written you everything concerning the Mass, and that is settled."

On July 12, Peters wrote that he did not know the length of the bagatelles and so could not tell whether they were to be printed separately or together; but he asked that a number be sent him together with word as to how many of such small pieces Beethoven had on hand, as he might take them all. As for songs, he would prefer to have some in the style of "Adelaide" or "Schloss Markenstein." The honorarium for the compositions which were to be sent would now amount to 200 or 300 florins at the 20 florin rate, but as he could not determine the exact amount he asked Beethoven to collect the amount from Meiss (Meisl) Brothers, bankers, on exhibit of receipt and bill of shipment. It was all the same to him whether he collected the money now or later; it was waiting and at Beethoven's disposal. In this manner, so convenient for Beethoven, he would make all his payments for manuscripts purchased. On August 3 Beethoven writes:

. . . I have not made up my mind as to the selection of songs and remaining marches and bagatelles, but everything will be delivered by the 15th of this month. I await your advice in the matter and will make no use at present of your bill of exchange. Of the bagatelles you will receive 4—in conformity with the established price that makes a sum of 360 fl. at the 20 florin rate. Be sure to calculate it exactly— I am not holding you to a higher sum than the others; on the contrary for the songs I have reckoned too little for my time is really too valuable— As soon as I know that the honorarium for *the Mass* and the other works is here all these songs can be delivered by the 15th— . . . .

Peters was prompt in his remittance of the money which was to be subject to Beethoven's order; Beethoven, though less prompt in collecting it, did so prior to his delivery of the manuscripts for which the money was to pay. Singularly enough, the incident which provides for us knowledge of the time when the money was received by Peters' agent served as evidence in Beethoven's excuse for drawing the money without keeping his part of the agreement. On July 25, about a fortnight after the date of Peters' letter of advice, Piringer, associate conductor of the *Concerts spirituels*, who was on terms of intimacy with Beethoven, wrote him as follows:

Domine Generalissime!

Victoria in Döbling—fresh troops are advancing! The wholesalers, Meisl Bros. here in the Rauhensteingasse, their own house, 2nd story, have received advices from Hr. Peters in Leipzig to pay several hundred florins to Herr Ludwig van Beethoven— I hasten on Degen's pinions[11] to convey this glad report to *Illustrissimo* at once.— Today is the first sad day in the Viennese calendar, because yesterday was the last day of the Italian opera.

This letter Beethoven sent to Peters from Baden on September 13 in evidence of his presumption that Piringer, who was a daily caller at the Steiner establishment, had gossiped about the relations between him and Peters. He was sorry that Peters had sent the money so early, but fearing talk he had collected the money. He would send all the little things soon. He had been pressed by the Cardinal, on whom he had to attend several times a week; and work had been forced upon him by the opening of the Josephstadt Theatre; also he wanted to write new trios to some of the marches and revise other works, but illness and too much other employment had prevented. "You see from this at least that I am not a composer for the sake of mere contemptible gain. . . . You will recall that I begged you to keep everything away from this man [Steiner]. Why? That I will reveal to you in time. I hope that God will protect me against the wiles of this wicked man Steiner."

Now there enters a new element into the story of the Mass which is introduced by Beethoven near the end of a letter to Peters dated "Vienna, November 22, 1822":

Dear Sir!

In yours of November 9, in which I believe I was reproached for my *seeming negligence*—the honorarium already sent and yet *nothing received*—how objectionable it seems. Yet I know that if we were together, we could be reconciled in a few minutes— Your order is already assembled except for the *choice* of songs; as a fee for attendance you will receive one more of them than the number agreed upon— I could send you several other bagatelles in addition to the four ordered; there are still nine or ten of them available. If you *would write to me about this right away* I could send them or as many more along with them as you want— Indeed my health has not been fully restored by the baths, yet on the whole I have progressed. Besides I am badly off here since somebody else selected rooms for me that are not suitable, something which is difficult to surmount and has slowed me up not a little in my affairs since things are hardly yet in order— This is the state of affairs with regard to the Mass: already I have finished *one* completely but another is *not yet* finished. There will always be *gossip* about such as us and you have been misled by it. *I do not yet* know which of the two you will receive— Pressed on all sides I must declare the opposite of "the spirit weighs nothing"— I greet you most heartily and hope that a relationship which is profitable and not dishonorable to *me* may exist in the future between us both.

Yours faithfully   Beethoven

The gossip against which Beethoven warned Peters, it is safe to assume, related to the compositions which the latter had purchased but not received;

---

[11] De,en was a popular aeronaut who had not long before excited the interest of Beethoven. TK, III, 62, n. 1.)

in great likelihood rumors about the Mass had reached Leipzig. Peters was in communication with Steiner and others; and that he knew that the Mass had been planned for the installation of Archduke Rudolph as Archbishop of Olmütz he had indicated when he expressed the belief that it was something "really excellent" because it had been composed for an occasion. The mass which Beethoven had promised to deliver by the end of July, 1822, could therefore have been none other than the Mass in D. It is deserving of mention, however, that there is evidence that Beethoven was thinking of more than one mass at the time—in fact that he had thoughts of three. In a sketchbook of the period is found a memorandum: "The *Kyrie* in the second mass with wind-instruments and organ only";[12] and in another place there are six measures of a theme for a *Dona nobis* with the superscription "Mass in C-sharp minor."[13] To this *Dona* there is still another reference or two of a later date; but that is all. It is likely that the second mass was intended for the Emperor, as we shall see later; Beethoven himself said that he had thoughts of a third.

Peters was getting importunate, and on December 20 Beethoven wrote to him that nothing intended for him was entirely ready; there had been delays in copying and sending, but he had no time to explain. The songs and marches would be sent "next week." There were six bagatelles instead of four, but if he insisted on four a separate arrangement would have to be made. He had so many applications for his works that he could not attend to them all: "Were it not that my income brings in nothing[14] I should compose only operas, grand symphonies, church music or at the outside quartets in addition." Of smaller works Peters might have variations for two oboes and English horn on a theme from *Don Giovanni*—"Da ci la mano" wrote Beethoven, meaning "Là ci darem la mano"—and for full orchestra a "Gratulatory Minuet."[15] He would like Peters' opinion about the complete edition.

During February and March, 1823, Beethoven finally sent on to Peters three songs ("Opferlied," "Bundeslied" and "Der Kuss"),[16] six bagatelles (from Op. 119) and three tattoos (Turkish music) and a march (WoO 18, 19, 20, 24). On March 4, 1823, Peters wrote, in answer to a letter of Beethoven's dated February 15, that he was distressed by the manuscripts that he had received and that he was sending back the three songs since they were not what he had asked for. His objections were that he had wanted extended songs with pianoforte accompaniment and "that I want to have good choice things from you."[17] Just when Beethoven received the songs back is not

[12] *II Beeth.*, p. 152. (TK, III, 63, n. 1.)

[13] *Ibid.*, pp. 541, 543. (TK, III, 63, n. 1.)

[14] Beethoven indulges in his propensity for puns: "Wäre mein Gehalt nicht ganz ohne Gehalt." (TK, III, 63, n. 2.)

[15] WoO 3. A composition written for a serenade given to Hensler, director of the Josephstadt Theatre, as will appear later. (TK, III, 64, n. 1.)

[16] Op. 121b (first version for 3 solo voices, chorus and small orchestra), Op. 122 and Op. 128. (TDR, IV, 260.)

[17] See Kurt Herbst, "Beethovens Opferlied Kompositionen," in *NBJ*, v, p. 142.

clear, since on the one hand, he was offering songs to Simrock in his letter of March 10, 1823, which must have been these three, the only ones yet unpublished; on the other hand, in the next and final letter to Peters of this year, dated March 20, 1823, he was giving instructions for two of these songs, which show that he believed them still to be in Peters' possession.

In this latest letter to Peters, after referring to the marches, bagatelles and Peters's request for a string and a piano quartet, Beethoven writes:—

As regards the Mass I will also send you a document which I beg you to sign, for in any event the time is approaching when you will receive one or the other. Besides yourself there are two other men who also desire each a mass. At present I am resolved to write at least three; the first is entirely finished, the second *not yet*, the third not even begun.— But in view of this I must have an understanding so that I may be secured in any case, you may have the Mass whenever you pay 1000 C.M. . . . .

So far as Peters is concerned the matter must be dropped for a space; he published none of the works sent to him and did not receive the Mass. One of the "two other men" was, in all likelihood, Artaria, Beethoven's old publisher. On August 22, 1822, Artaria received a letter which, as it seems to stand alone so far as the Mass is concerned, may well be printed in full:

Being just now overwhelmed with work, I can only say briefly that I have always returned your favors whenever possible. As regards the Mass I have been offered 1000 florins, C.M. for it. The state of my affairs do not permit me to take a smaller honorarium from you. All that I can do is to *give* you the *preference*. Rest assured that I do not *take a heller more* from you than has been *offered me by others*. I could prove this to you in writing. You may think this over but I beg of you to send me an answer by *tomorrow noon* as tomorrow is post-day and my decision is expected in other places— I will make a proposition to you concerning the 150 florins C.M. which I owe you, but the sum must not be deducted *now*, as I am in urgent need of the 1000 florins— In addition I beg of you to keep everything secret about the Mass. As always

your grateful friend Beethoven

Here *the* Mass (*Missa Solemnis*) is implied and not *a* mass from several. When Beethoven wrote this letter he had offered the Mass to Peters, earlier to Simrock and had indicated the same purpose to Schlesinger. Thus there were not less than four publishers who hoped to receive the Mass. Also he raised their hopes for works which were not ready or even hardly begun.

Because of these striking facts it is appropriate to consider Beethoven's personality and the circumstances under which he lived. The painstaking work that Beethoven put into the works of these late years came from his innermost heart and he never felt that he had done enough. While he was absorbed with this kind of work he was free of his cares and guided only by the demands of his art. In his long letter to Peters of March 20, 1823, already mentioned, Beethoven speaks of the necessity in his position of considering his own interests and adds: "It is another thing during the work itself, since I never think of gain, thank God, but only *how to compose*." These were his principles.

Then too there was his health and the duress already described which cramped the elasticity of his nature and diminished his delight in creating. "To begin a great work makes me shudder," he is once supposed to have said. So many big plans remained inexecuted and the completion of big works laid considerable claims on his time. So he wrote small pieces and resuscitated old, forgotten ones. Also his income had diminished due to the reduced payments on the pension supplied by his princely admirers and due to his limited productivity of the last few years;—consequently, he was in need of straight cash. His expenses included those for the care of his nephew and the cost of his stays at resorts for the care of his own health, and these compelled him to concern himself with his earnings. Hence came the necessity to get the highest possible fees for his works, for dealings unfortunately with many parties at once, and for acceptance of advance payments. His embarrassments compelled him to borrow money since the bank shares that he owned he no longer considered his own but an inheritance for his nephew and not to be touched. Thus, he owed money, among others, to Steiner and Artaria. To the former he owed nearly 3000 florins, as he wrote to his brother, and this explains not only the painful relations with Steiner but also Beethoven's wish to have his new works published by foreigners. To Artaria he owed 1000 florins; yet it will be remembered he wrote to the firm that the sum of 150 florins which he hoped soon to pay back on his debt must not now be deducted from a possible fee since he needed the whole amount; this sheds light on the extent of his financial cares.

These circumstances invite one's deepest sympathy; the noble impulses of his heart on all other levels and the reasons which necessitated his doing everything to better his affairs are well known; yet the conscientious reporter cannot ignore the actual, public facts and, hard as it is, cannot acquit Beethoven of the reproach that his conduct did not agree with the principles of strict honor and justice. These are dreary episodes in the history of Beethoven which nevertheless cannot be overlooked if he is to be wholly understood as a man; but how withdrawn they are from the heights reached by the works that he composed during these troubled times.

Beethoven finally borrowed money from his brother and asked his help in the sale of his works. This circumstance brings Johann van Beethoven back significantly into this history and invites an inquiry into his character and his conduct with reference to his famous brother. Something of his earlier history has been told in the chapters of this biography which deal with the incidents of the years 1808 and 1812. The brother had grown rich enough in the interim to buy some farm property near Gneixendorf and to make his winter residence in Vienna. There we find him in the spring of 1822 living in the house of his brother-in-law, a baker named Obermayer, at the intersection of Koth- and Pfarrgasse. Thenceforward for a number of years, because of his relationship to his famous brother, and also because of his idiosyncrasies, habits and public behavior (and to a smaller number, the conduct of his wife), he became a conspicuous and rather comical figure in Vienna. Gerhard von Breuning describes him thus:[18] "His hair was blackish-brown; hat well brushed; clothing clean but suggesting that of a man who wishes to be elegantly clad on Sundays; somewhat old-fashioned and uncouth, an effect which was caused by his bone-structure, which was angular and unlovely. His waist was rather small; no sign of embonpoint; shoulders broad; if my memory serves me rightly, his shoulders were a trifle uneven, or it may have been his angular figure which made him look unsymmetrical; his clothing generally consisted of a blue frockcoat with brass buttons, white necktie, light trousers (I think corn color), loose linen-thread gloves, the fingers too long so that they folded at the ends or stuck out loosely. His hands were broad and bony. He was not exactly tall of stature, but much taller than Ludwig. His nose was large and rather long, the position of his eyes, crooked, the effect being as if he squinted a little with one eye. The mouth was crooked, one corner drawn upwards giving him the expression of a mocking smile. In his garb he affected to be a well-to-do elegant, but the rôle did not suit his angular, bony figure. He did not in the least resemble his brother Ludwig."

Breuning also says in his book *Aus dem Schwarzspanierhause*, that he was sometimes seen driving in the Prater with two or four horses in an old-fashioned phaeton, either handling the reins himself or lolling carelessly in the seat with two gallooned servants on the box. Beethoven's friends used to ridicule his brother to his face. In a Conversation Book of early 1823 Count Moritz Lichnowsky writes: "Everybody thinks him a fool; we call him only the Chevalier . . . all the world says of him that his only merit is that he bears your name."[19] No doubt there was something, even a good deal, of the parvenu in Johann's character. He had neither the intellectual nor moral poise to fit him for the place which he thought he was entitled to fill by virtue of his wealth and his relationship to one of the most famous men of his age. Nor could he command respect from a social point of view. Also the indecent behavior of his wife must have been repugnant to Ludwig's circle of friends, and a memorandum found among Schindler's papers discloses that her conduct in Vienna was such that Beethoven again thought of invoking the police.

That Johann van Beethoven was fond of money is indicated in his remarks in the Conversation Books, when his advice to his brother is always dictated by financial considerations. If he lacked appreciation of his brother's real significance in art, he was proud of the world's appreciation of him, and if he could not have high regard for that high moral attitude in the matter which had brought condemnation on his sister-in-law and wife, he at least showed magnanimity in not trying to do his brother injury and being

[18] In a note to Thayer. (TK, III, 66, n. 1.)　　　[19] Schünemann, II, p. 396.

always ready to help him when he could. It is very likely that he was not at all musical and that his affectation of appreciation of his brother's works made him a fair subject for ridicule. In a conversation in 1824 the nephew relates that his uncle had been present at a chamber concert. Beethoven wanted to know what he was doing there, and the nephew replies: "He wants to acquire taste; he is continually crying *bravo*." So also Holz relates, in 1826, that Johann had certainly heard the Quartet in E-flat major ten times, yet when it was played in that year he said he was hearing it for the first time.

Exactly when Beethoven went to Oberdöbling in the summer of 1822 is not known, but he was there in July, and an endorsement on the Simrock letter of May 13 would seem to indicate that he was there in that month. His lodgings were in No. 135 Alleegasse. In the spring or early summer he wrote the following letter to Johann:

I was counting on seeing you—but in vain—on Staudenheim's orders I am still having to take medicine, and am not allowed to move about much— I beg you instead of going to the Prater today to come to me with your wife and daughter— I only wish that the benefits which are certain to result from our being together may be achieved without hindrance. I have enquired about lodgings; there are tolerably good ones to be had and you won't have to pay much more than before. From a purely financial point of view, how much can be saved on both sides without our having to sacrifice our pleasure— I have nothing against your wife, I only wish that she would see how much you too might benefit from being with me and that we need not be troubled by all the petty miseries of life.

Now farewell. I hope to see you for sure this afternoon, at which time we could take a drive to Nussdorf, which would do me a lot of good—

Your true brother Ludwig

Peace, peace be with us. God grant that the most natural tie between brothers be not unnaturally broken again. Besides, my life may not be of long duration. I say again that I have nothing against your wife, although her behavior towards me has struck me as strange several times of late. Besides I have been ailing for three and one half months and am very, yes extremely sensitive and irritable. But away with everything which *cannot promote* the object, which is that I and my good Karl maintain a moderate way of life, which is so necessary to me—You have only to look at my house here to see what happens, what it is like when sickly as I am I have to put myself *in the hands of strangers*, not to mention other matters which we have already discussed—

In case you come today, you can pick up *Karl, for this reason*, I am *enclosing* this unsealed letter to H. v. Blöchlinger which you can send off to him at once.—

Here there is no mention of business matters and hence it may be assumed that the letter dates from an early period in the reunion of the brothers. But business considerations prompted two long letters at the end of July which, except for passages concerning those negotiations with publishers about which the reader already knows, should be given in full. The first is dated July 26:

Dear brother!

Because I have been extremely busy and thoroughly uncomfortable with respect to my dwelling and my servants, both of whom are extremely awkward, I have not yet been able to write you. As for my health, it is better. I have been having to drink Johannes spring-water, take powder 4 times a day, and now I am supposed to go to Baden to take 30 baths; I will go there by August 6 or 7 if it is *possible* to do so. If you could only come for a few days to help me, yet the dust and the heat would be too much for you. If it weren't for that you could stay with me in Baden for some 8 days, ad tuum libitum . . . [Negotiations with Peters are summarized.] Also Breitkopf and Härtel have sent the Saxon Chargé d'Affaires to me concerning my works. Also I have received requests from Paris for my works and again from Diabelli in Vienna; in short, people are scrambling for my works; what an *unfortunate fortunate* man I am!!!— That *Berliner* has also turned up— If my health would return I might yet feather my nest.—

The Archduke Cardinal is here, I go to him twice a week. Though there is nothing to be expected from him in the way of magnanimity or money, I am on such a good and confidential footing with him that it would be extremely painful not to show him some agreeable attention. Also I do not think that his apparent niggardliness is his fault— Before I go to Baden, I need some clothes because I am really lacking in them, especially in shirts as you have already seen. Ask your wife what she thinks of this linen, it costs 48 x [kreutzer] V.S. per ell.— If you can come, please do unless this adds trouble for you. I will come to you with Karl in September if I don't go to Olmütz for the sake of the Cardinal, who wishes it very much— As for the house, since it is already taken so be it; now the question is whether it will also suit me![20]— The rooms lead into the garden, but just now garden air is the worst thing for me; then the entrance is through the *kitchen* which is very unpleasant and inconvenient—and now I must pay a quarter year's rent for nothing. Instead of this then, Karl and I, if possible, will arrive at your house in Krems and have a good old time until the money is again retrieved—that is, if I don't go to Moravia— Write me as soon as you receive this; give my greetings to your family. If I did not have to go to Baden, I would certainly have visited you during the coming month, but now things cannot be otherwise. Do come if you can, it would be a great relief for me.— Write at once— Farewell— I embrace you with all my heart

and am as ever your true brother Ludwig

On July 31, Beethoven writes:

Best little brother! Most high and mighty property holder!

Yesterday[21] I wrote to you when I was exhausted by much strain and business, and it may be hard for you to read because of a bad pen. First of all write me how often the post travels from you to me, from me to you. . . . I should be glad if you would write me whether you can spare me something so that I will not be prevented when the time comes from going to Baden, where I must stay for at least a month. You can see that there is no lack of safety here as you will get

---

[20] The house was in the Kothgasse, and because of Ludwig's indecision, Johann had decided evidently to go ahead on his own.

(TDR, IV, 272, n. 2.)

[21] Evidently Beethoven started this letter on July 27.

the 200 fl. paid back to you with thanks in September.[22] Please send the enclosed note[23] back to me immediately. Moreover, as a trades-man you are always a good counsellor. Likewise the Steiner people are pushing me into a corner. They wish to have in writing that I shall give all my works to them. They are willing to pay for each printed sheet; but I have explained to them that I will not enter into such an arrangement with them until they cancel the debt. For that I have offered them 2 works which I wrote for Hungary[24] and which can be considered as two small operas, from which they have already accepted 4 pieces. The debt amounts to about 3000 fl., but they have outrageously charged me interest, to which I do not agree. I have taken over from Karl's mother a part of her debt since I want to do everything I can for her insofar as it isn't against Karl's interest. If you were here, these things would soon be disposed of; it is only necessity that is forcing me to such transactions. It would be wonderful if you could come and visit Baden with me for 8 days, only you must write immediately what you think about it. Meanwhile get the kitchen and cellar well stocked; for presumably my little son and I will make our headquarters at your house and we have the noble resolve to eat you out of house and home. Naturally this is about our plans for September.

Now farewell, best little brother! Read the Gospel every day; concentrate on the Epistle of Peter and Paul; travel to Rome and kiss the Pope's toe. Sincere greetings to your family. Write soon, I embrace you with all my heart.

Your faithful brother Ludwig

I, secretarius embrace you with all my heart and hope to see you soon again. Karl

N.B. I am not enclosing the order for 300 fl. C.M. because I am afraid that something might happen to it.

The Saxon Chargé d'Affaires sent by Breitkopf and Härtel, mentioned in Beethoven's letter of July 26, was Georg August Griesinger, Haydn's first biographer, who had made Beethoven's acquaintance as a young man. On June 17 he wrote on behalf of the firm to Beethoven expressing Härtel's regret that the business connection which formerly existed had been discontinued and his desire to renew it with an opera. Griesinger gave his address and offered to meet him there or in a place of Beethoven's choosing. —*{Beethoven gave the following reply.

It was a pleasure to receive from you a few lines, and as soon as I come to the city I will visit you. Since I have been ailing for 5 months I have to be thrifty with the produce of my art— I was very glad to hear something from you, a man of such merit. (generally—and especially in the writing of Haydn's life)—

With the greatest respect
Yours sincerely Beethoven}*—

[22] Evidently a loan of 200 florins had already been broached to Johann. (TDR, IV, 273, n. 4.)

[23] A note from Peters informing Beethoven that because he did not yet know how many bagatelles he would want he was assigning him a sum of 300 florins.

[24] *König Stephan* and *Die Ruinen von Athen*. (TK, III, 70, n. 1.)

Mentioned also in Beethoven's letter of July 26 to Johann is his visits twice a week to Archduke Rudolph. The following note to his pupil probably belongs here:

I came home yesterday after I heard that I was not to have the favor of coming to Y. I. H. Yesterday the weather had already had a bad effect on me, hence I am obliged to remain at home today; I will make it good in the following weeks. I regret only that today I must deny myself the favor of seeing and being with Y. I. H.

There must now be recorded some of the facts connected with the visit to Beethoven of Friedrich Rochlitz, distinguished musical *littérateur* and first editor of the Leipzig *Allgemeine Musikalische Zeitung*. Rochlitz arrived in Vienna on May 24 and remained there till August 2. He wrote two letters to Härtel about his experiences in the Austrian capital, one of June 28 from Vienna and the other of July 9 from Baden. The latter contained his account of his meeting with Beethoven and is reprinted in Vol. IV of his *Für Freunde der Tonkunst*.[25] He had never seen Beethoven in the flesh and was eager for a meeting. A friend to whom he went (it is very obvious that it was Haslinger) told him that Beethoven was in the country and had grown so shy of human society that a visit to him might prove unavailing; but it was Beethoven's custom to come to Vienna every week and he was then as a rule affable and approachable. He advised Rochlitz to wait, and he did so until the following Saturday. The meeting was a pleasant one and enabled Rochlitz to study Beethoven's appearance and manner; but the interview was suddenly terminated by Beethoven in the midst of the visitor's confession of his own admiration and the enthusiasm which Beethoven's symphonies created in Leipzig. From the beginning Beethoven had listened, smiled and nodded; but after he had curtly excused himself on the score of an engagement and departed abruptly, Rochlitz learned that his auditor had not heard or understood a word of all that he had said. Rochlitz continues:[26]

"Some two weeks later I was about to go to dinner when I met the young composer Franz Schubert, an enthusiastic admirer of Beethoven. The latter had spoken to Schubert concerning me. 'If you wish to see him in a more natural and jovial mood,' said Schubert, 'then go and eat your dinner this very minute at the inn[27] where he has just gone for the same purpose.' He took me with him. Most of the places were taken. Beethoven sat among several acquaintances who were strangers to me. He really seemed to be in good spirits and acknowledged my greeting, but I purposely did not cross over to him. Yet I found a seat from which I could see him and, since he spoke loud enough, also could hear nearly all that he said. It could not

---

[25] Leipzig, 1832, IV, p. 352.

[26] Following is the translation, with slight modifications, from *Beethoven, Impressions of Contemporaries*, O. G. Sonneck, ed. (Schirmer, 1926), pp. 123ff.

[27] According to Deutsch this may have been the "Blumenstöckl" in the Ballgasse. See O. E. Deutsch, *Memoirs of Schubert* (New York, 1958), p. 304.

actually be called a conversation, for he spoke in monologue, usually at some length, and more as though by hapchance and at random.

"Those about him contributed little, merely laughing or nodding their approval. He philosophized, or one might even say politicized, after his own fashion. He spoke of England and the English, and of how both were associated in his thoughts with a splendor incomparable—which, in part, sounded tolerably fantastic. Then he told all sorts of stories of the French, from the days of the second occupation of Vienna. For them he had no kind words. His remarks all were made with the greatest unconcern and without the least reserve, and whatever he said was spiced with highly original, naïve judgements or comical fancies. He impressed me as being a man with a rich, aggressive intellect, an unlimited, never resting imagination."

After finishing his meal Beethoven approached Rochlitz and beckoned him into a little anteroom, where conversation was carried on with the help of a tablet which Beethoven produced. "He began by praising Leipzig and its music; that is to say the music chosen for performance in the churches, at concerts and in the theatre. Otherwise he knew nothing of Leipzig and had only passed through the city when a youth on his way to Vienna.[28] 'And even though nothing is printed about the performances but the dry records, still I read them with pleasure,' he said. 'One cannot help but notice that they are intelligent and well inclined toward all. Here, on the contrary. . . .' Then he started in, rudely enough, nor would he let himself be stopped. He came to speak of himself: 'You will hear nothing of me here.' 'It is summer now,' I wrote. 'No, nor in winter either!' he cried. 'What should you hear? *Fidelio?* They cannot give it, nor do they want to listen to it. The symphonies? They have no time for them. My concertos? Everyone grinds out only the stuff he himself has made. The solo pieces? They went out of fashion here long ago, and here fashion is everything. At the most Schuppanzigh occasionally digs up a quartet, etc.'[29] And despite all the exaggeration in what he said a modicum of reason and truth remains. At last he had relieved himself and harked back to Leipzig. 'But,' said he, 'you really live in Weimar, do you not?' He probably thought so because of my address. I shook my head. 'Then it is not likely that you know the great Goethe?' I nodded my head vigorously. 'I know him, too,' said Beethoven, throwing out his chest, while an expression of the most radiant pleasure overspread his face.

"'It was in Karlsbad[30] that I made his acquaintance—God only knows how long ago! At that time I was not yet altogether deaf, as I now am,

---

[28] This was undoubtedly the Berlin trip of 1796 about which Rochlitz knew nothing. (TDR, IV, 285, n. 1.)

[29] Rochlitz was probably helping out his memory here by drawing a bit on his fancy; Schuppanzigh was at this time still in Russia, having started on a tour through Germany, Poland and Russia in 1815, from which he did not return till 1823. (TK, III, 75.)

[30] They first met in Teplitz in 1812. However, since both went on to Karlsbad it is probable that they saw each other there too. (TDR, IV, 285, n. 5.)

though I heard with great difficulty. And what patience the great man had with me!' He told numerous little anecdotes and gave the most enjoyable details. 'How happy it all made me at the time! I would have died for him ten times over. Then, while I was still brimming with ardor, I thought out my music for his *Egmont*[31] and I did make a success of it, did I not?' . . . . 'Since that summer in Karlsbad I read Goethe every day, that is, when I read at all. He [Goethe] has killed Klopstock for me. You are surprised? And now you laugh? Ah ha! It is because I have read Klopstock. I carried him about with me for years while walking and also at other times. Well, I did not always understand him, of course. He leaps about so much and he begins at too lofty an elevation. Always *Maestoso*, D-flat major! Isn't it so? But he is great and uplifts the soul nevertheless. When I could not understand him I could sort of guess. If only he did not always want to die! That will come quickly enough. Well, at any rate, what he writes always sounds well. But Goethe—he is alive, and he wants us all to live with him. That is why he can be set to music. There is no one who lends himself to musical setting as well as he. . . .' "

At this point Rochlitz believed that the opportunity had arrived to present Härtel's proposal and wrote it out. According to a note added by Rochlitz, this was to write music for Goethe's *Faust* similar to that for *Egmont*. "He read it. 'Ha!' he cried and flung up his hand. 'That would be a piece of work! That might yield something!' He went on in this fashion for a time, picturing the thought to himself in a manner anything but inept, while, with his head thrown back, he stared at the ceiling. 'But,' he next began, 'for some time past I have been carrying about with me the idea of three other great works. Already I have hatched out much in connection with them, that is to say, in my head. These I must first get rid of: two great symphonies each different from the other, and each also different from all my other ones, and an oratorio. And that will be a long-winded affair; for you see, for some time past I find I no longer settle down to write so easily. I sit and think and think and what I have to say is all there, but it will not get down to paper. I dread beginning works of such magnitude. Once I have begun, then, all goes well. . . .' "

Most of this is in harmony with what we know from other sources. We have seen how laboriously Beethoven developed the works of large dimensions in this period; we know that he had thought of *Faust* as a subject for composition as early as 1808 and that it pursued him in his last years. But Härtel's proposition sent through Griesinger in the same year was for an opera, and it seems likely that the *Faust* idea was independent of it and possibly an original conceit of Rochlitz's. Rochlitz continues his description:

[31] False. *Egmont* was written in 1810, over two years before the time he met Goethe. Rochlitz, it seems, was again indulging his imagination. (TDR, IV, 286, n. 1.)

"Our third meeting was the merriest of all. He came here, to Baden, this time looking quite neat and clean and even elegant. Yet this did not prevent him—it was a warm day—from taking a walk in the Helenental. This means on the road that all travel, even the Emperor and the imperial family, and where everyone crowds past everyone else on the usually narrow path; and there he took off his fine black frockcoat, slung it across his shoulder from a stick, and wandered along in his shirtsleeves. He stayed from about ten in the forenoon to six o'clock in the evening. . . . During the entire visit he was uncommonly gay and at times most amusing, and all that entered his mind had to come out. ('Well, it happens that I am unbuttoned today,' he said and the remark was decidedly in order.) His talk and his actions all formed a chain of eccentricities, in part most peculiar. Yet they all radiated a truly childlike amiability, carelessness, and confidence in every one who approached him. Even his barking tirades—like that against his Viennese contemporaries, which I already have mentioned—are only explosions of his fanciful imagination and his momentary excitement. They are uttered without haughtiness, without any feeling of bitterness and hatefulness—and are simply blustered out lightly, good-humoredly, the offsprings of a mad, humorous mood. In his life he often shows—and for the sake of his own subsistence only too often and too decidedly—that to the very person who has grievously injured him, whom he has most violently denounced one moment, he will give his last thaler the next, should that person need it.

"To this we must add the most cheerful recognition of merit in others, if only it be distinctive and individual. (How he speaks of Handel, Bach, Mozart!) He does not, however, where his greater works are concerned, allow others to find fault (and who would have the right to do so?) yet he never actually overvalues them; and with regard to his lesser things is more inclined, perhaps, to abandon them with a laugh than any other person. He does this the more since once he is in the vein, rough, striking witticisms, droll conceits, surprising and exciting paradoxes suggest themselves to him in a continuous flow. Hence in all seriousness I claim he even appears to be amiable. Or if you shrink from this word, I might say that the dark, unlicked bear seems so ingenious and confiding, growls and shakes his shaggy pelt so harmlessly and grotesquely that it is a pleasure, and one has to be kind to him, even though he were nothing but a bear in fact and had done no more than a bear's best."

Rochlitz concludes by describing his parting with Beethoven, when he had "thrust our good Beethoven into the carriage": "This time my reflections did not turn only, as on the first time I met him, on the grievous complaint with which fate had afflicted Beethoven. After all, I realized that he also had his hours of great gladness and perfect happiness. In other hours, also good ones, he lived in his art or in his plans and dreams regarding it; the evil hours, however, are thrown into the bargain and he takes them, pours out his soul with regard to them and then forgets them. After all, who may claim to be any better off?"

Although little is known of the subsequent relation between Beethoven and Rochlitz, yet an appreciation of this spirited writer remained until the days of Beethoven's last illness when, in answer to a question, he explained that he would choose Rochlitz for his biographer.

Beethoven had a meeting with another man earlier in this year which is of even more interest. This man was Rossini. His operas had been on the current list in Vienna for several years, and with the coming of the composer in person, in the spring of 1822, the enthusiasm for him and his music had grown into a fanatical adoration. Beethoven had seen the score of *Il Barbiere* and heard it sung by the best Italian singers of the period. Moreover, he had a high admiration for the Italian art of song and a very poor opinion of German singers. Rossini was on his wedding trip, having but recently married Colbran, and his elegant manners and brilliant conversation had made him the lion of aristocratic drawing rooms in the Austrian capital. *Zelmira* had been written especially for the Vienna season, though it had been tried at the Teatro San Carlo in Naples in the preceding December. It had its first performance at the Kärnthnerthor Theatre on April 13[32] under the direction of Domenico Barbaja.

Several of Beethoven's utterances concerning the musician, who no doubt did much to divert the taste of the masses away from the German master's compositions, have been preserved. Seyfried recorded that in answer to the question, "What is Rossini?" Beethoven replied, "A good scene painter,"[33] and Seyfried also makes note of this utterance: "The Bohemians are born musicians, the Italians ought to take them as models. What have they to show for their famous conservatories? Behold their idol—Rossini! If Dame Fortune had not given him a pretty talent and pretty melodies by the bushel, what he learned at school would have brought him nothing but potatoes for his big belly!"[34] To Freudenberg at Baden in 1824 he remarked: "Rossini is a talented and a melodious composer; his music suits the frivolous and sensuous spirit of the times, and his productivity is so great that he needs only as many weeks as the Germans need years to write an opera."[35]

The Rossini craze was no doubt largely responsible for some of Beethoven's outbreaks concerning the taste of the Viennese, but on the whole he does not seem seriously to have been disturbed by it. Schindler cites him as remarking on the change in the popular attitude: "Well, they can not rob me of my place in musical history."[36] As for the Italian singers he thought so much of them that he told Karoline Unger that he would write an Italian opera for Barbaja's company.

---

[32] Archduke Rudolph wrote variations on one of the melodies from the opera, which Beethoven corrected. (TK, III, 77, n. 1.)

[33] *Studien*, Appendix, p. 24. (TDR, IV, 291, n. 3.)

[34] *Ibid.*, p. 39.

[35] Karl Gottlieb Freudenberg, *Erinnerungen eines alten Organisten* (Leipzig, 1872), p. 42. (TDR, IV, 291, n. 3.)

[36] *Biogr.*, II, p. 282. (TDR, IV, 291, n. 2.)

As for Rossini, he had heard some of Beethoven's quartets played by Mayseder and his associates, and had enjoyed them enthusiastically. It was therefore natural enough that he should want to visit the composer. Schindler says that he went twice with Artaria to call upon him, after Artaria had each time asked permission, but that on both occasions Beethoven had asked to be excused from receiving him—a circumstance which had given rise to considerable comment in Vienna. The story is not true, but that it was current in Vienna four years afterward appears from an entry in a Conversation Book of August 1826 where somebody asks: "It is true, isn't it, that Rossini wanted to visit you and you refused to see him?" There is no written answer. We repeat: the story is not true. Twice, at least, Rossini publicly denied it. In 1867 Dr. Eduard Hanslick visited him with two friends in Paris. Concerning the interview, Hanslick wrote:[37]

Suddenly, as if he intentionally wanted to call attention to something loftier, he asked if the Mozart monument at Vienna was finished? And Beethoven's? We three Austrians looked rather embarrassed. "I remember Beethoven well," continued Rossini after a pause, "although it is nearly half a century ago. On my visit to Vienna I hastened to look him up."

"And he did not receive you, as Schindler and other biographers assure us."

"On the contrary," said Rossini, correcting me: "I had Carpani, the Italian poet with whom I had already called upon Salieri, introduce me, and he received me at once and very politely. True, the visit did not last very long, for conversation with Beethoven was nothing less than painful. His hearing was particularly bad on that day and in spite of my loudest shoutings he could not understand me; his little practice in Italian may have made conversation more difficult."

This confirms what Rossini told Ferdinand Hiller in 1856:[38] "During my sojourn in Vienna I had myself introduced to him by old Calpani [*sic*]; but between his deafness and my ignorance of German, conversation was impossible. But I am glad that I saw him, at least."

The name of Franz Schubert was introduced in the account by Rochlitz and the impression created is that the younger composer was aware of the master's habits but knew and admired him from afar. In an earlier chapter was given the description by Anselm Hüttenbrenner of the gathering of composers, of whom Schubert was one, between 11 and 12 o'clock a few times a week at Steiner's store in the Paternostergässchen to exchange musical opinions. On April 19, 1822, the firm of Cappi and Diabelli announced their publication of Schubert's variations on a French song for pianoforte, four hands, which was "dedicated to Herr Ludwig van Beethoven by his Worshipper and Admirer Franz Schubert."[39] That this work made

[37] In an article in the *Neue Freie Presse* of July 21, 1867, reprinted in *Aus dem Concertsaal*, 2nd edition (Vienna and Leipzig, 1897), p. 594. (TDR, IV, 292, n. 3.)

[38] Ferdinand Hiller, *Aus dem Tonleben*

unserer Zeit (Leipzig, 1868), II, p. 49. (TDR, IV, 292, n. 4.)

[39] Otto Erich Deutsch, *Schubert, a Documentary Biography*, trans. by Erich Blom (London, 1946), p. 222.

Beethoven more aware of Schubert as a person and an artist is suggested by the following evidence from Kreissle's biography of Schubert: "It should be stated, however, that a gentleman still living at Vienna, an intimate and trusted friend of Schubert's [Herr Josef Hüttenbrenner],[40] shortly after the presentation of his musical work [the four-hand variations to Beethoven], heard from Schubert's own mouth that he certainly visited Beethoven, but that he was not at home, and that Schubert entrusted his variations to the care of the housemaid, or man-servant, and consequently that at that time he neither saw and still less spoke to Beethoven. Hüttenbrenner remarks further that Schubert subsequently heard with great pleasure of Beethoven's enjoying these variations and playing them frequently and gladly with his nephew Karl."[41]

On August 31, Beethoven wrote his brother that he was leaving for Baden the next day or at the most the day after next. In Baden he lived for awhile at the inn "zum goldenen Schwan," which is still standing and has a tablet commemorating his visit.

Here Beethoven began the work which was to call him back into public notice. This was the music for the opening of the Josephstadt Theatre, which the director of the theatre, Carl Friedrich Hensler, director also of the combined theatres of Pressburg and Baden, asked of him immediately after his arrival at the watering-place. Hensler (1761-1825) was a popular dramatist as well as manager and an old acquaintance of Beethoven's, by whom he was greatly respected. He had bought the privilege of the Josephstadt Theatre in Vienna. Carl Meisl, who was a Commissioner of the Royal Imperial Navy, had written two festival pieces for the opening, which had been set down for October 3, 1822, the name-day of the Emperor. The first piece was a paraphrase of Kotzebue's *Ruinen von Athen*, written for the opening of the theatre in Pesth in 1812, for which Beethoven had composed the music. Meisl took Kotzebue's text and made such alterations in it as were necessary to change *Die Ruinen von Athen* into *Die Weihe des Hauses*. Nottebohm's reprint in *Zweite Beethoveniana* (p. 385 *et seq.*) enables a comparison to be made with the piece as it left the hands of Meisl and the original. The new words did not always fit the music and caused Beethoven considerable concern. A choral dance:

> Wo sich die Pulse
> jugendlich jagen,
> Schwebet im Tanze
> das Leben dahin, etc.

[40] Brother of Anselm Hüttenbrenner.

[41] Heinrich Kreissle von Hellborn, *The Life of Franz Schubert*, trans. by Arthur D. Coleridge (London, 1869), II, pp. 263-64. Kreissle, in introducing the testimony, was answering Schindler's improbable story that at this visit the composers met, that hearing a criticism from Beethoven of his variations, Schubert was completely overwhelmed and lost control of himself until he had left Beethoven's house. Josef Hüttenbrenner's remarks (in answer to Ferdinand Luib) are given in O. E. Deutsch's *Memoirs of Schubert*, p. 75. See also Walter Nohl, "Beethoven and Schubert's personal Relations," in *MQ*, XIV (1928), pp. 553-62.

was introduced and to this Beethoven had to write new music, which he did in September. He also revised, altered and extended the march with chorus.[42] Beethoven wrote a new overture also, that known as *Die Weihe des Hauses*, putting aside the overture to the *Ruinen von Athen* because that play had served as a second piece, or epilogue, at Pesth. On a revised copy of the chorus "Wo sich die Pulse" Beethoven wrote: "Written towards the end of September, 1823, performed on October 3 at the Josephstadt Theatre." The 1823 should be 1822, of course, but singularly enough the same blunder was made on a copy of the overture and another composition, the *Gratulationsmenuett,* which was written about the same time. The explanation is probably that offered by Nottebohm,[43] viz.: that Beethoven dated the copies when he sent them to the Archduke. Beethoven's remark in a letter to Johann that he had finished the chorus with dances and would write the overture if his health allowed, also fixes the date of the composition of the overture in September. This Schindler confirms in this anecdote about the origin of the overture:[44] "Meanwhile September was come. It was therefore time to go to work on the new overture, for the master had long ago seen that the one to the *Ruinen von Athen* was for obvious reasons unsuitable. One day, while I was walking with him and his nephew in the lovely Helenenthal near Baden, Beethoven told us to go on in advance and join him at an appointed place. It was not long before he overtook us, remarking that he had written down two motives for an overture. At the same time he expressed himself also as to the manner in which he purposed treating them—one in the free style and one in the strict, and, indeed, in Handel's. As well as his voice permitted he sang the two motives and then asked us which we liked the better. This shows the roseate mood into which for the moment he was thrown by the discovery of two gems for which, perhaps, he had been hunting a long time. The nephew decided in favor of both, while I expressed a desire to see the fugal theme worked out for the purpose mentioned. It is not to be understood that Beethoven wrote the overture to the *Weihe des Hauses* as he did because I wanted it so, but because he had long cherished the plan to write an overture in the strict, expressly in the Handelian, style. . . . The newly organized orchestra of the Josephstadt Theatre did not receive it till the afternoon before the opening, and with innumerable mistakes in every part. The rehearsal which took place in the presence of an almost filled parterre, scarcely sufficed for the correction of the worst of the copyist's errors."

The overture and chorus written for the *Weihe des Hauses* are "occasionals" and were conceived and wrought out in a remarkably short time

---

[42] Published as Op. 114 and designated as "new" by Beethoven, though not a measure had been added, but only a few lines of text, and the choral music simplified. Steiner published pianoforte arrangements for two and four hands in 1822, and the score in 1826. (TK, III, 80, n. 1; cf. KHV, p. 330.)

[43] *II Beeth.*, p. 396. (TDR, IV, 301, n. 1.)

[44] *Biogr.*, II, pp. 7-8. (TDR, IV, 301.)

for that period in Beethoven's activities. The first was offered for publication to Steiner and, with other pieces, to Diabelli. The negotiations failed and the overture finally appeared from the press of Schott in 1825, with a dedication to Prince Galitzin.

Beethoven's stay in Baden was interrupted by the performance of the *Weihe des Hauses*, which took place, as projected, on October 3, the eve of the Emperor's name-day. All of the 400 reserved seats and boxes had been sold several weeks before. Beethoven had reserved the direction for himself and sat at the pianoforte, the greater part of the orchestra within view, his left ear turned towards the stage. He was still able to hear a little with that ear, as we know from the fact related by Schindler, that he was fond of listening to Cherubini's overture to *Medea* played by a musical clock which stood in a restaurant adjoining the Josephstadt Theatre. Kapellmeister Franz Gläser stood at his right, and Schindler, who had recently abandoned the law, led the first violins. At the dress rehearsal Fanny Heckermann sang timidly and dragged perceptibly in the duet. Beethoven observed this and called the singer to him, pointed out the places in which he wanted more animation, spoke some words of encouragement and advised her to follow the tenor, who was an experienced singer. He then had the number repeated and on its conclusion remarked: "Well done, this time, Fräulein Heckermann!"[45] The tenor was Michael Greiner, with whom Beethoven was acquainted, from Baden, and Fräulein Kaiser sang the part of Pallas. The rehearsal and the performance demonstrated plainly, Schindler says, that under no circumstances was Beethoven able longer to conduct large bodies of performers. The representation, despite the enthusiasm of the performers, stimulated by Beethoven's encouraging speeches, was not a success. Beethoven would take none of the fault to himself, however, though his anxiety led him to hold back the music despite the exertions of his two leaders, whom he admonished against too much precipitancy, of which Schindler protests they were not guilty. There were demonstrations of enthusiasm at the close and Beethoven was led before the curtain by Director Hensler. The work was repeated on October 4, 5 and 6.

Beethoven's return to Baden was on or before October 11, and he stayed in a house in the Magdalenahof, Frauengasse No. 85, belonging to Johann Grundgeyer, who was not only a merchant but also Master of the Baths, Magistrate, and Police Commissioner. This house also still stands and has a memorial tablet. Grundgeyer kept a log of house rentals in which is recorded in 1822 "Hr. v. Beethoven from Oct. 11 2 rooms and 1 kitchen, at 2 fl. 45 k. per day part-payment 20 fl. V.S. 27 finis." It is not known whether the sum of 27 florins was the whole sum or a final payment to be counted with the statement of 20 florins.[46] At any rate, Beethoven could not have been there for more than 2 or 3 weeks because soon he was to contribute

[45] *Ibid.*, p. 9.
[46] See Theodor Frimmel, "Beethoven im

Kurort Baden bei Wien," in *NBJ*, IV (1930), pp. 75-6.

to another musical event in Vienna. At this time Beethoven left his old dwelling on the Landstrasse and moved into quarters next to his brother's house in the Windmühle Vorstadt. Johann's house on the Kothgasse No. 61 was owned by his brother-in-law, the master baker Leopold Obermayer; Beethoven's rooms were in a house on the Oberepfarrgasse No. 60, owned by a certain Johann Ehlers.[47]

Beethoven's friendly feeling for Hensler gave rise to a new orchestral composition which was part of a tribute paid by the members of the company to their director on November 3, the evening before his name-day. After a performance of Meisl's drama *1722, 1822, 1922*, the audience having departed, the director was called to the festively decorated and illuminated stage, and surrounded by his company in gala dress. A poetical address was read to him by the stage-manager. After he had gone back to his lodgings, the orchestra and chorus serenaded him, the programme consisting of an overture to *The Prodigal Son* by Kapellmeister Drechsel, a concerto for flute by Kapellmeister Gläser, and what Bäuerle's *Theaterzeitung* called "a glorious new symphony" composed for the occasion by Beethoven, the whole ending with the march and chorus from Mozart's *Titus*. The "new symphony" was the *Gratulationsmenuett* of which mention has been made. Nothing is said in the accounts about Beethoven's presence at the serenade, and as *Fidelio* was performed that night at the Kärnthnerthor Theatre, his absence might easily be explained. On the next day Hensler gave a dinner in the property room of the theatre at 3 P.M. Beethoven, Gläser, Bäuerle, Gleich, Meisl, Hopp and others were present.[48] Beethoven had a seat directly under the musical clock. Gläser told Reischl[49] who provided the entertainment to set the clock to the overture to *Fidelio* and then wrote to Beethoven to listen, as he would soon hear it. Beethoven listened and then said: "It plays it better than the orchestra in the Kärnthnerthor."[50]

The *Gratulationsmenuett* was offered to Peters in the letter of December 20. Beethoven was evidently eager to realize quickly on a work which had cost him but little labor—the product of a period in which his fancy seemed to have regained its old-time fecundity and he his old-time delight in work. He offered it elsewhere and gave a copy (the one that he misdated) to

[47] In the *Verzeichniss aller in der Kaiserl. Königl. Haupt-und Residenz-stadt Wien mit ihren Vorstädten befindlichen Häuser*, arr. and ed. by Anton Behsel (Vienna, 1829) is indicated:

Windmühle neue (1823)
    Johann Ehlers   60 Polizei Bezirks-
                        direct: Mariahilf
    Leop. Obermayer 61 Gassen und Plätze:
                        Oberepfarrgasse

[48] Max Unger, "Vom geselligen Beethoven," *Österreiche Musikzeitschrift*, XII (1957), p. 92, supplies the following identifications: Franz Gläser, son of Beethoven's copyist, Peter Gläser,

and Theatre Kapellmeister; Adolph Bäuerle, author and editor of the *Wiener Allgemeine Theaterzeitung*; Joseph Alois Gleich, productive poet for the Josephstadt stage and scholar in the civil service; Carl Meisl, author of the *Weihe des Hauses*; Friedrich Hopp, author as well as actor. This anecdote was told to Thayer on October 28, 1859 by Hopp. (TK, III, 82, n. 1.)

[49] According to O. E. Deutsch, *Österreiche Musikzeitschrift*, XII (1957), p. 163, Wolfgang Reischl was landlord of the Josephstadt Theatre.

[50] See Schünemann, II, p. 293, for a similar account by implication.

Archduke Rudolph for his collection. Artaria published it in 1832 under the title "Allegretto" with a dedication to Karl Holz. The title on the autograph reads: "Tempo di Minuetto quasi Allegretto" (Allegro non troppo was originally written but then scratched out in favor of): "Gratulations-Menuett."

The revival of *Fidelio* which took place on November 3, after an absence from the stage of three years, was a benefit performance for Wilhelmine Schröder, then seventeen years old. Later as the famous dramatic singer, Madame Schröder-Devrient,[51] she was reputed to be the greatest of all the Fidelios; but she did not reach her full artistic stature until after Beethoven's death. Haitzinger sang Florestan, Zeltner Rocco, Forti Pizarro. Rauscher was Jacquino, Nestroy the Minister, Fräulein Demmer sang Marcelline and Fräulein Schröder, Leonore. Schindler tells a pathetic tale concerning the dress rehearsal. Together with his friends, mindful of the happenings in the Hall of the University in 1819 and in the Josephstadt Theatre only a short time before, Schindler advised Beethoven not to attempt to conduct the performance. He hesitated for a few days, then announced his intention to direct with the help of Umlauf. Schindler escorted him to the rehearsal. The overture went well, the orchestra being well trained in it, but at the first duet it became painfully manifest that Beethoven heard nothing of what was being sung on the stage. He slackened his beat and the orchestra obeyed; the singers urged the movement onward. Umlauf stopped the performance at the rappings on the jailor's lodge-gate but gave no reason to Beethoven. At the same place on the repetition there was the same confusion. Let Schindler continue the narrative: "The impossibility of going ahead with the author of the work was evident. But how, in what manner inform him of the fact? Neither Duport, the director, nor Umlauf was willing to speak the saddening words: 'It will not do; go away, you unhappy man!' Beethoven, already uneasy in his seat, turned now to the right now to the left, scrutinizing the faces to learn the cause of the interruption. Everywhere a heavy silence. Then he summoned me. I had approached near him in the orchestra. He handed me his notebook with an indication that I write what the trouble was. Hastily I wrote in effect: 'Please do not go on; more at home.' With a bound he was in the parterre and said merely: 'Out, quick!' Without stopping he ran towards his lodgings, Pfarrgasse, Vorstadt Leimgrube.[52] Inside he threw himself on the sofa, covered his face with his hands and remained in this attitude till we sat down to eat. During the meal not a word came from his lips; he was a picture of profound melancholy and depression. When I tried to go away after the meal he begged me not to leave him until it was time to go to the theatre. At parting he asked me

---

[51] She met the actor Karl Devrient in 1823 and was his wife for five years after which time the marriage was dissolved.

[52] The confusion in Schindler's address may be explained by the fact that the Oberepfarrgasse was renamed Leimgrubenstrasse. For this information I am indebted to Dr. Kurt Smolle.

to go with him next day to his physician, Dr. Smetana, who had gained some repute as an aurist."[53]

Some details of the representation may be learned from the account in the *Theaterzeitung* of November 9. The day was the name-day of the Empress; the square about the Opera-house was illuminated; the national hymn, "Gott erhalte Franz den Kaiser," was sung; the overture received such applause that it had to be repeated; the great duet and the canon quartet also, and the soprano and tenor were recalled at the end of the opera.

—Wilhelmine Schröder-Devrient wrote an account of her debut as Leonore at the request of Gustav Schilling[54] from which we quote in part:

"Under the guidance of my talented mother many of the traits in Leonore's character became clear to me; however I was still too young, too little developed within to have a full understanding of what took place in Leonore's soul, emotions for which Beethoven had conceived his immortal harmonies. At the rehearsals which were led by Umlauf who was then kapellmeister, the limits of my underdeveloped young voice soon became known and many things in my part were changed for me so that the effect did not suffer too much. The last rehearsals were set, when I learned before the dress rehearsal that Beethoven had asked for the honor of conducting the work himself in celebration of the day. On hearing this news a great fear came over me, and I also remember my frightful awkwardness which nearly drove my poor mother, as well as those who were working with me, to despair. But Beethoven sat in the orchestra and waved his baton over everyone's heads, and I had never seen the man before!— At that time the master's physical ear was already closed to all sounds. With a bewildered face and unearthly inspired eyes, waving his baton back and forth with violent motions, he stood in the midst of the performing musicians and didn't hear a note! If he thought it should be *piano* he crouched down almost under the conductor's desk and if he wanted *forte* he jumped up with the strangest gestures, uttering the weirdest sounds. With each piece our courage dwindled further and I felt as though I were watching one of Hoffmann's fantastic figures appear before me. The inevitable happened: the deaf master threw the singers and orchestra completely off the beat and into the greatest confusion, and no one knew any longer where they were. Beethoven, however, knew nothing of all this, and so with difficulty our rehearsal came to an end, with which he seemed to be well satisfied, for he laid down his baton with a cheery smile. But now it was impossible to entrust him with the performance, and Kapellmeister Umlauf had to perform the heart-rending task of pointing out to him that the opera could not be given under his direction. I am told that he resigned himself with a melancholy look upwards, and I found him at the performance on the following night sitting in the orchestra

[53] *Biogr.*, II, p. 11. (TDR, IV, 319, n. 1.)
[54] It was published as a contribution to *Beethoven-Album, ein Gedenkbuch dankbarer*   *Liebe und Verehrung für den grossen Todten* (Stuttgart, 1846).

behind Umlauf lost in profound thought. . . . Beethoven followed the whole performance with eager attention, and he looked as if he were trying to see from each of our gestures whether we had even half understood him.

"Even then they used to call me a little genius; and indeed on that evening a more mature spirit seemed to have come over me, for several touches of sheer genius shone forth from my performance which must not have escaped Beethoven, for the next day he came himself, the great master, to bring me his thanks and his congratulations. With hot tears I moistened the hand that he offered me, and in my joy, I would not have exchanged anything in the world for this praise from Beethoven's lips! He promised at that time to write an opera for me, but unfortunately it remained nothing but a promise."

The two accounts of the rehearsal, while agreeing in general, do not agree in detail. Schindler's direct participation in Beethoven's departure from the scene would seem to make his account the more likely to be correct. Elsewhere, however, Schindler, in declaring that Beethoven never saw Schröder-Devrient as Leonore,[55] shows an obvious lack of memory in recalling these days which lessens the reader's confidence in the exactness of his account. That Beethoven was at a performance is confirmed by a remark of the Darmstadt composer Ludwig Wilhelm Reuling in a Conversation Book of March, 1823: "I saw you in the theatre at the first performance of *Fidelio*.[56]

Fidelio was repeated on November 4 and also on November 26, December 2 and 17, and March 3 and 18, 1823. According to the *Modenzeitung*, November 12, 1822, "Beethoven attended the second performance, sitting in a box in the front tier." Louis Schlösser, who was at this performance, adds confirmation by telling how he saw Beethoven leaving the theatre in the company of Schindler and von Breuning.[57]

Following Schindler's narrative we learn that Beethoven's woeful experience at the rehearsal led to a resolution on his part to make another effort to be healed of his deafness. He went to Dr. Smetana, who prescribed medicaments to be taken inwardly, thereby indicating, as Schindler asserts, that he had no expectation of effecting a cure, but wanted only to occupy Beethoven's mind, knowing what to expect from so impatient, wilful and absent-minded a patient; for Beethoven was as unready to follow a physician's advice as a musician's, and was more likely to injure himself with overdoses of drugs than to invite the benefit which the practitioner hoped for by obedience to the prescription. The usual thing happened; not only with Dr. Smetana's treatment, but also with that of the priest, Pater Weiss, whom he had consulted some 18 years before and to whom he now returned. For a while he thought that the oil which the priest dropped into his ears was beneficial, and Pater Weiss himself expressed the belief that the left ear, at least, might

[55] *Neue Berliner Musikzeitung*, July 30, 1851.
[56] Schünemann, III, p. 86.
[57] The periodical, *Hallelujah*, IV (1885), p. 232. (TDR, IV, 318, n. 3.)

permanently be helped; but Beethoven grew skeptical, as he always did unless he experienced immediate relief, his work monopolized his attention, and despite the priest's solicitations he abandoned the treatment and yielded himself to his fate. Thenceforward no one heard him lament because of his deafness.

The compositions which were in Beethoven's hands at the close of the year were those which had occupied him in the earlier months. The Mass, several times completed but never complete so long as it was within reach, received what must now be looked upon as its finishing touches. Progress was made on the Ninth Symphony and the Diabelli Variations, and thought given to a quartet, perhaps several quartets.

The Bagatelles for Pianoforte grouped under Op. 119, some of which had been published a year before (Nos. 7-11), were finished; Nos. 1 to 6 were ready for the publisher by the end of 1822—the autograph manuscript bearing the inscription "Kleinigkeiten, 1822 Novemb." Nottebohm thinks that Nos. 2 to 5 were conceived between 1800 and 1804; a sketch for No. 5 (C minor, "Risoluto") is found among sketches made in 1802 for the Sonata in C minor, Op. 30; Lenz says sketches for No. 3 (in D, "a l'Allemande") are among sketches for the last movement of the "Eroica" Symphony; No. 6 (G major) is sketched on a sheet containing experimental studies for a passage in the *Credo* of the Mass; sketches for Nos. 2 and 4 are among suggestions of a melody for Goethe's "Erlkönig," WoO 131,[58] indicating an early period which cannot be determined.[59]

Beethoven offered a number of Bagatelles to Peters on June 5, July 6 and November 22; he sent six to the publisher on February 15, 1823. Peters returned them—Beethoven receiving them on March 19—with the remark that they were not worth the price asked for them and that Beethoven ought to consider it beneath his dignity to waste his time on such trifles; anybody could write them. Schindler says that Peters's action aggrieved Beethoven, which is easily believed.[60] On February 25, 1823, Beethoven sent the eleven Bagatelles to Ries in London with instructions to sell them as best he could. On May 7, 1823, six were offered to Lissner in St. Petersburg. At the end of 1823 they were published by Clementi in London and Schlesinger in Paris, the latter giving them the opus number 112. Sauer and Leidesdorf issued them in Vienna with the same opus number at the end of April, 1824.[61] The number 119 appears to have been assigned to the set after an agreement had been reached with Steiner concerning the works now numbered 112 to 118.

The last known song by Beethoven, "Der Kuss," was finished at this time,

---

[58] See KHV, pp. 593-94.

[59] The piece added to the set by Diabelli, in his later publication "12 Nouvelles Bagatelles," was an adaption of the pianoforte accompaniment of Beethoven's early song "An Laura" and clearly does not belong to the set.

(Cf. TDR, IV, 321.)

[60] *Biogr.*, II, pp. 44-5. (In his account Schindler confuses them with the set, Op. 126, bagatelles of a higher order and not composed at this time.) (TDR, IV, 322, n. 3.)

[61] KHV, pp. 345-46.

though written down practically as we know it in 1798. Sketches involving the few changes made are found among some for the overture, the *Weihe des Hauses* and the Ninth Symphony. The autograph is dated "December, 1822." In 1825 it was published by Schott and Cappi, numbered 121, and did not receive the number 128 until 1828.[62]

Schindler, in his list of vocal music for Beethoven's last period lists among others: "Op. 121b, 'Opferlied,' Poem by Matthison [*sic*]. For a solo voice with chorus and orchestra, published 1826 by Schott. Op. 122 'Bundeslied.' Poem by Goethe. For two solo voices and 3-part chorus with accompaniment of 2 clarinets, 2 horns and 2 bassoons, published 1826 by Schott. Both of the preceding songs were written in 1822 for the tenor Ehlers at a concert for his own benefit in Pressburg."[63] Beethoven had known Ehlers since 1814 at which time he sang in Treitschke's Singspiel *Die gute Nachricht*.[64] Thayer-Deiters dismissed Schindler's composition dates since the last version of "Opferlied," Op. 121b is written for a soprano and not a tenor, and was the work of the summer of 1824. But the discovery of Wilhelm Ehler's Akademie program by Viktor Papp[65] shows that Schindler was more accurate than at first supposed. On December 23, 1822, in Pressburg was given "eine grosse musikalisch deklamatorische Akademie" which included two of Beethoven's newest compositions: the *Gratulationsmenuett* and "Matthisson's Opferlied für drei Solostimmen und Chor, aus Freundschaft für den Concertgeber für diese Akademie komponiert." ("Matthisson's Opferlied for 3 solo voices and chorus composed for this *Akademie* out of friendship for the concert-giver.") This version, which Herbst calls No. 3,[66] is scored for soprano, alto and tenor solo and four-part chorus with accompaniment of 2 clarinets, 2 horns, violas and violoncellos, and was first performed in Vienna in April, 1824. It will be remembered that on February 15 Beethoven wrote Peters that he had sent him three songs, "Bundeslied," "Der Kuss" and "Opferlied." Since this version of "Opferlied" was completed before the end of the year it is fair to assume that "Bundeslied" was also, since Beethoven may well have intended it for Ehler's use, as Schindler records, and for some reason it was not used.

On September 2, Beethoven received a letter from Charles Neate, which was plainly an answer to an appeal which had been sent by the composer, concerning the publication in London of three quartets. Letters from Ries refer to the same quartets, which as yet existed only in Beethoven's intentions. Neate says that he had found it difficult to obtain subscriptions for the works. He thought, however, that he might still be able to raise 100 pounds, but could not get any money before the arrival of the works in London. There was also apprehension that the compositions would be copied in Vienna. Beethoven had referred to a quartet and possibly some successors

[62] *Ibid.*, p. 389.
[63] *Biogr.*, II, p. 152.
[64] See *A* 472.
[65] *Beethoven és a Magyarok* (Beethoven and the Hungarians) (Budapest, 1927), p. 122.
[66] See "Beethoven's Opferliedkomponisten," *NBJ*, v (1933), pp. 137-53.

in his correspondence with Peters, so that it is more than likely that a determination to return to the quartet field had been formed by Beethoven before the practical and material incentive came to him in the last month of the year from Prince Galitzin—the incentive to which we owe three of the last five quartets.

—⇥Prince Nikola[u]s Borissowit[s]ch Galitzin [Golizyn],[67] born in 1794 in Moscow, was an influential force in the musical life of St. Petersburg. He played the violoncello, and his wife (née Princess Helene Saltykow) was an admirable pianist. Prince Galitzin was an ardent admirer of Beethoven's music and had arranged some of his pianoforte works for strings. The first mention of his name was in a Conversation Book in the first half of April, 1820, when Kanne, in answer to some question writes "der Gallizin bor[i]s." This is followed by "wo wir so oft war[e]n" ("where we were so often"); to what this refers and its connection, if any, with the name of the prince is not known. (See Schünemann, II, p. 45.)⇥—

Then on November 9, 1822, the prince wrote the following letter to Beethoven:

Monsieur!

I take the liberty of writing you, as one who is as much a passionate amateur in music as a great admirer of your talent, to ask if you will not consent to compose one, two or three new quartets for which labor I will be glad to pay you what you think proper. I will accept the dedication with gratitude. Would you let me know to what banker I should direct the sum that you wish to get. The instrument that I am cultivating is the violoncello. I await your answer with the liveliest impatience. Could you please address your letter to me as follows

To Prince Nicolas de Galitzin at S. Petersburg care of Messrs. Stieglitz and Co. Bankers.

I beg you to accept the assurance of my great admiration and high regard.

Prince Nicolas Galitzin

—⇥Beethoven's reply was written in French in Karl's hand and the composer supplied the date and his signature:

Your Highness! Vienna January 25, 1823

I would not have failed to answer Your letter of Nov. 9 sooner if the multitude of my affairs had not prevented me from writing you. It was with great pleasure that I found that Your Highness is interested in works of my creation. You wish to have some quartets; since I see that you are cultivating the violoncello, I will take care to give you satisfaction in this regard. Inasmuch as I am constrained to live by the products of my mind, I must take the liberty of setting the honorarium for one quartet at 50 ducats. If this is agreeable with your Highness, I beg you to inform me soon and to direct this sum to the banker

---

[67] For the correct spelling of Galitzin's name and the information concerning his birth I am indebted to Miss Emily Anderson's "Two Letters from Beethoven to Prince Nikolas Galitzin," in *Festschrift Joseph Schmidt-Görg zum 60. Geburtstag*, ed. by Dagmar Weise (Bonn, 1957), pp. 1-9.

Hénikstein in Vienna; I bind myself to finish the 1st quartet by the end of the month of February or at the latest by the middle of March.

In expressing to you my real interest in your musical talent, I thank your Highness for the regards that you have been willing to indicate, in choosing me to increase, if it is possible, your love for music. I have the honor of being

Your Highness's very humble servant
Louis van Beethoven[68]

The smaller compositions completed in this year were:

Bagatelles for Pianoforte, Op. 119, Nos. 1-6. Nos. 2-5 were worked out from early sketches.

"Bundeslied" for Two Solo Voices and Three-part Chorus with accompaniment of 2 clarinets, 2 bassoons and 2 horns (Goethe), Op. 122. Revision of sketches of 1797.[69]

"Der Kuss" (C. F. Weisse), Op. 128. Revision of a sketch of 1798.

Gratulationsmenuett for Orchestra, WoO 3, for a Serenade for Carl Friedrich Hensler.

Music for the *Weihe des Hauses* (Meisl):
Overture in C, Op. 124.
March with Chorus, Op. 114 (revision of Op. 113, No. 6).
Chorus "Wo sich die Pulse," WoO 98.

"Opferlied" for Soprano, Alto, Tenor and Chorus with accompaniment of 2 clarinets, 2 horns, violas and violoncellos, third version (listed with Op. 121b in KHV).

Short Piece for Two Violins for Alexandre Boucher, WoO 34. Boucher (1778-1861) was a French violinist who called on Beethoven with a letter of introduction from Goethe. Beethoven wrote out this musical souvenir of seven measures on April 29.[70]

Progress on large works consisted of:

1821-2. Sonata for Pianoforte in C minor, Op. 111. On the first page of the fair copy Beethoven wrote: "January 13, 1822."

1819-23. Main work on the Thirty-three Variations on a Theme by Diabelli, Op. 120.

1819-22/23. Tentative completion of the *Missa Solemnis* in D major, Op. 123.

The publications of the year were:

By Breitkopf and Härtel:
Overture to *Fidelio* in E major.
By Schlesinger in Berlin and Paris:
Sonata for Pianoforte in A-flat major, Op. 110.
By Steiner:
"Meeresstille und glückliche Fahrt" for Chorus and Orchestra, Op. 112, dedicated to the author, J. W. von Goethe.

---

[68] *Ibid.*, p. 4, for the first printing of this letter. See also *A* 1123.

[69] Hans Boettcher, *Beethoven als Lieder-*

komponist (Augsburg, 1928), Table IV.

[70] See *FRBH*, I, pp. 57-8.

First continental editions:

By Artaria, Mechetti, Schlesinger, and Steiner:
   Twenty-five Scottish Songs with Accompaniment of Pianoforte, Violin and
   Violoncello, Op. 108, dedicated to Prince Anton Heinrich Radziwill.
By Simrock:
   Symphonies Nos. 1-3 *in score.*

CHAPTER XXXVI

THE YEAR 1823

SUBSCRIPTIONS FOR THE *MISSA SOLEMNIS*—MORE NEGOTIATIONS WITH ENGLAND—GRILLPARZER AND OPERA PROJECTS—PROGRESS OF THE NINTH SYMPHONY

THIS period in Beethoven's life was great in inspiration and creation. The great Mass was ready, needing only corrections and a few alterations. Work continued on the new symphony, and the stimulation to write some new string quartets, the big labor of the last years, was already upon him.

The progress of the Mass and the negotiations, still inconclusive, toward its publication have been sketched for the preceding years. Now at last it was possible for the work to reach its destination. It was intended, as we have long known, for Archduke Rudolph; since the plan was first formulated, four years had elapsed. On February 27, 1823, he wrote of his intention to pay him a visit and apologized that he had not written for such a long time:

... but I have been wanting to wait until I had sent the Mass; but then there were really terrible mistakes in it and to such an extent that *every part* had to be read over; it was delayed further by many other affairs that could not be put off, which led to still other circumstances to hinder me, for so much confronts a man when he least expects it. However, that I have had Y.I.H. continually in mind is shown by the copies of some new publications[1] that are being sent which have been ready for Y.I.H. for several months; but I did not want to send them on ahead of the Mass. This *last* is being bound and after that will be respectfully handed over by me to Y.I.H. ...

This took place on March 19, 1823, the evening before the anniversary day of the enthronement of the Archduke as Archbishop of Olmütz, for

[1] The overture and chorus for the *Weihe des Hauses* and the *Gratulationsmenuett*. (TDR, IV, 325, n. 2.)

which solemnization the Mass was supposed to have been ready. In the catalogue of the Rudolphinian Collection, now preserved by the Gesellschaft der Musikfreunde in Vienna, it is entered thus: "*Missa Solemnis.* Partitur. MS. This beautifully written MS. was delivered by the composer himself on March 19, 1823."

The plan to write the Mass for the installation ceremonies seems to have been original with Beethoven; it was not suggested by the Archduke or any of his friends, so far as has ever been learned. He began work upon it at once. ⸺Let us review the chronology here. In the first edition of his *Biographie*,[2] Schindler dates the beginning of the composition of the Mass as the winter of 1818-19. As mentioned earlier, Max Unger[3] has established the time more precisely as the first months of 1819 on the basis of the first sketches for the *Kyrie*, which follow those for the Diabelli Variations, in a sketchbook from the Wittgenstein Collection.⸺ Nottebohm's study[4] of the sketches led him to conclusions which may be summed up as follows: the movements were taken up in the order in which the various portions appear in the Roman missal, but work was prosecuted on several movements simultaneously. The *Kyrie* was begun shortly after the fact of the Archduke's appointment was known; the *Gloria* was completely sketched by the end of 1819, and the *Credo* in 1820. ⸺In the first of the three *Missa Solemnis* sketchbooks at the Beethovenhaus in Bonn, dated by Schmidt-Görg December, 1819-April, 1820,[5] there is evidence to amplify Nottebohm's generalization. Sketches for the *Credo* appear on the very first page of the forty-four page sketchbook, whereas there is still work on the close of the *Gloria* on page 31. There are also a few sketches for the *Sanctus*.⸺ The entire Mass was complete in sketchbook form in the beginning of 1822. But with the elaboration of the sketches the Mass was not really finished, for subsequently Beethoven undertook many changes. The *Allegro* molto which enters in the *Credo* at the words "et ascendit" is shorter in the autograph than in the printed edition. At the entrance of the words "et iterum" and "cujus regni" the autograph is in each case two measures shorter than in the printed score. In the autograph, and also in the copy which Beethoven gave to the Archduke, the trombones do not enter till the words "judicare vivos et mortuous." There are no trombones in the *Gloria*. The trombone passage which now appears just before the entrance of the chorus on "judicare" was formerly set for the horns. After the words "et mortuous" the trombones are silent until the end of the *Credo* in the autograph; they enter again in the beginning of the *Sanctus*, but are silent at the next *Allegro*. They occur in the *Benedictus*, but are wanting in the *Agnus Dei*. He made so many changes in the tympani part of the *Agnus Dei* that he wore a hole in the very thick paper. From

[2] [1840], p. 113.

[3] "Die Beethoven Handschriften der Familie W. in Wien," in *NJB*, VII (1937), pp. 167-68.

[4] *II Beeth.*, pp. 148-56. (Cf. TDR, IV, 326,

n. 3.)

[5] Joseph Schmidt-Görg, *Ein Skizzenbuch aus den Jahren 1819-20* (Bonn, 1952), pp. 15-16.

the nature of these supplementary alterations it is to be concluded that considerable time must have elapsed before they could all be made. Holding to the date on which the copy was delivered to the Archduke (March 19, 1823), the earliest date at which the Mass can have received its definitive shape as we know it must be set down as the middle of 1823. That he was sincere in his purpose to provide a mass for the installation ceremonies is to be found, outside of Schindler's statement, in a letter to the Archduke in which he says:

The day on which a high mass of my composition is performed at the ceremony for Y.I.H. will be to me the most beautiful in my life and God will enlighten me so that my poor powers may contribute to the glory of this solemn day.

Something was said at the beginning of Chapter XXIII of this biography concerning the views Beethoven entertained on the subject of religion and dogmatic and sectarian Christianity. His attitude towards the Roman Catholic Church becomes an almost necessary subject of contemplation in a study of the *Missa Solemnis*; but it is one into which the personal equation of the student must perforce largely enter. The obedient churchman of a Roman Catholic country will attach both less and more importance, than one brought up in a Protestant land, to the fact that he admonished his nephew when a lad to say his prayers and said them with him (as the boy testified in the guardianship proceedings), that he himself at least once led him to the door of the confessional,[6] that he consented to the summoning of a priest when *in extremis* and that he seemed to derive comfort and edification from the sacred function. It is not necessary, however, to go very deeply into a critical study of the Mass in order to say that while the composition shows respect for traditions in some portions and while it is possible to become eloquent without going beyond the demonstration contained in the music itself, in describing the overwhelming puissance of his proclamation of the fatherhood of God and belief in Him as the Creator of all things visible and invisible, the most obvious fact which confronts the analytical student is that Beethoven approached the missal text chiefly with the imagination and the emotions of an artist, and that its poetical, not to say dramatic elements were those which he was most eager to delineate.

One example of this may be found in the *Agnus Dei*. It was scarcely necessary for Beethoven to do so, but he has nevertheless given us an explanation of his singular treatment of the prayer for peace. Among the sketches for the movement is found the remark: "dona nobis pacem darstellend den *innern* und äussern Frieden" ("delineating internal and external peace"), and in agreement with this he superscribes the first *Allegro vivace*

[6] In a Conversation Book of 1820 we read this remark by Beethoven: "What I think of confession may be deduced from the fact that I myself led Karl to the Abbot of St. Michael for confession. But the Abbot declared that as long as he had to visit his mother, confession would be of no avail." (TDR, IV, 335, n. 1.) See Schünemann, I, p. 203.

in the autograph with the same words. In the later copy this phrase is changed to "Prayer for internal and external peace,"[7] thus showing an appreciation of the fact that the words alone contain the allusion to peace which in its external aspect is disturbed by the sounds of war suggested by the instruments. The petition for peace is emphasized by the threatening tones of military instruments accompanying the agonizing appeal for mercy sent up by the voices. The device is purely dramatic and it was not an entirely novel conceit of Beethoven's. When the French invaded Styria in 1796, Haydn wrote a mass "In tempore belli" in which a soft drum-roll entered immediately after the words "Agnus Dei" and was gradually reinforced by trumpets and other wind-instruments "as if the enemy were heard approaching in the distance."

By the end of 1822, Beethoven had made the plan of postponing the publication of the Mass in order to sell manuscript copies of it by subscription to the sovereigns of Europe. In the Library of the Paris Conservatory is an unpublished letter from Johann van Beethoven without address but apparently to the Paris publisher Pacini in answer to a request for quartets or quintets by his brother.[8] Johann answered that his brother could not oblige just now since he was working on a symphony, an opera and a big mass, asked the publisher for help in the sale of manuscript copies of this last work at the French court, and offered him a new trio for 2 violins and viola and a big overture.[9]

In the first week of the new year Beethoven sent his brother with a letter to Griesinger of the Saxon Legation asking him to give advice on the subject of subscription to the bearer of the letter, apologizing for not coming in person on the grounds of indisposition. Whether or not Griesinger came to his assistance we do not know, but within a fortnight work on the project had been energetically begun. Schindler was now called upon to write, fetch and carry as steadily and industriously as if he were, in fact, what he described himself to be—a private secretary. Among his papers in Berlin are found many billets and loose memoranda bearing on the subject, without date, but grouped as to periods by Schindler himself and provided with occasional glosses touching their contents. Beethoven took so much of his time in requisition, indeed, that he offered to pay him 50 florins after the collection of one of the subscription fees, but Schindler records that he never received them nor would he have accepted them. He was, as he informed the world

[7] *Il Beeth.*, pp. 151-52, 471-72. (TDR, IV, 352, n. 2.)

[8] Max Unger, "Die Beethovenhandschriften der Pariser Konservatorium-Bibliothek" in *NBJ*, VI (1935), p. 122. As Unger points out, Pacini is the likely recipient because there is in the same library the autograph of a letter from Beethoven to Pacini, dated April 5, 1823 which begins: "Monsieur! C'est mon Frère, qui me disait, que vous souhaitiés de

posseder quelquesunes de mes Compositions. . . ." See *ibid.*, p. 117; also *A* 1166.

[9] The symphony was of course the ninth, the opera a reflection of Beethoven's constant search for a good libretto, the big overture that to the *Weihe des Hauses*. But nothing is known of a trio for two violins and viola. This was either a mistake by Johann or an indication that Beethoven intended or was willing to write such a work.

for many years afterward on his visiting card, "L'Ami de Beethoven," and his very considerable and entirely unselfish labors were "works of friendship" for which he wanted no remuneration; but he was very naturally rejoiced when Beethoven presented him with several autograph scores, and we have seen how, after the death of Beethoven, Breuning gave him many papers which seemed valueless then but are looked upon as invaluable now. Moreover, he disposed of his Beethoven memorabilia to the Royal Library of Berlin for an annuity of 400 thalers—all of which, however, does not detract from the disinterestedness of his labors for Beethoven, alive, suffering and so frequently helpless.

The invitations to the courts were issued in part before the end of January. A letter to Schindler, evidently written in that month, asked him to draw out a memorandum of courts from an almanac in which the foreign embassies stationed at Vienna were listed. The invitations were posted on the following dates: to the courts at Baden, Wurtemburg, Bavaria and Saxony on January 23; "to the other ambassadors" (as Beethoven notes) on January 26; to Weimar on February 4; to Mecklenburg and Hesse-Darmstadt on February 5; to Berlin, Copenhagen, Hesse-Cassel and Nassau on February 6; to Tuscany on February 17, and to Paris on March 1. The invitation to the court at Hesse-Cassel had been written on January 23, but it was not sent because, as Schindler says, "it had been found that nothing was to be got from the little courts." The letter came back to Beethoven and its preservation puts in our hands the formula which, no doubt was followed in all the formal addresses. We therefore give it here:

The undersigned cherishes the wish to send his latest work, which he regards as the most successful of his intellectual products, to the Most Exalted Court of Cassel.

It is a grand solemn mass for 4 solo voices with choruses and complete grand orchestra in score, which can also be used as a grand oratorio.

He therefore begs the High Embassy of His Royal Highness, the Elector of Hesse-Cassel, to be pleased to procure for him the necessary permission of your Exalted Court.

Inasmuch, however, as the copying of the score will entail a considerable expense the author does not think it excessive if he fixes an honorarium at 50 ducats in gold. The work in question, moreover, will not be published for the present.

Vienna, 23 January, 1823.   Ludwig van Beethoven.

Only the signature was in Beethoven's handwriting. It is not known how many of these invitations were issued; Schindler's account goes only to the subscriptions received and even here it is not entirely accurate. There were ten acceptances. The first came from the King of Prussia. Prince Hatzfield acted in the matter for Berlin ----and Beethoven also invoked the aid of the King's Secretary, Friedrich Duncker.[10] Court Councillor Wernhard, Director of the Chancellery of the Embassy at Vienna, brought the report to

---

[10] Johann Friedrich Leopold Duncker, died 1842. See FRBH, I, 117.

Beethoven and asked him if he would not prefer a royal order to the 50 ducats. Without hesitation, Beethoven replied "50 ducats," and after Wernhard had gone he indulged in sarcastic comments on the pursuit of decorations by various contemporaries—"which in his opinion were gained at the cost of the sanctity of art."[11] Beethoven received the money, but the score was not delivered, owing, no doubt, to delay in the copying, and in July Prince Hatzfield felt compelled to remind the composer of his remissness. Prince Radziwill in Berlin also subscribed, but he did not receive his copy till more than a year later. On June 28, 1824, a representative of the Prince politely informed Beethoven that he had sent a cheque for 50 ducats to him with a request for a receipt and a copy of the score, but had received neither. Schindler says the fault lay with the copyists; in every copy many pages had to be rewritten.

On July 1, 1823, Beethoven wrote a long letter to the Archduke in which he reported on the progress of his subscription plan and asked for help in obtaining a subscription from the Grand Duke of Tuscany. Because of the light that this letter throws on the role of the Archduke as both patron and student, it is given in full:

Your Imperial Highness!

Since the departure of Y.I.H. I have been ailing for the most part, afflicted especially with severe pain in the eyes, which has improved only to the extent that for the last eight days I have been able with care to use my eyes again. Y.I.H. will learn from the enclosed receipt of June 27 that several pieces of music have been sent you. Since Y.I.H. seems to find pleasure in the Sonata in C minor, I believed that it would not be presuming too much to surprise Your Highness with the dedication. The variations have been copied for five or even six weeks at least, nevertheless it has been too much for my eyes to read through them all; in vain I looked forward to a complete recovery. So finally I let Schlemmer look them over, and although they do not look very elegant, yet they ought to be correct. The Sonata in C minor was printed in Paris and very badly; and since it was reprinted here, I took as much care as possible in correcting it.—

Soon I will send a beautiful printed copy of the variations. In regard to the Mass which Y.I.H. wished to see made more generally useful, the continuously poor state of my health for several years has compelled me to think of means for bettering my situation, more especially because of the heavy debts which I have incurred and also the fact that I had to forego the visit to England which I was invited to make. For this the Mass seemed suitable. I was advised to offer it to several courts. Hard as it was for me to do this I nevertheless did not think that I ought to subject myself to reproach by not doing it. I therefore invited several courts to subscribe for the Mass, fixed the fee at 50 ducats, as it was thought that this was not excessive, nor unprofitable, if a number of subscribers were to be found. Thus far, indeed, the subscription does me honor, their Royal Majesties of France and Prussia having accepted. Also a few days ago I received a letter from my friend Prince Galitzin in St. Petersburg, in which this truly amiable

[11] Schindler, *Biogr.*, II, p. 18. (TDR, IV, 358, n. 1.)

prince informs me that His Imperial Majesty of Russia has accepted and I should soon hear the details from the Imperial Russian embassy here. In spite of all this, however, although others have also become subscribers I have not yet received as much of a fee as I would from a publisher, but I do have the advantage that the work remains *mine*. The costs of copying are large and will be increased by the three new pieces[12] which are to be added, which I shall send to Y.I.H. as soon as I have finished them.—Perhaps Y.I.H. will not find it burdensome graciously to use your influence with H.R.H., the Grand Duke of Tuscany, so that His Highness also might take a copy. The invitation was sent some time ago to the Grand Duke of Tuscany through von Odelgha, his agent here, and O. solemnly assures me that the invitation will surely be accepted; but I am not entirely confident as several months have gone by and no answer has been received. Since the matter is already under way, it is only natural that as much as possible be done to attain the desired result. It was hard for me to undertake this, still harder for me to tell Y.I.H. of it or bring it to your notice, but *"Necessity knows no law"*—But I thank Him above the stars that I am beginning to use my eyes again. I am now writing a new symphony for England, for the Philharmonic Society, and hope to have it completely done in a fortnight. I can not yet strain my eyes for a long period, wherefore I beg Y.I.H. graciously to be patient in regard to Y.I.H.'s variations, which seem to me charming but need a more thorough study by me. Continue especially Y.I.H. to practice, jotting down briefly your ideas at the pianoforte. For this a little table alongside the pianoforte will be necessary. By this means not only is the creative fancy strengthened, but at the same time one learns to get ahold of the most remote ideas. It is also necessary to write without the pianoforte; and sometimes to develop a simple chorale melody with simple and again with varied figurations with counterpoint and again without. This will cause no headache to Y.I.H. but rather give you great pleasure at finding yourself absorbed in the art.—Gradually there comes the capacity to represent just what we wish and feel, an essential need in the case of men of noble mold—My eyes bid me stop.—All that is good and beautiful to Y.I.H. and in saying farewell may I be called the most faithful servant of Your Imperial Highness.

With deepest respect

L. v. Beethoven

This letter was written in Vienna, but from Hetzendorf he sent a postscript asking for help in a different quarter. Much to Beethoven's vexation and impatience the Saxon court was very tardy in its reply, or rather in subscribing, for at first the invitation was declined; but Beethoven was not thus to be put off by a court with which his imperial pupil was closely connected.

Should Your Imperial Highness wish to favor me with a letter, I beg of you to address it "to L.v. Beethoven in Vienna," from whence I receive all letters here safely through the post.—If convenient, will Y.I.H. graciously recommend the Mass to Prince Anton in Dresden, so that His Royal Majesty of Saxony might be induced to subscribe to the Mass, which will surely happen if Y.I.H.

---

[12] These pieces were to be an offertory, a graduale and a "Tantum ergo." (TK, III, 95, n. 1.) See Schünemann, III, p. 90.

were to show the slightest interest in the matter. As soon as I am informed that you have shown me this favor, I shall at once address myself to the Director General of the Theatre and Music there, who is in charge of such matters, and send him the invitation to subscribe for the King of Saxony which, however, I do not wish to do without an introduction from Y.I.H.—*My opera Fidelio* was performed with great success in Dresden at the festivities in honor of the visit of the King of Bavaria, all their Majesties being present. I heard all of this from the above-mentioned Director General, who asked me for the score through Weber and afterwards made me a handsome present in return.—Y.I.H. will pardon me for inconveniencing you by this request but Y.I.H. knows how little importunate I am as a rule. However, should there be anything objectionable to you in my request, anything the least unpleasant, you will understand as a matter of course that I would be no less convinced of your magnaminity and graciousness. It is not greed nor the desire for speculation, which I have always avoided, but necessity which compels me to do everything possible to extricate myself from this position. In order not to be too harshly judged, it is perhaps best to be frank. —Because of my constant illness, which prevented me from composing as much as usual, I am burdened with a debt of 2300 florins C.M. which can be liquidated only by extraordinary efforts. If things are improved for me by these subscriptions, for which there is every hope, I shall be able to get a firm foothold again through my compositions.—Meanwhile, may Y.I.H. be pleased to receive my frankness not ungraciously. If I were not apt to be blamed for not being as *active* as formerly, I would have kept silent as I have always done. As regards the recommendations, I am nevertheless convinced that Y.I.H. is always glad to do good *wherever possible* and will make no exception *in my case*—

The Archduke fulfilled Beethoven's wish concerning the Saxon Court, and wrote to the Director General v. Könneritz promising to send the invitation to the King. In a second letter dated July 25th Beethoven enclosed a letter to the King's brother, Prince Anton, which contained an invitation to the King.

These last efforts were successful: King Friedrich August subscribed for the Mass, and on July 31 Archduke Rudolph wrote to his music-master: "My brother-in-law Prince Anton has already written to me that the King of Saxony is expecting your beautiful Mass." On September 12, Prince Anton wrote to Beethoven that he had no doubt his royal brother would grant his wish, especially as he had spoken to him on the subject in the name of his brother-in-law, the Cardinal. The money must have arrived soon afterward, and Beethoven set Schindler's mind at ease by writing to him: "In order that evil report may not longer injure the poor Dresdeners too much, I inform you that the money reached me today, with all marks of respect."

The Grand Duke of Hesse-Darmstadt was appealed to directly under date of February 5; the letter, signed by Beethoven, was forwarded through the Hessian ambassador, Baron von Türckheim, a cultured art connoisseur and subsequently Intendant of the Grand Ducal Theatre in Darmstadt. The composer, Louis Schlösser was in Vienna at the time, and Baron von Türckheim, knowing that he wanted to make Beethoven's acquaintance, gave him the opportunity by asking him to carry the information that the invitation had been accepted to Beethoven, handing him the dispatch with the Grand Ducal seal affixed for that purpose. Schlösser went to Beethoven, "No. 60 Kothgasse, first story, door to the left." Beethoven read the document with great joy and said to Schlösser: "Such words as I have read do me good. Your Grand Duke speaks not only like a princely Maecenas but like a thorough musical connoisseur of comprehensive knowledge; it is not alone the acceptance of my work which rejoices me but the estimation which in general he places upon my works."[13]

No success was met with at the cultivated Court of Weimar, though here Beethoven invoked the assistance of no less a dignitary than Goethe. His letter to the poet is still preserved in the Grand Ducal archives and is worthy of being given in full:

Vienna, February 8th, 1823

Your Excellency!

Still living as I have lived from my youthful years in your immortal, never-aging words, and never forgetting the happy hours spent in your company, it nevertheless happens that I must recall myself to your recollection—I hope that you received the dedication to Your Excellency of "Meeresstille und glückliche Fahrt" composed by me. Because of their contrast, both seemed to me adapted for expression in music; how gladly would I know whether I have fittingly united my harmonies with yours. Advice too, which would be accepted as very truth, would be extremely welcome to me, for I love the latter above all things and it shall never be said of me veritas odium parit.—It is very possible that a number of your poems which must ever remain unique, set to music by me, will soon be published, among them "Rastlose Liebe."[14] How highly would I value some general observations from you on the composition or setting to music of your poems!— Now a request to Y.E. I have composed a Grand Mass which, however, I do not want to publish at present, but which is to be sent to the principal courts; the honorarium for the same is 50 ducats only. I have addressed myself in the matter to the Grand Ducal Weimarian Embassy, which has accepted the appeal to His Serene Highness and promised to deliver it. The Mass can also be used as an oratorio and everyone knows that the benevolent societies are suffering from the lack of such things!—My request consists in this, that Y.E. call the attention of His Serene Highness, the Grand Duke, to this matter so that His Highness may also subscribe. The Grand Ducal Weimarian Embassy gave me to understand that it would be very beneficial if the Grand Duke could be induced to regard the matter favorably in advance.—I have composed [geschrieben] so much but have *gained from it* [erschrieben] scarcely a thing.[15] Now I am no longer alone

---

[13] From Schlösser's *Persönliche Erinnerungen an Beethoven*, published in *Hallelujah*, VI (1885), Nos. 20 and 21. (TDR, IV, 362, n. 3.)

[14] Sketched in 1804 but unfinished. See *II Beeth.*, p. 575 and Hans Boettcher, *Beethoven als Liederkomponist*, p. vi. (Cf. TDR, IV, 364,

n. 2.)

[15] Beethoven is playing on words—"schrieben," to write or to compose, and "erschrieben" —to gain by writing. "Ich habe so vieles geschrieben, aber *erschrieben*—beinahe gar nichts."

but have for six years been father to the son of my deceased brother, a promising youth in his sixteenth year, wholly devoted to learning and already at home in the rich literature of ancient Greece. But in these regions such things cost a great deal and, in the case of young students, not only the present but also the future must be borne in mind; and as much as I formerly kept my thoughts directed aloft I must now also turn my gaze *earthwards*—My income is *worthless*[16]—My poor health has for several years made it impossible for me to make professional journeys or to seize upon the many opportunities which yield *profit!* Could I completely recover my health, I might expect other and better things. —Y.E. must not think that it is because I am asking a favor that I have dedicated "Meeresstille und glückliche Fahrt" to you—this was already done in May, 1822. I had not thought of this method of making the Mass known at that time—not till a few weeks ago.—The respect, love and esteem which I have cherished for the only and immortal Goethe since the days of my youth have remained with me. Feelings like this are not easily put into words, especially by a bungler *like myself*, who has always been bent only on making *tones* his own. But a singular feeling impels me to tell you this, inasmuch as I live in your works—I know that you could not refuse to help an artist who feels only too keenly how far *mere monetary reward* is from *his art.* Yet now he is compelled by *necessity because of others* to work and labor *for others*—The good is always plain to us and therefore I know that Y.E. will not deny my request—

A few words from you would fill me with happiness—

I remain, Your Excellency, with the sincerest and most unbounded respect,

Beethoven.

According to Schindler, who was surely in a position to know, no answer to this letter was ever received; nor did the Grand Duke subscribe. That the invitation reached its destination may safely be assumed from Beethoven's remark about the interest displayed in the plan at the embassy; but the document is not to be found in the archives.

It was an unfortunate time for Goethe, who was now 73 years old. The Swiss student, Frederic Soret records in his conversations with the poet, for February, 1823: "Goethe was very ill in the course of this month." From Goethe's own diaries during the month there is mention of bloodletting, fever and delirium, and at one point the physicians thought they would not be able to save him.[17] A spring of convalescence and a stay at Marienbad during June and July in which Goethe was absorbed by his infatuation for the youthful Ulrike von Levetzow ruled out his penning an answer to the composer.

Bavaria's story is a short one. In a Conversation Book towards the close of May, Schindler writes: "A negative answer has come from Bavaria." To the King of Naples, Beethoven sent a French copy of the letter of invitation practically identical with the formula, and also to the King of France. In

---

[16] "Mein Gehalt (income) ist ohne *Gehalt*" (without worth). The pun cannot be translated into English.

[17] Ludwig Lewisohn, *Goethe: The Story of*

a Man (New York, 1949), II, p. 320. See also Romain Rolland, *Goethe et Beethoven* (Paris, 1930), p. 96.

the latter case Cherubini was asked to be the intermediary. The draft of Beethoven's letter to him is still preserved among the Schindler papers in Berlin. Beethoven's interpolations in bad French are given without change:

Highly respected Sir!

It is with great pleasure that I embrace the opportunity to approach you in writing. In spirit I am with you often enough, inasmuch as I value your works more than all others written for the stage. However, the beautiful world of art must deplore the fact that for a considerable period no new theatrical work of yours of large dimensions has appeared, at least not in our Germany. Highly as your other works are esteemed by true connoisseurs, it is a veritable loss to art *not yet* to possess a new product of your great mind for the theatre. True art remains imperishable and the genuine artist feels sincere pleasure in real and great products of genius; and so I too am enraptured whenever I hear a new work of yours and feel as great an interest in it as in my own works.—In brief, I honor and love you—If it were not for my continual ill health I could see you in Paris, and with what extraordinary delight would I discuss artistic matters with you?! —And here I must add that to every artist and art-lover I always speak of you with enthusiasm, otherwise you might perhaps[18] believe, since I am about to ask a favor of you, this this was merely an introduction to the subject. I hope, however, that you will not attribute such low-mindedness to me—

My request is as follows: I have just completed a grand solemn Mass, and I desire to send it to the European courts, because for the present I do not wish to publish it. Through the French Embassy here I have forwarded an invitation to His Majesty the King of France to subscribe to this work. I know that if you would advise His Majesty to take the Mass, he would surely do so. Ma situation critique demande que je ne fixe seulement come ordinaire mes pensées aux ciel au contrairs, il faut les fixer en bas pour les necessites de la vie; whatever may be the fate of my request to you, I shall always love and honor you et vous resteres toujours celui de mes contemporains, que je l'estime le plus si vous me voulez faire une estréme plaisir, c'etoit si m'ecrireres quelques lignes, ce que me soulagera bien—l'art unie touta le monde, how much more then true artists, et peut etres vous me dignes aussi, de me mettre also to be counted amongst this number,

avec la plus haute estime,

votre ami e serviteur

Beeth.

The letter was despatched on March 15. Cherubini did not receive it, and as late as 1841 expressed his great regret at the miscarriage which, however, worked no harm to the enterprise. King Louis XVIII not only subscribed for the Mass but within less than a year sent Beethoven a gold medal weighing twenty-one Louis d'or, showing on the obverse side the bust of the King and on the reverse, within a wreath, the inscription: "Donnée par le Roi à Monsieur Beethoven." Duke d'Achâts, First Chamberlain of the King, accompanied the gift with the following letter:

---

18 According to TDR, IV, 368, this word is not clear. The present editor is grateful for Miss Anderson's correct reading (*A* 1154).

I hasten to inform you, Monsieur, that the King received with favor the gift of the Score of Your Mass set to Music and charged me to send you a gold medal of him in effigy. I am pleased to be able to transmit to you the evidence of His Majesty's satisfaction and I take this occasion to offer you the assurance of my respectful consideration.

First Chamberlain of the
King's Chamber
Duke d'Achâts

Tuileries, February 20, 1824

"This was a distinction," says Schindler, "than which one more significant never fell to the lot of the artist during his life";[19] but the biographer certainly is in error when he intimates that the medal was given in payment of the subscription price. Beethoven informed Archduke Rudolph that the King had accepted the invitation in his letter of July 1, 1823; the medal was received early in 1824, over eight months later. Beethoven's needs and the reply which he gave the messenger from Prussia when he offered a decoration instead of the 50 ducats, indicate plainly enough how he felt as to the remuneration. Evidently King Louis XVIII paid the money in the regular way and sent the medal as a special mark of distinction.

No subscription was received from the King of Naples. The negotiations with the Grand Duke of Tuscany were more successful, though they dragged on into the next year. They were a subject of discussion in the Conversation Book in which Count Lichnowsky, brother Johann and nephew Karl took part. From remarks there recorded it appears that an appeal was also made to Empress Maria Louisa, Duchess of Parma. Here the agent was again Odelgha and there was a plan to interest Countess Neuberg. Count Lichnowsky seems to have suggested the name of Maria Louisa and offered to write to Count Neuberg, whom he knew, on the subject. It looks also as if the case of the Grand Duke of Tuscany had been exceptional, in that the Mass had been forwarded before the subscription had been received; this at least might be the interpretation of a remark noted by Karl: "I shall go to Odelgha on Sunday. We must get to work, or they will keep the Mass and send nothing."

Schindler says that Beethoven sent a carefully written letter to the King of Sweden to accompany the invitation; but nothing came of it. The King of Denmark subscribed, but as we hear nothing of the particulars, it is most likely that everything went smoothly in his case.

Prince Galitzin was asked to make a plea to the Russian Court and reported in a letter to Beethoven, dated June 2, that the invitation had been accepted and the official notification would follow in due course through the Russian Embassy. The money came soon afterwards. On July 9, Schindler writes in a jocular vein, using a metaphor which had already done service in Beethoven's correspondence:

[19] *Biogr.*, II, p. 20. (TDR, IV, 369.)

I take pleasure in reporting to you herewith, that by command of the Emperor of all the Russias, 50 horsemen in armor are arrived here as a Russian contingent to do battle under you for the Fatherland. The leader of these choice troops is a Russian Court Councillor. Herr Stein, pianoforte maker, has been commissioned by him to quarter them on you. Rien de nouveau chez nos voisins jusqu'ici.

Fidelissimus Papageno.[20]

The director of the business affairs of the Russian Embassy, von Obreskow, appears to have made inquiry as to how the fee was to be paid. Beethoven instructs Schindler as follows:

The letter to H.v.Obreskow follows. Take it along with you and say concerning the money that only a receipt need be sent to me for which, as soon as I return it, the money can be paid to the bearer of the receipt.—As soon as I receive this money you will receive 50 fl. V.S. right away for your trouble. Say nothing more than necessary, for people only find fault with it. Also do not speak of the Mass as not being finished which is not true, for the new pieces are only additions—Don't trouble me with anything else—

Papageno's master wishes you well.

On the back of the page, Beethoven adds a postscript starting on the right hand side in which he employs a device for insertion commonly used in the sketchbooks. At the syllable *vi-* the text proceeds to the answering syllable *de* (on the left hand side) for the words to be inserted.

de if there is occasion,	I have indicated your address.
Always bear in mind	Tell them, but inconspicuously—*vi-*
that these same persons represent	in the appropriate place, how
Majesty itself.	France also simply
	sent you the money—

Impatience at the non-delivery of the Mass at the expected time must have been expressed by the Russian Embassy, for in a note which Schindler dates "in the winter of 1824," Beethoven says:

Mr. v. Schindler:
Here is the Paquett for the Russian Embassy. Please look after it at once—moreover say that I shall soon visit him in person, inasmuch as it hurts me that lack of confidence has been felt in me. I thank God I am in a position to prove that I do not deserve it in any way nor will my honor permit it!—

Prince Galitzin, meanwhile, also became a subscriber, and in a letter of August 3 proposed that the Mass be published by popular subscription at four or five ducats, as there were not many amateurs who could afford to pay 50 ducats for a written copy. "All that I can do," the Prince writes in conclusion, "is to beg you to put me down among your subscribers and to send me a

---

[20] "Papageno" was the name applied to Schindler in his notes when Beethoven wished to enjoin silence on his factotum; the allusion, of course, being to the lip-locked birdcatcher in Mozart's *Zauberflöte*. (TK, III, 102, n. 1.)

copy as soon as possible so that I may produce it at a concert for the benefit of the widows of musicians which takes place annually near Christmas." Plainly, the Prince's subscription was in the existing category; there was no other, and Beethoven, in view of the invitation to the courts, could not at once entertain the subject of a popular subscription for a printed edition. Galitzin also acceded to Beethoven's request that the 50 ducats already deposited in Vienna by him for a quartet be applied to the account of the Mass. He writes of September 23 (October 3): "I have just received your letter of the 17th and hasten to answer that I have instructed the house of Henikstein to pay you immediately the 50 ducats which I fancied had long ago been placed at your disposal." The bankers Henikstein sent the Prince Beethoven's receipt for the 50 ducats "which we paid to him on the order and account of Your Highness as fee for the Mass which we have forwarded through the High State Chancellery." The score was in the hands of Prince Galitzin on November 29, but the performance which he projected did not take place until April 6, 1824. It was the first complete performance of the Mass anywhere.

On June 21, 1823, Beethoven also sent a letter to the St. Petersburg Philharmonic Society announcing the completion of the Mass. He invited the interest of the "illustrious art connoisseurs of the Russian nation" and presented the usual opportunity: a manuscript copy of the Mass for the fee of 50 ducats.[21]

A special invitation to subscribe to the Mass was not extended to the Austrian court for reasons which, no doubt, were understood between Beethoven and Archduke Rudolph and which may have been connected with efforts which were being made at the time to secure a court appointment for the composer. At the request of Artaria, however, an invitation was sent to Prince Nikolaus Esterhazy. Beethoven had little confidence in the successful outcome of the appeal, probably with a recollection in his mind of the Prince's attitude toward him on the occasion of the production of the Mass in C in 1807. His lack of faith in the enterprise was justified; Esterhazy did not subscribe.

No invitation was sent to the English court, probably because Beethoven cherished a grudge in that quarter; but subscriptions were asked of two large singing societies—the Singakademie of Berlin and the Cäcilienverein of Frankfurt. Zelter was director of the Singakademie, and to him Beethoven writes on Feb. 8:[22]

My gallant fellow artist!

Let me make a request to you in writing, since we are so far apart that we cannot speak with one another. Unfortunately too writing can occur only occasionally —I have written a Grand Mass, which might also be performed as an oratorio

[21] See MacArdle & Misch, *New Beethoven Letters*, p. 421.

[22] For the corrected German version of this letter, I am indebted to the late Miss Anderson.

(for the benefit of the poor—as is the good custom that has been introduced), but I did not want to publish it in print in the ordinary way, but to give it to the principal courts only. The fee amounts to 50 ducats. Excepting the copies subscribed for, none will be issued, so that the Mass will be practically only in manuscript—However, there must be a passable number if the composer is to gain anything—I have sent a request from here to the Royal Prussian Embassy that His Majesty the King of Prussia might be inclined to take a copy, and have also written Prince Radziwill concerning his taking an interest in it—I ask of you that you do what *you* can in the matter. A work of this kind might also be of service to the Singakademie, for there is little to keep it from being performed by voices alone; but the more doubled and multiplied the latter in combination with the instruments, the more effective it would be—It might also be in place as an oratorio, such as is in demand for the Benevolent Societies—As I have been more or less ill for several years and therefore am not in the most splendid circumstances, I have had recourse to this means. I have written much—but *gained from it*—almost zero!—I am more disposed to send my glances upwards—but a man is compelled for his own and for others' sake to direct them downwards. But this too is part of man's destiny—With sincere regards I embrace you, my dear fellow artist.

Your friend Beethoven

The letter will be seen, on comparison with that written on the same day to Goethe, to be either a draft for the latter in part or an echo of it. There is the same pun on "geschrieben" and "erschrieben," the same lament about having to keep his eyes on the ground while desirous to keep them on higher things, the same reference to the value of the Mass for concert purposes on behalf of charity. As this last point is one which would naturally occur to the writer in addressing a musician and not at all naturally in an appeal to a poet, it is safe to say that the Zelter letter was written first. It is an unpleasant duty to call attention to a very significant difference between this letter and the invitation issued to the courts as well as the letter to Goethe. In the latter he distinctly says that the Mass will not be published in the ordinary way "for the present," thus reserving the privilege of printing it at a future time. To Zelter, and presumably to the Frankfurt society, he plainly intimates that there is to be no publication in the ordinary way at all. It is not a violent presumption that Zelter may have observed this discrepancy, which was of vital moment to his society, and that this may have caused the termination of the negotiations, which began auspiciously enough in a letter written by Zelter on February 22 in reply to Beethoven's. In this letter he said he was ready to purchase the Mass for the Singakademie at his own risk, provided Beethoven would adapt it to the use of the society—that is, arrange it for performance practically without instruments—a proceeding, he explained, which would make it practicable for all similar concert institutions. To this letter Beethoven replied on March 25:

. . . I have carefully considered your suggestion for the Singakademie. If it should ever appear in print I will send you a copy without pay. It is true that it might almost be performed *a la cappella*, but to this end the whole would have to be arranged. Perhaps you have the patience to do this.—Besides, there is already a movement in it which is entirely *a la cappella* and I am inclined to call this style the only true church style. I thank you for your readiness. From *such an honored* artist *as you*, I would never accept anything.—I honor you and desire only an opportunity to prove this to you in deed.

There the matter ended, so far as is known. The negotiations with the Frankfurt society were more successful. On May 19, 1823, J. N. Schelble, director, wrote saying: ". . . The hope of receiving a new composition from you, great master, inspires all the members and reinvigorates their musical zeal; I therefore request you as soon as it is convenient to you to forward a copy of your Mass to me. . . ."

There were, therefore, as appears from this account and the list of names sent in November, 1825, to the publishers of the Mass, ten subscribers, namely: the Czar of Russia, the Kings of Prussia, Saxony, France and Denmark, the Grand Dukes of Tuscany and Hesse-Darmstadt, Princes Galitzin and Radziwill and the Cäcilia Society of Frankfurt. Beethoven's receipts, 500 ducats, were very materially reduced, how much we cannot say, by the costs of copying. In this work his principal helper was a professional copyist named Schlemmer, who could best decipher his manuscript. But Schlemmer was sickly and died before the year was over; his successor was named Rampel, and seems to have caused Beethoven a great deal of annoyance; he probably was made to bear a great deal of the blame for the tardiness of the work, for which, also, the composer's frequent alterations were in part responsible.

The story of Beethoven's plan to get private subscriptions to the Mass has taken the reader well into the year 1823. This story has been related here in order to provide a necessary background for the understanding of Beethoven's other negotiations of the year, especially those concerning the publication of the Mass. It is now time to turn back and take up the other events of the year, presenting them as much as possible in chronological order.

On January 20 Beethoven wrote a little piece for voice and pianoforte in the album of Baroness Cäcilie v. Eskeles,[23] on the words of Goethe: "Der edle Mensch sei hülfreich und gut."[24]

The Symphony in D minor, on which he was working industriously, had been the subject of correspondence between himself and Ries (in London) for some time before the year opened. On July 6, 1822, Beethoven had inquired of his old pupil: "What would the Philharmonic Society be likely to offer me for a symphony?" Ries, evidently, laid the matter before the

[23] Wife of the Viennese banker, Baron Bernard v. Eskeles. See KHV, pp. 622-23 for clarification of dedicatee, long thought to be the daughter of v. Eskeles (Baroness Marie, since 1825 Countess Wimpffen).

[24] From the beginning of the last stanza of "Das Göttliche":

"Edel sei der Mensch,
   hülfreich und gut!"

directors of the society who, at a meeting on November 10, "resolved to offer Beethoven fifty pounds for a M.S. symphony."[25] Ries conveyed the information to Beethoven in a letter dated November 15. In a reply dated December 20, 1822, Beethoven writes:

My dear Ries!

Overwhelmed with work I could not answer your letter of November 15 until now—I accept with pleasure the offer to write a new symphony for the Philharmonic Society even though the honorarium from Englishmen cannot match that of other nations; for I myself would write gratis for the first artists of Europe, if I were not still poor Beethoven. If I were in London, what would I not write for the Philharmonic Society! For Beethoven can compose, God be thanked —though he can do nothing else in this world. If God gives me back my health, which at least has improved somewhat, I shall yet be able to comply with all the requests which have come from all parts of Europe, even from North America; and I might yet make my way in the world.

The request from North America was for an oratorio from the Handel and Haydn Society in Boston[26] and was made from an unidentified Boston banker to the Viennese banker Geymüller. In a Conversation Book of early April, 1823, Dr. Johann Bihler writes: "The oratorio for Boston?" and Beethoven answers: "I cannot write what I should like best to write, but that which the pressing need of money obliges me to write. This is not to say that I write only for money—when this period is past I hope to write what for me and for art is above all—Faust."[27]

A glimpse into the occupations, cares and perplexities which beset Beethoven at this period is given by the first letter in the series to Ries written in the new year—on February 5, 1823:

My dear good Ries!

I have no further news to give you about the Symphony; but meanwhile you may confidently count on receiving it, since I have made the acquaintance here of a very amiable and cultivated man, who holds an appointment in our Imperial Embassy at London.[28] He will undertake later to forward the Symphony to you in London, so that *it will soon be in London*. Were I not so poor that I am obliged to live by pen I would accept nothing at all from the P.Soc; as it is I must wait until the fee for the Symphony is deposited here.—But to give you an evidence of my affection for and confidence in the society I have already delivered the new Overture referred to in my last letter to the aforementioned gentleman of the Imperial Embassy. As he is to depart from here in a few days, he will deliver it to you in person in London. Goldschmidt will no doubt *know where you live, if not, please tell him*, so that this accommodating gentleman will not be obliged long to hunt for you—I leave to the Society all the arrangements about

[25] George Hogarth, *The Philharmonic Society of London* (London, 1862), p. 31. (TK, III, 110, n. 2.)

[26] See Charles C. Perkins, *History of the Handel and Haydn Society of Boston* (Boston, 1883), I, p. 87. (TK, III, 87.)

[27] Schünemann, III, p. 149.

[28] A man named Bauer, who is referred to by name in the next letter to Ries to be quoted. (TDR, IV, 382, n. 3.)

the Overture which, like the Symphony, it can keep for eighteen months. Not until after the lapse of that time shall I publish it. And now another request: my brother here, who keeps a horse and carriage, wanted to derive advantage from me and so, without asking me, he offered the Overture in question to a publisher in London named Boosey. Let him be told that at present it is impossible to say whether he can have the Overture or not, I will write to him myself. —It all depends on the Philharmonic Society. Say to him please that my brother made a mistake in the matter of the *Overture*—As to the other works which he wrote to him about, he may have them. He *bought* them of me in order to *profit* from them, as I now see—O frater! I beg of you to write to me as soon as possible after you have received the Overture whether the P. Soc. will take it, for otherwise I shall publish it soon—I have heard *nothing* of your Symphony dedicated to me. If I did not look upon the dedication as a sort of challenge for which I might give you revanche I should long ago have dedicated some work to you. *As it is,* I have always thought that I must first see your *work*; and how willingly would I show you my gratitude in some manner. I am deeply your debtor for so many proofs of your affection and for favors. If my health is improved by a bath-cure which I am to take in the coming summer I shall kiss your wife in London in 1824—

Ever yours

Beethoven

How Johann became involved with transactions concerning his brother's compositions becomes clear from a letter to Schott in the next year in which Beethoven says "I have given to my brother, to whom I am indebted for many kindnesses, instead of a sum of money which I owe him, the following works"; and he listed an overture (Op. 124), three songs and some bagatelles.[29] In his next letter to Ries on February 23, 1823, after referring again to the Symphony and the Overture, he informed him that he had sent two sonatas (Op. 110 and 111) and was sending eleven bagatelles (Op. 119) and asked Ries to traffic with them as shrewdly as possible. Had he received a dedication from Ries, he said, he would have at once inscribed the Overture to him.

On March 22 Ries was informed that the symphony would be finished in two weeks, and on April 25 that it would be received soon along with thirty-three variations (Op. 120) dedicated to his wife.

Not long afterward Beethoven wrote another letter to Ries which has been preserved only in part:

—in addition to these hardships I have many debts to pay, for which reason I would be glad to have the honorarium paid to me if you have disposed of the Mass. By then the London copy will have been made. There need be no scruples because of the few souverains who are to get copies of it. If a local publisher made no objections, there ought to be still fewer in London, since I bind myself in writing that not a note of it shall appear in print or otherwise—and, what is

---

[29] See *A* 1321. The bagatelles offered to Johann were his last set, Op. 126, composed at the end of 1823.

more the Revers is a guarantee for everything. Attend to everything soon for your poor friend; I await also your plan of travel. Things have become too awful. I am tormented by the Cardinal worse than before; if I don't go there, it is a crimen legis majestatis. As for payment, I must draw my wretched salary with the aid of a *stamp*— Since you apparently wish a dedication from me, how happy I am to gratify a wish from you, much happier than one from the *finest of fine gentlemen*, entre nous; the devil only knows how one can keep from falling into their hands. The dedication of the new symphony will be *to you*—I hope eventually to receive *yours* to me—

Bauer has herewith a new document for the King which is concerned only with the Battle of Vittoria, of which he has taken along a printed copy. There is no mention of the Mass. Be good enough to tell H. Bauer to open the old one in order to see its contents. H. Bauer does not have the Mass. The thing is for Bauer to open the letter to the King that he took from here, whereupon he will see what was written to the King about the Battle of Vittoria. *The enclosed communication holds to this in the same way*, but there is no longer mention of the Mass. Our amiable friend Bauer shall see only if he can get a butcher's knife or a tortoise for it. It is understood that the printed copy of the score of the Battle will also be given to the King—Bauer *returns here at the end of May.* Please then let him know *right away* that which concerns him—The present letter will cost you a lot of money, so subtract it from what you send me. I am so sorry to have caused you this trouble—God be with you—Best regards to your wife until I myself am there. Watch out, you think I am *old*, but I am a *young old man*—as ever your

Beethoven

Neither Ries received a dedication; the Ninth Symphony was dedicated to the King of Prussia and the Diabelli Variations to Antonie Brentano.

Of the earlier inaction of King George IV upon receiving the score of *The Battle of Vittoria* there has already been mention. Before leaving for England, Bauer visited Beethoven and an entry of his in a Conversation Book of middle February refers again to this matter:

I am of the opinion that the King had it performed, but perhaps nobody reminded him that on that account he ought to answer.

His next entry reads:

I will carry a letter to the King and direct it in a channel which will insure its delivery, since I cannot hand it over in person.[30]

The character of the address to the king can be guessed at from the following draft for an earlier letter which was found amongst Schindler's papers:

In thus presuming, herewith, to submit my most obedient prayer to Your Majesty, I venture at the same time to supplement it with a second.[31]

[30] Schünemann, III, p. 14.

[31] The first request, presumably, was to have been an invitation to subscribe to the Mass in D, and the letter to Ries shows that Beethoven decided subsequently to strike the King of England from his list. (TK, III, 112, n. 1.)

Already in the year 1813, the undersigned took the liberty, at the frequent requests of several Englishmen then living here, to send to Your Majesty his composition entitled "Wellington's Battle and Victory at Vittoria" which no one possessed at that time. The then Imperial Russian Ambassador, Prince Rasoumowsky, undertook to send the work to Your Majesty by a courier.

For many years the undersigned cherished the sweet wish that Your Majesty would graciously make known the receipt of his work to him; but he has not yet been able to boast of this happiness, and had to content himself with a brief notice from Herr Ries, his former worthy pupil, who reported that Your Majesty had been pleased graciously to deliver the work to the then Musical Director, Herr Salomon and Herr Smart for public performance in Drury Lane Theatre. This appears also from the English journals, which added, as did Herr Ries, that the work had been received with extraordinary favor not only in London but elsewhere. Inasmuch as it was extremely humiliating to the undersigned to learn all this from indirect sources, Your Majesty will surely pardon his sensitiveness and graciously permit him to observe that he spared neither time nor cost to lay this before Your Exalted Person in the most proper manner in order to provide a pleasure for Your Majesty.

From this the undersigned concludes, that it may have been improperly submitted to Your Majesty and inasmuch as the most obedient petition which is now submitted, enables him again to approach Your Majesty, he takes the privilege of handing to Your Majesty an accompanying printed copy of the Battle of Vittoria in score, which has been set aside for this highest purpose ever since 1815 and which has been retained so long because of the uncertainty felt by the undersigned concerning the matter.

Convinced of the lofty wisdom and graciousness which Your Majesty has hitherto shown toward art and artists to their appreciation and good fortune, the undersigned flatters himself that Your Majesty will graciously condescend to take all this in consideration and grant his most humble petition.

Convaincu de la haute Sagesse dont Votre Majesté a toujours su apprecier l'art ainsi que de la haute faveur qu'elle accorde a l'artiste le soussigné se flatte que Votre Majesté prendra l'un et l'autre en consideration et vaudra en grace condescendre a sa tres-humble demande.

a Vienne le 24 fevrier.[32]

Among the friends who were offering Beethoven advice in the handling of his affairs was Count Moritz Lichnowsky. According to Schindler, there was a difference of opinion between the count and the composer concerning the signing of an agreement with Steiner, whereupon Beethoven improvised the following canon[33] in the much frequented tavern "zur goldenen Birne":

"Written on Febr. 20 1823 in the coffee house zur Birn on the Landstrasse" [note by Schindler]

[32] According to Miss Anderson, *A*, p. 1005, n. 2, this was added to Beethoven's draft in another hand.

[33] From the Schindler papers (portfolio 1, no. 35) in the Berlin Library. Published in Hermann Hirschbach's *Musik-Krit-Repertorium*, I₁₀ (1844), p. 468. (TDR, IV, 388, n. 5.) See Ludwig Misch, *Beethoven Studies* (Norman, 1953), pp. 121-22. Misch's reading is used here except for his misprint on the final note of measure 4.

Bester Herr Graf   Sie sind ein Schaf!   Bester Herr Graf   Sie sind ein Schaf! Bester Herr Graf
[Best Mister Count You are a fool!]

Sie sind ein Schaf!   Bester Herr Graf   Sie sind ein Schaf!

Beethoven, however, was not always in such a gay mood; financial difficulties were now crowding in on him. First of all, the debt remained to his
friend Franz Brentano in Frankfurt. Meanwhile, Steiner, who may have
thought that consideration was no longer incumbent on him, now that
Beethoven was offering his works to other publishers, pressed him for the
money which he had lent him and threatened to sue him for the balance
of the debt. Beethoven presented a counter-claim and demanded that Steiner
publish a number of compositions which he had purchased but had not issued. Steiner, now the owner of the works, refused. At this time Beethoven
had no ready means at his disposal. He appealed to his brother Johann to go
security for him, but he refused. Then he consulted Dr. Bach, who advised
him to dispose of one of his shares of bank stock. Beethoven resisted this advice as long as he could, since he considered these shares not his own but
his nephew's, so he attempted instead to use them as security for a loan.
Schindler was called upon to act as agent in this matter, as is shown by the
following notes. The contents of the first part of this first one date Beethoven's trouble with Steiner as being in the early stages of the organization
of subscriptions for the Mass:

Very best optimus optime!
    I am sending you the calendar. All the local embassies are indicated by where
the paper is stuck in. If you would soon make me out a list of the courts from
this, then we could hurry things up. By the way, I ask you to *co-operate with him*
when my brother interposes; otherwise we might experience *pain* rather than *joy*—
    Try to find some philanthropist who will make me a loan on a bank share, so
that, first, I need not put too severe a strain on the generosity of my special friends
the B[rentanos] and may not myself be subjected to need because of the withholding of this money, due to the beautiful arrangements and precautions made
by my *dear* brother!—It would be lovely if you appeared at Mariahilf this afternoon around 3.30 or even in the forenoon—
    It must not be apparent to people that the *money* is needed—

In another note he writes:

Dear S,
    Do not forget the B.S. [bank share], it is highly necessary. I should not like to
be sued for no reason whatsoever. The conduct of my brother is worthy of him—
The tailor is coming today and I hope to hold him off with kind words.
                                            Very hastily yours

Schindler added the following note to the letter: "In 1823 the firm of Steiner and Haslinger had threatened Beethoven with a law suit in connection with his debt of 800 gulden V.S.; this happened before any honorarium had been received for the subscription copies of the Mass. Therefore it was necessary to sell a bank share in order to satisfy the creditors." ⟶In 1821 Beethoven was supposed to have begun paying semi-annual installments of 600 florins to Steiner, it will be remembered, and he must have been behind in his payments. However, if, as Schindler says, he sold a bank share, he should have realized about 1250 florins, V.S. on the sale, since, according to Steiner's letter to Beethoven of December 29, 1820, quoted previously, the capital amounted to 10,000 florins V.S. or 4000 florins C.M. Thus he could have liquidated the debt to Steiner with this money, if Schindler's figure of 800 florins is correct. That he did not do so completely, we shall see in the next chapter. Therefore, the inference is that he used it for other creditors as well. He was indebted to other publishers as we know, and even to such a tradesman as the tailor Lind, who had also threatened legal action against him.[34] The figure 800 is at variance with Beethoven's own description of the debt when he wrote on July 31, 1822, that it was about 3000 florins, plus interest. Thus, the picture remains confused, and only this much is certain, that he was deeply indebted,[35] and that this gave impetus to his plans for realizing profit from subscriptions for the Mass.

The Conversation Books of this period show that Schindler, despite his devotion to the master, was stubborn, and unlike the other close friends, dared express criticism or a contrary opinion as the following entries show: The first, in January:[36]

Don't be so undecided, my dear Master!—
now what do you wish me to do in regards to a bank share and how much is one worth?
I would arrange for it right away today in order to have done everything to achieve this purpose.

In April he writes:[37]

Don't think night and day about your debts, when you are well you'll pay them without any pain.—

It was while in this distressful state concerning his debts that he took the first step towards making his nephew his legal heir. On March 6, 1823, he wrote to Bach:

[34] See *A* 1128, 1129.
[35] See Max Unger, "Beethovens Konversationshefte als biographische Quelle," *DM*, Vol. 34, no. 12, pp. 380ff, for further discussion of Beethoven's debts before he had to sell his eighth bank-share.
[36] Schünemann, II, p. 325.
[37] *Ibid.*, III, p. 126.

Dear honored friend!

Death might come unannounced and give no time to make a legal will, there-fore I hereby attest with my own hand that I declare my beloved nephew Karl van Beethoven to be my universal heir and that after my death everything without exception *which can be called my property shall belong to him*—I appoint you to be his curator, and if there should be no testament after this you are also au-thorized and requested to find a guardian for my beloved nephew K. v. Beet-hoven—to the exclusion of my brother Johann van Beethoven—and secure his appointment according to law. I declare this writing to be valid for all time as being my last will before my death—I embrace you with all my heart—

Your true admirer and friend
Ludwig van Beethoven

The words excluding Johann from the guardianship were written on the third page of the document and on the first there was this later addition: "NB. In the way of capital there are 7 shares of bank stock, whatever else is found in cash is like the bank shares to be his." Shortly before his death he reiterated this bequest with modifications entailed by changed conditions.

In November, 1822, Anton Tayber, Imperial Court Composer, died; and this seemed a favorable opportunity for Beethoven to apply directly for the position. At the urging of Count Lichnowsky, this was done through the "Court Music-Count," Count Moritz Dietrichstein. Both proposed that Beethoven compose a mass for the Emperor. On February 23, 1823 Dietrich-stein wrote the following letter to Lichnowsky:[38]

Dear friend!

It would have been my duty long ago to reply to good Beethoven, since he came to me so trustfully. But after I had spoken with you I decided to break silence only after I had received definite information on the subject in question. I can now tell you positively that the post held by the deceased Tayber—who was not Chamber but Court Composer—is not to be filled again. I do not want to write to Beethoven because I do not like to disappoint a man whom I so sincerely respect, and therefore I beg of you when occasion offers to let him know the fact and then to inform me when and where I may meet him, as I have forgotten where he lives.

I am also sending you herewith the score of a mass by Reutter which Beet-hoven wished to see. It is true that H. M. the Emperor is fond of this style, but Beethoven, if he writes a mass, need not adhere to it. Let him follow the bent of his great genius and have a care only that the mass be not too long or too diffi-cult to perform;—that it be a *tutti* mass and have only short soprano and alto solos in the voices (for which I have two fine singing-boys)—but no tenor, bass or organ solos. . . . If he wishes he may introduce a violin, oboe or clarinet solo.

His Majesty likes to have fugues well worked out but not too long;—the *Sanctus* and *Osanna* as short as possible, in order not to delay the transubstantia-tion, and—if I may add something on my own account—the *Dona nobis pacem* connected with the *Agnus Dei* without marked interruption, and soft. In two

---

[38] See Schindler, *Biogr.*, II, pp. 29-31. (TDR, IV, 393, n. 1.)

masses by Handel (arranged from his anthems), two by Naumann and Abbé Stadler, this makes a particularly beautiful effect. These in brief, as results of my experience, are the things which are to be considered and I should congratulate myself, the court and art if our great Beethoven were soon to take the work in hand. . . .

On March 10 Dietrichstein sent Beethoven three texts for graduals and a like number for offertories from which to choose words to be used in the mass to be composed for the emperor. On the count's letter Beethoven wrote the memorandum: "Treat the gradual as a symphony with song—does it follow the Gloria?" Here we have some light on the subject which came up for thought during the account of Beethoven's negotiations with publishers for the Mass in D. It will be remembered that on one occasion he wrote to Peters that he had not made up his mind which mass he should have, and on another that he had three masses, two other publishers having asked for such works. Simrock's hopes, meanwhile, had been diverted from *the* mass to *a* mass. It would seem that Beethoven was much pleased with the interest manifested in his application by Count Dietrichstein, and looked with auspicious eye upon the latter's plan to put him into the Emperor's good books. There can scarcely be a doubt but that he gave considerable thought to the proposed mass while still at work on the Mass in D. He conceived the plan of accompanying the Kyrie with wind instruments and organ only in a "new mass," as he designates it,[39] and sketches for a *Dona nobis pacem* which have been found "for the mass in C-sharp minor"[40] point to a treatment which may be said to be in harmony, so far as can be seen, with Count Dietrichstein's suggestions.

Beethoven spoke of the "second" mass to others besides the publishers. Nothing came of it, however. He decided to postpone work on the mass for the Emperor, pleading the pressure of other obligations in the letter of thanks which he sent to Counts Lichnowsky and Dietrichstein. They and the Archduke Rudolph were greatly disappointed and, if Schindler is to be believed, the Archduke and Lichnowsky reproached him.[41]

In this period, too, the alluring vision of a new opera presented itself, haunted the minds of Beethoven and his friends for a space and then disappeared in the limbo of unexecuted projects. *Fidelio* had been revived on November 3, 1822, at the Kärnthnerthor Theatre. Its success was so great that the management of the theatre offered a commission to Beethoven for a new opera. Beethoven viewed the proposition favorably and his friends hailed it with enthusiasm, especially Count Moritz Lichnowsky. Beethoven's love for classic literature led him to express a desire for a libretto based on some story of the antique world. He was told that such were all worn thread-

---

[39] *II Beeth.*, p. 152. (TDR, IV, 395, n. 2.)
[40] *Ibid.*, pp. 541, 543. (TDR, IV, 395, n. 3.)
[41] Schindler bases his statements on alleged testimony of the Archduke's secretary Bau- meister, but there is no word of reproval in any of the letters of the two men which have been found. See *Biogr.*, II, p. 33. (TK, III, 117, n. 2.)

bare. In the Conversation Books we see what suggestions were offered by others: a text by Schlegel; Voltaire's tragedies; Schiller's *Fiesco*. Local poets and would-be poets were willing to throw themselves into the breach.

Friedrich August Kanne, editor of the musical journal published by Steiner and Co., wrote a libretto which Beethoven sent to Schindler with the following note:

I am sending you the book by K, which aside from the fact that the first act is lukewarm, has been so admirably written that it really doesn't require one of the first composers—I will not say that it would be just the most suitable things *for me*, but if I can rid myself of obligations to which I am bound, who knows what might happen—or can happen!

In haste your friend
Beethoven

Kindly let me know that you have received it.

Brother Johann writes in a Conversation Book at the end of January: "Spohrschild [*sic!*] visited me today, he sends his regards. And if you tell him to he will write an opera for you."[42] Johann Sporschil (or Sporschill), historian and publicist, was at that time ending his period of study in Vienna and had connections for a brief time with the composer. Beethoven evidently accepted his offer, for Sporschil set to work and composed a libretto in 2 acts, entitled *The Apotheosis in the Temple of Jupiter Ammon*,[43] which was apparently sent to Beethoven act by act. The result was a weak text concocted to serve as a substitute for the text to the *Weihe des Hauses* for which the music, it will be remembered, was drawn principally from the *Ruinen von Athen*. As other plans developed, Sporschil's piece was forgotten.

In the forefront of those urging Beethoven on to a new opera subject was Count Moritz Lichnowsky. In February he writes in a Conversation Book: "Recently I was with a certain Madam Neumann. 2 to 3 years ago she wrote a libretto, *Alfred the Great*, it is said to be very beautiful, I will bring it in 3 or 4 days"; and the count goes on to describe the work which contains, he has heard, a "fabulous spectacle."[44] At the same time he reports that he has been in touch with Grillparzer and writes a few pages later: "I am eager for an answer from Grillparzer. He has a beautiful command of language, a lot of fire and imagination and [is] qualified to write a big poetic work.... This would be something for a second opera.—If he writes something for you, his composition would be the winner."[45]

Franz Grillparzer (born in 1791) by this time was well known to the Viennese as a dramatic poet through his plays *Sappho, The Ancestress* and *The Golden Fleece*; he was now completing his tragedy *Ottokar*. —⟨Since

[42] Schünemann, II, p. 344.

[43] This libretto is among the Schindler papers in the Berlin State Library and has been published by Hans Volkmann, *Neues über Beethoven* (Berlin, 1904), pp. 67-72.

(TDR, IV, 397, n. 1.)

[44] Schünemann, II, pp. 395-96. Schünemann identifies the authoress as Marianna Neumann von Meissenthal (1768-1837).

[45] *Ibid.*, p. 397.

1813 he had had the security of a clerkship in the Lower Austrian revenue administration, and through the influence of his patron, Count Stadion, minister of finance, he was appointed poet to the Court Theatre in 1818. Already he and Beethoven had met several times, and, being musically educated, he admired the composer very highly. Beethoven's renewed interest in the poet, prompted by Lichnowsky, is shown in a note to Schindler: "I am asking you for Grillparzer's address; perhaps I will visit him myself."

Grillparzer has left us an account of his attempt to collaborate with Beethoven on an opera in his *Erinnerungen an Beethoven* (written in 1840).[46] According to this account it was Count Moritz Dietrichstein, director of both court theatres, who informed him that Beethoven was turning to him for a new libretto.[47]

"This request, I must confess, gave me no little embarrassment. Once I had the idea of writing a libretto, still remote enough in itself, I began to doubt if Beethoven who meanwhile had become completely deaf and whose latest compositions without detracting from their high worth possessed a quality of harshness, who to me seemed to be in conflict with the treatment of the singing voice; I doubted, I say, if Beethoven was still capable of composing an opera. The thought, however, of giving to a great man the opportunity for a work which would be at any rate of the first interest overcame all considerations and I agreed.

"From the dramatic material which I had set aside for future adaptation, there were two which, if necessary, would permit of operatic treatment. One was set in the realm of most intense emotion. But aside from the fact that I knew no lady singer who would be able to rise to the main role, I also did not want to give Beethoven the opportunity to step still closer to the extreme limits of music which lay nearby, threatening like precipices, in partnership with material that was semi-diabolical."

This was, as the Conversation Books show, *Drahomira,* a story drawn from Bohemian legendary history.[48] Schindler told Beethoven that the poet would adapt the subject for him, and Lichnowsky reported that the poet wanted to discuss the matter with him.[49] This was in late April. Thus *Drahomira* was considered seriously for a time along with a second subject about which Grillparzer writes: "When I choose the fable of Melusine, so far

---

[46] Grillparzer wrote his reminiscences as the result of reading Ludwig Rellstab's *Aus meinem Leben*. Grillparzer claimed that reference to his attempt at collaboration with Beethoven on an opera text was misrepresentative. The reference was a remark made by Beethoven to Rellstab in 1825: "It is so difficult to find a good libretto! Grillparzer promised me one, he had already written one, yet we couldn't really come to an understanding. I wanted something entirely different than he!" See Alf. Chr. Kalischer, *Beethoven und seine* *Zeitgenossen* (Berlin, 1908), iv, p. 165.

[47] Alfred Orel in his book *Grillparzer und Beethoven* (Vienna, 1941, p. 16), suggests that Lichnowsky, having sounded out both artists on the idea of collaborating, arranged to have the suggestion from an official source to Grillparzer, in view of Beethoven's pride and artistic conscience.

[48] Only sketches exist. Grillparzer has written "one of my earliest works, around 1809 or 1810." (TDR, iv, 399, n. 1.)

[49] Schünemann, iii, pp. 190, 200.

as possible I banished the reflective element and sought, by giving prominence to the chorus, creating powerful finales and treating the third act almost melodramatically, to adjust myself to the character of Beethoven's last period. I avoided a preliminary conference with the composer concerning the subject-matter, because I wanted to preserve the independence of my views. Moreover, it was possible to make alterations, and in the last instance it rested with him whether to compose the book or not. In order not to coerce him in the least I sent him the book by the same channel which had brought me the call. He was not to be influenced by personal considerations or embarrassed in any manner whatsoever."

The book appealed to Beethoven, but several conferences between him and the poet were necessary before it was brought into satisfactory shape. Grillparzer had excluded much of the material in the old legend which was unsuited to dramatic treatment, and strengthened the plot with conceits of his own invention. As soon as he had sent the text he went to Beethoven at Schindler's request. At first blush Beethoven was much pleased with the book, and he wrote Grillparzer a letter which delighted the poet. Grillparzer describes the visit to Beethoven at his lodgings in the Kothgasse which he made in company with Schindler:[50]

"I found him lying in soiled nightwear on a disordered bed, a book in his hand. At the head of the bed was a small door which, as I observed later, opened into the dining-room and which Beethoven seemed in a manner to be guarding, for when subsequently a maid came through it with butter and eggs he could not restrain himself, in the middle of an earnest conversation, from throwing a searching glance at the quantity of the provisions served—which gave me a painful picture of the disorder prevailing in his domestic economy.

"As we entered Beethoven arose from the bed, gave me his hand, poured out his feelings of good-will and respect and at once broached the subject of the opera. 'Your work lives here,' said he, pointing to his heart; 'I am going to the country in a few days and shall at once begin to compose it. Only, I don't know what to do with the hunters' chorus which forms the introduction. Weber used four horns; you see, therefore, that I must have eight; where will this lead to?' Although I was far from seeing the need of such a conclusion I explained to him that without injury to the rest of the book the hunters' chorus could be omitted, with which concession he seemed to be satisfied, and neither then nor later did he offer any objection to the text or ask that a change be made. He even insisted on closing a contract with me at once. The profits of the opera should be divided evenly between us, etc. I declared to him, and truthfully, that I had not thought of a fee or anything of the kind while at work. . . . Least of all was it to be the subject of conversation between us. He was to do with the book what he pleased—I

[50] Friedrich Kerst, *Die Erinnerungen an Beethoven* (Stuttgart, 1913), II, pp. 46-8.

would never make a contract with him. After a good deal of talk back and forth or rather of writing, for he could no longer hear speech, I took my leave, promising to visit him in Hetzendorf after he had settled himself there.

"I had hoped that he had given up all thoughts of business in regard to the matter; but a few days later my publisher, Wallishauser, came to me and said that Beethoven insisted upon the execution of a contract. If I could not make up my mind, Wallishauser suggested that I assign the property-right in the book to him and he would arrange with Beethoven, who was already advised of such a step. I was glad to get rid of the business, let Wallishauser pay me a moderate sum, ceded to him all the author's rights, and banished the matter from my thoughts. Whether or not they made a contract I do not know; but I would think so since otherwise Wallishauser would not have neglected to complain to me in his customary way about the money that he had risked."

Otto Jahn's notes of a conversation with Grillparzer state that Beethoven made a contract with Barbaja,[51] who was the *de facto* manager of the Kärnthnerthor Theatre, for 6,000 florins, V.S. (2,500 C.M.). Shortly afterward Barbaja abandoned the contract, saying to Beethoven that he knew that though he was bound by it he could not use the opera. Thereupon Beethoven tore up the document. On April 20, 1824, Duport[52] wrote to Beethoven that Barbaja had sent word from Naples that he would like to have an opera by Beethoven and would give time and terms as soon as he received assurance that his contract from the theatre would be extended from December 1. The extension was not granted. Schindler denied that a contract between manager and composer ever existed.

Unsatisfied with Meisl's revision of the *Ruinen von Athen*, Beethoven evidently turned to Grillparzer for an improved version of this text, for in early March Grillparzer writes in a Conversation Book:

I am making those changes which you consider necessary.

•~•

Please give me an approximate idea for the duet; for I am fitting my ideas with yours as regards what is supposed to be sung.

•~•

Perhaps this duet should have nothing other than Minerva's *joy* in contrast to Mercury's gloomy warnings.

•~•

I see that the invention of a new treatment is necessary; but it is not created at a moment's notice; the working out of it is much faster than the invention; thus naturally I must ask for time to consider it at home so that I can think it through.

---

[51] Domenico Barbaja was leaseholder of the theatre from 1822 to March, 1825, at which time he took it over.

[52] Louis Antoine Duport, formerly a dancer, was the real owner of the theatre at that time.

If I am to leave the book and my lines here with you, I ask you only to send it back by H. Schindler as soon as you don't need it anymore.—As for the idea of creating the illusion of the Greek epoch nowadays, the censor would give it an emphatic negative vote.

I believe that only that which is *completely sure* should be presented *publicly* even if something *great* is not immediately sent in to the world. This conviction cannot be contradicted. I mean—the power thereto to feel.

The result in relation to the cantata would then be: you have enough intrinsic worth here to hold on to book and material and to provide me with your observations which can be delivered; meanwhile I will be contemplating the material and so perhaps we will come to an understanding. In short the conclusion is: *deliberation*, and I won't do any work without first consulting you directly concerning the plan.[53]

Further conversations about opera plans with reference to both *Drahomira* and *Melusine* continued right up to the time that Beethoven moved to Hetzendorf in the middle of May. With consideration of the summer months the story of Grillparzer will be resumed.

A project which cropped out intermittently during 1823 was the writing of an overture on the musical motive suggested by the letters composing the name of Bach. The thought seems to have become fixed in his mind in 1822, though the device of using

as a motive in composition was at least as old as the Leipzig master's "Art of Fugue," and no doubt familiar to Beethoven. However, he was deeply engrossed in fugal writing at this period, and it is very likely, as Nottebohm suggests, that he conceived an overture on the motive as a tribute to Bach's genius.[54] Several sketches showing different forms of the theme appear in the books of 1823; and a collateral memorandum, "This overture with the new symphony, and we shall have a concert (*Akademie*) in the Kärnthnerthor Theatre," amongst sketches for the last quartets in 1825, shows that he clung to the idea almost to the end. Had Beethoven carried out all the plans for utilizing the theme which presented themselves to him between 1822 and 1825, there would have been several Bach overtures; unfortunately he carried out none.

On April 13, 1823, the boy Franz Liszt, who was studying with Carl Czerny and had made his first public appearance on the first day of the year,

[53] Schünemann, III, pp. 76-7. See also Kalischer, *op.cit.*, pp. 177-80.

[54] *II Beeth.*, pp. 577-80. (TDR, IV, 416, n. 1.)

gave a concert in the small Redoutensaal. A few days earlier he along with his father was presented to Beethoven by Schindler. There is an entry in a Conversation Book which, because of the handwriting and courtly language, was probably written by the father:

I have often expressed the wish to Herr von Schindler to make your high acquaintance and am rejoiced to be able now to do so. As I shall give a concert on Sunday the 13th I most humbly beg you to give me your high presence.[55]

The day before the concert, Schindler writes in a Conversation Book:

Little Liszt has urgently requested me humbly to beg you for a theme on which he wishes to improvise at his concert tomorrow. [Some words crossed out] humilime dominationem Vestram, si placeat scribere unum Thema—

He will not break the seal till the time comes.

The little fellow's free improvisations cannot yet, strictly speaking, be interpreted as such. The lad is a true pianist; but as far as *improvisation* is concerned, the day is still far off when one can say that he improvises.

Czerny Carl is his teacher.
Just eleven years.

Do come, it will certainly amuse Karl to hear how the little fellow plays.

It is unfortunate that the lad is in Czerny's hands—

After a brief change of subject Schindler returns to the conversation about Liszt:

Won't you make up for the rather unfriendly reception of the other day by coming tomorrow to little Liszt's concert?

It will encourage the boy. Will you promise me to come?[56]

According to Nohl who got the story from Liszt himself, Beethoven did attend the concert, went afterwards upon the stage, lifted up the prodigy and kissed him.[57] — At the concert, however, the theme upon which he

---

[55] Schünemann, III, p. 170.

[56] *Ibid.*, pp. 135-36.

[57] Ludwig Nohl, *Beethoven, Liszt und Wagner* (Vienna, 1814), p. 199. (TDR, IV, 417, n. 2.) Schindler's references to Liszt in his biography are unreliable since on the question of Beethoven's attendance at the concert he contradicts himself, claiming in the second edition (1845) that Beethoven was there and in the third edition (1860) that he was not. Schindler's increasing disapproval of Liszt appears to explain the contradiction. Liszt's

improvised was not one by Beethoven but a rondo theme of some 20 measures. According to the reviews the improvisation did not please.[58]

Amid the account of the negotiations concerning subscriptions to the Mass there was mentioned the name of Louis Schlösser who at this time was friendly with Beethoven and whose reception by him provides a fine example of the cordiality that Beethoven could offer to young artists. Louis Schlösser (1800-1886) was a violinist in the Darmstadt court orchestra and in the spring of 1822 he received a leave of several years in which to travel and broaden his knowledge through study with foreign artists. He went first to Vienna and then to Paris before returning to Darmstadt where he eventually became kapellmeister. His "Personal Reminiscences of Beethoven," an account written some 50 years later of his stay in Vienna, may be summarized here.[59] For months he was unsuccessful in his attempts to meet Beethoven. Finally on November 4, 1822, at the second performance of *Fidelio* he got his chance to see him at least from a distance. He was leaving the theatre with his friend Franz Schubert. "Together with us, three gentlemen, to whom I paid no further attention because their backs were turned to me, stepped out of a lower corridor; yet I was not a little surprised to see all those who were streaming by toward the lobby crowding to one side, in order to give the three plenty of room. Then Schubert very softly plucked my sleeve, pointing with his finger to the gentleman in the middle, who turned his head at that moment so that the bright light of the lamps fell on it and—I saw, familiar to me from engravings and paintings, the features of the creator of the opera I had just heard, Beethoven himself. My heart beat twice as loudly at that moment; all the things I may have said to Schubert I now no longer recall; but I well remember that I followed the Desired One and his companions (Schindler and Breuning, as I later discovered) like a shadow through crooked alleys and past high, gable-roofed houses, followed him until the darkness hid him from sight."

The opportunity to visit Beethoven was finally made by the Hessian Ambassador, Baron von Türkheim, as mentioned earlier, who gave Schlösser the commission of reporting to Beethoven the acceptance of the subscription to the Mass from that court. Climbing up the dark stairs to the first story of the Kothgasse No. 60, Schlösser turned as instructed to the door on the left. Finding no servant or maid, he opened the door which led into the kitchen "through which one had to pass to gain the living-rooms. . . . After repeatedly knocking in vain at the real living-room door, I entered and

---

own account of the meeting to his pupil, Ilka Horowitz-Barnay, which was made in 1875, the last year of his life, must also be used with caution because of the inaccuracies in detail. Frimmel believed that Nohl's account was essentially correct. See *Beethoven Studien*, II, pp. 93-105. Also Gerth Baruch, "Liszt and

Beethoven" in *Monthly Musical Record*, Vol. 66 (1936), p. 176.

[58] Schünemann, III, p. 135, n. 1.

[59] See footnote 13. For English translation see G. Schirmer's *Impressions of Contemporaries* (1926), pp. 132-48, from which we draw in part.

found myself in a rather commodious but entirely undecorated apartment; a large, four-square oak table with various chairs, which presented a somewhat chaotic aspect, stood in the middle of the room. On it lay writing-books and lead-pencils, music-paper and pens, a chronometer, a metronome, an ear-trumpet made of yellow metal and various other things. On the wall at the left of the door was the bed, completely covered with music, scores and manuscripts. I can recall only a framed oil-painting (it was a portrait of Beethoven's grandfather, for whom, as is known, he had a child-like reverence) which was the sole ornament I noticed. Two deep window-niches, covered with smooth paneling I mention only because in the first a violin and bow hung from a nail, and in the other Beethoven himself, his back to me, stood busily writing down figures and the like on the wood, already covered with scribblings."

Schlösser continues: "The deaf Master had not heard me enter, and it was only by stamping vigorously with my feet that I managed to attract his notice and he at once turned around, surprised to see a young stranger standing before him. Yet before I could address a single word to him, he commenced to excuse himself in the politest manner imaginable because he had sent out his housekeeper, and no one had been in attendance to announce me, the while quickly drawing on his coat; and then first asking me what I wished. Standing so near this artist, crowned with glory, I could realize the impression which his distinguished personality, his characteristic head, with its surrounding mane of heavy hair and the furrowed brow of a thinker, could not help but make on every one. I could look into those profoundly serious eyes, note the amiably smiling expression of his mouth when he spoke, my words always being received with great interest.

"My visit probably occurred shortly after he had eaten breakfast, for he repeatedly passed the napkin lying beside him across his snow-white teeth, a habit, incidentally, in which I noticed he often indulged. Steeped in my contemplation of him I entirely forgot the unfortunate man's total deafness, and was just about to explain my reason for being there to him when, fortunately, I recalled the uselessness of speaking at the last moment, and instead reverentially handed him the letter with its great seal."

Having expressed pleasure over the letter and the visit from him, Beethoven, continues Schlösser, "seized his ear-trumpet, so I explained the unbounded veneration accorded his genial works, with what enthusiasm they were heard, and what an influence the perfection of his intellectual creations had exercised on the cultural level of the day. Though Beethoven was so impervious to flattery of any kind, my words which came stammering from the depths of my soul, nevertheless seemed to touch him, and this induced me to tell him of my nocturnal pursuit of him after the performance of 'Fidelio.' 'But what prevented you from coming to see me in person?' he asked. 'I am sure you have been told any amount of contradictory nonsense; that I have been described as being an uncomfortable, capricious and arrogant person, whose music one might indeed enjoy, but who personally was to be avoided. I know these evil, lying tongues, but if the world considers me heartless, because I seldom meet people who understand my thoughts and feelings, and therefore content myself with a few friends, it wrongs me.'

"He had put down his ear-trumpet, for speaking into it agitated his nerves too greatly; his complaint, so he insisted, did not lie in the weakness of the auditory canals, but was seated in the intestines; his physicians in treating him had made a false diagnosis their point of departure, etc."

From then on, Schlösser wrote his questions on sheets of paper lying at hand. Beethoven spoke of particular passages in his works—would that Schlösser had preserved these remarks!—of the superficial art currents in Vienna, under Italian influence, the "speechlessness" of princely gentlemen. Then he asked Schlösser to show him his compositions, and after inviting him to a meal two days from then (March 3) he dismissed him with the greatest amiability. "Do not hesitate to avail yourself of me whenever I can be useful to you or be of service to you in any way," were his parting words.

On the morning of March 3, Beethoven surprised his admirer by mounting the four flights of steps to pay a return visit. Schlösser writes: "What I did and said in my first confusion I do not know; he, on the other hand, well aware of my embarrassment, at once began to speak: he had called, in order since it was such a pleasant day, to take me along for a little walk before dinner, and to improve the occasion by making the acquaintance of my lodgings, instruments, music and pictures of my parents, which I had mentioned to him. And he actually began to turn the pages of my copy-books of contrapuntal exercises, to look over my little hand-library, in which he found his favorites, Homer and Goethe, and I even had to submit to him a drawing of mine, and all of these things he examined attentively and praised." Beethoven's meal ended with coffee which he himself had prepared with a newly discovered machine, the construction of which he explained. Afterwards there was talk of his abandoned trip to England, his difficulties with the pension payments, *Fidelio* and the attempt to find a good new opera libretto, his new compositions; and as his guest left, he called out "To our next meeting!"

According to Schlösser, Beethoven was living "alternately in the delightful Helenenthal near Baden, where in Nature's open, his creative powers drew their richest nourishment among the hills and the heavily-laded woods, and where ideas, as he expressed himself, flowed to him in quantity. I visited him there, for he felt himself much indisposed: the germ of his future illness was even then present in his body, and yet I could not help but admire the strength of soul with which he fought against it. Nothing about him betrayed his suffering during our excursions in common through the surrounding country; the pictures of the landscapes captured completely his eyes and his feelings. . . ."

He continues: "Only a few weeks later we met in the *Kärthnerstrasse*. His keen eye discovered me first; and coming up to me he at once seized me by the arm with the words: 'If you can spare the time then accompany me to the *Paternostergassel*, to Steiner's (the music shop of Steiner and Haslinger) whom I want to give a good set-down. These publishers always have all sorts of excuses handy. When it comes to bringing out my compositions they would like to put it off until I am dead, because they think they would do a better business with them; but I shall know how to meet them.' (literally). At this encounter I had been so surprised at the very onset to find Beethoven, usually so careless about his attire, dressed with unwonted elegance, wearing a blue frock coat with yellow buttons, impeccable white knee-breeches, a vest to match, and a new beaver hat, as usual on the back of his head. I left him at the entrance to the shop, which was crowded with people while, thanking me for escorting him, he entered Mr. Steiner's office with the latter. I could not resist telling my teacher Mayseder, who lived in the neighborhood, about the striking metamorphosis of Beethoven's elegant appearance, an event which, however, caused Mayseder far less surprise than it had caused me, for he said with a smile: 'This is not the first time that his friends have taken his old clothes during the night and laid down new ones in their place; he has not the least suspicion of what has happened and puts on whatever lies before him with entire unconcern.' . . . I shall only add, to what has gone before, the last conversation I had with this profoundly serious thinker. One day I brought him a new, somewhat complicated composition I had written, and after he had read it he remarked: 'You have given too much, less would have been better; but that lies in the nature of heaven-scaling youth, which never thinks it possible to do enough. It is a fault maturer years will correct, however, and I still prefer a superfluity to a paucity of ideas.' 'What shall I do to find the right way and—how did you yourself attain that lofty goal?' I added, timidly. 'I carry my thoughts about with me for a long time, sometimes a very long time, before I set them down,' he replied. 'At the same time my memory is so faithful to me that I am sure not to forget a theme which I have once conceived, even after years have passed. I make many changes, reject and reattempt until I am satisfied. Then the working-out in breadth, length, height and depth begins in my head, and since I am conscious of what I want, the basic idea never leaves me. It rises, grows upward, and I hear and see the picture as a whole take shape and stand forth before me as though cast in a single piece, so that all that is left is the work of writing it down. This goes quickly, according as I have the time, for sometimes I have several compositions in labor at once, though I am sure never to confuse one with the other. You will ask me whence I take my ideas? That I cannot say with any degree of certainty: they come to me uninvited, directly or indirectly. I could almost grasp them in my hands, out in Nature's open, in the woods, during my promenades, in the silence of the night, at the earliest dawn. They are roused by moods which in the poet's case are transmuted into words, and in mine into tones, that sound, roar and storm until at last they take shape for me as notes.' "}⚐•⁓

At parting, Beethoven gave Schlösser a sheet containing a canon for six voices on the words, "Edel sei der Mensch, hülfreich und gut," with the inscription: "Words by Goethe, tones by Beethoven. Vienna, May, 1823." On the back he wrote: "A happy journey, my dear Herr Schlösser, may all things which seem desirable come to meet you. Your devoted Beethoven." Beethoven also gave Schlösser, who was going to Paris, a letter of introduction to Cherubini which accomplished his acceptance as a pupil of the Conservatoire.

Another small composition belonging to this time is the birthday cantata for Prince Ferdinand Lobkowitz (born April 13, 1797), son of Beethoven's benefactor, Prince Franz Joseph v. Lobkowitz. The autograph, now lost, was inscribed "Evening of April 12, 1823 before the birthday of his Ser. Prince Ferdinand Lobkowitz."[60] Karl Peters (tutor to the Lobkowitz family) gives this account of its origin: "The copy of a little cantata which he [Beethoven] wrote for me to be performed on the birthday of the Prince . . . was in reality written by him and most daintily tied together with blue ribbon. . . . The cantata consists only of a few reiterated words, we can hardly say, *composed* by himself, and originated when he heard of the approaching birthday festival of the Prince when visiting us. 'And is there to be no celebration?' he asked, and I answered him, 'No.' 'That will not do,' he replied; 'I'll hurriedly write you a cantata, which you must sing for him.' But the performance was never realized."

Our old friend Schuppanzigh, after an absence of seven years, returned to Vienna in 1823. ⁓•⚐{On April 26 Beethoven sent him a greeting in the form of a five-part canon, "Falstafferel, lass' dich sehen!" ("Falstafferel, let us see you!") In a Conversation Book at the end of April Schuppanzigh reports to Beethoven on many things, including fellow musicians:[61]

Ries is doing very well in London
Ries plagiarized too much from Beethoven
Everything, but with Ries too obviously

•⁓•

Field played beautifully

•⁓•

He should be heard playing Bethoven [*sic*!]
what a unique pleasure

•⁓•

Field is a very good man and his greatest admirer[62]

---

[60] Ludwig Nohl saw the autograph, which had passed from the family of Karl Peters to Dr. O. Zeithamer of Prague. See *Neue Briefe Beethovens* (Stuttgart, 1867), pp. 221-28.

(TDR, IV, 422, 423, n. 1.)
[61] Schünemann, III, pp. 177-78.
[62] Schuppanzigh heard the composer John Field play the piano in Russia. It will be

•~•

I have never heard the instrument handled as well by any other

•~•

. . . This Jewish lad Moscheles is causing a sensation in London, I cannot understand it at all.

•~•

Field is earning alot of money from lessons, nevertheless he never has 100 fl. because he uses it all drinking Champagne wine. Beethoven would like Field very
much because he is a real Falstaff.

•~•

Humel [*sic*] played a *quatre mains* with Field, a most perceptible difference, however was felt by both nonconnoisseurs and connoisseurs. The way Field played reminded me very much of him [Beethoven] Field played his concerto in C minor
very beautifully.}

On May 4 Schuppanzigh gave a concert at which Piringer conducted
the orchestra, and on June 14 the quartet meetings were resumed, with
Holz, Weiss and Linke as his associates.

The story of Diabelli and the Mass has been postponed until now
because it is intertwined with the last part of the story of the Diabelli Variations. Anton Diabelli, a partner in the firm of Cappi and Diabelli, invited
a number of composers to contribute a variation on a waltz theme of his
own for a collection to be entitled *Vaterländischer Künstlerverein* ("Native
Society of Artists"). The invitations were presumably made in 1819 since
the autograph of Carl Czerny's variation (in the Vienna National Library)
is dated "March 1821."[63] According to Schindler, Beethoven at first refused
the invitation.[64] However, by early 1819 Beethoven had made sketches for
four different variations, which come just before the preliminary sketches for
the *Kyrie* of the *Missa Solemnis*.[65] Beethoven in his letter to Simrock of
February 10, 1820, included mention of some "grand variations on a well
known 'Deutsche' which, however, I cannot promise you as yet. . . ." As
time progressed, Beethoven's conception of the work grew; according to
Schindler, he had in mind first six or seven, then twenty-five variations.
On June 5, 1822, he offered Peters "Variations on a waltz for pianoforte
alone (there are many) for the price of 30 ducats in gold." The main work,
then, was done in this year, and the full thirty-three variations were completed by March or April, 1823.

Meanwhile Beethoven had started negotiations with Diabelli concerning
the publication of both the Mass and the Variations. At some point during

---

remembered that Schuppanzigh and Beethoven
always addressed each other as "he."

[63] See Heinrich Rietsch, "Fünfundachtzig
Variationen über Diabellis Waltzer," in *BJ*, 1
(1908), p. 31.

[64] See *Biogr.*, II, pp. 34-5. (TDR, IV, 424,

n. 3.)

[65] The Wittgenstein sketchbook has 87
pages, of which pages 4-14 contain sketches
for what became Variations 11, 18, 19 and
32. See KHV, p. 348.

the growth of the latter, an agreement had been reached to publish the variations separate from the growing collection of variations of the other fifty composers. In the fall of 1822 Beethoven wrote the following letter to the publisher:⟩⟩⟨⟨⟩--

Dear D——!

Patience! I am still *not yet* living as a *human, much less* in a way that is suitable and necessary for me—The fee for the Variat. should be 40 ducats at the most if they are worked out on as large a scale as is planned; but if this should *not take place*, it would be set for *less*—Now more about the overture. Along with this I would be glad to give you seven numbers from the *Weihe des Hauses*. I have been offered a fee of 80 ducats for them. I would give you in addition a Gratulationsmenuett for full orchestra, in short, the overture and seven numbers from the Weihe des Hauses and the Gratulationsmenuett, all for 90 ducats—My housekeeper goes to the city today in the forenoon. Please give her for me an answer to my offer—I hope to be able to get to your Var. by the end of next week—Fare well excellent friend

Yours truly
B——n[66]

In March, 1823, Diabelli called Schindler into his shop and had a talk with him which is detailed in a Conversation Book. It is Schindler who is speaking:[67]

Diabelli called me today while I was passing and said to me that he would take the Mass and publish it in two months by subscription. He guarantees you the 1000 florins, as he says he has already told you. You can have as many copies as you want.

•∾•

So often I have wanted to ask you to take better care of your pocketbook. Was there much in it?
Diab. only asks of you that you let him know your decision within a few days, then he will have work begun at once and promises that everything shall be ready by the end of May. You, however, will not have any further care in the matter.

•∾•

I think the proposition a very good one, the more, because the work will be printed at once.

•∾•

Then decide the thing quickly, and settle with him right away.

Beethoven appeared to have doubts or scruples on the score of the invitations sent to the sovereigns.

---

[66] For a discussion of this letter see Sonneck, *Beethoven Letters in America*, pp. 16ff.   [67] Schünemann, III, pp. 87-8.

It will make no difference to the most exalted courts if printed copies are put out.

•∾•

Do you want the 1000 florins in cash at once or later—he assures me that they will be guaranteed to you; the business now is that you come to an understanding.

It appears, now, that Diabelli wanted to publish the three supplementary pieces (Gradual, Offertory and "Tantum Ergo") as well; but Beethoven still hesitated.

It would be best if you were to persuade Diab. to print the work at once, but wait a few months with the publication by subscription. Then you will not be compromised in the matter, nor he either.[68]

Later (there had plainly been another conversation between Schindler and Diabelli):

Diabelli agrees to wait until the tardy answers have been received before opening the subscription. But he is not willing to wait a whole year.[69]

And in April:

As to how you are agreed about it,—the only question is whether you give Diab. the privilege of announcing the subscription a month before he pays.

•∾•

It is his own wish not to take the Mass in hand until he has paid.[70]

And in another Conversation Book in April, Schindler writes:

Diab. told me also that he will pay for the Mass as soon as he receives it, but he would like to have it by July 1 in order to have it ready by the St. Michael Fair.[71]

Subsequently Diabelli asked for it by August 1 and then September 1. Beethoven was firm in his determination to keep faith with his subscribers. He writes to Schindler: "There are only two courses as regards the Mass, namely, that the publisher delay the publication a year and a day; or, if not, we cannot accept a subscription."

Meanwhile from another undated letter to Schindler it is shown that a contract had been made between them: "Nothing is to be changed in the Diabelli contract except that *the time* when he is to receive the Mass from me be left undetermined." Both works were involved and soon difficulties developed. Beethoven writes: "From my little book I see that you have doubts in the matter of the Mass and Diab., wherefore, I beg you to come soon, for in that case we will not give him the Var. either, as my brother knows somebody who wants to take them both. We are therefore in a position to talk to him."

This matter, in which Schindler acted as Beethoven's agent brought out the following:

[68] *Ibid.*, pp. 90-91. [69] *Ibid.*, p. 97. [70] *Ibid.*, p. 153. [71] *Ibid.*, p. 125.

Dear S.! ———

I wish that the business which is so disagreeable to you might be brought to a conclusion soon. Moreover I was not, *unfortunately*, completely *wrong* in not quite trusting Diab.— . . . .

To this letter Schindler provided the following note:

This concerns a contract between Diabelli and us concerning the Mass. Diab. spoke solely of plans for the work which were not only disadvantageous to the work but also damaging for the composer which I completely resisted, whereupon Diab. became very rude and declared that since the contract was as good as closed he would summon me before a court of law if the contract was broken off. This threat, however, did not help him at all; he had to take back the document.

Thus Diabelli was one more publisher *not* to receive the Mass; but he was to have the consolation of the publication of the thirty-three variations on his own theme. In the Conversation Books of April and May there is repeated reference to the shipment of a copy of the Variations to Ries in England and the dedicating of the work to Ries's wife. During this time, Diabelli had the manuscript, and there are remarks concerning the need of getting him to return it. Brother Johann urged that arrangements for the publication of the Mass and the Variations be made both in London through Ries and in Paris through Schlesinger.[72] Schindler agreed and urged particularly the shipment to London. At the end of April he writes:[73]

Your brother fears that Diab. will not want to give back the manuscript, but of course he must do so.

•~•

If you want to send the Variat. to London, it is high time to do so.

•~•

He is afraid only that they will arrive too late because Diab. will have published them in 3 weeks.

Variat. (with 2 *Schusterfleck*)[74] dedicated to Mada[me] Ries, etc.

•~•

That will please H. Ries very much.

On April 25, 1823, Beethoven wrote a letter to Ries in which he promises: "You will also receive in a few weeks 33 variations on a theme dedicated to your wife." Although the copy for Mme. Ries is dated April 30[75] there was

---

[72] *Ibid.*, p. 140.

[73] *Ibid.*, pp. 203, 205.

[74] According to Schindler, *op.cit.*, Beethoven made fun of Diabelli's theme and called it a *Schusterfleck*, that is a cobble or a cobbler's patch. Like *Vetter Michel* and *Rosalia* in the

musical terminology of Germany, a *Schusterfleck* is a tune largely made up of repetitions on different degrees of the scale of a single figure or motive. (TK, III, 127, n. 1.)

[75] See KHV, p. 349.

evidently a delay in the shipment as Beethoven says in a letter to Ries dated July 16: "By this time the variations have probably arrived.—I could not write out the dedication to your wife myself since I do not know her name."⅜—

On May 7 Beethoven offered the Variations for publication to Lissner in St. Petersburg. The Variations appeared from the press of Cappi and Diabelli in June[76] with a dedication to Mme. Antonia von Brentano;[77] not, it will be observed, to the wife of Ries. Had there been an English edition there would have been such a dedication, but it is another case in which an English publisher was disappointed in the conduct of the composer. Ries had complied with Beethoven's solicitations and secured a publisher. He closed an agreement with Boosey; but when the manuscript reached London, Boosey was already in possession of a copy of the Vienna edition and the work had also been printed in Paris. The copy made for London bore a dedication written in large letters by Beethoven to Madame Ries; but the printed copies were inscribed to Madame Brentano. Beethoven attempted an explanation and defence in a letter to Ries dated Baden, September 5:

You say that I ought to look about me for somebody to look after my affairs; now this was just what happened with the variat. which were looked after for me by my friends and Schindler. How? The variations were not to appear here until after they had been published in London, but everything went askew. The dedication to Brentano was intended only for Germany, as I was under obligation to her and could publish nothing else at the time. Besides, only Diabelli, the publisher here, got them from me. Everything was done by Schindler, a bigger wretch I never knew on God's earth—an arch-scoundrel whom I have sent about his business—I can dedicate another work to your wife in place of it. . . .

How much blame in this affair really attached to Schindler is not known; it seems pretty apparent that at the same time as Beethoven was fuming against him at home, he was doing duty in London as a whipping-boy. Beethoven, however, went right on calling for the help of the "arch-scoundrel."

After the labors and vexations of town life in the winter, the call of the country in the summer was even more than usually imperative, because the work which had long occupied Beethoven's mind—the Ninth Symphony—was demanding completion. His brother Johann had invited him to visit him on his estate near Gneixendorf, but he had declined. His choice for the summer sojourn fell upon Hetzendorf, a village not far from Vienna,

---

[76] They were advertised as published in the *Wiener Zeitung* on June 16. The Variations were republished in June, 1824, as Part 1 of Diabelli's *Vaterländischer Künstlerverein*, subtitled "Variations for the Pianoforte on a given theme composed by the most select composers and virtuosi of Vienna and the R. I. Austrian States." Part 2 consisted of 50 variations by 50 different composers.

[77] Mme. von Brentano was to have had the dedication of the Pianoforte Sonata in C minor (see letter to Maurice Schlesinger, February 18, 1823, *A* 1140); but then Beethoven changed his mind and decided to dedicate it to Archduke Rudolph (see letter to the Archduke, July 1, 1823, *A* 1203).

where he removed on May 17. After much hesitation, he finally decided upon a villa, surrounded by a beautiful park, which belonged to Baron Müller-Pronay. There was some haggling about the rent and some questioning about the post service—an important matter in view of the many negotiations with publishers, in all of which Schindler was depended on—but eventually all was arranged. Ill health marred the Hetzendorf sojourn. Beethoven's other ailments were augmented by a painful affliction of the eyes which called for medical treatment, retarded his work and caused him no small amount of anxiety. Complaints on this score began in April and were continued through July, on the 15th of which month he writes to the Archduke, "My eyes are better, but improvement is slow. . . . It would be more rapid if I were not obliged to wear glasses. It is an unfortunate circumstance and has delayed me in everything"; and later, when on a short visit to Vienna: "I have just heard that Y. I. H. is coming here tomorrow. If I cannot obey the wishes of my heart, please ascribe it to my eyes. I am much better, but I must not breathe the town air for many more days, for it would have an ill effect on my eyes." In August, very shortly before his departure for Baden: "I am feeling really badly and not only because of my eyes. I propose to drag myself to Baden tomorrow to take lodgings and in a few days will have to go there to stay. The town air has an injurious effect on my entire system and I hurt myself by going twice to my physicians in the city."

At this time Beethoven was continuing to supervise the copying of scores of the Mass, to which was added the unwelcome task of corrections in connection with the publications of the Diabelli Variations and the Pianoforte Sonata, Op. 111. Here is one of the many letters to Schindler from this period:

Samothracian L[umpenker]l![78]

How about the trombone part? It is certain that the fellow still has it—as he did not return it when he brought back the Gloria. There was so much to do in looking over the wretched scribbling that we forgot to take back the trombone part. If necessary I shall come to Vienna to the police—Here, for Rampel, is first the theme of the Var. which is to be copied for me on a separate sheet—then he is to copy the rest to Var. 13 or rather to the end of Var. 12, and so an end of this—

Get from Schlemmer what is lacking of the Kyrie—

Show him my postscript and herewith satis—for such H[auptlumpenkerl]s—there is nothing more to be done—

[78] Beethoven had a number of nicknames for Schindler besides *Papageno* with its various qualifications. One of these was *Lumpenkerl*; another *Hauptlumpenkerl*—Ragamuffin and Chief Ragamuffin. In this instance Schindler is a "Samothracian ragamuffin" and Schindler in a gloss tells us that the allusion was to the ancient ceremonies of Samothrace, Schindler being thus designated as one initiated into the mysteries of Beethoven's affairs and purposes. The injunction of silence was understood, of course. Count Brunsvik, Count Lichnowsky and Zmeskall were also initiates. (TK, III, 106, n. 1.)

Farewell—attend to everything—I am obliged to bind up my eyes at night and must be very sparing in my use of them. *Otherwise*, Smetana writes, I shall write but few more notes.

To Wocher, whom I shall visit myself as soon as I come to town, my best compliments, and have the var. been sent yet?

Good wishes

Postscript

Diabelli receives herewith the old and part of the new.

My eyes which are still worse rather than better make everything go slowly. As soon as Diabelli is ready with this, send it out to me whereupon he will get all the rest right away—The idea that one must have the manuscript in order to show ownership is a new one to me which I have never heard before; counter-evidence is already provided by the MSS which I have; several of these were engraved and then I received them back again—

I have been asked sometimes for a document concerning the property right of a work and D. can have this also—

D. could have claimed a copy, but you know what happened, the more since we wanted to hand over the Var. to D. as quickly as possible.

The unusual story of the publication of the Sonata in C Minor, Op. 111, has waited until now since it involves not only the Berlin and Paris edition published by Schlesinger *père et fils* but also reprints in Vienna by Diabelli and Leidesdorf. There was also an attempt to arrange an English edition which misfired, bringing additional humiliation to Ferdinand Ries. The sonata was first published at approximately the same time by the two Schlesinger firms, probably close to the beginning of the year 1823.[79] In the letter for Schlösser, dated May 6, at the time of his departure from Vienna, Beethoven writes: "Likewise ask Schlesinger . . . what the reason is that I have still received no copies of the Sonata in C minor." Schindler reports ". . . the Paris editions had to be sent twice to Vienna; on account of the extraordinary number of mistakes even in the second proof, the composer demanded that Op. 111 be sent once again to which the management of the firm did not wish to comply. Thereupon it seemed that the sky would collapse over our master."[80]

The *Wiener Zeitung* announced a sonata as "newly arrived" on May 27. Diabelli quickly obtained a printed copy of the sonata and planned a reprint in an attempt, like that of Sauer and Leidesdorf, to capture the business in Vienna. In a letter to Moritz Schlesinger, dated June 3, 1823, Beethoven made a list of errors in the French edition of the sonata and then referred to the two "pirated" editions as follows:

[79] The date is not established. Kinsky-Halm date it in one place as 1822 (p. 319), in another (p. 761) as April, 1823. However, if the reference by Count Lichnowsky to "2 Paris sonatas" in a Conversation Book of early February, 1823 (Schünemann, II, p. 353) is to this sonata (along with Op. 110) then Kinsky Halm's latter date is too late.

[80] *Biogr.*, II, p. 3.

By a remarkable accident someone sent to me here two copies as a curiosity to show how far one can go in the art of forgery; the one printed in Paris by you and the other here by Leidesdorf are so alike that one cannot tell the difference. Even the price is the same. It appears that you have played into the hands of your friends. Diabelli is now engraving it too, so I hear—therefore—although I have received no copy from you, I believe, nevertheless, that it is my duty to acquaint you with the new mistakes along with the old ones, and ask you please to have them corrected carefully.

As Sonneck points out,[81] Beethoven must have already made a set of *errata* before receiving a printed copy (old mistakes) and then received a copy from someone in Vienna ("I have received no copy from you), from which he listed new mistakes. Notes to Schindler, Diabelli and the Archduke give evidence as to how Beethoven felt about the faulty Schlesinger edition. Here was an opportunity, if he helped with the correcting, for the Diabelli reprint to provide a more accurate printing of the work. This, however, he did not admit to Schlesinger: "Diabelli is now engraving it too, so I hear."

In a letter to Schindler, which Beethoven has humorously divided into "Beginning," "Continuation," and "End," the last part is concerned with this problem:

End.

Inquire from the arch-scoundrel Diabelli if the French copy of the Sonata in C minor has been printed so that I may receive it for corrections. At the same time I have reserved four copies of it for myself, of which one is to be on fine paper for the Cardinal. If now he is his usual scoundrelly self, I will personally sing a bass aria to him in his store, so that it will resound in the store and from there to the Graben.[82]

Further mention of the *errata* was made in a letter from Beethoven to Diabelli[83] in which the composer suggested that Diabelli use the Paris copy as model for his publication, since there were additional mistakes in the other version (Sauer and Leidesdorf). He urged haste in producing the proofs, since he wished to correct them at once. He felt that the other two publishers deserved this treatment, although normally he would not do things in that way. The request for four copies, with one on special paper for the Archduke, was repeated.

The reprint of the sonata followed shortly afterward, as is shown by Beethoven's letter of July 1 to the Archduke previously quoted announcing the dedication of the sonata and the arrival of a reprint copy corrected by him from the French edition. As to the ethics of Beethoven's participation in

[81] O. G. Sonneck, *Beethoven Letters in America*, pp. 25-6.

[82] According to Miss Anderson, p. 1037, n. 1, there is a notation by Schindler on the autograph of this letter saying that Diabelli wrote to Beethoven and said that he would take down this bass aria, publish it and even pay him for it, whereupon Beethoven became more patient with him!

[83] First published in English translation by A. H. Fox Strangeways in *Music and Letters*, xv (1934), p. 16. See also A 1182.

this reprint of Op. 111, Sonneck makes this significant point: "Neither Schlesinger nor Beethoven could prevent Diabelli from reprinting the work. Once the damage was done to Schlesinger by Diabelli, the composer in Beethoven asserted himself and every instinct of artistic self-protection in him demanded that he undo the damage done to him as the creator of the Sonata by Schlesinger with so very faulty an edition."[84]

As for Beethoven's plan to have Ries arrange the publication in Britain of the last two pianoforte sonatas, Op. 110 and 111 (along with the Diabelli Variations), the situation is more difficult to understand. In 1820, he made an agreement with Schlesinger for the publication of three (Op. 109-111) sonatas, which presumably included rights to sell in England.[85] Already on February 25, 1823, Beethoven writes to Ries ". . . I hope you have already received both sonatas." Again on April 25 ". . . Take care only that the C minor sonata is engraved immediately; I guarantee to the publisher that it will not be published anywhere beforehand, also I will grant him property rights for England if need be, but it must be printed immediately. Since the other one in A flat, if already available in London, has nevertheless been printed with mistakes, he can announce this one then as a correct edition when he prints it." In view of the assurance of a correct version of the A flat Sonata and the guarantee of first printing of the Sonata in C minor, Beethoven must have intended to send Ries manuscript copies of both sonatas. While waiting for them to arrive, Ries had come to an agreement with Clementi as to the fee, just as he had with Boosey in connection with the Variations. Although in a Conversation Book in the beginning of May Schindler writes: "I am surprised that Ries has not mentioned anything about the sonatas. Wocher believes that he must have received them."[86] Ries implies in the *Notizen*[87] that they arrived with the Variations, which, as already mentioned, may have been as late as July. At any rate by the time the sonatas did arrive, Ries had the further humiliation "that the sonata [Op. 111] had already been printed in Paris!"

In his *Erinnerungen an Beethoven*, Grillparzer writes of his promise, after visiting Beethoven, to visit him in Hetzendorf. The poet kept his promise, going thither with Schindler. Part of his account may best be given in his own words: "We took a promenade and entertained each other as well as was possible half in conversation, half in writing, while walking. I still remember with emotion that when we sat down to table Beethoven went into an adjoining room and himself brought forth five bottles. He set down one at Schindler's plate, one at his own and three in front of me, probably to make me understand in his wild and simple way that I was master and should drink as much as I liked. When I drove back to town without Schindler, who remained in Hetzendorf, Beethoven insisted on accompanying me. He sat himself beside me in the open carriage but instead of going only

[84] Sonneck, *op.cit.*, p. 29.
[85] See letter of May 31, 1820. *A* 1024.
[86] Schünemann, III, p. 222.
[87] Page 123.

to the edge of the village, he drove with me to the city, getting out at the gates and, after a cordial handshake, starting back alone on the journey of an hour and a half homeward. As he left the carriage I noticed a bit of paper lying on the seat which he had just vacated. I thought that he had forgotten it and beckoned him to come back; but he shook his head and with a loud laugh, as at the success of a ruse, he ran the faster in the opposite direction. I unrolled the paper and it contained exactly the amount of the carriage-hire which I had agreed upon with the driver. His manner of life had so estranged him from all the habits and customs of the world that it probably never occurred to him that under other circumstances he would have been guilty of a gross offence. I took the matter as it was intended and laughingly paid my coachman with the money which had been given to me."[88]

Following are excerpts from a Conversation Book used during the visit to Hetzendorf. The first permits us to observe the poet's ideas on the music for his own libretto:

Are you still of the opinion that something else ought to be substituted for the first chorus of the opera?

.~.

Perhaps a few tones of the hunting-horns might be continued by an invisible chorus of nymphs.

.~.

I have been thinking if it might not be possible to mark every appearance of Melusine or of her influence in the action by a recurrent and easily grasped melody. Might not the overture begin with this and after the rushing Allegro the introduction be made out of the same melody.

.~.

I have thought of this melody as that to which Melusine sings her first song.

.~.

Drahomira

.~.

I will send you the plot of this Drahomira in writing.

Grillparzer made many observations concerning music and musicians which must have interested Beethoven even when he did not agree with him. Earlier he had asserted that on the whole the North Germans knew little of music—they would never produce anything higher than *Der Freischütz*. Now he writes of Italian opera:

Lablache, and in a degree Fodor, are better actors than the Germans ever had.[89]

---

[88] Thayer saw Grillparzer on July 4, 1860, and got from him a confirmation of both incidents here narrated. (TK, III, 120, n. 1.)

[89] Luigi Lablache was a well-known bass.

Josephine Fodor was first a pianist, then a singer. At this time she was singing at the Kärthnerthor Theatre.

Perhaps Mozart formed himself on Italian opera.

•⌣•

It's worse now. You would have trouble to find singers for your opera.[90]

Among the cheering incidents of the summer were the reports which reached him of the production of *Fidelio* under the direction of Weber in Dresden. Weber opened a correspondence on January 28. His diary shows that he continued it with letters dated February 18, April 7 and June 5, and that Beethoven's answers were dated February 16, April 10 and June 9.[91] Most unfortunately all these letters have disappeared, and the only hints we have as to their contents are from the draft for Weber's first communication discovered among the papers of the writer: "*Fidelio*. To Beethoven. The performance in Prague under my direction of this mighty work, which bears testimony to German grandeur and feeling, gave me an intimacy, as inspiring as it was instructive, with the essence through which I hope to present it to the public in its complete effectiveness here, where I have all possible means at my command. Every representation will be a festival day on which I shall be privileged to offer to your exalted mind the homage which lives in my heart, where reverence and love for you struggle with each other."

Weber had received the score of the opera on April 10 from Beethoven, who had to borrow it from the Kärnthnerthor Theatre, whose musical archives were in the care of Count Gallenberg. Through Schindler, Gallenberg sent word to Beethoven that he would send the score, provided two copies were on hand; if not, he would have a copy made. Schindler, reporting the message to Beethoven, adds that Gallenberg had said he thought Beethoven himself had the score: "But when I assured him that you did not have it he said that its loss was a consequence of your irregularity and many changes of lodgings." Nevertheless, Weber got the score and after fourteen rehearsals the representation took place with great success. Von Könneritz, Director-General of the Royal Chapel, reported the triumph to Beethoven and sent him a fee of 40 ducats. Beethoven, in acknowledging receipt on July 17, was emboldened "by the account which my dear friend Maria Weber gives me of the admirable and noble motives of Your Excellency" to ask his intercession with the Saxon court on behalf of the Mass in D, as has already been recorded in this chapter.

Another pleasant experience for Beethoven may be recorded here. In 1822 the Royal Academy of Music of Sweden had elected Beethoven to a foreign membership. The consent of the Austrian government was necessary to his

[90] Schünemann, III, pp. 398-400.

[91] Max Maria von Weber, *Carl Maria von Weber* (Leipzig, 1854), II, p. 466. (TDR, IV, 436, n. 4.) But according to Erwin Kroll, the known dates of Beethoven's answers are April 9 and June 9. See "Carl Maria von Weber and Beethoven," *NBJ*, VI (1935), p. 135.

acceptance of the honor and this seems to have been deferred an unconscionably long time; at least Beethoven's letters to the Academy and to King Charles XIV (whom as General Bernadotte, then French Ambassador at Vienna, he had known 25 years before) are dated March 1, 1823. When permission came he wrote notes to the editors of the newspapers *Beobachter* and *Wiener Zeitung*,[92] asking them to announce the fact of his election; these letters were to be delivered by Schindler, to whom Beethoven wrote instructions in the following note:

Very best L[umpen]k[er]l from Epirus no less than from Brundusium etc!

Give this letter to the Beobachter. His name must be written on it by you—At the same time ask him whether his daughter has progressed well on the pianof[orte] and whether I might perhaps be of service to her with a copy of my compositions?—I have written down *honorary member*, but I do not know whether this is right or whether just to put *as a foreign member, not knowing* about such things and *never* noticing.

You have also something to deliver to Bernardum non Sanctum concerning this story. But also ask Bernard about this rascal Rupprecht. Explain the chit-chat to him and ask how one can apply the leather to such scandalous people.

Ask both philosophical newspaper writers if this is an *appointment to Honorary or Dishonorary Membership?*—

I am eating at home, if you want to come, do so—

Beg pardon of Herr Beobachter that the letter looks so confused—There is really too much to be done.

Find out also whether a copy of the Beobachter can be bought.

This letter shows both that Beethoven was not always as indifferent to distinctions of all kinds as he sometimes professed and that in this busy and in many ways troubled period his humor had not left him.

About this time Franz Schoberlechner, a young pianist, appealed to him for letters of recommendation to be used on a concert tour. The letter reached Beethoven through Schindler, to whom he returned it with the curt indorsement: "A capable fellow has no need of recommendation other than from one good house to another." Schindler importuned him again and Beethoven answered: "It must be plain to you that I do not want to have anything to do with this matter—as for 'being noble' I think I have shown you sufficiently that I am that on principle; I even think that you must have observed that I have never been otherwise—Sapienti sat—" That ended the matter.

At this time, Beethoven was once again in a position to recommend a colleague, which he did gladly. When Kapellmeister Drechsler of the Josephstadt Theatre became a candidate for the post of second court organist, Beethoven recommended him enthusiastically to Archduke Rudolph, whom in a second letter he urged to remain firm notwithstanding the fact that

---

[92] Joseph Anton von Pilat was editor of the *Beobachter*, and Beethoven's friend J. K.   Bernard of the *Wiener Zeitung*. See *A* 1217, 1218.

Abbé Stadler had presented another candidate. Archduke Rudolph spoke to the emperor and Count Dietrichstein in favor of Drechsler, but in vain.

In his letters Beethoven referred to a canon, "Grossen Dank," which he said he had written for the Archduke and which he intended to hand him in person. A sketch for it has been found among those for the Ninth Symphony,[93] but there is no record of its having been received by the Archduke.

Beethoven's domestic affairs continued to plague him. While at Hetzendorf he had the services of a housekeeper whom he described as "the swift-sailing frigate" Frau Schnaps, in letters to Schindler. He had no end of trouble about his town lodging in the Kothgasse where Schindler was living, and was compelled to write long letters to his factotum on the subject. Here is one sent from Hetzendorf on July 2:

The continuous brutality of the landlord from the beginning and for as long as I have been in the house, calls for the help of the R.I. police. Go to them direct. As regards the storm windows, the housekeeper was ordered to look after them and particularly after the recent severe rain-storm to see if they were necessary to prevent rain from entering the room. But she found that it had neither rained in nor could rain in. Believing this, I put on the lock so that the brutal fellow could not open my rooms in my absence as he threatened to do—Tell them further how he behaved towards you and that he posted the bill without notice, which he has no right to do before St. James's day.—

He has also refused to give me a receipt from St. George's to St. James'[94] as this paper shows, because of the demand that I pay a charge for lighting of which I knew nothing. This abominable lodging without a *stove-flue* and with the most wretched sort of *main chimney* has cost me at least 250 florins V.S. for extra expenses above the rent, in order to make it habitable while I was there in the winter.

It was an intentional cheat, inasmuch as I never saw the lodgings in the first story but only in the second, for which reason many objectionable things remained unknown to me. I cannot comprehend how it is possible that *so shameful a chimney, ruinous to human health, can be tolerated by the government.* You remember how the walls of your room looked because of smoke, how much it cost to get rid of some, but not all, of the nuisance—The chief thing now is that he be commanded to take down the notice and to give me the receipt for the rent paid at any rate, since under no circumstances will I pay for that wretched lighting. Furthermore, I had other large expenses in order to make life endurable in that lodging—My sore eyes cannot yet stand the town air, otherwise I would go myself to the imperial police.

Yours faithfully

Lv.Beethoven

Schindler obeyed instructions. In a letter to Beethoven dated July 3rd, he reported that the police director, Ungermann, sent his compliments to Beet-

[93] *II Beeth.*, pp. 177-78.
[94] I.e., for the second quarter-year rental period, April 24-July 25.

hoven, granted all his wishes in advance, but advised him to pay the six florins for lighting to prevent a scoundrelly landlord from having any kind of hold upon him. The poster came down, but Beethoven had had enough and moved to new lodgings in the fall.

Beethoven's nephew Karl pursued his studies at Blöchlinger's Institute till August and then spent his vacation with his uncle at Baden. He made himself useful as amanuensis and otherwise, and his words are occasionally found among the notes of conversation. His mother remained in the background for the time being, which is providential, for Beethoven had trouble enough with his other sister-in-law, the wife of Johann, whose conduct reached the extreme of reprehensibleness in the summer of 1823, during a spell of sickness which threw her husband on his back. The woman chose this time to receive her lover in her house and to make a shameless public parade of her moral laxness. The step-daughter was not less neglectful of her filial duties.

Schindler, who in Beethoven's lodgings was living next door to Johann wrote a letter on July 3 from which we quote: "As I have been visiting him [Johann] three to four times a day since he took to his bed, and have entertained him by the hour, I have had an opportunity carefully to observe these two persons; hence I can assure you on my honor that, despite your venerable name, they deserve to be shut up, the old one in prison, the young one in the house of correction. . . . This illness came opportunely for both of them, to enable them to go their ways without trammel. These beasts would have let him rot if others had not taken pity on him. He might have died a hundred times without the one in the Prater or at Nussdorf the other at the baker's deigning to give him a look. . . . He often wept over the conduct of his family and once he gave way completely to his grief and begged me to let you know how he is being treated so that you might come and give the two the beating they deserve. . . . It is most unnatural and more than barbarous if that woman, while her husband is lying ill, introduces her lover into his room, prinks herself like a sleigh horse in his presence and then goes driving with him, leaving the sick husband languishing at home. She did this very often. Your brother himself called my attention to it, and is a fool for tolerating it so long." Further accounts of his sister-in-law's misconduct reached Beethoven's ears, and he was frank in his denunciation of her to his brother. Schindler was asked by Beethoven to lay the matter before the police, but he managed to postpone that step for the time being.[95]

Burdened with these difficult relationships, with physical suffering of different kinds, and with other vexations as well, Beethoven labored at Hetzendorf on the great work which, already begun, was supposed to be nearing its end: the *Symphony for England* or, as we are used to naming it,

[95] See *A*, p. 1042, n. 5, for further remarks by Schindler on this subject.

the Ninth Symphony. In his letter to Archduke Rudolph of July 1, already quoted, Beethoven writes: "I am now writing a new symphony for England, for the Philharmonic Society, and hope to have it completely done in a fortnight." The work claimed his attention to such a degree that he strove for solitude and wished if possible to see no one, not even Schindler.

This deep concentration on his big work resulted in much disturbance in his domestic affairs. "Completely preoccupied, he roamed through fields and pastures, sketchbook in hand, without giving a thought to the arranged hour for meals. When he returned he was repeatedly without his hat, which never happened formerly even in the moments of highest inspiration. Up to the middle of August were to be seen big notebooks with notations for his new work." So Schindler writes.[96] The ideas for the symphony had been growing in his mind for a long time before the writing out in this summer; otherwise he would not have been able to write Ries on April 25, 1823: "Right now I am not well because of many vexations that I have had to endure, yes even pain in my eyes! But do not worry; you will have the symphony soon; it is really this miserable situation alone that has been the fault." During the labor on this work there was room for nothing else in his mind; it was so ever-present with him that there was neither paradox nor hyperbole in his words "I am never alone when I am alone."

To the distractions already mentioned there came another which is related by Schindler: "Then the 'raptus' seized him to want to leave the beautiful villa of Baron Pronay and move to beloved Baden; the reason 'because the Baron made deep bows to him every time they met.'" Here Schindler cites the phrase "Humility of man towards man—it pains me" from the second letter to the "Immortal Beloved."

Beethoven may have formed the plan earlier in the year—probably had—but the Baron's excessive politeness helped to turn his departure into something like a bolt. Schindler continues:

"There appeared one morning his swift-sailing frigate, the good old housekeeper, in my room (it must be remembered that since September 1822 Beethoven had shared his room with me in the Pfarrgasse [Kothgasse], Vorstadt Leimgrube) and brought the message: the master feels that he is unable to work any longer in Hetzendorf and must depart from there; he expected me the next day to be with him at 5 o'clock in the morning so that I could help him in the search of a house in Baden. As evidence there were the following lines in his hand: 'Samothracian L—K— Come, the weather is just right. But it is better earlier than later, presto prestissimo, we are leaving from here.'

"This trip from Hetzendorf to Baden and the business there are among my most singular experiences with the great eccentric. Forthwith he began

[96] *Biogr.*, II, p. 51.

to reminisce over the long list of dwellings which he had already occupied there and their inconveniences and unpleasantnesses. There was only one of all that he had occupied which he now wanted; 'but the people have declared in years past that they do not want to take me [Beethoven] in again.' But such declarations had come from other houses there several times already. When we had arrived he requested me to proceed as a go-between to the desired house[97] and in his name to give a promise of better order and respect for other occupants (a chief cause of the complaint). This promise, however, received no attention. I was refused. My persevering friend was deeply troubled by this. Once again the bearer of the flag of truce was sent to the stronghold of the coppersmith with new assurances of good conduct. This time he found a willing ear. One specific stipulation, however, was made, that in order to have the room overlooking the street as in past years, Beethoven must provide it with window shutters. We tried in vain to learn the reason for this strange demand. Meanwhile, since the procurement of this requisite proved necessary for the prevention of bright sunlight for the composer's ailing eyes, this demand was willingly agreed to. A few days later the move took place."[98]

Schindler then gives the reason for the request. Beethoven was in the habit of scrawling all kinds of memoranda on his shutters in lead pencil—accounts, musical themes, etc. A family from North Germany had noticed this in the previous year and had bought one of the shutters as a curiosity. The thrifty smith had an eye for business and disposed of the remaining shutters to other summer visitors. When Beethoven was informed by an apothecary at Baden of this strange transaction, he broke into homeric laughter.

The day of Beethoven's move to Baden was August 13, as we learn from a letter to the Archduke on August 22. Excerpts from two letters to his nephew dated August 16 and 23 show his mood at this time. The first concerns his health and general state of mind:

At first I did not want to tell you anything until my health had improved *here*, which has not yet completely happened. I came here with catarrh and a cold, both severe for me, since the original trouble, moreover, has always been catarrhal, and I fear that this will soon cut through my life's thread or, what is worse, cut it *bit by bit*—Moreover my ruined belly must be restored by medicine and diet, and this I owe to the *faithful servants*! You can imagine how I am racing about, for only today did I again begin my service to the muses *purposefully* (after all *unpurposefully* would be unintentionally)—I *must serve them*, but that is not to be noticed—for the baths invite me at least to the enjoyment of beautiful nature, but nous sommes trop pauvres, et il faut écrire ou de n'avoir pas de quoi. . . .

[97] Rathausgasse No. 94, owned by the coppersmith Johann Bayer, where Beethoven stayed in the late summer of 1821.
[98] *Biogr.*, ii, pp. 52-3.

The second reflects the annoyance he felt at Schindler during this period:

. . . He was with me only a day here to take a lodging, as you know. He slept at Hetzendorf, and as he said, went back to the Josephstadt in the morning. Do not get to gossiping against him, it might work him injury, and is he not already sufficiently punished being *what he is*. It is necessary that I tell him the truth plainly, for his evil character, which is prone to trickery, needs to be handled seriously. . . .

At the same time he answered a letter from his brother Johann, now convalescing, in which he felt forced to speak out concerning the latter's family affairs:

Baden, August 19

Dear Brother:

I am rejoiced at your better health. As regards myself, my eyes are not entirely recovered and I came here with a disordered stomach and a frightful catarrh, the first due to the arch-pig of a housekeeper, and the second to a beast of a kitchen-maid whom I had once sent away but whom I took back—You should not have gone *to Steiner*. I will see what can be done. It will be difficult to do anything with the songs *in puris*, as their texts are German, but more likely with the overture.—

I received your letter of the 10th through the hands of the miserable scoundrel *Schindler*. You need only to give your letters directly to the post, from which I am certain to receive them, for I avoid this mean and contemptible fellow as much as possible—Karl cannot come to me before the 29th of this month when he will write you. You cannot be wholly unadvised as to what the two *canailles*, Lout and Bastard,[99] are doing to you, and you will have had letters on the subject from me and Karl, for, little as you deserve it I shall never forget that you are my brother, and a good angel will 'yet come to rid you of these two *canailles*, this former and present strumpet who slept with her fellow no less than three times while you were ill, and who, in addition to everything else, has your money wholly in her hands. O infamous disgrace, isn't there a spark of manhood in you?!!!—Now concerning another matter. You have my own manuscript of some pieces for the "Ruinen von Athen," which I want urgently because the copies of the score made for the Josephstadt lack several things which are to be found in these manuscript scores of mine. Since I am writing something similar, I want this most urgently, so write where I can get these manuscripts, I particularly ask this of you. About coming to you I will write another time. Ought I so to degrade myself as to associate with such bad company? Mayhap this can be avoided and we might yet pass a few days with you?! About the rest of your letter another time. Farewell. Unseen I hover over you and work through others so that these *canailles* shall not strangle you.—

As always your faithful

Brother.

[99] Meaning Johann's wife and step-daughter. (TDR, IV, 452, n. 1.) According to Anderson, *A*, p. 1081, n. 4, this passage and the one beginning "a good angel" through "spark of manhood in you" were deleted by another hand, though still legible. This is true also, at the close of the letter, of the adjective "bad" and the word "canailles."

It is interesting to read that he asked specifically for the original manu-script to the *Ruinen von Athen* "since I am writing something similar." There is no trace of what this composition was. Nohl questioned whether it might have been the opera *Melusine*.[100]

At Baden Beethoven's health improved. In a letter to the Archduke, dated August 22, he complained of a catarrhal trouble, the misery in his bowels and the trouble with his eyes, but adds: "Thank God, the eyes are so much improved that I can again use them considerably in the daytime. Things are going better also with my other ailments; more could not be asked in this short time." He was characteristically optimistic about the completion of his symphony as is shown in a letter to Ries dated September 5 in which he reports: "The score of the symphony has been completed by the copyists during the last few days and consequently Kirchhoffer and I are merely waiting for a good opportunity to send it off." At this time the symphony was not ready, let alone copied; but in his head it was far advanced and in July he was already working out the third movement. Franz Christian Kirchhoffer was a bookkeeper in the Ofenheimer wholesale firm in Vienna. Beethoven wrote several letters to him at this time and both now and later he acted as intermediary between Beethoven and Ries. On September 5 the composer wrote to Kirchhoffer that he would receive the score of the sym-phony in fourteen days at the most, but that what was really important now was the speedy delivery of the Mass to Ries. The letter ends: "As you can expect, Ries has hardly taken any action at all in this matter so far. Yet I think he will exert himself once the work is in London—Choose a day to come to Baden and you will be received by my Karl and myself with love and friendship."

There were several visitors to Beethoven at Baden in the summer of 1823 who have left accounts of their experiences. One was an Englishman, Edward Schulz, who published his story in the *Harmonicon* in January, 1824. Schulz visited Beethoven on September 28 in the company of Has-linger.[101] He describes it as a *dies faustus* for him and, as Schindler shrewdly observes, it must have also been one for Beethoven, since he managed to hear the conversations of his visitors without the aid of an ear-trumpet. He talked with great animation, as was his wont when in good humor, but says the English visitor, "One unlucky question, one ill-judged piece of advice—for instance, concerning the cure of his deafness—is quite sufficient to estrange him from you forever." He asked Haslinger about the highest possible note on the trombone, but was dissatisfied with the answer which he received; introduced his nephew and showed his pride in the youth's attainments by telling his guest that he might put him to "a riddle in Greek" if he liked. At dinner during a visit to the Helenthal he commented on the profusion of

100 Ludwig Nohl, *Beethoven's letzte Jahre* (Leipzig, 1877), p. 908. (TDR, IV, 453.)

101 Schulz had already paid a short visit to Beethoven in 1816. (TDR, IV, 456.)

provisions at dinner, saying: "Why such a variety of dishes? Man is but little above other animals if his chief pleasure is confined to the dinner-table." An excerpt from the letter will serve to advance the present narrative: "In the whole course of our table-talk there was nothing so interesting as what he said about Handel. I sat close by him and heard him assert very distinctly in German, 'Handel is the greatest composer that ever lived.' I cannot describe to you with what pathos, and I am inclined to say, with what sublimity of language, he spoke of the *Messiah* of this immortal genius. Every one of us was moved when he said, 'I would uncover my head, and kneel down at his tomb!' H. and I tried repeatedly to turn the conversation to Mozart, but without effect. I only heard him say, 'In a monarchy we know who is the first'; which might or might not apply to the subject. Mr. C. Czerny—who, by-the-by, knows every note of Beethoven by heart, though he does not play one single composition of his own without the music before him—told me, however, that B. was sometimes inexhaustible in his praise of Mozart. It is worthy of remark that this great musician cannot bear to hear his own earlier works praised; and I was apprized that a sure way to make him very angry is to say something complimentary of his Septetto, Trios, etc. His latest productions, which are so little relished in London, but much admired by the young artists of Vienna, are his favorites. His second Mass he looks upon as his best work, I understood. He is at present engaged in writing a new opera called *Melusine*, the words by the famous but unfortunate poet Grillparzer. He concerns himself but very little about the newest productions of living composers, insomuch, that when I asked about the *Freischütz*, he replied, 'I believe *one* Weber has written it.' You will be pleased to hear that he is a great admirer of the ancients, Homer, particularly his *Odyssey*, and Plutarch he prefers to all the rest; and of the native poets, he studies Schiller and Goethe in preference to any other; this latter is his personal friend. He appears uniformly to entertain the most favorable opinion of the British nation. 'I like,' said he, 'the noble simplicity of the English manners,' and added other praises. It seemed to me as if he had yet some hopes of visiting this country together with his nephew."

A few days after the one just recorded Beethoven received a visit from a man of much greater moment than the English traveller. The new visitor was Carl Maria von Weber. That the composer of *Der Freischütz* was unable in his salad days to appreciate the individuality of Beethoven's genius has already been set forth; and the author of the letter in the *Harmonicon* seems to have learned that Beethoven was disposed to speak lightly of Weber only a month before he received him with most amiable distinction at Baden. He was often unjust in his comments on even his most devoted friends, and we may believe that to Schulz he did speak of the composer as "one Weber," and at the same time accept the account which Max Maria von Weber gives of the reception of his father by Beethoven. From the affectionate biography written by the son, we learn that after the sensational success achieved by *Der Freischütz* Beethoven was led to study its score and that he was so astonished at the originality of the music that he struck the book with his hand and exclaimed: "I never would have thought it of the gentle little man (*sonst weiche Männel*). Now Weber must write operas; nothing but operas—one after the other and without polishing them too much. Casper, the monster, stands out here like a house. Wherever the devil puts in his claws they are felt." He learned to know *Euryanthe* later and was less impressed by it than by its predecessor. After glancing through it hurriedly he remarked: "The man has taken too much pains." Whatever may have been their earlier feelings and convictions, however, the representations of *Fidelio* at Prague and Dresden under the direction of Weber warmed their hearts towards each other. Weber had come to Vienna, bringing with him his pupil Benedict, to conduct the first performance of *Euryanthe*. On his visit in the previous year, when *Der Freischütz* was produced, he had neglected to call on Beethoven, but now some kindly words about *Euryanthe* spoken by Beethoven to Steiner being repeated to him, he made good his dereliction and, announced by Haslinger, drove out to Baden to pay his respects. In his diary Weber noted the visit thus: "The 5th, Sunday (October, 1823), at 8 o'clock, drove with Burger (Piringer), Haslinger and Benedict to Baden; abominable weather; Saw spring and baths; to Duport and *Beethoven*; received by him with great cordiality. Dined with him, his nephew and Eckschlager at the Sauerhof. Very cheerful. Back again at 5 o'clock." On the next day (though the letter is dated "October 5") Weber wrote an account to his wife as follows: "I was right tired but had to get up yesterday at 6 o'clock because the excursion to Baden had been appointed for half-past 7 o'clock. This took place with Hasslinger, Piringer and Benedict; but unfortunately the weather was atrocious. The main purpose was to see Beethoven. He received me with an affection which was touching; he embraced me most heartily at least six or seven times and finally exclaimed enthusiastically: 'Indeed, you're a devil of a fellow!—a good fellow!' We spent the afternoon very merrily and contentedly. This rough, repellant man actually paid court to me, served me at table as if I had been his lady. In short, this day will always remain remarkable in my memory as well as of those present. It was uplifting for me to be overwhelmed with such loving attention by this great genius. How saddening is his deafness! Everything must be written down for him. We inspected the baths, drank the waters, and at 5 o'clock drove back to Vienna."

Max Maria von Weber in his account of the incident says that Beethoven, in the conversation which followed his greeting of the "devil of a fellow," railed at the management of the theatre, the concert impresarios, the public, the Italians, the taste of the people, and particularly at the ingratitude of his nephew. Weber, who was deeply moved, advised him to tear himself away from his discouraging environment and make an artistic tour through

Germany, which would show him what the world thought of him. "Too late!" exclaimed Beethoven, shaking his head and going through the motions of playing the pianoforte. "Then go to England, where you are admired," wrote Weber. "Too late!" cried Beethoven, drew Weber's arm into his and dragged him along to the Sauerhof, where they dined. At parting, Beethoven embraced and kissed him several times and cried: "Good luck to the new opera; if I can I'll come to the first performance."

A generation later Sir Julius Benedict, who had also put his memory of those Vienna days at the service of Weber's son, wrote down his recollections for this work in these words:

"I endeavor, as I promised you, to recall the impressions I received of Beethoven when I first met him in Vienna in October, 1823. He then lived at Baden; but regularly, once a week, he came to the city and he never failed to call on his old friends Steiner and Haslinger, whose music-store was then in the Paternostergässchen, a little street, no longer in existence, between the Graben and the Kohlmarkt.

"If I am not mistaken, on the morning that I saw Beethoven for the first time, Blahetka, the father of the pianist, directed my attention to a stout, short man with a very red face, small, piercing eyes, and bushy eyebrows, dressed in a very long overcoat which reached nearly to his ankles, who entered the shop about 12 o'clock. Blahetka asked me: 'Who do you think that is?' and I at once exclaimed: 'It must be Beethoven!' because, notwithstanding the high color of his cheeks and his general untidiness, there was in those small piercing eyes an expression which no painter could render. It was a feeling of sublimity and melancholy combined. I watched, as you can well imagine, every word that he spoke when he took out his little book and began a conversation which to me, of course, was almost incomprehensible, inasmuch as he only answered questions pencilled to him by Messrs. Steiner and Haslinger. I was not introduced to him on that occasion; but the second time, about a week after, Mr. Steiner presented me to the great man as a pupil of Weber. The other persons present were the old Abbé Stadler and Seyfried. Beethoven said to Steiner: 'I rejoice to hear that you publish once more a German work. I have heard much in praise of Weber's opera and hope it will bring both you and him a great deal of glory.' Upon this Steiner seized the opportunity to say: 'Here is a pupil of Weber's'; when Beethoven most kindly offered me his hand, saying: 'Pray tell M. de Weber how happy I shall be to see him at Baden, as I shall not come to Vienna before next month.' I was so confused at having the great man speak to me that I hadn't the courage to ask any questions or continue the conversation with him.

"A few days afterwards I had the pleasure of accompanying Weber and Haslinger with another friend to Baden, when they allowed me the great privilege of going with them to Beethoven's residence. Nothing could be more cordial than his reception of my master. He wanted to take us to the Helenenthal and to all the neighborhood; but the weather was unfavorable, and we were obliged to renounce this excursion. They all dined together at one table at an inn, and I, seated at another close to them, had the pleasure of listening to their conversation.

"In the month of November, when Beethoven came to town and paid his daily visit to the Paternostergässchen, I seldom missed the opportunity of being one of the circle of young admirers, eager to show their reverence to the greatest musical genius as well as hoping to be honored by his notice. Among those whom I met upon this errand were Carl Maria von Bocklet, his pupil, Worzischek, Léon de St. Louvain, Mayseder, Holz, Böhm, Linke, Schuppanzigh, Franz Schubert and Kanne.

"On the morning after the first performance of *Euryanthe,* when Steiner and Haslinger's shop was filled with the musical and literary authorities, Beethoven made his appearance and asked Haslinger: 'Well, how did the opera go last night?' The reply was: 'A great triumph.' *'Das freut mich, das freut mich,'* he exclaimed, and perceiving me he said: 'I should so much have liked to go to the theatre, but,' pointing to his ears, 'I go no more to those places.' Then he asked Gottdank, the régisseur; 'How did little Sontag get on? I take a great interest in her; and how is the book—good or bad?' Gottdank answered the first question affirmatively, but as to the other he shrugged his shoulders and made a negative sign, to which Beethoven replied: 'Always the same story; the Germans cannot write a good libretto.' Upon which I took his little conversation book and wrote in it: 'And *Fidelio?*' to which he answered: 'That is a French and Italian book.' I asked him afterwards: 'Which do you consider the best librettos?'; he replied *'Wasserträger* and *Vestalin.'*"

Madame Marie Pachler-Koschak, with whom Beethoven had spent many happy moments in 1817, was among those who took the waters at Baden in the summer of 1823, but we are told she searched for him in vain, a fact which shows in what seclusion he must have dwelt some of the time at least. She was more fortunate when she returned in September to complete her cure; and when she left Baden she carried with her an autographic souvenir—a setting of "Das Schöne zum Guten," the concluding words of Matthison's "Opferlied."

Towards the close of October Beethoven returned to Vienna. We know the date approximately from Benedict's account, the first performance of *Euryanthe* having taken place on October 25. He removed to new lodgings ---⚡in the Landstrasse on the corner of the Bockgasse (now Beatrixgasse)[102] and the Ungargasse⚡---, where his nephew remained with him as long as he continued a student at the University. Here he worked at the Ninth Symphony, more particularly on the last movement.

[102] I am grateful to the late Dr. Kurt Smolle for this information.

The Bagatelles, Op. 126, belong to this period, though their completion fell in the next year. Taking up earlier sketches probably, Beethoven worked on them after the Ninth Symphony was practically complete in his mind and in the sketchbooks. Nottebohm had subjected them to a minute study[103] which leads him to the conclusion that the pieces were conceived as a homogeneous series, the numbers being linked together by key relationship. On the margin of a sketch for the first one Beethoven wrote "Cycle of Trifles" (*Kleinigkeiten*), which fact, their separation from each other (all but the first two) by the uniform distance of a major third, taken in connection with their unity of style, establishes a cyclical bond. When he offered them to Schott in 1824 he remarked that they were probably the best things of the kind which he had ever written. They were among the compositions which had been pledged to his brother, in whose interest he offered them to Schott. They were published by that firm in 1825.

After the conversations with Grillparzer at Hetzendorf on the subject of *Melusine,* there were many others with whom Beethoven discussed the opera and who came to him to tell him of their desire to see it written. Duport was greatly interested, wanted to read the book with care, and asked Beethoven's terms; Lichnowsky was willing to risk the financial outcome; "I will go security," he says in October, "for the money which you want for the opera. After selling the opera to the director you can still reserve the right of disposing of it at home and abroad." And again: "If you do not compose the opera, German opera is finished—everybody says that. After the failure of Weber's opera *Euryanthe* many sent the books back. Freischütz is not a genuine opera. If you can use me in any way, you know me and how sincere I am"; and still again, towards the end of November: "You will get incomparably more without a contract; if you want one, the director will make a contract with pleasure at once.— Talk it over with Grillparzer; it will also be all one to him.— Duport already asked about the opera several days ago." From other quarters Beethoven was urged to write to Duport after the latter had written to him.

In the late fall the composer wrote the following letter to the poet:

Honored Sir!

The management would like very much to know your conditions concerning your Melusine. So far they have spoken out on their own, and this is probably better than our applying pressure concerning the same—My domestic life has been in great disorder for some time, otherwise I would have looked you up already and made another invitation to visit—For the time being write your conditions to the management or to me and I will then forward them myself— Overburdened with work, I could neither pay you a visit earlier nor can I now. I hope this will happen sometime soon; my No. is 323.[104]

[103] *II Beeth.*, pp. 193ff. (TDR, IV, 477, n. 1.)

[104] Orel (*Grillparzer und Beethoven*, p. 130) notes that the house number was added in pencil after the writing of the letter. This was the house on the corner of the Ungargasse, No. 323, Landstrasse.

In the afternoon you will find me in the coffee-house opposite the Goldene Birne. If you want to come, please come *alone*, this importunate appendix of a Schindler, as you must have noticed in Hetzendorf, has long been extremely objectionable to me—otium est vitium—I embrace you heartily and honor you fully

Yours with all my heart
Beethoven

Grillparzer's visit was evidently at Beethoven's house on the Ungargasse, and the entries in the Conversation Book, which follow, were all written by Grillparzer:

The censor has banned my tragedy Ottokar.

It is not allowed even in print.

It applies very much to Austria.

Who takes the blame for Austria?

Unfortunately it is really patriotic.

No one can comprehend the reason for the ban.[105]
You have again taken up Melusine?

I have already appealed to the management twice but have had no answer.

I have already said that I was compelled to ask 100 ducats for it. Because as a matter of fact, all the profits of an opera-book remain with the theatre in which it is performed for the first time.

I could have made a spoken drama out of the same material which would have brought me three times as much.

I *must* ask so much in order to meet my obligations to Wallishauser.

For ordinary opera-books they pay up to 300 florins Convention Coin.

Have you already begun to compose?—Will you please write down for me where you want the changes made?

[105] *Ottokar* was performed for the first time on February 19, 1825.

Because then, nevertheless, the piece will have to begin with a *hunt*.

Perhaps the last tones of a vanishing hunters' chorus might blend with the introduction without having the hunters enter.

To begin with a chorus of nymphs might weaken the effect of the chorus at the close of the first act.

I am not quite versed in opera texts.

You want to deliver it to the theatre by September.

The direction wants to make a creditable showing in the eyes of the public.

Doesn't the text of the opera also seem too *long* to you? To whom are you thinking of giving the rôle of Raimund?

They are talking of a young tenor who may have made his debut by that time.

I believe his name is Cramolini; besides a handsome figure he is said to have a beautiful voice.[106]

It is said that the management is having him educated.

Forti is a little too gross.

Then I am to expect your suggestions as to alterations *in writing*. *Soon* perhaps? I am not busy at present.

I am ready for anything.

For a space there is talk about oratorio texts (*Judith*) and the possibility of musical expression in the case of Christ. Then the text of *Drahomira* is referred to, concerning which Beethoven seems to have asked. Grillparzer says:

[106] Luigi Cramolini (1805-1884) made his debut in *Ioconda* on February 27, 1824.

Drahomira

.~.

Great variety, great characters, effects.

.~.

The mother of St. Wenzelaus, the Duke of Bohemia.

.~.

One of her sons kills the other. She is herself a pagan, the better son is a Christian.

.~.

They still show the spot in Prague where she was swallowed up by the earth with horses and equipage.

.~.

After I have lost all hope *here* I shall send it to Berlin.[107]

There is much more talk in the Conversation Book about the opera, but neither sequence nor date can always be determined. Lichnowsky told him that the management of the theatre was willing to do anything asked of it and was negotiating with Grillparzer. Brother Johann says: "Grillparzer is coming tomorrow—that is no affair of yours.— You wrote to the management to make arrangements with the poet, and to this it was agreed; hence Grillparzer must make terms." In the same book Schickh, the editor, writes: "Why don't you compose Grillparzer's opera? Write the opera first and then we shall be in a position to wish you also to write a Requiem."

Grillparzer mentions in his *Erinnerungen* that Beethoven told him in Hetzendorf that his opera was ready (whether he meant in his head or in its essential elements in the numerous sketchbooks, the poet could not say), but after the composer's death not a single note was found which could indubitably be assigned to their common work. Why didn't Beethoven compose *Melusine*? Many reasons must be obvious to those who have followed this narrative closely: illness; vexation of spirit; loss of initiative; a waning of the old capacity to assimilate conceptions and ideas which did not originate in his own consciousness and were not in harmony with his own predilections.[108] Moreover, it was the period of his greatest introspection; he was communing more and more with his own soul, and separating himself more and more from all agencies of utterance except the one which spoke most truthfully and directly within him, and to which he entrusted his last revelations—the string quartet. *Melusine* was not composed, but the opera continued to occupy his attention at intervals until deep into the next year, and unless Holz is in error, some of his last labors were devoted to it.

The smaller compositions written in this year were:

---

[107] Orel, *op.cit.*, pp. 74-6.
[108] See Douglas Yates, *Franz Grillparzer* (Oxford, 1946), pp. 139-44, for further reasoning on this question.

Canons:
  "Bester Herr Graf, Sie sind ein Schaf!", WoO 183, written of Count Lichnowsky on February 20.
  "Edel sei der Mensch, hülfreich und gut" (Goethe), WoO 185, for Baroness Eskeles in early May.
  "Falstafferl, lass' dich sehen!", WoO 184, for Schuppanzigh on April 26.
  "Das Schöne zum Guten" (Matthisson), WoO 202, for Frau Pachler-Koschak on September 27.
  "Der edle Mensch sei hülfreich und gut" (Goethe), WoO 151, for Baroness Eskeles on January 20.
  Lobkowitz Cantata for Soprano, Chorus and Pianoforte, WoO 106, for the birthday celebration of Prince Ferdinand Lobkowitz (b. April 13, 1797) on April 12.

Progress on large works consisted of:

1819-22/23. *Missa Solemnis* for Four Solo Voices, Chorus, Orchestra and Organ, Op. 123, written for Archduke Rudolph of Austria, Cardinal-Archbishop of Olmütz and presented to him on March 19, 1823.
1822-4. Symphony No. 9 in D minor was the main labor of the year 1823. Sketches date back to 1817.
1819-23. Thirty-three Variations on a Waltz by Anton Diabelli, Op. 120.

The publications of the year were:

By Cappi and Diabelli:
  Variations for Pianoforte on a Waltz by Anton Diabelli, Op. 120, dedication to Antonie Brentano.
By Schlesinger in Paris and by Clementi in London:
  Sonata for Pianoforte in C minor, Op. 111, dedicated to Archduke Rudolph.[109]
By Clementi in London:[110]
  Eleven Bagatelles for Pianoforte, Op. 119.[111]
By Steiner:
  Overture to the *Ruinen von Athen*, Op. 113.

First printing in score:

By Simrock:
  Symphony No. 4 in B-flat major, Op. 60.

[109] The question of the chronology of the printings of the last sonata by different publishers is a controversial one. For a summary of this question see KHV, p. 319.
[110] See Alan Tyson, "The First Edition of Beethoven's Op. 119 Bagatelles" in *MQ*, Vol. 49 (1963), pp. 331-38.

[111] According to Kinsky-Halm (KHV, p. 347), opus number 119 was not assigned until the printing of Nottebohm's first *Verzeichniss* for Breitkopf and Härtel in 1851.

CHAPTER XXXVII

THE YEAR 1824

THE HISTORY OF THE NINTH SYMPHONY—ITS FIRST PERFORMANCE—CONTINUED NEGOTIATIONS WITH PUBLISHERS—PRINCE GALITZIN AND OPUS 127

THE year 1823 ended with Beethoven in his new lodging on the corner of the Ungargasse, occupied with work upon the Ninth Symphony, which was approaching completion, oppressed with anxiety concerning his health and worried about his brother's domestic affairs. His eyes continued to trouble him till late in March; Schindler cautioned him not to rub them, as that might increase the inflammation; Karl suggested buying a shade to protect them from the glare of the light; and when Count Brunsvik wanted to take him along with him to Hungary, Schindler advised him to take the trip, as it might be beneficial for his eyes.

About this time Beethoven took an unusually charitable attitude towards Karl's mother. She had been ill for some time as is shown by a remark by Bernard in a Conversation Book of February-March, 1823: "Have you heard nothing concerning your sister-in-law? My housekeeper has told me that she is sick and things are going very badly with her. The doctor has told it to her himself. He said that she could not pay for the medicine. You should have inquired before how the matter stands."[1] That Beethoven seems to have followed up this suggestion is shown by an undated letter to Bernard:

Dear Friend!

I beg of you before the day is over to make inquiries about Frau van Beethoven and if it is possible, to have her assured through her physician that from this month on *so long as I live* she shall have the enjoyment of the whole of her pension, and I will see to it that if I die first, Karl shall not need the half of her

[1] Schünemann, III, pp. 115-16.

pension— It was, moreover, always my intention to permit her to keep the whole of her pension as soon as Karl left the Institute, but as her illness and need are so great she must be helped at once. God has *never* deserted me in this heavy task and I shall continue to trust in Him. If possible I beg you to send me information to-day and I will see to it that my tenacious brother also makes a contribution to her—

Yours sincerely
Beethoven

Beethoven wrote to her on January 8, 1824, possibly in answer to an entreating letter from her:

Many affairs have prevented Karl and myself from sending you our good wishes for the New Year, but I know that, nevertheless, you expect nothing but the best wishes for your welfare from me as well as Karl—

Concerning your need, generally I would have been glad to help you out with a sum, but unfortunately I have too many expenses and debts and am still waiting for a certain amount of money and so am unable right now to prove to you my willingness to give you immediate help— Meanwhile I assure you herewith in writing that you can keep Karl's half of your pension from now on. We will hand over to you each month the receipt whereupon you can collect it yourself since there is indeed no shame (and I know that several of my acquaintances receive their pensions every month) in receiving it monthly. Should I be in a position later on to give you a sum from my bank for the improvement of your circumstances, it will certainly be done—the 280 fl. 25 kr. which you owe Steiner I have likewise taken over already as you have probably been told— Moreover, for some time you have not had to pay any interest on the loan—

You have received two months of pension from me through Schindler— On the 26th of this month or some time after that you will receive the pension payment for this month— Concerning your lawsuit I will soon have a discussion with Dr. Bach—

We wish you all possible good, Karl as well as myself—

Your most willing to help L. v. Beethoven

Beethoven seems to have regretted his magnanimity soon afterwards. In another letter to Bernard he writes:

Dear Bernard!

With so little time it is too much trouble for me to write to the doctor myself, to whom, however, I send best greetings herewith. Now briefly, what she has for sure, pension 406 fl. 30 kr. V.S. and the interest on 6700 fl. V.S. yearly adding to 335 V.S.; she is also to receive 480 fl. V.S. yearly from *Hofbauer*. Since, as I hear, the latter considers her child as his, *he is probably right*. And since she has become such a prostitute I believe that I and Karl even more should be sensitive to the guilt of *her bad behavior*. Hence if this 480 fl. of Hofbauer's is true, I believe she should not be given the whole other half of the pension. Perhaps such an eminent man as the doctor could clarify the thing; at any rate I do *not* want *to come into contact with her*. I am sending her herewith 11 fl. C.M. and ask you to deliver it to her via the *doctor* and further that she does not know from whence it comes.

But I request that she write a statement that she has received this— If all these things could be clarified, one could see what more is to be done for her; and I am ready to help all I can—

Your friend Beethoven⊱---

The nephew was now attending the philological lectures at the university and living in the winter and spring months with his uncle. He had left Blöchlinger's Institute in August, 1823, and matriculated at the university. He was active in the service of Beethoven, doing work as his amanuensis, carrying messages, making purchases, and so on; in fact Beethoven seems to have taken up more of his time than was good for his studies. Karl's involvement with the servants and household affairs is shown by the following excerpts in his hand from the Conversation Books: "Every time that you have trouble with the servants, I have to carry the blame for it; I don't know how I came to that." "If you had made decisions, everything would have been different long since." Beethoven loved his nephew tenderly and was unceasingly thoughtful of his welfare; but the jealousy of his affection led him to exercise a strictness of discipline over him which could not fail to become irksome to a growing stripling. He left him little liberty, and, yielding to a disposition prone to passion, he not seldom treated him with great severity. The youth appears in the Conversation Books as lively, clever and shrewd, and Beethoven, proud of his natural gifts of mind, was indulgent of his comments on others, permitting him apparently to speak lightly and discourteously of the men upon whose help and counsel he was obliged to depend. The result of Beethoven's extremes of harsh rebuke and loving admonition, of violent accusation and tender solicitude, was to encourage him in his innate bent for disingenuousness and deception, and he continued the course which he had begun as a boy of repeating words of disparagement touching those on whom his uncle leveled his criticisms, and of reporting, no doubt with embellishments of his own invention, the speeches which told of the popular admiration in which the great composer was held. By this species of flattery he played upon the weakness of his uncle and actually obtained an influence over him in the course of time which he exploited to his own advantage in various directions. He was naturally inclined to indolence and self-indulgence, and it is not strange that Beethoven's self-sacrifice in his behalf never awakened in him any deep sense of gratitude, while his unreasonable and ill-considered severity aroused a spirit of rebellion in him which grew with his advance towards manhood. Beethoven never seems to have realised that Karl had outgrown the period when he could be treated as a child, and it was a child's submission which he asked of him.

At the beginning of the year the pianist Friedrich Kalkbrenner was in Vienna; on January 25 he gave a recital in the small Redoutensaal. Schindler writes in a Conversation Book: "Did Hr. Kalkbrenner do you the favor of honoring you with a ticket to his concert? Otherwise he has not given out any." At the same time Moscheles had returned from his tour abroad to play in Vienna, but at this particular moment he was taken sick in Prague. Beethoven had heard a great deal about Kalkbrenner; Johann expressed the opinion that he played better than Moscheles; Schindler wrote down that he had scored a triumph. According to Karl, "Moscheles is said to have acknowledged that he did not grasp the meaning of your Variations at all."

Schuppanzigh gave repeated quartet performances at this time; Beethoven's Septet and F minor Quartet especially were received with great enthusiasm. At the performance on February 1 there were present several of Beethoven's friends such as Tuscher, Piringer and Wolfmayer.[2]

Grillparzer's opera-book was a frequent subject of conversation between Beethoven and his friends in the early months of 1824 as already mentioned, but petitions and advice were alike unfruitful. He did not go to work upon it nor yet upon a composition which presented a more urgent obligation. This was the oratorio which he had agreed to write for the Gesellschaft der Musikfreunde and on which he had received an advance of money in 1819. Here the fatal procrastination, though it may have been agreeable to Beethoven, was not altogether his fault. Bernard began the book, but seems to have put it aside after a few weeks.

Reference has already been made to the fact that in 1819 Oliva could not understand Bernard's inaction in the matter.[3] In April, 1820, Bernard himself writes: "I must finish the oratorio completely this month so that you can begin on it at Mödling."[4] His intentions were not carried out, however, for in August, 1820, somebody writes:

I have put it seriously to *Sanctus Bernardus* that it is high time that it be done, that Hauschka himself was urging a completion; he will finish it *this month, id est* in 5 days; and he will talk with you this evening at Cameel's[5]. . . . [two pages later] When I told Bernard that Hauschka had come to you about it he was embarrassed, it seems that he is throwing the blame on you.

•~•

He does not want to show his poetical impotency.[6]

--⚹At this time Beethoven had a sketch of the first part of the text which Bernard asked to be returned, with the promise that the oratorio text would be finished "in the following weeks."[7]⚹-- Finally towards the close of October, 1823, Bernard gave a copy of the complete text of the oratorio, which was entitled *Der Sieg des Kreuzes* ("The Victory of the Cross"), to Beethoven and also one to Sonnleithner for the Society. After waiting nearly three months, the directorate of the society at a meeting held on January 9, 1824, took action, the nature of which was notified to both Beethoven and Bernard.

[2] Johann Nepomuk Wolfmayer, rich Viennese merchant and music-lover to whom Beethoven was to dedicate his last quartet.
[3] Schünemann, I, p. 35.
[4] *Ibid.*, II, p. 55.

[5] *Ibid.*, p. 225. The writer is Oliva, according to Schünemann.
[6] *Ibid.*, p. 227.
[7] *Ibid.*, p. 240.

According to K. F. Pohl,[8] librarian of the society, Leopold v. Sonnleithner had proposed to the society that there be a performance of the Mass and the Ninth Symphony. Beethoven declared that he wished to give the proceeds of the second performance to the society "in case this would assume the expenses for copying and all other such incidentals." The society estimated the expenses as coming to 1842 florins; this was considered too great and the project was abandoned. Sonneck in his penetrating essay on this subject has rightly emphasized that this gesture on Beethoven's part was made before he received the reminder from the society on January 9 and should be borne in mind when reading the composer's answer to the society. As Sonneck puts it, "Beethoven, embarrassed by his predicament with Bernard's long delayed and unsatisfactory text, proposed a means for squaring his financial account with his creditors which they seriously considered."[9]

The society wrote to Bernard that as it had left the choice of the text which he was to compose to Beethoven, it could not say whether or not the society would make use of the poem which he had sent until Beethoven had set it to music, and the censor had given his sanction. He was also asked to co-operate with the society in stimulating Beethoven to finish the work "so long expected by the musical world."

The letter from the society to Beethoven follows:

Dear Sir!

When the Society of the Friends of Music of the Austrian Empire invited you to write an oratorio four years ago, which proposal you accepted along with its terms; it left to you the choice of a poem and a poet. Soon thereafter it was learned that H. Bernard had undertaken the writing of the poem. As often as we turned to you in this long interim and asked if you were already occupied with this work, we heard that the poem was not yet in your hands. We could not expect that a composer of your stamp should sketch the plan of his musical composition before he had been entrusted with the whole of the poem and had found it worked out and finished according to his wish; therefore we could only turn to H. Bernard and urge him on. Finally he handed in the complete poem to the society near the end of October, 1823, and explained that he had also given a copy over to you. Since on the one hand we could only make use of the text if you, the composer, not only have actually chosen it for composition but also have actually completed the composition; but on the other hand the resolve has been expressed repeatedly by you to deliver such a work to the society, which has been confirmed by the part-payment made on request; we request consequently Your Well-born to inform the society categorically whether you will set to music the poem delivered by H. Bernard and at what time we may hope to receive this work to which every friend of music and admirer of your great talent has been looking forward for such a long time with keen expectation.

Receive assurances of the most distinguished respect.

Beethoven wrote the following answer to the society on January 23:

[8] Karl Friedrich Pohl, *Die Gesellschaft der Musikfreunde* (Vienna, 1871), pp. 13-14.
[9] *Beethoven Letters in America*, pp. 95-7.

Dear Sirs!

Since I have been overloaded with business and still plagued continually by an eye trouble, please be good enough to excuse my late answer— Concerning the oratorio I hope that veritas odium *non* parit. *I did not* choose H. v. B[ernard] to write the text; I was assured that the Society had commissioned him— For [since] H. v. B. has been editing the newspaper, it has been difficult to confer with him much. It has become a long story, however, very irksome in fact for me, since H. v. B. had written nothing other than "Libussa" for music, which at that time had not yet been performed. I have known it, however, since 1809 and since that time it has become very much altered; thus I couldn't with full confidence view the undertaking with him as anything but difficult. On account of this I was forced all the more to hold out until I had the whole text; at one point I finally received the first part. But according to B's disposition it had to be changed again, and I had to give it back again, that much I remember. Finally I received the whole at the same time that the Society did, with other obligations having occurred which I could not fulfill because of earlier illness. I have now really had to hurry to keep my word, all the more since you know that I *unfortunately can live only from works that I write. But now a variety of passages have to be altered* in B's oratorio. I have already indicated some and soon will finish and then acquaint B with them. For, though I find the material good and the poem has some value, it cannot remain *as it is.* "Christus am Ölberg" was written by me in collaboration with the *poet* in 14 days, but that poet was musical and had written several things for music and I could consult him at any moment. Let us leave out of consideration *the value* of poems of this sort. We all know that allowances are to be made. The good lies here in the middle; but so far as I am concerned, I would rather set Homer, Klopstock, Schiller to music. If they offer difficulties to be overcome, *these immortal poets* at least are worthy of it— As soon as I am through with making changes in the oratorio with B, I shall have the honor to inform you of the fact and at the same time let the society know when it may with certainty count upon it. That is all I can say about it at present—Respecting the 400 fl. V.S., sent to me *without demand,* I would have sent them back long ago had I been able to foresee that the matter of this oratorio would last much longer than I had imagined. It was grievous to me not to be able to express myself on the subject. In this connection I had the idea of joining with the Society in a concert, in order to provide at least the interest on the sum. But neither Herr Schindler nor my brother was authorized to say anything on the subject, and it was farthest from my thoughts that it should be done *in such a manner.* Please inform H. L. v. Sonnleithner of this too. Also I heartily thank the Society for the offer of the platform and other aid which it proffered me. In due time I shall make use of this offer— I shall be glad to hear whether the Society wishes to make use of my works, among which is a new symphony, later on after my concert. The great Mass is really rather in the oratorio style and particularly adapted to the Society. I shall be especially pleased if my unselfishness and also my zealous desire to serve the Society in whose benevolent deeds in behalf of art I always take the greatest interest, are recognized— Please accept especially my high esteem for you, Sirs, with all respect

Ludwig van Beethoven

Beethoven was frequently urged to set to work on the music of *Der Sieg des Kreuzes*; but he was also advised not to compose it. Archduke Rudolph accepted the dedication of the poem and wrote to Beethoven telling him of the fact and expressing a wish that he would set it to music. But the editor Schikh said to him: "If I were Beethoven I would *never* compose the extremely tiresome text of his oratorio." Beethoven had expressed satisfaction with the subject and the quality of the lines; he discussed changes which he wished to have made with Bernard after he had had time to consider the work as a whole; he promised Hauschka in September that he would compose it as soon as he returned to the city, and asked him to pay Bernard his fee; but he never set seriously to work upon it, though at the end of the letter to Hauschka (which bears date September 23, 1824) he reiterated his promise so that he might, with mock solemnity, attest it by affixing his hand and seal.

The book of the *Sieg des Kreuzes* was based upon the ancient story of the apparition of the cross and the legend *"In hoc signo vinces"* to Constantine the Great, who had crossed the Alps into Italy and lay encamped confronting his enemy Maxentius before Rome. His daughter Julia, who was represented as wife to Maxentius, attempted to avert the battle, but the vision strengthened Constantine's resolve. Julia heard the angelic canticles which accompanied the apparition and was converted to the true faith, persisting in it to martyrdom, to which she was condemned by her husband. Maxentius also heard the voices, but his augurs (allegorical figures representing Hate and Discord) interpreted them to his advantage, whereas similar figures (Faith, Hope and Charity) inspired the Christian army. The battle scene was preceded by pious canticles on the one hand, harsh songs on the other; Constantine promised to raise the Cross on the forum in Rome, victory was celebrated with Christian hymns, "Hosanna!" and "Glory to God!" Beethoven's copy of the libretto has been preserved, and in it are indications that he made some heroic excisions. He permitted Faith, Hope and Charity to remain, but banished Hate and Discord. It is pretty plain that he found nothing inspiring in the work. Holz told Jahn that he said to him, "How could I get up any enthusiasm about it?" Schindler says that Beethoven's failure to set the book caused a rupture of the friendship which existed between him and Bernard. The directors of the Gesellschaft der Musikfreunde dropped the matter, neither importuning Beethoven more nor taking any steps to recover the money paid on account. The society afterwards elected him to honorary membership.

During the account of the oratorio project, we learned that the new symphony was ready or almost ready and that an *Akademie* had already been planned for a performance of the new work. Schindler, who was an eyewitness of events at this time, gives the termination date for the Ninth Symphony as February, 1824, and adds that the conclusion of the work had a cheering effect upon Beethoven's spirits. He no longer grudged himself occasional recreation and was again seen strolling through the streets of Vienna, gazing into the shop-windows through eye-glasses which dangled at the end of a black ribbon, and, after a long interregnum, greeting friends and acquaintances as they passed. The history of the work is far more interesting than that of any other of his compositions, with the possible exception of the Mass in D. Nottebohm has painstakingly extracted from the sketchbooks all the evidence which they afford, touching the origin and development of the work, and presented it in a chapter of his *Zweite Beethoveniana,*[10] and his conclusions have been adopted in the presentation of facts which follow.

Thoughts of a symphony to succeed the Symphonies in A and F major (Nos. 7 and 8) were in the composer's mind while he was making sketches for those two works in 1812; but the memoranda there found tell us only in what key the new symphony was to be; they are mere verbal notes: "2nd Sinfonie, D minor" and "Sinfonie in D minor-3rd Sinfonie."[11] A fugue-theme, identical, so far as the first three measures go, with that of the Scherzo of the Ninth Symphony, presented itself to him and was imprisoned in his notebook in 1815, being recorded among the sketches for the Sonata for Pianoforte and Violoncello in D, Op. 102.[12]

There is another sketch with a note[13] to show that Beethoven was thinking of a new symphony at the time, but the sketch cannot be associated with the Ninth Symphony.

The fugue-theme appeared again in 1817 in an altered form but with the same rhythmic outline.

According to Nottebohm, this was to be the main theme for the Fugue for five stringed instruments. The Fugue, Op. 137, was worked out, however, in D major on a different subject. Both versions of the D-minor theme reappeared in later sketches for the symphony, the composition of which really began when the beginning of the first movement was sketched. Of

---

[10] Pages 157ff. (TDR, v, 18, n. 2.)

[11] *Ibid.*, p. 111. (TDR, v, 18, n. 1.)

[12] There are several stories touching the origin of the fugue-theme of the Scherzo of the D minor Symphony, two of which may be given for what they are worth. Czerny says that the theme occurred to Beethoven while listening to the twittering of sparrows in a garden. Holz told Jahn that one evening Beethoven was seated in the forest at Schön-

brunn and in the gloaming fancied he saw all about him a multitude of gnomes popping in and out of their hiding places; and this stirred his fancy to the invention of the theme. (TK, III, 145, n. 1.)

[13] "Sinfonie at the beginning only 4 voices, 2 viol. viola, basso, amongst them forte with other voices and if possible bring in all the other instruments one by one and gradually." (TK, III, 145, n. 2.)

this fragments are found on loose leaves belonging to the year 1817. By the end of that year and the beginning of 1818 (presumably from September to May) extended sketches of the movement were made. The principal subject was definitely fixed, but the subsidiary material was still missing. The fugue-theme was assigned to the third movement. There was no suggestion of the use of Schiller's "Ode to Joy," but a plain intimation of an instrumental finale.

In 1818 a plan was outlined for the introduction of voices into the slow movement of a symphony which was to follow the Sinfonie in D. It is as follows:

Adagio Cantique.
Pious song in a symphony in the ancient modes—Lord God we praise Thee—alleluia—either alone or as introduction to a fugue. The whole 2nd sinfonie might be characterized in this manner in which case the vocal parts would enter in the last movement or already in the Adagio. The violins, etc., of the orchestra to be increased tenfold in the last movement, in which case the vocal parts would enter gradually—in the text of the Adagio Greek myth, *Cantique Ecclesiastique*—in the Allegro, feast of Bachus [*sic*].

It will be recalled that in 1822 Beethoven told Rochlitz that he had two symphonies in his mind which were to differ from each other. One difference at least is indicated here by the purpose to use voices in a movement to be written in the old modes. His well-known love for classic subjects, no doubt, prompted the thought of the "pious orgies" of a Pagan festival. Schiller's hymn was still absent from his mind. These sketches were all likewise excursions undertaken while Beethoven was chiefly occupied with the composition of the Pianoforte Sonata, Op. 106. What progress, if any, was made with the Symphony during the next four years can not well be determined. The work was interrupted by the composition of other works, notably the Mass in D, the last three Pianoforte Sonatas and the Overture, Op. 124.[14] It was not until the Mass and the Josephstadt music were finished in the sketches that he gave his attention to the Symphony.

In the sketches of 1822, there are evidences of considerable progress on the first movement, little if any on the Scherzo, the fugue-themes of 1815 and 1817 appearing in them almost unchanged. There is no hint as yet of the slow movement, but among the sketches appears the beginning of the melody of the "Ode to Joy" with the underlying words, assigned as a finale. The thought of using the Ode for a concluding movement had presented itself, but only tentatively, not as a fixed determination. Following this sketch, but of another date (to judge by the handwriting and the contents), comes a memorandum indicating that the symphony in mind (perhaps the one to be written for London) was to consist of four movements—the first (no doubt, though it is not mentioned) being the present first, the second in 2/4 time,

14 Nottebohm might well have added the Diabelli Variations.

the third (presumably) in 6/8, while the fourth was to be built on the fugal theme of 1817 and to be "well-fugued." The next recognizable sketch is for a Presto in 2/4 designated as a second movement and this is followed by the beginning of the first movement preceded by four measures in triple time marked "Alla Autrichien." A third sketch is marked as belonging to a "Sinfonie allemand." It is a new melody to the words beginning Schiller's Ode to be used in a chorus. The accompanying memorandum reads:

Sinfonie allemand after which the chorus

Freude   schöner   Götter = funken   Tochter   aus   E = ly = si = um

enters or also without variations. End of the Sinfonie with Turkish music and vocal chorus.

The last relevant sketch in the book of 1822 is a sort of thematic index to the symphony as it now lay planned in Beethoven's purpose:

The second movement was to be a fugued Scherzo with the theme of 1815, the fourth the Presto in 2/4 time which first appeared in this year, the fifth the "Ode to Joy." In the midst of these sketches appears the significant remark: "Or perhaps instead of a new symphony, a new overture on *Bach*, well fugued with 3——."[15]

The conclusions to be drawn from the sketches thus far are that, as was the case in 1812 when the Seventh and Eighth Symphonies were brought forth as a pair, Beethoven was again contemplating the almost simultaneous production of two symphonies. He did not adhere to the project long, so far as we can know from the written records, and the remark about the substitution of an overture on B-a-c-h probably marks the time when he began seriously to consider the advisability of abandoning what would then have been the Tenth Symphony. With the exception of a portion of the first movement, the Ninth Symphony was still in a chaotic state. Taken in connection with negotiations which had been concluded with the Philharmonic Society of London, it may be assumed, however, that the present Symphony in D minor was associated in Beethoven's mind with the English

[15] Nottebohm fills the hiatus with "Trombones? Subjects?" (TK, III, 147, n. 1.)

commission, and that the second, which he had thoughts of abandoning in favor of the overture, was to have been a "Sinfonie allemand." For a time, at least, Beethoven is not likely to have contemplated a choral movement with German words in connection with the symphony for the London Philharmonic Society: this was to have an instrumental finale. The linguistic objection would be invalid in the case of the German symphony, however, and to this was now assigned the contemplated setting of Schiller's poem.

Work now proceeded with little interruption (except that occasioned by the composition of the Variations, Op. 120), and most of the first half of 1823 was devoted to the first movement, which was nearly complete in sketch-form before anything of the other movements appeared beyond the themes which have already been cited. When the foundation of the work is firmly laid we have the familiar phenomenon of work upon two or three movements simultaneously. In a general way it may be asserted that the year 1823 saw the birth of the Symphony, though work was carried over into 1824. The second movement was complete in the sketches before the third—this was about August; the third before the fourth—about the middle of October. The second theme of the slow movement was perfected before the sketches for the first movement were finished. In a Conversation Book used in the fall of the year 1823 the nephew writes: "I am glad that you have brought in the beautiful andante." The principal theme of the movement appears to have been conceived between May and July, 1823, but it had to submit to much alteration before it acquired the lovely contours which we now admire. This was the case, too, with the simple folksong-like tune of the Finale.

Sketches for the Finale show that Beethoven had made considerable progress with the setting of Schiller's Ode before he decided to incorporate it with the Symphony. In June or July, 1823, he wrote down a melody in D minor which he designated "Finale instrumentale":

and which, transposed into another key and slightly altered, was eventually used in the finale of the Quartet in A minor, Op. 132. That it was intended for the Finale of the Symphony is proved by the fact that it is surrounded with sketches for the Symphony in D minor and Beethoven recurred to it twice before the end of the year; there was no thought of the quartet at the time.

When he began work on the Finale, Beethoven took up the choral part with the instrumental variations first and then attacked the instrumental introduction with the recitatives. Once the present "Joy" melody, as noted in the fall of 1822, was adopted, the tune underwent many transformations in the second part before its definitive form was established. Among the musical sketches occur several memoranda containing hints which were carried out in part, for instance: "Turkish music in Wer das nie gekonnt, stehle"; in sketches for the Allegro *all marcia*: "Turkish music—first pianissimo—a few sounds ppmo—a few rests—then the full strength"; a third: "On Welt Sternenzelt forte trombone blasts"; a fourth (in studies for the final chorus: "the height of the voices to be more by instruments" ("die Höhe der Stimmen mehr durch Instrumente") which may be interpreted to mean that Beethoven realized that he was carrying the voices into dangerous altitudes and intended to give them instrumental support.[16]

Other sketches indicate that Beethoven intended for a considerable time to write an instrumental introduction with new themes for the Finale. For this prelude there are a number of sketches of different kinds, some of them conceived while sketches for the first movement were still in hand. Before July, 1823, there are no hints of a combined vocal and instrumental bridge from the Adagio to the setting of the "Ode to Joy." After that month there are evidences that he had conceived the idea of introducing the "Joy" melody played upon wind instruments with a prelude in the recitative style, a reminiscence of the first movement and premonitory suggestions of the fundamental melody. This was the first step towards the eventual shape of the Finale. The lacking element was the verbal link which should connect the instrumental movements with the choral conclusion. This came after his return from Baden to Vienna. The sketches bear out Schindler's remark: "When he reached the development of the fourth movement there began a struggle such as is seldom seen. The object was to find a proper manner of introducing Schiller's Ode. One day entering the room he exclaimed 'I have it! I have it!' With that he showed me the sketchbook bearing the words, 'Let us sing the song of the immortal Schiller Freude,' whereupon a solo voice began directly the hymn, to joy."[17]

By grouping a number of sketches it is now possible to make a graphic representation of the ideas which passed through Beethoven's mind while seeking a way to bridge the chasm between instrumental and vocal utterances by means of a formula of recitative. The sketches are in parts illegible, in parts so obscure that Nottebohm and Deiters differ in their readings. Here

---

[16] *II Beeth.*, p. 186.   [17] *Biogr.*, II, p. 55. (TDR, v, 26.)

is Deiters' version; it may be compared with Nottebohm's in *II Beeth.*,
pp. 189ff. Over a portion of an instrumental recitative

(a)

occur the words: "No this would remind us too much of our despair"; other
sketches follow in the order here indicated:

Heute ist ein feierlicher Tag
[To-day is a solemn day]

mei ne Fru (Freunde?) die - ser sei ge - fei - ert
[my fri (friends?) let it be cele-brat - ed]

durchmit Gesang und [Tanz? Scherz?]
[with song and [Dance? Play?]]

O nein dieses nicht etwas
[O no not this something]
ist es was ich fordere
[is this what I ask]

anderes gefällig
[else pleasing]

etc.

There follows:

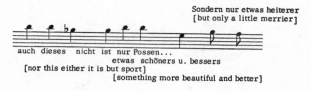

Then is introduced the Adagio theme and, further, the "Joy" theme:

These are taken up again:

---

[18] Beethoven connected this by a numeral to the above statement of the theme. He crossed out the preceding. (TDR, v, 30, n. 1.)

[19] Under this line Beethoven wrote "was ich. . . ."; then follow two words, "ich selbst," in pencil. (TDR, v, 30, n. 2.)

After stating the "Joy" theme, he takes up the following words:

Ha   dieses ist[es]   Es   ist nun   ge - fun - den
[Ha   this   it is   it   now is   dis-cov-ered]

Freu₋ - -

meilleur

Later comes the memorandum which Beethoven showed Schindler ("Lasst uns das Lied des unsterblichen Schillers singen, Freude, etc.") and then:

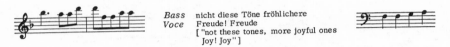

Bass   nicht diese Töne fröhlichere
Voce   Freude! Freude
       ["not these tones, more joyful ones
       Joy! Joy"]

The entire Symphony was finished in sketch-form at the end of 1823 and written out in score in February, 1824. Omitting from consideration the theme of the second movement, noted in 1815 and again in 1817 (probably with an entirely different purpose in mind), the time which elapsed between the beginning of the first movement (1817-1818) and the time of completion was about six and a half years. Within this period, however, there were extended interruptions caused by other works. Serious and continuous labor on the Symphony was not taken up until after the completion of the *Missa Solemnis*; it began in 1822, occupied the greater part of 1823 and ended in the early part of 1824. Beethoven, therefore, worked on the Symphony a little more than a year.

The idea of composing music to the Ode, it will be remembered, already existed in 1793 when Professor Fischenich wrote to Charlotte von Schiller; "He [Beethoven] proposes also to compose Schiller's 'Freude,' and indeed strophe by strophe." ──It is heard of again in a sketchbook of 1798, where there is a melodic phrase adapted to the words, "Muss ein lieber Vater wohnen."[20]── In 1808, Beethoven wrote the Fantasy for Piano, Chorus and Orchestra, Op. 80, in which he first essayed the idea of an orchestral beginning (introduced by a solo piano) leading to a concluding section with chorus; and in letters[21] he compared this work to the choral movement of the Ninth Symphony.[22] Amongst sketches for the Eighth Symphony there crops up a

20 *II Beeth.*, p. 479.

21 For instance, to Probst and to Schott, March 10, 1824.

22 The use of the song "Gegenliebe," composed in 1795, in the Choral Fantasy is striking both by its melodic resemblance to the "Joy" theme and by the similarity of treatment: the theme and variations stated first by the instruments, culminating in the statement by the chorus. (TDR, v, 47.)

melody for the beginning of the hymn amongst material used for the Overture, Op. 115, into which he appears at one time to have thought of introducing portions of it.[23] All these sketches, of course, preceded the melody of 1822, conceived for use in a "Sinfonie allemand." When Beethoven first took up the ode for setting it was to become a "durchkomponierte Lied," i.e., each stanza was to have an illustrative setting; when he planned to incorporate it in an overture he proposed to use only selected portions of the poem, for he accompanies the melodic sketch with the note: "Disjointed fragments like Princes are beggars, etc., not the whole"; and a little later: "disjointed fragments from Schiller's Freude connected into a whole."[24]

The questions which have been raised by the choral finale are many and have occupied the minds of musicians, professional and amateur, ever since the great symphony was first given to the world. In 1852 Carl Czerny told Otto Jahn that Beethoven had thought, after the performance, of composing a new finale without vocal parts for the work. Schindler saw the note in Jahn's papers and wrote in the margin: "That is not true"; but it must be remembered that there was a cessation of the great intimacy between Beethoven and Schindler which began not long after the Symphony had been produced, and lasted almost till Beethoven was on his deathbed. Schindler can not have been present at all of the meetings between Beethoven and his friends at which the Symphony was discussed. Nevertheless he is upheld, in a measure, by the fact (to which Nottebohm directed attention) that Beethoven, if he made the remark, either did not mean it to be taken seriously or afterwards changed his mind; for after keeping the manuscript in his hands six months he sent it to the publisher as we have it. Seyfried, writing in *Cäcilia* (Vol. IX, p. 236), faults Beethoven for not having taken the advice of well-meaning friends and written a new finale as he did for the Quartet in B-flat, Op. 130.[25] Even if one of the well-meaning friends was Seyfried himself, the statement has value as evidence that Beethoven was not as convinced as Czerny's story would have it appear that the choral finale was a mistake. Sonnleithner, in a letter to the editor of the *Allgemeine Musikalische Zeitung* in 1864,[26] confirmed Jahn's statement by saying that Czerny had repeatedly related as an unimpeachable fact that some time after the first performance of the Symphony Beethoven, in a circle of his most intimate friends, had expressed himself positively to the effect that he perceived

[23] Beethoven notes "Freude schöner Götterfunken Tochter Overture ausarbeiten" [*ausarbeiten*—to be worked out]. See *Beeth.*, p. 41. (TDR, V, 49, n. 1.)

[24] "Abgerissene Sätze wie Fürsten sind Bettler u.s.w." The phrase is probably a record of Beethoven's imperfect recollection of the line *"Bettler* werden Fürstenbrüder," which appeared in an early version of Schiller's poem where we now read "Alle Menschen werden Brüder." The thought lies near that

it was the early form of the poem, when it was still an "Ode to Freedom" (not "to Joy"), which first aroused enthusiastic admiration for it in Beethoven's mind. In a Conversation Book of 1824 Bernard says to Beethoven: "Instead of 'Beggars become brothers of princes' it reads in your text 'All men become brothers.'" (TDR, V, 49, n. 2.)

[25] Nottebohm (*II Beeth.*, p. 182) guesses that the advice came from Seyfried himself.

[26] April 6, 1864, pp. 245-46. (TDR, V, 65.)

that he had made a mistake [*Misgriff*] in the last movement and intended to reject it and write an instrumental piece in its stead, for which he already had an idea in his head. What that idea was the reader knows. That Beethoven may have had scruples touching the appropriateness of the choral finale, is comprehensible enough in view of the fact that the original plan of the Symphony contemplated an instrumental close and that Beethoven labored so hard to establish arbitrarily an organic union between the Ode and the first three movements; but it is not likely that he gave long thought to the project of writing a new finale.

For the chief facts in the story of the first performance of the D minor Symphony in Vienna we are largely dependent on Schindler, who was not only a witness of it but also an active agent. Beethoven was thoroughly out of sympathy with the musical taste of Vienna, which had been diverted from German ideals by the superficial charm of Rossini's melodies. He wanted much to produce his symphony, but despaired of receiving adequate support or recognition from his home public. His friends offered him encouragement, but his fear and suspicion that his music was no longer understood by the Viennese and he no longer admired, had grown into a deep-rooted conviction. The project of a concert at which the Mass in D should be performed had been mooted months before.

Since 1822, Beethoven had been acquainted with the young singers, Karoline Unger and Henriette Sontag. On September 8 of that year he wrote to his brother Johann, "Two singers visited us today and since they wanted by all means to kiss my hands and were really pretty, I proposed that they kiss my mouth." Judging from the Conversation Books he saw them a good deal in 1823, and they vied with one another in their expressions of devoted veneration for the master. Near the end of 1823, Schindler writes down: "If they do not come, it is merely the fault of jealousy, for Unger told me that she would come alone; but I replied that she should certainly bring Sontag along with her, it would give you twice as much pleasure: now I am curious [to see] whether it will happen."[27] Unger did come alone in December and again in January from which time springs the involvement of these two artists in the first performance of the new symphony. On January 25, 1824, Unger writes:

When are you going to give your concert? When one is *once* possessed by the devil, one can be content.

On a regular day in Lent, when 3 or 4 take place, would be best.

If you give the concert, I will guarantee that the house will be full.

Still a moody suspicion, which the lady thinks it her right to rebuke:

[27] Alfred C. Kalischer, *Beethoven und seine Zeitgenossen* (Leipzig, 1910), III, p. 213.

You have too little confidence in yourself. Has not the homage of the whole world given you a little more pride? Who speaks of opposition? Will you not learn to believe that everybody is longing to worship you again in new works? O obstinacy!

In this mood, Beethoven had turned to Count Brühl in Berlin and inquired whether or not a performance of the new Mass and Symphony might be given in that city, and Brühl had favored the plan. When news of this fact became known in Vienna, a number of Beethoven's friends addressed him in the following memorial:

To Herr Ludwig van Beethoven.

Out of the wide circle of reverent admirers surrounding your genius in this your second native city, there approach you today a small number of the disciples and lovers of art to give expression to long-felt wishes, timidly to prefer a long-suppressed request.

But as the number of spokesmen bears but a small proportion to the many who joyfully acknowledge your worth and what you have grown to be to the present as well as the future, so the wishes and requests are by no means restricted to the number of those who are like-minded with themselves and who, in the name of all to whom art and the realization of their ideals are something more than means and objects of pastime, assert that their wish is also the wish of an un-numbered multitude, their request is echoed loudly or in silence by every one whose bosom is animated by a sense of the divine in music.

It is the wish of those of our countrymen who reverence art to which we desire more especially to give expression; for though Beethoven's name and creations belong to all contemporaneous humanity and every country which opens a suscepti-ble bosom to art, it is Austria which is best entitled to claim him as her own. Among her inhabitants appreciation for the great and immortal works which Mozart and Haydn created for all time within the lap of their homes still lives, and they are conscious with joyous pride that the sacred triad in which these names and yours glow as the symbol of the highest within the spiritual realm of tones, sprang from the soil of their fatherland. All the more painful must it have been for you to feel that a foreign power has invaded this royal citadel of the noblest, that above the mounds of the dead and around the dwelling-place of the only survivor of the band, phantoms are leading the dance who can boast of no kinship with the princely spirits of those royal houses; that shallowness is abusing the name and insignia of art, and unworthy dalliance with sacred things is beclouding and dissipating appreciation for the pure and eternally beautiful.

For this reason they feel a greater and livelier sense than ever before that the great need of the present moment is a new impulse directed by a powerful hand, a new advent of the ruler in his domain. It is this need which leads them to you to-day, and following are the petitions which they lay before you in behalf of all to whom these wishes are dear, and in the name of native art.

Do not withhold longer from the popular enjoyment, do not keep longer from the oppressed sense of that which is great and perfect, a performance of the latest masterworks of your hand. We know that a grand sacred composition has been associated with that first one in which you have immortalized the emotions of a soul, penetrated and transfigured by the power of faith and superterrestrial light.

We know that a new flower glows in the garland of your glorious, still unequalled symphonies. For years, ever since the thunders of the Victory at Vittoria ceased to reverberate, we have waited and hoped to see you distribute new gifts from the fulness of your riches to the circle of your friends. Do not longer disappoint the general expectations! Heighten the effect of your newest creations by the joy of becoming first acquainted with them through you! Do not allow these, your latest offspring, some day to appear, perhaps, as foreigners in their place of birth, introduced, perhaps, by persons to whom you and your mind are strange! Appear soon among your friends, your admirers, your venerators! This is our nearest and first prayer.

Other claims on your genius have been made public. The desires expressed and offers made to you more than a year ago by the management of our Court Opera and the Society of Austrian Friends of Music had too long been the un-uttered wish of all admirers of art, and your name stimulated the hopes and expectations of too many not to obtain the quickest and widest publicity, not to awaken the most general interest. Poetry has done her share in giving support to these lovely hopes and wishes. Worthy material from the hand of a valued poet waits to be charmed into life by your fancy. Do not let that intimate call to so noble an aim be made in vain. Do not delay longer to lead us back to those departed days when the song of Polyhymnia moved powerfully and delighted the initiates in art and the hearts of the multitude!

Need we tell you with what regret your retirement from public life has filled us? Need we assure you that at a time when all glances were hopefully turned towards you, all perceived with sorrow that *the one* man whom all of us are compelled to acknowledge as foremost among living men in his domain, looked on in silence as foreign art took possession of German soil, the seat of honor of the German muse, while German works gave pleasure only by echoing the favorite tunes of foreigners and, where the most excellent had lived and labored, a second childhood of taste threatens to follow the Golden Age of Art?

You alone are able to insure a decisive victory to the efforts of the best amongst us. From you the native Art Society and the German Opera expect new blossoms, rejuvenated life and a new sovereignty of the true and beautiful over the dominion to which the prevalent spirit of fashion wishes to subject even the eternal laws of art. Bid us hope that the wishes of all who have listened to the sound of your harmonies will soon be fulfilled! This is our most urgent second prayer.

May the year which we have begun not come to an end without rejoicing us with the fruits of our petition and may the coming Spring when it witnesses the unfolding of one of our longed-for gifts become a twofold blooming-time for us and all the world of art!

Vienna, February, 1824.

Prince C. Lichnowsky	Abbé Stadler	Count Czernin, First
Artaria and Co.	von Felsburg, Court Sec.	Chamberlain
v. Hauschka	Count Ferd. von	Count Moritz v. Fries
M. J. Leidesdorf	Stockhammer	J. F. Castelli
J. E. von Wayna	Anton Diabelli	Prof. Deinhardtstein
Andreas Streicher	Count Ferd. v. Palfy	Ch. Kuffner
Anton Halm	Baron Ed. v. Schweiger	J. N. Nehammer, State
		Secretary

Steiner von Felsburg,	Carl Czerny	Dr. L. Sonnleithner
Bank Sequestrator	Count M. v. Lichnowsky	Steiner and Co.
Count M. v. Dietrichstein	v. Zmeskall	Lederer
Ig. Edler von Mosel,	Court Councillor	J. N. Bihler
R.I. Court Councillor	Kiesewetter	

The most active agent in securing signatures was Count Lichnowsky. It was published in Bäuerle's *Theater-Zeitung* and also in Kanne's journal. This publication and gossip to the effect that he had prompted both writing and printing, annoyed Beethoven greatly. He gave vent to his rage in a remark which he himself wrote in a Conversation Book: "Now that the thing has taken this turn I can no longer find joy in it. The atrocity of attributing such an act to me sickens me with the whole business and I am scarcely able to address even a few words to men of such intellectual prominence. Not a single critic can boast of having received a letter from me. I have never—" there his outburst breaks off; he did not finish the sentence in writing. Schindler tried to ease his mind! "Your fears are groundless," he wrote; "your honor has not been compromised—let that suffice you; nobody will accuse you of having been directly concerned in it." Court Secretary von Felsburg and J. N. Bihler, a tutor in the imperial household, waited upon Beethoven one afternoon to present the address, and talk over its suggestions. Beethoven said he wanted to read it when alone. Later Schindler went to him and found him with the letter in his hand. He was manifestly moved by its expressions and handed it to Schindler to read while he went to the window and gazed out for quite a while. Then he returned to Schindler, said briefly: "It is very beautiful!—it rejoices me greatly!" and when Schindler also had expressed his delight added: "Let us go out for a walk." During the walk he remained sunk in thought.[28]

The object had in view by the designers of the memorial was accomplished;—Beethoven was lifted out of his despondent mood and inspired with new determination. By March Schindler had been informed that the concert would be given in Vienna. He lauded Beethoven's decision and begged him not to distress himself with vain imaginings about the outcome—everything would go gloriously and everybody would esteem it an honor to participate. Expressions of satisfaction poured in on the composer from all quarters, and also offers of help. Beethoven's friends gathered together and discussed the details in the liveliest fashion—the time, the place, the programme, the choir and orchestra, who should sing the solos, the copying of the music in which Beethoven laid great stress on the supervision of the parts, the price of seats, the number of rehearsals. The concert season was drawing to a close and delay was hazardous; but delay there was, for Beethoven was vacillating, full of doubtings and suspicions, and there was a too great multiplicity of counsellors. Schindler was kept extremely busy; Lichnowsky and Schuppanzigh bestirred themselves mightily; brother

[28] *Biogr.*, II, p. 64.

Johann came to the fore with advice and suggestions, especially about the business administration; nephew Karl, much to Schindler's dissatisfaction, not only ran errands but volunteered his opinion on many topics. A page from a Conversation Book will disclose how the consultations with Beethoven were carried on—for Beethoven's consent to every step had to be obtained, which was a pity. In the following excerpt it is Schuppanzigh who is speaking to the composer, whom he, as was his wont, addresses in the third person—as was fitting to the dignity of "Mylord Falstaff."

How about his concert?

It is getting late, Lent will not last much longer.

He ought to give three movements [the Mass is meant, of course].

Under no circumstances a piano piece.

There are no piano players here.

He will need Buringer [Piringer] to provide the best dilettante, Sonnleithner to look after the singers, and Plachetka [Blahetka] for the announcements and bills.

He has offered himself.

Young Sonnleithner has all the amateur singers under his thumb.

Sonnleithner knows them too and understands it.

It would be a good idea *for him* [Beethoven] *to pay a visit to Duport to talk to him once more about me.*

The significance of the concluding remark will appear later. At another time Karl is reporting progress:

Piringer has said that he would undertake the appointment of the instrumentalists. Sonnleithner the chorus. Schuppanzigh the orchestra. Blahetka the announcements, tickets, etc. So everything is looked after. You can give two concerts. . . .

When will you have it announced?

Schuppanzigh is coming tomorrow. . . .

Blahetka offered to stamp the tickets, etc., but I think that all such matters ought to be [entrusted] to your brother. It would be safer. . . .

⋅~⋅

Piringer has enough to do with the choruses.

⋅~⋅

Piringer is a very capable man but not the man that Schuppanzigh is; in any event it would be unjust to disregard S., as he has taken so much pains and spurred on the others.

At first it was agreed that the place should be the Theater-an-der-Wien. The director, Count Palffy, who had signed the memorial, was willing to provide the theatre and all the forces, vocal as well as instrumental, for 1200 florins, let Beethoven have as many rehearsals as he desired and fix the prices of admission. But a difficulty presented itself at once. At the Theater-an-der-Wien Seyfried was kapellmeister and Clement leader of the orchestra. Beethoven wanted Umlauf to be general conductor of the concert and Schuppanzigh leader of the orchestra. Count Palffy was willing to sacrifice Seyfried, but not Clement—at least, he asked that if Clement was to be displaced it be done with as little injury to his feelings as possible. He therefore suggested that Beethoven write a letter of explanation to Clement, which he felt sure would solve the difficulty. Meanwhile Schindler had begun negotiations with Duport, director of the Kärnthnerthor Theatre. Duport was favorably inclined towards the enterprise and also towards Schuppanzigh; but troublesome questions of another kind were now precipitated— questions about prices of admission, the solo singers and the number of rehearsals. On all these points Beethoven was so irresolute that the project seemed likely to fall by the wayside; in which crisis the leading spirits thought themselves entitled to resort to a stratagem to give stability to the wavering mind of Beethoven. In at least one instance the Conversation Book record was given the appearance of a formal journal of proceedings. It was now planned that Lichnowsky, Schindler and Schuppanzigh should simultaneously call upon Beethoven as if by accident, turn the conversation on the points on which it was necessary for Beethoven to reach a decision and that his utterances should then be put into writing and he be asked, half in jest, half in earnest, to affix his signature to the document. The ruse succeeded for the nonce, but after the conspirators had gone away, Beethoven saw through the trick which had been played on him, and scenting treachery as was his wont, decided off-hand to abandon the concert. He issued his pronunciamento to the three friends in this characteristic fashion:

To Count Moritz Lichnowsky.
I despise treachery—
Do not visit me any more. There will be no concert—

To Herr Schuppanzigh.
Let him not visit me more. I shall give no concert.

To Schindler.
I request you not to come again until I send for you. There will be no concert.

The three friends refused to take umbrage at Beethoven's rudeness; the notes were not accompanied by a silken rope; they gave him time to get over his wrath and suspicion and then went on with the preparations for the concert. In the Conversation Book there appears a record of consultation which was opened formally by Schindler as follows:

Present:
Mr. L. van Beethoven, a *musikus*.
Mr. Count v. Lichnowsky, an amateur.
Mr. Schindler, a fiddler.
Not yet present today:
Mr. Schuppanzigh, a fiddler representing Mylord Fallstaff.

At this consultation Schindler reported an offer from Palffy to furnish the Theater-an-der-Wien, orchestra, lights, etc., *appertinenta* for 1000 florins, provided a second or third concert be given. At a moderate charge for admission (which would be necessary) he said the receipts would be 4000 florins, which would yield a profit of 2000 florins at the first concert and about 3000 at the second, when there would be no copying charges. The prices would not be so high as at the Redoutensaal. If Duport were to charge only 300 florins, there would still be a further charge of 300 florins for building the platform. Palffy wanted only his expenses. Would Beethoven authorize him [Schindler] and Lichnowsky to complete arrangements with Palffy? He need not be paid, and it would be possible to withdraw from the arrangement at any time. Haste was necessary, for a supervisor must be appointed—Umlauf or somebody else—so that rehearsals might begin. If Schuppanzigh were given too much to do and anything went ill, the conductor would lay the blame on insufficient study. From the record of a subsequent consultation (in March) the following excerpts are made:

Lichnowsky: It is right that the orchestra be doubled, but superfluous to engage more than are necessary; after Schuppanzigh and Umlauf know wha is at their service at the Wiedener Theatre we can tell what is needed.
Schindler: Lichnowsky says that a smaller orchestra is more effective at th Theater-an-der-Wien than a large one in the Redoutensaal.

• ⌒ •

You need not take all at the Theater-an-der-Wien, none at all if you do n need them, that is the arrangement with Palffy.
Lichnowsky: Unnecessary expenses must be avoided.
Schindler: You will not have to pay the forces at the Theater-an-der-Wien all—so that may be deducted.

• ⌒ •

The days of performance if agreeable to you would be the 22nd or 23rd or 24th of this month.

Lichnowsky: You will make money, and more if you give a second concert, for which you write a new duet. In the second concert when it will not be necessary that all the pieces be *new*, you will have the same symphony and two other Mass movements.

Schindler: The prices of admission will be considerably modified at 2 florins for the parterre, 2 florins for the gallery and 3 florins for the seats.

•∿•

You ought not to seek difficulties where there are none; if the worst comes to the worst, everything will be settled.

•∿•

I shall see Schuppanzigh today at noon; but before then Lichnowsky will go to Palffy tentatively to report your decision.

•∿•

The conversation continued (probably the next day):

Schindler: Schuppanzigh is greatly pleased that you have come to an understanding with Palffy. He will make use of the entire orchestra of the theatre. He is coming to the Redoutensaal today, as he hopes to find you there.

•∿•

The choruses at the theatre are also good; Schupp. says that the women's choir of the society is not of the best because they are all young girls; which is true. . . .

•∿•

The Baron[29] took the tempo just once again as fast, therefore your advice was highly important; not until the second time did it go well.

•∿•

Besides, the women's choir is thoroughly bad. Falstaff was also convinced and is now glad that nothing but the men's choir will be needed.

•∿•

The solo voices are much too weak for the room and too young

•∿•

The soprano singer is sixteen years old at the most.

•∿•

[29] Baron Eduard von Lannoy, one of the directors of the concerts by the Gesellschaft der Musikfreunde which took place in the Redoutensaal. (TDR, v, 76, n. 2.) On April 4 he conducted a concert with the following program: Haydn, Symphony in D; Paër, So-prano aria from *Griselda*; B. Romberg, First movement of Violoncello Concerto in G; Beethoven, *Opferlied* [3rd version]; Caraffa, Overture to *Le solitaire*; Mozart, Hymn "Preis dir, Gottheit, durch alle Himmel."

Palffy is sending you word through Prince Lichnowsky that he will send you his offer, which you already know, and the promise which he made, to-morrow in writing.

•◥•

You are choosing the lesser of two evils.

•◥•

Twenty to twenty-four for each part in the chorus are already on hand.

•◥•

Of the twelve violins for each part we today selected the six best, who are to be arranged in rank and file.

•◥•

The only wish that Palffy has, as he admitted to Lichnowsky today, is that Clement be handled as gently as possible so that his feelings may not be hurt. For this reason we all request you to write a billet to Clement and tell the truth as it is.

•◥•

But as there is no question but that he will come to the second concert, I suggest that the direction be then given to him. Schuppanzigh is agreed to this.

•◥•

And as Piringer of the Theater-an-der-Wien asserts that as a high R.I. offi-cial he cannot take part, Clement might take first place among the second violins at the first concert and Schuppanzigh at the second.

•◥•

Palffy certainly does not want you to take Clement, but only to take the trouble to write him a billet and tell him about the matter. He will certainly be agreeable.

•◥•

He [Schuppanzigh] has become much quieter and more *commode* since he was in Russia, for his paunch is already beginning to embarrass him.

•◥•

Böhm will play first violin.

•◥•

Piringer will not play at the An-der-Wien, which is all one to Schuppanzigh.

But matters were not so easily arranged with Clement as Schindler had imagined. He did not want to be deprived of the honor of playing at the concert, the orchestra of the Theater-an-der-Wien sided with him and declared that it would not play under Schuppanzigh. Schindler appealed to Count Palffy, who knew that though you can lead a horse to water you cannot make him drink. He said that he could command the men to play under Schuppanzigh, but he did not want to be answerable for the mischief which would result. Schindler advised Beethoven that if Palffy stood by Clement the contract for the Kärnthnerthor Theatre be closed with Duport. Up to late in April it was as good as settled that the concert would be given at the Theater-an-der-Wien, though Beethoven's fatal indecision left the point uncertain. With negotiations pending with both theatres, the Redoutensaal came up for consideration, and finally (it would seem as a consequence of advice by the Steiner firm), also a fourth locale. This was the Landständischer Saal, a small room in which the *Concerts Spirituels* took place. Lichnowsky, when he heard that Beethoven was considering such a step, hurried to him with representations that if the hall were taken there would be trouble with Palffy and he himself humiliated and embarrassed, since he had come to an agreement with the manager in his name. He as well as Schindler was sorely tried by the new turn of affairs and represented to Beethoven that the room was too small, holding only 500 persons, and that the court would not go there. But nephew Karl favored the hall because its choice would avoid the difficulties incident to the selection of either of the theatres. Lichnowsky and Schindler did not seek to hide their displeasure from Beethoven because of his willingness to take the advice of others (meaning, no doubt, brother Johann, nephew Karl and Steiner), in preference to theirs, but at length circumstances compelled him to abandon all other plans and agree to take the Kärnthnerthor Theatre. He considered the noon hour as the time for the concert, but Johann told him that an evening concert was worth 1500 florins more than one given in the daytime; he clung to the Landständischer Saal, but Schindler told him that on the day which had been fixed upon there was to be a concert at the Redoutensaal in which Sontag, Unger and the Italian singers would take part. "The girls" would therefore be unavailable for his concert and the court would, of course, go to the fashionable place and affair. As late as April 21, it was publicly announced that the concert would be given in the Theater-an-der-Wien, but at length Beethoven made up his mind, and Schindler was empowered to close with Duport for the Kärnthnerthor Theatre. Palffy yielded to the composer's wishes, but regretfully, saying that he would rather lose 1000 florins than the honor of having the concert in his house. It would seem as if it was the cabal in the orchestra against Schuppanzigh which ended Beethoven's irresolution. Beethoven now decided to take the Court theatre for 400 florins, chorus and orchestra being included as well as the lighting, with the privilege of one or two repetitions on the same terms in eight or ten days. In the letter of April 24 which Schindler sent to Duport, were named Sontag (soprano), Unger (alto), and Preisinger (bass) as solo singers, Umlauf and Schuppanzigh as leaders, the orchestra and chorus were to be augmented from the amateur forces of the Gesellschaft der Musikfreunde. There were to be 24 violins, 10 violas, 12 contrabasses and violoncellos, and the number of wind-instruments was to be doubled, for which reason room would have to be provided for the orchestra on the stage. Duport was requested to fix the date not later than

May 3rd or 4th and was informed that the reason why the agreement with Count Palffy had been cancelled was that the Theater-an-der-Wien was lacking in capable solo singers and that Palffy wanted Clement to lead the orchestra, whereas Beethoven had long before selected Schuppanzigh for the post. With a change of date to May 7 this arrangement was formally confirmed.

But many details remained to be settled, the most vexatious to Beethoven being the prices of admission. Beethoven wanted an advance on the regular tariff. Duport appealed to the Minister of Police, but permission to raise the prices was refused. In the selection of solo singers Therese Grünbaum had been considered, but she was eventually set aside in favor of Henriette Sontag, for whom Beethoven had a personal admiration (he could not know much, if anything, about her voice and art). Jäger had been suggested for the tenor part, but Anton Haitzinger was chosen because, in a spirit of professional courtesy, Jäger refused to take a part away from a Kärnthnerthor singer. Forti and Preisinger were rival candidates for the solo bass parts. The latter was considered the more musical of the two and better fitted for Beethoven's music, and was therefore selected. He took part in the rehearsals, and for him Beethoven made a change in the music of the recitative in the Symphony (Schindler gives it in his biography);[30] but at the last the *tessitura* of the part was found to be too high for him and Preisinger had to withdraw. It was impossible under the circumstances now to appeal to Forti, and the part was entrusted to Seipelt of the company at the Theater-an-der-Wien.

It was originally intended that the programme should consist of the new Overture (Op. 124), the Mass in D and the new Symphony; but realizing that this would make the concert unduly long Beethoven first decided to omit the *Gloria* of the mass, and after the rehearsals had already begun he curtailed the list still more by eliding the *Sanctus*. The large amount of copying involved was done by a staff of men some of whom worked, apparently, under the supervision of the widow of Schlemmer, Beethoven's favorite copyist who had died the year before. The composer angrily rejected Haslinger's suggestion that the chorus parts be engraved, but consented to have them duplicated by lithographic process. The church authorities were opposed to the performance of missal music in a theatre and the censor therefore withheld his approval of the programme. So, in April, at the suggestion of Schindler, Beethoven wrote a letter to the censor, Sartorius, in which he pleaded for his consent to the performance on the ground that he was giving the concert by request, had involved himself in costs by reason of the copying, there was no time in which to produce other novelties, and if consent were refused he would be compelled to abandon the concert and all his expenditures would have been in vain. The three ecclesiastical pieces which were to be performed were to be listed on the programme as hymns.

[30] II, pp. 77-8.

The letter failed of its mission; not until an appeal was made to Count Sedlnitzky, the Police President, through the agency of Count Lichnowsky, was the performance sanctioned.

The rehearsals were now in progress. Dirzka[31] was making good headway with the choruses and was satisfied; Schuppanzigh was holding rehearsals for the strings in the rehearsal-room of the Ridotto; the solo singers were studying under the supervision of Beethoven, sometimes in his lodgings, Umlauf assisting. Accustomed to Rossini's music, the principal singers found it difficult to assimilate the Beethovenian manner, especially as it is exemplified in the concluding movement of the symphony. They pleaded with the composer for changes which would lighten their labors, but he was adamant. Unger called him a "tyrant over all the vocal organs" to his face, but when he still refused to grant her petitions she turned to Sontag and said: "Well, then we must go on torturing ourselves in the name of God!"[32] The choirmaster requested that the passage in the fugue of the *Credo* where the sopranos enter on B-flat *in alt* be altered, because none of the singers could reach the note; but though Umlauf reinforced that argument, a refusal was the only reply. In only one alteration did Beethoven acquiesce;—he changed the concluding passage of the bass recitative, because Preisinger could not sing the high F-sharp; but Preisinger did not sing at all at the concert. The consequences of his obduracy were not realized by Beethoven at the concert, for though he stood among the performers and indicated the tempo at the beginning of each movement he could not hear the music except with his mental ear. The obvious thing happened;—the singers who could not reach the high tones simply omitted them. Duport had allowed two full rehearsals. There was to have been a third, but it was prevented by a rehearsal for a ballet. At the final meeting on May 6, Beethoven was "dissolved in devotion and emotion" at the performance of the *Kyrie*, and after the Symphony stationed himself at the door and embraced all the amateurs who had taken part.[33] The official announcement of the concert read as follows:

GRAND
MUSICAL CONCERT
by
HERR L. v. BEETHOVEN
which will take place
To-morrow, May 7, 1824
in the R. I. Court Theatre beside the Kärnthnerthor.

The musical pieces to be performed are the latest works of Herr Ludwig van Beethoven.

[31] Choral Director of the Kärthnerthor Theatre.
[32] See Schindler, *Biogr.*, ii, p. 76. (TDR, v, 89, n. 1.)
[33] The statement about the *Kyrie* was made by Holz to Jahn; that about the Symphony, by Fuchs. (TK, III, 164, n. 1.)

First: A Grand Overture

Second: Three Grand Hymns with Solo and Chorus Voices.

Third: A Grand Symphony with Solo and Chorus Voices entering in
the finale on Schiller's Ode to Joy.

The solos will be performed by the Demoiselles Sontag and Unger and
the Herren Haizinger and Seipelt. Herr Schuppanzigh has undertaken
the direction of the orchestra, Herr Kapellmeister Umlauf the direction
of the whole and the Music Society the augmentation of the chorus and
orchestra as a favor.

Herr Ludwig van Beethoven will himself participate in the general
direction.

Prices of admission as usual.

Beginning at 7 o'clock in the evening.

The overture was that to the *Weihe des Hauses*; the hymns were the
Kyrie, *Credo*, and *Agnus Dei* from the Mass in D. Duport had a hand in
the drafting of the announcement and wanted to include in it the statement that Beethoven would conduct with Umlauf. In a Conversation Book
Schindler reported the fact to Beethoven and added:

I did not know what to reply and so it was omitted this time.

•~•

You *could* surely conduct the overture alone.

•~•

It would put too severe a strain upon your ears and for that reason I would not
advise you to conduct the whole.

The theatre was crowded in every part except the imperial box; that was
empty. Beethoven had gone in person, accompanied by Schindler, to invite
the Imperial Family, and some of its members promised to attend; but the
Emperor and Empress had left Vienna a few days before and Archduke
Rudolph, who had naturally displayed interest in the affair, was in Olmütz.
But we hear of several of Beethoven's present and former friends seated in
various parts of the house;—poor, bedridden Zmeskall was carried to his
seat in a sedan chair. Some of the foremost musicians of Vienna were in
the band—Mayseder, Böhm, Jansa, Linke etc. The performance was far
from perfect. There was lack of a homogeneous power, a paucity of nuance,
a poor distribution of lights and shades. Nevertheless, strange as the music
must have sounded to the audience, the impression which it made was profound and the applause which it elicited enthusiastic to a degree.[34] At one
point in the Scherzo, presumably at the startling entry of the tympani at
the *ritmo di tre battute*, the listeners could scarcely restrain themselves, and
it seemed as if a repetition then and there would be insisted upon. To this

[34] From the review in the Lpz. *AMZ* (July 1, 1824), Vol. 26, p. 438.

Beethoven, no doubt engrossed by the music which he was following in his mind, was oblivious. Either after the Scherzo or at the end of the Symphony, while Beethoven was still gazing at his score, Fräulein Unger, whose happiness can be imagined, plucked him by the sleeve and directed his attention to the clapping hands and waving hats and handkerchiefs. Then he turned to the audience and bowed. The incident is variously related. Schindler and Fräulein Unger (the latter of whom related it to George Grove in London in 1869) say that it took place at the end of the concert. Thalberg, the pianist, who was present, says that it was after the Scherzo. A note among Thayer's papers reads: "November 28, 1860. I saw Thalberg in Paris. He told me as follows: He was present at Beethoven's concert in the Kärthner-thor Theatre 1824. Beethoven was dressed in black dress-coat, white neckerchief, and waistcoat, black satin small-clothes, black silk stockings, shoes with buckles. He saw after the Scherzo of the 9th Symphony how B. stood turning over the leaves of his score utterly deaf to the immense applause, and Unger pulled him by the sleeve, and then pointed to the audience when he turned and bowed. Umlauf told the choir and orchestra to pay no attention whatever to Beethoven's beating of the time but all to watch him. Conradin Kreutzer was at the P.F."

Did Thalberg describe Beethoven's dress correctly? Evidently not. In a conversation just before the concert Schindler writes: "We will take everything with us now; also take your green coat, which you can put on when you conduct. The theatre will be dark and no one will notice it. . . . Oh, great master, you do not own a black frock coat! The green one will have to do; in a few days the black one will be ready."

After the concert Beethoven's friends, as was natural, came together to exchange comments and felicitate him. From Schindler Beethoven received a report which is preserved in the Conversation Book. It gives us a glimpse of his own joy and the composer's happy pride in having been more enthusiastically greeted than the court:

Never in my life did I hear such frenetic and yet cordial applause.

•~•

Once the second movement of the Symphony was completely interrupted by applause.

•~•

and there was a demand for a repetition.

•~•

The reception was more than imperial

•~•

for the people burst out in a storm four times. At the last there were cries of Vivat!

•~•

The wind instruments did very bravely

•~•

not the slightest disturbance could be heard.

•~•

When the parterre broke out in applauding cries the 5th time the Police Commissioner yelled Silence!

•~•

The court only 3 successive times but Beethoven 5 times.

•~•

My triumph is now attained; for now I can speak from my heart. Yesterday I still feared secretly that the Mass would be prohibited because I heard that the Archbishop had protested against it. After all I was right in at first not saying anything to the Police Commissioner. By God, it would have happened!

•~•

He surely never has been in the Court Theatre. Well, Pax tecum!

Joseph Hüttenbrenner went with Schindler when he escorted the composer to his lodgings. On the following day Schindler wrote in the Conversation Book:

The whole audience was impressed, crushed by the greatness of your work.

•~•

In Paris and London the concert would certainly have yielded from 12 to 15 thousand florins; here it may be as many hundreds.

•~•

After yesterday you must now too plainly see that you are trampling upon your own interests by remaining longer within these walls. In short, I have no words to express my feelings at the wrong which you are doing yourself.[35]

•~•

When Karl comes home at noon, be so good as to instruct him [to come] after his lectures, this at five o'clock, to the box-office where I will be waiting for him. The box-office will be opened in his presence and he will receive the money.[36]

•~•

Then I will fetch him at the university at 5 o'clock.

•~•

Have you recovered from yesterday's exertions?

---

[35] Schindler is referring to a new invitation to Beethoven from Charles Neate to visit London (*Biogr.*, II, p. 89), which is discussed further in the next chapter.

[36] These excerpts prove that in his biography, Schindler's story of showing Beethoven the box-office report the evening of the concert must be false. (TK, III, 168.)

The financial results of the concert fell far short of Beethoven's expectations. The gross receipts were 2200 florins in the depreciated Vienna money, of which only 420 florins remained after paying the cost of administration and copying; and against this pitiful sum some petty expenses were still chargeable. Beethoven was not only disappointed; he was chagrined and thrown into a fuming ill-humor. He invited Schindler, Umlauf and Schuppanzigh to dine with him at the restaurant "Zum wilden Mann" in the Prater. The composer came with his nephew; "his brow was clouded, his words were cold, peevish, captious," says Schindler. He had ordered an "opulent" meal, but no sooner had the party sat down to the table than the "explosion which was imminent" came. In plainest terms he burst out with the charge that the management and Schindler had cheated him. Umlauf and Schuppanzigh tried to convince him that that was impossible, as every penny had passed through the hands of the two theatre cashiers, whose accounts tallied, and that though it was contrary to custom, his nephew had acted in behalf of his brother as comptroller. Beethoven persisted in his accusation, saying that he had his information from an entirely credible source. Thereupon Schindler and Umlauf abruptly left the room. Schuppanzigh remained behind just long enough to get a few stripes on his broad back and then joined his companions in misery. Together they finished their meal at a restaurant in the Leopoldstadt.[37]

It is more than likely that Beethoven's "credible" informant was his brother Johann. He was jealous of Schindler's participation in the composer's business affairs and probably took advantage of a favorable opportunity to strengthen Beethoven's chronic suspicion and growing distrust of what the composer himself looked upon as Schindler's officiousness. In the Conversation Book used at the meeting after the concert, Karl tells his uncle: "Schindler knows from an ear-witness that your brother said in the presence of several persons that he was only waiting for the concert to be over before driving S. out of the house."

Before the second concert Schindler received a letter which on its face shows that he had written Beethoven defending himself against the charges made. Beethoven's letter was as follows:

I do not accuse you of any wrongdoing in connection with the concert, but unwisdom and arbitrary actions have spoiled many things, besides I have a certain fear lest some great misfortune shall some time happen to me through you— Clogged drains often open suddenly, and that day in the Prater I thought you were offensive in several ways—Moreover, there are many times when I would rather try to repay the services which you perform for me with a little gift rather than with a *meal*; for I admit that often you disturb me very much. If you do not see a pleasant face you say at once: "Bad weather again today," for being commonplace yourself how can you help misunderstanding that which is not commonplace? In short I love my independence too much. There will be

[37] Schindler, *Biogr.*, II, p. 88. (TDR, v, 94.)

no lack of opportunities to invite you, but it is impossible to do so continually, inasmuch as thereby all my affairs are disarranged—Duport has consented to next Tuesday for the concert; for the Landständischen Saal, which I might have had for tomorrow evening, he again refuses to let me have the singers; he has also again turned to the police. Therefore please go there with the bill and learn if there is any objection to the second time—I would never have accepted the favors done me gratis and I will not in the future. As for friendship that is a difficult thing in your case; in no event would I like to entrust my welfare to you since you lack judgement and act arbitrarily, and I learned some time ago to know you from a side which is *not to your credit*; and so *did others*—I must confess that the purity of my character does not permit me to recompense mere favors with friendship, although I am ready willingly to serve your welfare—

B

A second concert had been contemplated from the outset, or at least since the opening of negotiations with Palffy. Schindler says[38] that Duport offered to pay all expenses and guarantee 500 florins Convention Money (1200 florins Vienna Standard) with the understanding that the profits should be divided equally between Beethoven and the exchequer of the theatre. But he wanted a change made in the programme. To this change, obviously designed as a concession to the popular taste, Beethoven seems to have given his consent. The concert took place on Sunday, May 23rd, at midday—half-past twelve o'clock, with the following program:

First: A Grand Overture [Op. 124]
Second: A new Terzetto, composed by Herr Ludwig van Beethoven, sung by
    Mad. Dardanelli, Herren Donzelli and Botticelli. ["Tremate, empi, tremate"]
Third: A Grand Hymn, sung by Dlles. Sontag, Unger, Herren Haizinger, Sei-
    pelt and assembled chorus. [Kyrie from the Mass in D]
Fourth: Aria, "Di tanti palpiti," sung by Herr David. [from Rossini's *Tan-
    credi*][39]
Fifth: A Grand Symphony with Solo and Chorus Voices entering in the
    Finale on Schiller's Ode to Joy.

The delightful weather lured the people into the open air, the house was not half full and there was, in consequence, a deficit of 800 florins. Nor was the popular demonstration of enthusiasm over the music as great as at the first concert, and Beethoven, who had not favored the repetition, was so disheartened that he was with difficulty persuaded to accept the 500 florins which Duport had guaranteed to him. He was also vexed to find his old trio, "Tremati, empi tremate," announced as a novelty (it was composed more than twenty years before, and had been performed in 1814), and so was Tobias Haslinger, who had bought but had not published it. Moreover,

[38] *Ibid.*, p. 73. (TDR, v, 96.)
[39] According to Schindler (*ibid.*, p. 74), this was transposed a few tones higher and sung almost throughout in a falsetto voice. Schindler says that Sontag also sang her favorite *aria di bravura* by Mercadante, but of this number there is no mention in the *affiche*. Schindler concludes: "This parody of the festive instance (the first concert) our master luckily did not hear." (Cf. TDR, v, 97.)

Haslinger had been overlooked in the distribution of complimentary tickets. Beethoven had to apologize to him for the oversight, which he protested was due to an inadvertence, and also to explain that the announcement of the trio as a new work was of Duport's doing, not his.

Meanwhile a copy of the Symphony was sent to the London Philharmonic Society, through Kirchhoffer; the date may be determined by Beethoven's receipt of £50 from Kirchhoffer "for my symphony delivered to him for the Philharmonic Society in London," dated April 27, 1824.[40]

One outcome of the concerts of May was the appearance of a new portrait of Beethoven. It was a lithographic reproduction of a crayon drawing made by Stephen Decker and was printed as a supplement to the *Wiener Allgemeine Musikalische Zeitung* edited by F. A. Kanne, on June 5, 1824. In this and two subsequent numbers of the journal (June 9 and 16) Kanne reviewed the concerts with discriminating appreciation, ending with an enthusiastic encomium of the composer. In 1827 Steinmüller made a plate of Decker's drawing for Artaria. Schindler and Frimmel agree in saying that the well-known portrait by Kriehuber is an imitation of Decker's drawing, which was made, as Kanne's journal stated, "a few days after his great concert in May, 1824."[41]

During the preparations for the concerts, thought was also given to the usual summer sojourn, and various places—Grinzing, Heiligenstadt, Penzing, Breitensee, Hietzing, Hetzendorf—were canvassed in consultation with Beethoven by his friends. His brother had again offered him a home on his estate and it was expected that Count Brunsvik would come for the concert and take Beethoven back with him to Hungary. In all of the excursions which were made in the vicinity of Schönbrunn in search of a summer home, Schindler accompanied the composer to see, to advise, to negotiate. The choice fell upon Penzing, where an apartment was found in the first story of the house numbered 43 belonging to a tailor in Vienna named Johann Hörr, who was rejoiced to have so distinguished a tenant. Beethoven took it for the summer beginning on May 1, for a rental of 180 florins, C.M. The lodgings were in all things adapted to his needs and Beethoven, entirely satisfied, moved into them soon after the second concert. An old couple lived in the parterre, but otherwise he was the only tenant of the house. But the house lay close to a footbridge over the little stream called the Wien Fluss and people crossing it frequently stopped to gaze into his rooms. He could have saved himself the annoyance by drawing the curtains, but instead he flew into a rage, quarreled with his landlord, against whom he recorded his anger by scrawling the epithet "Schurke" (rogue, wretch, scoundrel, etc.) under his name on the receipt, and removing to Baden (Gutenbrunn).

[40] The original is in the British Museum (Add. MS 33965, p. 174); it was first published by D. W. MacArdle, "Four Unfamiliar Beethoven Documents," *Music and Letters*, xxxvi (1955), p. 337.

[41] See Theodor Frimmel, *Beethoven in Zeitgenössischen Bildnis* (Vienna, 1923), pp. 57-8.

The move had taken place by May 27 on which date he wrote from Baden to the Steiner firm requesting some music paper.[42] He stayed there on and off until November; thus he was again paying rent for three lodgings at the same time.

The matter of the subscriptions for the Mass being disposed of (except so far as the deliveries of some of the scores was concerned), and the Symphony completed, Beethoven now had time, while getting ready for their performance, to think also of their publication. On February 5, 1823, Beethoven had assured Ries that the Philharmonic Society could keep the symphony for eighteen months before he would publish it; on January 15, 1825, he wrote Charles Neate assuring him that a year would elapse between the time the society had received the score and its publication. When Beethoven took up the matter of publication again he ignored Simrock, Peters and the Vienna publishers and turned to Schlesinger, Schott and Sons of Mainz and H. A. Probst of Leipzig.

On February 25 Beethoven offered to Moritz Schlesinger in Paris the Mass for 1000 fl. C.M., the Overture (Op. 124) for 50 gold ducats and the Symphony, not to be published until 1825, for 600 fl. C.M., and some new quartets later on.[43]

On the same day, in answer to a letter from Probst, he made an offer of some smaller works to test the publisher's interest with the assurance that if he were prompt he would offer larger works.[44] Probst received the letter on March 1 and answered at once. On March 10 Beethoven offered the Mass and the Symphony for the same prices that he had set for Schlesinger with the added stipulation that in recompense for the necessary delay in the publication of the latter he might have the piano arrangement gratis. Only a portion of this letter has been preserved, but the contents of the lost fragments can be gathered from Probst's answer under date March 22, in which he promised to deposit at once with Joseph Loidl and Co. one hundred imperial ducats to Beethoven's account, to be paid over on delivery of three songs with pianoforte accompaniment (two of them to have parts for other instruments, the third to be an arietta), six bagatelles for pianoforte solo, and a grand overture with pianoforte arrangement for two and four hands. What these works were may easily be guessed. After this business had been arranged to the satisfaction of both parties, Probst said, he would communicate his decision respecting the Mass. Beethoven wrote in July explaining his delay on the score that the compositions "had just been finished" but were now ready for delivery at any moment to Herr Loidl, to whom he requested that the money be sent. On August 10 Beethoven received word that the 100 ducats had already been sent to Loidl and Co. in Vienna. A letter written by Beethoven at this time has been lost, but a portion of its contents can be deduced from Probst's reply a week later—August 16. The Leipzig pub-

---

[42] See *A* 1293.   [43] See *A* 1267.   de Beethoven," *Revue de Musicologie*, VI
[44] See Charles Bouret, "Une lettre inédite   (1922), pp. 13ff. Also *A* 1266.

lisher admitted that his action in depositing the money to be delivered in exchange for the manuscript had been due to reports which had reached him concerning difficulties which another publisher had had with the composer. In purchasing manuscripts without examination he was departing from his established rule of action and he trusted to the admiration which he felt for the composer's genius that the latter had set aside works of excellence for him. He would gladly have published the Symphony, but was deterred by the danger of piracy which was peculiarly great in Austria. He promised a speedy and handsome publication of the works purchased.

The other publisher mentioned by Probst was probably Peters, for in a letter dated August 28 Beethoven promised Probst he would write soon to explain his dealings with "Herr Peters." He announced that he had sold the Mass to another publisher and that he had received an advance on the symphony, but that if Probst made up his mind quickly on the latter this other publisher might be persuaded to receive other works for this sum. The last known letter to Probst, which is one of the new letters printed by Miss Anderson,[45] is dated January 26, 1825. The smaller works, for which Probst had deposited the 100 ducats, belonged in reality to his brother, he wrote, as a security against a sum of money advanced to him. Beethoven gave two reasons why negotiations with Probst had come to grief; first, his brother was angry "that you wanted to have all the works tried out before you would pay for them"; and second, his brother had found better offers from other publishers. The only hope that Beethoven could hold out was the possibility of Probst's receiving some string quartets. Once again dealings with a Leipzig publisher had come to nothing.

Beethoven meanwhile had been approached by Schott and Sons or by the editor, Gottfried Weber, of their journal *Cäcilia* to find a Viennese correspondent for their magazine, of which they were going to send a copy. This was before March 10, 1824, for on that date Beethoven answered as follows:

Dear Sir!

I beg of you most respectfully to give my thanks to the E[ditoria]l S[taf]f of the C[äcili]a[46] for their attention. As for my unimportant self, how gladly would I serve them, were it not that I feel the greater calling compelling me to make myself known to the world through composition. However, I have given instructions to discover a reliable correspondent for you (which is very difficult here because of partisan feeling). If I find something noteworthy about myself (but oh heavens how difficult that is), I will be glad to have it communicated through this person; and, if you specifically require it and my almost incessant affairs allow, I will also make a communication myself—

As for my works for which you have made request, I offer you the following, but your decision must not be long in the making—a new grand solemn mass with solo voices and chorus parts and full orchestra. Difficult as it is to speak

---

[45] *A* 1347.
[46] The German "R—n der C——a" stands

undoubtedly for "Redaktion der Cäcilia" ("editorial staff of the Cäcilia").

of myself, still I consider it my greatest work; the honorarium would be 1000 fl. C.M.: a new grand symphony, which closes with a finale (like my fantasy with chorus but much bigger and more extended) with vocal parts for solos and choruses with words from Schiller's immortal, famous song "An die Freude." The honorarium is 600 fl. C.M. A new quartet for 2 violins, viola and violoncello, the honorarium 50 ducats in gold.—[47]

These matters are presented in accordance with your wishes. As the result of this report, do not judge me as commercially-minded; but as a true artist I cannot disdain competition, through it rather I am in a firm position to work faithfully for my muse and am able to provide in a noble way for many other people— Your answer concerning the works indicated would have to be made very soon.

Yours very truly

Beethoven

In an answer of March 24, the firm accepted the offer of the Quartet at once, but asked either a reduction of the fees for the Symphony and Mass, or permission to pay the money in installments at intervals of six months. Subsequently the firm offered to provide a guaranty for the deferred payments and to consider any proposition which Beethoven had to make. The two letters, dated respectively March 24 and April 10, remaining unanswered, Schott and Sons again wrote on April 19 and still again on April 27, introducing with the former letter Christian Rummel, Kapellmeister of the Duke of Nassau, and asking a contribution to *Cäcilia* in the latter. On May 20, in the midst of his preparations for the second concert, Beethoven replied and repeated his offer of the Mass and Symphony, but held the matter of the Quartet in abeyance. He asked that payment for the other works be made by bills drawn on a Vienna bank payable 600 florins in one month, 500 florins in two months and 500 florins in four months. On July 3 he also conceded the Quartet, which he promised to deliver inside of six weeks. With an answer from Schott on July 19, the business was concluded and, as an undated letter of Beethoven's shows, much to his gratification; the business methods of Schott and Sons were extremely satisfactory to him. But the year came to an end, and the Mainz publishers were still waiting for their manuscripts, while Beethoven was kept busy writing explanations in answer to their questions and requests.

Meanwhile, in a letter to the firm, written in November, he offered for publication the overture which had been performed at his concert [Op. 124], six bagatelles and three songs in behalf of his brother to whom they belonged, the price 130 ducats in gold. These were the works which Probst had agreed to purchase for 100 ducats and the money for which had been sent to Vienna. Schott agreed to buy them for 130 ducats and Beethoven wrote to his brother in Gneixendorf on December 10: "I inform you that Mainz will give 130 ducats in gold for your works; if Herr Probst will not pay as much, give them to Mainz, who will at once send a cheque to you as quickly as to me, these are really honest, not mean, business men. . . ."

[47] Quartet in E-flat, Op. 127, which, however, was not yet completed. (TDR, v, 102, n. 3.)

Johann promptly put himself in communication with Schott and Sons and graciously confirmed the sale of the works at 130 ducats, "Out of respect" for his brother.

Peters, who had been informed of the state of affairs concerning the Mass, evidently sent a complaint, or protest, to Beethoven, for on December 12, 1824, the latter writes:

Dear Sir:

Streicher has written you concerning a certain matter. I told him myself that this affair would run into difficulty, and this is what has happened. I inform you only that the whole affair concerning the Mass is off, since I have now promised it definitely to a publisher, and thus naturally the proposals made by Streicher cannot be carried into effect—You would have received a violin quartet already but for the fact that I had to give it to the publisher who got the Mass, since he expressly asked for this at the same time. But you will receive another one soon for sure, or I will make you an offer of a greater work from which the sum already received would then be subtracted. Only please have patience for a bit since I will certainly satisfy you—You *did wrong to yourself and to me*, and you are still doing the latter, as I hear, in accusing me of having sent you *inferior* works. Did you not yourself ask for songs, marches and bagatelles? Afterwards it occurred to you that the fee was too large and that a larger work might have been had for it. That you showed yourself to be a poor judge of art in this is proved by the fact that several of these works have been and will be published, and that such a thing has never happened to me before—As soon as I can I will liquidate my indebtedness to you, and meanwhile I remain

Yours truly
Beethoven

I am not now *in a position* to do this more quickly.

During the summer of 1824 Karl was continuing his philological studies at the university. On one of his visits to his uncle not long after the concerts the conversation proceeded from the progress of Karl's studies to the question of his choice of a career. Karl writes:[48]

I will not do anything without your consent and will, if you wish, continue to study, or even more begin something new.

•~•

You will find my choice rather strange, but I will speak freely, nevertheless, as I prefer to do. The profession which I would like to choose is not a *common* one. On the contrary, it *also* demands study; only of a different kind; and one that is to my liking, I believe.

•~•

Soldier

•~•

In no company at all[49]

•~•

[48] This conversation, and others between Karl and Beethoven of a personal nature, are in the appendix to Vol. V of TDR, pp. 506ff.

[49] Presumably Beethoven asked from whence he had gotten the idea.

The regulation is certainly very strict. And mathematics and the science of fortification are certainly not among the lowest.

Later on there is further conversation about Karl's studies which show, even though only Karl's side of the conversation is recorded, that there was conflict between them: Beethoven worried over Karl's effort and use of time; Karl answered that he was exerting himself to the utmost and not seeing anyone but his fellow student Erik with whom he read Greek and Latin.

On August 1 Beethoven wrote to his lawyer friend, Dr. Bach, concerning his nephew and his will:

Most worthy friend!
My heartfelt thanks for your kind recommendation here; I am really well taken care of—I must remind you of the part of my will concerning Karl. I think that I might have a stroke some day, like my worthy grandfather whom I take after. Karl is and remains the sole heir of all that I have and that may be found after my death. However, since one must leave something to one's relatives, even when they are quite uncongenial, my *brother* is to receive my French piano from *Paris*—Karl could bring the will on Saturday if it doesn't inconvenience you in any way—As far as Stein [Steiner] is concerned, he will be satisfied to have his debt completely paid off at the end of this month and at the end of September—For if something comes of the Mainz affair, it will take no longer than that, and the first 600 fl. should at any rate be paid back to two of the most generous human beings[50] who, when I was nearly desperate, kindly advanced me this sum without any interest whatsoever.

> With fondest wishes I embrace you.
> Respectfully your friend Beethoven

In September of this year the interest of Beethoven's old friend Andreas Streicher, whose wife was a visitor at Baden, seems to have been awakened in a marked degree, and he gave himself to the devising of plans to ameliorate the composer's financial position. In a letter dated September 5 he proposed: first, that six high-class subscription concerts be given in the approaching winter, which, with 600 subscribers, would yield after defraying costs a total of 4,800 florins C.M.; second, that the project for a complete edition of the compositions be revived, which, as he outlined it, he thought might yield a profit of 10,000 florins C.M. From Beethoven's letter of December 12 to Peters, it is clear that Streicher had also acted as intermediary for the composer with this firm.

Streicher tried to make himself useful in still another way. He suggested that manuscript copies of the Mass in D with pianoforte or organ accompaniment be sold to a number of singing societies. This project had already been attempted in the case of the Singakademie of Berlin and achieved in that of the Cäcilienverein of Frankfurt. In a letter from Streicher to the directors of the Gesangverein in Zürich, dated September 17, 1824, is enclosed a note

[50] Undoubtedly the Brentanos. (TDR, v, 154, n. 5.)

of authorization from the composer to Steiner, dated the day before, requesting that, owing to the cost of copying, etc., the price be 50 ducats. This was the same that he had asked of his royal subscribers for the full orchestral score. None of the projects came to execution, though the second, which lay close to Beethoven's heart, came up for attention once again at a later date.

Towards the end of September, Johann Andreas Stumpff, a native of Thuringia but a resident of London, was among the visitors at Baden who were admitted to intimate association with Beethoven. This was another Stumpff, not the one who came to Vienna in 1818 with a letter from Thomas Broadwood, and who tuned the new English pianoforte. He was a manufacturer of harps and an enthusiastic admirer of Beethoven's music. Anticipating a meeting with the composer, he had provided himself with a letter of introduction to Haslinger, whose help to that end he asked. He had also gotten a letter from Streicher, whose acquaintance he had made in London. He accomplished his end and wrote a long and enthusiastic account of his intercourse with Beethoven at Baden, whither Haslinger had accompanied him on his first visit.[51] He was received by Beethoven with extraordinary cordiality. The composer accepted an invitation to dinner, entertained his host at dinner in return, played for him on his Broadwood pianoforte (after Stein, at Stumpff's request, had restored its ruins), and at parting gave him a print of one of his portraits and promised to alight at his house if ever he came to London. Much of his conversation, which Stumpff records, is devoted to a condemnation of the frivolity and bad musical taste of the Viennese, and excessive laudation of everything English. "Beethoven," Stumpff remarks, "had an exaggerated opinion of London and its highly cultured inhabitants," and he quotes Beethoven as saying: "England stands high in culture. In London everybody knows something and knows it well; but the man of Vienna can only talk of eating and drinking, and sings and pounds away at music of little significance or of his own making." He spoke a great deal about sending his nephew to London to make a man of him, asked questions about the cost of living there and, in short, gave proof that an English visit was filling a large part of his thoughts. The incidents of the conclusion of the dinner which he gave to Stumpff may be told in the latter's words:

Beethoven now produced the small bottle. It contained the precious wine of Tokay with which he filled the two glasses to the brim. "Now my good German-Englishman, to your good health." We drained the glasses, then, extending his

[51] Stumpff's manuscript, which also covered the principal incidents of a trip through Germany, after his death came into the possession of his surviving partner, T. Martin, who permitted Thayer to transcribe all of it relating to Beethoven. Many of his observations parallel those made by Reichardt, Rochlitz, Schultz and other visitors, and their repetition here would add nothing to the story of Beethoven's life and manners; besides, the account is too long to be inserted in full. The reader who wishes to read all of it is referred to TDR, v, pp. 122ff. (TK, III, 181, n. 1.)

hand, "A good journey to you and to a meeting again in London."—I beckoned to him to fill the glasses again and hurriedly wrote in his notebook: "Now for a pledge to the welfare of the greatest living composer, Beethoven."—I arose from my chair, he followed my example, emptied his glass and seizing my hand said: "To-day I am just what I am and what I ought to be,—all unbuttoned." And now he unbosomed himself on the subject of music which had been degraded and made a plaything of vulgar and impudent passions. "True music," he said, "found little recognition in this age of Rossini and his consorts." Thereupon I took up the pencil and wrote in very distinct letters:

"Whom do you consider the greatest composer that ever lived?"

"Handel," was his instantaneous reply; "to him I bow the knee," and he bent one knee to the floor.

"Mozart," I wrote.

"Mozart," he continued, "is good and admirable."

"Yes," wrote I, "who was able to glorify even Handel with his additional accompaniments to *The Messiah*."

"It would have lived without them," was his answer.

I continued writing. "Seb. Bach."

"Why is he dead?"

I answered immediately "He will return to life again."

"Yes, if he is studied, and for that there is now no time."

I took the liberty of writing: "As you yourself, a peerless artist in the art of music, exalt the merits of Handel so highly above all, you must certainly own the scores of his principal works."

"I? How should I, a poor devil, have gotten them? Yes, the scores of *The Messiah* and *Alexander's Feast* went through my hands."

If it is possible for a blind man to help a cripple, and the two attain an end which would be impossible to either one unaided, why might not in the present case a similar result be effected by a similar coöperation? At that moment I made a secret vow: Beethoven, you shall have the works of Handel for which your heart is longing if they are anywhere to be found.

Stumpff relates that Beethoven's brother, who came into the room during his visit, seemed glad to greet him and begged him most amiably to call on him, as he desired to talk with him about a number of things. At parting, Beethoven accompanied Stumpff to the door and said: "That is my brother—have nothing to do with him—he is not an honest man. You will hear me accused of many wrong actions of which he has been guilty. Farewell!" Stumpff returned to London on December 6. He fulfilled his vow touching the gift of Handel's works two years later.

Czerny visited Beethoven in Baden, and a notice from him in Jahn's papers is interesting on account of a remark concerning Napoleon: "In 1824 I went with Beethoven once to a coffee-house in Baden where we found many newspapers on the table. In one I read an announcement of Walter Scott's *Life of Napoleon* and showed it to Beethoven. 'Napoleon,' he said, 'earlier I couldn't have tolerated him. Now I think completely otherwise.'"

In the latter part of the summer Beethoven accepted a commission from Diabelli for "a Sonata in F for Pianoforte, four hands." The project seems to have originated from the publisher, who asked for such a composition and specified the key in a letter dated August 7, 1824. Beethoven, in a letter dated August 24, agreed to compose the work for a fee of 80 ducats in gold, although a sonata for four hands was not in his line. He mentioned the composition and the fee which he was to receive for it in the draft for a letter to Schlesinger next year, but never wrote the work; nor have any certain traces of it been found in the sketchbooks.

Two notes to Haslinger in October show that a new element had entered into Beethoven's worries concerning his nephew. The first is dated "Baden, evening of October 6":

Dear Tobias!

I beg of you most fervently to inquire right away at the house in the Johannisgasse, into which we are going to move, whether Karl slept there yesterday and today, and, if he is at home, to give him this note immediately; if not, to leave it with the caretaker there to give to him—He has been away since yesterday and this evening neither he nor the housekeeper are here. I am alone with a person who can neither speak, read nor write, and I can find scarcely a thing to eat dining out—Once already I have had to go in from here to fetch Karl in Vienna; once he has gone somewhere it is hard to bring him away. I beg of you to notify me right away what you can. I would like to have had a few more peaceful days here; unfortunately I will have to return to the city on account of him. At any rate I beg of you to let no one know of this. God is my witness as to what I have had to endure already because of him. If there is no information from the caretaker in the Johannisgasse, then send someone to the Landstrasse, where I lived before, to ask the caretaker where Frau von Niemetz[52] lives, in order to find out there if he has been to her place or is coming there, so that she will direct him here at once.

Naturally I shall remunerate your servant as well as pay the cost of postage for the letters—Also I beg of you to take care of the letter to my Cain-brother—I beg of you to answer immediately whether or not he has been found.

Most hastily your friend   Beethoven

For God's sake an answer immediately.

The second letter dated "Baden, the day after the 6th Octob. 1824" determines the year date of the first. Touching is the expression of relief expressed in this letter, the first part of which is given here:

Best one!

Our Benjamin arrived here early today, on which account I am firing off 17 and a half cannons—Earlier events through no fault of his et sine mea culpa made me anxious, thank heaven everything goes well and opportunely at times despite my agitatos! With these wretched arrangements it is no wonder one gets anxious about a growing young man, and with it the poisoned breath dragons!—

. . . .

[52] The mother of Karl's friend Niemetz, who will be mentioned shortly.

Four years earlier at the Blöchlinger Institute, Karl had made the friendship of a fellow student named Niemetz. By now they were close friends and Karl invited him to join in one of his visits to Baden. The following discussion about Niemetz, in a Conversation Book, marked by Schindler "Fall of 1824 in Baden" has a particular interest in that it includes Beethoven's part in the conversation:

Beethoven: I am very ill pleased with your choice of this friend. Poverty certainly deserves sympathy, but not invariably. I would not want to be unfair to him but to me he is a burdensome guest, lacking completely in decency and manners, which belong in some degree to all well brought up youths and men.—Besides I suspect that his interests are more with the housekeeper than with me—Besides I love quiet; also the space here is too limited for several people since I am constantly busy, and he cannot engage my interest at all.—You still have a very weak character.

Karl: Concerning my choice, I believe that a close acquaintance of four years' duration is really sufficient to get to know a man from *all angles*, especially a boy who cannot possibly remain disguised for such a long time—Thus there cannot be a question of lack of conviction, but merely of the reasons which led me to it, and they are in a word: the very great similarity of character and tastes. If he has been unable to please you, you are free to send him away, but he has not deserved what you have said about him.

Beethoven: I find him rough and common. These are no friends for you.

Karl: If you find him rough, you are mistaken. In any event, I wouldn't have thought that he had given you the opportunity to think it. Also I do not intend to exchange him for another which would be a clear sign of weakness of character, for which you reproach me certainly with injustice; for of all the students at Blöchlinger's I have found *no one* but him who would have cheered up my own, often dreary home, and consequently I feel that I am gratefully indebted to him.

Beethoven: You are not yet in a position to discriminate.

Karl: It is really useless to quarrel over a subject, especially over a [person's] character concerning which I will never abandon my conviction, *so long as I can consider that I myself am not a bad man*, for if there is something good in *me*, he possesses it in at least as high a degree as I, and it would be unfair to be angry with him if you do not judge *me* likewise. For my part I will not stop loving him as I would my brother, if I had one.

Here Beethoven's part in the conversation stops; but this talk shows the boy, just turned eighteen, was in mature command of himself in these inevitable scenes with his uncle, which represented as they did two essentially different points of view.

At some point in the first part of November, Beethoven returned again to Vienna, where he took up his new residence—at 969 Johannesgasse, in a house owned by a family named Kletschka. From a relative of this family, Dr. Jurié v. Lavandal, Frimmel learned that Beethoven had quarrels with both the housekeeper and his nephew, which led to noisy scenes; further that "at times the deaf master pounded the piano (presumably out of tune) quite unmercifully." As a result of these disturbances, Frau Kletschka finally had to send her young daughter, Nanette, to her boarders to serve notice.[53] But here the story of Beethoven's dwellings is unclear. On the one hand it would appear that he remained at this address throughout the winter, since this address is given as late as April 18, 1825, in a letter from Beethoven to Dr. Braunhofer.[54] Yet from two sources we learn that Beethoven moved to the Krugerstrasse. The writer, Heinrich Friedrich Rellstab, describes his visit in early April, 1825, to see the composer "in the Krugerstrasse No. 767 on the fourth floor."[55] Meanwhile Gerhard von Breuning lists Beethoven's residence for the winter of 1824-25 as "Krugerstrasse 1009 (now 13) . . . second story."[56] Frimmel points out the fallacy of Rellstab's address since at that time there were no numbers under 1000 on the Krugerstrasse. Because of the expense it seems unlikely that Beethoven was once again occupying two dwellings at the same time. But it may well be that, having been ousted temporarily from the Johannesgasse and forced to live elsewhere, he was later allowed to return.

On November 17, 1824, as the autograph attests, Beethoven wrote a four-part canon on the words "Schwenke dich ohne Schwänke," which he sent to Schott and Sons for publication in the *Cäcilia,* where it appeared in April, 1825. There the title is "Canon on one who was called Schwenke." The person whose name has thus been perpetuated was the pianist and composer, Carl Schwencke.[57]

The state of Beethoven's health is suggested by the following letter to Archduke Rudolph, dated November 18, 1824:

Your Imperial Highness
Since I was ill when I returned here from Baden I was prevented from betaking myself, as I wished to do, to Y.I.H. because I was forbidden to go outside. Yesterday was the first day that I could walk in the free air again—Your gracious letter caught me just when I was confined to my bed. As I was in a state of perspiration at that moment, since my poor health resulted from a chill, it was impossible for me to get up, nevertheless I know that Y.I.H. is convinced that I never could neglect the regard due you—Tomorrow at noon I shall have the pleasure of paying my respects; moreover, means will not be lacking to arouse Y.I.H.'s musical spirit which can be nothing but beneficial for art—my refuge—God be praised—
Your Imperial Highness's truly most obedient servant Beethoven

The main composition of the year 1824 was the Quartet in E-flat, Op. 127, the history of which is inevitably wound up with the history of Prince Galitzin's request to Beethoven for three string quartets. The story is now taken up from where it was left off, at the end of the chapter for the year 1822. First, the time schedule of composition. Ideas for the work were

[53] *BJ,* I, p. 75; *FRBH,* II, pp. 462-63.
[54] *BJ,* I, pp. 74-5; see also *A* 1359. Miss Anderson identifies the writer of the address as nephew Karl.
[55] Kerst, II, p. 121.

[56] *Aus dem Schwarzspanierhause,* p. 45.
[57] Born in Hamburg in 1797, son of Christian Friedrich Gottlieb Schwencke, Director of Church Music and Cantor at the Johanneum in Hamburg. (TDR, v, 139.)

probably in the composer's head when he offered a quartet to Peters in June, 1822. The invitation from Galitzin in November, 1822 undoubtedly spurred the work forward, and in January, 1823 Beethoven agreed to write some string quartets. Then the composition and performance of the Ninth Symphony delayed work until the summer of 1824.[58] The main work was done in the second half of 1824 and the beginning of 1825, and the work was first performed on March 6, 1825. By this time there were also pre-liminary sketches for the first and last movements of the second quartet (Op. 132).[59]

Beethoven's letter to Prince Galitzin of January 25, 1823, has already been given, in which he accepted the invitation to write three string quartets. Galitzin replied on February 23;[60] he expressed his joy over Beethoven's acceptance, notified him that he had made the order to his banker, Stieglitz,[61] to make payment of 50 ducats for the first quartet, stated his eagerness to send 100 more for two more quartets, and instructed him in how to mail the music, urging him to tell no one about it so that he could receive a higher price from his publisher. As already mentioned, Beethoven asked the Prince to subscribe to the Mass and then asked him to permit the 50 ducats for the first quartet to be applied to the subscription for the Mass. Beethoven re-ceived this sum from Henikstein, Stieglitz' representative in Vienna, on October 22. A note from Henikstein to the Prince, dated October 25, 1823, shows that the Prince agreed to the redesignation of the money. Meanwhile, during the year, Galitzin was writing to Beethoven frequently concerning the arrival of the first quartet and news of the start of the second. At this time, however, his patience was tempered with understanding of the re-quirements of artists. In his letter of November 29, 1823, after expressing joy over the arrival of the manuscript of the Mass and enquiring about the pianoforte sonatas that he had been expecting, he says: "I am really impatient to have a new quartet of yours, nevertheless, I beg you not to mind and to be guided in this only by your inspiration and the disposition of your mind, for no one knows better than I that you cannot command genius, rather that it should be left alone, and we know moreover that in your private life you are not the kind of person to sacrifice artistic for personal interest and that music done to order is not your business at all."

On August 3, 1823, Prince Galitzin had first expressed his desire for the score of the Mass so that he could perform the work at St. Petersburg. When the score arrived, however, there was missing a page of the *Gloria,* a precaution that Beethoven had taken against his manuscript being stolen

---

[58] For sketches see *II Beeth.*, pp. 210ff., 534-46.

[59] *Ibid.*, pp. 547ff. See also pp. 180-81.

[60] The letters from Galitzin to Beethoven may be found in the Appendix of TDR, v, pp. 552ff. Of the letters from Beethoven to Galitzin, only three, plus one draft, have been found, out of a total of what must have been at least ten. See *A* 1123, 1244, 1292, 1405.

[61] Baron Ludwig Stieglitz was a banker in St. Petersburg.

while copied. Beethoven wrote a letter of apology and explanation to the Prince on December 13, 1823, with assurances that the missing page would soon arrive, and with further notices concerning the Gloria section.

In his answer of December 30, Galitzin indicated that his performance of the Mass would take place in February or Easter. Since the first fifty ducats from Galitzin had been reapplied to the Mass at Beethoven's request, the Prince now writes: "Let me know whether you need 50 for the 1st quartet, [if so] I will make it immediately available to you." In his next letter, dated March 11, 1824, Galitzin was more impatient and worried as to whether Beethoven was ill and consequently unable to fulfill his promises; he reiterated his wish that if Beethoven should need money, he should feel free to draw it on account with M. M. Stieglitz and Co.; and he announced that the performance of the Mass, which was a benefit for musicians' widows, would take place on April 7. Galitzin's next letter described what was in fact the first full performance in the world of the Mass in D. It deserves to be given in full:

Petersburg, April 8, 1824

Monsieur, I am eager to give you an account of the performance of your sublime masterpiece which we presented here to the public the night before last.[62] For several months I have been extremely impatient to hear this music performed, the beauties of which I foresaw from the score. The effect of this music on the public cannot be described and I doubt if I exaggerate when I say that for my part I have never heard anything so sublime; I don't even except the masterpieces of Mozart which with their eternal beauties have not created for me the same sensations that you have given me, Monsieur, by the Kyrie and Gloria of your Mass. The masterly harmony and the moving melody of the Benedictus transport the heart to a plane that is really blissful. This whole work in fact is a treasure of beauties; it can be said that your genius has anticipated the centuries and that there are not listeners perhaps enlightened enough to experience all the beauty of this music; but it is posterity that will pay homage and will bless your memory much better than your contemporaries can. Prince Radziwill, whom you know is a great amateur of music, arrived just a few days ago from Berlin and was present at the performance of your mass which he had not known before; he was enraptured with it just like myself and all those present.—I hope that your health is restored and that you are going to give us many more products of your sublime genius.—Excuse the nuisance that I often cause by my letters, but it is a sincere tribute from one of your greatest admirers.

P. Nicolas Galitzin

[62] Prince Galitzin was in error either in the dating of his letter or in the phrase "the night before last," for the performance took place on April 7 (April 7—New Style or Gregorian Calendar; March 26—Old Style or Julian Calendar). This date has been established by Boris Schwarz, who has found mention of the concert in two different Russian newspapers as having taken place on March 26th. This evidence supports the March 26 date (Old Style) given by the Lpz. *AMZ* (Vol. 26, May 27, 1824) in reporting the event and the April 7 date (New Style) mentioned by Prince Galitzin himself in his letter to Beethoven on March 11, 1824. See Boris Schwarz, "More Beethoveniana in Soviet Russia," *MQ*, Vol. 49, 1963, pp. 147-49.

Beethoven's next (and last surviving) letter to the Prince is dated "Vienna, May 26, 1824." The letter is in German for the probable reason, as Miss Anderson has pointed out,[63] that Galitzin, in a letter of May 5, 1823, specifically asked Beethoven for "a letter in German and in his own hand so that I may have the pleasure of owning an autograph letter of yours." The letter follows:

My dear and honored Prince!

So many of your charming letters unanswered!—[Please] attribute it only to the overwhelming load of business, and certainly not to neglect on my part— Having been entreated to give a few concerts in which I lost time and money; and to the shame of our present organization in Vienna, I had to be sacrificed to a former dancer Duport, who is lease-holder at the Kärthnerthor. Let me off from repeating a description of the vulgar details, which anyway would revolt and disgust you as it does me. But allow me to tell you that it was a waste for me of much time and money—Here I have learned that the Mass is going to be given in St. Petersburg as a great oratorio. My circumstances force me, since here they do nothing at all *for me*, but rather *against me*, to try a second subscription on this work, and in fact, as Y.E. once wrote me, to offer a printed copy of the score for 5 ducats in gold, which could be printed and delivered in a half year. I cannot send you this invitation until the next post—You will soon receive your quartet, promised so long ago to you, perhaps also the others. If only the inquiries and encouragements from all sides for big works were not so strong. The necessity of the time requires it, *poverty* is helped and aided thereby in every way, what an incentive for such works!—Since I can well imagine that you yourself employ works for this purpose, I will send Y.E. a new overture and a trio which was sung by three local Italians and performed excellently. Should you wish a new big symphony with a finale in which occurs chorus and solo parts, I would have a score of it copied. The cost would be nothing more than a reimbursement for the cost of copying—Perhaps it would be possible through your efforts to be able to have the mass dedicated to His Majesty the Emperor of Russia; perhaps such a generous monarch as the Russian Emperor would even settle on me a yearly pension for which I would first deliver all my big works to His Majesty and would also fulfill speedily His Majesty's commissions and thereby would be able to have helped suffering mankind—

Enclosed is an impression of the medal from His Majesty from France as a sign of his satisfaction with my mass. The medal weighs a half a pound in gold; and [has] Italian verses about me—which . . . the side of genius which outside is radiantly white, only the. . . .[64]

With all the esteem and devotion
from Your Highness's faithful Beetho[ve]n[65]

[63] Emily Anderson, "Two Letters from Beethoven to Prince Galitzin," in *Festschrift Schmidt-Görg* (Bonn, 1957), p. 5. The letter that follows is from her reading of the original autograph; *ibid.*, pp. 6-7.

[64] According to Miss Anderson (*ibid.*, p. 7, nn. 26, 27) there are two incompletions in the last sentence: in the first a word has been erased through smudging, in the second, the rest of the sentence is missing.

[65] It is impossible to match in English the omission of letters in the signature. "Ihre Du[rch]laucht mit aller liebe v. [Ve]rehrung verharre[nder] Beetho[ve]n."

Replying June 16, Galitzin accepted Beethoven's offer of the symphony, the overture and the trio. As regards the Mass, Galitzin answered that to secure permission to dedicate a work to the Emperor one must write to Count Nesselrode, and that he would be glad to distribute as many printed copies of the Mass as possible, but that the difficulty of its performance precluded a large sale. Considering the later history between Beethoven and Galitzin, the postscript is interesting: "If you ever find yourself in the least kind of difficulty, apply quickly to me. I will be only too glad to be able to be of help to you."

In his next letter, dated July 28, he offered the advice already advanced by Schindler, and doubtless by others: "Right now I am convinced that if you wanted to travel in Europe without any treasures other than your compositions, and without any recommendations other than your immortal masterpieces, you would take the world by storm. Your presence alone at Paris, London would eclipse everything else, and the concerts which you would give would not resemble those in Vienna." He was impatient now and mentioned that he had heard that Beethoven was working on a cantata by Bernard and on Grillparzer's *Melusine*. Two more letters were written by Galitzin before the end of 1824. Only the second of the two has survived and is dated December 5. In this letter Galitzin reported that upon his return from a trip he witnessed a flood that completely inundated St. Petersburg. He planned a second performance of the Mass for the benefit of the flood survivors for which he also wanted the scores of the symphony and overture. As regards the quartet, he announced that 50 ducats were being remitted to Count von Lebzeltern, minister of Austria, for remittance to Beethoven, after a delay which was not of his own making, and that Beethoven could expect it soon. This then was the second payment of 50 ducats and was specifically for the first quartet. Beethoven must have written to him in the fall concerning his poor health for Galitzin answers: "I am really very much vexed that you have suffered so from poor health, but suffering is an indispensable part of human life, and it seems that geniuses like yourself ought to impose on nature and force her to respect those like you who are distinguished from the rest of mankind."

By the end of the year the quartet was sent and was acknowledged by Galitzin on April 29, 1825, after having "performed it several times." In the chapter devoted to the year 1826, the story of Prince Galitzin and the Beethoven quartets is continued.⁂—

After offering "a new quartet" to Schott on March 10, 1824, Beethoven corresponded with the firm during the year and kept postponing the date of delivery. The Mass and the Symphony were received on January 18, 1825, but still not the quartet. Not until after the first performance on March 6 did the publishers receive the manuscript; on May 7, 1825, Beethoven wrote to them: "You will have received the Quartet by this time, it is the one that was promised to you. I could have an honorarium of 60 ducats from several publishers here, but I have put it off in order to keep my words with you." —⚹❀The compositions completed in this year were:

(1817) 1822-4. Symphony No. 9 in D minor, Op. 125.
1823-4.   Six Bagatelles for Pianoforte, Op. 126.
1824.   Canons:
           "Schwenke dich ohne Schwänke," WoO 187, for Carl Schwencke in November.
           "Te solo adoro" (Metastasio), WoO 186, for Carlo Evasio Soliva on June 2.[66]
           "Opferlied" for Soprano, Chorus and Orchestra (Matthisson), Op. 121b, final version.[67]
           Waltz in E-flat for Pianoforte, WoO 84, for the Viennese actor, Carl Friedrich Müller on November 21 (see publications).

The publications of the year were:

In the Berlin *Allgemeine Musikalische Zeitung* supplement, December 8: Piece in B-flat for Pianoforte, WoO 60.
In C. F. Müller's *Musikalisches Angebinde zum neuen Jahre,* a collection of forty waltzes by forty different composers:
Waltz in E-flat for Pianoforte, WoO 84.[68]
By Steiner:
Variations for Pianoforte, Violin and Violoncello on Wenzel Müller's Song, "Ich bin der Schneider Kakadu," Op. 121a.[69] ❀❀—

---

[66] Nothing is known of Beethoven's relation to the musician Carlo Evasio Soliva (*ca.* 1792-1853); see KHV, p. 689.

[67] See Hurt Herbst, "Beethovens Opferliedkompositionen" in *NBJ,* v (1933), pp. 137ff; KHV, p. 354; and *II Beeth.,* pp. 541-42.

[68] See Max Unger, "Zu den Erstdrucken einiger Werke Beethovens" in *Zeitschrift für*

Musik, Vol. 105 (1938), pp. 145-48.

[69] Steiner's opus number is simply Op. 121; the "a" had to be added because of Schott's printing in the following year of the final version of the "Opferlied" with the number 121—now designated as Op. 121b. According to Alan Tyson, the work was published about the same time by Chappell and Co. and Goulding and Co. in London. See his *The Authentic English Editions of Beethoven* (London, 1963), p. 121.

CHAPTER XXXVIII

THE YEAR 1825

ANOTHER INVITATION FROM LONDON— INCREASING TROUBLE WITH HIS NEPHEW—THE THREE GALITZIN QUARTETS COMPLETED

IN THE early part of 1824, thoughts of a visit to England had been re-vived by a letter from Charles Neate; it had been determined that the visit should be undertaken in the fall and that Schindler should accompany him. When nothing developed, Neate wrote another letter on December 20, 1824, bringing with it an invitation from the Philharmonic Society of London which kept the thought of an English visit alive in Beethoven's irresolute mind for a considerable space longer. Neate wrote in an extremely cordial vein. He had long wished to see Beethoven in England, he said, where he believed that his genius was appreciated more than in any other country; and now he had received the pleasant charge from the Philharmonic Society to invite him to come. He made no doubt but that in a short time he would earn enough money richly to compensate him for all the inconveniences of the journey. The Philharmonic Society was disposed to give him 300 guineas for conducting at least one of his works at each of the Society's concerts in the coming season, and composing a new symphony and a concerto which was to be produced during his visit but to remain the composer's property. As an additional pecuniary inducement he held out that Beethoven could give a concert of his own at which he would make at least £500, besides which there were many other avenues of profit open to him. If he were to bring along the quartets about which he had written, they would yield him £100 more, and he might therefore be sure of carrying back a large sum of money, enough, indeed, to make all the remainder of his life much pleasanter than the past had been. He told Beethoven that the new Symphony had arrived and the first rehearsal of it was set for January 17. He hoped that

Beethoven would be on hand to direct it at the first concert of the Society and trusted that a report that a copy of it was in Paris was not true.

Beethoven replied on January 15 and again on the 27th. The first letter follows:

Monsieur!

With the greatest pleasure I received your letter of—[December 20] through which you had the kindness to inform me that the Philharmonic Society, with its distinguished artists is inviting me to come to London. I am well satisfied with the conditions made to you by the society, but I wish to propose that besides the 300 guineas that it has promised me I be sent 100 more guineas for traveling expenses; for I need to buy a carriage; also I need to be accompanied by someone. You can see clearly that that is necessary; besides I beg you to let me know the inn at which I may stay in London. I will take a new quartet along with me.

As for the rumor that you wrote about, that there is a copy of the 9th Symphony in Paris, there is no foundation in it at all. It is true that this symphony will be published in Germany, but not before the year has come to an end during which time the Society will be playing it. On this point I must inform you again to have only small rehearsals of this composition, with the four string parts for example; for it is the only way to study well such a work; above all the choruses should be rehearsed. There are still some errors, a list of which I will send you by the next post.—

It seems to me that in the second movement of the Symphony it has been forgotten that at the repetition of the minore after the Presto one must begin again at the sign and continue without repetition right to the ferma, then one goes directly to the Coda.[1]

I beg you to reply as quickly as possible for I am being asked to write a big new composition which I will not begin, however, without hearing from you.[2]— I have to write all the time, not to accumulate wealth—only to provide for my needs.

Now I need to have assurance on this point.—I will be charmed to see you and to know that noble nation, England. I am your sincere friend,

Monsieur,
with the highest regards
Louis van Beethoven

To this letter Neate replied on February 1. He had conveyed the contents of Beethoven's letter to the directors of the Philharmonic Society and had now regretfully to report that they had declined to make any change in their offer. He was personally willing to give the advance asked, but the individual directors were not masters of their conduct in all things; they had to abide by the laws of the Society. He hoped that under the circumstances Beethoven would come; he was sure the trip would pay him, and the directors would impatiently await his presence at the second concert, it being already

---

[1] He wrote the same thing later to Schott. In the Complete Works Edition, the repetition of the Scherzo is completely written out.

(TDR, v, 161, n. 2.)

[2] This was the oratorio on Bernard's text *Der Sieg des Kreuzes*. (TDR, v, 161, n. 3.)

too late for the first. There was to be another rehearsal of the Symphony that evening.

Again Beethoven had to struggle with the question as to whether or not he should make the journey to London. He was strongly urged by his desire to earn a large sum of money. His friends pressed him with arguments in favor of the trip. Karl admonished him to make up his own mind without giving heed to the insatiable avarice of his brother, but reminded him that Neate had assured him he would make enough money to be free of care the rest of his life. Johann did not talk of the financial advantage alone but said that he would benefit physically, travel being good for the health. Apparently answering an objection of Beethoven's on the score of his age, Karl reminded him that Haydn also went to London when he was fifty years old—and he was "not so famous." Schuppanzigh burst out with his brusque third person singular: "I wish he would pick up enough courage to make the trip; he would not regret it." Who should accompany him? Schindler had been recommended by Neate, but his name does not occur in these conversations; instead there was talk of Schuppanzigh and young Streicher. But as it turned out, no one was to accompany him, nobody alight with him at either the house of Stumpff or the Hotel de la Sablonière in Leicester Square which Neate had recommended as a French house much visited by foreigners. His doubts, suspicions, fears for his health, anxiety about his nephew, his fatal indecision, prevailed. On March 19 he wrote to Neate that he would make the visit some other time—perhaps in the fall; two days later the Symphony was performed for the first time in London. From that time on there was no further mention of the trip.

In this same letter, however, Beethoven kept alive the idea of selling the quartets in England and wrote that he was satisfied with Neate's offer for them provided that he would be allowed to publish the quartets in a year and a half or two years. On May 25 he reaffirmed his satisfaction with the price already offered of £100 for three quartets but warned that the first quartet was much in demand by different artists and had already been promised them for their benefit; he urged Neate to let him know whether he was satisfied with his conditions, so that he could send the first quartet right away; he stipulated that the honorarium would not be due until he reported the completion of the other two quartets; and he urged haste because of the demands from publishers.

The absence of Ries's name in the negotiations with England is explained by the fact that he was no longer in London. He had purchased an estate in Godesberg, near Bonn, and removed thither in 1824. From there he wrote to Beethoven inviting him to visit him for awhile; he also made various enquiries concerning Beethoven's compositions, for which a word of explanation is needed. In 1817 there had come into being the Lower Rhenish Musical Festival. For the seventh annual meeting, which was to be held at Aix-la-Chapelle, Ries had been invited to be the conductor and he had accepted on

December 24, 1824. During that year reports of the Vienna performance of the Ninth Symphony had spread and it was desired to make the symphony a feature of the festival scheme. In January, 1825, Schott and Sons were asked if the score would be in print by May and replied in the negative on January 25th. Thereupon Ries, who at first was not enthusiastic about performing the symphony, was asked to write Beethoven for a manuscript copy. He also asked for the metronome markings of *Christus am Ölberg*, which was another work slated for performance. Beethoven's answer, which follows, is undated but undoubtedly was written in February:

Dear Ries!

You have pressed so for an answer that I can only tell you the most essential things now. I knew already from Kirchhoffer that you had left London. My very pressing situation has hardly given me the chance to write you anything at all. K[irchhoffer] took the Symphony which certainly won't be able to appear before the end of the summer. These sales at the moment are only preliminaries, the time which the London Philharmonic Society has stipulated will be held to completely.[3] Bremen has *never* received it. Nor did Paris as someone wrote me from London. How much one has to bear if one has the misfortune to become famous!

Now as to what you want. It will be a great pleasure to indicate the tempi of Christus am Ölberge for you by metronome, even though this indication of time is so unstable.—As for the symphony I will make you now a more general offer. My situation forces me to seek resolution of my *needs* [Nöthen] through my *notes* [Noten]. Would it be possible for you to arrange the affair *in this way?* I would send *you* my score of the symphony or a good copy, also a score of the Mass, and the overture which I wrote for the Phil. Society. Also I could give you several small things for orchestra, and for chorus. In this way such a society would be in a position to give two or three concerts instead of one. Perhaps 40 carolins would not be too much for it—I leave the whole matter to you. This concept does not come from *me* but from those who want to rescue me from my *needs* through my *notes*—I take the deepest interest in your property in Godesberg; no one could have a more envious joy over it than I whose deepest desires would be realized by such a property. However, it appears that my destiny is not to be quite the way I want it. Greet your old father heartily for me. I am overjoyed on account of his happiness. I embrace you heartily and hope to be able to write you more soon.

As always your true friend

Beethoven

You write soon too.

Beethoven consented to Ries's request and about March 11 sent the score of the first three movements but only the individual parts of the finale. This was explained in a letter to Ries dated March 19:

[3] In his letter to Neate on January 15, Beethoven promised that the symphony would not be published in Germany until the Society had had the score for a year. Actually it was not published by Schott until August, 1826.

My dear friend!

Just eight days ago, immediately after receiving your letter, the symphony was sent with the next mail-coach to go; three movements copied out in score and the Finale complete in individual parts. I only have *my own* score therefore I could only send you the parts of the Finale. But you will receive the score of the Finale by the mail-coach leaving eight days from now along with other works which I am sending. Along with the symphony there was sent an overture and an Opferlied with chorus, the latter apparently full of mistakes, however. But I will send you from here a list of the mistakes. Also there is still to be sent one contrabassoon part for the Finale of the symphony.[4]

This is all, dear friend, that I can tell you today; I am too pressed. I will thank you in writing myself for your fine proposals, but I cannot today on account of a burnt hand. All good wishes to your father and your wife. You will be satisfied by me in any case.

As ever your true friend   Beethoven

Ries waited in vain for the score of the finale and finally had to have one made from the parts. In a letter dated April 9, Beethoven explained more specifically that it was an approaching concert that prevented him from sending his score of the finale; at the same time he enumerated what was being sent: a revised copy of *Opferlied*, the chorusmaster's score of the symphony finale, and an overture in C, 6/8 time; by the next post the *Kyrie* and the *Gloria*, and an Italian Duet. He was still to send a grand march and chorus and might have added an overture which was yet unknown outside of Vienna, but thought he had sent enough. The overture in C was, of course, Op. 115; the march and chorus were from the *Ruinen von Athen*.

The performance took place on May 23, 1825, the second day of the festival, with the following program: 1. The Ninth Symphony 2. Mozart's *Davidde penitente* 3. Overture to *Die Zauberflöte* 4. *Christus am Ölberg*. The time was too short for the difficult music to be learned thoroughly and at the performance portions of the slow movement and the Scherzo of the Symphony were "regretfully" omitted, a fact that, it is to be hoped, was never known to Beethoven.[5] On June 9 Ries wrote a letter to Beethoven concerning the event. There were 422 performers in chorus and orchestra, and the popular reception of the music was enthusiastic enough to enable him to report to Beethoven that the performance had been a success; and

---

[4] The contrabassoon part is missing from the Aix-la-Chapelle score of the Ninth Symphony, so the part could never have been sent. See Otto Baensch, "Die Aachener Abschrift der neunten Symphonie" in *NBJ*, v (1933), p. 16.

[5] In the *Rheinische Flora* (No. 82, May 26, 1825), J. B. Rousseau writes: "At the performance the Scherzo was omitted, although

it had been rehearsed, because lack of time necessitated the abridgement. Other than that the orchestra executed all that was possible after removing countless difficulties in connection with the performance of this symphony." See Eugen Brümmer, *Beethoven im Spiegel der zeitgenössischen rheinischen Presse* (Würzburg, 1932), p. 52.

he sent him 40 Louis d'or as a fee. Ries recognized the symphony as a work without an equal and told Beethoven that had he written nothing else it would have made him immortal. "Whither will you yet lead us?" he asked. Very naturally, Beethoven had reported the negotiations touching a visit to England to Ries, who expressed his satisfaction that he had not accepted the engagement and added: "If you want to go there you must make thorough preparations. Rossini got £2500 from the Opera alone. If Englishmen want to do an extraordinary thing, they must all get together so as to make it worth while. There will be no lack of applause and marks of honor, but you have probably had enough of these all your life."

Mass and symphony had been delivered to Fries, the banker, on January 16, to be forwarded to Schott and Sons. Beethoven informed the firm by letter on January 22 and took occasion to deny the report that the Mass had been printed elsewhere. He was particularly anxious to remove doubt in connection with the Schlesingers: "Schlesinger is not to be trusted, for he takes where he can; both père et fils bombarded me for the Mass and other works, but I did not deign to answer either of them, since after thinking them over I had cast them out long before." The second section of the letter deserves to be given in full:

Schlesinger also wished to publish *all* my quartets and periodically to have from me each time a new one of these and pay me what I wished, but since this could hurt my plan of an edition of my complete works, I also left this unanswered. You might reflect upon this opportunity sometime for it is better to be done *by me* than after my death. I have received offers already about it and also plans, but these firms don't seem to me to be suited for such a big undertaking. I would rather put my trust in you. In general, I would prefer to be paid for it in one lump sum; I would indicate the usual unimportant corrections and supply for every category of works, as for example sonatas, variations, etc. a similar new work—Here are a pair of canons for your journal—three others will follow[6]— as a supplement to a romantic biography of Tobias Haslinger here in three parts. First part, Tobias discovers that he is the apprentice of the famous master Kapellmeister Fux—and holds the ladder for the master's Gradus ad Parnassum. Now since he is inclined towards pranks, he shakes and jogs it causing many who have already climbed up quite a way suddenly to break their necks etc. Now he bids farewell to us mortal men and returns to daylight in the time of Albrechtsberger. 2nd part. The Nota cambiata, which already existed with Fux becomes used regularly by A[lbrechtsberger], the appoggiaturas used to the utmost, the art of creating musical skeletons is worked to extremes etc. Tobias like a caterpillar spins himself anew into a cocoon and then he unfolds himself again and appears in this world for the third time. 3rd part. His wings, hardly grown, waft him to the Paternostergässel: he becomes the Paternostergässel Kapellmeister. A graduate of the appoggiatura school, he retains nothing from it but the *change*,[7]

[6] The pair of canons were those on Hoffmann and Schwencke. See KHV, WoO 180 and 187. There is no evidence that the three others were sent. (Cf. TK, III, 190, n. 2.)

[7] A pun on the word *Wechsel*—i.e. *Wechselnote* (appoggiatura) and *Wechsel* (change).

and so he brings forth the friend of his youth and finally becomes a member of several *empty*[8] societies etc. If you ask him about this he will certainly allow this biography to be printed.

Very hurriedly

Yours

Beethoven

The Schotts did not notice that Beethoven had wanted the prior consent of Haslinger, and published the facetious biographical sketch in the April issue of *Cäcilia* with only minor changes, followed it with the two canons entitled "Upon one who is called Schwenke" and "Upon one who is called Hoffmann," and added Beethoven's own signature. In a letter dated February 5 Beethoven had urged Schott as a joke to ask Haslinger for *"my romantic biography of him"* and added: "That is the way to handle this fellow, a *Viennese* without heart. He is the one *who advised me not to deal with you*." He went on to describe Steiner as a "rascally fellow and skinflint," and Haslinger as a "weakling" whom he made useful to himself in some things.

However, after hearing of the printing in *Cäcilia*, Beethoven dictated the following letter to Schott on August 13:

Dear Sir!

I observed with astonishment in the 7th issue of Cäcilia, p. 205, that, along with the canons, you published a joke, sent in a friendly manner, which can easily be taken for a biting insult, although indeed this was not my purpose at all. To offend anyone has always been inconsistent with my character.

Concerning myself as an artist, I am not known as one to become aroused about anything written about me from the point of view of my art. Concerning myself, however, as a man, I must react entirely differently.

You should have seen at first glance that the whole biographical sketch of my respected friend Herr Tobias Haslinger was only a *joke* and could not be meant otherwise, since I wanted, as my letter said, to heighten the joke even more by a request to him on your part for permission to publish his biography. Well, it appears that it was my flighty and often illegible handwriting which gave rise to the misunderstanding.

The contributions, which you yourself requested to be sent, would have corresponded perfectly to my purpose if you had inserted just the two canons, the titles of which show sufficiently that they couldn't easily be connected with a biography of Haslinger; but I could not have dreamt that you would misuse private correspondence and put such a joke before the public, the absurdities of which, which you chose to insert at the beginning (for example, line 2 "2 canons which as supplements I . . . etc."),[9] cannot be explained at all. The word "empty"

---

[8] The pun is untranslatable: "geleert" literally "emptied," as opposed to "gelehrt" (learned). This is a pun he used several times in his correspondence.

[9] Schott's article is entitled "Canons along with mention of their occasion by Ludwig van Beethoven" and begins: "It gives me pleasure to send from here a few canons to Cäcilia and its readers which I have written as supplements to a humorous romantic biography of the local Herr Tobias Hasslinger. . . ."

["geleert"], which applies to the whole of the humorous outline, could have been permitted in a group which was having an amusing conversation but in public it would never have occurred to me to put it in place of "learned" ["gelehrt"].

That was pushing the jest too far!

In the future I will know enough to guard against new misunderstandings being caused by my writing.

I expect you to print this in the Cäcilia without delay and without additions or deletions. For the affair consists of just what I have explained here, and must not be interpreted in any other way.

Vienna, August 13, 1825   L. van Beethoven

[In Beethoven's own handwriting]

I am counting with complete certainty upon your inserting this statement in the Cäcilia right away.

Yours sincerely

Beethoven

It does not appear that this communication was ever printed, neither does it appear that Beethoven took the matter so greatly to heart as his letter was calculated to make the public believe, had it been printed. On August 10 he wrote to his new friend Karl Holz: "I hear with amazement that the Mainz street-boys really abused my joke! It is contemptible; I assure you it was not at all my intention. What I meant was to have Castelli write a poem along these lines, but just under the name of the musical Tobias, with music by me. Since it has *so happened*, it must be accepted as a dispensation from heaven, it will form a companion-piece to Goethe's Bahrdt *sans comparaison* with all other authors. But I believe Tobias himself has wronged *them* somehow—Voila the revenge! It is better anyhow than to fall into the jaws of some monster[10]—I can't shed tears over it but must laugh like—" To his nephew he wrote: "It was not right for Mainz to do a thing like that, but as it is done it will do no harm. The times demand strong men to castigate these petty, tricky, miserable little fellows—much as my heart rebels against doing a man harm. Besides it was only a joke and I never thought of having it printed." Haslinger may have felt incensed at the publication, but he eventually accepted it in an amiable spirit and it did not lead to any rupture of friendship between the two men.

In a letter to Schott, dated January 26, 1825, which was concerned primarily with corrections of the Mass in D, Beethoven wrote a post-script indicating passages in the *Agnus Dei* where the appoggiaturas had been written incorrectly as eighth notes rather than sixteenth notes. It ends thus: "From this you can observe what copyists I am left with now; the fellow is a stupid Bohemian, a pandour, doesn't understand a thing; at first he writes quarters in the appoggiaturas, then finally eighths. Since I was no longer supervising [the work] I noticed this as it was being hastily wrapped."

[10] The remark was made for the sake of a play on words: "Rache" (revenge) and "Rachen" (jaws). (TK, III, 191, n. 1.)

This was probably the copyist Wolanek against whom the composer had railed repeatedly. In delivering some uncompleted manuscripts by messenger some time before Easter, Wolanek ventured a defense of his dignity in a letter which, though couched in polite phrases, was nevertheless decidedly ironical and cutting:[11]

To Herr Ludwig v. Beethoven!

Since I cannot add the finale to the score until Easter and you will no longer need it at this time, I am sending over the complete parts along with what has already been begun for your favorable disposition.

I remain gratefully obliged for the honor rendered by your employment of me; as for more concerning the discordant behavior towards me, I can only regard it smilingly as a good-natured outburst to be accepted. In the ideal world of tones there are so many dissonances, shouldn't they exist also in the real world?

My one comfort is the firm conviction that had Mozart and Haydn, those celebrated artists, been hired as your copyists they would have shared a fate similar to mine.

I request only not to mix with those common copyists who consider themselves happy to be able to maintain their existence by being treated as slaves.

At any rate be assured that I will never have the least bit of cause to blush in front of you on account of my behavior.

Respectfully yours Ferd. Wolanek

Beethoven read the letter, and, in a rage, drew lines across its face from corner to corner. Then in letters two inches long he scrawled over the writing the words: "Dummer, Eingebildeter, Eselhafter Kerl"—("Stupid, Conceited, Asinine Fellow"). That was not enough. There was a wide margin at the bottom of the sheet, just large enough to hold Beethoven's next ebullition: "Compliments for such a good-for-nothing, who pilfers one's money?—better to pull his asinine ears." Then he turned the sheet over. A whole page invited him—and he filled it up the middle with "Dirty Scribbler! Stupid Fellow! Correct the blunders which you have made in your ignorance, insolence, conceit and stupidity, this would be more to the purpose than to try to teach me, which is as if a *Sow* were to try to give lessons to Minerva." The margins were still available: on the right—"*Do you do honor* to Mozart and Haydn by never mentioning *their names*." On the left; "It was decided yesterday and even before then *not to have you* write *any more* for me."[12]

—The story of the events leading up to the first performance of the E-flat Quartet has been set forth in detail by Alfred Ebert[13] and may be summarized here. In January, 1825, Schuppanzigh was starting another

[11] The letter implies that Beethoven had already treated him to an outburst of temper. (Cf. TDR, v, 175-76.)

[12] According to Unger, these outbursts were never sent in the form of a letter ("Beethovens Handschrift," Heft 4 of *Veröffentlichungen*

des Beethoven-Hauses in Bonn).

[13] "Die ersten Aufführungen von Beethovens Es-dur Quartett (Op. 127) im Frühling 1825" in *DM*, Vol. 9, No. 13 (1910), pp. 42-63, 90-106.

subscription series of quartet concerts and was anxious to have his quartet (Holz, 2nd violin; Weiss, viola; Linke, cello) give the first performance of the work at the opening concert. In a Conversation Book he writes:

If he [Beethoven] has a mind to hand me the quartet for a performance, that is, so I can make it known, there may be a big difference in my present subscription.

In E-flat

He allows me then to be the one to make it known?

Beethoven affirmed the question to the delight of Schuppanzigh, who must have assumed that the quartet was ready, for the following notice appeared on January 20 in Bäuerle *Theaterzeitung*:

The famous musical artist Herr Schuppanzigh will continue his popular quartet performances but in the small *Vereinssaal beim roten Igel*. The first concert is on Sunday, January 23; the most distinguished of the new musical works are: the new renowned double quartet by L. Spohr as introduction, a new quintet [*sic*!] by Ludw. van Beethoven (still in manuscript) and in conclusion by common request the most famous and popular Septet by the same artist.

Schuppanzigh rushed this into print no doubt because he knew how easily Beethoven's decisions could be altered. His fear was justified. At the urging of Johann and Karl, Beethoven had promised the quartet to Linke for a benefit concert. The conflict was discussed and Beethoven was persuaded to let Linke have it first and then let Schuppanzigh perform it as often as he liked. Thereupon Schuppanzigh was invited to lunch to learn the decision. Schuppanzigh writes:

This affair with the quartet is accursed.

That doesn't matter; he can also give it to Linke. His music can be heard more often than once.

I wouldn't say anything if it were not already in the newspaper.

I cannot call it off.

He makes nothing of it.

Linke has said nothing about it to me. If he had spoken to me I would not have asked him for it.

I have said it myself[14] to Linke and he hasn't said a word about it.

---

[14] That Schuppanzigh is performing the music.

But he certainly hasn't promised him because that isn't his habit; he has perhaps given him a half-consent, still that is not yet a solemn promise.

⚬~⚬

I recall that Linke spoke to me of a quartet in A Minor which is supposed to be concertante for the cello.[15]

⚬~⚬

It is no disadvantage for Linke if he gives it to him now too.

Schuppanzigh succeeded in swinging the decision back in his favor, and Linke was given the hope of getting the A Minor Quartet, which was realized in the fall. In the meantime he was annoyed and held Schuppanzigh responsible for the change. However, by the middle of January the quartet still was not ready so that for his first concert Schuppanzigh had to substitute the Quartet in F Minor, Op. 95.

During January and February there was also much conversation concerning another set of spring concerts of Beethoven's works, in which the name of Schuppanzigh played a prominent part. Karl, who seemed consistently to take sides against Schuppanzigh argued for Ferdinand Piringer, now director of the *Concerts spirituels*: "Piringer demands nothing.—And you must give Schuppanzigh a third of the total of all those concerts." There was similar talk concerning the sale of tickets, the program, and the locale of the concert. Schuppanzigh meanwhile was worried not only about the delay in starting rehearsals for these concerts—which were never to materialize—but also the delay in receiving the new quartet for the second concert on March 6. In the middle of February he asks: "How is the quartet getting on?"

No Conversation Books from this time to the time of the concert have survived[16] to clarify just when Schuppanzigh actually received the parts. However there is a letter[17] from Beethoven to the violinist in which he mentions the fact that the quartet is now his to perform from this moment "until the second Sunday." Since the March 6th concert took place on a Sunday, this could mean that the quartet was sent less than two weeks before performance. In any case, in view of what happened at the performance, and afterwards, it is clear that Schuppanzigh did not have enough time for proper rehearsing of such a difficult work.✦—

Beethoven was greatly concerned with the outcome, and, as if at once to encourage and admonish the players, he drafted a humorous document and sent it to the quartet for signature. The statement is in another hand[18] and signed by Beethoven. The signatures of the players follow in pencil:

[15] This remarkable statement was made when Beethoven was working on the first and last movements of Op. 132. In the summer of 1825, Holz wrote in a Conversation Book: "The violoncello has very many so-called grateful passages in the new quartet."

[16] In the same Conversation Book referred to above, Johann writes (21 pages later):

"When you have the quartet copied, you will have part of it copied here." Two pages later: "In any case it is safest if you take some pages out and have them copied here or at my house."

[17] See A 1350.

[18] According to Thayer (TDR, v, 179, n. 2), this is in Karl's handwriting. However,

Best ones!

Each one is herewith given his part and is bound by oath and indeed pledged on his honor to do his best, to distinguish himself and to vie each with the other in excellence.

Each one who takes part in the affair in question is to sign this sheet.

Schuppanzigh	Beethoven
Weiss	
Linke	Schindler secretarius

The grand master's accursed violoncello.

Holz

The last, but only in signing.

The performance took place on March 6, and the result was disappointing. The music was not understood either by the players or the public and was all but ineffective. Schuppanzigh was held responsible and his patience must have been severely taxed by Beethoven's upbraidings and his determination to have an immediate repetition by other players. Schuppanzigh defended himself as vigorously as possible and was particularly vexed because Beethoven cited his brother's opinion of the performance—that of a musical ignoramus. He wanted to play the Quartet a second time, but told Beethoven that he had no objections to the work being handed over to Böhm; yet he protested with no little energy, that the fault of the fiasco was not his individually, as Beethoven had been told. He could easily master the technical difficulties, but it was hard to arrive at the spirit of the work: the ensemble was faulty, because of this fact and too few rehearsals. Beethoven decided that the next hearing should be had from Böhm, and though Schuppanzigh had acquiesced, he harbored a grievance against the composer for some time.

Joseph Böhm[19] had been leader of the quartet concerts in Vienna during Schuppanzigh's long absence. He has left an account of his connection with the work as follows:

... The affair did not come off well. Schuppanzigh, who played first violin, was weary from much rehearsing, there was no finish in the performance, the quartet did not appeal to him, he was not well disposed towards the performance and the quartet did not please. Few were moved, it was a weak *succès d'estime.*

When Beethoven learned of this—for he was not present at the performance—he became furious and let both performers and the public in for some harsh words. Beethoven could have no peace until the disgrace was wiped off. He sent for me first thing in the morning—In his usual curt way, he said to me. "You must play my quartet"—and the thing was settled.—Neither objections nor doubts could prevail; what Beethoven wanted had to take place, so I undertook the difficult task.—It was studied industriously and rehearsed frequently under Beethoven's own eyes: I said Beethoven's *eyes* intentionally, for the unhappy man was so

---

Miss Anderson (III, 1182, n. 5) identifies it as Schindler's hand. This is further borne out by Schindler's signing the document as "secretarius."

[19] Böhm (1795–1876) became a professor of violin playing at the Vienna Conservatory in 1819, a member of the Imperial Orchestra in 1821. He was a teacher of Joseph Joachim.

deaf that he could no longer hear the heavenly sound of his compositions. And yet rehearsing in his presence was not easy. With close attention his eyes followed the bows and therefore he was able to judge the smallest fluctuations in tempo or rhythm and correct them immediately. At the close of the last movement of this quartet there occurred a *meno vivace*,[20] which seemed to me to weaken the general effect. At the rehearsal, therefore, I advised that the original tempo be maintained, which was done, to the betterment of the effect.

Beethoven, crouched in a corner, heard nothing, but watched with strained attention. After the last stroke of the bows he said, laconically, "Let it remain so," went to the desks and crossed out the *meno vivace* in the four parts.

The quartet was performed finally and received with a real storm of applause. Now Beethoven was satisfied. Steiner, who had attended one or more of the rehearsals, was particularly enraptured by it and at once offered to buy it for publication for 60 ducats—a fact which Beethoven did not fail to report to Schott and Sons when he sent the manuscript to them. --◦◦§{The work was played three times by Böhm with the other three members of the Schuppanzigh quartet: once for a small audience, twice a few days later for a larger audience in an evening concert on March 23. Then Böhm asked Beethoven's permission to use the quartet in a benefit concert for himself, which he clearly deserved.}§◦--- On April 28 Bäuerle's *Theaterzeitung* made a report on Schuppanzigh's concert, the details of which are already known, and on Böhm's, which follows: ". . . then a steadfast patron of art and noble connoisseur brought about a new performance of this quartet by the above named man with the substitution for first violin of Herr. Prof. Böhm, since this group in the meantime had played the new quartet for a small group of art lovers with particular success. This professor now performed the wonderful quartet, twice over on the same evening, for the same very numerous company of artists and connoisseurs in a way that left nothing to be desired, the misty veil disappeared and the splendid work of art radiated its dazzling glory. Although Prof. Böhm had a lighter touch, yet this composition was heard from a master; if it was also imperfect yet it was so performed that one had to recognize an artist familiar with Beethoven's spirit; but he has provided a productive growth to his fame through the playing three times of this uncommonly difficult quartet. Such artistic trials of strength are the greatest gain for the art especially if, as here, the loser himself doesn't yield; for every impartial person must confess that Herr Schuppanzigh could not play *this* composition better in so short a time, whether he should not or could not have postponed that performance is another question which may be answered by someone better informed, if he dares to do so."

--◦◦§{The quartet had been given one performance by Schuppanzigh, three performances by Böhm already with a fourth one for his benefit in early

[20] The mark is *Allegro con moto* in the Complete Works Edition; *Allo. commodo* in others. (TK, III, 193, n. 1.)

April; on April 15 and again in the latter part of April Joseph Mayseder performed the work with his own group at private concerts in the house of Dembscher, an official or agent of the war department of the Austrian Government. ⸭⸺ The quartet by now received what Holz described as a "réparation d'honneur."[21] Beethoven was completely satisfied and, no doubt, went to work on its successor with a contented mind.

It has now become necessary to pay attention to the new friend of Beethoven whose name has already been mentioned—the successor of Schindler, as he had been of Oliva, in the office of factotum in ordinary. This was Karl Holz, a young man (he was born in 1798) who occupied a post in the States' Chancellery of Lower Austria. He had studied music with Glöggl in Linz; yet Schuppanzigh also called him his pupil. He was a capable violinist and had already been for some time a member of Böhm's quartet group; then upon Schuppanzigh's return from Russia in 1823, he became a second in the latter's quartet. He seems to have come into closer contact with Beethoven early in the spring of 1825, probably when, having to conduct a performance of the B-flat Symphony at a concert in the Redoutensaal, he asked an audience of the composer in order that he might get the tempi for that work. Though not a professional musician, he gave music lessons, later occasionally conducted the *Concerts spirituels* and eventually became the regular director of these affairs. Emboldened by the kindness with which he was first received he gradually drew nearer to the composer and in August, 1825, an intimate friendship seemed imminent, as is indicated by Beethoven's remark in a letter, dated August 24, to his nephew: "It seems as if Holz might become a friend." He was good at figures, a quality which made him particularly serviceable to Beethoven (who was woefully deficient in arithmetic)[22] at a time when he was dealing with foreign publishers and there was great confusion in money values and rates of exchange. He was also a well-read man, a clever talker, musically cultured, a cheery companion, and altogether an engaging person. All these qualities, no less than the fact that he was strong and independent in his convictions and fearless in his proclamation of them, recommended him to Beethoven, and he does not seem to have hesitated to take advantage of the fact that he entered the inner circle of Beethoven's companions at a time when the composer had begun to feel a growing antipathy to Schindler. He promptly embraced the opportunity which his willing usefulness brought him, to draw close to the great man, to learn of him and also to exhibit himself to the world as his confidential friend. He was not obsequious, and this pleased Beethoven despite the fact that he

[21] In a Conversation Book these comparisons were made: *Karl*: "Mayseder plays more brilliantly, Böhm more expressively." *Holz*: "I believe that Mayseder would play it better.—He conducts the other three while Böhm lets it conduct itself." (TDR, v, 183, n. 2.)

[22] There are pitiful proofs in the Conversation Books that simple sums in addition were more than he could master and that on his deathbed he studied the mysteries of multiplication. (TK, III, 194, n. 1.)

himself was not indisposed to play upon his friends for his own purposes "like instruments," as he himself once confessed.

In a short time Holz made himself indispensable and acquired great influence over the composer. He aided him in the copying of his works, looked into the affairs of nephew Karl and reported upon them, advised him in his correspondence, and directed his finances at a time when he was more than ordinarily desirous to acquire money so that he might leave a competency on his death to his foster-son. In time Beethoven came to entrust weighty matters to his decision, even the choice of publishers and his dealings with them. His prepossessing address, heightened by his independence of speech, made it less easy to contradict him than Schindler. Moreover, the recorded conversations show that he was witty, that he had a wider outlook on affairs than Beethoven's other musical advisors, that his judgements were quickly reached and unhesitatingly pronounced, even concerning composers and art forms. It is astonishing, for example, that he was allowed to express a very bold opinion, contrary to Beethoven's, about Mozart. His speeches were not free from frivolity nor always from flattery, but he lived at a time and among people accustomed to extravagant compliments, and there can be no doubt of his reverence for Beethoven. In April Holz said to him: "I am no flatterer, but I assure you that the mere thought of Beethovenian music makes me glad, first of all, that I am alive."[23] He wanted to be Beethoven's friend, and Beethoven recognized how valuable he was to him, so their friendship gradually became closer.

We owe much of our knowledge of the relations between Beethoven and Holz to Schindler's statements as they appear in his biography,[24] two articles which appeared in the *Kölnische Zeitung* in 1845, and among the glosses on the Conversation Book. But many of his utterances show ill-feeling, which is not unfair to trace back to a jealousy dating back to the time when Holz crowded Beethoven's "Secretary sans Salary" out of Beethoven's service and good graces. There was no open rupture between Beethoven and Schindler, but a feeling of coolness and indifference which grew with the advancement of the younger man in the favor of the composer. The results of Beethoven's fellowship with a cheery companion were certainly not so great as Schindler says, nor so evil and grievous as he intimates. Beethoven was accustomed to drink wine from youth up, and also to the companionship which he found in the inns and coffee-houses of Vienna. It was, moreover, undoubtedly a charitable act to drag him out of his isolation into cheerful company. We know that he was so accustomed to take wine at his meals that his physicians found it difficult to make him obey their prohibition of wine and heating spices when he was ill. Beethoven's table habits were thus described by Holz to Jahn: "He was a stout eater of substantial

[23] J. G. Prodhomme, *Cahiers de Conversation de Beethoven* (Paris, 1946), p. 346.

[24] Vol. II, pp. 107-110; 323-30. (TDR, v, 186.)

food; he drank a great deal of wine at table, but could stand a great deal, and in merry company he sometimes became tipsy (*bekneipte er sich*). In the evening he drank beer or wine, generally the wine of Vöslau or red Hungarian. When he had drunk he never composed. After the meal he took a walk."

Beethoven's letters to Holz bear witness to his fond regard for the man. His name, which in German signifies "wood" and in the literature of the Church also "cross," provided Beethoven with a welcome chance to indulge his extravagant fondness for punning. Thus, in the composer's jovial address book, not distinguished by reverence in anything sacred or profane, Holz becomes "Best Mahogany," "Best Splinter from the Cross of Christ," "Best lignum crucis." —The tone of the letters, unlike those to Schindler, was always respectful and even upon occasion conciliatory, as is shown by the beginning of the following note: "Dear Friend! You can be assured that I am not thinking any more of the recent incident and that this will never change my feelings of gratitude towards you."[25]— Holz had his entire confidence, and when the great catastrophe of 1826 came, Holz was the strongest prop upon which he leaned.[26]

The E-flat Quartet had been successfully brought forward, a pause had been reached in the correspondence with Schott and Sons and Neate, a summer home for Beethoven was in prospect, and considerable progress had been made in the draft for the second quartet designed for Prince Galitzin, when an illness befell Beethoven which kept him within doors, and for a portion of the time in bed, from about the middle of April to the middle of May, 1825. In the middle of April Schindler writes: "I believe that this is the result of your exertions in recent days and the disorder in your way of living.— —Dear master, think of the future. What will be the result of your working at night? Otherwise it would never have happened."

Beethoven had been told by his physician that he was in danger of an inflammation of the bowels, and as such Beethoven described his ailment in letters to Piringer and to Schott and Sons.[27] Dr. Staudenheim had been in attendance on him before and had insisted upon strict obedience to his prescriptions. Beethoven sent for him again and was apparently unsuccessful in getting him to come to his house where he was confined, for he writes down: "Braunhofer Bauernmarkt No. 588." —The distinguished Viennese doctor, Anton Braunhofer, had been giving medical attention to Beethoven periodically since 1820. On April 18 he received the following letter from the composer:

My honored friend,

   I am feeling poorly and hope you will not deny me your help since I am suf-

[25] Letter of April 26, 1826.
[26] For a study of Holz see Walter Nohl, "Karl Holz in seinem Verhältnis zu Ludwig van Beethoven" in *Neue Musik-Zeitung*, Vol. 46 (1925), p. 180.
[27] See *A* 1368 and 1370.

tering great pain. Is it possible for you to visit me as early as today, this I beg of you from the bottom of my heart—

With everlasting gratitude and respect, your

Beethoven[28]

Dr. Braunhofer proved to be even less considerate of the patient's wilfulness than his predecessor, he was so blunt and forceful in his demands for obedience that Beethoven was somewhat awed, and beneficial results followed.[29] Dr. Braunhofer did not want to "trouble" Beethoven for long with medicines, but he gave orders for a strict diet.

No wine, no coffee; no spices of any kind. I'll arrange matters with the cook.

Then I will guarantee you full recovery which means alot to me, understandably, as your admirer and friend.

A sickness does not disappear in a day. I shall not trouble you much longer with medicine, but you must adhere to the diet, you'll not starve on it.

Braunhofer was encouraged that his patient's fever had already lessened, and Karl reminded the composer that the prohibition of spirits had also been ordered under Staudenheim. Braunhofer continues:

You must do some work in the daytime so that you *can sleep at night*. If you want to get entirely well and live a long time, you must live according to nature. You are very liable to inflammatory attacks and were close to a severe attack of inflammation of the bowels; the predisposition is still in your body.

I will give you a powder—

I'll wager that if you take a drink of spirits, you'll be lying weak and exhausted on your back in a few hours. . . .

The doctor inspired him with courage and hope, and admonished him to keep quiet and patient. In dry weather he was to take walks, but even after going to Baden he must take no baths as long as the weather remained damp and symptoms of his illness remained.

When you have been in Baden for awhile, it will be better, and should there be a recurrence, let me know. When are you going?

Do not forget the bit of music, just something unimportant, what matters is that it is your handwriting.

[28] The address "Johannisgasse No. 969 im 4ten Stock, rechts die Tür" is given in another hand, identified by Miss Anderson as that of Karl. See *A* 1359.

[29] For fuller details of the diagnosis and treatment, see Walter Nohl, "Beethoven und sein Arzt Anton Braunhofer," *DM*, Vol. 30, No. 12 (1938), pp. 823ff.

You should be striving to get to the country soon.

It will give you fresh air, the walks here are too fatiguing.

In the country you can have natural milk.

In the beginning of May Beethoven's condition had improved sufficiently for him to make the long-planned move to Baden, which he did on May 7. On May 13 he wrote to Dr. Braunhofer the following humorous note in the form of a dialogue between doctor and patient:

Esteemed Friend!

D: How is the patient?

Pat: We are in bad health—still very weak, and are belching and so forth. I think that a stronger medicine is going to be necessary, but one which is not binding—By now surely I should be allowed to drink white wine diluted with water, for that mephitic beer is simply revolting to me—my catarrhal condition is as follows: I spit up rather a lot of blood, apparently only from the windpipe. But often it streams out of my nose, as happened frequently last winter as well. There is no doubt that my stomach has become terribly weakened and that my whole system suffers generally from this. I know my nature well enough to know that on its own my strength would hardly be able to be restored.

D: I will help first by being a Brownian then a Stollian.[30]

Pat: I should be glad to have some strength again so that I could be at my desk. Do think this over—*Finis.*

As soon as I come to the city I will see you. Just tell Karl when I can find you. However, it would be helpful to me if you could suggest to Karl what is still to be done. I took the last medicine only once and then lost it—

With respect and gratitude

Your friend Beethoven

Dok - tor sperrt das Tor dem Tod, No - te hilft auch aus der Noth
[Close the door 'gainst Death I plead, Doctor, notes will help in need]

Dok - tor sperrt das Tor dem Tod, No - te hilft auch aus der Noth
[Close the door 'gainst Death I plead, Doctor, notes will help in need]

Written on May 11, 1825 in the Helenthal, Baden on the second Antons Brücke on the way to Siechenfeld.

Beethoven[31]

[30] Two schools of medical thought were represented by the Scottish Doctor John Brown (1735-17?8) and the Viennese Doctor Maximilian Stoll (1742–1787). Brown attributed sickness to the sensitivity of the organs; Stoll thought in pathological and anatomological terms, which was unusual at that time.

[31] On a Tuesday, May 31, Beethoven wrote to his nephew that he planned to come to the city the next Saturday, June 4. On this trip he wrote out another canon for Braunhofer with the words "I was here, Doctor, I was

Despite the humorous manner of expression, it is clear that Beethoven took his condition seriously and longed to get working again. This happened soon thereafter; on May 17 he wrote to his nephew, "I am beginning to write a bit again." The work taken up was the A Minor Quartet, the progress of which had been interrupted by the illness. In a Conversation Book used in May or June, 1825, Beethoven writes: "Hymn of Thanksgiving to God of an Invalid on his Convalescence. Feeling of new strength and reawakened feeling."[32] As will appear, these words, slightly modified, formed the title of a newly planned second movement to the quartet, the "Song of Thanksgiving in the Lydian mode."

It was while Beethoven was ill in Vienna that Ludwig Rellstab made several visits to him, of which he has left enthusiastic reports.[33] He was 26 years old at the time and had made a mark as essayist and poet; the chief object of his journey to Vienna from Berlin, on which he set out on March 21, was to see the composer. He reached the Austrian capital in the last days of March or the first days of April. His account of the meeting is like many others except that it is written with literary elegance, albeit with that excessive fervor, that *Überschwänglichkeit*, which is characteristic of German hero-worshippers. —Further, Rellstab admitted himself that while he had a clear memory of what had happened in the large he could not remember the words of the conversation literally. The details of his text thus cannot pretend to be accurate.— Zelter had given him a letter of introduction in which he mentioned that Rellstab wanted to write the libretto of an opera to be set by the composer. After Beethoven had warmly greeted his visitor and expressed delight with Zelter's letter, this subject was broached and Beethoven expressed his pleasure at the prospect of getting an opera-book from Rellstab, since it was not easy to get a good poem. He mentioned past difficulties with Grillparzer, since the poet wanted one thing, and he another. Rellstab then quotes Beethoven as saying: "I care little what genre the works belong to, so the material be attractive to me. But it must be something which I can take up with sincerity and love. I could not compose operas like *Don Juan* and *Figaro*. They are repugnant to me. I could not have chosen such subjects; they are too frivolous for me!"

Rellstab had had it in mind to write an opera-book for Weber and had pondered over many subjects, and he now gave a list of these to Beethoven— "Attila," "Antigone," "Belisarius," "Orestes" and others. Beethoven read the names thoughtfully and then apologized for the trouble he was causing his visitor. Rellstab, seeing an expression of weariness in his face, took his departure, after saying that he would send him a specimen of his handiwork.

---

here." On the autograph is written: "On June 4th in the evening when I found that my honored friend Braunhofer was not at home—Beethoven." See KHV, p. 693.

[32] "Dankhimne eines Kranken an Gott bei seiner Genesung Gefühl neuer Kraft und wiederwachtes Gefühl." (TDR, v, 266-67.)

[33] *Aus meinem Leben* (Berlin, 1861), ii, pp. 224ff. (TDR, v, 196, n. 4.)

In a Conversation Book used in the middle of April there is further talk between Rellstab and Beethoven about opera, but the notes, which are fragmentary, give no indications of Beethoven's views.

The most interesting incident of the meetings occurred at a subsequent visit. Rellstab had told that he had been deeply moved (he dared not express a more specific opinion on the subject, being in doubt himself) by the Quartet in E-flat, which he had heard performed twice in succession.[34] He continues: "Beethoven read and remained silent; we looked at each other mutely, but a world of emotions surged in my breast. Beethoven, too, was unmistakably moved. He arose and went to the window, where he remained standing beside the pianoforte. To see him so near the instrument gave me an idea which I had never before dared to harbor. If he—Oh! he needed only to turn half way around and he would be facing the keyboard—if he would but sit down and give expression to his feelings in tones! Filled with a timid, blissful hope, I approached him and laid my hand upon the instrument. It was an English pianoforte by Broadwood. I struck a chord lightly with my right hand in order to induce Beethoven to turn around; but he seemed not to have heard it. A few moments later, however, he turned to me, and, seeing my eyes fixed upon the instrument he said: 'That is a beautiful pianoforte! I got it as a present from London. Look at these names.' He pointed to the crossbeam over the keyboard. There I saw several names which I had not before noticed—Moscheles, Kalkbrenner, Cramer, Clementi, Broadwood himself. . . . 'That is a beautiful gift,' said Beethoven looking at me, 'and it has such a beautiful tone,' he continued and moved his hands towards the keys without taking his eyes off me. He gently struck a chord. Never again will one enter my soul so poignant, so heartbreaking as that one was! He struck C major with the right hand and B as a bass in the left, and continued his gaze uninterruptedly on me, repeated the false chord several times in order to let the sweet tone of the instrument reverberate; and the greatest musician on earth did not hear the dissonance! Whether or not Beethoven noticed his mistake I do not know; but when he turned his head from me to the instrument he played a few chords correctly and then stopped. That was all that I heard from him directly."

Rellstab had planned a short excursion to Hungary and then intended to leave Vienna for his home. Fearful that he might not see Beethoven on his return to the city he went to him to say farewell: "Beethoven spoke very frankly and with feeling. I expressed my regret that in all the time of my sojourn in Vienna I had heard, except one of his symphonies and a quartet, not a single composition of his in concert,[35] why had *Fidelio* not been given? This gave him an opportunity to express himself on the subject of the taste

---

[34] It was probably the performance by Böhm. (TK, III, 201, n. 1.)

[35] As Ebert points out (*DM*, Vol. 9, No. 3, p. 106) this was not Vienna's fault. The B-flat Symphony was played on April 4, and on April 14, the Symphony in A. Schuppanzigh's group performed the quartets, and many concerts started with Beethoven overtures.

of the Vienna people. 'Since the Italians [Barbaja] have gotten such a strong foothold here the best has been crowded out. For the nobility, the chief thing at the theatre is the ballet. Nothing can be said about their appreciation of art; they have sense only for horses and dancers. We have always had this state of things. But this gives me no concern; I want only to write that which gives me joy. If I were well it would be all the same to me!' "

On his departure Beethoven, who had been absent from his lodgings when Rellstab called for his final leavetaking, sent him a letter to Steiner and Co., containing a canon on the words from Matthisson's *Opferlied* of which he had made use on at least one earlier occasion ("Das Schöne zu dem Guten").

During the summer at Baden, there was increasing tension between Beethoven and his nephew. However, before describing this, an account should be given of the composer's relationship to Karl during the early part of the year, in order to give a background for the growing preoccupation of his mind during these months. In the winter of 1824-25 Karl was still pursuing his studies in philology at the University of Vienna. The summer before, he had unsuccessfully tried to persuade his uncle to let him enter the army and abandon the career which had been chosen for him, which was probably that of a professor of languages. In the spring of 1825 Karl again was trying to make a shift in his studies. He wanted to enroll in a training school for a mercantile career, and this time he was successful in persuading his uncle. An early reference to the change occurs in a Conversation Book entry in March:[36]

I wanted to ask you whether perhaps you would not mind if I went to the Italian Opera today because it is the last opera. If I had known yesterday I would have stayed at home in order not to go to the theatre two days in succession. Meanwhile, of course, I am neglecting nothing, and when I once go to the Polytechnic Institute, this will happen very seldom anyhow. But if this is not all right with you, we will drop it. Otherwise I will go in the fourth balcony where it costs 30x.

Beethoven's reluctance in giving his consent to this change is shown by an entry of Karl's in early April:

You know that I will not oppose you if you *wish* me to continue to study; but I really feel that I will progress much better there since in times past I have lost interest. Nevertheless I will never forget my Greek but continue with it consistently and industriously, the more since I am far enough along in it so that reading it is no longer a strain for me but rather a pleasure.

In a letter to Karl Peters[37] Beethoven expressed his opposition to the plan, and took the attitude that Karl dreaded the university examinations because of "false modesty" rather than lack of ability. However, he said that he would agree to the change if Peters thought it best. The decision was finally

---

[36] All Conversation Book entries concerning Beethoven and Karl's relationship are found in the appendix to TDR, v, 510ff.
[37] See *A* 1360.

made, and Karl's conciliatory attitude towards his uncle at this time is shown by a Conversation Book entry written during the spring:

I am earnestly resolved to continue with zeal on the way that we have chosen; also I see that the subjects are not unpleasant at all. Some of them, for instance history and mathematics, in so far as they affect merchants will be given as well if not better than at the university. Thus it will undoubtedly go well.—

Karl entered the Polytechnic Institute about Easter, 1825, and Beethoven arranged to have the vice-director, Dr. Reisser, appointed as co-guardian in place of Peters, with whom he took counsel as he also did, in great likelihood, with Stephan von Breuning. There were two great admirers of Beethoven's music at the Institute, Reisser and Dr. Ignaz von Sonnleithner, one of the teachers. Karl was placed under the supervision of a government official named Schlemmer, who lived in the Alleegasse adjacent to the Karlskirche, and with whom the lad took lodgings. According to reports from Dr. Reisser and Karl himself, he made a good beginning in his studies, although he was hampered by the fact that he had entered late in the term and therefore had a good deal of back work to cover. A special tutor was engaged to help him with this.

—After Beethoven's move to the country, Karl was expected to visit his uncle in Baden on Sundays and holidays, but conflict on this point soon developed. Furthermore, now that the two were separated, Beethoven worried about Karl's whole way of life and sought to keep tight control over him, despite the fact that the young man was nearly nineteen. In an undated letter to Schlemmer, Beethoven voiced the suspicion that Karl mingled with bad company in the evenings. He continues: "I request you hereafter to watch out and under no pretext to let him outside of the house at night unless you have received something through Karl in writing from me."

Of Karl's feelings we learn mainly from the Conversation Books; of Beethoven's, from a remarkable series of letters that he wrote to his nephew from Baden, most of which are in the Berlin State Library. In a Conversation Book entry Karl showed the strain he was feeling from the demands on his time made both by his uncle and by his studies. Beethoven had evidently come to Vienna on business. Karl writes:

It is impossible to get everything done today if I also have some things to attend to with you. But I will take some things along because we are very much overloaded and on Sundays have to write out everything that has been presented during the whole of the week.

◦~◦

I really would like to go out with you today but it is almost impossible to do much out there because it is so much trouble to take along all the books and papers that I need; besides since I must go along with you to see about the lodging, there remains but little time for me.

◦~◦

Thus I think I will meet you somewhere around 12 o'clock and walk with you to the house and to the other places and eat with you. But then not come out till tomorrow so that I can make the most of having an evening to myself; for you do not realize *how much* there is to write and to study in order to satisfy the wishes of the professors and especially Reisser who watches me, moreover, very attentively.

⋅∿⋅

The day after tomorrow I could then come back early and be with you all day tomorrow.

⋅∿⋅

The work doesn't progress as fast as one would think.

And Karl goes on to elaborate in detail the number of subjects and the work for their preparation.

The first series of notes from Beethoven to Karl, written in May, were concerned with the poor weather, his feelings of weakness, household matters about which he asked Karl's help, and mentions of his projected weekend visits. On May 22, however, only fifteen days after his move, there was an abrupt change in the tone of Beethoven's letters upon his hearing that Karl had been seeing his mother. He writes:

Until now [it was] only conjecture although someone assured me that there were secret dealings again between you and your mother—Am I to experience once again the most abominable ingratitude? No, if this bond is to be broken, so be it, but you will be despised by all impartial men who hear of this ingratitude. . . . Shall I get involved again in these vulgarities? No, never again—in God's name if the Pactum weighs upon you—I turn you over to Divine Providence. I have done my job and upon this I can appear before the mightiest of all judges. Do not be afraid to come to me tomorrow, I can still presume, God grant, that *nothing of this* is true, for if it were truly your unhappiness would be unending, lightheartedly as my rascally brother and your—mother would take this matter—

I am expecting you for sure—along with the old woman.[38]

At the end of the next letter, written nine days later, Beethoven was still bitter:

. . . —God is my witness, I dream only of being completely removed from you and from this wretched brother and this abominable family to which I am attached—God grant me my wish, for I *cannot* trust *you* any more—

Unfortunately your Father or better not your Father

[38] Probably the housekeeper. Throughout the summer correspondence Beethoven complains about the ineptitude of his two servants. The housekeeper is referred to as "the old witch," "the old woman," "the old beast," etc., and her helper as "the wench," "Satanas," etc.

One more letter from the earlier part of the summer deserves to be cited in full, containing as it does one of Beethoven's references to death:

Baden, June 9, 1825

I wish at least that you would come here Saturday, I ask for an answer to no avail—God be with you and with me

as always your faithful Father

I have written to H. v. Reissig[39] to ask you to come here on Saturday. The carriage leaves Vienna around six o'clock and in fact *from the Kugel auf der Wieden.* Consequently you have only to get some work or study done before so that you will not lose anything by this. I am sorry to cause you this trouble— In the afternoon around five o'clock you will return again by the same carriage to Vienna. It is paid for already beforehand. In the morning you can shave here and also get a shirt and necktie in order to arrive there conveniently—Farewell, although I am sulky with you it is not without reason, and I would have liked not to have spent so much in order to have given to the world an *ordinary man*— I hope to see you without fail—Moreover *if the intrigues have already developed,* explain yourself openly and naturally and you will find one who is concerned consistently with what is good.

The lodging was advertised in the newspaper again on Tuesday. If you were unable to do anything, at least someone else could have written if by chance you were unwell—I would rather *not have to think anything else*—You know how I live here, with the cold weather to boot. The continual solitude weakens me even more, for often through my weakness I am really on the verge of feebleness. Oh do not pain me more; the man with the scythe will not be giving me much more time.

If you were to find a good lodging for me in the Alleegasse I would take it.

That Beethoven was becoming increasingly concerned over Karl's life in Vienna is further shown by the fact that he discussed these matters with his friends and asked their aid. On June 10 he wrote to Bernard asking him to see something of Karl since he was worried about his behavior and feared that he was becoming involved again with his mother. He informed Bernard that Reisser was the new co-guardian and said that since he had never met him he was not sure he would be co-operative. Therefore, he asked Bernard to call upon Reisser, to present him with Beethoven's qualifications as guardian, and to inform him that Blöchlinger had never allowed "her" at his house.

In September, at the time of the preparations for the first performance of the Quartet in A Minor, there are some entries by Karl Holz in the Conversation Books which suggest the role he was playing as Beethoven's helper:

On Sunday I was with Karl in order to give him your note; it was evening and I learned from the maid that he had gone out in the early morning and had not come back home to eat—

╍╍

[39] Beethoven means Reisser, the co-guardian. During the summer he frequently makes this mistake.

I have a plan to attach him closer to myself, I would like to win him over to my side; perhaps in this way I will learn to know him and his way of life more easily;

•~•

then I will dissuade him in a friendly manner—

•~•

I have lured him into going to a beer house with me because I [wanted] to see if he drinks much; but that does not appear to be the case. Now I will invite [him] at some point to play billiards; then I will see immediately if he has already been practising a long time—

•~•

What harm can come to him if he goes through the city from the Alservorstadt—

•~•

What do other young people do about it?

•~•

I think rather that you should give him something periodically for his efforts and the hardships he endures—

•~•

but no money[40]

•~•

I told him also that he is not supposed to go often into the Josephstadt—

•~•

His reason is because it doesn't cost anything.

•~•

I also told him that his uncle would be more inclined to give him money if [he] listened to some classic pieces at the Burg a few times each month—

•~•

I told him also that I would speak with you about this; he didn't want that.

•~•

He has gotten the love of money from your brother.

The letters continued through the summer alternating between tenderness and reproach. With the young man's sense of money he had no patience whatever, and insisted upon a strict accounting for every florin which he allowed him. In September he was enraged when he heard that Karl had resorted to borrowing from the servants:

... You also borrowed again last Sunday 1 fl. 15 kr. from the housekeeper, that vulgar old kitchen-wench—It was long ago forbidden—Everywhere it is the

[40] Considering the context, Holz may very well have meant "but no money has been given him."

same. I should have gotten along two years with the frock-coat. True, I have the bad habit of wearing an old coat at home, but Herr Karl, oh fie the shame of it, and why? The money-bag Herr L. v. B—n is here only for this purpose—

On the other hand, Beethoven apparently trusted Karl enough to delegate to him not only minor household errands, but important correspondence and negotiations. Throughout this summer's correspondence, along with the scoldings and the reproaches, there are instances of Beethoven's instructing Karl what to do about letters to Galitzin, Peters and Schlesinger, and of his using Karl to represent him in financial transactions.[41]

In early October the letters became even more emotional. On the 5th of the month Beethoven writes from Baden:

Precious, dear son!
I have just received your letter. Filled with anxiety I had today determined to hasten to Vienna—God be thanked, it is not necessary. Do but obey me, and love and happiness of the soul paired with human happiness will be at our side; and you will unite an intensive inner existence with the external, but it were better that the *former* dominate the *latter*—il fait trop froid—I shall see you on Saturday then. Write whether you are coming in the morning or the evening so that I may hasten to meet you—
I embrace you and kiss you a thousand times not as my *prodigal but as my newly born son*—I wrote to Schlemmer. Do not think harshly on that account— I am still so filled with anxiety[42]——My anxiety and my worry over finding you again will show you that your father is full of love.

Ayez la bonté, de m'envoyer a *bottle for lighting* with *matches* from Rospini ou en porte avec vous puisque de celle de Kärtnerthor on ne peut pas faire usage—

Beethoven moved from Baden into the Schwarzspanierhaus, his final residence, on October 15, a Saturday. His letters to Karl during those final ten days in Baden alternate between instructions for moving possessions into the new rooms from the brother's apartments (where they had been stored over the summer) and violent reproaches for his conduct.[43] The following excerpt from a letter dated October 12 shows his state of mind:

I wish that you would stop such *selfishness at my expense. It does as little credit to me as it does towards setting you on the right and proper course.* Continue this way and you will rue the day! Not that I shall die sooner, however much this may be your desire; but while I am alive I shall separate myself completely from you, although I shall not abandon you for this reason or withdraw my support—Look for the fool who has been so sanctified and *so rewarded by you daily*. The worst part is the results that *will come to you* because of your behavior. Who will believe or trust you after hearing what has happened and how you have inflicted mortal wounds upon me and wounded me daily?

[41] See the following letters: *A* 1394, 1400, 1401, 1402, 1413, 1414 and 1437.
[42] According to TDR, v, p. 548, n. 1, a piece of the autograph has been torn off at this place.
[43] See the following: *A* 1440, 1441, 1442, 1444.

The point was made in this and all of these last letters, that he was counting on seeing something of his nephew on Saturday, October 15, when he was coming to Vienna. In another letter, just before he had made the move, he reminded Karl: "It pained me especially that you came out so late on Sunday[44] and hurried off again so early." Then came the move and with it an additional emotional outburst written from Vienna:

My precious son!

Go no further—Come but to my arms, not a harsh word shall you hear. O God, do not rush away in your misery. You will be received as lovingly as ever. What to consider, what to do in the future, these things we will talk over affectionately. On my word of honor no reproaches, since they would in no case do good now. Henceforth you may expect from me only the most loving care and help—Do but come—Come to the faithful heart of

your father Beethoven
Volti sub[ito]

Come home immediately upon receiving this.
Si vous ne viendres pas
vous me tûerès surement
  lisés la lettre et restés
a la maison chez vous, venes
de m'embrasser votre pere
vous vraiment adonné soyes
assurés, que tout cela resterà
entre nous.[45]
Only for God's sake come back home today. It might bring you who knows what danger. Hurry, Hurry.

Karl had clearly absented himself and it can be presumed that he had gone to his mother. At this point the correspondence stops, and the only other letter of the autumn is a matter-of-fact note concerning payment of money to Frau Schlemmer, and a request for some of his nephew's time for some letter-writing.[46] In November the Conversation Books show new points of conflict which are taken up in the next chapter.

During the summer Beethoven received a number of visitors whose meetings with the composer have been recorded either by themselves or in the Conversation Books.

Karl Gottfried Freudenberg, a young musician who afterwards became Head Organist at Breslau and wrote a book of reminiscences entitled *Erinnerungen eines alten Organisten*, visited Beethoven in July of the year and has left a record which is none the less interesting because its lack of literary flourish is offset by succinct reports of the great composer's estimate of some of his contemporaries, and his views on ecclesiastical music. Beethoven, according to Freudenberg, described Rossini as a "talented and a

---

[44] October 9.
[45] According to TDR, v, p. 549, this French part is written on the outside of the letter under Karl's address, and the final sentences are on the top margin of the letter.
[46] *A* 1447.

melodious composer; his music suits the frivolous and sensuous spirit of the time, and his productivity is such that he needs only as many weeks as the Germans do years to write an opera." He said of Spontini: "There is much good in him; he understands theatrical effects and the musical noises of warfare thoroughly"; of Spohr: "He is too rich in dissonances, pleasure in his music is marred by his chromatic melody"; of Bach: "His name ought not to be Bach [brook] but Ocean, because of his infinite and inexhaustible wealth of combinations and harmonies. He was the ideal of an organist." This led Beethoven into the subject of music for the church. "I, too, played the organ a great deal in my youth," he said, "but my nerves could not stand the power of the gigantic instrument. I place an organist who is master of his instrument, first among virtuosi." Pure church music, he remarked, ought to be performed only by voices, unless the text be a *Gloria* or something of the kind. For this reason he preferred Palestrina to all other composers of church music, but it was folly to imitate him unless one had his genius and his religious beliefs; moreover, it was practically impossible for singers to-day to sing the long-sustained notes of this music in a cantabile manner.

The visit of Karl August Reichardt, afterwards Court Organist in Altenburg, seems to have been brief, and it is safe to presume that the young man received scant encouragement to remain long, for his talk was chiefly about himself, his desire to get advice as to a good teacher and to have Beethoven look at some of his music.

Otto de Boer was a member of the Academy of Fine Arts in Amsterdam. To gain an audience with Beethoven, he probably had used his predicate as a member of this academy, which had already elected Beethoven as one of its honorary members. This man from Holland must have diverted the composer with his broken German, which looks no more comical in the Conversation Book that it must have sounded; but a canon without words[47] which he carried away with him on August 3rd may be said to bear witness to the fact that he made a good impression on Beethoven, to whom he gave information concerning the state of music in Holland.

Carl Czerny spent some time in Baden. From his written entries it is apparent that he was urged by his erstwhile teacher to get an appointment and to compose in the larger forms. Beethoven was curious to know how much Czerny received for his compositions and Czerny told him that he attached no importance to his pieces, because he scribbled them down so easily, and that he took music from the publishers in exchange.

There is an autograph of a piece for pianoforte of thirteen measures, belonging to Mr. Louis Kramer of Syracuse, N.Y., with the inscription: "Comme un souvenir à Sarah Burney Payne par Louis van Beethoven le 27 Septembre, 1825."[48] This was the daughter of the famous music his-

[47] See KHV, p. 476 (WoO 35).
[48] See O. E. Albrecht, *A Census of Auto-* graph *Music Manuscripts of European Composers in America* (Philadelphia, 1953), p. 30.

torian, Dr. Charles Burney, and she was probably the author of a contribution to the *Harmonicon*, 1825, entitled "A visit to Beethoven."

Beethoven's greatest desire now must have been the completion of the order from Prince Galitzin for three quartets. As we already know, the first one, in E-flat, was finished and already performed. The sketches for the second one, in A minor (as established by Nottebohm)[49] date back to 1824. The work was originally to have the customary four movements; labor on it was interrupted by the illness of April and then the plan for the middle movements was changed to include the "Song of Thanksgiving in the Lydian mode," the short march before the last movement, and the minuet. The work was finished by August at the latest. The passage in eighth-notes in the second part of the second movement is practically a quotation from one of the German dances[50] written at least twenty-five years before, with the bar lines shifted so that the change of harmony occurs on the up-beats of the measures. Mentioned already are the references to the Song of Thanksgiving in the Conversation Books; in the original score it is inscribed "Sacred Song of Thanksgiving of a Convalescent to the Divinity, in the Lydian Mode. N.B. This piece has always B instead of B-flat," and in the second section in D major, simply "Feeling new strength." As has already been mentioned in the history of the Ninth Symphony, the principal theme of the last movement was originally conceived for the finale of that work. Immediately after the completion of this quartet, Beethoven set to work on the third quartet for Prince Galitzin. The story of this work comes later, while events must now be told which lead to the first performance of the second Galitzin quartet.

The quartet was to have its first public performance in a benefit concert for the cellist Linke after it had first been given a private hearing. Holz took the responsibility of having the work copied speedily and sent to Beethoven for corrections. The following letter from Beethoven to Karl shows that this arrangement did not result in his always being free of worry:

Dear Son!   Baden on Aug. 11

I am worried to death about the quartet, namely the 3, 4, 5 and 6th movement,[51] Holz has taken them along. The first measures of the 3rd movement have been left here, that is to say 13 in number—*I hear nothing from Holz*—I wrote him yesterday. Usually he writes. What a terrible misfortune if he should have lost it. *Just between us, he is a hard drinker.* Give me reassurance as quickly as possible —you can find out Linke's address at Haslinger's. Haslinger was here today, was very friendly, brought the periodicals and other things and begged for the new quartets. Don't engage in idle talk, it leads to vulgarities—But for God's sake give me some peace of mind concerning the quartet; what a terrible loss. The main ideas have been written on nothing but small scraps of paper, and I shall never be able to write out the whole thing again in the same way.

Your true father.

---

[49] *II Beeth.*, pp. 547ff.
[50] KHV, p. 448, WoO 13, No. 11.

[51] In its final form the quartet had only five movements.

I also point out to you that the coming *Sunday and Monday* are both holidays, thus you can arrange accordingly. With this opportunity you could perhaps [drive] here with me *Saturday* in the evening if I come in. Thus you gain the whole morning.

The idea of presenting the Quartet in A minor first for a small private gathering appears to have originated in Beethoven's own circle of friends, and apparently Beethoven wanted to have this at his own house. This had to be given up, however, in view of the difficulty for the audience of coming out to Baden for the occasion. Before coming to this, there were some other important visits which Beethoven received at this time, some of which are related in part to this performance.

The visit of the Danish composer, flautist and director, Friedrich Kuhlau, led to a right merry feast, for a description of which Seyfried found a place in the appendix of his *Studien*. The party consisted of Beethoven, the piano-maker Conrad Graf, Haslinger, Holz, Kuhlau, and the oboe teacher, Joseph Sellner. That the boundaries of good taste in conversation and story-telling may have been a bit strained is an inference from the fact that several pages of the Conversation Book containing the recorded relics of the affair are missing. After a promenade through the Helenenthal in which Beethoven amused himself by setting all manner of difficult tasks in hill-climbing, the party sat down to dinner at an inn. Champagne flowed freely, and after the return to Beethoven's lodgings, red Vöslauer, brought from his closet or cellar, did its share still further to elevate the spirits of the feasters. Beethoven seems to have held his own in the van of the revel. He wrote a canon in the Conversation Book with B-A-C-H as an opening motive and the words "Kühl, nicht lau" ("Cool, not lukewarm")—a feeble play on the Danish musician's name, but one which served to carry the music.[52] The next day Kuhlau confessed to Schlesinger that he did not know how he had gotten home and to bed; Beethoven's post-festal reflections may be gathered from the letter which accompanied a copy of the canon, which he sent to Kuhlau by the hands of Holz:

Baden, September 3, 1825

I must admit that the champagne went too much to my head also, yesterday, and that again I was compelled to experience that such things retard rather than promote my capacities. For easy as it usually is for me to meet a challenge of the instant, I do not at all remember what I wrote yesterday.

In handing over letter and canon to Holz for delivery he wrote to him that he had scarcely reached home before it occurred to him that he might have written down a lot of nonsense the day before.

On September 4 Beethoven received a visit from the Paris publisher, Moritz Schlesinger. He had seen Kuhlau in Vienna the day before and learned of their merry meeting and the canon that Beethoven had written on

[52] KHV, p. 693, WoO 191. The letters B-A-C-H in German represent the notes B-flat, A, C, B-natural.

Kuhlau's name. Schlesinger reported that Kuhlau was answering with a canon on B-A-C-H, and he asked permission to publish both canons in the journal put out by the Schlesingers in Berlin.

The publisher then came to the point of his visit; he wanted to publish the two new quartets. In mid-July Beethoven had written to Adolf Schlesinger in Berlin,[53] mentioning "two new grand violin quartets" and offering them for 80 ducats each. He could only have meant the A minor, Op. 132, and the B-flat major, Op. 130, not yet composed. Schlesinger was eager to know of the quartets; he asked if he could attend a rehearsal of the A minor quartet. His pertinacity on this matter evidently aroused Beethoven's suspicions, and his pride revolted at the thought that a publisher should ask to hear a work of his which he proposed to buy. Karl assured him that Schlesinger only wanted the privilege of hearing the new works of the master, and suggested that he might also be given a chance to hear the quartet which had already been sold to Schott.[54] Schlesinger also expressed his interest in becoming a sort of dealer *en gros* in Beethoven's products; besides the new quartets, he wanted to publish a Complete Edition, to begin with the chamber pieces, to which end he wanted still another quartet and three quintets. Schlesinger also tried to awaken the composer's literary ambition by offering to republish in the Berlin *Musikzeitung* whatever Beethoven might write to the Mainz journal about the joke on Haslinger. He suggested further that Beethoven ought really to write some essays on what a symphony and an overture ought to be and on the art of the fugue, of which he was the sole repository. He knew how to approach genius on its most susceptible side! He encouraged Beethoven to go to England, where he was so greatly admired. He reported that Cherubini had said to his pupils at the Conservatoire in Paris: "The greatest musical minds that ever lived or ever will live, are Beethoven and Mozart."[55]

At dinner, at Schlesinger's suggestion, the company drank the healths of Goethe and Cherubini. Again Schlesinger urged Beethoven to go to London:[56] "I repeat again that if you will go to England for three months I will engage that, deducting your traveling expenses, you will make 1000 pounds, or 25000 florins V.S. at least, if you give only two concerts and produce some new music. . . . The Englishmen are proud enough to count themselves fortunate if Beethoven would only be satisfied with them." When the toast to Cherubini was drunk, Schlesinger took occasion to satisfy the curiosity of Beethoven touching the status of the composer whom he most admired among living men: "Cherubini has now received the title of Baron from the government as well as the order of the Legion of Honor. It is a proof of the recognition of his talent, for he did not seek it. Napoleon, who

---

[53] See *A* 1403.
[54] Op. 127, in E-flat.
[55] On the margin Schindler records his doubt that this remark was ever made.

(TDR, v, 238, n. 1.)
[56] The following two quotations were taken by Krehbiel from Thayer's papers and are not included in TDR.

appreciated him highly, once found fault with one of his compositions and Cherubini retorted: 'Your Majesty knows no more about it than I about a battle.' Napoleon's conduct was contemptible. Because of the words that I have quoted he took away all of Cherubini's offices and he had nothing to live on. Nevertheless, he did an infinite amount of good for popular culture. If Napoleon, instead of becoming an insatiable world conqueror, had remained First Consul, he would have become one of the greatest men that ever existed."

It was about this time, also, that Karl told his uncle an anecdote to the effect that Cherubini, when asked why he did not compose a quartet, replied: "If Beethoven had never written a quartet, I would write quartets; as it is, I cannot."

Schlesinger had his way about hearing the new quartet, for it was rehearsed at his rooms at the tavern "zum Wilden Mann" on Wednesday, September 7, preparatory to its performance to a small group (which may have been a sort of dress rehearsal) on the 9th. Beethoven had originally wanted the players to come to his lodging at Baden, but in a letter to Karl dated September 6, he had agreed that this was impractical and suggested they all meet at Schlesinger's. Meanwhile, arrangements for the rehearsals had been made independently of Beethoven, and on the 8th Holz arrived in Baden to report to him the progress of the rehearsal the day before. He mentioned the fact that Karl was present, and also Wolfmayer and Tobias Haslinger, for Wolfmayer "at the Adagio wept like a child" and "Tobias scratched his head when he heard the quartet; he certainly regrets that the Jew Steiner did not take it." He continued about the arrangements for the performance the next day, which was to take place at noon, and stated that the innkeeper had arranged for them to have a larger room. This took place as scheduled, and on September 11 the quartet was performed for a larger group, also at "zum Wilden Mann."

During these days, Beethoven was concerned about making the final arrangements with Schlesinger concerning the purchase of the quartet. In the same letter to Karl referred to above, he urged him to make haste to complete the financial transactions with Schlesinger as he wished to return the money he owed to Peters, and later stated that he could not wait any longer—if Schlesinger wished to hear a rehearsal first, he could not have the quartet. Earlier in the letter he says "Entre nous il est pourtant juif." The negotiations were evidently completed by September 10, as there is a receipt of that date to Schlesinger for 80 ducats received. However, there is mention of two quartets both in this document and in a rough draft of an agreement written by Schlesinger in French, dated September 4th.[57] On the receipt the two quartets are referred to as "Opp. 132 and 134 12th and 17th quartets." Schlesinger had originally been interested in Op. 132,

[57] Unger, *Beethoven und seine Verleger*, p. 91. See also Anderson, III, Appendix G, Nos. 16 and 17.

in A minor, and Op. 130, in B-flat major. What he finally received was Op. 132 and the Quartet in F major, Op. 135, both published after Beethoven's death.—

We have an account of both the September 9 and September 11 occasions at "zum Wilden Mann" from the English visitor whom Beethoven received at this time. This was Sir George Smart, who, in the summer of 1825, made a tour of Germany in company with Charles Kemble. He was with Mr. Kemble when that gentleman made the agreement with Weber for *Oberon*, but his "principal reason for the journey," as he himself put it, "was to ascertain from Beethoven himself the exact times of the movements of his characteristic—and some of his other—Sinfonias." By the "characteristic" symphony Smart meant the ninth, which he had directed at its first performance in London on March 21, 1825. Sir George recorded the incidents of his meetings with Beethoven in his journal, from which the following excerpts are taken:[58]

"On the 7th of September, at nine in the morning, I called on Mayseder, who received me most politely. . . . We conversed about Beethoven's Choral Symphony; our opinion agrees about it. When it was performed here Umlauf conducted it and Kletrinski and Schuppanzigh were the leaders. All the basses played in the recitative, but they had the story that it was written for Dragonetti only.

"Friday, September 9th. . . . We then went to Mecchetti's music shop, they, too, are publishers, and bought three pieces for Birchall. . . . Mr. Holz, an amateur in some public office and a good violin player, came in and said Beethoven had come from Baden this morning and would be at his nephew's—Karl Beethoven, a young man aged twenty—No. 72 Alleegasse . . . . At twelve I took Ries[59] to the hotel Wildemann [*sic*] the lodgings of Mr. Schlesinger, the music seller of Paris, as I understood from Mr. Holz that Beethoven would be there, and there I found him. He received me in the most flattering manner. There was a numerous assembly of professors to hear Beethoven's second new manuscript quartette, bought by Mr. Schlesinger. This quartette is three-quarters of an hour long. They played it twice. The four performers were Schuppanzigh, Holz, Weiss, and Lincke. It is most chromatic and there is a slow movement entitled 'Praise for the recovery of an invalid.' Beethoven intended to allude to himself I suppose for he was

[58] Thayer visited Sir George in February, 1861, and received from him permission to make a transcript of all the entries in his journal touching the meetings with Beethoven, also supplementing them with oral information. The journal remained in manuscript for forty years after Sir George's death and then was edited by H. Bertram Cox and C. L. E. Cox. It was published under the title *Leaves from the Journal of Sir George Smart* (Long- mans, Green and Co., London, 1907). The excerpts quoted here are from the published book, and, according to Krehbiel, show signs of having been revised after Thayer made his transcript. See Smart (edition above), pp. 104-105, 108-109, 111, 113-15. (TK, III, 206, n. 1.)

[59] Not the composer but a pianoforte maker of Vienna. (TK, III, 207, n. 1.)

very ill during the early part of this year. He directed the performers, and took off his coat, the room being warm and crowded. A staccato passage not being expressed to the satisfaction of his eye, for alas, he could not hear, he seized Holz's violin and played the passage a quarter of a tone too flat. I looked over the score during the performance. All paid him the greatest attention. About fourteen were present, those I knew were Boehm (violin), Marx ('cello), Carl Czerny, also Beethoven's nephew, who is like Count St. Antonio, so is Boehm, the violin player. The partner of Steiner, the music seller, was also there. I fixed to go to Baden on Sunday and left at twenty-five minutes past two. . . .

"Saturday, September 10th. . . . I called for the music at Artaria's for Birchall, for which I paid, and on our return found a visiting-card from Earl Stanhope and also from Schlesinger of Paris with a message that Beethoven would be at his hotel to-morrow at twelve, therefore of course I gave up going to Baden to visit Beethoven, which he had arranged for me to do. . . . In the morning Mr. Kirchoffer called to say he should invite me to his house. It was he who, through Ries, had the arrangement of procuring the Choral Symphony for our Philharmonic Society.

"Sunday, September 11th. . . . From hence I went alone to Schlesinger's, at the 'Wildemann,' where was a larger party than the previous one. Among them was L'Abbé Stadler, a fine old man and a good composer of the old school, to whom I was introduced. There was also present a pupil of Moscheles, a Mademoiselle Eskeles and a Mademoiselle Cimia,[60] whom I understood to be a professional player. When I entered Messrs. C. Czerny, Schuppanzigh and Lincke had just begun the Trio, Op. 70, of Beethoven, after which the same performers played Beethoven's Trio, Op. 79[61]—both printed singly by Steiner. Then followed Beethoven's quartette, the same that I had heard on September the 9th and it was played by the same performers. Beethoven was seated near the pianoforte beating time during the performance of these pieces. This ended, most of the company departed, but Schlesinger invited me to stop and dine with the following party of ten: Beethoven, his nephew, Holz, Weiss, C. Czerny, who sat at the bottom of the table, Lincke, Jean Sedlatzek—a flute player who is coming to England next year, and has letters to the Duke of Devonshire, Count St. Antonio, etc.—he has been to Italy—Schlesinger, Schuppanzigh, who sat at the top, and myself. Beethoven calls Schuppanzigh Sir John Falstaff, not a bad name considering the figure of this excellent violin player.

"We had a most pleasant dinner, healths were given in the English style. Beethoven was delightfully gay but hurt that, in the letter Moscheles gave me, his name should be mixed up with the other professors. However he soon got over it. He was much pleased and rather surprised at seeing in the

[60] Presumably Antonia Cibbini, née Kože-luch, who was among those who attended the performance of the quartet. (Cf. TDR, v, 245.)

[61] Undoubtedly Op. 97 which was published by Steiner. Artaria published the Op. 70 trios in Vienna.

oratorio bill I gave him that the 'Mount of Olives' and his 'Battle Symphony' were both performed the same evening. He believes—I do not—that the high notes Handel wrote for trumpets were played formerly by one particular man. I gave him the oratorio book and bill. He invited me, by his nephew, to Baden next Friday. After dinner he was coaxed to play extempore, observing in French to me, 'Upon what subject shall I play?' Meanwhile he was touching the instrument thus

to which I answered, 'Upon that.' On which theme he played for about twenty minutes in a most extraordinary manner, sometimes very fortissimo, but full of genius. When he arose at the conclusion of his playing he appeared greatly agitated. No one could be more agreeable than he was—plenty of jokes. He was in the highest of spirits. We all wrote to him by turns, but he can hear a little if you halloo quite close to his left ear. He was very severe in his observations about the Prince Regent never having noticed his present of the score of his 'Battle Symphony.' His nephew regretted that his uncle had no one to explain to him the profitable engagement offered by the Philharmonic Society last year."

Smart accepted Beethoven's invitation to visit him at Baden on September 16, and at this meeting accomplished the specific purpose of his visit to Vienna by getting Beethoven to give him the tempo of various movements from his symphonies, by playing portions of them on the pianoforte. He wrote on Beethoven's slate in French, a language which he said Beethoven spoke fluently, in order to get Beethoven's intentions as to the performance of the work. Asked about the recitative for instruments in the last movement, Beethoven's reply was: "The recitative in strict time."[62] Smart objected, that so played, it was not a recitative nor had words to recite. Beethoven replied, "he called it so," and finally closed the discussion with "I wish it to go in strict time." This from a composer was of course decisive.[63]

Though he had been warned not to write in Beethoven's book, Sir George did not, or was not always able to, obey the injunction. A considerable portion of the conversation at the meeting is preserved in a Conversation Book

[62] The exchange between Beethoven and Smart concerning the recitative is based on Thayer's notes from his conversations with Sir George Smart in London in 1861. (TK, III, 208, n. 2.)

[63] The question of how the bass recitatives ought to be played had already been discussed when the rehearsals for the concert of 1824 were in progress, as is shown by Schindler's entries in a Conversation Book in March of that year: "How many contrabasses are to play the recitative?— Will it be possible?

All!— There would be no difficulty in strict time, but to give it in a singing style will make careful study necessary.— If old Kraus were still alive we could let the matter go unconcernedly, for he directed 12 contrabasses who had to do what he wanted.— Good; then just as if words were under it?— If necessary I will write words under it so that they may learn to sing." (TK, III, 208, n. 2.) For more concerning the 1824 performance, see Leopold Sonnleithner, AMZ, April 6, 1864, pp. 245-46.

which covers three dates, September 16, 19 and 24. From this book some excerpts are made here, since they bear on the subject which filled so large a place in the plans of Beethoven for several years, and were in his mind up to the time of his death—the English tour. Other matters bearing on points of history which have been or may be mentioned, are included. The nephew had translated for Beethoven the announcement of the Ninth Symphony as it appeared on the programme of the Philharmonic's concert of March 21, viz.: "New Grand Characteristic Sinfonia, MS. with vocal finale, the principal parts to be sung by Madame Caradori, Miss Goodall, Mr. Vaughn and Mr. Phillips; composed expressly for this Society." No doubt Beethoven gave expression, as he frequently had done, to his admiration for the English people and possibly also for their national hymn, for Karl translates the stanza:

> Long may he reign!
> May he defend our laws,
> And ever give us cause
> To sing with heart and voice:
> God save the king!

The one-sided conversation proceeds:

Smart: You understand English writing?

⁓

Extremement bien

⁓

Winter me dit que on l'intention de donner Fidelio a music.

⁓

Karl: He would like to know the tempi of the finale of the last symphony. Haven't you it here?
How long have you worked on the symphony?

⁓

How long does it last?—1 hour and 3 minutes

⁓

¾ hour

⁓

We are now going to take a walk.

According to Smart's journal, Beethoven now ordered dinner "with his funny old cook," told his nephew to look after the wine, and the party of five took a walk. "Beethoven was generally in advance humming some passage. . . ." Holz talked to Beethoven now about Schlesinger, telling him that it was the publisher's purpose to print the quartets in succession, which would postpone the appearance of the thirteenth for two years, and advised Beethoven hereafter to make immediate publication a condition of purchase.

He suggested that if he were to threaten not to compose the quintets under the circumstances it might help. The conversations continued:

Karl: He asked why you had not come before now; he said the 300 pounds of the Philhar. Society were not to be looked upon as the principal thing. For that you needed only to appear 2 or 3 times in the orchestra and make money with your own concerts.

∾

He said that in a short time you could make at least 1000 pounds and carry it away with you.

∾

You can do better business with the publishers there than here.

∾

And you'll find 1000 friends, Smarth [*sic*] says, who will do everything to help you.

∾

. . . We'll wait till the year is over before going to England.

∾

. . . You'll not leave London so quickly if we are once there.

∾

Others are living there too, like Cramer, etc.

∾

In two years at least 50,000 florins net. Concerts.

∾

I am convinced that if you were to want to go away from here they would do everything to keep you here.

We shall let Smart conclude the story of the meeting.[64] "On our return [from the walk] we had dinner at two o'clock. It was a most curious one and so plentiful that dishes came in as we came out, for, unfortunately, we were rather in a hurry to get to the stage coach by four, it being the only one going to Vienna that evening. I overheard Beethoven say, 'We will try how much the Englishman can drink.' *He* had the worst of the trial. I gave him my diamond pin as a remembrance of the high gratification I received by the honour of his invitation and kind reception and he wrote me the following droll canon as fast as his pen could write in about two minutes of time as I stood at the door ready to depart.

Ars lon-ga   vi-ta bre-vis

[64] Smart, *op.cit.*, p. 124. A facsimile of the autograph of the canon is given.

'Written on the 16th of September, 1825, in Baden, when my dear talented musical artist and friend Smart (from England) visited me here. Ludwig van Beethoven.'"

Smart left Vienna on his return journey to London soon after September 18th. Schlesinger remained a short time longer in which time he saw Beethoven again. In the conversations there is talk of another performance of the quartet at which Holz played first violin[65] since Schuppanzigh was absent, and also a performance that included the quartets both in A minor and E-flat. This last took place probably on September 26 on which day Beethoven writes the following:[66]

Si non per portas   per mu-ros   per mu-ros per muros

I wish for you the most beautiful bride, my worthy one, and I take this opportunity to ask you to remember me to Hr. Marx in Berlin [and see] that he doesn't expect too much of me and leaves me a way out through the back door.[67]

After securing the A minor Quartet and an assurance that he should also have that in B-flat (he had offered to deposit 80 ducats with a Viennese banker against its completion and delivery and Beethoven had accepted his offer), Schlesinger said that he would purchase the first of the three quartets from Schott and Sons so as to have all three for his Complete Edition. Karl, in reporting the fact to Beethoven, expressed his belief that the Schotts would sell for fear that if they did not Schlesinger would reprint the work in Paris without permission. The latter made a strenuous effort to get the autograph score of the A minor, but had perforce to content himself with a copy. Holz represented to Beethoven that the autograph would be an asset for Karl in the future, and Karl was of the same opinion; he supported Holz's assertion with the argument that such "Capitalien" grew more valuable with age and that he was sure Schlesinger would get 30 ducats for the manuscript. Beethoven expressed indifference as to which publisher got the works so long as he was promptly paid. In a letter to Holz of August 24, he writes:

[65] Later Beethoven grew merry at his expense and wrote a canon in the Conversation Book to the words "Holz, Holz geigt die Quartette so, als ob sie Kraut eintreten!" ("Holz fiddles quartets the way they mash vegetables!"), WoO 204. (Cf. TDR, v, 250.)

[66] The canon also appears in a sketchbook in the midst of work on the fugue of the Quartet in B-flat. See *II Beeth.*, p. 11. For solutions to the canon see TDR, v, 249, n. 1; L.

Misch, *Beethoven Studies*, pp. 126-28; and Carl Dahlhaus, "Zwei Rätselkanons von Beethoven" in *Musica*, IX (1955), pp. 500-01.

[67] In 1824, Adolf Berhard Marx (1795-1806) with Moritz's father founded the *Berliner Allegemeine Musikalische Zeitung*, which, during its seven years of existence, championed Beethoven's music. Beethoven is obviously referring to these writings in this letter.

... It is immaterial which hellhound gnaws my brains, since it must needs be so, only see that the answer is not delayed too long. The hellhound in L[eipzig] can wait and meanwhile entertain himself with Mephistopheles (the editor of the L[eipsiger]Musikal[ische] Zeitung) in Auerbach's Cellar. He will soon be plucked by the ears by Beelzebub, the chief of devils. ...

The Leipzig "hellhound" thus consigned to Beelzebub was, of course, Peters.

The house into which Beethoven moved on October 15 is fully described and pictured in Gerhard von Breuning's book *Aus dem Schwarzspanierhause.* It derived its name from the fact that it had been built by the Benedictines of Spain. In it Beethoven occupied four rooms on the second floor, besides a kitchen and servants' quarters.[68] One of the most important results of Beethoven's removal to these quarters was a reestablishment of the intimate relations which had existed for so many years with the friend of his youth Stephan von Breuning, a Councillor in the War Department of the Austrian Government, who lived hard by. Though there had been no open rupture between him and Beethoven an estrangement had existed from the time when von Breuning had advised against Beethoven's assumption of the guardian-ship over his nephew. They had met occasionally *ad interim*, but it was not until they became neighbors that the intimate friendship which had existed in earlier years was restored. A beginning in this direction was made when, on a visit to Vienna in August, Beethoven met the Breuning family in the street. It was necessary that changes be made in the lodgings and while waiting for them Beethoven became a frequent visitor at the Breunings, dining with them frequently and sometimes sending them a mess of fish, of which he was very fond. Madame von Breuning meanwhile looked after the fitting out of his kitchen and saw to the engagement of his servants. Concerning the relations which existed between Beethoven and her father's family, Marie, a daughter of Stephan von Breuning, wrote many years after (in a memorandum for Thayer):

"My mother once met Beethoven when on her way to the Kaiserbad on the Danube; he accompanied her for the rather long distance from the Rothes Haus, where she lived. She spent about an hour in the bathhouse (the bath being a warm one) and on coming out was surprised to find Beethoven waiting to accompany her home. She often said that he was always gallant towards women and had paid court to her for a while.

"She related, too, that his animated gestures, his loud voice and his indifference towards others surprised the people in the street, and that she was often ashamed because they stopped and took him for a madman. His laugh was particularly loud and ringing.

"My mother often and repeatedly deplored the fact that she had never heard him play—but my father, in his unbounded tenderness, always replied

[68] In a letter to Dr. Braunhofer, dated February, 1826, Beethoven refers to this address as "Meine Wohnung, Schwarzspanier 2ter Stock, No. 201 Links." See Anderson, p. 1278, n. 3.

when she expressed a desire to hear him: 'He doesn't like to do it, and I do not want to ask him because it might pain him not to hear himself.'

"Beethoven repeatedly invited my mother to coffee, or, as the Viennese say, *zur Jause*; but my mother almost always declined, as his domestic arrangements did not appear altogether appetizing.

"My mother often said to my father that Beethoven's habit of expectorating in the room, his neglected clothing and his extravagant behavior were not particularly attractive. My father always replied: 'And yet he has a great deal of success, especially with women.'

"Beethoven often told my mother that he longed greatly for domestic happiness and much regretted that he had never married."

Beethoven was fond of Stephan von Breuning's son Gerhard, whom, because of his attachment to his father, he dubbed *Hosenknopf* (Trousers-button) and because of his lightness of foot Ariel. He once had the boy play for him, criticized the position of his hands and sent him Clementi's Method as preferable to Pleyel's which the lad was using.

There can be no doubt that the renewed association with von Breuning frequently turned his thoughts to his old home and his boyhood friends in the Rhine country, and his delight must have been keen when at the end of December he received letters from Wegeler, whom he had not seen since he left Vienna twenty-eight years before, and his wife, who had been Eleonore von Breuning. They were tender letters, full of information about their family, each other, friends and relations—real home letters telling of births, marriages, careers and deaths. One would think that they ought to have been answered at once, but Beethoven did not find the time or occasion to write a reply until the next year; thus they will be given in full in a later chapter.

After the private performances in September, the Quartet in A minor received its first public performance in November, advertised on October 27 in the *Sammler* as follows: "L. van Beethoven's newest Quartet in A minor will be performed on Sunday, November 6, 1825 in the Music Society's room at the 'rother Igel' in a benefit concert for Herr Joseph Linke. Also Beethoven's great Trio in B-flat major for pianoforte, violin and 'cello will be presented with Hr. Carl Maria von Bocklet on the piano part."[69] The concert was a great success and reports of it were given to Beethoven by Holz and Nephew Karl. Schuppanzigh received permission to perform the quartet again on November 20.

On November 29, 1825, Beethoven was one of fifteen men elected to honorary membership in the Gesellschaft der Musikfreunde by the directors, Cherubini, Spontini, Spohr, Catel and Weigl being among them. The election was confirmed by the society on January 26, 1826, but the diploma

[69] Concerning the confusion between Bocklet and Würfel in the Conversation Books, see TDR, v, pp. 259-60.

was not issued until October 26, and thus reached Beethoven's hands only a few months before his death.

On November 25, Beethoven wrote to Schott and Sons promising to send them the metronome marks for the Mass in D soon, telling them to print the list of subscribers before the dedication, asking delay in the matter of the dedication of the Ninth Symphony, and requesting that the publication of both works be postponed three months. He gives the title of the Mass as follows:

MISSA

composita, et
Serenissimo ac Eminentissimo Domino Domino
Rudolpho Joanni Caesareo Principi et Archiduci Austriae S.R.E.
tit. S. Petri in monte aureo Cardinali et Archiepiscopo Olomucensi
profundissima cum veneratione dedicata
a
Ludovico van Beethoven

On the same day, he wrote to Peters in Leipzig to the effect that his recent letters had not been definite and certain. He wanted a specific statement that the amount which he (Beethoven) had received as an advance was 360 florins. If Peters was willing to take a quartet for that sum he would send him one soon; if not, and if he preferred to have the money, he would return it to him. "If you had done this at once you might have had two quartets; but you cannot ask me to be the loser. If I wanted to draw the strings together tighter I could ask a larger price. . . . I will send nothing for examination." This, then, was Beethoven's ultimatum: Peters must pay 360 florins for the Quartet or receive back the money advanced three years before. Peters asked for the money and it was paid over to Steiner and Co. on his order on December 7.

Among the musicians who visited the composer at this time may be mentioned Theodore Molt, a man evidently of German birth and now a music teacher in Quebec, who was making a European tour. He gained the privilege of telling Beethoven to his face how greatly he admired him, then asked the favor of a souvenir which he could carry back on a journey of "3,000 hours" as a precious keepsake. For him, on December 16, Beethoven wrote the canon, "Freue dich des Lebens."[70]

Among the performances of Beethoven's works in these last months not already mentioned were the Mass in C in the Karlskirche on September 18 attended by Sir George Smart, the D major Trio in another Schuppanzigh concert on November 13 in which the Bohemian composer, Wilhelm Würfel

---

[70] From Thayer's notebook of 1857: "Circumstance related to me by the son of Mr. Molt. When Mr. Molt called upon Beethoven, December 16, 1825 (B's birthday), Beethoven showed him some verses he had just written complimentary to a young lady and fell into such enthusiasm talking about her that he passed entirely from his musical conversation. Verses poor enough, Mr. Molt said. Mr. Molt also described the meanness of the rooms in which B. lived." (TK, III, 211, n. 1.)

played the pianoforte, the *Eroica* on November 27, the Choral Fantasy, the E-flat Trio on December 11 played by A. Halm, and finally the Septet, which again created great enthusiasm. In this last the players were Schuppanzigh, Weiss, Linke, the double bass player Metzer, the clarinetist Friedlowsky, the horn player Herbst, and the bassoonist Mittag. Mittag related to Thayer the following anecdote. Going home one evening, he stepped into a tavern known as "Zum Dachs" to drink a glass of beer. Smoking was not allowed in the place and there were few guests. In a corner, however, sat Beethoven in an attitude of one lost in thought. After Mittag had watched him a few minutes he jumped up and called to the waiter: "My bill!" "Already paid!" shrieked the waiter in his ear. Mittag, thinking that Beethoven ought not to be left alone, followed him without betraying himself and saw him enter his house safely.

The great contributions which Beethoven made to music in the year 1825 were the quartets in A minor, Op. 132 and in B-flat major, Op. 130, already mentioned above. In March Beethoven had written to Neate that the first of the three quartets which he thought of bringing to London was completed (Op. 127 in E-flat), that he was at work on the second and that it and the third would be finished "soon." As we know, the A minor Quartet was not completed until midsummer because of Beethoven's illness, and upon its completion he set to work immediately on the third of the quartets, that in B-flat. On August 24 he mentioned in letters to Karl Holz and nephew Karl that he expected to finish the quartet by the end of the month, or at most in twelve days. It was not completed until November, however, and during this month Beethoven himself writes in the Conversation Book: "Title for the Quartet," and a strange hand adds: "3ième Quatuor. Pour deux Violons, Viola et Violoncello composé aux désirs de S. A. Monseigneur le Prince Nicolas Galitzin et dédié au même," to which Beethoven adds: "par L. v. B."

Schlesinger had negotiated for this quartet along with that in A minor, it will be remembered, but it was sold to Artaria; in January, 1826, Holz writes: "The Quartet will be printed at once; thus the third Quartet will appear before the first two." This was not the case, as the first of the Quartets, Op. 127, appeared in June, 1826, and the third of the Quartets, Op. 130 in B-flat, did not appear until May, 1827, from the press of Artaria. However, the fact that it did appear before the second Quartet, Op. 132 in A minor, which Schlesinger did not publish until September, 1827, accounts for its having received the earlier opus number. It had its first public performance in March, 1826, and will be further discussed in the next chapter. The Fugue in B-flat, Op. 133, originally formed the finale of the work but was put aside after the first performance; and the present finale, which was composed in Gneixendorf in 1826, was substituted.

Two trifles which kept company wtih the Quartets in this year were a Waltz in D and an Écossaise in E-flat for pianoforte, which were published in a collection of light music by C. F. Müller. There are several allusions to the oratorio commissioned by the Gesellschaft der Musikfreunde in the Conversation Books of 1825, in one of which Grillparzer is mentioned as a likely author for another book; but so far as is known no work was done on *Der Sieg des Kreuzes,* though Bernard did shorten the book.

In a Conversation Book at the very end of the year, in the midst of remarks about New Year's greetings, Beethoven wrote the following:

It is very interesting that the opening idea for the Quartet in C-sharp minor should appear before the close of 1825.[71] Underneath Beethoven writes: "Only the praise of one who has enjoyed praise can give pleasure." —a relic, no doubt, of some of the composer's classic readings.[72]

---⊰⊱The compositions of the year may be divided into large works and trifles.

Large works:
Quartet for Strings in E-flat, Op. 127, completed in February.
Quartet for Strings in A minor, Op. 132, completed by August.
Quartet for Strings in B-flat major, Op. 130, first version (with the fugue, later to be separated as Op. 133, as finale) completed in November.
Trifles:
Canons:
"Ars longa, vita brevis," WoO 192, second setting, for Sir George Smart on September 16.
"Ars longa, vita brevis," WoO 193, third setting, date and occasion unknown.
"Doktor sperrt das Tor dem Tod," WoO 189, for Dr. Anton Braunhofer, on May 11.
For two instruments, WoO 35, for Otto de Boer, on August 3.
"Freu' dich des Lebens," WoO 195, for Theodore Molt, on December 16.
"Gott ist eine feste Burg," WoO 188, written perhaps for the album of the Courlander, Colonel von Düsterlohe,[73] on January 12.
"Ich war hier, Doktor," WoO 190, for Dr. Anton Braunhofer, on June 4.
"Kühl, nicht lau," WoO 191 for Friedrich Kuhlau, on September 3 (see *A* 1427).
"Si non per portas," WoO 194, for Moritz Schlesinger, on September 26 (see *A* 1433).
Ecossaise in E-flat for Pianoforte, WoO 86 (see publications).

[71] According to Kinsky-Halm, work began on Op. 131 shortly after the conclusion of the composing of Op. 130, i.e., November, 1825. See KHV, p. 397, also *II Beeth.*, Section 1.

[72] Laudari a viro laudate—[Naevius;] Loetus sum laudari me, inquit Hector, opinor apud Naevium, abs te, pater, a laudato viro—[Cicero ad fam. xv, 6]; Cum tragicus ille apud nos ait magnificum esse laudari a laudato viro, laude digno, ait.—[Seneca, Epist. 102, 16.] (TK, III, 217, n. 1.)

[73] See Hans Volkmann, "Beethoven als Epigrammatiker," in *DM*, Vol. 7, No. 13 (1908), p. 29n.

Piece for Pianoforte, WoO 61a, for Sarah Burney Payne, September 27.
Waltz in D for Pianoforte, WoO 85 (see publications).

The publications for the year were:

By Sauer and Leidesdorf:

For C. F. Müller's collection of dances, *Ernst und Tändeley*: Ecossaise in E-flat for Pianoforte, WoO 86.

For C. F. Müller's collection of waltzes, *Seyd uns zum zweytenmal will-kommen!*: Waltz in D for Pianoforte, WoO 85.

By Schott in Mainz:

"Bundeslied" for Two Solo Voices and Chorus and accompaniment of two clarinets, two bassoons and two horns (Goethe), Op. 122.

"Der Kuss" (Weisse), Op. 128.

"Opferlied" for Soprano, Chorus and Orchestra (Matthisson), Op. 121b.

Overture to *Die Weihe des Hauses*, Op. 124, dedicated to Prince Nikolas Galitzin.

Six Bagatelles for Pianoforte, Op. 126.

By Schott in *Cäcilia*, No. 7.

Two Canons: "Hoffmann, sei ja kein Hofmann," WoO 180, and "Schwenke dich ohne Schwänke!", WoO 187.

By Steiner:

Grand Overture in C major ("zur Namensfeier"), Op. 115, dedicated to Prince Anton Radziwill.

CHAPTER XXXIX

THE YEAR 1826 THROUGH THE AUTUMN

DIFFICULTIES WITH PRINCE GALITZIN—
THE NEPHEW'S ATTEMPT AT SUICIDE—
GNEIXENDORF—THE LAST COMPOSITIONS

THE year which witnessed the last of Beethoven's completed labors, and saw what by general consent might be set down as the greatest of his string quartets, that in C-sharp minor, Op. 131, beheld also the culmination of the grief and pain caused by the conduct of his nephew. The year 1826 was a year of awful happenings and great achievements; a year of startling contradictions, in which the most grievous blows which an inscrutable Providence dealt the composer as if utterly to crush him to earth, were met by a display of creative energy which was amazing not only in its puissance but also in its exposition of transfigured emotion and imagination.

There was a good deal of talk concerning the performance of Beethoven's works at the beginning of the year, at the Schuppanzigh evening concerts and the *Concerts spirituels,* etc. The new Quartet in B-flat major, Op. 130, was ready to be rehearsed; and at the home of the rich music-lover Dembscher, an agent of the Austrian War Department, there were quartet parties with Mayseder as first violin, at which the A minor Quartet was played. There was talk of new compositions—oratorios on the old text by Bernard and on a new one by Kuffner, the opera on Grillparzer's *Melusine,* a requiem, and a new symphony. Beethoven's thoughts, however, were not with such things but in the congenial region of the string quartet. Having fulfilled his commission for Prince Galitzin by writing the Quartets in E-flat, A minor and B-flat, he had started to work on the Quartet in C-sharp minor, to which we return later in the chapter. That he could continue to write amidst all the disturbing circumstances of this year in the higher and purer regions of chamber music was a source of admiration and wonder to his friends.

{ 973 }

The figure which stands out in the highest relief throughout the year beside that of the composer is that of Holz, whose concern for his welfare went into the smallest detail of his unfortunate domestic life and included also a major part of the labors and responsibilities caused by the tragic outcome of the nephew's attempt at self-destruction. Schindler appears at intervals, but with jealous reserve, chary of advice, waiting to be asked for his opinion and pettishly protesting that after it once had been given it would not be acted upon. Stephan von Breuning appears in all the nobility of his nature; and in the attitude and acts of Brother Johann, there is evidence of something as near affectionate sympathy and interest as Beethoven's paradoxical conduct and nature invited of him. Among the other persons whom the Conversation Books disclose as his occasional associates were Schuppanzigh, Kuffner, Grillparzer, Abbé Stadler and Matthias Artaria, whose talk was chiefly about the affairs in which they were concerned.

The year was not far advanced before Beethoven's health was bothering him again; it was the old abdominal complaint of the year before. Near the end of January he was not feeling well; he complained of pains in the bowels and found locomotion difficult. He suffered also from his eyes, and Johann recommended that he use an eye lotion. Dr. Braunhofer was called and made the familiar injunctions. Beethoven was advised to abstain from wine for a few days and also from coffee, which he was told was injurious because of its stimulating effect on the nerves. The patient was advised to eat freely of soups, and small doses of quinine were prescribed. On February 23 the doctor received the following note from his patient:

Honored friend!
How indebted I am to you for your care of me. I have obeyed your orders as much as possible; wine, coffee, everything according to your order. It is difficult to judge right away to what extent there are results in these few days. The pain in my back is not great, but the malady is still there. Therefore I think that I will have reason to use the medicines which you sent me today (the cost of which, however, I don't know)—Do not forget your own interests on account of others. I am very sorry not to be able to prescribe something for you in return and must leave you to your own resources—I hope to see you as soon as possible—
    Yours gratefully
     Beethoven

In another note to Braunhofer at this time, Beethoven refers to his trouble as "rheumatism or gout." Frequent visits from the doctor and admonitions from his friends to be cautious continued until March, during which month he appeared to improve and, according to the Conversation Books, take an interest again in musical events and other things that were going on in the world.

The event that was personally important to Beethoven at this time was the first performance of his Quartet in B-flat—his "Leibquartett" it is once called in the Conversation Books. Schuppanzigh and his fellows had taken in hand. They found the concluding fugue extremely troublesome, but ιe Cavatina entranced them at once; Schuppanzigh entered a record against ιy change in it. The performance took place on March 21, 1826. The second and fourth movements had to be repeated, but the fugue proved a *crux* as, no doubt, the players had expected it would. Some of Beethoven's friends argued that it had not been understood and that this objection would vanish with repeated hearings; others, plainly a majority, asked that a new movement be written to take its place. Johann van Beethoven told the composer that the "whole city" was delighted with the work. Schindler[1] says that the *Danza alla tedesca*, one of the movements which was demanded a second time, was originally intended for another quartet, presumably that in A minor. Schuppanzigh's high opinion of the Cavatina was shared by many and also by Beethoven himself. Holz said that it cost the composer tears in the writing and brought out the confession that nothing that he had written had so moved him; in fact that merely to revive it afterwards in his thoughts and feelings brought forth renewed tributes of tears.

The doubts about the effectiveness of the fugue felt by Beethoven's friends found an echo in the opinions of the critics. Matthias Artaria, the publisher, who seems in this year to have entered the circle of the composer's intimate associates, presented the matter to him in a practicable light. He had purchased the publishing rights of the Quartet and after the performance he went to Beethoven with the suggestion that he write a new finale and that the fugue be published as an independent piece, for which he would remunerate him separately. Beethoven listened to the protests unwillingly, but, "Vowing he would ne'er consent, consented" and also requested the pianist Anton Halm, who had played in the B-flat Trio at the concert of March 21 to make the four-hand pianoforte arrangement for which there had already been inquiries at Artaria's shop. Halm accepted the commission and made the arrangement, with which Beethoven was not satisfied; "You have divided the parts too much between *prim* and second," he remarked to Halm,[2] referring to a device which the arranger had adopted to avoid crossing of hands—giving passages to the right hand which should logically have been given to the left, the effect being the same to the ear but not to the eye. Nevertheless, Halm presented a claim for 40 florins to Artaria for the work, and was paid. Beethoven then made an arrangement and sent it to Artaria ——via Holz, to whom he sent a note beginning with the salutation "Best Wood of Christ!" in which he asked Holz to give the arrangement to Artaria, hoping that he would take it and give Beethoven 12 ducats for the work. He concludes: "However, Hr. M. knows anyhow that we gladly and often are at his service without payment and shall be —but the present service which I rendered him is too menial not to have to

---

[1] *Biogr.*, Part II, p. 116. See Nottebohm *Beeth.*, p. 53. (TDR, v, 293, n. 1.)

[2] Halm's personal explanation to Mr. Thayer. (TK, III, 224, n. 1.)

insist on compensation—Appointing you now Executor in this matter, I beg of you, honorable Sir, to receive everything."[3]

To this Artaria demurred and asked Beethoven for Halm's manuscript. Beethoven sent it via Holz with instructions to get back his own arrangement in return for it. At the same time he told Artaria that while he did not ask that Artaria publish his work, he was under no obligation to give it to him; he might have it for the twelve ducats.[4] Artaria reconciled himself to the matter and paid Beethoven his fee on September 5. The arrangement which Artaria announced on May 10, 1827, as Op. 134 (the original score being advertised at the same time as Op. 133) was Beethoven's.

There was talk of other performances of the Quartet. Schuppanzigh was indisposed to venture upon a repetition, but Böhm and Mayseder were eager to produce the work at one of their quartet parties at Dembscher's house. But Dembscher had neglected to subscribe for Schuppanzigh's concert and had said that he would have it played at his house, since it was easy for him to get manuscripts from Beethoven for that purpose. He applied to Beethoven for the Quartet, but the latter refused to let him have it, and Holz, as he related to Beethoven, told Dembscher in the presence of other persons that Beethoven would not let him have any more music because he had not attended Schuppanzigh's concert. Dembscher stammered in confusion and begged Holz to find some means to restore him to Beethoven's good graces. Holz said that the first step should be to send Schuppanzigh 50 florins, the price of the subscription. Dembscher laughingly asked, "Must it be?" ("Muss es sein?") When Holz related the incident to Beethoven he too laughed and instantly wrote down the following canon:

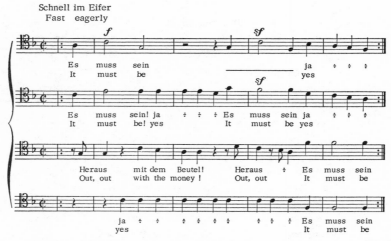

Schnell im Eifer
Fast eagerly

Es muss sein / It must be ... ja / yes

Es muss sein! ja / It must be! yes ... Es muss sein ja / It must be yes

Heraus mit dem Beutel! / Out, out with the money! ... Heraus / Out, out ... Es muss sein / It must be

ja / yes ... Es muss sein / It must be

[3] See Sonneck, *Beethoven Letters in America*, pp. 77-8.

[4] Beethoven wrote out a canon for Holz, "Da ist das Werk," WoO 197 (KHV, p. 698), with the text: "Here is the work. Bring back the sum—one, two, three, four, five, six, seven, eight, nine, ten, eleven, twelve ducats."

Out of this joke in the late fall of the year grew the finale of the last of the last five quartets, that in F major, Op. 135, to which Beethoven gave the superscription: "Der schwer gefasste Entschluss" ("The difficult resolution"). The story that the phrases: "Muss es sein? Es muss sein," and "Der schwer gefasste Entschluss" had their origin in a scene frequently repeated when Beethoven's housekeeper came to him of a Saturday for the weekly house-money, was spread by Schindler, who was familiar in a way with the Dembscher incident, but assigned it to the Quartet in E-flat. Holz was an actor in the scene and is the better witness, being confirmed, moreover, by the Conversation Book. The joke played a part in the conversations with Beethoven for some time.

Schuppanzigh's attempt to have another benefit concert (*Akademie*) came to nothing. A morning concert in the Augarten, which Schuppanzigh hoped to give on May 1st, finally took place on May 11. Several things by Beethoven were played: an overture, March with chorus from the *Ruinen von Athen,* one of the violin Romances, and perhaps *Adelaide.*[5] The concert went well; the overture and march were particularly liked, and Schuppanzigh played, besides the Romance, a piece by Kreutzer. Among the operas performed during the year was *Fidelio,* with Nanette Schechner in the title role. She made her debut on May 22, 1826, at the Kärthnerthor Theatre in Joseph Weigl's *Schweitzerfamilie.* Both Holz and Schindler reported to Beethoven concerning her singing with high praise and compared her favorably with Milder-Hauptmann. Schechner wanted very much to meet the composer at this time, but her wish was not to be fulfilled until February of the next year.

With the Quartet in B-flat, Beethoven had completed the three works of its kind which he had been commissioned to compose by Prince Nikolas Galitzin. He had taken three years to perform the task, but in the end the patience of his patron had been nobly rewarded. Meanwhile the Prince had been privileged to shine in the musical circles of St. Petersburg as one who stood peculiarly close to the greatest of living composers. During the delay, Prince Galitzin's conduct was in the highest degree honorable. In his letters he was most generous in his offers of assistance, practically giving Beethoven *carte blanche* to draw on his bankers in case of need. After the first performance of the *Missa Solemnis,* for which he had been primarily responsible, he presented his copy of the written score to the Philharmonic Society of St. Petersburg. He was so proud of his collection of Beethoven's music that he applied to the composer himself to help him make it complete. Too eager to wait for the publishers, he commissioned Beethoven to have copies made for him of new works, like the Ninth Symphony and the overture to the *Weihe des Hauses,* at his expense. He entertained the idea of repeating in St. Petersburg the concert which Beethoven had given in Vienna, at which the Symphony had received its first performance. For awhile he contemplated

[5] The Conversation Books mention a performance of the song by Hoffmann, but Thayer believed that this referred to the concert on March 21. (TDR, v, 306, n. 1.)

a repetition of the Mass. His first payment of 50 ducats for the first quartet in October, 1823 had been transferred, at Beethoven's request, to his subscription for the Mass. A second payment of 50 ducats, which was sent on December 5, 1824, was clearly for the first quartet. The work was sent to the Prince at the beginning of 1825, and Beethoven received a letter of grateful acknowledgement, written on April 29.

After an exchange of letters in June,[6] there is a break in the correspondence until the beginning of 1826. In the summer of 1825 Beethoven had two overtures, *Zur Namensfeier* and the *Weihe des Hauses,* sent to the Prince with a dedication to his patron on the latter. The A minor Quartet, Op. 132, had received its first public performance on November 6, 1825 in Vienna. That the Prince had heard of this performance is shown by his next letter:

St. Petersburg, January 14, 1826

Dear, respected Monsieur van Beethoven,

I am much at fault for not having yet acknowledged the receipt of the overtures which you had the kindness to send me. I was waiting for the shipment of the quartet to express my thoughts all at once. Since that time I have been very ill and then I was obliged to make a trip into the heart of Russia. All these circumstances and unexpected changes here have prevented me from writing to you up until now. I have just read in the musical Gazette of Leipzig that the new Quartet in A minor was performed in Vienna, and I am so impatient to get acquainted with this new masterpiece that I beg you to send it to me by post, like the preceding one, without further delay.

I will remit the amount of 75 ducats to M. Stieglitz to be remitted to you by M. Fries; 50 for the quartet and 25 for the overture which is magnificent and which I thank you very much for dedicating to me. The Leipzig journal referred to your new quartet in such flattering terms that I could not be more impatient to get acquainted with it. Would you forward it as soon as possible, for soon I am leaving for the coronation in Moscow, and then I will send you my address.

I wish you a good and happy new year.

Your devoted friend
Prince Nicolas Galitzin[7]

The A minor Quartet was sent in February, the B-flat Quartet shortly thereafter, as we shall see. But Beethoven waited in vain to be paid for them, and this was a matter of concern to him and those close to him during the months to come.

Holz knew a courier named Lipscher who often went to St. Petersburg, and he volunteered in January to obtain his services if the money did not

---

[6] On June 4 Beethoven had written of ill-health. A letter from the Prince dated June 21 ends: "I will have forwarded immediately the 460 silver florins which are coming to you, very happy to be able to contribute something for the betterment of your circum-stances." There is no record of such a sum having been received.

[7] The Galitzin correspondence covered in this chapter, and the conversations relating to it, are drawn from TDR, v, Appendix II, pp. 567ff.

arrive soon. In March Johann suggested that his brother write another letter, which he himself would post, for fear that the last quartet had never been received.

In May, Holz writes in the Conversation Books:

The courier Lipscher, who took the third quartet and was supposed to bring back the money, has written from Petersburg: he went to the home of the Prince, who excused himself, he had no time, he could come another day; Lipscher then went 5 or 6 times but was never received; all kinds of excuses were given. A so-called blue note for 5 f.[lorins] given to a servant helped him finally to get through to the Prince again; he was embarrassed again, fumbled through his scores and finally said that Lipscher might come to him before his departure for Vienna and receive the money.

The fellow believes it is nothing more than a Russian trick!

But he adds that he is not to be put off so easily; he thinks that he will be here in 4 to 5 weeks. And it is certain now that he has received the 2nd Quartet.[8]

At about this time Schindler makes the following entry:

The affair with Galitzin is becoming serious and I wish you a happy outcome.

If you had followed my advice, you would have sent at most *one* quartet and then stopped.

You have never let yourself be deceived by flattery except by this princely braggart.

In June, Holz writes:

The courier Lipscher has written: "7 times I went to see the scamp, the last time it turned out that he had left for the coronation in Moscow—merely a Russian trick."

Several couriers have told me that there has been little action from the embassy; it does not want to have a quarrel with this gentleman.

Lipscher advised Beethoven to turn to the banker Stieglitz in Vienna, who could exert more pressure than the Embassy. Karl urged his uncle to do the same. On August 13 Stieglitz answered a letter of August 2 from Beethoven reporting that the Prince was not at home but probably near Koslow in the Tambow region and that the matter would be attended to upon his return.

Finally in November a letter arrived:

[8] The second of the last two: *i.e.*, B-flat Quartet.

$^{10}\!/_{22}$ November, 1826

My dear and respected Monsieur van Beethoven!

You must think I am very inconsistent and fickle to let so much time go by without writing you especially since I have received from you two new master-pieces of your immortal and inexhaustible genius. But the unhappy circumstances that I find myself in, partly from great losses which have brought me several bankruptcies, partly from other considerations that I cannot explain to you, have drawn me away from my usual occupations.

Now I am living in the country in the heart of Russia, and in a few days I will be leaving for Persia to participate in the war there. Before this I will definitely dispatch the sum of 125 ducats to be remitted to you, and I can only offer you my thanks for your masterpieces and my excuses for having taken so long to give you any sign of life. Please let me keep on hearing from you, it means a lot to me. Always write to me at the old address, and tell me, I beg of you, what new things you are composing.

Accept the esteem and regard of one of your greatest admirers.

Pce Nicolas Galitzin

Since this letter was written before his return to St. Petersburg, it shows that he had received both of the last two quartets before his trip and that he recognized his debt to be 50 ducats for each of those quartets and 25 ducats for the dedication of the overture *Weihe des Hauses*. On the outside of this letter there is a notation, probably written by Breuning: "Inquiry sent on January 10, 827 concerning this matter to the banking house, Stieglitz and Company, requesting the delivery of the sum of 125 ducats or a report." Stieglitz answered this inquiry on January 18 reporting that he had sent another reminder to the Prince in Koslow. A final appeal to Stieglitz was written on March 21, 1827, which Beethoven signed on his deathbed. There the matter rested until after his death. The story of later negotiations is told in the Appendix (H).

Now we turn to Beethoven's current relations with his publishers. He was on friendly terms with Matthias Artaria, who had taken the B-flat Quartet and the Fugue and, unlike others, did not delay in preparing them for publication. He visited Beethoven, met him at inns, and wanted him to come to his own quarters. But in the course of a month there was some trouble between the two, possibly in connection with the afore-mentioned piano arrangements of the Fugue. Artaria wanted the "new" Quartet in C sharp minor, but Beethoven decided to give it to Schott.

Serious misunderstandings continued between Beethoven and the firm of Steiner and Haslinger. Perhaps there was still ill-will on Beethoven's part because of Steiner's behavior in the matter of the debt, which had now been settled; the same on Steiner's part was easy to understand since Beethoven was no longer giving him his new works but bringing them out with other publishers, some of whom were foreigners. Steiner had lost out on the bid-ding for the B-flat Quartet. Also it had been a year ago that the joke on Haslinger had been printed in Schott's magazine, *Cäcilia*. Beethoven frequently needed music from Steiner's firm and was slow in returning it. On the other hand foreign correspondents were using Steiner's as an address with which to get their letters through to Beethoven, and it often happened that they remained there for weeks at a time. Already by the end of January Beethoven requested Schott to communicate with him through Artaria rather than Steiner in order to avoid delay. It is likely that Holz exercised an unfavorable influence here, for he did not care for Steiner and did not miss opportunities to slander him. At the same time, he sought to alienate Steiner from Beethoven and made pronouncements to him concerning Beethoven's way of using people.

The following stern note to Haslinger introduces a new cause for strife.[9]

I report to you that neither the Overture[10] nor the "Elegischer Gesang"[11] need further corrections, also that the titles are correct. But concerning the march with chorus[12] and the vocal terzetto,[13] the faulty notes of before are now indeed correct, but the titles are still not the way I myself indicated. Since this affair has been going on for 6 weeks, and I have many examples in connection with this where I could not overcome your obstinacy, I have handed both titles in their original form to His Honor the Censor, about which I hereby serve you notice.

Vienna, April 9, 826   Ludwig van Beethoven

I wanted to inform you of the above as a favor so that you may prepare for it. For I will *never* allow these works to appear with the titles which you have set up.

Beethoven's principal worry was in the wording of the title of the piano-vocal score of the Terzett, published in February, which implied that the work was originally scored for piano accompaniment.

At Holz's urging Beethoven sent him with the following note[14] to the Censor's office, the head of which was the Book Censor, Councillor Sartorius:

Highly honored Censor!

I am threatened by an edition of several of my works, wherein, out of resentment towards me, mistakes indicated by me have not been corrected. The titles are of such a barbaric nature that they would bring disgrace to Vienna. Therefore I request your honor that these works not be allowed to be advertised until I with my own signature have confirmed that these works appear in proper condition.

In the Conversation Books there is much discussion of the affair. In April it is presumably Holz who writes:

He [the censor] cannot recall if Haslinger had already received permission of the censor to publish this.

[9] Taken from Unger, *Ludwig van Beethoven und seine Verleger*, No. 94. See also *A* 1480.
[10] To *König Stephen.*
[11] Op. 118.
[12] Op. 114.
[13] Op. 116.
[14] Unger, *op.cit.*, p. 22. See also *A* 1479.

If this has already happened, it would not be easy to remedy; on the contrary, he would have resolved it already.

•~•

If it has already happened, we still have the foreign newspapers to whom we can place it in the proper light.

During the summer of 1826 Tobias Haslinger had become the sole owner of the firm when Steiner retired. In the Conversation Book of September, the matter comes up again and Holz writes:

Today Tobias showed [me] the proof-impression of the new title for the Terzett: I discovered a new mistake right away. The printer placed "vor tutti orchestra" well but left out "estratto per il cembalo."

•~•

It is to be fixed by the day after tomorrow.

•~•

This way one would think one was buying the whole score.

Finally the correction was made according to Beethoven's wishes, and he asked Haslinger to announce this in the newspapers. Beethoven had always maintained a friendly personal relationship with Haslinger, and despite Holz's antagonism this was now resumed, as is shown by letters of this same month, in which Beethoven returns to the old, characteristically mischievous tone.[15]

There was greater confidence in the firm of Schott at Mainz, who continued to bring out Beethoven's new compositions. The E-flat Quartet, Op. 127, appeared in March, 1826, and the Ninth Symphony by the end of August. Schott also received the next work, the C-sharp minor Quartet, Op. 131.

Holz said that when he once remarked to Beethoven that the one in B-flat was the greatest of the three quartets (Op. 127, 130, 132) the composer replied: "Each in its way. Art demands of us that we shall not stand still. You will find a new manner of voice treatment (part writing) and thank God there *is less lack of fancy than ever before*."[16] Afterward he declared the C-sharp minor Quartet to be his greatest. The first form of the fugue-theme in this work, as has been noted, was written down in a Conversation Book in the last days of December, 1825. The quartet was the main work of the next month, and indeed for the first half of 1826 with interruptions only from sickness, preparations for the performance of the B-flat Quartet, and the four-hand arrangement of the Fugue (Op. 133). Before the end of

15 See *A* 1522, 1526, 1530.
16 From Holz's recollections (Wilhelm von

Lenz, *Eine Kunststudie* [Hamburg, 1860], v, p. 217.) (TDR, v, 318, n. 2.)

January the variation theme appears in a Conversation Book in Beethoven's hand:

It is likely that a goodly portion of the work was written within a month and ready for the copyist, for in January Holz suggested that something from the work in hand be tried. Whether or not it was ever played in public in the lifetime of the composer cannot be said with certainty.[17] Schindler says positively that it was not performed by Schuppanzigh. On March 28 Beethoven wrote to Schott and Sons in Mainz and established the price of a quartet "*of this kind* at least 80 gold ducats."[18]

In another letter to Schott, dated May 20, Beethoven complained of ill health and pressing affairs which prevented him from completing the quartet until now. He restated the fee of 80 ducats, but said that he was willing to be paid in two installments. On July 12 he wrote that the quartet was ready for delivery upon receipt of the draft of the second installment of the fee. The score was turned over to Schott's agent in Vienna on August 12. On the copy Beethoven had written: "Put together from pilferings from one thing and another" ("Zusammengestohlen aus Verschiedenem diesem und jenem"). Because this had alarmed the publishers, Beethoven writes on August 19: "I report to you that the score was delivered to Frank 7 days ago. You wrote me that the quartet must be an original one. I felt rather hurt, so as a joke I wrote on the copy that it was put together from pilferings. Nevertheless, it is *brand new*—." It was published by Schott and Sons in June, 1827, after Beethoven's death.

The quartet was originally to be dedicated to his friend and admirer, Johann Wolfmayer, as was indicated in a letter to Schott on February 22, 1827. Then on March 10 he wrote again to change the dedication to Baron Joseph von Stutterheim, Lieutenant Field-Marshal, who had made a place for Karl in his regiment.

Now we turn to the projects which the composer's friends tried unsuccessfully to persuade him to undertake. First, there was Bernard's *Der Sieg des Kreuzes* which Beethoven had promised to write for the Gesellschaft der Musikfreunde. At the end of 1825 Kanne's advice had been sought and he recommended an abbreviation of the text. Hauschka gave his approval to the revision. In April Kuffner told Beethoven that he had read Bernard's oratorio book but could not find in it even a semblance of an oratorio, much less half-good execution. These protests could only strengthen Beethoven's distaste for the text. At any rate the plan was definitely laid aside. According to Holz, he never worked earnestly on the subject and yet, at the same time,

[17] In a letter to Schott at the end of September, 1826, Beethoven writes of a projected performance "for the benefit of an artist" (Joseph Böhm?) of which there is no record. See *A* 1531. (TDR, v, 318, n. 1.)

[18] See *A* 1472.

showed his intention to write no more "Opern" and piano pieces, but only oratorio. Holz further relates that Beethoven, in reference to his last sonatas, which he called his last but also the best that he had written for piano, said: "It is and remains an inadequate instrument. In the future I shall write in the manner of my grand-master Handel annually only an oratorio or a concerto for some string or wind instrument, provided I have completed my tenth symphony (C minor) and my Requiem."[19]

Perhaps there was something of personal equation in Kuffner's judgement of the Bernard text, for he was ready to write not only one but even two oratorio texts if Beethoven would but undertake their composition. He presented the plan of a work to be called "The Four Elements," in which Man was to be brought into relationship with the imposing phenomena of Nature. Meanwhile, there was discussion of the subject of Saul. Holz relates that "Beethoven had given much study to Handel's *Saul* and read a lot about the music of the ancient Hebrews; he wanted to write choruses in the old modes." In April the conversation was lively on the subject. Kuffner was to revise the text for Beethoven; he was already thinking of a place for the performance. Kuffner intended in his treatment of the story of Saul to make it a representation of the triumph of the nobler impulses of Man over untamed desire. Kuffner set to work; and Holz brought a few sections of the text to the composer. In a Conversation Book he says:

I must take back this one in Kuffner's handwriting by the day after tomorrow. I will take care of your copy.

·~·

I copied this quickly from Kuffner.

·~·

Here there might be a chorus in the Lydian mode as you wanted to bring one in.

Holz urged that it would be a shame if this mode were heard only in a quartet.[20] In May he brought greetings from Kuffner, who was now at work on it body and soul. He also explained that Kuffner intended to treat the chorus as an effective agent in the action, for which purpose it was to be divided into two sections, like the dramatic chorus of the Greek tragedians. Kuffner was sufficiently encouraged to write the book and Holz says that Beethoven finished the music of the first part "in his head." If so, it stayed there, as far as the sketchbooks bear testimony.

His friends also urged him to compose a Requiem mass and such a composition belongs in the category with the oratorio as a work which he had been paid to undertake. Among the ardent admirers of Beethoven and most zealous patrons of the Schuppanzigh Quartets was Johann Nepomuk Wolfmayer, a much respected cloth merchant. One of the methods chosen by Wolfmayer to show his appreciation of the composer was occasionally to

[19] From Holz's recollections to Frau Linzbaur, in Nohl, *Beethoven, Liszt and Wagner*, p. 112. (TDR, v, 326, n. 1.)
[20] Op. 132, third movement.

have a new coat made for him which he would bring to Beethoven's lodgings, place upon a chair and then see to it that an old one disappeared from his wardrobe. We have already heard a similar story from Mayseder. It is said that Wolfmayer sometimes had difficulty in getting the composer's consent to the exchange, but always managed to do it. Early in the second decade of the century Wolfmayer commissioned Beethoven to write a Requiem for him and —offered him 100 ducats as honorarium.[21] Beethoven promised, but never set to work: though Holz says he was firmly re-solved to do so and, in talking about it, said that he was better satisfied with Cherubini's setting of the Mass for the Dead than with Mozart's. A requiem, he said, should be a memorial of the dead and have nothing in it of the noises of the last trumpet and the day of judgement.[22]

There was still talk of an opera, and the matter was constantly being broached by different members of his circle. Brother Johann urged opera as the most remunerative enterprise to which he could now apply himself. The serious von Breuning also advised him to write an opera right away. Duport, director of the Court Opera, sent word through Holz and Johann that conditions were favorable for an opera to be written and that Grill-parzer's *Melusine* would be acceptable to him.

Beethoven evidently had expressed the intention or wish to the older Schlesinger to write an opera for Berlin. This information was passed on to the General Intendant of the Berlin Theatre, Count von Brühl, who wrote a letter to Beethoven on April 6.[23] First he expressed the honor it would bring his stage to have a work written for it by such an artist as Beethoven; then he added that Schlesinger had given him Grillparzer's *Die schöne Melu-sine* which, although full of good things was too close in subject matter to *Undine*, an opera by de la Motte Fouqué and E. T. A. Hoffmann, which had already appeared on his stage.[24] He closed with the hope that Beethoven and Grillparzer would collaborate on another subject. This letter was evidently never answered.

An adaptation to operatic uses of Goethe's *Claudine von Villa Bella* was discussed, apparently with favor, but Kanne, who was designated to take the adaptation in hand, was afraid to meddle with the great poet's drama. So nothing came of the Berlin project or of *Melusine*, though Grillparzer talked it over again with Beethoven and told Holz that though he was not inclined to attach too great importance to it, yet he thought it would be hard to find an opera text better adapted to its purpose than it, from a musical and scenic point of view. To Schindler, Beethoven once held out a prospect that "something would come" of the idea of music for *Faust* which Rochlitz had implanted in Beethoven's mind; but it shared the fate of opera and oratorio.

[21] See *FRBH*, ii, p. 466. (Cf. TDR, v, 329, n. 1.)

[22] From O. Jahn's memoranda from Holz. See Nohl, *op.cit.*, p. 111. (TDR, v, 329; also

see n. 2.)

[23] See *DM*, Vol. 3, No. 12, p. 437. (TDR, v, 330, n. 1.)

[24] July, 1816.

The sketchbooks bear witness, though not voluminously, to other works of magnitude which were in Beethoven's thoughts in this year but never saw completion. These were a symphony and overture. In a book used towards the end of 1825, containing sketches for the last movement of the Quartet in B-flat, there is a memorandum of a *Presto* in C minor, ¾ time, and of a short movement in A-flat, *Andante*, which Schindler marked as belonging to "the tenth symphony."[25]

There are also much longer sketches for an overture on B-a-c-h, in the midst of which Beethoven had written: "This overture together with the new symphony and we shall have a new Akademie in the Kärnthnerthor."[26] Schindler published the sketches of the symphony in Hirschbach's *Musikal-isch-kritisches Repertorium* of January, 1844, and started the story of an uncompleted tenth symphony. Lenz says that Holz wrote to him that Beethoven had played "the whole of the Tenth Symphony" for him on the pianoforte, that it was finished in all of its movements in the sketches, but that nobody but Beethoven could decipher them. Holz, however, made no such broad statement to Otto Jahn, a much more conscientious reporter than Lenz. To Jahn he said that there was an introduction in E-flat major, a soft piece, and then a powerful *Allegro* in C minor, which were complete in Beethoven's head and which he had played to him (Holz) on the pianoforte. This is very different from an entire symphony. In the letter to Moscheles dictated to Schindler on March 18, 1827, bearing a message of thanks to the Philharmonic Society of London for money sent during his illness, the composer says that he will bind himself "to compose for it [the Society] either a new symphony, which lies already sketched in my desk, or a new overture or something else which the Society would like."[27]

[25] *II Beeth.*, pp. 11-12.

[26] Sketches for an overture on B-A-C-H also appear in 1823 and 1824.

[27] From the reading given in *Beethoven als Freund der Familie Wegeler-v. Breuning*, ed. S. Ley (Bonn, 1927), pp. 232-34.

Among Beethoven's intimate friends was Abbé Stadler, an old man and an old-fashioned musician, the horizon of whose aesthetic appreciation was marked by the death-date of his friend Mozart. Castelli says that he used to call Beethoven's music "pure nonsense"; certain it is that he used to leave the concert-room whenever a composition by Beethoven was to be played. Schuppanzigh offered as an excuse for him that he had a long way to go to get home, and it does not appear that Beethoven ever took umbrage at his conduct. Holz, telling Beethoven in February, 1825, that as usual he had left the room when an overture by Beethoven was about to be played, added: "He is too old. He always says when Mozart is reached, 'More I cannot understand.'" But once he stayed and not only listened to a Beethoven piece but praised it. It was the Trio for Strings, Op. 9, which had been composed nearly a generation before! Holz becomes sarcastic: "One might say A.B.C.D. (*Abbé cédait*)." Stadler now had occasion to court Beethoven's favor, or at least to betray the fact that even if he could not appreciate his music he yet had a vast respect for his genius and reputation. In 1825, Gottfried Weber had written an essay, which was published in the *Cäcilia* journal, attacking the authenticity of Mozart's *Requiem*. The article angered Beethoven, as is evidenced by his marginal glosses on the copy of the journal which he read, now in the possession of the Beethoven-Haus in Bonn. The glosses are two in number: "Oh you arch ass!" and "Double ass!" Such a disposition of an attack on the artistic honor of his friend did not suffice Stadler. He published a defense of Mozart, *Vertheidigung der Echtheit des Mozartschen Requiems*, and sent a copy to Beethoven, who acknowledged it thus:

on the 6th of Feby., 1826

Respected and venerable Sir!

You have done a really good deed in securing justice for the manes of Mozart by your truly exemplary and exhaustive essay. Both lay and profane, and all who are musical or who can in any way be accounted such must give you thanks—

Either nothing or a great deal is required to broach such a subject as H[err] W. has done. When it is also considered, as far as I know, that such a one has written a book on composition and yet tries to attribute such passages as

to Mozart, and if one adds to it an example of W[eber]'s own crudities such as

we are reminded by H.W.'s amazing knowledge of harmony and melody of the old and dead Imperial composers Sterkel, Haueisen,[28] Kalkbrenner (the father), André (certainly not the other one) and so forth.

Requiescant in pace—But I am particularly grateful to you, my honored friend, for the happiness you have given me in sending me your essay. I have always counted myself among the greatest admirers of Mozart and shall remain so until my last breath—

Reverend Sir, *your blessing very soon*—

With sincere regards, venerable Sir, I remain your faithful

Beethoven

The concluding supplication recalls an anecdote related by Castelli in his memoirs: Beethoven and Abbé Stadler once met at Steiner's. About to depart, Beethoven knelt before the Abbé and said: "Reverend Sir, give me your blessing." Stadler, not at all embarrassed, made the sign of the cross over the kneeling man and, as if mumbling a prayer, said: "Nutzt's nicht, so schadt's nix" ("If it does no good, 'twill do no harm"). Beethoven thereupon kissed his hand amid the laughter of the bystanders. Jahn heard the same story from Fischoff.

Though direct evidence is lacking, it seems obvious to associate the following three-part canon (see WoO 178) with this amusing anecdote:

A remark in a Conversation Book of 1826 indicates that Stadler had urged Beethoven to write a mass. Holz says:

If Stadler tells you to write a mass it is certain that something will be done for it. He knows best of anybody which way the wind blows.

•~•

He has Dietrichstein and Eybler in his pocket.

•~•

[28] See *A* 1468; I am indebted to Miss Anderson for the reading of this name.

You are well cared for if Stadler favors it.

The conversations of Holz also provide a fleeting glimpse of Schubert in this year. Holz told Beethoven that he had seen the young composer with some one (perhaps Artaria or Mosel) and that the two were reading a Handel score together.

He [Schubert] was very amiable and thanked me for the pleasure which Mylord's [Schuppanzigh's] Quartets gave him; he was always present.

•~•

He has a great gift for songs.

•~•

Do you know the Erlkönig?

•~•

He spoke very mystically, always.

Friedrich Wieck, father of Clara Schumann, spent several hours with Beethoven, having been presented by Andreas Stein, the pianoforte maker. He told about the visit long afterward in a letter to his second wife, which was reprinted in the *Signale* No. 57, in December, 1873, from the *Dresdener Nachrichten.* Beethoven gave his guest wine (to which Wieck was not accustomed), improvised for him for over an hour and talked voluminously about, ". . . musical conditions in Leipzig—Rochlitz—Schicht—Gewandhaus—his housekeeper—his many lodgings, none of which suited him—his promenades—Hietzing—Schönbrunn—his brother—various stupid people in Vienna—aristocracy—democracy—revolution—Napoleon—Mara—Catalani —Malibran—Fodo—the excellent Italian singers Lablache, Donzelli, Rubini and others, the perfections of Italian opera (German opera could never be so perfect because of the language and because the Germans did not learn to sing as beautifully as the Italians)—my views on pianoforte playing— Archduke Rudolph—Fuchs in Vienna, at the time a famous musical personality—my improved method of pianoforte teaching, etc. . . . ."

Wieck said that the meeting was in Hietzing in May, and that Beethoven played upon the pianoforte "presented to him by the city of London"—three obvious mistakes, since Beethoven was not in Hietzing in May, but in Vienna, and the Broadwood pianoforte, which was not presented to him by the city of London but by Thomas Broadwood, was in the hands of Graf for repairs in May.

Different proposals for Beethoven's move to the country were already being offered early in the year. In February Johann invited him again to his country house. It is not surprising that Beethoven did not consider it at this time. He was waiting for the money from Prince Galitzin and Karl writes: "If the sums of money should come, you could probably go to the country." Among many possibilities was a move to Ischl.[29] In May Beethoven writes:

[29] In June Karl writes: "I have enquired about Ischl, it is 32 miles from here." (TDR, v, 343, n. 2.)

"It is best to go to Ischl." In June and July there is talk of the baths there which are beneficial to those suffering from gout. Holz offered also to find a house in Baden for him. It had been planned to make a move for the summer, but the place had not yet been decided upon when an event took place which suddenly changed all such thoughts: an attempt by Karl to take his life.

Let us take up the history of Beethoven and his nephew from where we left off. As we have seen, in 1825 Karl had transferred from the University to the Polytechnic Institute. He lived in the Alleegasse with Schlemmer and as a rule came at midday to his uncle's, in whose circle he played an active role. He reported on many things that were happening in the outside world, also on musical and literary developments. He continued to be active in his uncle's affairs (plans, publishers, money), wrote letters for him and ran errands. Holz writes in a Conversation Book, "He has sensible opinions," and again mention is made of his "good talents."

However, since he had enrolled late in the term at the Institute, Karl employed a tutor to help him, and apparently still needed his help a year later. At the time of the change to the Institute, Beethoven made the remark that the expense of the tutor, along with the board at Schlemmer's, would amount to 2000 florins a year.[30] Entries in the Conversation Book of 1825 show that the matter was under discussion and that Beethoven had registered his disapproval of the tutor to Schlemmer, for Karl writes:

I have spoken to Schlemmer about it too. He denied ever having said that; also, since he was not informed about it, he couldn't know to what extent I need him or not.

•~•

My class hours are all distributed. My tutor comes early, from 8.30 to 9.30. Then lectures from 9 to 12. In the afternoon lectures from 3 to 5. I have an hour from 5 to 6.

•~•

In the evenings I do all my assignments.

•~•

Thus after 5. It is always just like today. But it will be a quarter hours later.

Later, there appears in Schlemmer's hand:

I can assure you that as yet he has never stayed away overnight. Also I must tell you that your nephew is at home daily in the evening, and that he goes out early only if it is time for school. But if he were going out to play, then it would have to be instead of school. Otherwise he is at home and he cannot play. In the time that he has been here he has been changing his ways favorably. He said today at lunch that the tutor was not really satisfied, he is negligent in his studies.

[30] See TDR, v, p. 523.

Karl writes:

The lessons are not difficult for me, also I could not have taken up any *earlier* what I am taking with *him* because we take up only those studies which are being given in college.

•~•

From my lessons with him I save several hours in which I would have had to work alone for myself.

To another complaint Karl answered: "I would be glad if you would inform yourself; each day the professors are bound to know when I leave since the names are read out. Also H. Reisser sees me daily." Around New Year's Day, 1826, Holz writes: "I have already spoken with Reisser; he says that Karl is behaving himself the way you would expect from a reasonable person.

Karl complains again of his schedule and amount of work: "There is now a great deal to do; and it is frightful to give up Sundays."

At about this time there came up the question of a carnival ball to which Karl wanted to go. Holz spoke approvingly of it and intended to accompany Karl to it, but apparently had to dissuade Beethoven from doing the same:

Nevertheless you would be most embarrassed if you were obliged to let people gape at you.

•~•

I will go with him to a regular ball.

•~•

I would be afraid, if I were alone with him, he might run away, and I would not know where.

•~•

If there is a ball in the Apollo Room, the so-called Ball of the Reformists, you would be noticed there less probably than elsewhere which would certainly be [more] agreeable to you.

The old mistrust of Karl's misuse of free time led to renewed complaints of any long periods of absence. In February Beethoven must have expressed the desire that Karl come to live with him again, for at this time the nephew writes in a Conversation Book:

You go ahead and do what you think is best. I believe simply that the distance[31] would cause a great loss of time, instead of my being, as I am now, a few minutes from home and able to study.

•~•

In the summer we will not feel the distance as much.

•~•

But it is the *last* year; then we need never be separated any more.

[31] *I.e.*, from the Institute.

Beethoven gave in, but the mistrust remained, and the conflict between them grew. The alternation between strong reproaches, moral sermons and excessive emotional expressions of love served only to diminish bit by bit Beethoven's authority over the boy, and as a result Karl saw less and less of his uncle. Beethoven felt this keenly and asked his brother Johann to find out the reason. At the beginning of March Johann writes in the Conversation Book:

Today I spoke with him earnestly about why he had been to see you so little.

•~•

His answer was approximately as follows. He would very much like to be with you but he fears the frequent rows and reproaches for his mistakes of the past, also the frequent rows with the servants. However, please do not reproach him with this; otherwise he would no longer be candid with me. From here, however, I think that only you can draw him to yourself completely.

•~•

I suppose on account of his frequently poor appearance; I have spoken bluntly to him about it but he consistently denies everything.

Johann then advised his brother to write important letters himself, so that no one else would know their contents. He offered to post them himself. He continues: "In 4 months Karl will be ready with everything, then you must urge him to go immediately into a local or foreign business house, for otherwise he will become a lout [ein Lump] and will let himself live off of you as long as you are living; then he could idle away his time."

Johann advised that in the latter case the guardianship should be placed in the hands of Dr. Bach, because "You are as little able as I to be always running after him." In these conversations we also find Schindler once again, to whom Beethoven had voiced his fears. Schindler replies: "I am sorry to hear it, what all are we to live through with Karl, if it goes on like this." And he advised Beethoven not to depend upon Holz in the management of this affair.

Meanwhile Karl explained again how much work he had to do—for example, "The professors assign so much work over the holidays that one can scarcely get it done. The fair copying is the most disagreeable part because it takes alot of time,"—and its effect on his visits and his participation in outside events. In June he writes: "There is much to be done because the examinations are soon." Holz adds: "Now Karl does not have much longer to study."

Another form of duress came from the uncle's suspicion of the nephew in money matters. Beethoven asked to see the receipts of last month's payment to Schlemmer and expressed misgivings over Karl's demands for funds. Karl writes:

If the receipt is not in my room, Schlemmer can give it to me along with the receipt for this month.

⋅~⋅

It will show up all right.

⋅~⋅

When I go walking and have a drink and the like. I don't have any other expenses.

This last answer from Karl must have been to a demand from his uncle as to how he used money, and must be weighed against a statement by Schlemmer in the Conversation Books, and later again by Breuning, that the principal reason that circumstances had become intolerable for Karl was that he was heavily in debt.

There were violent scenes, evidently in Karl's rooms which deeply embittered him. Shortly afterwards his uncle visited him again to break down his obstinacy. Here follows Karl's part of the dialogue, which shows what tension had been reached over Beethoven's persistence:

You consider it insolence if, after you have upbraided me for hours undeservedly, this time at least, I cannot turn from my bitter feeling of pain to jocularity. I am not so frivolous as you think. I can assure you that since the scene on Sunday in the presence of this fellow I have been so depressed that the people in the house noticed it. The receipt for the 80 florins which were paid in May I now positively know, after a search at home, that I gave you, as I already said on Sunday; it must and no doubt will be found.

⋅~⋅

If I continue to work while you are here it is not in a spirit of insolence, but because I believe that you will not be offended if I do not permit your presence to keep me from my labors, which are now really piling up on me, all the more since we see each other *here,* where there is time, enough to talk over all needful things. You are mistaken, too, when you think that I wait for your coming to *become industrious.* You also seem to accept as *my views* what I repeat to you as the opinions of *others* as, for example, the word of *Haslinger* and the twaddle of Frau Passy.

⋅~⋅

I know very well what to think of such gossip, but did consider it my duty to inform you about it.

⋅~⋅

I hope that what I have said will serve to convince you of my real views and feelings and put an end to the strain which has existed of late between us, though not on my side by any means.

At one point, judging from a recorded remark by Holz, Karl seems to have raised his hand in physical violence against his uncle. Holz writes:

I came in just as he took you by the breast.

⋅~⋅

At the door, as he was coming out.

It is the only allusion to the incident in the book and we know none of the particulars; but it and other scenes of tumult and the utterances which they provoked must have inspired the dreadful conflict of emotions which finds expression in a letter written at this time:

If for no other reason than that you obeyed me, at least, all is forgiven and forgotten; more today by word of mouth, very quietly—Do not think that I am governed by anything but thoughts for your well-being, and from this point of view judge my acts—Do not take a step which might make *you* unhappy and shorten *my* life—I did not get to sleep until 3 o'clock, for I coughed all night long—I embrace you cordially and am convinced that soon you will no longer *misjudge* me; I thus judge your conduct yesterday—I expect you without fail today at one o'clock—Do not give me cause for further worry and apprehension— Meanwhile farewell!

Your real and true Father

We shall be alone, for I shall not permit H.[32] to come—the more so since I do not wish anything about yesterday to be known. Do come—do not permit my poor heart to *bleed any longer*.

The subjects discussed in the Conversation Books continued to be the same: the securing of a position for Karl, the proximity of the examination, the pile of work, done partly with the tutor, the difficulty of coming to see Beethoven as often as the uncle wished. Karl told him specifically that he could not come in the evening. Was it merely work in the evening that detained him? His uncle felt uninformed about how he spent his evenings and in whose company. There was the usual suspicion of the company he kept and of his desire to gamble,[33] to which there was now added talk of his taking flight. Beethoven inquired about him often—too often according to Reisser. He was to be seen in the vestibule of the Polytechnic Institute at noontime waiting to escort his nephew home arm in arm.

At this time Karl was also seeing his mother, which, of course, was directly contrary to Beethoven's wishes. There he saw his friend, Niemetz, with whom his mother had become acquainted. At this time Beethoven wrote a short note to Holz:

Please come as soon as possible, thereupon we can arrange everything. It is no small matter, he wanted to go away again early today.

Most hurriedly

Your Beethoven

The force of circumstances had made Karl sullen and angry. Schindler writes in the Conversation Book that once when he was admonished by his teachers at the Institute and reminded of his duty to his uncle he replied, "My uncle! I can do with him what I want, some flattery and friendly gestures make things all right again right away." According to Holz, Karl said

---

[32] Holz. (TDR, v, 349, n. 2.)
[33] In the Conversation Book, Schindler writes of seeing Karl gambling in coffee-houses with coachmen and mere common people "with whom he often dealt with dishonorably in games." (TDR, v, 351, n. 2.)

that he could wrap his uncle around his finger. A note to Niemetz was sub-sequently found in which Karl writes: "I had to write you in such a great hurry from fear and worry of being discovered by the old fool."

In the last days of July, Beethoven was notified that Karl had disappeared and was intending to take his life. Evidently Karl had left the house leaving a hint of his purpose. Schlemmer learned of this, and from him Holz, who went to report to Beethoven. They both went to Schlemmer's house where Holz writes out:

I will fetch the police.

•〜•

Still he must be moved away from here. He certainly will not take the examination.

•〜•

Shall I have Schlemmer fetched?

Then Schlemmer reports:

The story in brief, since you have heard it already from Hr. Holz: I learned today that your nephew intended to shoot himself before next Sunday at the latest. As to the cause I learned only this much, that it was on account of his debts, but not completely, only in part was he admitting that they were the consequences of former sins.

•〜•

I looked to see if there were signs of preparations; I found in his chest a loaded pistol all right, together with bullets and powder. I tell you this so that you may act in this case as his father. The pistol is in my keeping.

•〜•

Be lenient with him or he will despair.

To the question of possible debts to him, Schlemmer answers: "I have been paid completely—up to the present month, but not yet for August."
Holz questions further, while looking through papers:

This is not his handwriting, yet everything is paid for till the end of July.

•〜•

There is still a great deal more to be learned.

Holz then went to the Institute to find Karl and returned to report:

He is not staying here.

•〜•

I could not detain him; he said he would come again to Schlemmer's, but he wanted to get his papers from a friend, meanwhile I talked with Reisser.

•〜•

I said that I could not wait more than a quarter of an hour.

Beethoven apparently rebuked him for letting his ward out of his sight. He answers:

He would have run away from you just the same.

.~.

I think that if he has made up his mind to injure himself, no one can prevent him.

.~.

He has till September 3 to make up his examinations.

Holz evidently continued his search among Karl's papers: "Here is 30 x more for the rest of Schlemmer's board. He [Karl] said to me, 'What good will it do you to detain me? If I do not escape today, I will at another time.'"

Subsequently Schlemmer writes:

I will unload the gun. My wife has the second pistol.

.~.

Because I was not at home when it was found.

A new suspicion now seized upon the mind of Beethoven. For some reason, though he may also have uttered it orally, he wrote it down in the book: "He will drown himself." Probably he did not want the bystanders to know his thoughts, and the fear was therefore committed to the written page for the instruction of Holz. What else was said at the same time we do not know, for the book here shows a mutilation; some pages are missing. Perhaps Schindler removed them in later years to save the integrity of his account; or they may have been torn out by Beethoven himself when, some weeks later, Holz advised him to look through his books against their possible demand for examination by the police magistrate; they might contain references to affairs which he did not want to bring into public discussion. The missing pages might have helped us in the chronology of the story, but the main facts are before us without them. It was resolved first to go to the house of Niemetz, who it was thought might be privy to Karl's intentions, and then if necessary, to call in the help of the police.

Meanwhile Karl, having given Holz the slip, went straight to a pawnbroker and pledged his watch. From Holz's subsequent account we know that this took place on a Saturday—i.e. July 29th. With the money he bought two new pistols, powder and balls. He did not dare go to his lodgings for the pistols which he had in readiness for the contemplated deed, and the new ones were therefore necessary. For him the circumstance proved fortunate. He drove out to Baden, and spent the night in writing letters. One was to his uncle, and this he enclosed in one to his friend Niemetz. The next morning, it being a Sunday, he climbed up to the ruins of Rauhenstein, in the lovely Helenenthal which his uncle loved so well, and there discharged both pistols toward his left temple. He was a bungler with firearms. The first bullet flew past harmlessly; the second ripped up the flesh and grazed the bone, but did not penetrate the skull. Holz said afterwards that, had he taken with him the pistols which he was obligated to leave at his lodgings, he would have been a dead man; their barrels were charged with powder and ball to above the middle. A teamster came upon him lying among the ruins and, no doubt at his request, carried him to his mother's house in the city.

It was there that Beethoven found him. And to his uncle's questions he answers:

It is done. Now, only a surgeon who can hold his tongue. Smetana, if he is here.

Do not plague me with reproaches and lamentations; it is past. Later all matters may be adjusted.

She has sent for a doctor, but he is not at home. Holz will soon bring another one.

Then Beethoven asks: "When did it happen?" and the mother writes the answer:

He has just come. The teamster carried him down from a rock in Baden and has just driven out to you. . . . I beg of you to tell the surgeon not to make a report or they will take him away from here at once, and we fear the worst.

There is a bullet in his head on the left side.

Smetana was the physician who had treated Karl when he was a boy at Giannatasio's school. Beethoven knew him as a friend. To him he writes:

Most honored Herr von Smetana,
    A great misfortune has happened, which Karl accidentally inflicted upon himself. I hope that he can still be saved, especially by you if you come quickly. Karl has a *bullet* in his head; how, you shall learn—But quick, for God's sake, quick.
                        Yours respectfully,
                                Beethoven
In order to give help quickly, it was necessary to take him to his mother's, where he now is. The address follows herewith.

Holz took this letter for delivery but, before he left, a surgeon named Dögl had been called in. Returning, Holz had a message from Smetana saying that Dögl was a capable practitioner and that in order not to compromise him he would not come unless Dögl desired to see him in consultation. Karl expressed himself as satisfied and the case was left for the time being in Dögl's hands.

Beethoven went home, but Holz remained some time longer. The matter had to be reported to the police and Holz thought it best to do this himself, as he wanted to be able to inform Beethoven what the consequences of the young man's act were likely to be in case of his recovery. He learned, and so reported, that there would be a severe reprimand and thereafter police surveillance. He also told Beethoven that, after he had left, Karl had said, "If only he would not show himself again," and "If he would only quit his reproaches!" He had also threatened to tear the bandage from the wound if another word were spoken to him about his uncle.

On August 7th,[34] the day being a Monday, the wounded youth, who by his act was in the hands of the law, was removed from his mother's house to the general hospital by the police authorities. If Beethoven was forced to leave the would-be suicide in the hands of his mother for an entire week it was most likely because the police authorities commanded it; he did not yield her a day after her son came out of the hospital.

Meanwhile Holz reported regularly on Karl's condition:

Four of the most skillful doctors come four times daily.

．～．

He is getting unfailing care.

．～．

As yet there is no fever, but if it should come, then there would be a dangerous crisis.

．～．

The Magistrate as a criminal court is now concerned with this.

Under the Austrian code an attempt at suicide was an offence against the Church and guilty persons were remanded to the care of priests who imparted religious instruction until a profession of conversion could be recorded.

The priest will be sent by the Magistrate, you need not concern yourself with this any more.

．～．

He will not be released until he has passed a complete examination in religious instruction and has been completely converted, so that there is no longer fear of a relapse.

．～．

In such cases the police treat the misguided one with the greatest possible forbearance in order not to arouse stubbornness.

．～．

But custody must not be as a punishment but as a means of security for himself.

[34] The date was obtained by Thayer from the records of the hospital on September 22, 1862. F. Helm, then Director of the hospital, certified to the fact of reception, treatment and discharge, but stated that no history of the case could be found in the records. (TK, III, 260, n. 1.)

The instruction was administered to Karl by a Redemptorist, and since the Liguorian penances were proverbially strict, Holz inspired the hope in Beethoven that Karl's secret would be discovered by the priest. "These Liguorians are like leeches," is one of his remarks to the composer while Karl was lying at the hospital.

Strenuous efforts were made by Beethoven through Holz and others to discover what direct cause had led the misguided young man to attempt to end his life. The inquiries made of him at the hospital during the weeks spent there brought scarcely more information from his lips than the first question asked by his mother. Schindler seems to have been persuaded that it was his failure to pass the examinations at the Institute; but this theory is not tenable. Aside from the fact that he had till September 3 to make up his neglected studies, he never himself advanced this as an excuse nor an explanation, but explicitly denied it. In the hospital he told Holz that it would have been easy for him to make himself fit to pass, but that, having made up his mind to do away with himself long before, he had not thought it worthwhile to continue his studies. "He said that he was tired of life," Holz reports to Beethoven, "because he saw in it something different from what you judiciously and righteously could approve." He also phrased it thus: "Weariness of imprisonment." To the examining police magistrate Karl said that his reason for shooting himself was that Beethoven "tormented him too much," and also "I grew worse because my uncle wanted me to be better." To Beethoven's question if Karl had railed against him, Schlemmer replied: "He did not rail, but he complained that he always had trouble." Holz's explanation many years after to Otto Jahn was that "Beethoven was rigorous to excess in his treatment and would not allow him the slightest extravagance." There is a memorandum in the Conversation Books which discloses that Beethoven received specific reports about his conduct, and noted them for reference: "One night in the Prater.—2 nights did not sleep at home." Beethoven stinted him in the matter of pocket-money, and the scores of reckonings in the Conversation Books show how close was the watch kept upon every kreutzer placed in his hands. So he had recourse to borrowing and no doubt, though the fact does not appear in the books, he went into debt at the places he frequented for pleasure. When he shot himself he had paid his lodging bill for the month but owed his tutor. In a Conversation Book there was talk of a sale of books, which did not belong to Karl but to his uncle. Since this constituted a penal offense, a bad conscience along with fear of punishment could have been providing further pressure before the catastrophe. Beethoven, in his efforts to find an explanation that was excusable on moral grounds, wanted to advance a cause of mental disturbance. In his hand appears a note in a Conversation Book: "Mental aberration and insanity; the heat too—afflicted with headaches since childhood."

Stephan von Breuning's son, Gerhard, has described the shattering effect of this attempted suicide upon Beethoven.[35] "The pain which he received from this event was indescribable; he was cast down as a father who has lost his much-loved son. My mother met him on the Glacis completely undone. 'Do you know what has happened? My Karl has shot himself!' 'And—is he dead?' 'No, it was a glancing shot, he is still living, there's hope that he can be saved;—but the disgrace that he has brought upon me; and I loved him so.'" Evidently Gerhard was sent to the master soon after, for he writes in a Conversation Book: "You must come to us for all your meals so that you will not be alone."

The occurrence was soon noised about the city and much sympathy was expressed for Beethoven, as Holz took occasion to inform him. He told him of an invitation from Schuppanzigh, who was delighted when he received Beethoven's acceptance. Holz writes: "He has also invited Wolfmeyer [*sic*] who is overjoyed to be able to see you once again; but My Lord[36] asks that you accept this invitation not for Sunday but for Monday since Wolfmayer is prevented on Sunday from appearing anywhere. Wolfmayer will bring the drinks."

Schindler wrote[37] that the blow bowed the proud figure of the composer, and that he soon looked like a man of seventy. To add to his suffering he was compelled to learn that many persons placed part of the blame for the rash act upon him.

The surgical section in which Karl was placed in the hospital was under the care of a Dr. Gassner, whose assistant, Dr. Seng, had supervision over Karl. He related the following subsequently to Gerhard von Breuning:[38] "In the late summer of 1826 there came to me one day during my inspection a man in a gray coat whom at first glance I took to be a simple peasant. He asked me in a dull voice, 'Are you Assistant Doctor Seng? I was referred to you in the reception office? Is my nephew with you, the dissolute fellow, the scoundrel,' etc. After learning the name of the patient, I answered in the affirmative and told him that he was lying in a room in the three-florin ward, was bandaged for gunshot wound, and asked if I could direct him to him. Whereupon he said, 'I am Beethoven.' And, while I led him to him, he spoke further, 'I did not really want to visit him for he does not deserve it, he has given me too much vexation, but . . .' and then he continued to talk about his nephew's conduct and how he was altogether too spoiled, etc.—But I was astonished to have these things expressed to me by the great Beethoven, and I promised him that I intended to give his nephew the best possible care."

There was no delay in discussing plans for the future of the boy. In fact, prompt decision was necessary, for it was the penal aspects of the case

---

[35] *Aus dem Schwarzspanierhause*, p. 78. (TDR, v, 360.)

[36] Schuppanzigh.

[37] *Biogr.*, II, p. 127. (TDR, v, 360, n. 1.)

[38] *Aus dem Schwarzspanierhause*, p. 79 (TDR, v, 361, n. 1.)

which held the greatest terrors for Beethoven. Shortly after Karl had been put into the hospital, Holz writes:

Here you see ingratitude as clear as the sun; why do you want further to restrain him. Once with the military, he will be under the strictest discipline, and if you want to do anything more for him you need only make him a small allowance monthly. A soldier at once.

•‿•

Do you still doubt? This is a marvelous document.

It seems likely that this last remark may have been called out by the letter written by the nephew on the eve of his attempt—a letter which has never been found.

Holz also urged him to give up the guardianship. He pointed out that it would be the Magistrate's responsibility to find a replacement and that Beethoven, relieved of his duties, would be free to decide what more, if anything, he would want to do for the boy. He reported: "It is not hatred of you which he feels, but something entirely different." After reminding Beethoven of the sacrifices he had made, Holz writes: "If your good nature had not so often got the better of your firmness you would have driven him away long ago."

As court councillor in the war department, Stephan von Breuning's opinion had especial weight. "A military life will be the best discipline for one who cannot endure freedom; and it will teach him how to live on little," is one of Breuning's first utterances. As we shall see, this opinion, shared by Schindler and Holz, prevailed. As for the guardianship, Dr. Bach joined these three in advising Beethoven to relinquish it, but there was no immediate change as Karl's cure took its course.

To return to other matters, in July, 1826, Schott was ready with the Ninth Symphony, but in a letter of July 26 Beethoven asked him to delay the despatch of the printed score to the King of Prussia, to whom it was dedicated, until he had had the opportunity to send the monarch a manuscript copy, which, he said, would have no value after the publication. The question of who should receive this dedication had been under consideration since April, 1823, when Beethoven had written to Ferdinand Ries promising him the dedication. A year later, in a Conversation Book, Ries was still a candidate along with the Kings of France and Prussia and Emperor Alexander of Russia. The latter died on December 1, 1825; in a letter to Schott, dated January 28, 1826, Beethoven indicated that he was to have received the dedication but that now new arrangements were to be made.

When Beethoven finally decided that the symphony should be dedicated to the King of Prussia, he obtained permission from Prince Hatzfield, the Prussian Ambassador, to do so. On March 28 Beethoven informed Schott that on that very day he had received word from the Ambassador of His

Royal Majesty's acceptance.[39] >— At the end of September the presentation copy was ready; Beethoven wrote the title-page, and the score was handsomely bound by Steiner and Co.[40] It was placed in the hands of Dr. Spicker, the King's librarian, with the following letter:

Your Majesty:

It is a piece of great good fortune in my life that Your Majesty has graciously allowed me to dedicate the present work to you.

Your Majesty is not only the father of your subjects but also protector of the arts and sciences; how much more, therefore must I rejoice in your gracious permission since I am also so fortunate as to count myself a citizen of Bonn and therefore one of your subjects.

I beg of Your Majesty graciously to accept this work as a slight token of the high reverence which I give to all your virtues.

Your Majesty's
Most obedient servant
Ludwig van Beethoven

The King's acknowledgement was as follows:

In view of the recognized worth of your compositions it was very agreeable for me to receive the new work which you have sent me. I thank you for sending it and hand you the accompanying diamond ring as a token of my sincere appreciation.

Berlin, November 25, 1826.   Friedrich Wilhelm
To the composer Ludwig van Beethoven

Schindler says that when the case containing the King's gift was opened it was found to contain, not a diamond ring as the letter had described it, but one set with a stone of a "reddish" hue, which the court jeweler to whom it was shown appraised at 300 florins, paper money. Beethoven was very indignant and was with difficulty dissuaded from sending it back to the Prussian Ambassador; eventually he sold it to the jeweler at the value which he had set upon it. Whether or not the ring was the one really sent from Berlin or one which had been substituted for it (as was suspected in some quarters) has never been determined.

After Karl's attempt to end his life, with its crushing effect upon the composer, the friends, Holz in particular, made many efforts to divert Beethoven's mind from his disappointment and grief. They accompanied him on brief excursions into the country which he loved so passionately and which had been closed to him, for the customary happy seasons, by his nephew's act. Again did his brother offer him a haven at Gneixendorf in August, only to receive the curt answer: "I will not come. Your brother?????!!!! Ludwig."

Meanwhile Beethoven was far from idle. He had begun a new quartet, in F major, and Schlesinger, *père*, who had come from Berlin, negotiated with him for its publication. He had the new finale for the B-flat Quartet on his

---

[39] See *A* 1472.
[40] See *A* 1526 for his humorous instructions to Haslinger regarding this matter.

mind and, as will appear later, several other works occupied him. With Schlesinger he talked about the Complete Edition and some military marches which the King of Prussia was to pay for, as they were to be written for the Royal Band.

Meanwhile a recurring subject of conversation during the summer was the question of Karl's future. As has been mentioned, Breuning, Holz and Schindler favored placing him in the army, while Dr. Bach urged that he be sent off at once to some business house in Trieste, Milan or Hamburg.

In a discussion with his uncle in the hospital Karl writes:

My present condition is still such that I would ask you to make as little mention as possible of what has happened and cannot be altered. If my wish concerning a military career can be fulfilled I will be very happy, in any case I consider it the thing in which I could live and be satisfied. So I ask you to employ the means you think best and above all to see to it after my recovery that I get away from here as soon as possible.

•◥•

With the reminder that I chose this career out of desperation, I am asking you not to be hindered from taking the necessary measures; I am sufficiently composed to be able to reflect calmly and my desire for *this* object will always remain the same.

•◥•

As a cadet in the regiment I could also hope for promotion soon.

•◥•

The same way in which so many have gone.

There was also the immediate question of where Karl would go when he first left the hospital. During the investigation by the court, Holz kept Beethoven informed about all the proceedings and discussions with the counsel in charge. He reported that while Beethoven's management of the affair would be respected fully, the question of where young Beethoven should stay in the future could present difficulties. There was the possibility that he would wish to be with his mother, which the court viewed as a natural response to instinct. At one point Beethoven, after considering the possible measures that might be taken by the court and the police, writes: "My only intent was that he improve; if he is abandoned now, something terrible could still happen."

Beethoven was unalterably opposed to the nephew's being with the mother for even a day. In an interview with Karl he brought the subject up and began to berate her as usual, but the young man interrupted him:

I do not want to hear anything that is derogatory to her; it is not for me to be her judge. If I were to spend the little time I shall be here with her, it would be only a small return for all that she has suffered on my account. Nothing can be said about a harmful influence on me even if it should happen, if for no other reason than the shortness of the time.

•❧•

In no event shall I treat her with greater coldness than has been the case heretofore, whatever may be said on the subject.

He repeated his desire for the new career and his wish to leave Vienna as soon as possible. He made clear that his mother would offer no objection to the military career: "All the less, therefore, can I deny her wish to be with me during these days, as I shall in all likelihood not be here again soon. It is self-evident that this will not prevent you and me from seeing each other as often as you wish."

Very reluctantly Beethoven gave his consent that his nephew should become a soldier. But he spilled out his feelings to Holz, who was in Baden, in a letter of September 9, reiterating his dislike of the army as a career. His first thought was to send Karl to a military institute and have him graduated as an officer. This proved impracticable. Meanwhile Breuning, in pursuance of his own plan, consulted Baron von Stutterheim and persuaded him to give the young man a cadetship in his regiment. Having carried the day with his plan, Breuning agreed to accept the guardianship, which had been laid down by Reisser. Beethoven now set down his terms for the cadetship in a pencilled note which, though lacking an address, was undoubtedly for Breuning: "I believe that there are three points to be observed with Karl. First, he is not to be treated as a culprit, which would have exactly the opposite result from what we want; second, in order to become promoted to a higher rank, one cannot live too modestly and meanly; third, too great a limitation on his eating and drinking might have a harsh effect upon him. I am not trying to obstruct you."

Now the plans for this disposition were made. He was to be presented to von Stutterheim as soon as he was discharged from the hospital, take the oath of service the next day, and leave Vienna for Iglau, where von Stutterheim's regiment was stationed, within five or six days. Breuning, as guardian, now found himself confronted by a serious embarrassment. Where should the young man be sent while the preparations for his entry into the military service were being made? Karl did not want to go to his uncle's, nor did von Breuning want to send him there, and he frankly tells Beethoven the reason: "If he were here you would talk to him too much and that would cause new irritation; for he testified in the police court that the reason why he had taken the step was because you harassed him too much."

Beethoven, on the other hand, was still fearful that the magistrate might allow him to go to his mother's, and to guard against this he wrote two letters to that official, a man kindly disposed to him, whose name was Czapka. These letters follow:

1.

Sir!

I earnestly beg of you, since my nephew will be well in a few days, to direct that he be not permitted to leave the hospital with anybody but *myself and Hr. von Holz*. It must not possibly be allowed that he be near his mother, that utterly depraved person. My solicitude and my request are justified by her bad and wickedly malicious character, the belief that she often tempted Karl to lure money from me, the probability that she divided sums with him and was also in the confidence of Karl's dissolute companion, the notice which she attracts with her illegitimate daughter, *the father of whom is still being sought*, and the likelihood that at his m[other]'s home he would make the acquaintance of women who are anything but virtuous. Even the habit of being in the company of such a person cannot possibly lead a young man to virtue—While I recommend this concern to you, I meanwhile send you my best greetings, and only want to point out that, although this has been a very painful affair, I am very glad to have made the acquaintance of a man of such excellent intellect.

With sincere respect to your honor,

Your obedient servant Beethoven

2.

Sir!

Hofrat von Breuning and I have given mature consideration to what is to be done and have found that at this point it is inevitable that Karl spend a few days with me (while waiting here to leave for the army). His talk is caused by emotions resulting from the impression made on him by my reprimands when he had the idea of making an end to his life. However, after this period he showed himself to be still affectionate towards me. I assure you that for me mankind even in misfortune will always remain sacred. A warning from you would be very effective, also it would not hurt to give him to understand that he will be watched unseen while he is with me—

Please accept my very sincerest regards to you and consider me a warm friend, who wants to do good whenever possible.

Sincerely Beethoven

Late in September Beethoven's brother was again in Vienna. He repeated his offer to give the composer a temporary home and his nephew a harbor of refuge at Gneixendorf. This time Beethoven accepted. Karl was discharged from the hospital on September 25. Johann urged haste both on account of his business affairs and on account of Karl's status. But three days were needed to dispose of the business of finishing the corrections in the manuscript copy of the Ninth Symphony for the King of Prussia, and complete other correspondence. Thus it was on September 28 that Beethoven and his nephew set off for Gneixendorf with Johann for what was supposed to be a visit of a week. A night was passed at a village en route, and Johann's estate was reached in the afternoon of the next day—the 29th—but not too late for the composer to walk through the fields with his brother to take a look at the property. The next day the walk was extended to the vineyards on the hill in the forenoon and to Imbach in the afternoon. There Karl pointed out to his uncle some historical monuments: "This is the cloister where Marga-rethe, Ottokar's wife, died; the scene occurs in Grillparzer's piece." Thus, with other excursions the next day, life at Gneixendorf began.

Gneixendorf was a little village on a high plateau of the Danube valley about an hour's walk from Krems. It was a mean hamlet, with only one street and that narrow, rough and dirty. The houses were low huts. Wasser-hof, the Beethoven estate, lay opposite the village, and was reached by a wagon road which ran a large part of the way along the edge of a ravine, which had been made by torrents cutting into the clay soil. The plateau was almost treeless but covered with fields and vines. There were two houses on the estate, both large and handsome, each with its garden and surround-ing wall, and separated from each other by a road. Beethoven's rooms were on the east side of the house, which was a strongly built two-story stone and mortar structure, and, unless the surrounding trees interfered, had a magnificent view of the Danube valley stretching to the distant Styrian mountains.[41] Johann van Beethoven's possessions compassed nearly 400 acres, most of which he leased to tenants. A lover of hills and forests like Beet-hoven must have found the flat expanses of Wasserhof dreary and monoto-nous in the extreme, yet the distant view of the Danube seems to have com-pensated him in a measure, for in a letter to Schott, dated October 13, he writes: "The scenes among which I am sojourning remind me somewhat of the Rhine country which I so greatly long to see again, having left them in my youth."

Johann had made repeated efforts to persuade his brother to come to Gneixendorf ever since he had acquired the estate in 1819. In 1823 Beethoven wrote: "He always wants me to come to his people—*non possibile per me.*" The obstacle was Johann's wife, about whose behavior, it will be remem-bered, Beethoven had become very concerned in 1823. Urged on by Ludwig, Johann had made himself master of his household, for he wrote in a Con-versation Book of 1824: "My wife has surrendered her marriage contract and entered into an obligation permitting me to drive her away without notice at the first new acquaintance which she makes." Beethoven perhaps suggested that he do this very thing, for Johann continued: "I cannot do that. I cannot know but that some misfortune might befall me." Then Karl: "Your brother proposes that you spend the four months at his place. You would have four or five rooms, very beautiful, high and large. Everything is well arranged; you will find fowl, oxen, cows, hares etc. Moreover, as regards the wife, she is looked upon as a housekeeper only and will not disturb you. . . . You will scarcely see the woman. She looks after the house-keeping and works."

Beethoven was sick when he went to Gneixendorf. He had not recovered from his illness of the early months of the year when Karl attempted to kill himself, and this was not calculated to improve the physical or mental condi-

[41] The description is based on that made by Thayer when he visited Gneixendorf in 1860. (TK, III, 239, n. 1.)

tion of so nervous and irritable a being as he. He had never been a comfortable or considerate guest or tenant at the best, and his adaptability to circumstances was certainly not promoted by the repugnance which he felt towards his sister-in-law and his want of honest affection for his brother.

Concerning his life in Gneixendorf, a number of interesting details were told in an article entitled "Beethoven in Gneixendorf," published in the *Deutsche Musikzeitung* in 1862,[42] some of which are worth reciting again. One day Johann went to Langenfeld and Beethoven and other people from Gneixendorf went with him. The purpose was to visit a surgeon named Karrer, a friend of the brother. The surgeon was absent on a sick-call, but his wife, flattered by a visit from the landowner, entertained him lavishly. Noticing a man who held himself aloof from the company, sitting silently on the bench behind the stove, and taking him for one of her guest's servants, she filled a little jug with native wine and handed it to him with the remark: "He shall also have a drink." When the surgeon returned home late at night and heard an account of the incident he exclaimed: "My dear wife, what have you done? The greatest composer of the century was in our house to-day and you treated him with such disrespect!"

Johann had occasion to visit the syndic Sterz in Langenlois on a matter of business. Beethoven accompanied him. The conference lasted a considerable time, during all of which Beethoven stood motionless at the door of the official's office. At the leave-taking Sterz bowed often and low to the stranger, and after he was gone asked his clerk, named Fux, an enthusiastic lover of music, especially of Beethoven's; "Who do you think the man was who stood by the door?" Fux replied: "Considering that you, Mr. Syndic, treated him with such politeness, his may be an exceptional case; otherwise I should take him for an imbecile (*Trottel*)." The consternation of the clerk may be imagined when told the name of the man whom he had taken for an idiot.

Johann's wife had assigned Michael Krenn, son of one of her husband's vinedressers, to look after Beethoven's wants. At first the cook had to make up Beethoven's bed. One day, while the woman was thus occupied, Beethoven sat at a table gesticulating with his hands, beating time with his feet, muttering and singing. The woman burst into a laugh, which Beethoven observed. He drove her out of the room instanter. Krenn tried to follow her, but Beethoven drew him back, gave him three 20-kreutzer pieces, told him not to be afraid, and said that hereafter he should make the bed and clean the floor every day. Krenn said that he was told to come to the room early, but generally had to knock a long time before Beethoven opened the door. It was Beethoven's custom to get up at half-past 5 o'clock, seat himself at a table and write while he beat time with hands and feet and sang. This frequently stirred Krenn's risibles, and when he could no longer restrain his laughter he used to leave the room. Gradually he grew accustomed to it.

[42] Pages 77ff. The article was based largely on information gathered by Mr. Thayer at Gneixendorf in 1860 and had been submitted to him for revision. (TK, III, 241, n. 1.)

The family breakfast was eaten at half-past 7 o'clock, after which Beethoven hurried out into the open air, rambled across the fields shouting and waving his arms, sometimes walking very rapidly, sometimes very slowly and stopping at times to write in a sort of pocketbook. This book he once lost and said: "Michael, run about and hunt my writings; I must have them again at any cost." Michael luckily found them. At half-past 12 Beethoven would come home for dinner, after which he went to his room until about 3 o'clock; then he roamed over the fields until shortly before sunset, after which he never went out of doors. Supper was at half-past 7, and after eating he went to his room, wrote till 10 o'clock and then went to bed. Occasionally Beethoven played the pianoforte, which did not stand in his room but in the salon. Nobody was permitted to enter his rooms except Michael, who had to put them in order while Beethoven was out walking. In doing so he several times found money on the floor, and when he carried it to its owner, Beethoven made him show him where he had picked it up and then gave it to him. This happened three or four times, after which no more money was found. In the evening Michael had to sit with Beethoven and write down answers to questions which he asked. Generally Beethoven wanted to know what had been said about him at dinner and supper.

One day the wife of the landowner sent Michael to Stein with 5 florins to buy wine and a fish; but Michael was careless and lost the money. He came back to Gneixendorf in consternation. As soon as Frau van Beethoven saw him she asked for the fish, and when he told her of the loss she discharged him from her service. When Beethoven came into dinner he asked at once for his servant and the lady told him what had happened. Beethoven grew fearfully excited, gave her 5 florins, and angrily demanded that Michael be called back at once. After that he never went to table any more but had his dinner and supper brought to his rooms, where Michael had to prepare breakfast for him. Even before this occurrence Beethoven scarcely ever spoke to his sister-in-law and seldom to his brother. Beethoven would have liked to have taken Michael with him to Vienna.

Two old peasants told the owner of Wasserhof in 1862 stories which confirm Krenn's account of Beethoven's unusual behavior in the fields. Because of his unaccountable actions they at first took him for a madman and kept out of his way. When they had become accustomed to his singularities and learned that he was a brother of the landlord they used to greet him politely; but he, always lost in thought, seldom if ever returned their greetings. One of these peasants, a young man at the time, had an adventure with Beethoven of a most comical nature. He was driving a pair of young oxen, scarcely broken to the yoke, from the tile-kiln toward the manor-house when he met Beethoven shouting and waving his arms about in wild gesticulations. The peasant called to him: *A bissel stada!* ("A little quieter") but he paid no attention to the request. The oxen took fright, ran down a steep hill and the peasant had great difficulty in bringing them to a stand, turning them and getting them back on the road. Again Beethoven came towards them, still shouting and gesticulating. The yokel called to him a second time, but in vain; and now the oxen rushed towards the house, where they were stopped by one of the men employed there. When the driver came up and asked who the fool was who had scared his oxen the man told him it was the proprietor's brother. "A pretty brother, that he is!" was the answering comment.

The Quartet in F (Op. 135) was completed at Gneixendorf and was to be published by Moritz Schlesinger. ❧It will be recalled that in September, 1825, Schlesinger was hoping to receive two quartets, Op. 130 and 132, but was given only the latter. This had apparently caused a misunderstanding between them, which is clarified in a letter dated April 22, 1826.[43] Beethoven was hastening to answer a letter that Schlesinger had written him on April 13th, so that the rupture could be healed. He informed Schlesinger that "another new quartet will be finished in two or three weeks at the latest." This refers to Op. 135, about which Beethoven was already thinking. He asked for 80 gold ducats to be paid immediately. Then he explains, "I see from your letter that you misunderstood what I wrote, for I gave the quartet not to my brother but to Matthias Artaria." This of course refers to Op. 130.❧

When work began on the quartet cannot be determined precisely. In July Beethoven referred to the work to Holz, for the latter writes:

In what key?

⁓

But that will be the third in F. There is still none in D minor.

⁓

It is singular that there is none among Haydn's in A minor.

It is probable that the first sketches for the quartet and the canon "Muss es sein?" were written about the same time. But it cannot be determined whether or not the motif of the canon was destined from the first for the finale of the quartet. It may have been in Beethoven's mind for that purpose and the sudden inspiration on hearing the story of Dembscher's query "Muss es sein?" may have gone only to the words and the use of them with the music for the canon. That the quartet was to be shorter than the others was known before Beethoven left Vienna. Holz once said to Beethoven before the departure that Schlesinger had asked about the quartet and that he had replied that Beethoven was at work upon it and added "You will not punish him if it is short. Even if it should have only three movements it would still be a quartet by Beethoven, and it would not cost so much to print it."[44]

[43] See A 1481.

[44] Holz told Jahn that Schlesinger had bought it for 80 ducats and sent 360 florins in payment; whereupon Beethoven had said: "If a Jew sends circumcised ducats he shall have a circumcised quartet. That's the reason why it is so short." (TK, III, 245, n. 1.)

—◦❧{In a letter to the Paris publisher at this time Beethoven mentioned the difficulty he had had in completing the quartet, expressed by the motto "Es muss sein" etc., and lamented that for lack of a copyist he had had to write out the parts himself.[45] The date of the autograph is October 30, 1826. On this day his brother took the music to Vienna.}❧◦—

On October 13 the composer wrote a merry letter to Haslinger, addressed in music as "First of all Tobiasses,"[46] announcing that the quartet was finished. He wanted his help in delivering it to Schlesinger's agent, Tendler and Manstein, and in finding a way to persuade Schlesinger to pay him in gold as the other publishers did. On the same day he also wrote to Schott and Sons enclosing the metronome marks for the Ninth Symphony, which the Conversation Book shows had been dictated to Karl before the departure from Vienna.

The new finale for the Quartet in B-flat was also completed in Gneixendorf, though it, too, had been worked out almost to a conclusion in Vienna. It was delivered by Haslinger on November 25 to Artaria, who gave him 15 ducats for it. Schuppanzigh gave it a private performance in December and told Beethoven that the company thought it exquisite (*köstlich*) and that Artaria was overjoyed when he heard it.

—◦❧{In September, 1824, Beethoven wrote two different letters to Diabelli concerning the completion of a quintet. In the one he promised the quintet in a little over six weeks for 100 gold ducats; in the other he promised a flute quintet.[47] Nothing more is known of a quintet at the time. But in November, 1826, according to Nottebohm, there were sketches for the first movement of a string quintet in C major on a page originally to be used for the new finale of Op. 130. There were also sketches for other movements.[48] In the catalogue of Beethoven's posthumous effects No. 173 was "Fragment of a new Violin Quintet of November, 1826, last work of the composer."[49] Diabelli's firm bought the 24-measure fragment and published it in pianoforte arrangement, two and four hands, with the title "Ludwig van Beethoven's last Musical Thought, after the original manuscript of November, 1826," and the remark "Sketch of the Quintet which the publishers, A. Diabelli and Co., commissioned Beethoven to write and purchased from his relics with proprietary rights." This last suggests that the fragment was connected with the correspondence of 1824 although there are no signs of a flute.}❧◦— The published work is a short movement in two divisions, having a broad theme of a festal character, Andante maestoso and a polonaise rhythm.

—◦❧{The compositions for the year 1826 may be divided into big works and trifles or fragments.

45 See *A* 1538, 1538ª.
46 WoO 205ᵏ.
47 See *A* 1310, 1313.
48 See *Beeth.*, pp. 79ff., and *II Beeth.*, p. 522. Holz told Jahn that the first movement

of a quintet in C for strings, which Diabelli had bought for 100 ducats, was finished in the composer's head and the first page written out. (TDR, v, 407, also n. 1.)
49 WoO 62, KHV, p. 508.

Big works:

1825-6. Quartet for Strings in C-sharp minor, Op. 131, completed in July.

1826. Arrangement of the Great Fugue (Op. 133) for Pianoforte, four hands, Op. 134.

Quartet for Strings in F major, Op. 135, completed in October.

New Final Movement to the Quartet for Strings in B-flat major, Op. 130.

Trifles and fragments:

Beginning of a Quintet for strings in C major, WoO 62.

Canons:

"Da ist das Werk," WoO 197, to Holz in the beginning of September.

"Es muss sein," WoO 196, for Ignaz Dembscher, in April.

"Signor Abate," WoO 178, probably for Abt. Maximilian Stadler.

"Wir irren allesamt," WoO 198, for Karl Holz in early December.

The works that were published during the year were:

By Schott:

Quartet for Strings in E-flat major, Op. 127, dedicated to Prince Nikolas Galitzin (string parts in March, score in June).

Symphony No. 9 in D minor, Op. 125 ("Sinfonie mit Schluss-Chor über Schillers Ode: 'An die Freude' für grosses Orchester, 4 Solo- und 4 Chor-stimmen"), dedicated to King Friedrich Wilhelm III of Prussia (both in score and in parts in August).

By Steiner:

"Tremate, empi tremate" for Soprano, Tenor, Bass and Orchestra (Bettoni), Op. 116, in February.

March with Chorus from the *Ruinen von Athen*, Op. 114, in April.

Overture to *König Stephan*, Op. 117, in July.

By Haslinger, who took over the Steiner firm:

Elegischer Gesang, for Four Voices and String Quartet, Op. 118, dedicated to Baron Johann von Pasqualati, in July.

CHAPTER XL

DECEMBER, 1826–1827

THE RETURN FROM GNEIXENDORF TO VIENNA— THE FINAL ILLNESS—DEATH AND BURIAL

THE Conversation Books add nothing to the picturesque side of the account of Beethoven's sojourn in Gneixendorf as it has been drawn from other sources. They indicate that there were some days of peace and tranquility, and that not only Johann, but his wife and nephew also, were concerned with making the composer comfortable and providing him with such diversion as place and opportunity afforded. Several times there was mention of trips in the carriage, such as to nearby Krems where there was some sort of city life; yet travel was not always possible, as was mentioned once, because the carriage was in need of repair. Johann had business which took him occasionally to Vienna. According to Karl he had two years left to pay for his estate. Beethoven was supplied with writing materials from Krems by his nephew, who also found there the opportunity to play billiards. Johann met Holz and Linke in Vienna; the latter was anxious to have the new finale for the B-flat Quartet for an *Akademie*. The money for this movement was in the hands of the baker, Leopold Obermayr, brother of Johann's wife, Therese. Beethoven accepted Therese's offer to go to Vienna and bring the money back to him.

Karl did not neglect his piano-playing; he had brought along four-hand Marches by Lannoy to play with his uncle. "Karl plays very well" writes Therese at one point. But there were also strong scenes between uncle and nephew as could be expected. Karl had to hear frequent reproaches and in conversations was put on the defensive. For example:

You ask me why I do not talk.

Because I have had enough.

Yours is the right to command, and I must endure it all.

•〜•

I can only regret that I can give no answer to anything you have said today, since I know of nothing better to do than to listen and to remain silent as is my duty. You must not consider this insolent.

There was little mention of Beethoven's illness. Johann stressed the improvement of his eyes and attributed it to the good air on his estate. According to Gerhard von Breuning,[1] Stephan had been worried, after receiving a letter early in Beethoven's stay at Gneixendorf, that Beethoven was in danger of becoming very ill, possibly dropsical. Referring to an earlier time, Johann writes: "Because of poorly prepared food he would eat nothing at lunch except soft-boiled eggs, but then he would drink more wine so that he often suffered diarrhoea; thereby his belly became bigger and bigger, and he wore a bandage over it for a long time." In the beginning of December he lost his appetite and complained of thirst and abdominal complaints. There had been mention of "edematous" feet. These were clear manifestations of an existing liver disease.

In this condition, it can be imagined how sensitive he became to the increasingly cold weather in Gneixendorf, and how he must have longed for his customary way of living. But the Conversation Books do not make clear Beethoven's attitude on this score beyond occasional complaints about the food. Meanwhile Johann was becoming increasingly concerned about the effect of this life upon his nephew. To avoid an argument with his brother, he wrote him a letter on the subject near the end of November:

My dear Brother:
I can not possibly remain silent concerning the future fate of Karl. He is abandoning all activity and, grown accustomed to this life, the *longer* he lives as at present, the more difficult it will be to bring him back to work. At his departure *Breuning* gave him a fortnight in which to recuperate, and now it is two months.— You see from Breuning's letter that it is his decided wish that Karl *shall hasten* to his calling; the longer he is here the more unfortunate will it be *for him*, for the harder it will be for him to get to work, and it may be that we shall suffer harm.
It is an infinite pity that this talented young man so wastes his time; and on whom if not *us both* will the blame be laid? For he is still too young to direct his own course; for which reason it is your duty, if you do not wish to be reproached by yourself and others hereafter, to put him to work at his profession as soon as possible. Once he is occupied it will be easy to do much for him now and in the future; but under present conditions nothing can be done.
I see from his actions that he would like to remain with us, but if he did so it would be all over with his future, and therefore *this* is *impossible*. The longer we hesitate the more difficult will it be for him to go away; I therefore adjure you— make up your mind, do not permit yourself to be dissuaded by Karl. I think it ought to be *by next Monday*, for in no event can you wait for me, inasmuch as I

---

[1] *Aus dem Schwarzspanierhause*, p. 84. (TDR, v, 410, n. 2.)

cannot go away from here without *money*, and it will be a long time before I collect enough to enable me to go to Vienna.

On the back is written in pencil, perhaps after some conversation:

Let us leave this until the day you go.

⸱◟⸱

An old woman.

⸱◟⸱

She has her share and will get no more.

According to Schindler,[2] Ludwig took his brother's suggestions with bad grace; and before his departure from Gneixendorf there was an exceedingly acrimonious quarrel between the brothers, growing out of Ludwig's demand that Johann make a will in favor of Karl, thus cutting off his wife.[3]

The question of returning to Vienna was now discussed with Karl, whose attitude is shown by the following entry:

I cannot argue against it since we have been here longer than was planned; but *Breuning* himself has said that I cannot go to the Field-Marshal until I am able to appear without any visible sign left of what happened to me, because he wants to overlook the whole affair. This is almost accomplished now except for a little bit which really won't take much more time; therefore I believe that we should stay until next week at least. If I had pomade here then it would be unnecessary. Besides, the longer we remain here, the longer can we remain together, since once we are in Vienna, I naturally will have to leave right away." [The conversation turned to expenses, for Karl writes]: "As regards expenses, wood is so cheap that it is inconceivable that your brother should be at any considerable cost, for you can heat a long time with a cord and he is already overpaid."

Johann's recorded statements vary concerning the financial arrangements with his brother. Once in a Conversation Book he says: "You do not need money here"; and further on: "If you want to live with us you can have everything for 40 florins C.M. a month, which makes 500 f. for a whole year"; and again: "You will need only half of your pension." In another place he writes:

You can be here for 8 months, from March to November, then you will not need such large quarters, and in spring and summer it is much prettier here.

⸱◟⸱

I will charge nothing for the first fortnight; I would do more if I were not so hard pressed with taxes.

Karl's remarks show that at this time Beethoven was paying for his room. Inasmuch as some of Johann's offers to his brother were made immediately

---

[2] In a note attached to the letter. (See TDR, v, 412.)

[3] This happened naturally. Therese van Beethoven died on November 20, 1828 at Wasserhof; Johann died in Vienna on January 12, 1848. After costs, over 42,000 florins passed into his nephew's hands.

after this, it shows that Beethoven all along had been tempted by the possibility of a longer and perhaps permanent stay in Gneixendorf.

During this period of decision there was great strain between uncle and nephew. Beethoven asks:

What is the matter? Why are you hanging your head now? Isn't the truest devotion even with its shortcomings enough?

.∽.

The idea of going from here continues to pain you and I have also taken this into consideration.

Apparently this was followed by further strong reproaches, for Karl writes:

Did you see me speak a word? Hardly—for I was not disposed at all to speak, everything that you say about me needs no refutation. So I beg of you once and for all to leave me alone. If you want to go, good.

.∽.

If not, good again.

.∽.

But I beg of you once more not to torment me as you are doing; you might regret it, for I can endure much, but too much I cannot endure. You treated your brother in the same way today without cause. You must remember that other people are also human beings.

.∽.

These everlastingly unjust reproaches!

.∽.

Why do you make such a disturbance? Will you let me go out a bit today? I need recreation. I'll come again later.

I only want to go to my room.

.∽.

I am not going out, I want only to be alone for a little while.

.∽.

Will you not let me go to my room?

An entry by Therese suggests Beethoven's state of mind when Karl had been gone from the house: "Do not be concerned. He will certainly come home by 1 o'clock. It seems that he has some of your rash blood. I have not found him angry. It is you that he loves, to the point of veneration."

It must be assumed that the Monday referred to in Johann's letter was Monday, November 27; but several days must have elapsed between this date and the time when Beethoven and Karl set out on the fateful journey to Vienna. A determination seems to have been reached when the Conversation Book shows Johann as saying: "If you are to start on Monday the carriage must be ordered on Sunday." There is no recorded conversation touching the use of Johann's carriage, which, shortly before, had carried Johann's wife to Vienna, and which was to carry its owner there as soon as he could make a satisfactory adjustment of his financial affairs. That means of conveyance were discussed is proved by Johann's remark and also by a report made by Karl to the composer: "There is no postchaise to Vienna, but only to St. Pölten. . . . From here there is no opportunity except by a stagecoach."

Exactly how the travelers set out is not clear. In the first edition of his *Biographie*[4] Schindler writes: "This return journey, which that late in the year could not be made in one day, took place in an open carriage since, as Beethoven himself assured me, his brother denied him the use of his closed carriage." In the third edition he states that "his pseudo-brother denied him his closed town-carriage for the trip to nearby Krems, therefore he had to get there in an open calash."[5] Schindler was not at Gneixendorf; and his known antipathy to Johann makes the testimony the harder to evaluate.

Dr. Wawruch, Beethoven's attending physician during the illness which ended in his death, writes:[6] "Oppressed by the sad prospect of a gloomy future, being helpless in the case of sickness in the country, he longed to return to Vienna and used for his trip home the most wretched vehicle of the devil, a milkwagon, as he humorously put it."

Beethoven arrived in Vienna on Saturday, December 2, and as there is a reference to only one night spent in transit (as there had been one on the journey from Vienna to Gneixendorf), it is likely that he left Gneixendorf early in the morning of Friday, December 1. Dr. Wawruch continues: "That December was raw, damp, cold and frosty; Beethoven's clothing anything but adapted to the unfriendly season of the year, and yet he was urged on by an eternal unrest and a gloomy foreboding of misfortune. He was compelled to spend a night in a village tavern where, besides wretched shelter, he found an unwarmed room without winter shutters. Towards midnight he experienced his first fever-chill, a dry hacking cough accompanied by violent thirst and cutting pains in the sides. When seized with the fever he drank a few measures of ice-cold water and longed, helplessly, for the first rays of the morning light. Weak and ill, he permitted himself to be lifted into the *Leiterwagen* and arrived, at last, weak, exhausted and without strength, in Vienna." Wawruch derived his information from Beethoven, possibly in part also from Karl, the only witness from whom a succinct and absolutely correct account was to have been expected; unhappily the tale, which Karl must have been called upon to tell many times, was never reported.

It was Saturday, December 2, then, that Beethoven arrived in Vienna from Gneixendorf and went to his lodgings in the Schwarzspanierhaus. The first thing to be done was to get a doctor. According to Johann, Beethoven

---

[4] [1840], p. 179. (TDR, v, 415, n. 1.)
[5] [1860], II, p. 131. (TDR, v, 415, n. 1.)
[6] Dr. Wawruch wrote a history of Beethoven's illness entitled "Ärztlicher Rückblick

auf Ludwig van Beethovens letzte Lebensepoche" (dated May 20, 1827) which was first published by Aloys Fuchs in the *Wiener Zeitschrift*, April 30, 1842. (TDR, v, 419, n. 2.)

himself wrote to his old doctor, Braunhofer, who gave as his reason for not coming that the distance was too great.[7] Then Dr. Staudenheim was sent for; he promised to come but failed to do so. Then Dr. Wawruch of the General Hospital was called, and came directly. "I was not called until the third day," he writes in his report. It was apparently Holz who sent for him, and he did so on December 5, the day recorded by Karl in a Conversation Book as being the time of Wawruch's first visit. Evidently Holz had hastened to Beethoven upon receiving the following note:

Your official Majesty!

Immediately after my arrival, which occurred a few days ago, I wrote to you, but the letter was mislaid. Thereupon I became unwell so that I decided it would be better to stay in bed—Therefore I shall be very glad if you will come to see me. It will be less inconvenient for you now since everyone has come back from Döbling to the city—

Finally I will just add

Wir ir - ren al - le samt nur je - der ir - ret an - derst.
[We all err only each in a different way.]

As always your friend

Beethoven

The Conversation Book records the following in the handwriting of Holz:

I have had Professor Wawruch called for you; Vivenot[8] is himself sick. I do not know Wawruch personally, but he is known here as one of the most skilful physicians.

He is Bogner's doctor.

He is professor in the hospital.

He will come after dinner.

Wawruch came and introduced himself with the following words in a Conversation Book: "One who greatly reveres your name will do everything possible to give you speedy relief. Prof. Wawruch." Then in his presence the necessary questions to the patient were written out by Karl, including probably the question of the abdominal complaint.[9] Wawruch's report continues: "I found Beethoven afflicted with serious symptoms of inflammation of the lungs. His face glowed, he spat blood, his respiration threatened suffo-

---

[7] Walter Nohl suggests that the reason for Dr. Braunhofer's excuse was that his past experience with Beethoven helped him to diagnose that the patient was in the last stages of his illness and that he did not want to be the doctor in charge at the composer's death. See "Beethoven und sein Arzt Anton Braunhofer,"

DM, Vol. 30, No. 12 (1938), p. 828.

[8] Dominik Vivenot was a medical consultant in Vienna (see *A*, III, p. 1261, n. 2).

[9] According to TDR, v, 419, n. 1, certain pages at this point were removed, presumably by Schindler.

cation and a painful stitch in the side made lying on the back a torment. A severe counter-treatment for inflammation soon brought the desired relief; his constitution triumphed and by a lucky crisis he was freed from apparent mortal danger, so that on the fifth day he was able, in a sitting posture, to tell me, amid profound emotion, of the discomforts which he had suffered. On the seventh day he felt considerably better, so that he was able to get out of bed, walk about, read and write."

Andreas Wawruch was born in 1771 in Nemtschütz in Moravia. At Olmütz he was a student of theology, but before consecration to the priesthood he came to Vienna as tutor and there decided to abandon the church for medicine. In the course of time he became assistant and also son-in-law to Professor Hildebrand, the director of the General Hospital. Thence he went to Prague as professor of general pathology and pharmacology and, returning to Vienna, became professor of special pathology and medical clinics in the surgical department of the hospital. He was an amateur violoncello player and an ardent admirer of Beethoven's music. He died in 1842.

Wawruch's report thus far shows that Beethoven had weathered an attack of pneumonia. Before its continuation, account may be made of one or two letters.

Beethoven's old friends, Franz and Eleonore Wegeler, had written him almost a year ago, and now he finally answered. All three letters deserve to be given.[10] They begin the closing chapter to a friendship which, along with that of Stephan von Breuning, was one of the earliest and one of the most tender.

Coblenz, December 20, 1825

My dear old Louis!

I cannot have one of the 10 Ries children travel to Vienna without recalling memories of you. If you have not received a long letter every 2 months within the 28 years since I left Vienna, you may consider your silence on top of mine as the cause. This is not right at all, and all the less now when we older people want to live so much in the past and delight ourselves to the utmost with scenes of our youth. To me at least my acquaintance and childhood friendship with you, which was limited but blessed because of a good mother, is a very bright point in my life which I contemplate with pleasure and with which I become completely preoccupied when traveling. Now I look up to you as a hero and am proud to be able to say: I was not without influence on his development; he confided in me his wishes and dreams; and when later he was so frequently misunderstood, I knew well what he wanted. Thank God that I have been able to talk with my wife and now more recently with my children about you; yet the house of my mother-in-law was more your house than mine, especially after you lost your own noble mother. Just speak to us once again: yes, I think of you in your gay and in your dark moods! Is it that man is happy, even if he has such a great stature

[10] See Stephan Ley, *Beethoven als Freund der Familie Wegeler—v. Breuning* (Bonn, 1927), pp. 53-9. The editor is grateful to the publishers, H. Bouvier and Co., for granting permission for these translations.

as yours, still but one time in his life, namely in his youth; the rocks of Bonn, Kreuzberg, Godesberg, the Baumschul etc. have been a sounding board for you from which you have been able joyfully to shape many ideas.

Now I will tell you something about myself, about us in order to give you an example of how you must write me in reply.

After my return from Vienna in 1796, things went rather badly for me; for several years I had to live from my practice alone, and this lasted for some years in the poorest environment until I could support myself. Then I became a salaried professor and married in 1802. A year later I received a daughter, who is still living and who has married well. With much genuine intelligence she has the cheerfulness of her father and likes best to play Beethoven sonatas. This gift perhaps is not to her credit but simply hereditary. In the year 1807 a boy was born to me, who is now studying medicine in Berlin. Four years from now I will send him to Vienna, will you receive him? Concerning the family of your friend, my father died on Jan. 1, 1800 in his 70th year. Concerning that of my wife, the school-teacher died four years ago at the age of 72, and Aunt Stockhausen von der Ahr in the same year aged 73. Mama Breuning is 76, and our uncle in Kerpen 85 years old. The latter is still enjoying life and speaks often of you.— Mama and the aunt moved again to Cologne; they lived in the house of their parents, which they occupied again after 66 years, then had it newly built etc. I myself celebrated my 60th birthday in August in the company of some 60 friends and acquaintances, among whom were some of the foremost people of the town.— Since 1807 I have been living here, have a fine house now and a beautiful place. My superiors are satisfied with me and the King gave me decorations and medals. Lore and I are pretty well.

Now I have brought you up to date all at once with our situation; if you want to continue it, please write.—Of our acquaintances Court Councillor Stupp died three weeks ago, Fischenich is Councillor of State in Berlin; Ries and Simrock are two fine old men, but the latter is in much weaker health than the former.

Two years ago I was in Berlin for a month; there I made the acquaintance of the Director of the Singakademie, H. Zelter, a very genial man and extremely frank. The people there consider him uncivil. Hub. Ries in Cassel introduced me to Spohr. You see I am still in communication with artists.

Why haven't you avenged the honor of your mother when, in the Encyclopedia and in France, you were set down as a love-child? The Englishman who wished to vindicate you gave this slander a box in the ears, as we say in Bonn, and [showed that] your mother [would have had to] carry you for 30 years since the King of Prussia, your alleged father, had been dead since 1740.——Won't you ever stop seeing the Stephens steeple? Has traveling no attraction for you? Don't you ever want to see the Rhine again?—All the warmest regards from Frau Lore as well as myself.

Your ancient friend Wglr.

Enclosed was a note from Eleonore Wegeler:

For so long a time dear Beethoven!

It was my wish that Wegeler should write to you once again—now that this wish is fulfilled, I must still add a few words—not only to bring myself more vividly to your memory but to repeat the important question: do you have no

desire to see the Rhine and your birthplace once again?—You will be most welcome as our guest at any time and at any hour—and this would give Weg. and me the greatest joy—Our Lenchen is grateful to you for so many happy hours—listens so gladly to our stories about you—knows all the small details of our happy youth in Bonn—of the quarrels and reconciliations—How happy she would be were she able to see you! Unfortunately the girl has no musical talent but through great industry and perseverance she has progressed to the point where she can play your sonatas, variations and the like; and since music continues to be the greatest relaxation for Weg., she has given him many happy hours through this. Julius does have musical talent, but until now has neglected it—and just in the last half year he has been learning the violoncello with pleasure and delight—Since he has a good teacher in Berlin, I am confident that he will continue to learn—Both children are big and like their father—also with the gay, cheerful frame of mind which thank heaven Weg. still hasn't completely lost— —He gets great pleasure in playing the themes of your variations, the old ones are his favorites but he has been practising alot and with unbelievable patience on a new one—your Opferlied stands at the top—He never enters the living room without going to the piano—still, dear Beethoven! if you could see the way the lasting memory of you lives on with us—Just tell us once that it means something to you and that you haven't completely forgotten us—If it were not so difficult to satisfy our greatest desire, we would already have made a visit to our brother in Vienna which would certainly have included the pleasure of seeing you—But such a trip is not possible now since our son is in Berlin—Weg. has told you how things are with us—We would be wrong to complain—Even the most difficult period was easier for us than for 100 others—the greatest luck is that we are healthy and the children are good and well—Neither of them have ever given us any trouble and we are of good cheer—Lenchen has experienced just one great grief—that was when our poor little boy died—a loss which none of us will ever forget. Goodbye, dear Beethoven, and think of us with kind, friendly thoughts—
Eln. Wegeler

Beethoven's reply, a long time in coming, was dictated to Karl:

Vienna, 7th 10br.[11] 826
My old beloved friend!
I cannot convey the pleasure which the letters from you and your Lorchen gave me. Truly an answer should have followed with the speed of an arrow; but I am after all somewhat negligent as a writer because I think that the better people know me without it. I often form an answer in my head, yet when I want to write it down in most cases I throw the pen away because I am incapable of writing the way I feel. I remember all the love that you have constantly given me; for example how you had my room whitewashed and gave me such a pleasant surprise;—thus it was with the Breuning family. If we were separated one from another that was the force of circumstances; each had to follow the object of his goal and try to reach it; but the eternally firm and unshakeable principles of the

[11] Wegeler in his *Notizen* (p. 49) interpreted "10br." to mean October and subsequent editors agreed until Miss Anderson pointed out that this was an abbreviation of "December." See *A*, p. 1321, n. 3. This resolved satisfactorily one of the great puzzles of the year 1826.

good bind us together ever fast. Unfortunately I cannot write you today as much as I should like since I am bed-ridden and must limit myself to answering some points of your letter. You write that somewhere I am referred to as a natural son of the deceased King of Prussia; this was already mentioned to me a long time ago. But I have made it a principle never to write anything about myself nor to reply to anything written about me. Therefore I gladly leave it to you to make known to the world the honesty of my parents, and my mother in particular.— You write of your son. It goes without saying that if he should come here, he will find in me a friend and father; and whenever I am in a position to serve him or help him in anything, I shall do it with joy.

I still have the silhouette of your Lorchen from which I am reminded how dear to me still is everything good and lovely from my youth.

I will write briefly of my diplomas: I am an honorary member of the Royal Society of Sciences in Sweden, as well as in Amsterdam, and am also an Honorary Freeman of Vienna.— A short time ago a certain Dr. Spiker took my last big symphony with choruses to Berlin; it is dedicated to the King, and I had to write out the dedication in my own hand. Earlier I had sought permission from the Embassy to be allowed to dedicate the work to the King, which he then gave me. At Dr. Spiker's instigation I had to supply a corrected manuscript copy myself with the corrections in my own hand, the same to be delivered to the King since it is supposed to go to the Royal Library. Something has been said to me in this connection about the Order of the Red Eagle, Second Class.[12] What the outcome will be I do not know, for I have never sought for such marks of honor. But at my present age they could not be unwelcome for several reasons—After all I still live by the saying, Nulla dies sine linea; and if I let my muse sleep, it is so that she may reawaken with renewed strength. I hope still to bring some great works into the world and then as an old child end my earthly course somewhere amongst good men—You will soon receive some music through the Brothers Schott in Mainz—The portrait you will find enclosed is indeed an artistic masterpiece, yet it is not the latest one to be done of me.—Of the marks of honor which I know give you joy, I can report also that a medal was sent to me from the deceased King of France with the inscription: Donné par le Roi à Monsieur Beethoven; which was accompanied by a very courteous note from the Premier Gentilhomme du Roi, the Duc de Chartres—

My beloved friend! rest content now, for the memory of the past has taken hold of me; and not without many tears first will you be receiving this letter. The beginning has now been made and soon you will get another letter; and the more often you write me, the more pleasure you will give me. On account of our friendship no kinds of demands are needed, and so goodbye. I beg of you to embrace and kiss for me your dear Lorchen and your children and thereby think of me. God be with you all!

As ever your faithful friend who reveres you

Beethoven

A few days later Beethoven wrote to Schott and asked that the scores of the *Opferlied, Bundeslied*, the song "Bei Chloe war ich ganz allein," Op. 128 and the last bagatelles, Op. 126, be sent at his expense to Wegeler. A

---

[12] Third class is what is talked about in the Conversation Books. (TK, III, 244, n. 1.)

final exchange of letters between these old friends took place in February of the next year.

Dr. Wawruch visited Beethoven daily from December 5th to 14th and on one day he came twice. His report continues: "But on the eighth day I was alarmed not a little. At the morning visit I found him greatly disturbed and jaundiced all over his body. A frightful choleric attack (*Brechdurchfall*) had threatened his life in the preceding night. A violent rage, a great grief because of sustained ingratitude and undeserved humiliation, was the cause of this mighty explosion. Trembling and shivering he bent double because of the pains which raged in his liver and intestines, and his feet, thitherto moderately inflated, were tremendously swollen. From this time on dropsy developed, the segregation of urine became less, the liver showed plain indication of hard nodules, there was an increase of jaundice. Gentle entreaties from his friends quieted the threatening mental tempest, and the forgiving man forgot all the humiliation which had been put upon him. But the disease moved onward with gigantic strides. Already in the third week there came incidents of nocturnal suffocation; the enormous volume of collected water demanded speedy relief and I found myself compelled to advise tapping in order to guard against the danger of bursting."

At this point we may consider who was in attendance to the sick man. A servant, Thekla, who had apparently come from Gneixendorf (as her name appears in the Conversation Book used there) in the midst of the preparations for the operation was found to be dishonest and was eventually dismissed. There was, however, his reliable housekeeper Sali, who looked after his bodily needs. She is mentioned frequently by Gerhard von Breuning in his *Aus dem Schwarzspanierhause*, and had been found for Beethoven by Gerhard's mother over a year before. The composer's brother had arrived in Vienna about December 10 and thereafter was in regular attendance. As an apothecary he felt he could contribute to the decisions concerning the choice of food for his brother. The Conversation Books show that Karl was closely involved with Dr. Wawruch's care of the patient. In mid-December there are scattered entries in Karl's hand:[13]

The doctor has allowed rice-soup . . .

You may eat fruit.

Dr. Wawruch's visits: on the 5th of December one time, on the 6th of December 2 times, on the 7th-14th once per day.

[Later] The maid says that you have been drinking water at night, that will not do you any good.

[13] Stephan Ley, *Aus Beethovens Erdentagen* (Bonn, 1948), pp. 207-208.

During the enema you must hold your breath, otherwise it will run out. . . .

•~•

Take a breath.

•~•

Do not hold your breath, draw it in.

•~•

Hold it in hard, but longer.

•~•

Now hold on, then the enema will work.

Since Holz was now married, his visits were not as numerous, but he still found time to look after the correction and publication of the last compositions and to collect the composer's annuity. Schindler found his way back to the composer's side within a fortnight and seems, at least at first, to have been given more menial labors to carry out. Stephan von Breuning's visits were interrupted by illness and official labors, but his son, the thirteen-year-old Gerhard, frequently lent a gracious touch to the scene by his familiar mode of address, his gossip about his father's domestic affairs and his suggestions of intellectual pabulum for his august friend. He was a daily message-bearer between the two households and brought provisions such as soup from his family's kitchen. Other friends visited too, and from the city began to come expressions of sympathy.

After Dr. Wawruch had reached his decision, Dr. Staudenheim was called in consultation and he confirmed the attending physician's opinion as to the necessity of an operation. Beethoven was told; "after a few moments of serious thought he gave his consent." Wawruch had retained Dr. Seibert, principal surgeon (Primärwundarzt) at the hospital to perform the operation, which took place on December 20. Those present were Johann, Karl and Schindler. Beethoven's sense of humor did not desert him. When, the incision having been made, Dr. Seibert introduced the tube and the water spurted out, Beethoven said: "Professor, you remind me of Moses striking the rock with his staff." Wawruch writes in the Conversation Book:

Thank God it is happily over!

•~•

If you feel ill you must tell me.

•~•

Did the incision give you any pain?

•~•

From today the sun will continue to ascend higher.

•~•

God save you! [This in English]

•~•

Lukewarm almond milk.

•~•

Do you not now feel pain?

•~•

Continue to lie quietly on your side.

•~•

We shall soon measure off the water.

•~•

Five measures and a half.[14]

•~•

I hope that you will sleep more quietly tonight.

•~•

You bore yourself like a knight.

The operation made necessary renewed care and a close watch on the patient's diet. He was allowed to drink almond milk, but not in too great quantities, and also only a little coffee. During this period he had to remain in a near-lying position while it was being determined whether a second operation would be necessary.

One joyful event brightened the solitary gloom of the sick-chamber in the middle of December. From Johann Andreas Stumpff, of London, Beethoven received the 40 volumes of Dr. Arnold's edition of the works of Handel which the donor had resolved to send Beethoven on his visit in 1824. Gerhard von Breuning pictures the joy of Beethoven at the reception of the gift, which he described as royal compared with that of the King of Prussia.[15] One day the boy was asked to hand the big books from the pianoforte where they rested to the bed. "I have long wanted them," said the composer to his faithful little friend, "for Handel is the greatest, the ablest composer that ever lived. I can still learn from him." He leaned the books against the wall, turned over the pages, and ever and anon paused to break out into new expressions of praise. Von Breuning places all these incidents in the middle of February, 1827, but his memory was plainly at fault. The books arrived in December, for Stumpff preserved the receipt for them, a letter and Reichard's *Taschenbuch für Reisende*, which is dated "December 14, 1826." The gift was sent through the son of Stumpff's friend Streicher.[16]

---

[14] In his report Dr. Wawruch writes: "The liquid amounted to 25 pounds but the after-flow was certainly five times as much." (TDR, v, 431, n. 1.)

[15] *Aus dem Schwarzspanierhause*, pp. 94-5.

(TDR, v, 424.) The disappointing ring referred to in the preceding chapter had arrived only a few days before.

[16] See *A*, p. 1433 (19).

Just before the first operation (around December 19), Beethoven received a visit from Johann Baptist Jenger, who had been an official in the Chief Command at Graz. He brought two letters from Beethoven's old friend, Marie Pachler-Koschak. The first, written on August 15, 1825, was a letter of recommendation for Jenger who, upon being transferred to Vienna, was anxious to meet Beethoven; it closed with an invitation to come for a summer visit to the Pachler-Koschak country estate outside of Graz. This warm letter had become lost and then was found again; thereupon Frau Pachler wrote a second, dated November 5, 1826, reiterating the invitation for the present year. Too late! By the time he received the letters such an excursion was out of the question. On December 29 Dr. Jenger wrote a letter to Frau Pachler of his visit, from which we quote:

. . . I was startled as I entered his room, where everything lay pell-mell, as though in a storehouse. He himself lay in bed suffering terribly and since he had not shaved in 3 weeks, you can easily imagine, gracious lady, how he appeared. He greeted me in a very friendly manner and I had to sit on the bed with him. I wrote out the necessary information and delivered both of your letters which he read through attentively and enjoyed thoroughly. Afterwards he asked me to convey his hearty thanks to you, esteemed and gracious lady, and to add that he would write to you himself—as soon as he was able—then he spoke of your especial musical talents with great joy and concluded that it would have been more sensible for him to have gone to you in Graz than to his brother in Upper Austria. Nevertheless he hopes some time soon to see you in Graz, which perhaps will happen next year and about which I shall be advising him frequently, and perhaps I shall be making the trip there with him.

Eight days ago he was tapped for the first time because he was suffering from dropsy in the chest. It has not been successfully stopped and therefore he will have to be tapped soon again. Would to God he were already healthy again!

Stephan von Breuning had called on Beethoven shortly after his arrival, and the work of making a soldier of Karl was begun at once. There were formal calls to be made upon Lieutenant Field Marshal Stutterheim and other officers, a physical examination to be undergone, uniforms to be provided, the oath of service to be taken, and his monthly allowance to be fixed. The Conversation Books show that these preparations were expected to occupy only a few days; instead, they dragged themselves through the month of December. Breuning's illness was no doubt a contributing factor.

In early December, Karl writes:

You are wrong if you think that I have begun to vacillate.

◦─◦

On the contrary I am glad that the affair has ended the way I wanted it to and will never regret my decision.

A few days later he reports on a visit to Stutterheim:

He was very nice after all and said that before my departure I should come to see him again. The actual entrance into military service will take place the day after tomorrow.

.~.

I will ask about it this afternoon.

.~.

I shall be here for 5 to 6 days more. We cannot go together in any case because the doctor has told me that within the next 6 days you are not allowed to go out.

Around December 19th he writes: "I am already entered. Today I must go to the regiment doctor Von Gulay whose certificate is necessary, and tomorrow again to the Lieutenant Field Marshal." After the first operation, at which Karl was present, as already mentioned, he writes:

A uniform is ready.

.~.

On Saturday [December 23] I will get everything; but tomorrow there is much to be done; your brother must buy the necessary things with me; it is high time; after the holidays I must go to the regiment in Iglau.

.~.

Soon I must ask you for some money because I had to promise a present to the tailor. Today everything will be ready.

Then Johann writes: "Now you need not buy anything more, for he has everything." Later Karl writes:

I must go again to the Lieutenant Field Marshal.

.~.

On the 2nd of January.

.~.

Stage-coach.

.~.

[Johann] The trip takes 2 days with 15 to 20 fl.

After saying his good-byes and New Year greetings, Karl left for Iglau on January 2, 1827. There is no record of the parting, and it is safe to assume that it passed off without emotional demonstration of any kind. But Beethoven's thoughts went swiftly towards his self-assumed duty of providing for the young man's future. The very next day he wrote the following letter to Dr. Bach:

Vienna, Wednesday January 3, 1827

Before my death I declare Karl van Beethoven, my beloved nephew, my sole and universal heir of all the property which I possess in which is included chiefly seven bank shares and whatever money may be on hand.—If the laws prescribe a modification in this I beg of you as far as possible to turn it to his *advantage.*—I appoint you his *curator* and ask you along with his guardian, Hofrat von Breuning, to take the place of a father to him—God preserve you—A thousand thanks for the love and friendship which you have shown me.—

Ludwig van Beethoven

After the close of the letter there is noted the following: "This will of Herr Ludwig van Beethoven, which has *today* been brought to court by Dr. Bach and made known in his presence, (is) to be preserved and copies made—By the Viennese Magistrate, March 27, 827. Schütz"

Thus the will was read immediately after Beethoven's death, and the testamentary disposition, to which we return later. Beethoven had his letter to Bach sent to Breuning to read, who answered as follows:

Dearest friend!

I am still too weak to write much to you, but I think that the following few words from a candid heart should be said to you. Since through Gerhard you have told me that I should read the letter to Hr. Dr. Bach, I have done so and return it to you for the time being with the following observations. That you name Karl as heir in the event, hopefully far distant, that we all leave this life, is appropriate considering your way of thinking and what you have already done for him. But Karl has shown himself up until now to be very reckless, and one doesn't know how his character will shape itself at present; thus I would be of the opinion that for his own good and for the security of his future you limit his power to dispose of capital either during his whole life or at least for a few years more until he has become 24 years old, the age of his majority. In any case he would have enough yearly income at hand and the limitation would protect him from the consequences of reckless actions before he reaches maturity. Speak about this with Hr. Dr. Bach, whom I should think it would be best for you to have visit you. He will arrange everything in the simplest way; I should be glad to be able to talk with you or with Dr. Bach about my observations, for I fear that a mere time limitation will not keep Karl from contracting debts which he will have to pay subsequently from his whole inheritance.

I embrace you warmly.

Beethoven received a letter from his nephew in Iglau on January 13, which begins:

My dear Father,

I have received your letter written by Schindler, I ask only that in the future you include the date so that I can estimate the speed of the post. Concerning your state of health I am glad to know that you are in good hands; I too, had felt some distrust of the treatment of your former (or perhaps present?) physician; I hope improvement will follow.

He reported about his situation in the regiment, asked for money and for the flute part of the Pianoforte Concerto in B-flat (Op. 19), which one of the officers of the regiment wished to play. A postscript reads: "Do not think that the little privations to which I am now subjected have made me dissatisfied with my lot. On the contrary, rest assured that I am living in contentment, and regret only that I am separated so far from you."

{ 1027 }

Communications from the young man were not many, and Schindler's rebukes and complaints in the Conversation Books about his undutifulness were probably only a reflex of Beethoven's moods and utterances. One cause of dissatisfaction was the fact that a letter to Smart had been sent to him for translation and was not promptly returned. But he acknowledged the receipt of money towards the end of February, and on March 4th he wrote another letter, which has been preserved:

My dear Father,

I have just received the books that you sent me and thank you very much for them.

You will have gotten the translation of the letter to Smart; I don't doubt that it will have favorable results.

Just today a cadet, who had been in Vienna on a furlough, returned to his battalion; and he reports having heard that you had been saved by a frozen punch and are feeling well. I hope that this last is true no matter what the means may have been.

There is little new about myself to tell; the service goes its usual way with the difference only that the weather is much milder, thus the watches also are easier.

Write me very soon about the state of your health; also please give my hearty greetings to H. Hofrat [von Breuning]. I kiss you.
                    Your loving son Charl.
P.S. Please stamp your letters because I have to pay alot of postage here for which I hardly have enough from my account.

Karl van Beethoven never saw his uncle in life again, nor even in death, for he was not present at the funeral—as indeed in those days of tardy communication and slow conveyance he could not be.[17]

As the year 1826 ended, Beethoven's friends were discussing with Dr. Wawruch the necessity of a second tapping. The surgeon Seibert evidently advised a postponement of the operation. There were now signs of Beethoven's dissatisfaction with his doctor. According to Gerhard von Breuning,[18] Wawruch's visits were ungraciously received; when his name was announced, Beethoven would turn his face to the wall and exclaim, "Oh, the ass!" Schindler tried to sustain the patient's faith in the skill of his physician. In a Conversation Book[19] he writes:

He understands his profession, that is well known, and he is right in following a safe course.

•～•

I have a great deal of confidence in him, but I cannot speak from experience. But he is known as an able man—esteemed and appreciated by his students.

•～•

[17] According to Sterba, *op.cit.*, p. 300, Karl did hurry to Vienna, but arrived too late and always regretted it. Concerning Karl's later life, see Appendix I.
[18] *Op.cit.*, p. 90. This sentence does not appear in TDR (see TK, III, 283).
[19] Dated January 5th to 8th by Stephan Ley, whose order of entries is followed. See *Aus Beethovens Erdentagen*, p. 212.

But as we are here concerned with a *carum caput*, my advice from the beginning has been to take into consultation a physician whose familiarity with your constitution comes from *medical treatment*.

Then you always have an appetite?

And then Hr. Seibert is really right if he still postpones the second operation, for then it will probably make a 3rd unnecessary. Yet it is better and wiser if you still don't lose faith in your doctor, for after all he has already done a great deal.

Then Gerhard von Breuning writes:

How are you? . . .

Has your belly become smaller?

You are supposed to perspire more. . .

How was your enema?

You should take several

Have you read Walter Scott already?

Would you perhaps like to read some Schiller. The world history by Schröckh?

Descriptions of summer travel?

I will bring them to you tomorrow.

The second operation took place on January 8, according to Schindler, who was present. There were no complications; the tapping was accomplished without difficulty, and Dr. Seibert reported that the water was clearer and the outflow greater than the first time. Ten measures were drawn off.

Before the year's end Schindler was putting in his voice for more medical advice. He writes:[20]

Yesterday I urged your brother earnestly to hold a medical council of men who have known your constitution longer.

[20] *Ibid.*, p. 211.

Staudenheim, Braunhofer and Malfatti, three capable men whose judgement is not to be rejected.}╼─

On January 11, according to Jenger in a letter written the next day to Frau Pachler, the desired council of physicians took place and included Dr. Malfatti,[21] who "prescribed for B. nothing hereafter but frozen fruit punch and rubbing of the abdomen with ice-cold water, a remedy with which Malfatti is said to have completely cured a similar patient." It had become an ardent wish of Beethoven's that Malfatti undertake his case, but Malfatti had refused, pleading professional ethics, but no doubt actuated by reasons of a more personal character. Many years before, probably as early as 1813, he had been not only Beethoven's physician but also his friend; indeed he was an uncle of the Therese Malfatti to whom the composer once made an offer of marriage. He had what is easy to imagine to have been the experience of all the medical men who undertook the care of the great man. Beethoven was ever a disobedient and irritable patient. He became dissatisfied with Dr. Malfatti's treatment and commented upon it and him in such a manner as to cause a serious and lasting estrangement. Ten years had elapsed between this incident and the time when Beethoven's longing went out towards his one-time professional friend.[22] Before introducing the following account it should be emphasized that, although Malfatti introduced a new treatment, he did not want to have any discord with Dr. Wawruch, and the latter remained in charge of the case until the end.

Dr. Wawruch, after describing Beethoven's lack of appetite and loss of fluids writes:

"Then Dr. Malfatti, who thenceforth supported me with his advice, and who, as a friend of Beethoven's of long years' standing understood his predominant inclination for spirituous liquors, hit upon the notion of administering frozen punch. I must confess that the treatment produced excellent results for a few days at least. Beethoven felt himself so refreshed by the ice with its alcoholic contents that already in the first night he slept quietly throughout the night and began to perspire profusely. He grew cheerful and was full of witty conceits and even dreamed of being able to complete the oratorio 'Saul and David'[23] which he had begun.

"But this joy, as was to have been foreseen, did not last long. He began to abuse the prescription and applied himself right bravely to the frozen punch. The spirits soon caused a violent pressure of the blood upon the brain; he grew soporous, breathed stertorously like an intoxicated person, began to

[21] According to remarks by Johann in the Conversation Book, either Staudenheim or Braunhofer was also present. See TDR, v, 444.

[22] It was in April, 1817, according to a letter (June 19, 1817) from Beethoven to the Countess Erdödy.

[23] Schindler denies that Beethoven worked on the oratorio of *Saul and David* during his last illness. Thayer in a note directs attention to the fact that Beethoven was confessedly deeply absorbed in Handel's scores, which he had received only a short time before. (TDR, v, 445, n. 3.)

wander in his speech, and a few times inflammatory pains in the throat were paired with hoarseness and even aphony. He became more unruly, and when, because of the cooling of the bowels, colic and diarrhoea resulted, it was high time to deprive him of this precious refreshment."

Schindler now tried to effect a reconciliation between Dr. Malfatti and Beethoven. His account, which was printed in the *Frankfurter Konversationsblatt* of July 14, 1842, is clearly prejudiced against Dr. Wawruch's treatment: "Never shall I forget the harsh words of that man which he [Dr. Malfatti] commissioned me to bear to the friend and teacher who lay mortally ill, when after the second operation (January 8) I repeatedly carried to him the urgent requests of Beethoven that he come to his help or he should die. Dr. Wawruch did not know his constitution, was ruining him with too much medicine.[24] He had already been compelled to empty 75 bottles, without counting various powders, he had no confidence in this physician, etc. To all of these representations Malfatti answered me coldly and drily: 'Say to Beethoven that he, as a master of harmony, must know that I must also live in harmony with my colleagues.' Beethoven wept bitter tears when I brought him this reply, which, hard as it was, I had to do, so that he might no longer look for help to that quarter.... Though Malfatti finally took pity on poor Beethoven and abolished Wawruch's medicine bottles at once and prescribed an entirely different course of treatment, despite the pleadings of the patient he refused to remain his *ordinarius* and visit him often. On the contrary, he came only at long intervals, and contented himself with occasional reports from me as to the sick man's condition. He was not willing even to send one of his assistants to Beethoven and consequently Dr. Wawruch remained his daily visitor in spite of Beethoven's protests."

We learn more about Schindler's attempt to bring Beethoven and Malfatti together from his letter to the composer of January 19:

My great master!
Since I have a rehearsal today at half past eight from which I cannot be absent, I must report the result in writing of my second visit to Malfatti.

He is coming to you today at half past nine. Knowing perfectly well that the professor has a lecture until ten, I told him [Malfatti] that we are inviting him [Wawruch] to come at half past nine. In order that we don't get into a pickle, you just have to offer the excuse to Malf. that today for the first time you have learned from the Professor that because of his lecture he couldn't come before ten o'clock. Malf. has a meeting in the city at ten o'clock; therefore you have the opportunity that you want to speak with him alone—

What I am asking you, however, is to make a complete reconciliation with him concerning the past for it still rankles with him to a certain extent; only today he again gave me to understand that he could not forget this planned of-

---

[24] What this medicine might have been is known only in part: in the Conversation Books there is mention of almond milk and a salep drink.

fense, as he called it.—Some words of explanation from you will get everything to rights and bring it back on the old, friendly track.

Around two o'clock I shall have the honor of being with you again. Meanwhile summa cum reverentia

Your obliging

Ant. Schindler

A reconciliation took place. Beethoven no doubt, in the warm glow of a recovered friendship, gave the physician a full measure of confidence and hailed in him much more than the ordinary professional leech. It is also safe to assume that Malfatti knew from the beginning that a cure was impossible and strove at once for temporary relief, which in Beethoven's case was the surest of means for cheering him up and reanimating hope within him. By administering frozen punch he stimulated the jaded organs more successfully than Wawruch had succeeded in doing; at the same time he warned against excess in its use and forbade the patient taking it in a liquid form. But this was only at the beginning; when he saw the inevitable end approaching he waived all injunctions as to quantity. Schindler says: "The quantity of frozen punch permitted in the first weeks was not more than one glass a day. Not until after the fourth operation (February 27th), when it was seen that the case was hopeless, were all restrictions removed. The noble patient, feeling the marked effects of a doubled and even trebled allowance meanwhile, thought himself already half saved and wanted to work on his tenth symphony, which he was allowed to do to a small extent."

Schindler then included a note written to him by the composer:

Miracles! Miracles! Miracles! The highly learned gentlemen[25] are both defeated! Only through Malfatti's science shall I be saved! It is necessary that you come to me for a moment this forenoon.

The reiteration of the words "miracles" is indicated by the usual musical sign of repetition ·/·. There is no date in Beethoven's handwriting, but Schindler has endorsed it: "Beethoven's last lines to Schindler on March 17, 1827." The endorsement is of later date and marks another obvious error of memory. Wawruch says that Beethoven abandoned hope after the fourth tapping; Johann van Beethoven records that the physicians declared him lost on March 16. It is hardly possible that Beethoven wrote this note after he himself had abandoned all hope of recovery. More likely the pathetic document is an outburst of jubilation on feeling the exhilaration consequent on Malfatti's prescription, as mentioned in Wawruch's report.

Gerhard von Breuning, prejudiced as he was against Dr. Wawruch, was yet far from unqualified in his praise of Malfatti. He says:[26] "But the usually brilliant physician seems to have been little inspired in the presence of Beethoven. The frozen punch which he prescribed on his first visit to restore

[25] Probably Wawruch and Seibert, according to Schindler. (TDR, v, 449, n. 1.)
[26] *Aus dem Schwarzspanierhause*, p. 92.

the tone of the digestive organs, excessively weakened by Wawruch's overload of medicaments, had, indeed the desired restorative effect; but it was too transient. On the other hand a sort of sweat-bath prescribed a few days after the second [*sic*—should be "third"] operation was so obviously injurious to the patient, filled with longing and hope, that it had to be abandoned after the first application. Jugs filled with hot water were arranged in a bath-tub and covered thickly with birch leaves on which the patient was seated, all of his body but the head being covered with a sheet. Malfatti hoped for a beneficial action upon the skin and to put the organs into a productive perspiration. But the very opposite effect resulted. The body of the patient, which had been emptied of water by the scarcely completed tapping, attracted the moisture developed by the bath like a block of salt; it swelled visibly in the apparatus and in a few days compelled the introduction anew of the tube into the still unhealed puncture."

Von Breuning's account of the bath is to be compared with an entry from a Conversation Book of January 27-28.[27]

The dry hay-seed bath is supposed to make you perspire, and Malfatti says that this must be tried now since the internal medicine is not having the desired effect. . . .

It is nothing but hayseed in two piles placed on warm jugs; however the first bath is to last no longer than a half an hour.

On January 25 (the date is fixed by a remark of Johann's in the Conversation Book) Schindler had brought word to Beethoven that the mother of the singer Fräulein Schechner had sent for him that morning to tell him about two remedies which had proved efficacious in the case of her father, who had also been afflicted with dropsy. One of these was Juniper berry tea, the other a vapor bath from a decoction, the ingredients of which were a head of cabbage, two handfuls of caraway seeds and three handfuls of hayseed (*Heublumen*). These remedies had been prescribed by the physician of the late King of Bavaria and had worked a cure in the case of Madame Schechner's husband when he was 70 years old. Dr. Malfatti seems to have been told of these remedies and to have prescribed the bath, which, it is said in the Conversation Books, he recognized at once as a cure used by Dr. Harz, the Royal Physician mentioned.

The third tapping took place on February 2nd. Malfatti received the report of the operation from the surgeon. Schindler writes:

I am just wondering whether Malfatti won't want to check up today on the condition of your liver and belly. It would therefore be very good as a matter of caution if Hr. Seybert were sent for at 5 o'clock. He said naturally that he wants to see you again today.

[27] Ley, *op.cit.*, p. 214.

Perhaps to check up. The water is going through the liver.

•~•

Then the well-being of the liver is the key to the whole sickness.

•~•

You have been able to gain strength again since this.

•~•

It would be good in every way if he were here because perhaps he has checked up on everything. So he can give Malfatti the best information about it.

Thus there was talk now of the liver among Beethoven's friends. But it is not possible to determine how long before it had occurred to them that this organ was the seat of the trouble.

Among other friends who visited Beethoven during this period, the Conversation Books show Tobias Haslinger, Piringer, later Schikh, Streicher, Bernard, and the singer, Nanette Schechner. This last arranged through Schindler at the end of February, a short visit to tell the composer of her great admiration for his music. She described her successes in *Fidelio* in Munich, and stated that it was through singing in *Adelaide* that she had won her way to the operatic stage.[28]

On February 1 there came to the composer a cheery letter from his old playmate Wegeler, calling to his mind some of his early flames—Jeanette Honrath and Fräulein Westerholt—and playfully outlining a plan by which the old friends might enjoy a reunion: He would send, he said, one of his patients to Carlsbad and go there with him as soon as Beethoven should arrange also to go there for his convalescence. Then, after a three weeks' trip through South Germany, there should be a final visit to the home of their childhood. And, as before, Eleonore sent a postscript emphasizing the pleasure of the reunion. Beethoven answered the letter on February 17; he told his old friend that he was surprised that he had not received through Stephan von Breuning a letter of December 10 and a portrait bearing the same date, and that he would soon be receiving this portrait and some music through Schott.

Zmeskall, faithful to the old friendship, a bound prisoner to his room through gout, sent greetings and inquiries through Schindler. From his sick-bed Beethoven wrote a short answer, dated by Zmeskall February 18:

A thousand thanks for your sympathy. I do not despair. The most painful feature is the cessation of all activity. No evil without its good side—May heaven

[28] Some reminiscences of Schechner's sometime fiancé, the tenor Ludwig Cramolini, were published in the *Frankfurter Zeitung* of September 29, 1907, in which he describes this visit as one made by both himself and his friend during which he sang *Adelaide* and she an aria from *Fidelio* with Schindler at the piano. He dates the visit, however, mid-December, 1826. (Cf. TDR, v, 307, n. 1.) See BJ, II, pp. 373-79.

but grant you relief in your painful existence. Perhaps health is coming to both of us and we shall meet again in friendly intimacy.

Warm regards from your old sympathizing friend.

Beethoven

Though Beethoven had received the Handel scores in December, he does not seem to have had an opportunity to enjoy Stumpff's gift thoroughly until he turned to them for intellectual refreshment on his bed of pain. He had signed the receipt for them in December, but it was not until his thoughts turned to his English friends in the hope of pecuniary relief that he wrote a letter to Stumpff under date of February 8.

Most worthy friend!

What great joy was given to me by your sending the works of Handel as a present—for me a royal present!—This my pen cannot describe. An article about it, which I enclose, was even printed by the newspaper.[29] Unfortunately I have been laid up with the dropsy since the 3rd of December. You can imagine in what a situation this places me! Generally I live from the proceeds of my brain only, and thus provide all things for myself and my Karl. Unhappily for a month and a half I have not been able to write a note.

My salary suffices only to pay my semi-annual rent, after which there remains only a few hundred florins. Remember also that it cannot yet be determined when my illness will be over and I again will be able to sail through the air on Pegasus under full sail. Doctor, surgeon, everything must be paid—

I recall right well that several years ago the Philharmonic Society wanted to give a concert for my benefit. It would be fortunate for me if they would come to this decision now. I might still be saved from the poverty which now confronts me. On this account I am writing to Mr. S[mart]. And if you, dear friend, can do anything towards this end I beg of you to cooperate with Mr. S. A letter will also be written about this to Moscheles and if all my friends unite I believe that something can be done for me in this matter.

Concerning the Handel works for H. Imperial Highness, the Archduke Rudolph, I cannot as yet say anything with certainty. But I will write to him in a few days and remind him of it.

I thank you again for your glorious gift, at the same time I beg of you to tell me if I can be of any service to you here; this I would do with all my heart— I present once again to your sympathetic nature my situation here which I have described to you and meanwhile I wish you everything that is good and beautiful. I send you my best regards.

Very respectfully yours,

Beethoven

Stumpff had already been informed of Beethoven's illness by Streicher. It is evident that he went at once to Smart and Moscheles, and knowledge of Beethoven's condition and request was communicated to the directors of the Philharmonic Society forthwith. Beethoven, meanwhile, had written to both Smart and Moscheles, enclosing the letter of the former in the letter to

[29] The newspaper article was printed in the *Modenzeitung*. (TDR, v, 459, n. 3.)

the latter; but the quick and sympathetic action of the Society was no doubt due primarily to the initiative of Stumpff, for the letters could by no means have reached London when the directors held a meeting on February 28. Mr. Dance presided, and those present, as recorded in the Society's minutes, were F. Cramer, Horsley, Moralt, Dragonetti, Neate, Dizi, Beale, T. Cooke, Sir G. Smart, Welsh, Latour, Spagnoletti, Calkin, J. B. Cramer, Cipriani Potter and Watts. The minutes continue:

It was moved by Mr. Neate, and seconded by Mr. Latour:

"That this Society do lend the sum of One Hundred Pounds to its own members to be sent through the hands of Mr. Moscheles to some confidential friend of Beethoven, to be applied to his comforts and necessities during his illness."

Carried unanimously.

Both Stumpff and Moscheles wrote the good news to Beethoven the next day. A portion of Moscheles's letter appears in his translation, or rather paraphrase, of Schindler's biography.[30] In it he said: "The [Philharmonic] Society resolved to express their good will and lively sympathy by requesting your acceptance of 100 pounds sterling (1,000 florins) to provide the necessary comforts and conveniences during your illness. This money will be paid to your order by Mr. Rau, of the house of Eskeles, either in separate sums or all at once as you desire."

He added an expression of the Philharmonic Society's willingness to aid him further whenever he should inform it of his need of assistance. Meanwhile Beethoven's impatience was so great that, having found Smart's address among his papers, he wrote to him a second letter on March 6th, being able now to mention the fact of the fourth tapping on February 27th and to utter the apprehension that the operation might have to be repeated— perhaps more than once. On March 14th he was still without the answer of his English friends and he wrote again to Moscheles telling him of the two letters sent to Smart, urging action and concluding with

Whither is this to lead, and what is to become of me if this goes on for some time?—Truly, a hard lot has befallen me! But I yield to the will of fate and only pray that God in His divine will so order it that as long as I have to endure this death in life I may be protected against want. This will give me strength to endure my lot, hard and terrible though it may be, with submission to the will of the Most High.

So, my dear Moscheles I again bring my affairs to your attention and remain with the greatest respect

Your friend

L. v. Beethoven

Hummel is here and has already made me a few visits.

Scarcely was this letter sent when the letters of March 1st arrived from London. The impression that they made will be recorded later.

---

[30] Moscheles, *Life of Beethoven*, II, pp. 68-9.

Schindler says that the appeal to London, which had been suggested by Beethoven, had been discussed with the composer by himself and Breuning, who agreed in questioning the advisability of the step which, they said, would make a bad impression if it became known. They reminded Beethoven of his bank-shares, but he protested vigorously against their being touched; he had set them apart as a legacy for his nephew which must not be encroached upon.[31]

There are evidences outside of the importunate letters to London that Beethoven had frequent spells of melancholy during the period between the crises of his disease, which culminated in the third operation on February 2, and the fourth. Some of them were, no doubt, due to forebodings touching the outcome of his illness; some to the anxiety which his financial condition gave him (more imaginary than real in view of the easily convertible bank-shares), and some presumably to disappointment and chagrin at the conduct of his nephew, who had not answered his letter to Iglau. Breuning explained that the negligence might be due to Karl's time and attention being engrossed by the carnival gaieties at the military post, and warned Beethoven that to give way to melancholy was to stand in the way of recovery. We learn this from the Conversation Books which also give glimpses of friendly visits calculated to divert the sick man's mind and keep him in touch with the affairs of the city, theatre and the world at large. Doležalek, Schuppanzigh, and apparently Linke also, came in a group; Beethoven showed them the Handel scores and the conversation ran out into a discussion of international politics. Moritz Lichnowsky made a call and entertained him with the gossip of the theatres. Gleichenstein made several visits, and once brought with him his wife and son. The Countess was a sister of Therese Malfatti, and was disappointed when Beethoven did not recognize her. About the middle of February Diabelli gave Beethoven a print-picture of Haydn's birthplace, which he had published; Beethoven showed it to his little friend Gerhard von Breuning and said: "Look, I got this today. See this little house, and in it so great a man was born!"

Sometime in February—it was probably at the time when Beethoven's mind was so fixedly bent on obtaining help from London—Schindler was either ill or suffering from an accident which kept him for a brief space from Beethoven's bedside. The composer sent him a gift—a repast evidently—and a letter of sympathy which Schindler endorsed as being "in the month of Febr. 1827."

Concerning your accident, since it has already taken place, so soon can we see each other—I can send things to you through someone without any trouble—accept this—Here is something—Moscheles, Cramer—if you have not already received another letter. There is new reason to write on Wednesday, and present him anew with my heartfelt entreaty. If you are still not well by then, one of my [servants] can attend to the posting of it against the receipt—

[31] See *Biogr.*, II, p. 138.

Vale et fave—there is no need for assurance of my sympathy in your accident—
Do take *this meal from me* which has been given from the bottom of my heart—
Heaven be with you.

Your sincere friend

Beethoven

Schindler remarked of this letter that the broken sentences and gaps in his ideas showed that Beethoven was not always thinking connectedly during these days.

More pathetic than even this letter is the picture of the sufferer in his sick-room at the time of the fourth operation on February 27. So wretched were his surroundings that it is scarcely possible to avoid the conviction that not poverty alone but ignorance and carelessness were contributory to the woeful lack of ordinary sick-room conveniences. Gerhard von Breuning wrote[32] that after the operation the fluid which was drained from the patient's body flowed half-way across the floor to the middle of the room; and in the Conversation Books there is mention of saturated bedclothing and a suggestion by the physician that oilcloth be procured and spread over the couch. Beethoven now gave up hope. Dr. Wawruch says: "No words of comfort could brace him up, and when I promised him alleviation of his sufferings with the coming of the vitalizing weather of spring he answered with a smile: 'My day's work is finished. If there were a physician who could help me "his name shall be called Wonderful!"' This pathetic allusion to Handel's *Messiah* touched me so deeply that I had to confess its correctness to myself with profound emotion." The incident so sympathetically described bears evidence of veracity on its face; Handel's scores were always in Beethoven's mind during the last weeks of his life.

Among Beethoven's visitors in February was Wolfmayer, whose coming must have called up a sense of a long-standing obligation and purpose in the composer's mind.[33] On February 22nd he dictated a letter to the Schotts asking that the Quartet in C-sharp minor be dedicated to "my friend Johann Nepomuk Wolfmayer." The letter then proceeds:

Now, however, I come with a very important request.—My doctor has ordered me to drink very good old Rhine wine. To get a thing of that kind unadulterated is not possible at any price. If, therefore, I were to receive a small number of bottles I would show my gratitude to you in the Cäcilia. I think something might be done for me at the customs so that the transport would not cost too much.—As soon as my strength allows you shall receive the metronome marks for the Mass, for I am now just in the period when the fourth operation is about to be performed.—The sooner, therefore, that I receive the Rhine wine, or Moselle, the more beneficial it will be to me in my present condition; and I beg of

---

[32] *Op.cit.*, p. 104.

[33] It will be remembered that Wolfmayer had commissioned him years before to write a requiem, and had paid him for it. (TK, III, 296, n. 1.)

you most heartily to do me this favor for which I shall be under grateful obligation to you.

With the greatest respect I remain your very devoted

Beethoven

On March 1st he repeated his request:

I am under the necessity of becoming burdensome to you again, inasmuch as I am sending you a packet for the Royal Government Councillor Wegeler at Coblenz, which you will have the kindness to transmit from Mainz to Coblenz. You know without more ado that I am too unselfish to ask you to do all these things gratuitously.

I repeat my former request, namely, concerning *old white Rhine wine or Moselle*. It is infinitely difficult to get any here which is genuine and unadulterated, even at the highest price. A few days ago, on February 27, I had my fourth operation, and yet I am unable to look forward to my complete recovery and restoration. Pity your devoted friend who has the highest esteem for you.

Beethoven

On March 8 the Schotts answered that they had forwarded a case of twelve bottles of Rüdesheimer Berg of the vintage of 1806, via Frankfurt, but in order that he might receive a slight refreshment, they had sent that day four bottles of the same wine, two pure and two mixed with herbs, to be used as a medicine which had been prescribed for his disease. Before the wine reached Vienna, on March 10 Beethoven wrote again to the Schotts:

Gentlemen!

According to my letter the Quartet was to be dedicated to one whose name I have already sent to you. Since then there has been an occurrence which has led me to make a change in this. It must be dedicated to Lieut. Field-Marshal von Stutterheim to whom I am deeply indebted. If you have already engraved the first dedication I beg of you, by everything in this world, to change it, and I will gladly pay the cost. Do not accept this as an empty promise; I attach so much importance to it that I am ready to make any compensation for it. I enclose the title. As regards the shipment to my friend, the Royal Prussian Government Councillor v. Wegeler in Coblenz, I am glad to be able to relieve you wholly. Another opportunity has offered itself. My health, which will not be restored for a long time, pleads for the wines which I have asked for and which will certainly bring me refreshment, strength and health.

I remain with the greatest respect

Your very devoted Ludwig van Beethoven

A few days later Beethoven finally received the great gift from London and dictated the following acknowledgement to Schindler:

Vienna, March 18, 1827

My dear good Moscheles:

I cannot describe to you in words with what feelings I read your letter of March 1. The generosity with which the Philharmonic Society almost anticipated my petition has touched me in the innermost depth of my soul.—I beg you, therefore, my dear Moscheles, to be the agent through which I transmit my sincerest thanks to the Philharmonic Society for the particular sympathy and help.

I found myself constrained to collect at once the entire sum of 1,000 florins C.M., as I was in the unpleasant position of being about to borrow money, which would have brought new embarrassments.

Concerning the concert which the Philharmonic Society has resolved to give for my benefit, I beg the Society not to abandon this noble purpose, and to deduct the 1,000 florins already sent to me from the proceeds of the concert. And if the Society is disposed graciously to send me the balance, I will pledge myself to return my heartiest thanks to the Society by binding myself to compose for it either a new symphony, which lies already sketched in my desk, or a new overture or something else which the Society would like.

May heaven very soon restore me to health, and I shall prove to the generous Englishmen how greatly I appreciate their interest in my sad fate.

Your noble act will never be forgotten and I shall follow this with special thanks to Sir Smart and Mr. Stumpff.

Farewell! With kindest remembrances

    From your friend who highly esteems you

                Ludwig van Beethoven[34]

My kindest regards to your wife.

I have to thank you and the Philh. Society for a new friend in Mr. Rau. Please deliver to the Philh. Society the metronome marks of the Symphony. Here are the indications.

Metronome indications of tempi for Beethoven's last symphony, Op. 125.[35]

Allegro ma non troppo	88 = ♩
Molto vivace	116 = ♩·
Presto	116 = ♩·
Adagio tempo 1mo	60 = ♩
Andante moderato	63 = ♩
Finale presto[36]	96 = ♩·
Allegro ma non troppo	88 = ♩
Allegro assai	80 = ♩
Alla Marcia	84 = ♩·
Andante maestoso	72 = ♩
Adagio divoto	60 = ♩
Allegro energico	84 = ♩·
Allegro ma non tanto	120 = ♩
Prestissimo	132 = ♩
Maestoso	60 = ♩

Schindler relates[37] that Beethoven on March 24 whispered to him, "write

[34] For the corrected reading of the post-script the present editor is indebted to Ley's version, which is based on the autograph: *Beethoven als Freund der Familie Wegeler— v. Breuning*, p. 234.

[35] To here in Schindler's hand, according to Ley (*loc.cit.*), the rest in another hand. After the first tempo mark there is added,

apparently by Moscheles, "e un poco mae-stoso"; the "1mo" after "Adagio tempo" is crossed out and the words "molto e cantabile" substituted.

[36] In a letter to Schott on October 13, 1826, this section is given the mark "66=♩·."

[37] *Biogr.*, II, p. 141.

to Smart and Stumpff," and that he would have done so on the morrow had Beethoven been able to sign his name.

The history of the Philharmonic Society's benefaction may properly be completed at this point. The money, as is to be seen from Beethoven's acknowledgement, was collected by the composer at once. Herr Rau, of the banking house of Eskeles to whom it had been entrusted, called upon Beethoven immediately on receiving advices from London. It was on March 15, and two days later he enclosed Beethoven's receipt (dated March 16) in a letter to Moscheles which the latter transmitted to Mr. W. Watts, Secretary of the Philharmonic Society. Rau writes:

I have with the greatest surprise heard from you, who reside in London, that the universally admired Beethoven is so dangerously ill and in want of pecuniary assistance, while we, here at Vienna, are totally ignorant of it. I went to him immediately after having read your letter to ascertain his state, and to announce to him the approaching relief. This made a deep impression upon him, and called forth true expressions of gratitude. What a satisfactory sight would it have been for those who so generously relieved him to witness such a touching scene! I found poor Beethoven in a sad way, more like a skeleton than a living being. He is suffering from dropsy, and has already been tapped four times; he is under the care of our clever physician Malfatti, who unfortunately gives little hope of his recovery.

How long he may remain in his present state, or if he can at all be saved, can not yet be ascertained. The joyous sensation at the sudden relief from London has, however, had a wonderful effect upon him; it made one of the wounds (which since the last operation had healed) suddenly burst open during the night, and all the water which had gathered since a fortnight ran out freely. When I came to see him on the following day he was in remarkably good spirits and felt himself much relieved. I hastened to Malfatti to inform him of this alteration and he considers the event as very consolatory. He will contrive to keep the wound open for some time and thus leave a channel for the water which gathers continually. Beethoven is fully satisfied with his attendants, who consist of a cook and housemaid. His friend and ours, Mr. Schindler, dines with him every day and thus proves his sincere attachment to him. S. also manages his correspondence and superintends his expenses. You will find enclosed a receipt from Beethoven for the 1,000 florins (or 100 pounds). When I proposed to him to take half of the sum at present, and to leave the rest with Baron Eskeles, where he might have it safely deposited, he acknowledged to me openly that he considered this money as a relief sent him from heaven; and that 500 florins would not suffice for his present want. I therefore gave him, according to his wish, the whole sum at once, Beethoven will soon address a letter to the Philharmonic Society by which he means to express his gratitude. I hope you will again accept my services whenever they can be of any use to Beethoven. I am, etc.

In a letter, dated March 24, Schindler wrote to Moscheles:[38]

... In short, care and anxiety vanished at once when the money arrived, and he said quite happily, "Now we can again look forward to a comfortable day once

[38] The correct reading of these excerpts is drawn from Ley, *op.cit.*, pp. 236-37.

in awhile"; for there were only 340 fl. V.S. left in the cash-box, and we had economized for some time in the amount of beef and vegetables, which, more than anything else, made him suffer. The other day, it was Friday, his favorite dish of fish was cooked so that he could nibble from it. In short, his delight on receiving this noble gift from the Phil. Society resembled that of a child. Also a large so-called easy-chair had to be procured, which cost 30 f. V.S. in which he could stay at least a half hour per day so that his bed could be properly made up ... whatever remains of the 1000 f. we want to apply towards a respectable burial, without commotion, in the . . . [churchyard[39]] at Döbling where he ever delighted to roam. . . . Two days after your letter there came one from the worthy H. Stumpf, who also praised yours in the highest terms, all of which affected Beethoven so much. . . . Numerous times during the day he exclaimed, "May God reward them all a thousandfold."

Baron Pasqualati, Beethoven's old friend, in whose house he had lived for a long time, also made an effort to contribute to the composer's physical comfort and well-being. There are several little letters in which Beethoven acknowledges the receipt of contributions from his cellar and larder. One of these has been endorsed by a strange hand as having been sent or received on March 6. It reads:

Most honored old friend!
Hearty thanks for your health-gift; as soon as I have found out which of the wines is the most suitable I will let you know, but I shall abuse your kindness as little as possible. I am rejoicing in the expectation of the compotes and will appeal to you often for them—Even this costs me an exertion—Sapienta pauca—
Your grateful friend

Beethoven

And a little while afterwards he writes:

Honored friend!
I beg you again today for a cherry compote, but without lemons, entirely simple; also I should be glad to have a light pudding, almost like gruel—my good cook is not yet adept in food for the sick. I am allowed to drink *champagne*, but for the time being please send a champagne glass with it—Now as regards the wine: at first Malfatti wanted it to be only Moselle, but he asserted that there was none genuine to be obtained here. He therefore himself gave me several bottles of Krumpholz-Kirchner† and claims that this is the best for my health since no Moselle is to be had.—Pardon me for being a burden and ascribe it to my helpless condition.

Most respectfully your friend

Beethoven

Others who sent him gifts of wine were Streicher and Breuning, and, as we see from the above letter, Malfatti himself. Why should the doctors any

---

[39] Here there is a hole in the autograph. The English translation of this letter in Moscheles's *The Life of Beethoven* (II, p. 321) supplies the word "churchyard."

† Gumpoldskirchner, a wine made near Vienna. See *A*, III, p. 1343, n. 1.

more deny him what he liked; his days were numbered. Concerning the last few days of his life the Conversation Books provide no clue.

Beethoven's preoccupation with the works of Handel has already been mentioned. He also received great pleasure from the compositions of Schubert with which he became acquainted through Schindler. ---≈¶In the first edition of his biography Schindler writes:[40] "And how much Beethoven respected the talent of gifted Franz Schubert, which he really began to know only on his final sick-bed because previously certain people had lacked trust in him and belittled his name! After he had come through me to know the 'Ossian's Gesänge,' 'Die Bürgschaft,' 'Die junge Nonne,' 'Die Grenzen der Menschkeit' etc., he cried out with inner emotion, 'Truly a divine spark dwells in Schubert!' "¶---

Schindler at one time had expressed the opinion that Schubert was a greater song-composer than Beethoven and excited criticism thereby. As a defense of his opinion he wrote an article which was published in the *Theaterzeitung* (May 3, 1831):

"As the illness to which Beethoven finally succumbed after four months of suffering from the beginning made his ordinary mental activity impossible, a diversion had to be thought of which would fit his mind and inclinations. And so it came about that I placed before him a collection of Schubert's songs, about 60 in number, among them many which were then still in manuscript. This was done not only to provide him with a pleasant entertainment, but also to give him an opportunity to get acquainted with Schubert in his essence in order to get from him a favorable opinion of Schubert's talent, which had been impugned, as had that of others by some of the exalted ones. The great master, who before then had not known five songs of Schubert's, was amazed at their number and refused to believe that up to that time (February, 1827) he had already composed over 500 of them. But if he was astonished at the number he was filled with the highest admiration as soon as he discovered their contents. For several days he could not separate himself from them, and every day he spent hours with Iphigenia's monologue, 'Die Grenzen der Menschheit,' 'Die Allmacht,' 'Die junge Nonne,' 'Viola,' the 'Müllerlieder,' and others. With joyous enthusiasm he cried out repeatedly: 'Truly, a divine spark dwells in Schubert; if I had had this poem I would have set it to music'; this in the case of the majority of poems whose material contents and original treatment by Schubert he could not praise sufficiently. Nor could he understand how Schubert had time to 'take in hand such long poems, many of which contained ten others,' as he expressed it. . . . What would the master have said had he seen, for instance, the Ossianic songs, 'Die Bürgschaft,' 'Elysium,' 'Der Taucher' and other great ones which have only recently been published? In short, the respect which Beethoven acquired for Schubert's talent was so great that he now wanted to see his operas and pianoforte pieces; but his illness had now become so

[40] Page 256.

severe that he could no longer gratify this wish. But he often spoke of Schubert and predicted of him that he 'would make a great sensation in the world,' and often regretted that he had not learned to know him earlier."

The remark about Schubert recorded in both of Schindler's writings was evidently made more than once. In a letter from Anslem Hüttenbrenner to Ferdinand Luib of February 21, 1858, we find: "Beethoven said of Schubert one day: 'That man has the divine spark!' "[41] In another letter to Luib written two days later, Hüttenbrenner writes:[42] "But this I know positively, that about eight days before Beethoven's death Prof. Schindler, Schubert and I visited the sick man. Schindler announced us two and asked Beethoven whom he would see first. He said: 'Let Schubert come first!' "

Another incident recorded about Beethoven by Gerhard von Breuning deserves to be told here:[43] "One time, as so often happened when I came, I found him sleeping. I sat down on the bed, keeping quiet in order not to awaken him from a sleep that was hopefully giving him strength. I turned the pages of a Conversation Book that was lying on the bed still in use in order to find out who had been here during that time and what had been said. And I found there among other things the entry: 'Your Quartet which Schuppanzigh played yesterday did not please'—When he awoke a short time later, I held this passage before his eyes and asked him what he had to say about it. 'It will please them some day' was the laconic reply which he gave me and to clinch the argument he added knowingly that he wrote only as he thought best and would not permit himself to be deceived by the judgement of the day, ending: 'I know that I am an artist.' "

On March 20, Beethoven signed a document with Schindler and Stephan von Breuning which handed over to Schott the sole copyright and ownership of the C-sharp minor Quartet, Op. 131. It was enclosed in Schindler's letter to Schott of April 12th. On March 21st Beethoven wrote the final appeal to Stieglitz and Co., already mentioned, for the sum of 125 ducats owed him by Prince Galitzin.

In a letter which Schindler wrote to Moscheles, forwarding Beethoven's, he said: "Hummel and his wife are here; he came in haste to see Beethoven once again alive, for it is generally reported in Germany that he is on his deathbed. It was a most touching sight last Thursday to see these two friends meet again."[44] The letter was written on March 14 and the "last Thursday" was March 8th. We have an account of this meeting in Ferdinand Hiller's "Aus dem Ton-Leben unserer Zeit."[45] Hiller was then fifteen years old and had come to the Austrian capital with Hummel, who was his teacher. Hummel had heard in Weimar that Beethoven was hopelessly ill and had

[41] See O. E. Deutsch, *Memoirs of Schubert* (New York, 1958), p. 66.

[42] This letter was among Mr. Thayer's papers. (TDR, v, 480.) See Deutsch, *loc.cit.*

[43] *Aus dem Schwarzspanierhause*, p. 95.

(TDR, v, 480, n. 1.)

[44] See Ley, *op.cit.*, p. 230.

[45] *Neue Folge* (Leipzig, 1871), pp. 169ff. (TDR, v, 481, n. 1.)

reached Vienna on March 6; two days later he visited his dying friend. Hiller writes:

"Through a spacious anteroom in which high cabinets were piled with thick, tied-up parcels of music we reached—how my heart beat!—Beethoven's living-room, and were not a little astonished to find the master sitting in apparent comfort at the window. He wore a long, gray sleeping-robe, open at the time, and high boots reaching to his knees.[46] Emaciated by long and severe illness he seemed to me, when he arose, of tall stature; he was un-shaven, his thick, half-gray hair fell in disorder over his temples. The expression of his features heightened when he caught sight of Hummel, and he seemed to be extraordinarily glad to meet him. The two men embraced each other most cordially. Hummel introduced me. Beethoven showed him-self extremely kind and I was permitted to sit opposite him at the window. It is known that conversation with Beethoven was carried on in part in writing; he spoke, but those with whom he conversed had to write their questions and answers. For this purpose thick sheets of ordinary writing-paper in quarto form and lead-pencils always lay near him. How painful it must have been for the animated, easily impatient man to be obliged to wait for every answer, to make a pause in every moment of conversation, during which, as it were, thought was condemned to come to a standstill! He always followed the hand of the writer with hungry eyes and compre-hended what was written at a glance instead of reading it. The liveliness of the conversation naturally interfered with the continual writing of the visitor—I can scarcely blame myself, much as I regret it, for not taking down more extended notes than I did; indeed, I rejoice that a lad of fifteen years who found himself in a great city for the first time, was self-possessed enough to regard any details. I can vouch with the best conscience for the perfect accuracy of all that I am able to repeat.

"The conversation at first turned, as is usual, on domestic affairs,—the journey and sojourn, my relations with Hummel and matters of that kind. Beethoven asked about Goethe's health with extraordinary solicitude and we were able to make the best of reports, since only a few days before the great poet had written in my album. Concerning his own state, poor Beet-hoven complained much. 'Here I have been lying for four months,' he cried out, 'one must at last lose patience!' Other things in Vienna did not seem to be to his liking and he spoke with the utmost severity of 'the present taste in art,' and 'the dilettantism which is ruining everything.' Nor did he spare the government, up to the most exalted regions. 'Write a volume of penitential hymns and dedicate it to the Empress,' he remarked with a gloomy smile to Hummel, who, however, made no use of the well-meant advice. Hummel, who was a practical man, took advantage of Beethoven's condition

[46] Hüttenbrenner told Thayer that when Hummel came, Beethoven said, "I cannot re-ceive him in bed," immediately got up, put on a sleeping robe, and received him with due respect. (TDR, v, 481, n. 2.)

to ask his attention to a matter which occupied a long time. It was about the theft of one of Hummel's concertos, which had been printed illicitly before it had been brought out by the lawful publisher. Hummel wanted to appeal to the Bundestag against this wretched business, and to this end desired to have Beethoven's signature, which seemed to him of great value. He sat down to explain the matter in writing and meanwhile I was permitted to carry on the conversation with Beethoven. I did my best, and the master continued to give free rein to his moody and passionate utterances in the most confidential manner. In part they referred to his nephew, whom he had loved greatly, who, as is known, caused him much trouble and at that time, because of a few trifles (thus Beethoven at least seemed to consider them), had gotten into trouble with the officials. 'Little thieves are hanged, but big ones are allowed to go free!' he exclaimed ill-humoredly. He asked about my studies and, encouraging me, said: 'Art must be propagated ceaselessly,' and when I spoke of the exclusive interest in Italian opera which then prevailed in Vienna, he gave utterance to the memorable words: 'It is said *vox populi, vox dei*. I never believed it.'

"On March 13 Hummel took me with him a second time to Beethoven. We found his condition to be materially worse. He lay in bed, seemed to suffer great pains, and at intervals groaned deeply despite the fact that he spoke much and animatedly. Now he seemed to take it much to heart that he had not married. Already at our first visit he had joked about it with Hummel, whose wife he had known as a young and beautiful maiden. 'You are a lucky man,' he said to him now smilingly, 'you have a wife who takes care of you, who is in love with you—but poor me!' and he sighed heavily. He also begged of Hummel to bring his wife to see him, she not having been able to persuade herself to see in his present state the man whom she had known at the zenith of his powers. A short time before he had received a present of a picture of the house in which Haydn was born. He kept it close at hand and showed it to us. 'It gave me a childish pleasure,' he said, 'the cradle of so great a man!' Then he appealed to Hummel in behalf of Schindler, of whom so much was spoken afterwards. 'He is a good man,' he said, 'who has taken a great deal of trouble on my account. He is to give a concert soon at which I promised my cooperation. But now nothing is likely to come of that. Now I should like to have you do me the favor of playing. We must always help poor artists.' As a matter of course, Hummel consented. The concert took place—ten days after Beethoven's death—in the Josephstadt-Theater. Hummel improvised in an obviously exalted mood on the Allegretto of the A major Symphony; the public knew why he participated and the performance and its reception formed a truly inspiring incident.

"Shortly after our second visit the report spread throughout Vienna that the Philharmonic Society of London had sent Beethoven £100 in order to ease his sick-bed. It was added that this surprise had made so great an impression on the great poor man that it had also brought physical relief. When we stood again at his bedside, on the 20th, we could deduce from his utterances how greatly he had been rejoiced by this altruism; but he was very weak and spoke only in faint and disconnected phrases. 'I shall, no doubt, soon be going above,' he whispered after our first greeting. Similar remarks recurred frequently. In the intervals, however, he spoke of projects and hopes which were destined not to be realized. Speaking of the noble conduct of the Philharmonic Society and in praise of the English people, he expressed the intention, as soon as matters were better with him, to undertake the journey to London. 'I will compose a grand overture for them and a grand symphony.' Then, too, he would visit Madame Hummel (she had come along with her husband) and go to I do not know how many places. It did not occur to us to write anything for him. His eyes, which were still lively when we saw him last, dropped and closed to-day and it was difficult from time to time for him to raise himself. It was no longer possible to deceive one's self—the worst was to be feared.

"Hopeless was the picture presented by the extraordinary man when we sought him again on March 23rd. It was to be the last time. He lay, weak and miserable, sighing deeply at intervals. Not a word fell from his lips; sweat stood upon his forehead. His handkerchief not being conveniently at hand, Hummel's wife took her fine cambric handkerchief and dried his face several times. Never shall I forget the grateful glance with which his broken eye looked upon her."

The consultations between Beethoven and his legal advisers, Bach, Breuning and others, concerning the proper disposition of his estate by will, which had begun soon after Karl's departure for Iglau, had not been brought to a conclusion when it became apparent to all that it was high time that the document be formally executed. Dr. Bach does not seem to have been consulted at this crisis; haste was necessary, and on March 23 von Breuning made a draft of a will which, free from unnecessary verbiage, set forth the wishes of the testator in three lines of writing. Beethoven had protested against the proposition of his friends that provision be made that Karl should not be able to dissipate the capital or surrender any portion of it to his mother. To this end a trust was to be created and he was to have the income during life, the reversion being to his legitimate heirs. With this Beethoven declared himself at length satisfied; but when Breuning placed the draft before the dying man, who had yielded unwillingly, he copied it laboriously but substituted the words "natural" for "legitimate." Schindler says[47] the copying was a labor, and when Beethoven finished it and appended the signature he said: "There; now I'll write no more." Breuning called his attention to the fact that controversy would ensue from his change in the text, but Beethoven insisted that the words meant the same thing and there should be no change. "This," said Schindler, "was his last contradiction."

[47] *Biogr.*, II, pp. 146-47. (TDR, v, 484, n. 1.)

Hiller's description of the last visit of Hummel pictures the condition of the dying man on this day, and Schindler's statement that it was laborious for Beethoven to copy even the few words of the will is pathetically verified by the orthography of the document which, *verb. et lit.*, is as follows:[48]

Mein Nefffe Karl Soll allein Erbe sein, das Kapital meines Nachlalasses soll jedoch Seinen natürlichen oder Testamentarischschen Erben zufallen—

Wien am März 1827

luwig van Beethoven

According to Gerhard von Breuning,[49] signatures were necessary to several documents—the will, the transfer of the guardianship of the nephew to von Breuning and the letter of January 3, which also made a testamentary disposition of Beethoven's property. These signatures were all obtained with great difficulty. After von Breuning, Schindler and the dying man's brother had indicated to Beethoven, who lay in a half-stupor, that his signature was required, they raised him as much as possible and pushed pillows under him for support. Then the documents, one after the other, were laid before him and von Breuning put the inked pen in his hand. "The dying man, who ordinarily wrote boldly in a lapidary style, repeatedly signed his immortal name, laboriously, with trembling hand, for the last time; still legibly, indeed, but each time forgetting one of the middle letters—once an *h*, another time an *e*."

On the day which saw the signing of the will, Beethoven made an utterance, eminently characteristic of him. The date is fixed as March 23rd by Schindler's letter to Moscheles of March 24th[50] in which he says: "He feels the end coming for yesterday he said to me and H. v. Breuning, 'Plaudite, amici, comoedia finita est.' "[51] —Gerhard von Breuning writes of this scene:[52] "At the time of my visit to Bockenheim, Schindler told me that Beethoven had called out these words as the doctors were taking their leave after a long consultation, and my memory affirms this reminiscence positively.[53] I recollected most definitely that my father, Schindler and I were present when he spoke the words, and that he expressed these words in his favorite sarcastic-humorous manner as though to imply: nothing can be done. . . ."

When Beethoven's friends saw the end approaching, they were naturally desirous that he receive the spiritual comfort which the offices of the Roman

---

[48] The editor has followed the reading of Max Unger. See "Beethovens letzte Briefe und Unterschriften" in *DM*, Vol. 34, No. 5 (1942), p. 157.

[49] *Aus dem Schwarzspanierhause*, pp. 105-107.

[50] Ley, *op.cit.*, pp. 235-37.

[51] A common closing line in classical Roman comedy.

[52] *Op.cit.*, pp. 104-105.

[53] Breuning emphasized the date and the occasion to refute a statement in Dr. Wawruch's report and in Schindler's letter to *Cäcilia* (April 12, 1827) that the remark was made after taking the sacrament on March 24. Wawruch was not present; and Schindler, who was there, had already written to Moscheles that it was on March 23rd. In his letter to *Cäcilia* Schindler does not write of the remark on March 24th as one *repeated* from the day before, when it is known to have been made. (Cf. TK, III, 304-305.)

Catholic church offer to the dying, and it was equally natural that Beethoven, brought up as a child of the Church though careless of his duties towards it, should, at the last, be ready to accept them. Johann van Beethoven relates that a few days after the 16th of March, when the physicians gave him up for lost, he had begged his brother to make his peace with God, to which request he had acceded "with the greatest readiness." Confirmation of this is found in Dr. Wawruch's report. Wawruch, it will be remembered, had, at the beginning of his studies, intended to enter the priesthood. At the crisis described by Johann he says he called Beethoven's attention to his impending dissolution "so that he might do his duty as a citizen and to religion." He continues: "With the greatest delicacy I wrote the words of admonition on a sheet of paper (for only so were we able to communicate one to another). Beethoven read the writing with unexampled composure, slowly and thoughtfully, his countenance like that of one transfigured; cordially and solemnly he held out his hand to me and said: 'Have the priest called.' Then he lay quietly lost in thought and amiably indicated by a nod his 'I shall soon see you again.' "

Schindler's account, in a letter to the *Cäcilia* dated April 12, 1827, and printed in that journal in May, is as follows: ". . . As the business of the will had been settled, so far as was possible, the previous day, there remained with us only one ardent wish—to reconcile him with heaven and to show the world at the same time that he had ended his life a true Christian. The Professor in Ordinary [Wawruch] therefore wrote and begged him in the name of all his friends to receive the Holy Sacrament; to which he replied quietly and firmly [*gefasst*], 'I wish it.' The physician went away and left us to care for it."

In 1860 Hüttenbrenner wrote:[54] "It is not true, as has been reported, that I begged Beethoven to receive the sacrament for the dying; but I did bring it about at the request of the wife of the music-publisher Tobias Haslinger, now deceased, that Beethoven was asked in the gentlest manner by Herr Johann Baptist Jenger and Frau van Beethoven, wife of the landowner, to strengthen himself by receiving Holy Communion. . . . On the day of her brother-in-law's death Frau v. Beethoven told me that after receiving the viaticum he said to the priest, 'I thank you, ghostly sir! You have brought me comfort!' "

Hüttenbrenner is confirmed by Johann van Beethoven, who wrote in his brief review of his brother's last illness that when the priest was leaving the room Beethoven said to him, "I thank you for this last service." According to Nohl,[55] Beethoven received the viaticum in the presence of Schindler, von Breuning, Jenger and Therese, the wife of his brother Johann.

About one o'clock on March 24th the special shipment of wine and wine

[54] In a letter to Thayer which was found among Hüttenbrenner's posthumous papers and printed in the "Gratzer Tagespost" of October 23, 1868. (TDR, v, 488, n. 3.)

[55] *Beethoven*, III, p. 783. Nohl gives no sources. (TDR, v, 489, n. 2.)

mixed with herbs came from Mainz, and Schindler placed the bottles upon the table near the bed. Beethoven looked at them and murmured, "Pity, pity—too late!" He spoke no more. A little of the wine was administered to him in spoonfuls at intervals, as long as he could swallow it. Towards evening he lost consciousness and the death-struggle began. It lasted two days. "From towards the evening of the 24th to his last breath he was almost continually *in delirio*," wrote Schindler to Moscheles.[56] We have a description from Gerhard von Breuning:[57] "During the next day and the day following the strong man lay completely unconscious, in the process of dissolution, breathing so stertorously that the rattle could be heard at a distance. His powerful frame, his unweakened lungs, fought like giants with approaching death. The spectacle was a fearful one. Although it was known that the poor man suffered no more it was yet appalling to observe that the noble being, now irredeemably a prey to the powers of dissolution, was beyond all mental communication. It was expected as early as the 25th that he would pass away in the following night; yet we found him still alive on the 26th—breathing, if that was possible, more stertorously than on the day before."

Anselm Hüttenbrenner, who was a witness of Beethoven's death, writes:[58] "When I entered Beethoven's bedroom on March 26, 1827 at about 3 o'clock in the afternoon, I found there Court Councillor Breuning, his son, Frau van Beethoven, wife of Johann van Beethoven, landowner and apothecary of Lenz, and my friend Joseph Teltscher, portrait painter. I think that Prof. Schindler was also present."

Gerhard von Breuning says that Beethoven's brother was in the room, and also the housekeeper Sali; Schindler adds a nurse from Dr. Wawruch's clinic. No doubt all were present at one moment or another; they came and went as occasion or duty called. Hüttenbrenner says that Teltscher began drawing the face of the dying man, which grated on Breuning's feelings and he made a remonstrance, whereupon the painter left the room. Then Breuning and Schindler went away to choose a spot for the grave. Hüttenbrenner continues: "Frau van Beethoven and I only were in the death-chamber during the last moments of Beethoven's life. After Beethoven had lain unconscious, the death-rattle in his throat from 3 o'clock in the afternoon till after 5, there came a flash of lightning accompanied by a violent clap of thunder, which garishly illuminated the death-chamber. (Snow lay before Beethoven's dwelling.) After this unexpected phenomenon of nature, which startled me greatly, Beethoven opened his eyes, lifted his right hand and looked up for several seconds with his fist clenched and a very serious, threatening expression as if he wanted to say: 'Inimical powers, I defy you! Away with you! God is with me!' It also seemed as if, like a brave commander, he wished to call out to his wavering troops: 'Courage, soldiers!

---

[56] On April 4, 1827. See Ley, *op.cit.*, p. 239.
[57] *Aus dem Schwarzspanierhause*, p. 108. (TDR, v, 489.)
[58] In a letter to Thayer dated August 20, 1860. (TDR, v, 490, n. 1.)

Forward! Trust in me! Victory is assured!'[59] When he let the raised hand sink to the bed, his eyes closed half-way. My right hand was under his head, my left rested on his breast. Not another breath, not a heartbeat more! The genius of the great master of tones fled from this world of delusion into the realm of truth!—I pressed down the half-open eyelids of the dead man, kissed them, then his forehead, mouth and hands.—At my request Frau van Beethoven cut a lock of hair from his head and handed it to me as a sacred souvenir of Beethoven's last hour. Thereupon I hurried, deeply moved, into the city, carried the intelligence of Beethoven's death to Herr Tobias Haslinger, and after a few hours returned to my home in Styria."

—It is not clear that Hüttenbrenner was accurate in his identification of his companion at the death scene. Two months before writing the above, he had referred to the woman in question as "Karl's mother."[60] But Thayer learned from Karl's wife that his mother "could not have been present at Beethoven's death, as it was a matter of complaint with her that no news of his dying condition reached her until after all was over. Dr. Breuning also thinks that she could not have been there, for he has no recollection of ever having seen either of the sisters-in-law of Beethoven." Stephan Ley[61] suggests logically that the other person was the maid, Sali, whom Hüttenbrenner mistook for "Frau van Beethoven."—

When Breuning and Schindler left the dying man in the care of Hüttenbrenner and "Frau van Beethoven," they went to the cemetery of the little village of Währing, and selected a place for Beethoven's grave in the vicinity of the burial plot of the Vering family, to which Breuning's first wife had belonged. Their return was retarded by the storm. When they reentered the sick-room they were greeted with the words: "It is finished!" The immediate activities of the friends were now directed to preparations for the funeral, the preservation of the physical likeness of the great composer and, so far as necessary, the safeguarding of his possessions. In respect of the latter Gerhard von Breuning tells of a painful incident which happened on the day after Beethoven's death.

Breuning, Schindler, Johann van Beethoven and Holz were met in the lodgings to gather up the dead man's papers, particularly to look for the

[59] Thayer visited Hüttenbrenner in Graz in June, 1860. The transcript in Thayer's notebook of Hüttenbrenner's oral recital is more sententious and dramatic: "At this startling, awful peal of thunder, the dying man suddenly raised his head from Hüttenbrenner's arm, stretched out his own right arm majestically— 'like a general giving orders to an army.' This was but for an instant; the arm sunk back; he fell back; Beethoven was dead." (TK, III, 307, n. 2; 308, n. 1.)

[60] See H. E. Krehbiel, *Music and Manners in the Classical Period* (New York, 1898), p. 204. Krehbiel has published in this book

the complete transcript of Hüttenbrenner's remarks to Thayer in June, 1860. (Cf. TK, III, 307, n. 2.)

[61] *Wahrheit, Zweifel und Irrtum in der Kunde von Beethovens Leben* (Wiesbaden, 1955), pp. 41-2. Here Ley also discusses the close of a short piece by Johann on his brother's last sickness and death, now in the Beethovenhaus in Bonn. It is not known for whom Johann wrote, but his claim that Beethoven died in his arms is in direct contradiction to Hüttenbrenner's account. Ley believes it was a fabrication; Johann's vanity from the fame of his brother was well known.

seven bank-shares which the will had given to the nephew. In spite of strenuous search they were not found, and Johann let fall an insinuation that the search was a sham. This angered von Breuning and he left the house in a state of vexation and excitement. He returned to the lodgings in the afternoon and the search was resumed. Then Holz pulled out a protruding nail in a cabinet, whereupon a drawer fell out and in it were the certificates. In later years Holz explained to Otto Jahn: "Beethoven kept his bank-shares in a secret drawer, the existence of which was known only to Holz. While Beethoven lay dying his brother in vain tried to find out where it was." On a copy of this memorandum,[62] Schindler wrote: "First of all after the death, Johann van Beethoven searched for the shares, and not finding them cried out: 'Breuning and Schindler must produce them!' Holz was requested to come by Breuning and asked if he did not know where they were concealed. He knew the secret drawer in an old cabinet[63] in which they were preserved." With the certificates were found the letter to the "Immortal Beloved" and the portrait of the Countess von Brunsvik.[64]

On March 27th, an autopsy[65] was performed by Dr. Johann Wagner in the presence of Dr. Wawruch. In order to facilitate an examination of the organs of hearing, the temporal bones were sawed out and carried away. Joseph Danhauser, a young painter who chanced to be in Vienna, received permission from Breuning to make a plaster cast of the dead man's face. This he did on March 28, but the cast has little value as a portrait, inasmuch as it was made after the autopsy, which had greatly disfigured the features. On the same day, Danhauser made a drawing of the head of Beethoven, which he reproduced by lithographic process. This picture bears the inscription: "Beethoven, March 28, drawn at his death-bed, 1827," and to the left, "Danhauser." This drawing, too, was made after the autopsy. For a bust which he modeled, the artist made use of the cast taken by Klein in 1812. Danhauser never came in contact with Beethoven alive.

The funeral took place at 3 o'clock in the afternoon of March 29th. It was one of the most imposing functions of its kind ever witnessed in Vienna.[66] Breuning and Schindler had made the arrangements. Cards of invitation were given out at Haslinger's music-shop. ⸺In the Archives of the Vienna Supreme Court there is a document containing a full account of Beethoven's funeral. The material was transcribed by Andreas Zeller, "bürgl. Magistradtischer Konducktansager des bürgl. Grundt Alservorstadt und Breidenfeld" (Director of ceremonies for Alservorstadt and Breitenfeld) and published by Robert Franz Müller:[67]

[62] Preserved among Thayer's papers. (TK, III, 310, n. 1.)

[63] Schindler writes "cash-box" (*Biogr.*, I, p. 97); Breuning "writing-case" (*Schwarzsp.*, p. 112). (TDR, v, 493, n. 1.)

[64] See Appendix C for list of Beethoven's estate.

[65] See Appendix B.

[66] See *Aus dem Schwarzspanierhause*, p. 113; Hiller's *Aus dem Tonleben*, pp. 177ff.; *Der Sammler*, April 14, 1827; Seyfried's *Beethovens Studien*, appendix, pp. 50ff. (TDR, v, 494, n. 2.)

[67] *Beethovens Begräbnis* in *Reichspost*, Vienna, March 26, 1925, p. 2.

"Beethoven died on Monday, March 26, 1827 about 5.45 P.M. Two men kept the death watch. On Tuesday morning Dr. Johann Wagner dissected the corpse. Then it was clothed and laid in a polished oak coffin which rested on ball-shaped gilded supports. On the cover was constructed a gilded cross. The head of the deceased, adorned with a wreath of white roses, rested on a white silk pillow. The face, framed with gray curls, was very lifeless because of the dissection. The folded hands grasped a wax cross and a large lily. And near the body a large lily was placed on the right side and on the left. Over the coffin was spread a coverlet half pulled back. The bier stood in the room in which he died, with his head facing the 'composition room' [music room]. There were eight candles burning on both sides of the coffin. On a table at the foot stood a crucifix and holy water for aspersion together with ears of corn. The good faithful Sali, the Master's maid, tirelessly received the many who wished to pay their last respects to the deceased.

"Thursday was the time of departure. Andreas Zeller, the director of ceremonies, had given out the last gate ticket on the day before. Around noon he stepped into the room and distributed to the invited guests rose bouquets with white silk stitches. They were placed on the left sleeve. Near 3 o'clock poems by Castelli and Seidl were given out as keepsakes.[68] In the morning by order of Breuning Mathias Mann with 5 others had cleaned the roomy court. In this area were gathered Barbaja's singers of the Italian Opera. Before 3 o'clock the house-gate was closed, the court filled to overflowing, and outside the crowd stormily demanded entrance. The military assistance from the Alser Barracks, procured by Breuning, was hardly able to ward off the crowd. Even the schools were closed.

"At 3 o'clock the coffin was closed, carried down and placed in the court. The pall, ordered by Anton Schindler from the 2nd Civil Regiment, was spread over the coffin, the cross was adorned with a 'very beautiful' wreath, and the Evangelical book and the 'very beautiful' civic crown set up. The contour of the coffin was hidden by a group of wreaths. Nine priests from the Schottenstifte blessed the dead. Thereupon Barbaja's court singers sang a funeral song: a chorale by B. Anselm Weber.[69] The singers were Eichenberger, Schuster, Cramolini, Müller, Hofmann, Rupprecht, Borschitzky, and Anton Wranitzky from the orchestra. These singers also carried the coffin into the church.[70] Now the door was opened; the crowd was so jammed that only with the greatest difficulty was the director of ceremonies and his helpers able to organise the procession. Even those standing near the deceased became pressed from their places of honor behind the coffin. From here hung down broad white silk bands. The ends of the pall (not the points) were taken by the eight Kapellmeister—to wit, Eybler, Hummel, Kreutzer, Seyfried on the right; Gänsbacher, Gyrowetz, Weigl, Würfel on the left—the honor escort

---

[68] See *Aus dem Schwarzspanierhause*, pp. 119-22.

[69] From his opera *Wilhem Tell*.

[70] Trinity Church of the Minorites in the Alserstrasse.

of the sleeping master. They carried candles wrapped in crepe. On both sides of the coffin came the torchbearers: Anschütz, Bernard, Blahetka, Joseph Böhm, Castelli, Karl Czerny, David, Grillparzer, Konrad Graf, Grünbaum, Haslinger, Hildebrandt, Holz, Kaller, Krall, Lannoy, Linke, Mayseder, Meric, Merk, Mechetti, Meier, Paccini, Piringer, Rodicchi, Raimund, Riotte, Schoberlechner, Schubert, Schickh, Schmiedl, Streicher, Schuppanzigh, Steiner, Weidmann, Wolfmayer, and others, with lily bouquets adorning their shoulders. The torches were decorated with flowers.

"Now the procession, which had been formed with so much trouble, started to move, beginning with the carriers of the crosses decorated with flowers. Members of welfare institutions followed. Behind them strode the trombonists: the Blöch brothers, Weidl and Tuschka. Then followed Assmayer's choir with the singers Tiebe, Schnitzer, Gros, Sykora, Frühwald, Geissler, Rathmayer, Kokrement, Nejebse, Ziegler, Perschl, Leidl, Pfeifer, Weinkopf and Seipelt. They sang the *Miserere*, the refrain of which was blown by the trombonists. This *Miserere* was the work specified as music for All-Souls' Day, which Beethoven had written at Linz in 1812 at Glöggl's request. During the evening of March 26th and 27th Seyfried arranged it for voices. *Amplius lava me*[71] was also sung. The parish crucifer was followed by the nine priests from the Schottenstifte, striding slowly before the coffin. The cross-carriers, priests, corporation, and director of ceremonies wore rose bouquets. Behind the coffin in the middle of the boisterous crowd followed Johann and Johanna [? Therese?] van Beethoven, Stephan and Gerhard v. Breuning, Hofrat v. Mosel, the students of Drechsler, Kapellmeister of St. Anna, the pupils of the Conservatory, and numerous friends and admirers of the deceased. At the end of the procession came the 'very lovely ceremonial carriage' pulled by 4 horses which had been ordered from the office of Kirchenmeister of St. Stephan Cathedral. Thus the procession reached the Alsergasse. Gerhard von Breuning (prone to exaggeration) estimated the crowd at 20,000; the *Sammler* at 10,000. When the procession turned into the Alsergasse, a brass band played the 'Marcia funebre' from Op. 26. The church was filled to capacity; the soldiers on duty did not want to admit anyone after the coffin had been carried in. The relatives and friends of the master succeeded only with difficulty to get inside the church. Those who had fainted from the pressure of the crowd were taken across to the hospital.

"The inside of the church shone with candle-light. Zeller's receipt for the cost of lighting the three main altars showed that the town wax dealer had supplied 6 1/2 lbs.[72] But Johann Wolfmayer had candles at all altars, wall brackets, and chandeliers lit at his own expense. The nine priests from the Schottenstifte sang the *Libera* by Seyfried. Then the bier was carried by the bearers, led by the trombonists and priests and followed by the funeral

---

[71] Also written by Beethoven for Glöggl and arranged for voices by Seyfried. The singers and trombonists alternated in the performance. See WoO 30, Nos. 1 and 3.

[72] Cf. with the receipts for wax listed by Ley, *Aus Beethovens Erdentagen*, pp. 239-40.

guests. It was taken through the nave and to the door. The ceremony was over.

"After the religious service the ceremonial carriage took the coffin. A part of the crowd was dispersed but thousands closed in on the procession going slowly along the hospital street. It crossed the Alserbach by the Namentur, passed by the almshouse and the brick-kiln, reached the Währing line, crossed it, reached the right bank of the Währing Brook and went along the brook to the village parish church. The minister, Johann Hayek and a second priest were waiting there. The procession stopped; the coffin was carried into the church and blessed by both of the priests, candles were burning on three altars. After the ceremony the parish singers sang the *Miserere* [motets] and the *Libera*. . . . Now the bearers again took the bier. Many people were still following the procession, the village school-children were there, supervised by the school assistants; then came the local poor people. Before the coffin went the priests, the sacristan, and the acolyte with the censer. The funeral guests followed the coffin accompanied by the prayer leader. The Währing master of ceremonies arranged the procession. With the brook on the right and a slope falling gently on the left, the funeral procession approached the fields of the parish cemetery[73] amid the sound of bells. Before the gates—the present gates were added later—the bearers put their load down. Before the coffin stepped the great tragedian, Heinrich Anschütz, and delivered the gripping obituary by Grillparzer.[74] Thereupon a poem by Schlechta was passed out. And now the great man joined the other dead. The priests consecrated the tomb and blessed the corpse for the last time. By the last light of the spring day the coffin was lowered into the earth. . . . Tobias Haslinger had brought three laurel wreaths which Hummel placed on the grave. According to an old custom, those standing near threw earth on the grave and the torches were extinguished."

In its report *Der Sammler* said: "The crowd was so great that after the roomy court of Beethoven's residence could no longer hold it the gates had to be closed until the procession moved. The coffin containing the corpse of the great composer had been placed on view in the court. After the clergy were come to perform their sacred office, the guests, who had been invited to attend these solemn functions—musicians, singers, poets, actors—all clad in complete mourning, with draped torches and white roses fastened to bands of crape on their sleeves, encircled the bier and the choristers sang the *Miserere* composed by the deceased. Solemnly, sublimely the pious tones of the glorious composition floated upwards through the silent air. The scene was imposing. The coffin, with its richly embroidered pall, the clergy, the distinguished men who were giving the last escort to their colleague, and the multitude round about—all this made a stupendous picture."

[73] Friedhof.   [74] See Appendix A.

On April 3rd Mozart's *Requiem* was sung at the Church of the Augustinians,[75] under the direction of Lablache. On April 5th a further observance was made with a performance of the Cherubini *Requiem* at the Karlskirche. The grave in the cemetery at Währing was marked by a simple pyramid bearing the one word

BEETHOVEN

It fell into neglect, and on October 13th, 1863, the Gesellschaft der Musikfreunde of Vienna caused the body to be exhumed and reburied. On June 21st, 1888, the remains of Beethoven and Schubert were removed to the Central Cemetery in Vienna, where they now repose side by side.

FINIS

[75] According to the report in Landau's *Erste poetische Beethoven-Album* (Prague, 1877), dated March 29, 1827, the *Miserere* and *Libera me* were again performed at the close of the performance by popular request. See Kerst, pp. 239-40.

APPENDIX A

FRANZ GRILLPARZER'S FUNERAL ORATION[1]

STANDING by the grave of him who has passed away we are in a manner the representatives of an entire nation, of the whole German people, mourning the loss of the one highly acclaimed half of that which was left us of the departed splendor of our native art, of the fatherland's full spiritual bloom. There yet lives—and may his life be long!—the hero of verse in German speech and tongue; but the last master of tuneful song, the organ of soulful concord, the heir and amplifier of Handel and Bach's, of Haydn and Mozart's immortal fame is now no more, and we stand weeping over the riven strings of the harp that is hushed.

The harp that is hushed! Let me call him so! For he was an artist, and all that was his, was his through art alone. The thorns of life had wounded him deeply, and as the cast-away clings to the shore, so did he seek refuge in thine arms, O thou glorious sister and peer of the Good and the True, thou balm of wounded hearts, heaven-born Art! To thee he clung fast, and even when the portal was closed wherethrough thou hadst entered in and spoken to him, when his deaf ear had blinded his vision for thy features, still did he ever carry thine image within his heart, and when he died it still reposed on his breast.

He was an artist—and who shall arise to stand beside him?

As the rushing behemoth spurns the waves, so did he rove to the uttermost bounds of his art. From the cooing of doves to the rolling of thunder, from the craftiest interweaving of well-weighed expedients of art up to that awful pitch where planful design disappears in the lawless whirl of contending natural forces, he had traversed and grasped it all. He who comes after him will not continue him; he must begin anew, for he who went before left off only where art leaves off. Adelaide and Leonora! Triumph of the heroes of Vittoria—and the humble sacrificial song of the Mass!—Ye children of the voices divided thrice and four times! heaven-soaring harmony: "Freude, schöner Götterfunken," thou swansong! Muse of song and the seven-stringed lyre! Approach his grave and bestrew it with laurel!

He was an artist, but a man as well. A man in every sense—in the highest. Because he withdrew from the world, they called him a man-hater, and because he held aloof from sentimentality, unfeeling. Ah, one who knows himself hard of heart, does not shrink! The finest points are those most

[1] This translation is drawn from *Beethoven—Impressions of Contemporaries* (G. Schirmer: New York, 1926), pp. 229-31, with a few minor changes to correspond with the version upon which it is based in Grillparzer's Collected Works Edition (see Franz Grillparzer [Gesammelte Werke, Vol. 5] *Autobiographisches Studien*, R. Backmann ed., pp. 420-22, Bergland, Vienna, 1952). A slightly different version of the poem is to be found in Gerhard von Breuning's *Aus dem Schwarzspanierhause*, pp. 116-19, from a copy which his father had received from the poet.

easily blunted and bent or broken. An excess of sensitiveness avoids a show of feeling! He fled the world because, in the whole range of his loving nature, he found no weapon to oppose it. He withdrew from mankind after he had given them his all and received nothing in return. He dwelt alone, because he found no second Self. But to the end his heart beat warm for all men, in fatherly affection for his kindred, for the world his all and his heart's blood.

Thus he was, thus he died, thus he will live to the end of time.

You, however, who have followed after us hitherward, let not your hearts be troubled! You have not lost him, you have won him. No living man enters the halls of the immortals. Not until the body has perished, do their portals unclose. He whom you mourn stands from now onward among the great of all ages, inviolate forever. Return homeward therefore, in sorrow, yet resigned! And should you ever in times to come feel the overpowering might of his creations like an onrushing storm, when your mounting ecstasy overflows in the midst of a generation yet unborn, then remember this hour, and think, We were there, when they buried him, and when he died, we wept.

APPENDIX B

AUTOPSY[1]

March 27, 1827

THE corpse was very emaciated, especially in the limbs, and sown over with black Petechien; the abdomen, which was unusually dropsied, was distended and stretched.

The external ear was large and irregularly formed, the scaphoid fossa but more especially the concha was very spacious and half as large again as usual: the various angles and sinuosities were strongly marked. The external auditory canal was covered with shining scales, particularly in the vicinity of the tympanum, which was concealed by them. The Eustachian tube was much thickened, its mucous lining swollen and somewhat contracted about the osseous portion of the tube. In front of its orifice and towards the tonsils some dimpled scars were observable. The principal cells of the Mastoid process, which was large and not marked by any notch, were lined with a vascular mucous membrane. The whole substance of the Os petrosum showed a similar degree of vascularity, being traversed by vessels of considerable size, more particularly in the region of the cochlea, the membranous part of its spiral lamina appearing slightly reddened.

The facial nerves were of unusual thickness, the auditory nerves, on the contrary, were shrivelled and destitute of neurina; the accompanying arteries were dilated to more than the size of a crow quill and cartilaginous. The left auditory nerve much the thinnest, arose by three very thin greyish striae, the right by one strong clearer white stria from the substance of the fourth ventricle, which was at this point much more consistent and vascular than in other parts. The convolutions of the brain were full of water, and remarkably white; they appeared very much deeper, wider, and more numerous than ordinary.

The Calvarium exhibited throughout great density and a thickness amounting to about half an inch.

The cavity of the Chest, together with the organs within it, was in the normal condition.

In the cavity of the Abdomen four quarts of a greyish-brown turbid fluid were effused.

The liver appeared shrunk up to half its proper volume, of a leathery consistence and greenish-blue color, and was beset with knots, the size of a bean, on its tuberculated surface, as well as in its substance; all its vessels were very much narrowed, and bloodless.

---

[1] See Waldemar Schweisheimer, *Beethovens Leiden* (Munich, 1922), pp. 185-86. See also Seyfried's *Beethoven: Studies*, translated by Henry H. Pierson (Leipzig, 1853), pp. 43-44 from which the major part of the translation was drawn.

The Spleen was found to be more than double its proper size, dark-colored and firm.

The Pancreas was equally hard and firm, its excretory duct being as wide as a goosequill.

The Stomach, together with the Bowels, was greatly distended with air. Both Kidneys were invested by cellular membrane of an inch thick, and infiltrated with a brown turbid fluid; their tissue was pale-red and opened out. Every one of their calices was occupied by a calcareous concretion of a wart-like shape and as large as a split pea. The body was much emaciated.[2]

(Signed) Dr. Joseph Wagner
Assistant in the Pathological Museum

[2] For a recent medical summary of Beethoven's case history, see S. J. London, M.D., "Beethoven, Case Report of a Titan's Last Crisis," *Archives of Internal Medicine*, Vol. 113 (1964), pp. 442-48.

APPENDIX C

BEETHOVEN'S ESTATE

1. LEGAL INVENTORY AND ASSESSMENT[1]
    ON AUGUST 16, 1827
of musical effects and books belonging to the estate of the musician Ludwig van Beethoven, deceased on March 26, 1827, in Vienna at the Schwarzspanierhaus No. 200.

Present:
Brandstätter (Ferdinand), Municipal Secretary
v. Ortowitz (Franz), Commissary ("Sperr-Commissär")
Ohmeyer, substituting for Dr. Bach as Trustee
Hotscherer (Jacob), R.I. "Hof-Concipist" and Guardian (of the nephew)
                    In addition
    to those especially invited hereto:
Czerny (Carl), composer and petitioned witness
Piringer (Ferdinand), R.I. "Hofkammer-Registr.-Dir.-Adjunct"
Haslinger (Tobias), licensed Art and Music dealer
                    And both treasurers
Artaria (Dominik), licensed Art and Music dealer
Sauer (Ignaz), former   "   "   "   "

Works Spoken For
    For Count Lichnowsky
1 volume of Bach's Inventions and Preludes copied
6 volumes of Handel's works, bound

    For H. Schindler
Mass by Beethoven in D written as 3 Hymns

    Herr von Zmeskall
Gluck's Iphigenie auf Tauris
Orpheus und Eurydice is salable

    Herr v. Kuffner
Text for a Cantata. 1st section. Saul kehrt nach glänzenden Siegen etc.

    For the R.I. Court Theatre
Libretto to Fidelio
    "   " der edelste Mann

---

[1] Thayer, *Chron. Verzeichniss*, pp. 173-82.

H. v. Piringer
Fux's Gradus ad Parnassum

Steiner and Co.
Complete original score of the 7th Symphony in A
Siegessymphonie von der Schlacht bei Vittoria. Original score
Finale of the 8th Symphony. F major
Der heilige Augenblick. Cantata in score
Parts for a Cantata written out and score for the choral director in 2 packages

---

Artaria and Co.
belonging to same because H. v. Beethoven had borrowed them.
6 volumes of Metastasio's works
Score of the ballet Prometheus
Rondo, primo Amore for voice
Trio for 2 oboes and English horn
Overture to Fidelio
Andante Vivace with song
Sonata for pianoforte

F. Starke, Kapellmeister
No. 175. Trifles for pianoforte for Starke's Klavierschule

No. 204. Reutter. Count Lichnowsky

AUCTION CATALOGUE

I

Beethoven's Own Notes and Notebooks

No.		Appraised Fl.	Kr.	Sold Fl.	Kr.
1	Notes and notebooks	1	—	1	15
2	" " "	1	—	1	15
3	" " "	1	—	1	15
4	" " "	1	—	1	16
5	" " "	1	—	1	15
6	Notebook	1	—	1	15
7	"	1	—	1	30
8	Notes	1	—	1	25
9	"	1	—	1	15
10	" and sketches	1	—	1	15
11	Notebook	1	—	2	12

No.		Appraised Fl.	Kr.	Sold Fl.	Kr.
12	Notes and sketches	1	–	1	15
13	Notes	1	–	1	16
14	"	1	–	1	15
15	"	1	–	1	15
16	"	1	–	2	06
17	Notebook	1	–	2	50
18	Notes	1	–	1	22
19	"	1	–	1	30
20	"	1	–	2	10
21	Notebook	1	–	2	02
22	"	1	–	3	–
23	Notes	1	–	} 3	01
24	Notebook	1	–		
25	Notes	1	–		
26	"	1	–	1	30
27	"	1	–	1	30
28	Notebooks	1	–	2	10
29	Notebook	1	–	2	36
30	Notes	1	–	} 2	03
31	2 Notebooks	1	–		
32	Notebook	1	–	2	03
33	Notes	1	–	2	–
34	"	1	–	1	30
35	Notebook	1	–	2	44
36	Notes	1	–	1	30
37	"	1	–	1	15
38	"	1	–	1	15
39	Notes and Notebook	1	–	1	30
40	Notebook	1	–	2	–
41	Big notebook	1	–	2	–
42	Notes	1	–	1	–
43	Notebook and notes	1	–	1	–
44	"	1	–	1	30
45	2 Notebooks	1	–	} 2	30
46	Notes	1	–		
47	Notebook	1	–	1	10
48	Notes (Notirungen)	1	–	1	10
49	Notebook (Notirbuch)	1	–	1	10
50	Book of Notes (Notirungsbuch)	1	–	1	10
51	Prompter's part from the opera Fidelio, 2 acts, copy with notations in own hand	2	–	2	30

II

Used Sketches, Fragments and Works Unfinished In Part Still Unpublished and Written in Own Hand

No.		Appraised Fl. Kr.		Sold Fl. Kr.	
52	Quartet sketches	2	–	2	36
53	Sketches	2	–	2	30
54	Quartet sketches	2	–	2	30
55	Completed sketches and pieces	3	–	3	30
56	Completed sketches	3	–	3	01
57	Quartet sketches	2	–	3	–
58	Italian Ariettes	2	–	} 6	30
59	Sketches for a quintet still unknown	2	–		
60	Used sketches	2	–		
61	Copy of the Pianoforte Trio Op. 1, arranged as a quintet anonymously	1	–	1	–
62	Copy of Trio No. 2	2	–	3	–
63	Mass sketches	2	–	3	–
64	Quartet sketches, bagatelles for p.-f.	2	–	2	30
65	Sketches for a Pianoforte Concerto	2	–	} 3	–
66	Bagatelles	2	–		
67	Vocal piece with orchestra completed but not wholly orchestrated	3	–	9	30
68	Song	1	–	1	16
69	Sextet	2	–	2	30
70	Original songs	3	–	3	30

III

Autographs of Printed Works

No.		Appraised Fl. Kr.		Sold Fl. Kr.	
71	Sonate for Pianoforte	–	30	2	33
72	Manuscript printed by Simrock	1	–	1	24
73	2 pianoforte trios together in one copy belonging to Breitkopf	2	–	3	40
74	An die Hoffnung, song		20	1	30
75	Gesang der Nachtigal, song	–	10	1	–
76	Manuscript for pianoforte and other instruments, apparently Scottish songs	1	–	1	30
77	Quartet piece belonging to Schott		30	1	–
78	Quartet piece	1	–	3	03
79	" "	–	30	1	06
80	Finale of the Pastoral Symphony in score	1	30	2	06

No.		Appraised Fl. Kr.		Sold Fl. Kr.	
81	Score of the 4th Symphony 1st piece	1	30	5	–
82	A piece from the opera Fidelio in score	–	40	2	06
83	Abendlied	–	30	1	15
84	Fugue in a quartet	–	30	3	–
85	Fantasy-Sonata	–	45	1	40
86	Sonata for pianoforte and violin	–	45	2	59
87	Kyrie of the 1st Mass in score	1	–	1	24
88	March from Fidelio. Score	–	40	1	40
89	Pianoforte Concerto in E-Flat. Score	2	–	3	45
90	Variations for pianoforte	1	–	1	30
91	Sonata for p.-f. and violoncello	1	–	2	30
92	54th Sonata for pianof., not complete	–	30	–	36
93	Romance for violin. Score	–	30	3	45
94	Quartet piece	–	40	–	52
95	Violin-quartet piece, belonging evidently to Schlesinger	5	–	5	–
96	From Leonore a piece in score	–	20	–	24
97	4th Symphony in score	4	–	5	–
98	Scottish songs	–	40	1	–
99	Songs	–	40	–	48
100	Opferlied. Score	–	40	1	–
101	Sonata for pianoforte	1	–	1	30
102	Violin-quartet piece	4	–	4	–
103	Christus am Oelberg. Score	6	–	7	–
104	Gloria from the First Mass. Score	3	–	5	55
105	5th Symphony. Score	5	–	6	–
106	Andante from the Pastoral Symphony. Score	3	–	1	18
107	Bagatelles for pianoforte	1	–	2	03
108	Finale of the Concerto in E-Flat. Score	2	–	2	20
109	Festival overture in score	2	–	2	30
110	Quintet for violin	2	–	2	30
111	Pieces from Egmont	–	20	–	50
112	Quartet by Haydn in score, copied by Beethoven	–	40	1	–
113	Symphony in score	4	–	5	–
114	Fugue by Sebastian Bach transcribed for quartet by Beethoven	–	30	–	40
115	Concerto for Pianoforte in C major. Score	3	–	4	13
116	Sonata for Pianoforte in A-Flat	1	–	2	–
117	Fragment for a quartet	–	45	1	36
118	Finale of the Quartet in C-sharp minor	1	–	1	20
119	Quartet pieces	2	–	3	–
120	Sketches for a pianoforte sonata	1	–	2	05
121	Variations for pianoforte	1	20	2	–
122	Original score of the Septet	3	–	18	–
123	Quartet piece	–	40	1	–
124	Sonata for pianoforte and flute	1	–	1	30

No.		Appraised Fl. Kr.		Sold Fl. Kr.	
125	2nd Pianoforte Concerto in score	3	–	4	–
126	Last Mass in score	6	–	7	–
127	Quartet piece	–	40	1	–
128	Song to Chloe	–	30	1	06
129	Two Finales to the opera Leonore in score	4	–	5	–
130	Two quartet pieces	1	30	5	10
131	Two vocal pieces	1	–	2	48
132	Agnus Dei in score	1	30	2	–
133	Songs of Gellert	–	30	1	–
134	Songs of Goethe	–	30	1	20
135	Two sonatas for pianoforte	1	30	2	–
136	Piece from a sonata for p.-f. and violin	–	30	–	45
137	Entr'actes to Egmont	2	–	3	–
138	Sonata for pianoforte and violoncello	–	45	1	30
139	Quintet in E-Flat	1	–	2	30
140	Sonatas for pianoforte and violin	1	30	3	12
141	Concerted pieces (or concertos) for pianoforte	5	–	4	–
142	Der Wachtelschlag	–	30	2	–
143	Chorus from Die gute Nachricht	–	40	4	30
144	Copy in another hand of the Eroica Symphony in score with notations in own hand	3	–	3	10
145	Copy in another hand of the Overture to Egmont in score (1810)	1	–	1	09
146	Copy in another hand of the Chorus of Ruinen von Athen	–	40	1	–
147	Copy in another hand of the Triumphal March to Tarpeja in parts written out	1	–	1	45
148	Copy in another hand of the Choral Fantasy in score	1	–	1	20

IV

Remaining Original Manuscripts of Ludwig van Beethoven, Incomplete, Written in Own Hand, Not Yet Printed

No.		Appraised Fl. Kr.		Sold Fl. Kr.	
149	Contrapuntal essays, apparently by other masters, with his own notations. 5 packages.	10	–	74	–
150	Recitative and vocal piece with orchestra in score	5	–	6	03
151	Italian Songs, apparently unknown	3	–	4	–
152	Complete movement of a violin quintet	3	–	4	–
153	Complete vocal piece, Prüfung des Küssens	5	–	6	–
154	Italian Duet in score	5	–	6	12
155	Canon and four-voiced song	2	–	2	30
156	Several songs, appear unknown	1	30	1	45
157	Two complete small pieces for p.-f. from his early period	1	–	1	–

No.		Appraised Fl. Kr.		Sold Fl. Kr.	
158	Song and sacred movement	1	–		
159	Two tattoos in score	5	–	6	36
160	Fragment of an unknown trio for pianoforte	1	–	1	20
161	Original cadenza to the 1st Concerto in C major (only the ending is missing)	–	20	–	45
162	March for wind band	2	–	2	20
163	Two songs	1	–	1	12
164	Ruinen von Athen in score, incomplete	10	–	8	–
165	Sketches, apparently for a quartet or voices	2	–	2	20
166	Three original movements of a quartet for pianoforte, 2 violins and violoncello	3	–	4	06
167	Complete vocal work	6	–	9	03
168	Scene and Aria, Italian in a copy of another hand, but the original of 1796	2	–	5	10
169	Some numbers from König Stephen in autograph and some in copy	5	–	3	–
170	Collection of unknown and in part completed movements	3	–	6	36
171	2 complete manuscripts from the 12th year of the composer—a fugue and a concerto for pianoforte	2	–	2	–
172	Pianoforte movements	2	–	3	09
173	Fragment of a new violin quintet of November, 1826, last work of the composer	10	–	30	30
174	Canon in two voices	–	20	1	–
175	(Starke)				
176	Trifles, complete for the p.-f.	3	–	2	–
177	Rondo with orchestra for the p.-f., unknown	10	–	20	–
178	Marches for orchestra, uncertain whether some are known	5	–	10	50
179	Unknown trio for p.-f. and flute and bassoon, earlier work while still in Bonn	8	–	20	–
180	Orchestral piece with chorus, unknown	5	–	6	–
181	Minuets for orchestra, together with a copy	3	–	8	06
182	Movement of an unknown violin concerto	2	–	10	–
183	Song, unknown	1	–	3	50
184	Pianoforte pieces with accompaniment, in part unknown	2	–	6	31
185	Easy caprice for the pianoforte, unknown	1	–	20	30
186	Sehnsucht, song, apparently unknown	1	–	–	48
187	Aria with pianoforte accompaniment, complete	2	–	3	24
188	Song with five-part accompaniment, complete	2	–	8	43
189	Symphony by Haydn in B-Flat, score appears to be by Haydn	3	–	3	30

V

Copied Parts to Beethoven Works

No.		Appraised Fl.	Appraised Kr.	Sold Fl.	Sold Kr.
190	For the last Symphony	3	–	3	30
191	For Christus am Oelberg	2	–	2	30
192	For the Symphony in A major	2	–	3	–
193	Chorus parts to Schiller's Lied an die Freude	1	–	1	12
194	Wellington's Battle	1	30	1	45
195	Overture to Leonore	1	–	3	–
196	Two packages for the overture at the performance in the Josefstadt Theatre (Op. 124)		30	–	40
197	For two symphonies, 2 packages	–	20	–	40
198	For the Mass	–	30	1	–
199	For a Symphony, dances, march music written by different composers	–	30	–	40
200	Madrigals by Lughini, together with 17 different pieces	–	30	1	–
201	18 different pieces	–	20	–	24
202	Leonore by Paër, score	1	–	1	20
203	Copy of a violin quartet in score by Beethoven and sold to H. Schlesinger, along with 19 different pieces	1	30	2	50
204	Reutter, Cantata, Parnassa, Score	1	–	1	–
205	24 different pieces	–	30	–	35
206	13 " "	–	20	–	30
207	Bach's Kunst der Fuge	–	30	1	03
208	17 different pieces	–	20	–	40
209	Beethoven's Symphony in B-Flat and several pieces from Fidelio in score, Copies	1	–	4	30
210	Fanisca by Cherubini. Score "in 4 Livr."	3	–	4	40
211	21 different pieces	–	30	4	50
212	Fidelio in score, complete along with libretto	8	–	15	–
213	Overture in score.—3 and 4 varied songs by Haydn— along with 17 different pieces	1	–	2	10
214	Pianoforte Concerto by Beethoven in score with some corrections in own hand, along with 10 different pieces	1	–	2	–
215	15 different pieces	1	–	3	45
216	Mozart's Zauberflöte in score	3	–	5	36

VI

Printed Music

No.		Appraised Fl.	Kr.	Sold Fl.	Kr.
217	Beethoven's Wellington's Victory at Vittoria in score	1	–	4	–
218	The same work	1	–	4	30
219	Beethoven's Mass in score along with 25 different pieces	–	30	3	06
220	18 different pieces	–	30	1	30
221	Messiah by Handel and Mozart Le deux petits Savoyards by Dalairac Idomeneo by Mozart in pianoforte score Mozart's Requiem in score	2	–	7	30
222	Beethoven's Christus am Oelberg in score Fidelio in Pianoforte-score Le Cadi dupé (Gluck). Score	2	–	3	15
223	Beethoven's Symphonies in score Nos. 1,2. Giulio Sabino by Sarti Preindel Gesanglehre	1	–	3	03
224	Haydn's Creation in score	3	–	4	–
225	Haydn Mass No. 3. Score " " " 1. " Beethoven's Christus am Oelberg. Score.	1	30	4	–
226	Beethoven's Fidelio in Pianoforte score Select collection of Irish Melodies by Beethoven. 2 volumes. Edinburgh	2	–	15	49
227	Mozart. Don Juan in score along with 15 other pieces	2	–	8	34
228	Mozart. Cosi fan tutte in score, along with 9 different pieces	1	–	6	12
229	Beethoven. Christus am Oelberg in score Fugue by Reicha and Medea by Cherubini in score	2	–	12	–
230	Mozart. Titus in score, along with 10 different pieces	1	–	3	–
231	Haydn. Seasons in score Dalairac. "La Soirée orageuse." Score Salieri. "Les Danaides." Score	2	–	7	12
232	The Mount of Olives by Beethoven Mozart's quartets in score Felix in score Valentine de Milan by Mehul. Score	2	–	8	40
233	Beethoven. Leonore and Christus am Oelberg in pianoforte score along with 6 different pieces	1	–	5	03
234	Symphony by Beethoven, Op. 125, in score, along with 12 different pieces	1	–	7	03

No.		Appraised Fl. Kr.		Sold Fl. Kr.	
235	Bach's Kunst der Fuge, along with 12 different pieces	1	–	2	32
236	Handel's Keyboard suites, along with 15 different pieces	–	40	2	18
237	Beethoven. Symphony, Op. 125, in score along with 15 different pieces	1	30	7	06
238	Intermezzo, La Serva Padrona by Paisiello / 2 Entr'Actes from Egmont by Beethoven along with different music	1	–	1	–
239	Handel's works in 40 calf-bound volumes, London edition	50	–	102	–
240	(crossed out)				
241	Handel's Julius Caesar	1	–	2	10
242 243 244	(crossed out)				
245	Handel's Alexander's Feast. Score. Ms.	1	30	2	–
246	Choruses from Handel's oratorios	–	30	–	40

VII

Books on Music

No.		Appraised Fl. Kr.		Sold Fl. Kr.	
247	Knecht's Orgelschule and Bach's Art das Klavier zu spielen	1	–	3	40
248	A package of musical newspapers	–	30	3	15
249	Camphuysens Rymens Amsterdam 1647 / Collection of Songs / Riepel's Tonordnung / " Contrapunkt } 5 volumes folio / " Setzkunst	1	30	2	–
250	Kirnberger's works, 6 volumes / Koch. Harmonie / Vogler. Choralsystem / Turk. Organist	1	–	2	40
251	Works of Haydn in score. 14 volumes. 8 parts.	2	–	14	03
252	Traite de la Fugue by Marburg and divers other pieces	1	–	1	37

Clavier, bought by Spina   181 fl.
Medals
2 violins   33 fl.

2. Sale of Beethoven's Mss. and Musical Library.[2]

[2] From the *Harmonicon*, April, 1828, as reprinted in Schindler, *The Life of Beethoven*, ed. by Moscheles, II, pp. 373-76.

Vienna, March 16, 1828

The sale of the lamented Beethoven's MSS. and musical library, which lately took place here, excited uncommon interest among the lovers of music, amateurs as well as professional men. The following are the heads under which the articles were arranged in the catalogue:—

1. Fragments from Beethoven's musical portfolio, consisting of noted paper, scraps of various themes, &c. 2. Fragments and sketches in a more complete form. 3. Autographs of scores already published. 4. Autographs of unpublished music. 5. Copies of various Symphonies, Choruses, Overtures, Masses, &c., corrected by the composer's own hand. 6. Printed music and theoretical works. 7. A small collection of works of general literature. 8. A small collection of musical instruments. The contest for several of the articles was warm and spirited, particularly between the well-known music-sellers Artaria, Haslinger, and Steiner. More than forty works, unknown to the public, were brought to the hammer, the greater part of which are productions of Beethoven's earlier years. No doubt the present possessors will, ere long, afford the world an opportunity of enjoying these works of the lamented master. We observed that the greater proportion of them became the property of Artaria, after a severe contest with his brother publishers; several fetched extraordinarily high prices. Besides a great many other articles, Beethoven's last work, an unfinished Quintett, begun in November, 1828, fell to the lot of Diabelli, who triumphantly bore it away, at a very high price, from a host of competitors. The same gentleman also became possessor of a Solo-Capriccio, of a Rondo for pianoforte and orchestra, and of the English pianoforte which Beethoven had received as present from the Messrs. Broadwood. The gold medal which the composer had the honour to receive from Louis XVIII on receiving the copy of one of his grand masses was bought by some anonymous collector. But by far the most interesting article of the whole sale fell to the lot of M. Haslinger—the collection of contrapuntic exercises, essays, and finished pieces, which Beethoven wrote while under the tuition of his master, the celebrated Albrechtsberger, all in his own handwriting, with the interlineal corrections of that master, and his remarks on the margin. It is in five thick volumes, which were evidently preserved with great care. The struggle for the possession of this invaluable relic—the fruit of Beethoven's first studies—was long and spirited; but the stamina of M. Haslinger brought him through; after many a fiercely-contested round, he was at length declared the victor, none of his antagonists coming to time. We are happy to be able to state that this collection of studies, so interesting to the whole musical world, is immediately to be placed in the hands of Kapellmeister Seyfried, who is to prepare it for the press. M. Haslinger also became the fortunate possessor of a pianoforte Trio, consisting of an Allegro, Adagio, Finale, and Variations, composed while Beethoven filled the place of organist in Cologne; of a short Sonata for four hands; of several songs and other vocal pieces; of a small collection, entitled *Zapfenstreiche*

für Türkische Musik; of two violins, with the possessor's seal on each; and lastly, of Beethoven's copy of the works of Handel, Dr. Arnold's edition, in forty volumes folio. The latter, as is well known, was presented to the lamented composer by his friend M. Stumpff, of London, the possession of which tended so much to soothe Beethoven during his last protracted illness. The mind and talents of Handel were kindred to his own, and he was seen for hours hanging over these volumes in rapture and forgetting his sufferings. Two other competitors contended warmly for this prize—M. Gläser of Gotha, and Mr. Schenk, the well-known composer of *Der Dorfbarbier*; but M. Haslinger still retained his honours as champion of the field. We must, however, observe, that, warm as the opposition was between these different opponents, the contest was still conducted with becoming respect—not to say with a certain solemnity due to the relics of the mighty dead. Some of the prices given astonished even the most enthusiastic admirers of the composer, and are the most satisfactory proofs of the deep zeal and love for the art predominant among us.

3. A Record of Beethoven's Estate

According to Fischhoff's notarized copy found in the estate of O. Jahn (taken from Thayer's papers).[3]

The auction was held November 5, 1827, at 1149 Kohlmarkt, rear part of the building, third story, under the direction of Anton Gräfer, the appraiser. Total intake 1140 florins 18 C.M.

[stamp]

Legal [or an account of?] inventory and appraisal of the estate of Ludwig van Beethoven, composer, No. 200 in the suburb of Alser, who died March 26, 1827, a week ago, having left a will.

Cash:

After the death of the departed were found				
bills	1215 florins (C.M.)			
coupons			600 (V. S.)	
total	1215	"	600	"

of which 650 florins were entrusted to the guardian of the under-aged nephew, Herr Hofrat von Bräuning [*Sic!*], for funeral and other expenses. 565 florins (C.M.) and 600 florins (V.S.) remained for deposit.

Bank Shares:

One share of the National Bank of Austria, no. 2, page 3099, dated July 13, 1819, with a coupon number 28624, payable to Ludwig van Beethoven, at

[3] See TDR, v, pp. 579-83.

the rate of exchange according to the market report of March 26, 1827, being the date of his death

1063 fl.—

with eight coupons of the first half-year period, 1827.

One share of same, no. 3, page 3099, dated same, with coupon number 28625, payable to same, at same rate of exchange

1063 fl.—

with eight coupons of the first half-year period, 1827.

One share of same, no. 4, page 3099, dated same, with coupon number 28626, payable to same, at same rate of exchange

1063 fl.—

with eight coupons of the first half-year period, 1827.

One share of same, no. 5, page 3099, dated same, with coupon number 28627, payable to same, at same rate of exchange

1063 fl.—

with eight coupons of the first half-year period, 1827.

One share of same, no. 6, page 3099, dated same, with coupon number 28628, payable to same, at same rate of exchange

1063 fl.—

with eight coupons of the first half-year period, 1827.

One share of same, no. 7, page 3099, dated same, with coupon number 28629, payable to same, at same rate of exchange

1063 fl.—

with eight coupons of the first half-year period, 1827.

One share of the National Bank of Austria, no. 8, page 3099, dated July 13, 1819, with coupon number 28630, payable to Ludwig van Beethoven, at same rate of exchange

1063 fl.—

with eight coupons of the first half-year period, 1827

total   7441 fl.—

Outstanding Subsidies:

From the privy office of His Majesty, from the private treasury of His Royal Highness Archduke Rudolf the sum for the period March 1 through March 26, 1827, of an annual grant of 600 fl. C.M.   43 fl. 20

From the electoral Lobkowitz treasury the sum for the same period, of an annual grant of 700 fl. V.S. or 280 fl. C.M.

66 fl. 53

From the royal Kinsky main treasury of Archduke Rudolf at Prag the sum for the period from March 1 through March 26, 1827, of an annual grant of 1200 fl. V.S. or 480 fl.

34 fl. 40

total   144 " 53

Valuables:

1 oval-shaped ring set with emerald, brilliants and rose diamond		90 fl.		—
1 gold medallion with a picture of Ludwig XVIII 41 #		164 "		—
1 silver watch		8 "		—
1 " serving spoon	C. 10½ Loth.[4]	10 "	30	—
1 " ladle	" 4½ "	4 "	15	—
8 " tablespoons	" 27½ "	27 "	30	—
5 " teaspoons	" 4½ "	4 "	30	—
1 " salt cellar	" 5¾ "	5 "	45	—
		total 314 "	30	—

The above listed cash, bank shares and valuables were handed over to the court.

Clothing and Personal Linens: C.M.

2 cloth swallow-tailed coats, 2 spencers, 2 Prince Alberts, 1 blue cloth overcoat	15 fl.
16 assorted knee stockings and 8 pair of trousers	6 " —
2 hats, 6 pair of boots, 3 pair of suspenders, 6 razors, 2 small pistols, 1 cane, 1 dressing gown	6 " —
14 shirts, 20 undershirts, 20 ascots and handkerchiefs, 18 pair of socks, 8 night shirts, 14 pair of underpants, 6 night caps	10 "
	total 37 " —

Household Linens and Furnishings:

2 tablecloths, 10 napkins, 10 handtowels, 6 bed sheets, 4 slip covers	4 " —
2 hardwood bedsteads including a paillasse and 4 mattresses, 7 pillows, 1 light blanket, 3 old quilts, 1 fur cover	12 " —

In the First Room:

4 small hardwood tables, 8 leather chairs, 3 hardwood chests of drawers, 1 night stand, 2 softwood stools, 1 fire screen, 1 writing desk	6 " —
2 mirrors in gilded frames, 2 pair of window curtains, 2 money boxes	2 " —

In the Second Room:

2 old tables, 2 old chairs, 1 hardwood desk, 1 hardwood cupboard, 1 softwood cabinet, 1 night stand, 3 softwood stools, 1 pair of curtains.	6 " —

[4] Loth=*circa* 1½ oz. in Troy Weight.

In the Third Room:

1 leather easy chair, 1 old sofa, 1 trunk, 2 pair of curtains   4 " —

In the Kitchen:

14 china plates, some earthenware, 1 tin cup, several glasses, bottles, and bowls   4 fl. —

4 brass candleholders, 1 brass mortar, 1 copper tub, 1 rotisserie, assorted iron pots and pans, and the usual kitchen furnishings   6 " —

Maelzel's metronome   8 " —

1 piano by John Broadwood and Son of London in mahogany case   100 " —

        total 152 " —

Instruments:

1 cello	by Father Zuaneri	40 " —
1 viola	" Vinc. Reschner	10 " —
1 violin	" Josef Zuaneri	16 " —
1 "	" Nikolaus Amati	12 " —
	total	78 " —

Printed Music, Manuscripts and Music Books:

According to the record which accompanies the auction papers these were appraised at   480 " 30

Books:

According to the record which accompanies the auction papers these were appraised at 45 fl. 58 kr. V.S., or in C.M.   18 " 20

Accordingly the inventory of the estate is appraised at nine thousand eight hundred eighty-five florins 13 kr. C.M.

        9885 fl. 13 kr. C.M.

        six hundred florins V.S.

        600 fl. V.S.

Cash	1215 fl.	600
Bank Shares	7441 "	
Outstanding Subsidies	144 "	53
Valuables	314 "	30
Clothing and Personal Linens	37 "	
Household Linens and Furnishings	156 [*sic*]	
Instruments	78 "	
Printed Music and Manuscripts	480 "	30
Books	18 "	20
total	9885 "	13 600

Vienna, October 4. In witness thereof the following:

Dro Bach curator

Jacob Hotschevar (personal signature) as guardian of the under-aged Karl van Beethoven and as witness

Jos. Leop. Krembs (personal signature) as witness

Franz Horny (personal signature) as witness

Fred. Prandstätter (personal signature)

Ignaz Schleicher (personal signature)

Franz Deimal (personal signature) appraiser of jewels

Franz Anton Hausmann (personal signature) appraiser

G. S. Ferdinand Leichtl (personal signature) appraiser of watches

Tobias Sponagl (personal signature) public appraiser

Seb. Zimmermann (personal signature) public appraiser

Martin Stuss (personal signature) appraiser

The town violin makers

APPENDIX D

FIRST PUBLICATION OF WORKS AFTER
BEETHOVEN'S DEATH

THIS list excludes: 1) arrangements by others, unless available in print in no other form; 2) first complete score editions if the work has already been published in parts; and 3) canons.

After 1825.

By Gombart in Augsburg: "An die Geliebte" (Stoll), WoO 140.

1827.

By Matthias Artaria:

Fugue for String Quartet, Op. 133, dedicated to Cardinal Archduke Rudolph of Austria.

The same arranged for Pianoforte Four Hands, Op. 134, dedicated to Cardinal Archduke Rudolph of Austria.

String Quartet in B-Flat major, Op. 130, dedicated to Prince Nikolas von Galitzin.

By Cappi and Czerny: March in D for Military Band, WoO 24, in pianoforte transcription.

By Haslinger: Fugue for String Quintet, Op. 137.

By Schlesinger:

String Quartet in A minor, Op. 132, dedicated to Prince Nikolas von Galitzin.

String Quartet in F major, Op. 135, dedicated to Johann Wolfmayer.

By Schott:

Missa Solemnis for Four Soloists, Chorus and Orchestra, Op. 123, dedicated to Cardinal Archduke Rudolph of Austria.

String Quartet in C-sharp minor, Op. 131, dedicated to Baron Joseph von Stutterheim.

1828.

By Artaria: Three Piano Quartets (1785), WoO 36.

By Diabelli: Rondo a capriccio for Pianoforte, Op. 129.

1829.

By Diabelli: Rondo for Pianoforte and Orchestra, WoO 6, with realisations by Czerny from Beethoven's indications.[1]

1830.

By Artaria: Octet for Wind Instruments, Op. 103.

By Diabelli: Rondino for Eight Wind Instruments, WoO 25.

By Dunst:

Piano Sonata, incomplete, WoO 51, dedicated to Eleonore von Breuning.

Trio for Pianoforte, Violin and Violoncello, WoO 38.

Trio for Pianoforte, Violin and Violoncello, WoO 39, dedicated to Maximiliane Brentano.

[1] See KHV, p. 436.

1832.

By Artaria: Gratulationsmenuett for Orchestra, WoO 3.

In I. v. Seyfried's *Beethovens Studien*, p. 329: "Im Arm der Liebe ruht sich's wohl," WoO 159.

1836.

In *Wiener Zeitschrift für Kunst, Literatur und Mode*, No. 10, supplement: Cadenza to the First Movement of Mozart's *Concerto for Piano-forte and Orchestra in D minor*, K. 466; WoO 58, No. 1.

1837.

By Diabelli: "Seufzer eines Ungeliebten" (Bürger), WoO 118 and "Die laute Klage" (Herder), WoO 135.

By Haslinger: "Der glorreiche Augenblick" for Four Solo Voices, Chorus and Orchestra (Weissenbach), Op. 136.

1838.

By Haslinger: Overture "Leonore No. 1," Op. 138.

1839.

By R. Schumann in the *Neue Zeitschrift für Musik*, vi, supplement: "Gesang der Mönche" for Three Men's Voices from Schiller's "Wilhelm Tell," WoO 104.

1840.

By Haslinger: Triumphant March to Christoph Kuffner's tragedy, *Tarpeja*, WoO 2a.

1843.

In *Allgemeine Wiener Musikzeitung*, Vol. 3 (November 23): "Der edle Mensch sei hülfreich und gut" (Goethe), WoO 151.

1844.

By Haslinger: "Gedenke mein," WoO 130.

1846.

By Artaria: "*Die Ruinen von Athen*, Ein Fest- und Nachspiel, mit Chören und Gesängen, zur Eröffnung des Theaters in Pesth, verfasst von August von Kotzebue, Musik von Ludwig van Beethoven," Op. 113.

1852-53.

By Breitkopf and Härtel. Two earlier versions of Marzelline's Aria, "O wär ich schon mit dir vereint" from *Fidelio* (Op. 72, No. 1) as a supplement to O. Jahn's edition of *Leonore*, Op. 72, version 2 in pianoforte transcription [*see* 1956 and 1960].

1854.

By Breitkopf and Härtel: Leonore Overture No. 2 for Orchestra. (A shortened version had already been published in 1842.)

1858.

By Ewer in London: *Hochzeitslied* for mixed voices, WoO 105, version 2 (with new words by John Oxenford).

1860.

By Peters in Leipzig and Berlin: Twelve Folk Songs arranged for one and several voices, violin, violoncello and pianoforte, WoO 157. (First appearance in print of Nos. 1, 4, 6, 7, 10, 12; of No. 3 in the original arrangement.)

1864.

By Breitkopf and Härtel in the Complete Works Edition:

Series 2

No. 6. March in D for Military Band, WoO 24.

No. 7. Twelve Minuets for Orchestra, WoO 7.

No. 8. Twelve German Dances for Orchestra, WoO 8.

(These pieces had appeared previously only in pianoforte transcription in 1827, 1797 and 1798 respectively.)

Series 9

Cadenza to the Third Movement of Mozart's *Concerto for Pianoforte and Orchestra in D minor*, K. 466; WoO 58, No. 2.

Series 20

No. 4. Music for A. v. Kotzebue's Festspiel, *König Stephan* or *Ungarns erster Wohltäter*, Op. 117. (The overture was published by Steiner in 1826.)

No. 5. "Es ist vollbracht" for Bass, Chorus and Orchestra (Treitschke), WoO 97. (Published in pianoforte transcription in 1815.)

No. 6. "Germania" for Bass, Chorus and Orchestra (Treitschke), WoO 94. (Published in pianoforte transcription in 1814.)

1865.

In *Niederrheinische Musikzeitung* (September 23): "Das liebe Kätzchen" and "Der Knabe auf dem Berge" (KHV, p. 665).

1866.

In Thayer's *Chronologisches Verzeichniss*, No. 98: "Graf, Graf, liebster Graf," WoO 101.

1867.

In *Neue Briefe Beethovens*, ed. by L. Nohl:

No. 33. "Für Elise am 27 April zur Erinnerung von L. v. Bthvn," Piece for Pianoforte in A minor, WoO 59. (The autograph with the above inscription belonged to Therese Malfatti, who presented it to a Fräulein Bredl in Munich. Nohl saw it in the latter's possession.)

No. 255. "Lobkowitz-Cantate" for Soprano, Chorus and Pianoforte Accompaniment, WoO 106.

No. 290. Souvenir for Otto de Boer, WoO 35.

1872.

By Rieter-Biedermann (Lpz. and Winterthur): "Musik zu einem Ritter-Ballet," WoO 1, in pianoforte transcription by F. Dulcken.

1873.

In Gustav Nottebohm's *Beethovens Studien*, pp. 207-21:

Settings of texts by Metastasio:

"Bei labbri che Amore" for Soprano and Tenor, WoO 99, No. 1.

"Fra tutte le pene" for Soprano, Alto, and Tenor, WoO 99, No. 3b.

"Fra tutte le pene" for Soprano, Alto, Tenor and Bass, WoO 99, No. 3c.

"Guira il nocchier" for Soprano, Alto, Tenor and Bass, WoO 99, No. 5a, Version in B-flat.

"Per te d'amico aprile" for Soprano, Alto and Bass, WoO 99, No. 9.

1879.

By Schreiber in Vienna: Fragment of a Concerto in C major for Violin and Orchestra, WoO 5.

1880.

In Grove's *Dictionary of Music and Musicians,* Vol. 2, p. 205: "Sonatina per il Mandolino," WoO 43, No. 1.

1888.

By Breitkopf and Härtel in the Complete Works Edition, Vol. 25:

No. 1. *Cantata on the Death of Emperor Joseph the Second* for Soprano and Bass, Chorus, and Orchestra (Averdonk), WoO 87.

No. 2. *Cantata on the Elevation of Leopold the Second to Imperial Rank* for Soprano, Tenor and Bass, Chorus and Orchestra (Averdonk), WoO 88.

No. 3. Chorus for the Festspiel *Die Weihe des Hauses* for Soprano, Chorus and Orchestra (Meisl), WoO 98.

No. 4. *Chorus for the Allied Princes* with Orchestra (Bernard), WoO 95.

No. 5. "Opferlied" for Soprano, Alto, Tenor, Chorus and Small Orchestra (Matthisson), third version (first version of Op. 121b).

No. 6. Two Arias for Bass and Orchestra: "Prüfung der Küssens," WoO 89, and "Mit Mädeln sich vertragen" (Goethe), WoO 90.

No. 7. Two Arias for Umlauf's Singspiel, *Die Schöne Schusterin* (Stephanie le jeune), WoO 91: (1) for Tenor and Orchestra; (2) for Soprano and Orchestra.

No. 8. "Primo amore" for Soprano and Orchestra, WoO 92.

No. 9. Music for Duncker's drama, *Leonore Prohaska* for Chorus and Orchestra, WoO 96.

No. 10. "Abschiedsgesang" for Three Men's Voices (Seyfried), WoO 102.

No. 12. "Ich, der mit flatterndem Sinn" (Gleim), WoO 114.

No. 14. "Der Gesang der Nachtigall" (Herder), WoO 141.

No. 15. "Man strebt die Flamme zu verhehlen" (for Frau von Weissenthum), WoO 120.

No. 16. "O care selve" (Metastasio), WoO 119.

No. 17. "An Minna," WoO 115.

No. 19. "Trinklied (beim Abschied zu singen)," WoO 109.

No. 20. "Klage" (Hölty), WoO 113.

No. 21. "Elegie auf den Tod eines Pudels," WoO 110.

No. 23. "Musik zu einem Ritterballett" for Orchestra, WoO 1.

No. 24. March No. 2 in F for Military Band, WoO 19.

No. 25. March (Zapfenstreich) in C for Military Band, WoO 20.

No. 26. Polonaise in D for Military Band, WoO 21.

No. 27. Ecossaise in D for Military Band, WoO 22.

No. 29. March for 2 Clarinets, 2 Horns, 2 Bassoons, WoO 29.

No. 30. Three Equale for Four Trombones, WoO 30.

No. 31. Trio for Pianoforte, Flute and Bassoon, WoO 37.

No. 33. Adagio for Mandolin and Cembalo, WoO 43.

No. 34. Two Bagatelles for Pianoforte: No. 1 in C minor, WoO 52; No. 2 in C major, WoO 56.

No. 36. Allegretto for Pianoforte, WoO 53.

No. 37. "Lustig—traurig" for Pianoforte, WoO 54.

No. 39. Six Ecossaises for Pianoforte, WoO 83 (presumably transcriptions from Twelve Ecossaises for Orchestra, WoO 16), *see* 1806-1807.

No. 43. Ecossaise for Pianoforte. (This is a pianoforte transcription of an Ecossaise for Military Band, WoO 23.[2])

No. 44. Allemande for Pianoforte, WoO 81.

No. 46. Fugue for Organ, WoO 31.

1890.

By Breitkopf and Härtel in the Complete Works Edition, Vol. 25, supplement: Concerto for Pianoforte and Orchestra in E-flat, WoO 4.

In *Grove's Dictionary of Music and Musicians*, Vol. 3, p. 424: "Lob auf den Dicken" for Three Solos and Chorus, WoO 100, musical joke on Ignaz Schuppanzigh.

1893.

In *Deutscher Kunst- und Musikzeitung*, No. 6: Piece for Pianoforte (for Ferdinand Piringer), WoO 61.

1901.

In Theodor von Frimmel's *Ludwig van Beethoven* (Berlin), p. 65: Piece for Two Violins (for Alexandre Boucher), WoO 34.

In Alexander W. Thayer's *Ludwig van Beethovens Leben*, Vol. 1, 2nd edition as a supplement: Duo for Two Flutes (for J. M. Degenhart), WoO 26.

1902.

In *Die Musik*, 1/12, pp. 1078-79 and 1081-82:
"Que le temps me dire" (Rousseau), first version, WoO 116.
"Plaisir d'aimer," WoO 128.

In *Die Musik*, 1/12 as a supplement:
Adagio for Mechanical Instrument, WoO 33, No. 1.

1905.

By Breitkopf and Härtel, edited by Erich Prieger: *Leonore (Fidelio)* Opera in Three Acts, first version, Op. 73, in pianoforte transcription.

1906.

By Heugel in Paris: Twelve Minuets for Orchestra, WoO 12.[3]

1907.

By Breitkopf and Härtel: Eleven Viennese Dances for String and Wind Instruments, WoO 17.

1909.

In *Beethoven Briefe an N. Simrock* (Berlin), ed. by Leopold Schmidt, Appendix IV: Sonatina for Pianoforte, WoO 50.

1908-10.

By Brandstetter in Leipzig: *Leonore (Fidelio)*, Opera in Three Acts, Op. 72, in score.

1912.

By C. F. Peters: First Movement of "Duett mit zwei obligaten Augengläsern" for Viola and Violoncello, WoO 32.

In *Der Merker*, III/12 as a supplement: Sonatina for Mandolin and Pianoforte, WoO 44, No. 1.

[2] According to KHV, p. 461, this edition was based on a transcription by Czerny first published in his "Musikalischen Pfennig-magazin," Vol. 1, p. 108.

[3] Published in pianoforte transcription in 1903. (*See* 1955.)

1914.

By Breitkopf and Härtel: Variations on "Là ci darem la mano" from Mozart's *Don Giovanni* for Two Oboes and English Horn, WoO 28.

1916.

In the Catalogue of the Heyer Museum in Cologne, ed. by G. Kinsky, IV, music supplement, pp. 3-5: "An Laura" (Matthisson), WoO 112.

1920.

In G. Becking's *Studien zu Beethovens Personalstil* (Leipzig): Scherzo for Mechanical Instrument, WoO 33, No. 2.

1925.

In L. Schiedermair's *Der junge Beethoven* (Leipzig), pp. 425-426: "Punschlied," WoO 111.

1927.

By Breitkopf and Härtel in *Der Bär* (Leipzig), p. 158: "Hochzeitlied für Giannarasio del Rio" (Stein), version 1 in C, WoO 105.

1929.

By Strache: Twelve German Dances for Orchestra, WoO 13, in pianoforte transcription.

1933.

By Schott: Six Minuets for Two Violins and Bass, WoO 9.

1935.

In *Zeitschrift für Musik*, CII/11, pp. 1201-1203: "Que le temps me dure" (Rousseau), WoO 116, versions 1 and 2.

1936.

In *Schweizerische musikpädagogische Blätter*, XXV/15, pp. 226-28: "Quella cetra ah pur tu sei," for Soprano, Alto, Tenor and Bass (Metastasio), WoO 99, No. 10a.

1938.

By Schott: Introduction to Act II (and Triumphant March, *see* 1840) presumably for Christoph Kuffner's Tragedy, *Tarpeja*, WoO 2b.

1939.

By Eulenberg in Leipzig: "Nei giorni tuoi felici," Duet for Soprano and Tenor and Orchestra (Metastasio), WoO 93.

1940.

By Schott: Five Pieces for Mechanical Instrument, WoO 33, in pianoforte transcription. (For No. 1 in original form, *see* 1902; for No. 2, 1920.)

In *Sudetendeutsches Musikarchiv,* No. 1: Andante with Variations for Mandolin and Pianoforte, WoO 44, No. 2.

1941.

By Breitkopf and Härtel: Twenty-three Folk-Songs for Voice and Pianoforte, with accompaniment of Violin and Violoncello, WoO 158. (Inaccurate edition of No. 19 in *DM*, 2/6 [1902], supplement, pp. 2-4. First printing of No. 17 in *Veröffentlichungen des Beethoven-Hauses*, V [Bonn, 1928], plates I-V.)

In *Die Musik,* 33/7, p. 243: "Gia la notte s'avvicina," for Alto, Tenor and Bass (Metastasio), WoO 99, No. 4b.

1945.

In *Jahrbuch der Literarischen Vereinigung Winterthur*, pp. 247-54: "Un lieto brindisi" for Soprano, Two Tenors and Bass with Pianoforte Accompaniment (Bondi), WoO 103.

1949.

By Brucknerverlag in Wiesbaden: "No, non turbati" for Soprano and String Orchestra (Metastasio), WoO 92a.

In *Österreichische Musikzeitschrift* 4/1-2: "Traute Henriette," Hess *Verzeichnis*, No. 151.

1952.

By Breitkopf and Härtel: Romance cantabile for Pianoforte, Flute and Bassoon and small Orchestra (fragment) Hess *Verzeichnis*, No. 13.

By Peters: Second Movement of "Duett mit zwei obligaten Augengläsern" for Viola and Violoncello, WoO 32.

1953.

In *Atlantis* (Vol. 1953), pp. 212-13: "Nei campi e nelle selve" for Soprano, Alto, Tenor and Bass (Metastasio) in two versions, WoO 99, No. 7.

In *Eidgenössisches Sängerblatt*, 17/12, p. 145: "Ma tu tremi" for Soprano, Alto and Tenor (Metastasio), WoO 99, No. 6.

1953-54.

In *Beethoven Jahrbuch*, pp. 251-74: "Zapfenstreich Nr. 1," WoO 18, and "Zapfenstreich Nr. 3," WoO 19, in revised versions.

1955.

By Nagel (Musik-Archiv No. 183): Twelve Minuets for Orchestra, WoO 12, original version.

In *Musik im Unterricht* (November), supplement: "Feuerfarb' " (Mereau), version 1, Op. 52, No. 2.

1956.

In *Rivista Santa Cecilia*, 5/4: "O wär ich schon mit dir vereint," earlier version (in C minor) of Marzelline's Aria from *Fidelio* (Op. 72, version 1, No. 1) in score.

In *Musica* 10/6: "Der freie Mann" (Pfeffel), WoO 117.

1959.

By Breitkopf and Härtel in *Supplement I* to the Complete Works Edition: Settings of texts by Metastasio:
"Chi mai di questo core" for Soprano, Tenor and Bass, WoO 99, No. 2.
"Fra tutte le pene" for Tenor and Bass, WoO 99, No. 3a.
"Guira il nocchier" for Soprano, Alto and Bass, WoO 99, No. 5b.
"Guira il nocchier" for Soprano, Alto, Tenor and Bass (version in C), Hess *Verzeichnis*, No. 230.
"Quella cetra ah pur tu sei" for Soprano, Tenor and Bass, WoO 99, No. 10b.
"Quella cetra ah pur tu sei" for Soprano, Alto, Tenor and Bass, WoO 99, No. 10c.
"Scrivo in te" for Soprano and Tenor, WoO 99, No. 4.
"Sei mio ben" for Soprano and Tenor, Hess *Verzeichnis*, No. 231.

1960.

By Breitkopf and Härtel in *Supplement II* to the Complete Works Edition: "O wär ich schon mit dir vereint," earlier version (in C major) of Marzelline's Aria from *Fidelio* (Op. 72, version 1, No. 1) in score.

In *Supplement III*: Rondo for Pianoforte and Orchestra, WoO 6, original version (without Czerny's additions; *see* 1829).

1961.

In *Supplement IV*: Part II ("Seigessymphonie") of the Battle Symphony for Orchestra, Op. 91, original version for Mälzel's "Panharmonikon."

1962.

In *Supplement V*: "Opferlied" (Matthisson) version 1, Hess *Verzeichnis* No. 145.

"La tiranna," WoO 125.

"Hochzeitslied" (Stein), version 2 in A, WoO 105. See 1858.

Earlier versions of "Busslied" (Gellert), Op. 48, No. 6; "Lied aus der Ferne" (Reissig), WoO 138; "Wonne der Wehmut" (Goethe), Op. 83, No. 1.

"Dimmi, ben mio," version 2, Op. 82, No. 1.

Corrected versions of "Der Knabe auf dem Berge" and "Das liebe Kätzchen" (see 1865); "Neue Liebe, neues Leben" (Goethe), WoO 127.

Pianoforte transcriptions by Beethoven of "Freudvoll und leidvoll" (Goethe), simple and elaborated versions,[4] Op. 84, No. 4; "Opferlied" (Matthisson), Op. 121b; "Bundeslied" (Goethe), Op. 122.

---

[4] The simpler version was first published, but with mistakes, by Max Unger in *Zeitschrift für Musik* 102/11 1935 as a supplement.

APPENDIX E

DOCUMENTS PERTAINING TO THE FIRST PROJECTS FOR A BEETHOVEN BIOGRAPHY
(FROM 1826 TO SCHINDLER'S *BIOGRAPHIE*)

I. In the Beethovenhaus, Bodmer Collection:

"With pleasure I give my friend, Karl Holz, the assurance which has been asked of me, that I consider him competent to write my eventual biography, assuming that such a thing should be desired, and I repose in him the fullest confidence that he will give to the world without distortion all that I have communicated to him for this purpose.

Vienna, August 30, 1826,   Ludwig van Beethoven"

Holz never did write the biography; and after seventeen years he gave over this right to write "an authentic biography of Beethoven with the best documentation" to his friend Dr. Gassner in Carlsruhe in a note dated "Vienna, November 4, 1843."[1] No biography was forthcoming.

II.

The first biography of Beethoven was written by Joh. Aloys Schlosser, a man who hardly knew Beethoven, immediately after his death and rushed into print a few months later. The 93-page book, however, is dated Prague, 1828.

From Thayer's *Ludwig van Beethovens Leben*, 1st edition, ix:

"After Beethoven's death a certain Jacob Hotschevar became the 'legally appointed guardian of Beethoven's nephew and sole heir.' With the publication of Schlosser's wretched little 'biography' of the composer (which begins with the assertion of 1772 as the year of his birth and the naming of his father as Anton v. B.), Hotschevar sent a statement to Bäuerle's Theaterzeitung (Oct. 6, 1827) in which he said that 'we are entitled to expect soon a biography of Beethoven that is worthy of his great artistic talent.' "

In this report he included the remark that "the recently published biography [of Schlosser] . . . was filled with a variety of fundamental inaccuracies."[2]

III. From Schindler's *Biographie*, 1st edition, pp. 1-7:

"When in the course of the illness from which he had been suffering a full four months Ludwig van Beethoven was discussing with Hofrat von Breuning and me the biographies of the Greek Plutarch, Breuning used

---

[1] Schindler, *Biogr.*, II, pp. 326.

[2] See Adolf Sandberger, *Ausgewälte Auf-*   *sätze zur Musikgeschichte* (Munich, 1924), pp. 12-13.

the long awaited opportunity to ask Beethoven—seemingly without any further intentions—whom of his contemporaries he would choose as his biographer. Without hesitation he answered, 'Rochlitz, should he outlive me.' And furthermore he said, quite certainly it can be expected that after his departure, too, many busy pens would be quick to entertain the world with a large number of tales and anecdotes about him; this, indeed, seems to be the lot of all men who have exercised some influence upon their times. And thus it be his sincere wish that whatever be said of and about him in the future *remain unflinchingly true to fact in every respect, even if this or that person feel himself implicated, or even his own person* [Beethoven] *be implicated.* . . .

"Already resigned to his lot, Beethoven read with great attention and anticipation what his older friend Breuning had now written. Then he said very quietly, 'Here and there you see various papers scattered about. Take them and put them to their best use; but in all things remain true to fact. I am making you both responsible for this and therefore write to Rochlitz.'

"Our wishes were fulfilled thus, that he himself supplied us with necessary clues and other information on the papers. What further happened at the bedside of our beloved friend was that in accordance with his wishes I was to gather up all his correspondence, Breuning all other papers, among which was the first score of the opera *Fidelio*. This we quickly did.

"After Beethoven's death we had already decided to express jointly to Herr Hofrat Rochlitz the wish of our late friend. But then Breuning became ill, and two months later he followed his younger friend into the realm beyond. In many respects it was an unexpected death, which placed me—especially with respect to the common efforts centering around Beethoven—in an unpleasant situation. Soon thereafter Breuning's widow entrusted me with the papers which her late husband had kept. And thus it was my duty to turn, alone, to Hofrat Rochlitz, which I did September 12, 1827. On September 18 he replied as follows:

Never have the eccentricities and rather rough edges in Beethoven's nature hid from my eyes the nobility and grandeur of his character. And if I met with him but a few times while I was in Vienna, 1822,—but always in an atmosphere of candor and confidence—this was merely the result of the burdens which lay heavily upon him and made all conversation so difficult. That, together with a recognition of his genius and great merit as an artist, was also the reason for following, to the best of my abilities, the course of his intellectual and private life from an early age to the time of his death, to the extent that it is reflected in his works. And since from time to time I used every opportunity to collect information concerning his public life, I considered myself not entirely incapable of being his biographer when I first learned of his death. Indeed, I had planned to execute the project in this fashion, that Beethoven's life, like that of Maria von Weber, comprise the main section in the third volume of my book, *For Friends of Music*. To this plan are now added your promise of assisting me with materials and the wish, of which you informed me, of Beethoven himself. From all this

I ask you to judge whether or not I be inclined to carry out the request which you, as well as the various other friends of Beethoven, make of me. And thus it saddens me all the more that, in spite of all this, I am unable to do so. My life, which from earliest times has been filled with almost uninterrupted strenuous activity, has begun to take rather harsh revenge upon me. I am now finally forced to accept an almost total change of my previous habits. Most important in this modification of my life is that I spend much less time working at my desk. Lest I should again find such work necessary, or, to be more exact, tempting, I shall not undertake any new and significant assignments. Thus I am necessitated to abandon the thought of fulfilling both your wish and mine. I shall not tell you how deeply it hurts me to have to give you this answer; but one must accept those things which necessity sends.—Do accept my thanks for your trust and confidence, etc. . . .

"Despite this unambiguous rejection I dared to present my plea to Hofrat Rochlitz once again, this time placing special emphasis upon my assistance in this undertaking; for quite aside from the materials which I was keeping for his use, I was still in possession of many important facts which I had accumulated in the course of my long association with Beethoven,—facts which no other person possessed or ever could possess, for they were my exclusive experiences with that great man.

"As early as October 3, 1827, Herr Hofrat Rochlitz honored me with an answer of which I quote only the following:

Sir, first of all let me thank you for Beethoven's will, which you sent me. I can not describe to you how greatly the unmistakable, tender and childlike goodness delighted me, how deeply the painful suffering of that good soul moved me. Most assuredly this document will have a similar effect upon all who come to know it, outright evil people being an exception. Whenever he will be discussed not as an artist but as a human being, I do not know that anything more favorable and convincing can be said in support of the departed. The request which you repeat for a second time I cannot accept, and it is of no avail for either of us if I add "unfortunately!"

"In view of this explanation, and keeping the former resolve of not handing over to anyone the papers which were in my possession in mind, I made no further moves and now decided to await time and circumstance."

APPENDIX F

BEETHOVEN'S "IMMORTAL BELOVED"

T H E name "Immortal Beloved" comes from the second postscript to an undated letter written by Beethoven to an unknown lady.[1] The original, "unsterbliche Geliebte," has been almost consistently translated "immortal beloved," but Miss Anderson in *The Letters of Beethoven* points out that "eternally beloved" is a more accurate translation.[2] The letter was discovered by Holz who, with Stephan von Breuning and Johann van Beethoven, was searching for Beethoven's bank-shares. The letter was first in Schindler's possession and then was transferred to the Berlin State Library. It was first published in the first edition of Schindler's biography of Beethoven in 1840.

Schindler's book was the start of what is now a large and varied literature concerning this famous letter which has been primarily concerned with two unknown facts: the date of the letter and its recipient, if indeed the letter was ever sent at all. To support the various theories the letter and its two postscripts supply, along with the content and tone of the writing as a whole, we have the following clues: 1) The letter was written on July 6th in the morning, the first postscript Monday evening, July 6th, and the second postscript in the morning of July 7th; 2) "My journey was a fearful one; I did not reach here until 4 o'clock yesterday morning. Lacking horses the post-coach chose another route. . . . The coach must needs break down on the wretched road. . . . Esterhazy, traveling the usual road here, had the same fate with eight horses that I had with four"; 3) ". . . not till tomorrow will my lodgings be definitely determined upon"; 4) "Letters must be posted very early in the morning on Mondays—or on Thursdays—the only days on which the mail-coach goes from here to K."; 5) "I have just been told that the mail-coach goes every day—and I must close at once so that you may receive the letter at once."

With no existing envelope to establish the year by postal mark, the evidence must rest on the proposition that Beethoven was not absent-minded when he wrote "Evening, Monday, July 6th"; July 6th fell on a Monday in the years 1795, 1801, 1807, 1812, and 1818. Following is a summary of conclusions reached in the more important writings on the subject of this letter.

Date	Author	Publication	Date Assigned	Recipient
1840	Schindler	*Biographie*, 1st ed.	1806	Giulietta Giucciardi
		Written from an Hungarian bathing-place.		
1860	Schindler	*Biographie*, 3rd ed.	1801-3?	Giulietta Giucciardi

[1] See pp. 533ff. [2] *A*, I, p. 376, n. 1.

Date	Author	Publication	Date Assigned	Recipient
1865	Nohl	*Briefe Beethovens*	1800	Giulietta Giucciardi

The Countess Giulietta had married Count Gallenberg by 1801.

| 1879 | Thayer-Deiters | *Ludwig van Beethovens Leben*, Vol. 3, 1st ed. | | |
| | | | 1806[8] | Therese von Brunsvik |

In the summer of 1806 Beethoven was in Hungary and in Silesia. Thayer believed that Beethoven's correspondence with Gleichenstein concerning plans for marriage were to be dated in 1807 and were, along with the love-letter, connected with Countess von Brunsvik.

| 1909 | La Mara (Marie Lipsius) | *Beethovens Unster- bliche Geliebte* | 1807 | Therese von Brunsvik |

Publication of Therese's Memoirs. Discussion with descendants of Brunsvik and Giucciardi-Gallenberg families. "K" stands for the Brunsvik castle Korompa.

| 1909 | W. A. Thomas- San Galli | *Die Unsterbliche Geliebte Beethovens* | 1812 | Amalie Sebald |

With the elimination of every year but 1812 as the date of the letter, Teplitz is established as the location of the writer and Karlsbad is suggested as the location of its recipient. Beethoven's letter to Breitkopf and Härtel on July 17 establishes Beethoven's time of arrival as July 5. The fact that he is not on the guest lists until July 7 is explained by the passage in the first note: "not till tomorrow will my lodgings be definitely determined upon." In the same letter he instructs the publishers to send some of his works to Amalie Sebald, whose Berlin address he is able to give. Fanny del Rio's diary in 1816 mentions a love of five years ago "a union with whom he [Beethoven] would have considered the greatest happiness of his life"; Beethoven met Amalie Sebald in 1811.

| 1910 | A. de Hevesy | *Petites Amies de Beethoven*[4] | 1801 | Unknown |

Discussion of Therese's diary. The "Louis" mentioned by Therese ("I have chosen you among millions of men, Louis" etc.) is identified as Count Louis "Guillaume" Migazzi from references in the correspondence of her nephew, Ferdinand Deym.

| 1910 | W. A. Thomas-San Galli | | 1812 | Therese von Brunsvik |

Beethoven und die unsterbliche Geliebte: Amalie Sebald, Goethe, Therese Brunsvik und anderes

---

[8] In Volume 2 (1872), pp. 178-80, Thayer has not yet arrived at the proposition that Beethoven could have misdated the parts of the letter. The implication here is that the year must have been 1807.

[4] Cf. A. de Hevesy, *Beethoven. Vie intime* (Paris, 1927).

In 1812 Therese was staying with her sister Josephine at the Castle Wittschap near Iglau in Moravia. Beethoven may have journeyed to Teplitz by way of either Iglau or Prague, where Therese could have been visiting relatives at the time, for the meeting which preceded the writing of the letter.

1910 M. Unger   1812 Unknown
       Auf Spuren von Beethovens Unsterblicher Geliebten[5]
Goethe's diary records rain almost daily between July 8 and 18, occasionally till the end of the month, and heavy rain for July 3 and 4. This would account for the wretchedness of road conditions. The details of the postal schedule between Teplitz and Karlsbad are identical to those mentioned in the letter. If Amalie were the recipient, Beethoven would not have missed the chance to give her in person the music that he asked Breitkopf and Härtel on July 17 to send to her in Berlin. The passage in Fanny del Rio's diary cannot refer to the "Immortal Beloved" because of the sentence, "It had never reached a confession, but he could not get it out of his mind!" The letter itself constitutes a full confession. The tone of the notes to Amalie Sebald in September, 1812, is incompatible with that of the letter to the "Immortal Beloved." The similarity in style and use of expression between the letter of July 6-7 and that written on July 17, 1812, to Emilie M. provides a further argument for the year 1812.

1911 Thayer-Deiters Revised by H. Riemann   1812 Unknown
       Ludwig van Beethovens Leben, Vol. 3
Confirmation of San Galli's and Unger's arguments for the year 1812.

1920 La Mara (Marie Lipsius)   1807 Josephine von Brunsvik Deym
       Beethoven und die Brunsviks
An attempt to relate the letter to the "Immortal Beloved" with the correspondence of 1804 and 1805 between members of the Brunsvik family which express alarm over the developing relation between Beethoven and Josephine.

1921 Thayer-Deiters   1807 Therese von Brunsvik
       The Life of Ludwig van Beethoven, Revised by H. E. Krehbiel, Vol. 1.
Krehbiel upholds Thayer's theories despite the existence of modern research on the problem and adds a postscript concerned principally with La Mara's "Beethovens Unsterbliche Geliebte" of 1909.

1927 O. G. Sonneck   1812 Unknown
       The Riddle of the Immortal Beloved
A confession of love had occurred shortly before the letter was

---

[5] Cf. M. Unger, "The Immortal Beloved," *MQ*, XIII (1928), pp. 249-59.

written. Since Beethoven was in Prague from July 2 to part of July 4, it is most likely that this confession occurred in Prague and that the lady left for Karlsbad at about the same time that Beethoven left for Teplitz. The passage from the third note, "Oh God, why is it necessary to part from one whom one so loves and yet my life in V [Vienna] is now a wretched life—your love makes me at once the happiest and the unhappiest of men—at my age I need a steady, quiet life,—can that be under our conditions?", suggests that the lady's permanent residence was also Vienna.

1928 R. Rolland   1812 Therese von Brunsvik
    Beethoven-les grandes époques créatrices. De l'Héroique
        à l'Appasionata
    From a study of Therese's diary, made possible by Dr. Marianne de Czeke,[6] Rolland concluded that the years 1809-1813 were a period of crisis in the relation between Beethoven and Therese. If the letter was indeed written to her, her subsequent devotion of her life to philanthropy would dictate that she return the letter to its writer.[7]

1947 K. Smolle   1812 Therese von Brunsvik?
    Beethovens Unsterbliche Geliebte
    After the publication of the three parts of "Immortal Beloved" letter in Schindler's biography, Therese wrote in her diary (February, 1846): "They must have been addressed to Josephine whom he loved passionately"; was this a cover-up of her own love for Beethoven, which she wished to conceal because of personal pride or wounded love?

1954 S. Kaznelson   1812 Josephine von Brunsvik-Deym-Stackelberg
    Beethovens ferne und unsterbliche Geliebte
    Josephine married her second husband, Count Stackelberg on February 13, 1810. They bought property in Witschapp, Moravia. A lawsuit developed over the contract for payment, which Stackelberg lost. According to Therese von Brunsvik's Memoirs, this and other business reverses threatened the couple with financial ruin. The state of affairs destroyed their marriage relationship. Stackelberg blamed both sisters, Josephine and Therese, for the financial crisis caused by the legal decision against them, made a scene, and left them at the end of May or early June, 1812. According to Therese, they did not see him again until December 4 when he made an unexpected visit. With the marriage broken, Therese took the four Deym children as well as the two Stackelberg children to Dornbach for the summer; Josephine was left in Vienna alone. There are no entries in Therese's diary between

[6] See Dr. Marianne Czeke, *Brunsvik Teréz Gróf nö Naplói és Feljégyzései*; I. Kötet (Budapest, 1938).

[7] Cf. R. Rolland, "La Lettre de Beethoven à l'Immortelle Aimée," *La Revue musicale*, VIII (1927), No. 11, pp. 193-204.

June 9 and August 6, 1812. On April 9, 1813, Josephine gave birth to a daughter, Minona. Since Stackelberg was not with Josephine for over ten months before this date, he could hardly have been the father. Was not this child then the result of a love between Josephine and Beethoven in July, 1812, nine months earlier.[8]

Documentation is given for the identification of the Esterhazy who was "travelling the usual road here." Rolland had already identified him as Prince Paul Esterhazy, son of Nicholas.[9] In 1810 he was appointed Austrian ambassador to Dresden. On June 30, 1812, a message with his signature is sent from Prague. The next message is written from Teplitz on July 8, in which Prince Paul informs his minister, Count Metternich, that he is leaving for Dresden.

From this summary of the more significant discussions of the love letter it emerges that 1812 has now been accepted by all serious students of the problem as the year in which the letter was written, and that the identity of its recipient remains completely in doubt.

In 1927, O. G. Sonneck wrote his "The Riddle of the Immortal Beloved," which has already been listed, as a supplement to the English edition of Thayer's biography. His conclusions, still valid today, form an appropriate ending to the consideration of this problem in Beethoven biography.[10]

"To sum up and conclude: unless Fanny Giannatasio del Rio's ears tricked her, Beethoven in September, 1816, loved as on the first day her whom he had met five years before. But, he said, there had been no confession of love. *It follows that she can not have been the 'Immortal Beloved,'* for the reason that a mutual confession of love fairly shouts at one from out of the letter to the 'Immortal Beloved.' There must have been two women who at about the same time filled Beethoven with love. Who they were, we do not know but, if my argument is correct, then *not one love-riddle* confronts us *but two.*

"The coincidence that approximately five years prior to September, 1816, Beethoven met Amalie Sebald, prevents us from dismissing her peremptorily as one of the two. Psychologically it is quite possible that Amalie from the very first day of their acquaintance struck deep into Beethoven's heart, that this sentiment remained more or less one-sided on his part, that he sought her, without finding her, that delicacy and diffidence forbade him to press his suit and that, while their mutual tender affection drew them closer together during the last few days at Teplitz, time flew by without a mutual confession—and then it was too late. Thus, though Beethoven may have had Amalie Sebald in mind during that reminiscent conversation of September, 1816, *she was not the 'Immortal Beloved.'* Contrariwise, if he then

[8] For a vigorous refutation of this argument see J. Schmidt-Görg, *Dreizehn unbekannte Briefe an Josephine Gräfin Deym geb. v. Brunsvik* in *Veröffentlichungen des Beethovenhauses in Bonn,* Neue Folge, III (1957), pp. 38-9, n. 41.

[9] See also M. Unger, *Auf Spuren,* p. 20, n. 1.

[10] Pages 66-7. Copyright, 1927 by G. Schirmer, Inc. Used by permission.

was thinking of the 'Immortal Beloved,' he did not have in mind Amalie Sebald. Furthermore, when he jotted down his despairing confession that 'in this way with A, everything goes to ruin,' he may well have meant Amalie Sebald in the manner suggested by me as conjuring up a conflict between her and the 'Immortal Beloved.' If not, then the *A* stands for the initial of the name of the 'Immortal Beloved' herself and the remark simply expressed the presentiment of disaster for his relations with her. The task then would be to discover a woman other than Amalie Sebald with the initial *A* in her name to whom all circumstantial evidence, whether of a chronological, topographical or psychological nature, would apply. She would have to be a woman who probably lived, as did Beethoven, in Vienna, who was in *K.* during the same week that Beethoven wrote his 'Immortal Beloved' letter at Teplitz on July 6-7, 1812, whom he perhaps met between July 2-4, 1812, at Prague and whom he expected to see again, probably at Teplitz. Until that woman is discovered, the answer to the question 'who was Beethoven's "Immortal Beloved?"' will remain: *Unknown*. And many of us will not regret this at all in these days when privacy is fast becoming obsolete and publicity of private affairs a curse."

To Sonneck's wise conclusion the editor should add the following: as has already been mentioned at the beginning of Chapter 26, the initial from the Fischoff Manuscript, mentioned above, is also in doubt—there is no general agreement that it is to be read as *A*; the hope of a solution following Sonneck's formula is thus no longer to be sustained, and the mystery of the "Immortal Beloved" remains that much further from being solved.

APPENDIX G

DOCUMENTS AND COMMENTS IN THE MÄLZEL CASE

(The documents in the controversy between Beethoven and Mälzel together with Thayer's comments on them appear in TDR, III in Appendix II and in TK, II on pp. 272-76 as footnote 2.)

I

Deposition

OF MY OWN volition I had composed a Battle Symphony for Mälzel for his Panharmonica without pay. After he had had it for a while he brought me the score, the engraving of which he had already begun, and wanted it arranged for full orchestra. I had previously formed the idea of a Battle (Music) which, however, was not applicable to his Panharmonica. We agreed to perform this work and others of mine in a concert for the benefit of the soldiers. Meanwhile I got into the most terrible financial embarrassment. Deserted by the whole world here in Vienna, in expectation of a bill of exchange, etc., Mälzel offered me 50 ducats in gold. I took them and told him that I would give them back to him here, or would let him take the work with him to London in case I did not go with him—in which latter case I would refer him to an English publisher who would pay him these 50 ducats. The *Akademien* were now given. In the meantime Mälzel's plan and character were developed. Without my consent he printed on the placards that it was *his property*. Incensed at this he had to have these torn down. Now he printed: "Out of friendship for his journey to London"; to this I consented, because I thought that I was still at liberty to fix the conditions on which I would let him have the work. I remember that I quarrelled violently with him while the notices were being printed, but the time was too short—I was still writing the work. In the heat of my inspiration, immersed in my work, I scarcely thought of Mälzel. Immediately after the first *Akademie* in the Universitätssaal, I was told on all sides by trustworthy persons that Mälzel was spreading the news far and wide that he had loaned me 400 ducats in gold. I thereupon had the following printed in the newspaper, but the newspaper writers did not print it as Mälzel is on good terms with all of them. Immediately after the first *Akademie* I gave back to Mälzel his 50 ducats, telling him that having learned his character here, I would never travel with him, enraged for good reason because he had printed on the placards, without my consent, that all the arrangements for the *Akademie* were badly made and his bad patriotic character showed itself in the following expressions: I [*unprintable*], if only they will say in London that the public here paid 10 florins: not for the wounded but for this did I do this—and also that I would not let him have the work for London except on conditions concerning which I would let him know. He now asserted that it was a *gift of friendship* and after the second *Akademie* had this expression printed in the newspaper without asking me about it in the least. Inasmuch as Mälzel is a coarse fellow, entirely without education, or culture, it may easily be imagined how he conducted himself toward me during this period and increased my anger more and more. And who would force a gift of friendship on such a fellow? I was now offered an opportunity to send the work to the Prince Regent. It was now impossible to *give him the work unconditionally*. He then came to you and made proposals. He was told on what day to come for his answer; but he did not come, went away and performed the work in Munich. How did he get it? *Theft* was impossible—Herr Mälzel had a few of the parts at home for a few days and from these he had the whole put together by some musical handicrafts-man, and with this he is now trading around in the world. Herr Mälzel promised me hearing machines. To encourage him I composed the Victory Symphony for his Panharmonica. His machines were finally finished, but were useless for me. For this small trouble Herr Mälzel thinks that after I had set the *Victory Symphony* for grand orchestra and *composed the Battle for it,* I ought to have him the *sole owner* of this work. Now, assuming that I really felt under some obligation for the hearing machines, it is cancelled by the fact that he made at least 500 florins convention coin, out of the Battle stolen from me or compiled in a mutilated manner. He has therefore paid himself. He had the audacity to say here that he had the battle; indeed he showed it in writing to several persons—but I did not believe it, and I was right, inasmuch as the whole was *not compiled by me* but by *another.* Moreover, the honor which he credits to himself alone might be a reward. *I was not mentioned at all by the Court War Council,* and yet everything in the two *Akademien* was of my composition. If, as he said, Herr Mälzel delayed his journey to London because of the Battle, it was merely a hoax. Herr Mälzel remained until he had finished his patchwork(?), the first attempts not being successful.

Beethoven m. p.

II

Explanation and Appeal to the Musicians of London
by Ludwig van Beethoven

Herr Mälzel, who is at present in London, on his way thither performed *my Victory Symphony and Wellington's Battle at Vittoria* in *Munich* and, according to report, will also give concert performances of it in London as he was also willing to do in Frankfort. This leads me publicly to declare: that I never under any circumstances yielded or gave these works to Herr Mälzel, that nobody possesses a copy of them, and that the only one which I gave out was sent to His Royal Highness, the Prince Regent of England.

The performance of these works on the part of Herr Mälzel, therefore, is a fraud on the public, inasmuch as according to this explanation he is not in possession of them, or if he is in possession of them an infringement on my rights, as he has obtained them in an illegal manner.

But even in the latter case the public will be deceived, for that which Herr Mälzel will give them to hear under the title: *Wellington's Battle at Vittoria and Victory Symphony,* must obviously be a spurious or mutilated work, since he never received anything of these works from me except a single part for a few days.

This suspicion becomes certainty when I add the assurance of musicians of this city whose names I am empowered to mention in case of necessity, that Herr Mälzel said to them on leaving Vienna that he was in possession of the work and showed them parts of it, which, however, as I have already proved, could be nothing else than mutilated or spurious parts.

Whether Herr Mälzel is capable of doing me such an injury?—is answered by the circumstance that he had *himself* announced in the newspapers as the *sole* undertaker of my *Akadamien for the benefit of the soldiers wounded in the war* given here in Vienna, at which only works of mine were performed, without an allusion to my name.

I therefore call upon the musical artists of London not to suffer such an injury to me, their colleague, by a performance arranged by Herr Mälzel of the *Battle of Vittoria* and the *Victory Symphony,* and to prevent such an imposition on the London public in the manner set forth.

Vienna, July 25, 1814.

III

Certificate

We, the undersigned, certify in the interest of truth and can vouch under oath if necessary: that there were several conferences between Herr Louis van Beethoven and the Court Mechanician, Herr Mälzel of this city, at the house of the undersigned, Dr. Carl v. Adlersburg, the which had for their subject the musical composition called: "The Battle of Vittoria" and the visit to England; at these, Herr Mälzel made several propositions to Herr van Beethoven to secure the work aforementioned, or at least the right of first performance for himself. But as Herr Mälzel did not appear at the last meeting arranged for, nothing came of the matter, the propositions made to the former not having been accepted by him. In witness thereof.

Vienna, October 20, 1814

	Joh. Freiherr v. Pasqualati,
[L.S.]	*K. K. priv. Grosshändler.*
	Carl Edler von Adlersburg,
[L.S.]	*Hof- und Gerichts-Advocat*
	K. K. Öffentlicher Notar.

The so-called "Deposition" is, in truth, nothing more than an *ex-parte* statement prepared for the use of his lawyer by a very angry man, in whom a tendency to suspicion and jealousy had strengthened with advancing years and with the increase of an incurable infirmity. Mälzel's contra-statement to his lawyer is lost. He had no young disciple planning with zeal to preserve it and give it, with his version of the story, to posterity.

No one who is ignorant of Schindler's honestly meant, but partisan representations, or who, knowing them, can disabuse his mind of any prejudgment thence arising, can read Beethoven's statement without misgivings; all the more, if the facts proved by Moscheles and Stein—tacitly admitted, though utterly suppressed, in the document—are known to him. Nor will he be convinced by all the force of the harsh language of denunciation, that Mälzel did not act honestly and in good faith, when he called the "Victory" his property.

There is nothing in the first part of the statement that requires comment; though in passing it may be observed, that the pathos of "deserted by the whole world here in Vienna" would be increased if one could forget the Archduke, the Brentanos, the Streichers, Breitkopf and Härtel, Zmeskall, and others. It must be borne in mind (in Beethoven's favor) that the paper was written several months after the events of which it speaks; that it was drawn up at a time when its writer was excessively busy; that it bears all the marks of haste and want of reflection; that it was obviously intended for his lawyer's eye alone; that there is evident confusion of memory as to times and events; and that—be it repeated—it is the *ex-parte* statement of an angry man. Take the "400 ducats in gold"; here Beethoven's memory must have played him false, certainly as to the time, probably as to the substance of what he heard from the "trustworthy persons." Mälzel could have had no possible motive to utter so glaring a falsehood; but every motive not to do so. A few weeks later, he might and very probably did assert, that the damages to him arising from the sacrifice of the "Victory" as a piece for his Panharmonicon, from the expense of his prolonged stay in Vienna, from the loss of the holiday season in Munich, from the time, study and labor spent in experiments on Beethoven's ear-trumpets, and from his exclusion from all share in these profitable concerts, which he alone had made possible— that these damages were not less than 400 ducats. Nor does such an estimate appear to be a gross exaggeration. "I therefore had the following printed in the newspaper," continues Beethoven. If the passage which follows be what he desired to have printed, the reasons why the editors refused are sufficiently obvious; if they had cherished no regard for Mälzel and had believed him in the wrong, they must have suppressed such a communication for Beethoven's own sake.

The character of Mälzel—drawn in a few dark lines by his opponent—has no bearing on the real point at issue; it may, however, be observed as remarkable, that Beethoven alone made the discovery, and this not until—after some years of close intimacy and friendship—he had quarrelled with him. There are not many, who having so sagaciously planted and seen the harvest gathered in by another—who, smarting under the disappointment, and irritated by the loss of so much time, pains and labor—would sit down quietly, exhibit Job's patience, and refrain from all expressions of feeling not suited to a lady's boudoir. Nor is it to be supposed that Mälzel acted this Christian part; but then, Beethoven was hardly the man to cast the first stone at the sinner.

The sudden resolution to send the "Wellington's Victory" to the Prince Regent of England, was obviously part and parcel of the proceedings against Mälzel, the object being to defeat there any production of the work by him. Beethoven himself was the only loser by it. The prince never said "thank you" for it.

In the argument against the correctness of Mälzel's copy of the work, Beethoven is, to say the least, unfortunate. His opponent may have had, from *him,* only single parts (in the second paper it stands "a single part"!); but the circumstances were such that Mälzel could have had no difficulty in obtaining temporary use of most, if not all, the parts. Also there were plenty of "musical handicraftsmen" amply capable, after so many rehearsals and public performances, of producing a copy in the main correct.

It is painful to one who loves and reveres the memory of Beethoven, to peruse the closing passages of this document; it is, fortunately, not necessary to comment upon their character. It was not necessary for Beethoven to speak of Mälzel's share in the composition of the work, in the first of these papers; the opposing lawyer would attend to that; but was it just and ingenuous to suppress it entirely in the appeal to the London musicians? Schindler asserts that this appeal prevented Mälzel from producing it. It *could* have had no such effect. The simple truth is, that in those days for a stranger like Mälzel to undertake orchestral concerts in London would have been madness. The new Philharmonic Society, composed of all the best resident musicians, had hardly achieved an assured existence.

The third paper is testimony to a single fact and is so impartially drawn, so skilfully worded, as not to afford a point for or against either of the parties. Schindler closes his history of the affair thus: "The legal proceedings in Vienna were without result, however, the defendant being far away and his representatives knowing how to protract the case unduly, whereby the plaintiff was subjected to considerable expense and ever new annoyances. For this reason our master refrained from prosecuting the case further, since meanwhile the facts had become widely known and had frightened the false friend from making new attempts. The court costs were divided evenly by the litigants. Mälzel never returned to Vienna, but at a later period appealed in a letter to the friend whom he had swindled when he thought that he needed his recommendation for the metronome. This letter, dated Paris, April 19, 1818, is here. In it he represents to Beethoven that he was at work for him upon a hearing machine for use in conducting; he even invited him to accompany him on a journey to England. The master expressed his satisfaction with the metronome to the mechanician; but he never heard more concerning the machines."

Now Schindler's own account of the first two occasions when he spoke with Beethoven, copied into the text, partly with a view to this, shows that he could have no personal knowledge of the Mälzel affair, except its issue; and an examination of his pages proves further that his account of it is but a paraphrase of Beethoven's statement. His own words, written in a Conversation Book, demonstrate that the greater portion of the above citation is nonsense; for those words inform us that Mälzel returned to Vienna in the autumn of 1817; that, then and there, peace was made between the parties, and the old friendship restored; and that thereupon they passed a jovial evening together in the "Kamehl," where Schindler himself sang soprano in the "Ta, ta, ta" canon to the bass of Mälzel! What is the historic value of a narrative so made up and ending with such an astounding lapse of memory?

Mälzel spent his last years mostly in Philadelphia and other American cities. A few men of advanced years are still living there, unless recently passed away—[Thayer is writing in the eighth decade of the nineteenth century]—who retain an affectionate and respectful memory of him as a gentleman and man of culture; they will rejoice in this, at the least, partial vindication of their old friend. Candor and justice compel the painful admission that Beethoven's course with Mälzel is a blot—one of the few—upon his character, which no amount of misrepresentation of the facts can wholly efface; whoever can convince himself that the composer's conduct was legally and technically just and right, must still feel that it was neither noble nor generous.

Mälzel died suddenly on July 21, 1838, on an American brig, while on a voyage between the United States and the West Indies.

APPENDIX H

THE LATER HISTORY OF PRINCE GALITZIN'S PAYMENTS[1]

AT THE time of Beethoven's death, Prince Galitzin owed Beethoven 100 ducats for two string quartets and 25 ducats for the dedication to the Overture, *Weihe des Hauses.* On March 20, 1829, Hotschevar as guardian of Karl van Beethoven appealed to the Imperial Chancellery to ask the Embassy at St. Petersburg to collect the debt of 125 ducats from the Prince. Galitzin demanded an explanation, but after repeated requests from Karl agreed to pay 50 ducats in two installments of 20 and 30 ducats each. The sums were paid, the latter, as Karl's receipt shows, on November 9, 1832. Karl continued to make representations to the Prince touching a balance of 75 ducats still due and on June 2-14, 1835, Galitzin promised to pay the sum, not as a balance due on his business transactions with Beethoven, but as a memorial *pour honorer sa mémoire, que m'est chère.* Even now the money was not paid, but after a controversy had broken out between Schindler and the Prince over the former's charge that Beethoven had never been paid for the Quartets,[2] Galitzin sent the 75 ducats on October 13-25, 1852,[3] and Karl complaisantly acquiesced in the Prince's request and signed a receipt for the money, not in payment of the debt, but as a voluntary tribute to the dead composer.

The following is Krehbiel's "bit of history derived chiefly from Mr. Thayer's papers."

In the course of time Schindler's partly erroneous statement that the debt which Galitzin owed Beethoven at the time of his death was all on account of the quartets[4] was magnified into the statement made by Heinrich Döring (in his biography) and Brendel (in his *Geschichte der Musik*) that the Prince had "cheated" the composer out of the fee for the Quartets. Prince Nikolas Galitzin had withdrawn to his distant estates in Russia, but at his instigation the cudgels were taken up in his behalf by his son, Prince George, who, stirred into indignation by Döring's biography in particular, sent that writer the following letter: "I can not and do not want to know anything of the past, all the less since it will certainly not be expected of me to contradict the proofs produced by him (his father). But as by the publication of your article you have made the question for me one of the day, I, as a man of honor must do my duty to put an end to these misunderstandings. I have deposited the sum of 125 ducats which you bring in question with Mr. Kaskel, banker in Dresden, for the heirs of Beethoven, and from you, my dear Sir, I expect the necessary information in this matter, since you must have acquainted yourself with the necessary facts while writing your notice. You

[1] From TDR, v, pp. 571-78, and TK, III, pp. 229-31.

[2] See *Biogr.* 2nd ed., p. 163. In the third edition the statement was withdrawn.

[3] See the letter from Prince Galitzin to Karl, dated April 16, 1852, in TDR, v, pp. 573-75.

[4] *Biogr.* 1st ed., pp. 162-63.

must admit that hereafter I reserve the right to treat this question as a personal one! In case the family of Beethoven has died out there will be no other disposition of the money deposited with Banker Kaskel than to pay it over to a charity or some other cause which may be directly associated with the name and works of the famous artist. Dresden, July 15-3, 1858."

Karl van Beethoven, sole heir of the composer, had died three months previously, leaving a widow and children, who were his heirs. Prince George's money seemed like a gift of Providence to the widow, who hastened, as soon as she read the letter in a musical journal, to write to Holz as the friend of the dead composer to collect the money for her and express her gratitude to Prince George.[5] Holz complied with part of her request in a letter full of obsequiousness in which he accused Schindler of scandalmongering and offered to provide the Prince with evidence of that gentleman's rascality.[6] But he did not collect the money, which lay still untouched in the vaults of Kaskel in 1861, when Madame van Beethoven, having made a vain application to Prince George, addressed a letter to Kaskel asking whether the money was still deposited with him or had been withdrawn by Prince George. In the latter event she stated that she wanted to contradict a statement circulating by the public press that the heirs of Beethoven had received the gift. Kaskel referred her to Ad. Reichel, a musical director in Dresden and a friend of the Prince, through whom, indeed, the deposit had been made. On April 28, 1861, she wrote to Reichel, reviewing the facts in the case and stating her desire to apply the money, in case it was given to her, to the musical education of her youngest daughter, Hermine van Beethoven, then 8 years of age. Kaskel also wrote to Reichel, sending him Madame van Beethoven's letter and saying that as he had not heard anything from Prince Galitzin for several years he intended to turn the money over to the Municipal Court of Dresden in order to spare himself all further correspondence in the matter. Kaskel wrote to the Prince on May 7, 1861, asking him to prescribe a disposition of the money, for, if Kaskel carried out his determination to send it to the court, it would be frittered away. He urged that the money be given to Madame van Beethoven.

This revival of interest in the subject was evidently due to Mr. Thayer's activity in behalf of the widow and her daughter. Mr. Thayer was in London in 1860 and evidently took up the matter with the Prince. He makes no mention of the subject in his notice written for Grove's "Dictionary" (Art. "Galitzin"); but among his letters the present writer found the following letter, evidently written on the eve of his departure from England in February, 1861.

"Dear Mr. Thayer. Prince Galitzin has asked me to remit to you the enclosed letters, praying you kindly to act for him in the affair, as you will soon be on the spot. He begs you, however, to bear in mind the necessity of proving that the

[5] See TDR, v, pp. 576-77.   [6] *Ibid.*, p. 577.

money for these Quartets has not been paid (I fear an impossibility!); but how-ever vexatious this may be to poor Mad. v. B. everyone must defer to the obstacle to her having the money: in the awkward light in which it places the Prince's father. From what I can gather from his conversation he will be most satisfied to have the money appropriated for the purpose you suggested: the M.S.S. At all events Prince G. is quite content to leave the matter in your hands. Wishing you a pleasant journey and a speedy return, believe me, dear Mr. Thayer, Yours sincerely Natalia Macfarren."

The editor's [Krehbiel's] efforts to learn the ultimate disposition of the money deposited with Kaskel have been in vain. Mr. Thayer's papers con-tain no hint of the steps which may have been taken after Mrs. Macfarren's appeal to Prince George; the banking house of Kaskel is gone out of exist-ence; Nephew Karl's daughter, Hermine, is dead. For three years, from 1866 to 1869, she was a student in the pianoforte and harmonium classes of the Conservatory at Vienna, and it seems likely that Mr. Thayer suc-ceeded in having the Dresden deposit applied to her education; but if so he left no memorandum of that fact amongst the papers which have come under the editor's eyes.

APPENDIX I

KARL AND HIS DESCENDANTS

IN HIS article, "The Family van Beethoven," published in the Musical Quarterly,[1] Donald W. MacArdle has presented an admirably complete history of the composer's family and a thorough bibliography on the subject. His collection of material has been a primary source for this appendix.

At the time of his uncle's death, Karl van Beethoven was enrolled in Archduke Ludwig's 8th Infantry Regiment under Baron von Stutterheim at Iglau in Moravia. He hurried to Vienna upon hearing the news but arrived too late for the funeral.

In 1832 he resigned from the army and in August of that year married Caroline Naske. After two years as an administrator of a farm in Niklowitz, he received an appointment as frontier commissioner, which he held for two more years. In 1848 his uncle Johann died. Since Johann's wife, Therese, had already died twenty years before, Karl received the entire estate of his uncle, which amounted to 42,123 florins. He was now the beneficiary of the estates of both his uncles and was able to live the last ten years of his life in comfortable circumstances. He died on April 13, 1858.

Karl's widow was left with five children, one son and four daughters. The youngest daughter was Hermine, who has already been mentioned in connection with the later Galitzin payments in Appendix H. From the marriages of these daughters there were twelve children. The name of Beethoven was continued through Karl's son, Ludwig, who was born on March 8, 1839. In a codicil to his will dated March 23, 1827, Beethoven had indicated that the capital to his estate was to be used by Karl's "natural or testamentary heirs." Thus, from 1858, the year of Karl's death until 1874, the date of her last withdrawal, Caroline received financial support from this source. According to her daughters, she also received help from a pension provided by music-lovers in Vienna as well as from royalties from foreign theaters. She died in 1891.

Karl's son, Ludwig, married Marie Nitche in 1865. He had a varied career which became less and less distinguished as it developed: non-commissioned officer in the army, employee in the Chancellery of the German Order, traveling correspondent or salesman in various cities where, increasingly, he came afoul of the law, and finally, ordinary swindler. According to Sandberger,[2] Richard Wagner gave him introductions in Munich in 1868 and 1869 which led to his wheedling over a thousand florins from King Ludwig. His activities during the next three years, which included his trading in a variety of fictitious Beethoven memorabilia, led to his imprisonment in 1872

[1] MQ, xxv, No. 4 (1949), pp. 528-50.
[2] Adolph Sandberger, "Beiträge zur Beet-hoven-Forschung" in *Archiv für Musikwissenschaft*, Vol. 2 (1920), p. 398.

for a term of four years. Nothing definite is known about his life hereafter, but MacArdle has found clues that indicate that he may have come to the United States and been employed as a foreman-inspector on the Pacific Railroad.

Ludwig had a son, Karl Julius Maria, who was born in 1870. He spent most of his childhood in Belgium where he became a journalist. At the beginning of World War I he was living in England with his mother and an adopted brother. Then the family returned to their native Munich, and Karl enrolled in the army. In 1917, he died in an army hospital in Vienna, the last in the composer's branch of the family to bear the name Beethoven.

GENERAL INDEX

Index of Vienna Residences by Year

1816	Baden, 646
1817	Heiligenstadt, 672
	Nüssdorf, 674
1818	Mödling, 698ff.
1819	Mödling, 725, 742
1820	Mödling, 761, 764
1821	Unterdöbling, 776
	Baden, 777
1822	Oberdöbling, 797
	Baden, 798, 806-08
1823	Hetzendorf, 857-58, 867
	Baden, 867ff.
1824	Penzing, 913
	Baden, 913-14
1825	Baden, 946ff.
1826	no summer lodgings
(late September)	Gneixendorf, 1005ff.

INDEX TO COMPOSITIONS

A. INSTRUMENTAL MUSIC

I. WORKS FOR ORCHESTRA ALONE

SYMPHONIES

FOR OBOE

Concerto, fragment, 126-27, 144-45

FOR PIANOFORTE, VIOLIN, AND CELLO

Concerto in C (Op. 56), 351-52, 362, 365, 406, 429, 431

FOR PIANOFORTE, FLUTE, AND BASSOON (AND CHAMBER ORCHESTRA)

Romance in E minor, fragment (Hess *Verzeichnis* No. 13), 130, 174

III. WORKS FOR BAND

Ecossaise in D (WoO 22), 502
Ecossaise in C (WoO 23), 503
March in F (WoO 18), 475, 478, 502, 745, 793
March in F (WoO 19), 502, 793
March in C (WoO 20), 502, 793
March in D (WoO 24), 659, 793
March in B-flat (WoO 29). *See* Chamber Music without Pianoforte
Polonaise in D (WoO 21), 502

IV. CHAMBER MUSIC WITH PIANOFORTE

QUINTETS

For Pianoforte and Winds (Op. 16), 145, 191, 197, 201, 204, 298, 350, 640; arranged for Pianoforte and Strings, 198

QUARTETS

Three Quartets for Pianoforte and Strings (WoO 36), 72, 82, 123, 176

TRIOS

Three Trios for Pianoforte and Strings (Op. 1), 121, 123, 124, 148, 164, 165, 171, 175, 178, 179; No. 2, 148, 198; No. 3, 121, 171; transcription for String Quintet (Op. 104), 678-79, 692, 745
Two Trios for Pianoforte and Strings (Op. 70), 435, 450-51, 479, 962, 969
Trio for Pianoforte and Strings ("Archduke," Op. 97), 484, 507, 521, 577, 623, 636, 660, 962, 968; B's performance of, 577ff.
Trio for Pianoforte and Strings (WoO 38), 123, 132
Trio for Pianoforte and Strings in one movement (WoO 39), 492, 531, 548
Trio for Pianoforte, Clarinet, and Violoncello (Op. 11), 214, 217, 218, 257, 277
Trio for Pianoforte, Flute, and Bassoon (WoO 37), 124, 132
Variations for Pianoforte and Strings (Op. 44), 124, 132, 266-67, 362
Variations for Pianoforte and Strings on Wenzel Müller's "Ich bin der Schneider Kakadu" (Op. 121a), 659, 928
Transcription for Pianoforte, Clarinet, and Cello (Op. 38), of Septet (Op. 20), 265-66, 342, 392
Transcription for Pianoforte and Strings of Symphony No. 2 (Op. 36), 392

DUOS

V. CHAMBER MUSIC WITHOUT PIANOFORTE

OCTETS

PIANOFORTE TWO HANDS

VI. WORKS FOR VOICES *A CAPPELLA*

VII. CANONS

VIII. MISCELLANEOUS